Benefits for Migrants Handbook

8th edition

Rebecca Walker, Timothy Lawrence and Deborah Gellner

D0242715

Child Poverty Action Group works on behalf of the one in four children in the UK growing up in poverty. It does not have to be like this: we work to understand what causes poverty, the impact it has on children's lives, and how it can be prevented and solved – for good. We develop and campaign for policy solutions to end child poverty. We also provide accurate information, training and advice to the people who work with hard-up families, to make sure they get the financial support they need, and carry out high profile legal work to establish and confirm families' rights. If you are not already supporting us, please consider making a donation, or ask for details of our membership schemes, training courses and publications.

Published by Child Poverty Action Group
30 Micawber Street
London N1 7TB
Tel: 020 7837 7979
staff@cpag.org.uk
www.cpag.org.uk

A CIP record for this book is available from the British Library.

ISBN: 978 1 910715 09 3

Child Poverty Action Group is a charity registered in England and Wales (registration number 294841) and in Scotland (registration number SC039339), and is a company limited by guarantee, registered in England (registration number 1993854). VAT number: 690 808117

Cover design by Colorido Studios
Typeset by David Lewis XML Associates Ltd
Content management system by Konnect Soft
Printed by CPI Group (UK) Ltd, Croydon CR0 4YY

The authors

Rebecca Walker is a freelance trainer and and writer on welfare rights.

Timothy Lawrence is a solicitor specialising in immigration and asylum work at Southwark Law Centre in London.

Deborah Gellner is a solicitor at the Asylum Support Appeals Project.

Acknowledgements

The authors would like to thank everyone who has contributed to this book and all the authors of previous editions.

Thanks are particularly due this year to Henri Krishna, Fiona Ripley, Kelly Smith, Marie-Anne Fishwick and everyone at the Asylum Support Appeals Project.

We would also like to thank Alison Key for editing and managing the production of the book, Katherine Dawson for compiling the index and Kathleen Armstrong for proofreading the text.

The law covered in this book was correct on 1 July 2016. It includes regulations laid and judgments delivered up to this date.

Contents

Abbreviations   x

Part 1   Introduction
Chapter 1   How to use this book   3
1. About this *Handbook*   3
2. Checking the rules that affect you   5
3. Finding the relevant law   6
4. Immigration advice   7

Part 2   Immigration law
Chapter 2   Immigration and nationality law: overview   11
1. Immigration and nationality law   11
2. The main types of immigration status   13
3. British nationality   15
4. Immigration and nationality applications   16
5. Appeals and other remedies   18
6. Deportation   20

Chapter 3   Leave to enter or remain   21
1. Leave to enter or remain   21
2. Time-limited leave   23
3. Indefinite leave   23
4. Employment   24
5. Recourse to public funds   25
6. Sponsorship   26

Chapter 4   Asylum and human rights   31
1. Asylum seekers   31
2. Refugee leave and humanitarian protection   32
3. Stateless people   34
4. Leave for human rights and compassionate reasons   34
5. Fresh applications   38

Chapter 5   European Economic Area nationals and their families 40
1. The European Economic Area states   40
2. Rights of admission and residence   40
3. Documentation   41
4. Exclusion and removal   41

Chapter 6   Checking your immigration status   43
1. Introduction   43
2. British nationals and people with the right of abode   43
3. People with leave to enter or remain   44
4. People without leave   49
5. Asylum seekers   49
6. European Economic Area and Swiss nationals   50
7. Passport issues   50

Part 3   Benefits and immigration status
Chapter 7   People subject to immigration control   55
1. Introduction   55
2. The effect of immigration status on benefits and tax credits   56
3. Who is a 'person subject to immigration control'   57

Chapter 8   People subject to immigration control and benefits   65
1. Benefits and tax credits affected by immigration status   65
2. People subject to immigration control who can be entitled   66
3. Partners and children who are subject to immigration control   73

Chapter 9   Asylum seekers and refugees   78
1. Asylum seekers   78
2. Benefits and tax credits for people granted leave   79
3. Integration loans   82

Part 4   Benefits and residence rules
Chapter 10   Residence and presence rules: overview   89
1. Introduction   90
2. Presence   91
3. Past presence   92
4. Living in for three months   92
5. Residence   95
6. Ordinary residence   96
7. Habitual residence   100
8. The right to reside   101

Chapter 11   Habitual residence and the right to reside   104
1. The habitual residence test   104
2. 'Habitual residence in fact'   110
3. The right to reside   115

Chapter 12   Who has a right to reside   122
1. Introduction   122
2. Non-European Economic Area nationals   123
3. British, Irish and Commonwealth citizens   123

4. European Economic Area nationals   124
5. Croatian, A2 and A8 nationals   127
6. Initial right of residence   132
7. Jobseekers   133
8. Workers   140
9. Retaining worker status   146
10. Self-employed people   153
11. Retaining self-employed status   157
12. Self-sufficient people and students   159
13. Family members of European Economic Area nationals   164
14. Derivative residence rights   175
15. Permanent right to reside   184

Chapter 13   Residence and presence: rules for individual benefits   201
1. Means-tested benefits   201
2. Bereavement benefits   205
3. Child benefit and guardian's allowance   207
4. Disability and carers' benefits   208
5. Industrial injuries benefits   212
6. Contribution-based jobseeker's allowance and contributory   213
   employment and support allowance
7. Maternity allowance   215
8. Retirement pensions   215
9. Social fund funeral and winter fuel payments   216
10. Tax credits   218

Part 5   Benefits while abroad
Chapter 14   Going abroad   225
1. Introduction   225
2. How your benefits and tax credits are affected   227

Chapter 15   Going abroad: rules for individual benefits   233
1. Means-tested benefits   233
2. Bereavement benefits   243
3. Child benefit and guardian's allowance   243
4. Disability and carers' benefits   245
5. Incapacity benefit, severe disablement allowance and maternity   249
   allowance
6. Industrial injuries benefits   250
7. Contribution-based jobseeker's allowance and contributory   251
   employment and support allowance
8. Retirement pensions   253
9. Statutory payments   254
10. Tax credits   255

Part 6   **European co-ordination rules and international agreements**

Chapter 16   **European Union co-ordination rules**   261
1. Introduction   261
2. Who is covered   264
3. Which benefits are covered   268
4. Principles of co-ordination   271

Chapter 17   **International agreements**   291
1. Reciprocal agreements   291
2. Council of Europe conventions and agreements   299
3. European Union co-operation and association agreements   300

Part 7   **Claims and getting paid**
Chapter 18   **Delays**   307
1. Dealing with delays   307
2. Waiting for a decision on a claim   308
3. Delays when challenging a decision   322
4. Delays getting paid   328

Chapter 19   **National insurance numbers**   335
1. The national insurance number requirement   335
2. Obtaining a national insurance number   337
3. Common problems   340

Chapter 20   **Providing evidence**   345
1. General points about evidence   345
2. Evidence of immigration status   351
3. Evidence of residence rights   353
4. Types of evidence   354

Part 8   **Support for asylum seekers**
Chapter 21   **Asylum support**   369
1. Introduction   369
2. Support for asylum seekers   371
3. Temporary support   377
4. Support for failed asylum seekers   378
5. Support for people on temporary admission, temporary release or immigration bail   387
6. Support from your local authority   388

Chapter 22   **Applying for asylum support**   396
1. Applying for section 95 support   396
2. Making a decision on your application   397
3. Applying for section 4 support   404

Chapter 23   Payment and accommodation   408
1. Section 95 support   408
2. Section 4 support   413
3. Recovery of support   416

Chapter 24   Appeals   420
1. Introduction   420
2. The right to appeal   421
3. How to appeal   421
4. Decisions the First-tier Tribunal can make   430

Part 9   Other sources of help
Chapter 25   Other sources of help   439
1. Council tax reduction   439
2. Local welfare assistance schemes   443
3. Healthy Start food and vitamins   444
4. Education benefits   447
5. Free milk for children   449
6. Community care support from the local authority   449
7. Support under the Children Act 1989   450
8. NHS healthcare   451
9. Other financial help   453

Appendices
Appendix 1   Glossary of terms   459
Appendix 2   Information and advice   467
Appendix 3   Useful addresses   473
Appendix 4   Useful publications   485
Appendix 6   Passport stamps and other endorsements   491
Appendix 7   Abbreviations used in the notes   503

Index   511

Abbreviations

AA	attendance allowance	IS	income support
ARC	application registration card	JSA	jobseeker's allowance
ASAP	Asylum Support Appeals Project	MA	maternity allowance
ASU	Asylum Screening Unit	MP	Member of Parliament
BIA	Border and Immigration Agency	NASS	National Asylum Support Service
CA	carer's allowance	NI	national insurance
CABx	Citizens Advice Bureaux	OISC	Office of the Immigration Services
CJEU	Court of Justice of the European		Commissioner
	Union	PC	pension credit
CTC	child tax credit	PIP	personal independence payment
DLA	disability living allowance	REA	reduced earnings allowance
DWP	Department for Work and Pensions	SAL	standard acknowledgement letter
EC	European Community	SAP	statutory adoption pay
ECJ	European Court of Justice	SDA	severe disablement allowance
EEA	European Economic Area	SMP	statutory maternity pay
EFTA	European Free Trade Association	SPP	statutory paternity pay
ESA	employment and support	SSP	statutory sick pay
	allowance	SSPP	statutory shared parental pay
EU	European Union	TFEU	Treaty on the Functioning of the
FSU	Further Submissions Unit		European Union
HB	housing benefit	UC	universal credit
HMCTS	HM Courts and Tribunals Service	UK	United Kingdom
HMRC	HM Revenue and Customs	UKBA	UK Border Agency
IB	incapacity benefit	UKVI	UK Visas and Immigration
ICE	Independent Case Examiner		

Part 1

Introduction

Chapter 1

How to use this book

This chapter covers:
1. About this *Handbook* (below)
2. Checking the rules that affect you (p5)
3. Finding the relevant law (p6)
4. Immigration advice (p7)

1. About this *Handbook*

This *Handbook* is designed to be used by migrants and their advisers wanting advice on entitlement to social security benefits and tax credits. By 'migrants' we mean people, including British citizens, who have come or returned to Great Britain from abroad and people who have left Great Britain temporarily or to live abroad.

The law determining benefit entitlement for migrants is complex and frequently changing. As a result, migrants are often refused benefits and tax credits to which they are entitled, or not paid for family members when they should be.

This *Handbook* explains the different requirements that must be satisfied in order to be entitled to benefits and tax credits, so that you can understand whether or not you satisfy them and effectively challenge incorrect decisions.

This *Handbook* covers the rules that are most likely to affect migrant claimants and their families, and the practical problems that can arise. It is not a complete guide to the benefit rules and should be used together with general guides, such as CPAG's *Welfare Benefits and Tax Credits Handbook*.

European law after the UK referendum

The European law that is described in this *Handbook* has not changed as a result of the UK vote to leave the European Union (EU). European law will continue to apply in the UK until the UK formally leaves the EU. This requires the UK to officially notify the European Council of its intention to leave, and then negotiate the terms of departure over a period of up to two years (or longer if both sides agree).[1] See CPAG's online service and *Welfare Rights Bulletin* for updates.

How this book is organised

The book is split into parts, and related chapters are grouped under these parts. For a description of the information covered in each part, see below. For the chapters included in each part, see the table of contents on pv.

Part 1 is an introduction to this *Handbook*.

Part 2 gives an overview of immigration law to help you identify your immigration status and understand the immigration terms that appear in the rest of this *Handbook*. **Note:** immigration law is complex and frequently changing. If you are unclear about your, or a member of your family's, immigration status, or the effects of claiming a benefit or tax credit, you should obtain advice from a specialist immigration adviser (see p7).

Part 3 covers the way your, and your family member's, immigration status affects your entitlement to benefits and tax credits. If you and all the people included in your claim are European Economic Area (EEA) nationals, the rules in this part do not apply to you.

Part 4 covers the residence and presence requirements for all benefits and tax credits and how you satisfy them, including details on how you satisfy the 'right to reside' requirement if you or your family member are an EEA national.

Part 5 explains the way your entitlement to benefits and tax credits is affected if you, or a family member who is included in your claim, go abroad.

Part 6 describes the way in which the European Union social security co-ordination rules and international agreements on social security can assist you either to satisfy entitlement conditions in the UK or to be paid UK benefits abroad.

Part 7 covers some issues that can be particularly problematic for migrants – delays, satisfying the national insurance number requirement and providing evidence to show you meet the immigration, residence and presence rules.

Part 8 covers the rules on asylum support for people who have made an application for asylum in the UK.

Part 9 gives an overview of other possible sources of help that may be available to migrants.

Finding information

The two most efficient ways of finding information in this *Handbook* are to use the contents page or the index.

The contents shows the structure of the book and lists the parts, the chapters and the sections within each chapter.

The index contains entries in bold type, directing you to the general information on the subject or to the page(s) where the subject is covered more fully. Sub-entries under the bold headings are listed alphabetically and direct you to specific aspects of the subject.

Throughout this *Handbook* the text is referenced with the source of information, given in footnotes which are at the end of each chapter. For more information on finding the relevant law, see p6.

2. **Checking the rules that affect you**

As the rules are complicated, it is helpful to approach them systematically.

If you are not a European Economic Area (EEA) national (see p40), or if anyone you could include in your claim is not an EEA national, work through the following steps.

- **Step one:** be clear about your immigration status and that of anyone you could include in your claim. See Chapter 6 for help in determining on what basis you are in the UK. If you are unsure about your immigration status, get specialist immigration advice (see p7).
- **Step two:** check whether you are defined as a 'person subject to immigration control' (see Chapter 7). If you are not, your immigration status does not affect your benefit entitlement, but you must still satisfy any rules on residence and presence. **Note:** your partner's immigration status may still affect your entitlement (see Step five below).
- **Step three:** if you are defined as a 'person subject to immigration control', check whether the particular benefit or tax credit is one that excludes people subject to immigration control (see p57). If it is not, your immigration status does not affect your benefit entitlement, but you must still satisfy any rules on residence and presence.
- **Step four:** if the benefit you want to claim is one from which people subject to immigration control are generally excluded, check whether you come into an exempt group. These vary between the different benefits and tax credits (see p66). Even if you are in an exempt group, you must still satisfy all the other conditions of entitlement, including the residence and presence requirements.
- **Step five:** if you cannot claim the benefit you want, but you have a partner who may be able to include you in her/his claim, or if you can but have a partner or child who is subject to immigration control, check the rules on partners and children (see p73).
- **Step six:** if you or a member of your family have leave to enter or remain in the UK on condition that you do not have recourse to 'public funds', check whether any claim for benefits or tax credits could affect your/their immigration status (see p59).
- **Step seven:** if you are an asylum seeker or are dependent on an asylum seeker, you may be entitled to asylum support (see Chapter 21).

If you are an EEA national, or you are not an EEA national and your immigration status does not exclude you from entitlement, work through the following steps.

- **Step one:** check the residence and presence requirements for the benefit or tax credit you want to claim (see Chapter 13).
- **Step two:** if you are required to be 'habitually resident', check whether you are exempt from, or satisfy, this requirement (see Chapter 11).
- **Step three:** if you are required to have a right to reside, check how this test operates for the benefit or tax credit you want to claim (p115) and check whether you have a right to reside (see Chapter 12).
- **Step four:** if you are claiming a disability or carer's benefit check Chapter 16 to see whether you are covered by the European Union (EU) social security co-ordination rules. If you are, check whether the UK is the 'competent state' to pay these benefits.
- **Step five:** if you do not satisfy the residence and presence rules, the EU co-ordination rules may assist you. The ways they may assist are explained for each benefit and tax credit in Chapter 13 and an overview of the way the rules operate and who they apply to is covered in Chapter 16.

If you are entitled to benefit and want to know if you can continue to be paid when you, or someone who is included in your claim, go abroad, see Chapter 14 for an overview of the rules and Chapter 15 for the specific rules for individual benefits and tax credits. If you are going to another EEA country, the EU co-ordination rules may assist. Chapter 15 covers the ways they may assist for each benefit and tax credit, and an explanation of the way the rules operate and who they apply to is covered in Chapter 16.

3. **Finding the relevant law**

The complexity of the rules that specifically affect migrants means that it can be useful to refer to the relevant law not only when you are challenging a decision, but also when you make your claim. In order to ensure that the decision maker makes the correct decision on your claim, it may be helpful to provide an accompanying letter, setting out the legal requirement that you must satisfy and the way(s) in which you satisfy it. This may require you to set out more law – eg, relating to your immigration status, your right to reside, or the way the European Union co-ordination rules operate. You should also submit evidence that the law cited applies to you.

However, this does not guarantee that the correct decision will be made. If you are refused benefit when you believe you are entitled to it, you should challenge the decision. In any challenge, wherever possible, try to set out the relevant legal requirements and explain clearly how you meet them, citing the relevant law as appropriate and providing as much evidence as you can to show you meet the requirements.

This *Handbook* provides references to the law (both legislation and caselaw) and to guidance, to help you trace the source of the information given in the text.

- Find the information in the book relevant to the legal requirement you must satisfy and the text on how you satisfy it that applies to you.
- Find the footnote for that information and check the footnote text at the end of the chapter for the legal reference.
- Check Appendix 7 for an explanation of the abbreviations used in the references.
- See Appendices 2 and 4 for where to find the law and guidance online and for other useful sources of information.
- See Chapter 20 for information about providing evidence to show you satisfy legal requirements.

For a useful introduction to using legal sources, see CPAG's *Welfare Benefits and Tax Credits Handbook*.

Note: the law referred to in this *Handbook* applies in Great Britain. The equivalent law in Northern Ireland is often very similar and, in most cases, has the same effect. Many of the differences are due to the fact that the legislation and the administrative and adjudicating bodies in Northern Ireland are named differently. However, there are several instances in which the law in Northern Ireland is entirely different – eg, because a particular benefit can not yet be claimed.

Where there are differences in Scotland or Wales, either currently in force or expected in future, these are noted in this *Handbook*.

4. **Immigration advice**

If you are unsure about your immigration status, or that of anyone you could include in your claim, get specialist advice from your local law centre, Citizens Advice Bureau (CAB) or other advice agency that gives immigration advice (see Appendix 2).

Anyone who gives immigration advice must be:

- a solicitor, barrister or legal executive, or supervised by such a person;
- registered by the Office of the Immigration Services Commissioner (OISC); *or*
- an adviser with an organisation that is exempt from registration. For example, CABs are exempt, but only to give basic immigration advice.

It is a criminal offence for someone not covered by one of the above groups to give immigration advice.

Every OISC registered or exempt advice agency should display a certificate issued by the OISC to show it meets the OISC standards.

A list of all OISC registered and exempt advisers and advice organisations is on the OISC website, which also includes details of how to make a complaint about an immigration adviser.

Notes

1. About this *Handbook*
1 Art 50 Treaty on the European Union

Part 2

Immigration law

Part 2

Immigration law

Chapter 2

Immigration and nationality law: overview

This chapter covers:
1. Immigration and nationality law (below)
2. The main types of immigration status (p13)
3. British nationality (p15)
4. Immigration and nationality applications (p16)
5. Appeals and other remedies (p18)
6. Deportation (p20)

1. Immigration and nationality law

The right to live, work and settle in the UK is regulated and controlled by a complex system of laws. These are amended frequently.

Sources of law

The main UK Acts of Parliament that are concerned with immigration and nationality law are:
- Immigration Act 1971;
- British Nationality Act 1981;
- Immigration Act 1988;
- Asylum and Immigration Appeals Act 1993;
- Asylum and Immigration Act 1996;
- Human Rights Act 1998;
- Immigration and Asylum Act 1999;
- Nationality, Immigration and Asylum Act 2002;
- Asylum and Immigration (Treatment of Claimants, etc.) Act 2004;
- Immigration, Asylum and Nationality Act 2006;
- UK Borders Act 2007;
- Borders, Citizenship and Immigration Act 2009;
- Immigration Act 2014;
- Immigration Act 2016.

These Acts are supplemented by;
- statutory instruments (regulations);
- the Immigration Rules;
- government policies.

You can find the original (as enacted) and revised versions of Acts of Parliament and statutory instruments at www.legislation.gov.uk, although more recent revisions may not be included.

The Immigration Rules and most government policies concerning immigration can be found on the Home Office UK Visas and Immigration website at www.gov.uk/government/organisations/uk-visas-and-immigration.

The UK has also signed various international treaties and conventions, which guarantee certain rights. These include the:
- European Convention for the Protection of Human Rights and Fundamental Freedoms 1950 (the 'European Convention on Human Rights'), incorporated, in part, into UK law by the Human Rights Act 1998;
- 1951 Convention Relating to the Status of Refugees and its 1967 Protocol, commonly referred to as 'the Refugee Convention';
- 1954 Convention Relating to the Status of Stateless Persons and the 1961 Convention on the Reduction of Statelessness;
- European Council Directive 2003/9/EC, laying down minimum standards for the reception of asylum seekers ('the Reception Directive');
- European Council Directive 2004/83/EC on minimum standards for the qualification and status of third-country nationals or stateless people as refugees or as persons who otherwise need international protection, and the content of the protection granted ('the Qualification Directive');
- European Council Directive 2004/38/EC on the right of citizens of the European Union and their family members to move and reside freely within the territory of the member states ('the Citizens' Directive');
- 2005 Council of Europe Convention on Action Against Trafficking in Human Beings.

Caselaw of the tribunals and higher courts in the UK and Europe is also important in immigration and nationality law. Much of this can be accessed free of charge on the British and Irish Legal Information Institute website at www.bailii.org.

Relevant institutions

The **Home Secretary** (Secretary of State for the Home Department) is responsible for the **Home Office**. The department within the Home Office that deals with immigration control is currently called **UK Visas and Immigration (UKVI)**.

Immigration officers are generally responsible for processing people who arrive at the various UK ports of entry and for arresting, detaining and enforcing the removal of people from the UK. They have powers of search, entry, seizure and arrest of those suspected of having committed a criminal offence under immigration law, and may arrest and detain people who are liable to be detained in order to enforce their departure from the UK under immigration law.

Entry clearance officers stationed overseas are responsible for immigration control prior to entry to the UK, and now mainly operate behind commercial organisations responsible for the initial processing of applications. They decide whether to give **entry clearance** or **visas** to applicants under the Immigration Rules (see Chapter 3). They also decide whether to issue **family permits** (visas granted to family members of European Economic Area nationals – see Chapter 5).

Civil servants in UKVI are mainly responsible for deciding immigration and nationality applications made in the UK. Some applications made from outside the UK are also referred to civil servants in UKVI by visa officers stationed overseas.

HM Passport Office is the executive agency of the Home Office responsible for issuing UK passports and for administering the civil registration process in England and Wales – eg, births, deaths, marriages and civil partnerships.

Police officers are responsible for registering certain people who require leave to enter and remain in the UK, arresting people suspected of having committed a criminal offence under immigration law, and arresting and detaining people who are liable to be detained in order to enforce their departure from the UK under immigration law.

Judges of the **Immigration and Asylum Chambers of the First-tier Tribunal and the Upper Tribunal** are responsible for hearing and determining appeals against decisions made by entry clearance officers, immigration officers and the Secretary of State, applications for bail and most immigration-related judicial review applications.

Judges of the **Social Entitlement Chamber of the First-tier Tribunal** are responsible for determining appeals against decisions refusing asylum support.

Judges of the **Court of Appeal and UK Supreme Court** hear appeals from the Upper Tribunal, and judges of the **High Court** continue to decide applications for judicial review of certain types of decisions by the Home Secretary and her/his officers and the Upper Tribunal.

Cases may also be brought in the **Court of Justice of the European Union** if the matter concerns European Union law (which now includes asylum issues) and in the **European Court of Human Rights** if the matter concerns the European Convention on Human Rights.

2. The main types of immigration status

There are four main types of immigration status in the UK. You may be a person:
* with the right of abode. This includes British citizens (see p15);
* with leave to enter or remain (see Chapter 3);

- with a right to reside as a national of the European Economic Area (EEA) or as a family member of an EEA national (see Chapter 5);
- without status – eg, if you:
  - have entered the UK illegally;
  - previously had leave to enter or remain, but no longer have any such leave;
  - have made an asylum or human rights application when you sought to enter the UK – ie, at the port (see Chapter 4).

If you are without status, you might be given temporary admission, temporary release or bail (see below).

Note: the term 'person subject to immigration control' is important for establishing someone's entitlement to social security benefits. It has a specific meaning that is explained on p57.

Temporary admission, temporary release and bail

If you make an application for leave to enter or remain at a port of entry or while in the UK at a time when you do not have leave (including an application for asylum or on human rights grounds), you may be given temporary admission to the UK until your application is decided. If you have been detained, you may be granted temporary release or bail. Temporary admission or temporary release may also be given if:

- you were refused leave in the UK, but you have remained; *or*
- you have remained in the UK after your limited leave to enter or remain expired;
- you entered the UK illegally and have subsequently come to the attention of the immigration authorities.

Temporary admission, temporary release and bail are best understood as alternatives to detention. This type of status may continue if you have been refused asylum or another type of application, including if you have made a new application or further submissions that you would like considered as a fresh asylum and/or human rights application (see p38).

If you were given temporary admission at a port of entry, you are considered to be 'lawfully present in the UK', unless and until that status is withdrawn from you. This can be significant in relation to the requirement to have lawfully resided in the UK for a specified period of time to become eligible for citizenship or for indefinite leave to remain on the grounds of long residence. It can also be relevant to your eligibility to claim benefits.

Temporary admission or release usually means you have conditions imposed on you. These can include a requirement to live at a specified address, to report to an immigration officer at a specified time and place, and not to engage in paid or unpaid employment. There are criminal penalties if you do not adhere to these conditions, and failing to do so can make it more likely that you will be detained.

If you have temporary admission, temporary release or bail, you should have been issued with a notice informing you of your status and any conditions that apply.

Note: in certain circumstances, UK Visas and Immigration must provide accommodation to people with, or applying for, temporary admission, temporary release and bail (see p387).

3. **British nationality**

You can acquire British nationality:
- at birth, depending on the date and place of your birth, and on the nationality/citizenship and immigration and/or marital status of your parents; *or*
- on adoption; *or*
- by applying to the Home Secretary for naturalisation or registration; *or*
- as the result of legislative change.

Note: the examples given in this *Handbook* of how British citizenship may be acquired are basic. British nationality law is complex and there are many other routes that are not covered here.

There are six different forms of British nationality, only one of which (British citizenship) gives the right of abode in the UK (see below). A British national may be a:
- British citizen;
- British overseas territories citizen;
- British subject;
- British protected person;
- British national (overseas);
- British overseas citizen.

Some of the above forms of British nationality are rare and can no longer be acquired. In time, only British citizenship and British overseas territories citizenship will exist.

Multiple nationalities

Although some legal systems do not allow dual or multiple nationality or citizenship, UK law permits you to be a British national and a national of any number of other countries.

British nationals and the right of abode

'The right of abode' gives you the freedom to live in and to come to and go from the UK.

All full British citizens have the right of abode, but most people who have some other form of British nationality do not. Some Commonwealth citizens also have the right of abode, including people who are British nationals and not British citizens. However, it has not been possible to gain the right of abode since 1983 without also being a British citizen.

British nationals who do not have the right of abode generally require leave to enter or remain in the UK, but may have certain advantages over other foreign nationals in relation to applications for full British citizenship.

Acquiring British citizenship at birth

Most people, except children of diplomats or 'enemy aliens', born in the UK before 1 January 1983 automatically acquired British citizenship on that date.[1]

If you were born in the UK on or after 1 January 1983, you only acquired British citizenship if, at the time of your birth:

- your mother was a British citizen or was 'settled' in the UK – eg, she had indefinite leave to remain or permanent residence;[2] or
- your father was a British citizen or was 'settled' in the UK. If you were born before 1 July 2006, you could only gain citizenship from your father in this way if your parents were married, either at the time or subsequently. Since 1 July 2006, this restriction has no longer applied. If you were born before this date and did not acquire British citizenship because your parents were not married, you may now be able to register as a British citizen.

From 1 January 1983, a child born overseas acquires British citizenship if either parent is a British citizen, unless that parent is her/himself a British citizen by descent – eg, because s/he was also born overseas.[3] The same provisions as above apply to unmarried British fathers of children born abroad.

---

4. **Immigration and nationality applications**

Applying from outside the UK

You must obtain entry clearance before travelling to the UK to seek entry for most purposes.

Nationals of countries or territories listed in Appendix 1 of the Immigration Rules are known as **'visa nationals'**. If you are a visa national, you must obtain a visa before travelling to the UK for any purpose (unless you are a refugee – see Chapter 4).

Nationals of all other countries (**'non-visa nationals'**) may apply to an immigration officer at the port of arrival for entry for certain purposes, mainly for short-term visits. If you intend to stay for a longer period, you must usually obtain entry clearance before travelling.

Note: a European Economic Area (EEA) family permit is a visa issued to a non-EEA family member of an EEA national. However, it is not always necessary to obtain a family permit before being admitted to the UK. See p41 for more details.

An exempt vignette is issued to people, such as diplomats, who are exempt from the requirements of the Immigration Act 1971.

In most countries, you can apply for entry clearance online. In some countries, you must complete a printed application form. All applicants must attend a visa application centre in person. There is not a centre in every country in the world, so some applicants must travel to a different country to apply. Most applicants must have their fingerprints and facial image (known as 'biometric information') recorded at the visa application centre.

If you wish to apply for British nationality from outside the UK, you must usually send your application to UK Visas and Immigration (UKVI) in the UK.

Applying from within the UK

UKVI is responsible for processing applications made by people in the UK:
- for leave to remain in the UK, including for asylum;
- to extend their leave to remain or vary their leave to remain – ie, to change the type of leave or the conditions attached to it;
- for confirmation of their right to reside as an EEA national or the family member of an EEA national;
- for British nationality.

Some types of application can be made online from within the UK, but all applications must be supported by original documents.

Certain types of application must usually be made in person at a specified location. These include applications for asylum (except those made under Article 3 of the European Convention on Human Rights for health reasons) and further asylum and/or human rights submissions from someone who has previously applied for asylum unsuccessfully. Other types of application may also be made in person. A 'premium service' is available, with a shorter processing time (applications are sometimes dealt with on the same day), at an increased cost.

A fee is charged for most in-country applications. Exceptions to this include:[4]
- an application for leave to enter or remain for asylum reasons, including applications made under Article 3 of the European Convention on Human Rights for health reasons;
- an application for leave to enter or remain by a child who is being provided with assistance by a local authority;
- an application for limited leave to enter or remain by a victim of trafficking (in limited circumstances only);
- an application for limited leave to enter or remain for certain purposes if UKVI accepts that the applicant is destitute or that other exceptional circumstances

apply. In these circumstances, you must complete an application form for a fee waiver and provide evidence.

In addition, 'NHS surcharge' fees are charged for many applications for limited leave to enter or remain. Exceptions include applications for:[5]

- indefinite leave to enter or remain;
- entry clearance for leave to enter for six months or less;
- a child under 18 who is being looked after by a local authority;
- leave to enter or remain for asylum reasons, including applications made under Article 3 of the European Convention on Human Rights for health reasons;
- leave to remain which relates to someone being identified as a victim of human trafficking;
- leave to remain outside the Immigration Rules with access to public funds under the Home Office policy known as the 'destitution domestic violence concession' (see p35);
- entry clearance or leave to remain as the dependant of a person who benefits from certain other exemptions.

The standard surcharge fee is £150 a year per person for students and each of their dependants and £200 a year per person for everyone else.

See Chapter 25 for more information on NHS entitlement for those with leave to enter or remain.

5. **Appeals and other remedies**

Appeals to the First-tier Tribunal

The First-tier Tribunal (Immigration and Asylum Chamber) is a judicial authority that is independent of the UK government.

You can appeal to the First-tier Tribunal against either an 'immigration decision' (see below) or a 'European Economic Area (EEA) decision' (see p19). You can also apply to the First-tier Tribunal for bail from immigration detention.

Only the following are 'immigration decisions':[6]

- a decision by the Secretary of State that you can be removed from the UK where you have made a claim that you cannot be removed because of the Refugee Convention or because you are eligible for humanitarian protection;
- a decision by the Secretary of State to refuse a human rights application you have made (including an application made from abroad);
- a decision by the Secretary of State to revoke your leave to enter or remain as a refugee or as a person eligible for humanitarian protection.

'EEA decisions' are only decisions under the Immigration (European Economic Area) Regulations 2006 that concern:[7]

- a person's entitlement to be admitted to the UK;
- a person's entitlement to be issued with, have renewed or not to have revoked, a registration certificate, a residence card, a derivative residence card, a document certifying permanent residence or a permanent residence card;
- a person's removal from the UK; *or*
- the cancellation of a person's right to reside in the UK.

You can also appeal against a decision to deprive you of British citizenship.[8]

In certain circumstances, the Secretary of State has powers to prevent you from appealing until after you have left the UK or to prevent you from appealing altogether.

For example, if you are being deported (see p20) and wish to appeal on grounds that do not include a claim for asylum, you may be denied a right to appeal from within the UK (unless to do so would be contrary to your human rights). **Note:** the government plans to extend this power to all non-asylum human rights appeals cases, but at the time of writing, regulations to bring this into force had not been laid. You may also be refused a right of appeal from within the UK if the Secretary of State (lawfully) considers your chances of succeeding in an appeal are hopeless.

You may be prevented from appealing altogether if you could have raised the grounds on which you wish to appeal when given an earlier opportunity to state your case but you chose not to do so.

In most cases, you must pay a fee when you appeal. This does not currently apply if you are appealing against a decision to remove you from the UK and you are receiving legal aid, you are a child being supported by a local authority or if you apply to the Tribunal and are accepted as requiring a fee remission because you are unable to pay.

If you win your appeal, UK Visas and Immigration (UKVI) decides whether this means you must be granted leave or, in EEA law cases, whether your right to reside must be confirmed by issuing you with an appropriate document. Delays can occur while this is being considered (see p47).

Administrative review

If a decision has been made about you by UKVI that is not an 'immigration decision' or an 'EEA decision' (see above), you may be able to apply to the Home Office for an administrative review. This is not carried out by an independent body. Examples of such decisions include a decision to refuse you entry clearance or to refuse you leave to enter or remain where you have not made an asylum, humanitarian protection or human rights claim.

Judicial review

If a decision has been made about you that does not have a right to appeal, you may be able to challenge its lawfulness by applying for a judicial review to the Upper Tribunal or to the Administrative Court, depending on the nature of the decision. This includes a decision to uphold a refusal after an administrative review.

The Administrative Court also hears applications for bail from people in immigration detention if the grounds for bail cannot be considered by the First-tier Tribunal – ie, if they relate to the lawfulness of the detention.

6. **Deportation**

'**Deportation**' is a procedure under which a person without the right of abode (see p15) is removed from the UK and excluded from re-entering for as long as the deportation order remains in force. Deportation is most often used when someone has been convicted of a serious criminal offence or is considered to be a persistent offender, but anyone whose presence is deemed by the Secretery of State to not be conducive to the public good is liable to be deported.

Deportation is not the same as '**administrative removal**', which is the procedure for removing someone who has entered the UK illegally or breached her/his conditions of leave – eg, by overstaying.

If you are being considered for deportation you may, whether or not you have leave to enter or remain, be detained, given temporary admission, or released or bailed with conditions. See p14 for further information.

Notes

3. British nationality
1 s11 BNA 1981
2 s1 BNA 1981
3 s2 BNA 1981

4. Immigration and nationality
applications
4 Immigration and Nationality (Fees) Regulations 2016, No.226
5 Immigration (Health Charge) Order 2015, No.792

5. Appeals and other remedies
6 s82 NIAA 2002, as amended by IA 2014
7 Reg 2(1) I(EEA) Regs
8 s40A BNA 1981

Chapter 3

Leave to enter or remain

This chapter covers:
1. Leave to enter or remain (below)
2. Time-limited leave (p23)
3. Indefinite leave (p23)
4. Employment (p24)
5. Recourse to public funds (p25)
6. Sponsorship (p26)

1. Leave to enter or remain

You are likely to require leave to enter or remain in the UK unless you have:
- the right of abode. This includes British citizens (see p15);
- a right to reside as a national of the European Economic Area (EEA), or as a family member of an EEA national (see p40).

The Immigration Rules set out the circumstances in which leave to enter or remain can be granted for various purposes, including for study, employment and business, family connections, long residence, human rights and asylum. They also stipulate the duration of the leave and any conditions attached to it, the circumstances in which leave will be refused, curtailed or revoked, and the criteria for deporting people whose presence in the UK is considered to be against the public interest – eg, if someone has committed a serious criminal offence.

Changes to the Immigration Rules must be notified to Parliament, but there does not need to be any debate before the changes take effect. The Rules are currently extremely lengthy, complicated and difficult to navigate. A consolidated version is published on the UK Visas and Immigration (UKVI) website at www.gov.uk/government/organisations/uk-visas-and-immigration. The website also contains policy guidance that explains the Immigration Rules. The explanation given in the guidance is not always followed by tribunals and courts, but the guidance must usually be followed by UKVI decision makers and you can therefore rely on it if it is beneficial in your case.

Note: leave may also be granted outside the Immigration Rules (see p38).

Conditions of your leave

Leave to enter or remain in the UK may be given subject to a limited number of conditions. If you breach the conditions attached to your leave, you may commit a criminal offence, your current leave could be curtailed or revoked, and future applications for leave could be refused. You could also be detained and removed from the UK.

The conditions that may be attached to leave granted under the Immigration Rules that is subject to a time limit are:

- a condition about residence;
- a requirement to register with the police and/or report to the Home Office;
- restrictions on your taking employment or studying (see p24);
- a requirement to maintain and accommodate yourself and any dependants without having recourse to 'public funds' (see p25).

Who is exempt from the usual conditions

Some people are exempt from some of the usual conditions attached to permission to enter and remain in the UK. The main categories of people who are exempt are seamen and women, aircrew, diplomats and members of the UK or visiting armed forces.[1]

EEA and Swiss nationals and their family members have separate rights and conditions of entry and residence in the UK (see Chapter 5).

Nationals of some other non-EEA states also have special rights to establish themselves or provide services in the UK for economic purposes under agreements of 'association'. The most notable of these has been an agreement between the European Community (EC) and Turkey (see below).

Turkish nationals

Turkish nationals can establish themselves in the UK for economic purposes under an agreement of 'association' between the EC (as it was at the date of the agreement) and Turkey.

This EC-Turkey association agreement of 12 September 1963 is known as the 'Ankara Agreement'. Its purpose was to promote a move towards abolishing the restrictions on people who wished to move between Turkey and the EC in order to establish themselves or provide services. This was to be achieved by certain Association Council decisions[2] and by prohibiting the introduction of new national restrictions that were less favourable than those in force on the 'relevant date'. In the case of the UK, this is 1 January 1973, the date the UK joined the EC. The Immigration Rules in effect on 1 January 1973 were less restrictive in certain respects than the current ones. Turkish nationals can therefore have any relevant applications considered under these old, less restrictive, Immigration Rules.[3]

2. **Time-limited leave**

Leave may be granted for a limited period of time. Depending on the requirements in the Immigration Rules, you may be able to have it extended or varied (switched) to another category.

Note: any time-limited leave is automatically extended beyond the date it is due to expire if you make a valid application to extend or vary the leave before the expiry date. Your leave is extended until UK Visas and Immigration (UKVI) makes a decision on your application and, if this is refused, until any appeal rights or rights to administrative review are exhausted (see p47).[4] Leave is not extended if you appeal or apply for administrative review against a refusal of leave to remain and you did not have leave to enter or remain at the time you applied.

UKVI can take several years to process some applications (eg, those from people who have applied to extend leave given outside the Immigration Rules for human rights reasons) and appeals can take many months, sometimes years, before they are determined. This can cause problems when you need to satisfy others that your leave has been extended in this way.

Note: in certain circumstances, the Secretary of State has powers to prevent you from appealing until after you have left the UK. For example, if you are liable to deportation (see p20), you can be prevented from appealing until after you have left the UK if it would not breach your human rights to have an appeal from overseas. **Note:** the government plans to extend this power to all non-asylum human rights appeals cases, but at the time of writing, regulations to bring this into force had not been laid.

3. **Indefinite leave**

Indefinite leave to enter or remain in the UK is leave without a time restriction. Indefinite leave is sometimes referred to as 'settlement'.

There are no conditions (eg, on employment and claiming 'public funds' – see p25) attached to indefinite leave.[5] However, you may still be classed as a 'person subject to immigration control' for benefit purposes and therefore restricted from claiming benefits for a specific period of time if the leave was given on the basis of an undertaking by a sponsor that s/he would be responsible for your maintenance (see p61). Your sponsor may also be liable to repay any benefits claimed and may face criminal penalties (see p28). If you have been granted entry clearance or leave to enter on the basis of a maintenance undertaking, this is not stated on the document issued to you confirming this, and this may need to be checked with a decision maker. If you are in any doubt about whether the decision maker is correct, get specialist advice.

Indefinite leave can lapse if you are absent from the UK for too long (see below). It can also be revoked (see below).

If you have indefinite leave, you can leave the UK and return without your leave lapsing if:

- you wish to return to settle in the UK; *and*
- you have not been away from the UK for more than two years, unless there are special circumstances – eg, a previous long period of residence; *and*
- you did not receive any assistance from public funds towards the cost of leaving the UK. **Note:** 'public funds' in this context is the scheme that allows people to be reimbursed the costs of resettling in their country of origin. It does *not* refer to the fact that you may have claimed benefits and other public funds while in the UK (see p25).[6]

Your indefinite leave may be revoked for reasons including if:

- you become liable to deportation (see p20); *or*
- the leave was obtained by deception.

Note: if you have been granted indefinite leave to enter the UK, your visa shows an 'expiry' or 'valid until' date. This is the date by which your entry clearance must be presented to enter the UK for the first time, after which you have indefinite leave and the date becomes irrelevant.[7]

4. **Employment**

Certain types of leave are granted with a condition prohibiting employment. For example, visitors are usually prohibited from working. Other types of leave limit the employment you may do to a certain number of hours in a week (eg, if you are given leave as a student), or for a specific period of employment or business activity. This may be described as 'authorised' work. The details of what is authorised may be found in the relevant government policy, published on the UK Visas and Immigration (UKVI) website.

If you have been given leave for specific employment (eg, under tier two of the points-based system – see p28 – or, in the past, under a work permit) or a specific activity (such as self-employment, or as a writer, composer or artist), you can only work in the employment or undertake the activity for which you were given leave. If you wish to change employment, you must apply to UKVI for permission.

Since 27 January 1997, employers have been required to check that all new employees have the right to work in the UK and can be prosecuted for employing a migrant who cannot lawfully work. The law on the employment of migrant workers has changed several times since this date and the checks an employer must make (or should have made) depend on the date the worker was first employed by the employer. The application of such checks might raise race discrimination issues. If you think you have been treated unfavourably by an employer or potential employer, get specialist advice.

Note: since 1 December 2014, some landlords must check that you have the right to live in the UK before letting a property to you. This includes landlords who take in lodgers or sub-let property.

5. **Recourse to public funds**

Leave to enter or remain for certain purposes is only granted if you can show that you and your dependants can, and will, be adequately maintained and accommodated without recourse to public funds.

In addition, when leave is granted that is subject to a time limit, a condition prohibiting you from having recourse to public funds is usually imposed. This now includes most limited leave to enter or remain for family or private life reasons granted under Article 8 of the European Convention on Human Rights (see p34). If you have such a condition on your leave to remain, it is stated on the document issued to you confirming the leave.

If you breach this condition, you may commit a criminal offence, your current leave could be curtailed or revoked, and future applications for leave could be refused. You could also be detained and removed from the UK and/or refused citizenship on character grounds.

What are public funds

'**Public funds**' for the purposes of the Immigration Rules are:[8]
- attendance allowance;
- carer's allowance;
- child benefit;
- child tax credit;
- council tax benefit (now abolished);
- council tax reduction;
- disability living allowance;
- income-related employment and support allowance;
- housing benefit;
- income support;
- income-based jobseeker's allowance;
- pension credit;
- personal independence payment;
- severe disablement allowance;
- social fund payments;
- universal credit;
- working tax credit;
- housing and homelessness assistance;
- local welfare assistance.

Only the above are public funds; nothing else counts under the Immigration Rules, including other social security benefits and education. NHS services are not public funds under this definition, but they are restricted (see p451).

Note: in certain cases, you can still claim benefits defined as public funds without breaching the condition not to have recourse to public funds. This applies if you come into one of the exempt groups who can claim these benefits, despite being a 'person subject to immigration control' (see p66).[9]

6. **Sponsorship**

Who is a sponsor

The Immigration Rules define a sponsor as the person in relation to whom you are seeking leave to enter or remain as a spouse, fiancé/e, civil partner, proposed civil partner, unmarried partner (including same-sex partner) or dependent relative.

Your sponsor must usually demonstrate that s/he is able to maintain and support you in the UK without recourse to public funds. Parents must fulfil a similar role in the case of child applicants.[10] Support by third parties is permitted for some types of application,[11] but not for most 'family' applications.

Financial requirements

For most family applications, your sponsor must have a minimum specified annual income in order for you to be given leave to enter or remain as her/his family member.[12] The amount increases depending on the number of children in the family. A sponsor who is getting attendance allowance (AA), disability living allowance (DLA), personal independence payment (PIP), carer's allowance, industrial injuries disablement benefit and certain military and veteran payments does not have to have income above this threshold.

If your sponsor has more than a certain amount of savings, these can be used to make up any shortfall in her/his annual income.

Your own income, savings and prospective income, and (in most cases) any support from a third party, are disregarded entirely.

Adequate maintenance

For leave to be granted under decreasingly few other parts of the Immigration Rules, including some family cases, you must show that you can, and will, be maintained adequately without recourse to public funds. Whether or not there is adequate maintenance depends on the number of people who need maintaining and the income of the person or family unit concerned. The standard of adequacy currently required is that the income of the family as a whole must be equal to or greater than the amount an equivalent family would receive from income support

(IS) if all the family members were entitled to have recourse to public funds. The use of this benchmark has been justified as necessary to prevent immigrant families or communities having a lower standard of living in the UK than the poorest British citizens.[13] However, the minimum income requirement used in most other cases is significantly higher than that.

Note: support from third parties can be counted for some types of applications not made under Appendix FM of the Immigration Rules.[14]

AA, DLA and PIP claimed by a sponsor can be included when establishing whether a family's income is the same or higher than the IS amount.[15] It is arguable that the same approach should be applied to industrial injuries disablement benefit, and severe disablement allowance and its replacement employment and support allowance. You should obtain specialist advice if this might be an issue.

Adequate accommodation

In most cases, in order to be given leave to enter or remain as a family member, a certain standard and/or type of accommodation must be available to you.

There must be adequate accommodation for you and any dependants, without your having recourse to public funds and which the family owns or occupies exclusively.

The accommodation must not be overcowded. The Housing Act 1985 contains statutory definitions of overcrowding in a 'dwelling house'. A 'dwelling house' includes both a privately owned house and one owned by a local authority. A house is overcrowded if two people aged 10 years or older of the opposite sex (other than husband and wife) have to sleep in the same room, or if the number of people sleeping in the house exceeds that permitted in the Act, which specifies the number of people for a given number of rooms or given floor area.

The Immigration Rules often require that the accommodation must be owned or occupied 'exclusively' by the family unit concerned. A separate bedroom for the exclusive use of the applicant and sponsor is sufficient to meet this requirement, so a family may live in shared accommodation, sharing other rooms (such as a kitchen and bathroom) with other occupants.[16]

If your circumstances change

If you needed to satisfy financial, maintenance or accommodation requirements under the Immigration Rules before your leave was granted, your leave may be curtailed and/or a further application refused if you or your sponsor do not continue to meet these requirements throughout the period of leave granted.[17] **Note:** this only applies if your leave is subject to a time limit – ie, it does not apply if you have been granted indefinite leave to enter or remain (see p23). UK Visas and Immigration (UKVI) might discover that your circumstances have changed if, for example, you or your sponsor make a claim for social security benefits.

In addition, it appears that if you have been issued with a biometric residence permit (see p47), you must notify UKVI as soon as reasonably practicable if you know (or suspect) that a change in your circumstances means that you no longer qualify for leave under the Immigration Rules.[18] It is unclear whether this only applies to time-limited leave to remain or also to indefinite leave to remain.

If a change in your circumstances means you might not meet the requirements for the leave you have been granted, you should get specialist advice urgently.

See p35 if a qualifying relationship has ended because of domestic violence.

Maintenance undertakings

A sponsor may be asked to give a written undertaking to be responsible for your maintenance and accommodation, or for your care, for the period of leave granted and any further period of leave to remain that you may be granted while in the UK.[19] Undertakings are often requested for:

- dependent relatives, although not for children under 16 years coming for settlement;
- students relying on a private individual in the UK.

The benefit authorities sometimes mistakenly assume that every person referred to as a 'sponsor' will have given such an undertaking, but this is not the case. The definition of 'sponsor' is wider than this and not all sponsors are required to give a written undertaking.

If you have been granted leave to enter or remain as a result of a maintenance undertaking, you are excluded from claiming benefits.[20] If you subsequently claim benefit while in the UK, your sponsor may be required to pay back the value of the benefit claimed.[21] This restriction applies until you have been in the UK for five years since the date of the undertaking or the date of entry. If your sponsor dies, the restriction lapses immediately.

A maintenance undertaking may be enforceable, even if it is not formally drafted, and vice versa.[22] In one case, a formal declaration that a sponsor was able and willing to maintain and accommodate was held not to amount to an undertaking, as it did not include a promise to support.[23]

Unlike the condition not to have recourse to public funds, a maintenance undertaking is not stated on the document issued to you when your leave to enter or remain is granted.

Sponsorship under the points-based system

For some categories in the Immigration Rules, points are awarded to someone applying for leave to enter or remain for having various attributes and levels of income and/or savings. This is different from points-based schemes in other countries, as all the categories in the Immigration Rules require applicants to have all the attributes for which points are notionally awarded and so, in reality, the UK system is a points-based system in name only.

There are five 'tiers', or categories, of purpose under which leave may be granted under this system. These are:

- tier one: entrepreneurs, investors and exceptionally talented people – eg, scientists, engineers and artists;
- tier two: skilled workers with a job offer (usually only for occupations in which UKVI recognises there is a shortage of appropriately skilled workers available in the UK and European Economic Area labour market);
- tier four: students;
- tier five: youth mobility (previously called 'working holidays') and temporary workers – eg, for short-term creative or sporting events.

Note: tier three is not currently in use.

If you are applying under any tier, you must usually be sponsored by an employer or educational institution. The sponsor must hold a certificate of sponsorship. This is a unique reference number that the sponsor issues to you to enable you to remain in the UK, as opposed to an actual certificate or document.

Sponsors must report to UKVI any significant changes in the sponsored person's circumstances, suspicions that s/he is breaching the conditions of her/his leave or significant changes in the sponsor's own circumstances – eg, if s/he stops trading or becomes insolvent.

Notes

1. Leave to enter or remain
1 s8 IA 1971
2 Association Council decisions 2/76 and 1/80
3 Art 41.1 Additional Protocol to the Ankara Agreement; *R (Veli Tum and Mehmet Dari) v Secretary of State for the Home Department*, C-16/05 [2007] ECR I-07415

2. Time-limited leave
4 The extension of leave while a right of appeal can be exercised only applies within the time limit for appealing and when an out-of-time appeal has been accepted.

3. Indefinite leave
5 s3(3)(a) IA 1971
6 paras 18-19 IR

7 See UKVI policy guidance ECB9.4, at www.gov.uk/government/publications/entry-clearance-vignettes-ecb09

5. Recourse to public funds
8 para 6 IR
9 SS(IA)CA Regs, as amended by Social Security (Croatian) (Amendment) Regulations 2013, No.1474; para 6B IR

6. Sponsorship
10 para 297 and Appendix FM IR
11 *Mahad (previously referred to as AM) (Ethiopia) v Entry Clearance Officer* [2009] UKSC 16, 16 December 2009
12 Appendix FM IR

13 *KA (Pakistan)* [2006] UKAIT 00065;
    approved in *AM (Ethiopia) and Others
    and Another v Entry Clearance Officer*
    [2008] EWCA Civ 1082, 16 October
    2008
14 *Mahad (previously referred to as AM)
    (Ethiopia) v Entry Clearance Officer* [2009]
    UKSC 16, 16 December 2009
15 *MK (Somalia) v Entry Clearance Officer*
    [2007] EWCA Civ 1521, 28 November
    2007
16 Ch8, s1, annex F IDI. This includes
    information on the minimum size of a
    room and a table showing the
    maximum number of people allowed for
    any specific number of rooms.
17 paras 322(4)-23 IR
18 Reg 18 Immigration (Biometric
    Registration) Regulations 2008,
    No.3048
19 para 35 IR
20 s115(9)(c) IAA 1999
21 para 35 IR; ss78, 105 and 106 SSAA
    1992
22 *R (Begum)* [2003] *The Times*, 4
    December 2003
23 *Ahmed v SSWP* [2005] EWCA Civ 535

Chapter 4

Asylum and human rights

This chapter covers:
1. Asylum seekers (below)
2. Refugee leave and humanitarian protection (p32)
3. Stateless people (p34)
4. Leave for human rights and compassionate reasons (p34)
5. Fresh applications (p38)

1. Asylum seekers

Applying for asylum

Someone who has applied for recognition as a refugee or as a person requiring international protection in the UK is commonly called an **'asylum seeker'**.

Asylum applications to UK Visas and Immigration (UKVI) can be made on one or more of the following grounds:

- under the Refugee Convention (see p12);
- under Article 3 of the Human Rights Convention (see p12). This prescribes that no one shall be subjected to torture or to inhuman or degrading treatment or punishment;
- under the Qualification Directive (see p12).

The most common other Human Rights Convention Article raised in immigration cases is Article 8, which protects a person's right to enjoy private and family life without unnecessary or disproportionate interference (see p34).

'Temporary protection' is a separate and specific category of leave introduced by the Qualification Directive. It is intended to be given to people following a declaration by the European Union (EU) Council in recognition of a mass influx of displaced people. There have been no such declarations since the Directive came into force.

The definition of an asylum seeker for the purpose of support and accommodation (see p371) is limited to people who have applied under the Refugee Convention and/or Article 3 of the Human Rights Convention – eg, an application based only on Article 8 does not make someone an asylum seeker for asylum support purposes.[1] However, in certain situations, UKVI can provide accommodation to people who are subject to immigration control who are not asylum seekers (see p387).

An asylum seeker may have applied for asylum at a port of entry before passing through passport control, or from inside the country, having entered the UK illegally or with leave for a different purpose under the Immigration Rules.

Note: if you delay making an in-country asylum application, your entitlement to asylum support may be affected (see p371).

If your asylum application is refused or withdrawn, and you have not successfully appealed, you may be able to make a fresh application (see p38).

Detention and removal

Many asylum seekers are given temporary admission while their asylum application is considered, but a significant number have been detained while their application is considered, in the expectation that their application will be considered quickly and they can then be quickly removed from the UK if refused. Other asylum seekers are detained waiting for removal to a third country (ie, not the UK or their country of nationality), which is deemed to be responsible for considering their application.

If you are a failed asylum seeker, you can be detained without a time limit, provided the purpose of the detention is your removal from the UK and there is some prospect of that.

Permission to work

If you are an asylum seeker who has not received a decision on your initial application for asylum after one year, and the delay was not your fault, you can apply to UKVI for permission to work.[2]

However, the work you can do is restricted to a shortlist of skilled occupations for which UKVI recognises there is a shortage of workers available in the UK. So, in practice, this is of no benefit to most asylum seekers.

2. **Refugee leave and humanitarian protection**

If you are an asylum seeker who is recognised by UK Visas and Immigration (UKVI) as a refugee or as being in need of humanitarian protection, you are granted refugee leave or humanitarian protection leave respectively.

Refugees and humanitarian protection

A 'refugee' is someone who, owing to a well-founded fear of being persecuted because of race, religion, nationality, membership of a particular social group or political opinion, is outside the country of her/his nationality, and is unable to or, owing to such fear, is unwilling to avail her/himself of the protection of that country.

A person in need of **'humanitarian protection'** is someone who does not qualify as a refugee, but there are substantial grounds for believing that if s/he were returned to her/his country of origin, s/he would face a real risk of suffering serious harm. A person could, for example, face a risk of serious harm for reasons other than race, religion, nationality, membership of a particular social group or political opinion.

An initial five years' leave to remain is usually granted, with the option of applying for indefinite leave shortly before this leave expires.

During the limited five-year period, your leave can be reviewed and revoked. A review may be triggered if:

- you are a refugee, but your actions bring you within the scope of the 1951 Refugee Convention 'cessation clauses' – eg, if you travel back to your country of origin without a reasonable explanation;[3] or
- there is a 'significant or non-temporary' change in the conditions in your country of origin (or part of the country) that means your continuing need for protection is now placed in doubt and a formal declaration of the change is made by the responsible state authority.

Family reunion

If you have been given refugee or humanitarian protection leave, your spouse, civil partner or, in some circumstances, your unmarried partner, and dependent children under 18 who formed part of your family unit prior to your departure from your country can apply to be reunited with you in the UK. This is commonly called 'family reunion'. There are no maintenance and accommodation requirements that must be met.

Successful family reunion applicants are granted leave in line with your leave, but they may not be granted refugee or humanitarian protection as they are not necessarily recognised as refugees. The leave granted will expire at the same time as yours, and therefore may be limited leave of up to five years or indefinite leave.[4]

Exclusions

You can be excluded from refugee status or humanitarian protection status if:

- you have committed a crime against peace, a war crime, a crime against humanity or a serious non-political crime outside the UK before being admitted as a refugee; or
- you have been guilty of acts that are contrary to the purposes and principles of the United Nations. This could include being involved in terrorism or encouraging others to do that.

If you are excluded from refugee or humanitarian protection status for these reasons or your application is 'certified' (see below), but you cannot be removed to your home country for human rights reasons (eg, because you face a risk of torture), you may be granted restricted leave (see p37).

Your application can be 'certified' if you have committed a serious offence – eg, if you have been sentenced to 26 months (for refugee status) or 12 months (for humanitarian protection) in prison.

If you cannot be excluded, but your presence is considered to be undesirable, the Home Office may grant leave for shorter periods than five years and/or with a slower route to settlement.

3. **Stateless people**

A stateless person is defined by international law as someone who is 'not considered a national by any state under the operation of its law'.[5] On 6 April 2013, the UK introduced a provision in the Immigration Rules to recognise and grant leave to remain to certain stateless people.[6] Before this date, stateless people could obtain travel documents, but could not obtain leave. If you are recognised as being stateless in the UK, you can still obtain a stateless person's travel document.

4. **Leave for human rights and compassionate reasons**

Leave granted for Article 8 of the Human Rights Convention reasons

Article 8 of the European Convention on Human Rights guarantees enjoyment of private and family life without unnecessary or disproportionate interference. You may be able to rely on this Article if you have family in the UK and/or have lived in the UK for some time and developed ties here. If UK Visas and Immigration (UKVI) is considering removing you from the UK and this would disrupt (interfere with) these aspects of your life (eg, it would separate you from a loved one), under Article 8 you should only be removed if it is necessary and reasonable in the particular circumstances of your case. Since 9 July 2012, the Immigration Rules have set out the circumstances in which UKVI accepts it must allow you to stay in the UK for private and family life reasons if you do not satisfy the requirements of any other part of the Rules – eg, the minimum income requirement in family cases (see p26).[7] UKVI also accepts that there are some cases that fall outside the Rules but where it must grant leave in order to comply with Article 8.

From 9 July 2012, leave is given for periods of no longer than 30 months, potentially leading to indefinite leave after 10 continuous years. This is twice the length of time in which a family member can become eligible for settlement under other parts of the Immigration Rules. UKVI policy is to grant you leave subject to a condition that you do not have recourse to public funds, unless there are exceptional circumstances that you have raised in the application for leave. It is possible to apply for this condition to be lifted if there has been a change in your circumstances, or if the circumstances were not known to UKVI at the time the leave was granted.[8] UKVI policy is that 'exceptional circumstances' only exist if you are destitute or if you are a parent on a low income and there are particularly compelling reasons relating to the welfare of your child.[9]

Note: whether you are granted leave within or outside the Rules may have affected your eligibility for homelessness assistance or housing allocation by a local authority, even if you were allowed to claim public funds. The government intends to correct this anomaly, but if this an issue for you, get specialist housing law advice.

If you are a carer or sibling of a child who is a British citizen, you may have immigration rights under Article 8 of the European Convention on Human Rights, the Immigration Rules and/or under European Economic Area (EEA) law (see Chapter 12). There are potential advantages and disadvantages of relying on one or the other of these rights for your being able to obtain permanent settlement in the UK in the longer term. In addition, if you have rights under Article 8 or the Immigration Rules, you might be able to access public funds, but not if you rely on EEA law.

Note: before 9 July 2012, leave to remain given for Article 8 reasons was granted outside the Immigration Rules and was called **'discretionary leave'** (see p36).

Leave granted in cases of domestic violence

If you are granted leave to enter or remain in the UK as a spouse, unmarried partner (including a same-sex partner) or civil partner of a British citizen, or of a person with indefinite leave to enter or remain in the UK or a member of HM Forces who has served for at least four years, you must usually complete a probationary period of limited leave in the UK with your partner before you can apply for indefinite leave to remain, in order to settle in the UK permanently with your partner. The probationary period is currently five or 10 years. However, you may be able to apply for indefinite leave to remain earlier than this if your relationship has broken down as a result of domestic violence.[10]

You might have limited leave for a probationary period, which has been granted with a condition that you do not have recourse to public funds. Or you might have no leave because the probationary period has expired without your applying for further leave. In either situation, you can apply for a short period of limited leave (with no restrictions on public funds) under what is known as the 'destitution domestic violence' concession.[11]

If successful, you are granted limited leave to remain for three months with access to public funds, during which time you can apply for indefinite leave to remain under the domestic violence rule. If you do so, your 'destitution domestic violence' leave is extended until your application (and any appeal or administrative review) has been decided (see p47).

Note: the Home Office appears to restrict indefinite leave on domestic violence grounds to people who were granted leave to enter or remain under provisions in the Immigration Rules, as opposed to those granted leave outside the Rules, and also to exclude those whose leave to enter or remain was granted as a spouse, unmarried partner (including a same-sex partner) or civil partner of a person who has limited leave to remain for any purpose, including for refugee, humanitarian protection or human rights purposes. However, there may be scope for challenging these restrictions, and you should get specialist immigration advice if you are affected.

Discretionary leave

Discretionary leave is granted:
- in medical cases. The threshold for leave on this basis is high: an applicant's illness must have 'reached such a critical stage (ie, he is dying) that it would be inhuman treatment to deprive him of the care which he is currently receiving and send him home to an early death unless there is care available there to enable him to meet that fate with dignity';[12]
- if returning you would breach the European Convention on Human Rights – eg, if the government of the country to which you would need to go if you were not granted leave in the UK would flagrantly deny your rights to a fair trial under Article 6 of the Convention or your rights to enjoy family and private life. This is different to cases where the UK government would breach your rights by removing you or refusing to grant you leave to enter or remain in the UK;
- in other exceptional circumstances specified in UKVI enforcement policies;
- if you have been identified as a victim of trafficking within the meaning of Article 4 of the Council of Europe Convention on Action Against Trafficking in Human Beings and your personal circumstances are so compelling that it is considered appropriate to grant some form of leave;
- if you are an unsuccessful asylum seeker, but it is considered appropriate to grant leave to you (the scope of this is unclear);
- under transitional arrangements, if you have been previously granted discretionary leave.

Note: from 9 July 2012, discretionary leave is no longer granted for reasons relating to Article 8 of the European Convention on Human Rights (see p34) or to unaccompanied children. Both categories are now included in the Immigration Rules.

If you have been granted discretionary leave, you can have access to public funds (see p25) and are entitled to work.

Discretionary leave is normally granted for a period of 30 months, with the possibility of a further 30-month extension period. After you have had 10 continuous years of this type of leave, you can apply for indefinite leave to remain, unless you do not satisfy the indefinite leave rules – eg, because of a criminal conviction or a recent out-of-court settlement such as a caution or for a county court debt. The previous policy was normally to grant discretionary leave for three years, with the possibility of being able to apply to extend this, and of indefinite leave to remain after six continuous years. If you were granted leave before 9 July 2012, the previous policy continues to apply to you, with the benefit of a shorter required period before you can apply for indefinite leave to remain. The exception to this is if you were granted discretionary leave before 9 July 2012 because you were excluded from refugee or humanitarian protection leave but could not be removed from the UK for human rights reasons. In this case, the restricted leave policy now applies to you (see below).

If you apply to have your discretionary leave extended, or for indefinite leave to remain after completing the required period of time, your case is 'actively reviewed'. This means your circumstances are reviewed and leave is only extended if there have been no significant changes or criminality.

Unaccompanied minors

In the case of an unaccompanied child, limited leave may be granted within the Immigration Rules for up to 30 months or until the child is 17 and a half, whichever is the shorter period. At 17 and a half years, if s/he is not eligible for settlement, the child's case is actively reviewed on her/his application for further leave, and this may well be refused.

Restricted leave

If you are excluded from refugee or humanitarian protection leave (see p32) for the reasons outlined on p33, but you cannot be removed from the UK for human rights reasons (eg, because you face a risk of torture if you were to be removed), you may be granted restricted leave. The previous policy was to grant discretionary leave for short periods.

Restricted leave is usually only granted for a maximum of six months at a time, with restrictions:
- on your employment or occupation in the UK;
- on where you can reside;

- requiring you to report to an immigration officer or UKVI at regular intervals;
- prohibiting your studying at an educational institution; *and*
- prohibiting your doing voluntary work with children and/or vulnerable adults.

If you knowingly fail to comply with any restrictions imposed, you may commit a criminal offence.

Exceptional leave

Exceptional leave was replaced by humanitarian protection and discretionary leave in 2003. It was granted for similar reasons but also under blanket policies to applicants from countries experiencing civil or military upheaval.

Leave outside the Immigration Rules

It is possible to be given leave outside the Immigration Rules in special or unusual situations that would not otherwise be covered, including in Article 8 cases (see p34).

If you are given leave to enter or remain outside the Immigration Rules for compassionate reasons, UKVI policy is to grant the leave subject to a condition of no public funds, unless there are exceptional circumstances. The policy is as for leave granted for human rights reasons described on p34.

If you or a member of your family applied for asylum before July 2006, instead of refugee or humanitarian protection leave, you may have been granted indefinite leave to remain or discretionary leave under the asylum 'legacy' case resolution exercise. This was intended to deal with a backlog of unresolved cases that were identified at the time by the Home Secretary.

5. **Fresh applications**

If you made an asylum and/or human rights application that was unsuccessful and a decision was made to remove you from the UK, including if you appealed against such a decision and were unsuccessful, you must make further submissions to UK Visas and Immigration (UKVI) if you want to avoid being removed. The submissions must usually be made in person.

If it refuses to grant leave, UKVI should consider whether the further submissions amount to a 'fresh application' – ie, an application that is significantly different to the failed one and which has a realistic prospect of leading to leave being granted (including as the outcome of an appeal). If it decides that there is no fresh claim, you may be removed without an appeal and your only remedy is judicial review. It might take many months or years before a decision is reached and you might only be notified of the decision when you are detained for imminent removal.

If you are a failed asylum seeker, UKVI must usually provide you with accommodation if you have made further submissions that have yet to be considered and you would otherwise be destitute (see p371). The definition of a failed asylum seeker for these purposes includes someone who has made a refugee application and/or an application under Article 3 of the Human Rights Convention, which protects against torture and inhuman or degrading treatment.[13] It is likely that the definition also includes someone who has made a failed application for humanitarian protection. You may also be eligible to receive accommodation if you have been given temporary admission, temporary release or if you are seeking bail (see p387).

Notes

1. Asylum seekers
1 s94(1) IAA 1999
2 Art 11 EU Dir 2003/9; paras 360-61 IR

2. Refugee leave and humanitarian protection
3 Art 1C(1)-(6) 1951 Convention Relating to the Status of Refugees
4 Part 11, paras 352A-FJ IR and policy instructions

3. Stateless people
5 1954 Convention Relating to the Status of Stateless Persons
6 Part 14 IR

4. Leave for human rights and compassionate reasons
7 See Appendix FM: exception and para 2764DE IR
8 See www.gov.uk/government/uploads/system/uploads/attachment_data/file/286132/change-condition.pdf
9 The policy is contained in the IDI, 'Family Life (as a Partner or Parent)' FM 1.0a, and 'Partner and ECHR Article 8 Guidance', FM 8.0, which has been amended on several occasions.
10 paras 289A-C IR
11 www.gov.uk/government/publications/application-for-benefits-for-visa-holder-domestic-violence

12 *N (FC) v SSHD* [2005] UKHL 31

5. Fresh applications
13 s94(1) IAA 1999

Chapter 5

European Economic Area nationals and their families

This chapter covers:
1. The European Economic Area states (below)
2. Rights of admission and residence (below)
3. Documentation (p41)
4. Exclusion and removal (p41)

---

1. The European Economic Area states

The European Economic Area

The '**European Economic Area**' comprises the member states of the European Union (EU) plus the European Free Trade Association (EFTA) countries Norway, Liechtenstein and Iceland.

The current member states of the EU are: Austria, Belgium, Bulgaria, Croatia, Cyprus, Czech Republic, Denmark, Estonia, Finland, France, Germany, Greece, Hungary, Ireland, Italy, Latvia, Lithuania, Luxembourg, Malta, Netherlands, Poland, Portugal, Romania, Slovenia, Slovakia, Spain, Sweden and the UK.

Switzerland has a separate bilateral agreement with the EU.

---

2. Rights of admission and residence

If you are a European Economic Area (EEA) or Swiss national, you have an absolute right to be admitted to the UK (except for public policy, public security or public health reasons – see p41), provided you produce an identity card or passport, or you can otherwise prove your status.[1]

Certain family members of an EEA or Swiss national have similar rights to be admitted to the UK. In limited circumstances, these rights also apply to family members of British citizens, including of British citizen children.

These rights and the rights of EEA and Swiss nationals and their family members to reside in the UK are covered in detail in Chapter 12.

British citizens are also EEA nationals, but the rights of residence described here only apply to family members of British citizens in limited circumstances (see Chapter 12).

3. Documentation

If you are a European Economic Area (EEA) or Swiss national and have a right to reside in the UK, you have the right to be issued with a registration certificate by the Home Office. If you have acquired permanent residence, you have the right to be issued with a document certifying this. These documents are in the form of a vignette (sticker) fixed on a card booklet, separate from your passport.

If you are the family member of an EEA or a Swiss national and have a right to reside in the UK, you have the right to be issued with a residence card, or a permanent residence card if you have permanent residence. Alternatively, you may have been issued with a family permit entry visa before travelling to the UK. Each of these is usually a vignette (sticker) fixed in your passport.

If you have a right of residence derived from a relationship with an EEA or Swiss national, you have the right to be issued with a derivative residence card. Again, this is usually a vignette (sticker) fixed in your passport. Biometric residence permits may replace these documents for non-EEA national family members in the future.

Note: the above documents are declaratory. It is not necessary to obtain such a document in order to have the rights recognised by it, and the period of validity should not to be regarded as a grant of permission to reside for that period – ie, the fact that you hold a valid residence card or registration certificate does not necessarily mean that you continue to have the rights recognised by the Home Office at the time the document was issued.

4. Exclusion and removal

If you are a European Economic Area (EEA) or Swiss national, the family member of an EEA or Swiss national, or a person with a right of residence derived from a relationship with an EEA or Swiss national, you can be refused admission to the UK, refused a right to reside, refused the documentation associated with such rights and removed from the UK for public policy, public security or public health reasons.[2]

A decision made on public policy, public security or public health grounds must:

- not be taken for the economic benefit of the UK;
- be 'proportionate';
- be based exclusively on the conduct of the individual concerned, which must represent a genuine, present and sufficiently serious threat, affecting one of the fundamental interests of society;
- be for reasons that relate to your case in particular, rather than being intended to deter others;
- not be justified by a person's previous criminal convictions alone; *and*
- only be made after taking into account the person's age, state of health, family and economic situation, her/his length of residence in the UK, her/his social and cultural integration in the UK, and the extent of her/his links with her/his country of origin.

If you have permanent residence (acquired after five years' continuous lawful residence), the grounds for exclusion must be 'serious'.[3] An EEA or Swiss national aged under 18 cannot be excluded or removed unless it is in her/his best interests or her/his removal is imperative on grounds of public security.[4] Similarly, an EEA or Swiss national who has resided in the UK for 10 years cannot be excluded or removed except on imperative grounds of public security.[5]

You may be prevented from re-entering the UK if you have been removed in the preceding 12 months on the grounds of not having a right to reside. The stated aim of this is to avoid someone repeatedly exiting and re-entering the UK, getting a new three-month period of residence each time.[6]

If UK Visas and Immigration thinks you are involved in a 'marriage of convenience' or other fraud, you may be refused entry, or have your right to reside taken away.[7]

Notes

2. Rights of admission and residence
  1 Reg 11 I(EEA) Regs

4. Exclusion and removal
  2 Reg 19(5) I(EEA) Regs
  3 Reg 21(3) I(EEA) Regs
  4 Reg 21(4)(b) I(EEA) Regs
  5 Reg 21(4)(a) I(EEA) Regs
  6 Reg 21B I(EEA) Regs
  7 Reg 21B I(EEA) Regs

Chapter 6

· ·

Checking your immigration status

This chapter covers:
1. Introduction (below)
2. British nationals and people with the right of abode (below)
3. People with leave to enter or remain (p44)
4. People without leave (p49)
5. Asylum seekers (p49)
6. European Economic Area and Swiss nationals (p50)
7. Passport issues (p50)

1. Introduction

This chapter explains how to check your immigration status in order to establish your entitlement to social security benefits.

You can usually identify your immigration status in the UK from your passport and any endorsements in it by the UK immigration authorities (eg, stamps, stickers or vignettes) or, increasingly, from your biometric residence permit.

Note: some people's status (or nationality) may have changed since the passport, endorsement or card was issued. In addition, some people do not hold any of these.

If your immigration status is uncertain, you should contact a specialist adviser. A list of advisers and organisations is included in Appendix 2.

Note: anyone who gives immigration advice must be professionally regulated. For further details, see p7.

2. British nationals and people with the right of abode

If you are a British national, you can apply to HM Passport Office for a **UK passport** (see Appendix 6, Figure 1). However, not all British nationals have been issued with a passport and your British nationality does not depend on your being a passport holder.

UK passports are issued to all British nationals, not just British citizens, and it is important to distinguish between the different types of British nationality when checking your immigration status (see p15). Your passport specifies the type of British nationality you have. Holders of UK passports who have the right of abode in the UK are described as: 'British citizens or British subjects with the right of abode in the UK'.

Note: UK passports may also be issued to people whose right of abode is awaiting verification. The passport contains the endorsement: 'The holder's status under the Immigration Act 1971 has not yet been determined.'

If you have been granted British citizenship after applying to register or naturalise, you will have been issued with a certificate confirming this (see Appendix 6, Figure 2).

If you have the right of abode in the UK and are also a national of another Commonwealth country, you may have a **certificate of entitlement** endorsed in a passport issued by that country (see Appendix 6, Figure 3).

Although rare, a **certificate of patriality** issued under the Immigration Act 1971, and which was valid immediately before 1 January 1983, is regarded as a certificate of entitlement unless the holder no longer has the right of abode – eg, if you have renounced this, or if there has been independence legislation.[1]

Some people with the right of abode in the UK may hold a **confirmation of 'right of abode' document**. This was a non-statutory document issued for a brief period before the commencement of the Immigration Act 1988 to dual nationals with the right of abode who had opted to travel on non-British passports.

If you do not hold a passport or certificate confirming your British citizenship or right of abode, you may be able to prove that you have this status in some other way – eg, by producing a birth certificate showing that you were born in the UK before 1983. If your claim to British citizenship or the right of abode is complicated, you may need to prove descent from your parents and/or grandparents, and/or marriage to a person and that person's place of birth, ancestry and/or nationality status at specific times. If this applies to you, it may be helpful to get specialist advice to check your citizenship and/or right of abode.

3. **People with leave to enter or remain**

Entry clearance confirming leave to enter

Entry clearance is endorsed by a sticker (known as a '**vignette**') placed in a person's passport or travel document, or by data stored digitally in an identity card and government database (see p47).

The vignette endorsement may be designated as a visa (for visa nationals, stateless people and refugees), entry clearance (for non-visa nationals and British nationals other than British citizens) or a family permit (for dependants of European Economic Area nationals).

Two types of vignette are now issued. Which is used depends on the type of entry clearance given. Both include a photograph of the holder (see Appendix 6, Figure 9). Older versions look similar, but without a photograph (see Appendix 6, Figure 8). Even older ones were a smaller sticker, signed and date-stamped by an official (similar to the leave to remain endorsement vignette shown in Appendix 6, Figure 8).

Accompanying dependants whose details were included in the main applicant's passport might have received their own vignettes, fixed in the main applicant's passport.

Entry clearance granting you leave to enter allows you to enter the UK at a port without having to demonstrate that you satisfy the requirements of the Immigration Rules (unless you commit an act of fraud or there is a material change in circumstances). The vignette endorsement is usually date-stamped on entry (see Appendix 6, Figure 10) and confirms that you have been granted leave to enter the UK, often for the remaining period of validity stated on the vignette.

In some circumstances, an immigration officer can vary or extend your leave on your arrival in the UK.

The date the entry clearance first becomes valid is usually the same as the date of authorisation. As the holder, you may present yourself for initial entry under the entry clearance at any time during its validity. However, entry clearance officers have the discretion to defer the date the entry clearance first becomes valid for up to three months after authorisation if, for example, you wish to delay travelling to the UK.

If you are granted entry clearance, you may travel to, and remain in, the UK for the purpose for which it was granted. You may be able to travel in and out of the UK repeatedly, provided your entry clearance remains valid. However, if entry clearance has been authorised for multiple journeys to the UK of a fixed duration (eg, under the visitor category of the Immigration Rules), the duration of each visit is limited to a maximum of six months. This limitation is stated on the vignette under the heading 'duration of stay'.

If you have been granted indefinite leave to enter the UK, your visa shows an 'expiry' or 'valid until' date. This is the date by when the entry clearance needs to be presented to enter the UK for the first time, after which you have indefinite leave and the date becomes irrelevant.[2]

If you have presented the entry clearance at a port, there should be an ink stamp showing where and on which date that occurred. The date when the entry clearance was presented is the date when the entry clearance took effect as indefinite leave.

If you are granted entry clearance with a vignette for leave to enter on certain conditions (eg, as a student on condition that you do not work except in authorised employment and do not have recourse to public funds), these should be stated on the endorsement (see Appendix 6, Figure 9). However, if you have been granted entry clearance for leave to enter on the basis of a sponsorship undertaking (see p28), the reference on the vignette may be the name of the family member whom you are joining and there may be no indication that a sponsorship undertaking has been given. This is often misunderstood by the benefit authorities.

Leave to enter without entry clearance

Nationals of some countries cannot enter the UK for any purpose without first obtaining entry clearance (visa nationals). Others can apply at the port of entry for leave to enter for some of the purposes provided for under the Immigration Rules.

It is sometimes difficult to identify the purpose for which an endorsement of leave to enter has been given if someone made an application at the port of entry. If limited leave has been granted, the endorsement may be an **ink stamp**, stating the duration of the leave period for which leave is granted and the conditions (if any) attached to the leave (see Appendix 6, Figure 8). Each stamped endorsement by an immigration officer granting leave to someone without entry clearance should be accompanied by a rectangular date stamp, showing when the leave was granted.

The example shown in Appendix 6, Figure 8 is the endorsement usually made in the passport of someone given leave to enter at a port of entry as a visitor or student on a short course (of six months or less). The endorsement shows that leave has been granted on condition that the holder does not engage in any employment or have recourse to public funds.

If you are returning to the UK and already have indefinite leave to enter or remain, you may simply be given a date stamp on being readmitted.

If you leave the UK and return during a period of leave that has been given for more than six months, an immigration officer may endorse a grant of leave to enter with the same conditions, using an ink stamp stating this.[3]

Some people, usually Commonwealth citizens, who entered the UK before the Immigration Act 1971 came into force may have received an ink stamp on entry with no conditions attached. These people are referred to as 'freely landed'. They may have been treated as having been given indefinite leave to enter or remain when the 1971 Act came into force and might have retained this status by remaining resident in the UK (see p23).

Leave to remain granted in the UK

The UK **residence permit** replaced all former stamp and ink endorsements for permission to stay in the UK for longer than six months. The permit is a vignette, similar in appearance to that used to endorse entry clearance (see p44), and includes a photograph of the holder (see Appendix 6, Figure 8).

Previously, leave may have been endorsed using a smaller vignette sticker or by a rectangular stamp accompanied by a pentagonal date stamp (see Appendix 6, Figure 8).

If you were granted leave to remain on certain conditions (eg, as a student on condition that you do not work except in authorised employment and do not have recourse to public funds), these should be stated on the permit (see Appendix 6, Figure 9). However, if you were granted leave to remain on the basis of a sponsorship undertaking (see p28), this is not stated on the permit.

Biometric residence permits

Biometric residence permit cards for foreign nationals are now replacing the vignette (sticker) endorsements and other UK immigration status documents (see Appendix 6, Figure 5). You are issued with one as an alternative to having a sticker or ink stamp endorsement placed in your passport, which is not endorsed with your immigration status at all.

A biometric residence permit is a plastic card, the same size as a debit or credit card, which bears the holder's photograph, name, date of birth, nationality and immigration status. An electronic chip attached to the card holds digitised biometric details, including fingerprints, a facial image and biographical information (including name, and date and place of birth).

The card also shows details of your immigration status and entitlements in the UK, including what kind of leave you have and whether you can work. A database holds a record of the biometrics of every person to whom a card has been issued, so these can be cross-checked.

If you have the new identity card, you may need to inform UK Visas and Immigration (UKVI) of specified changes in your circumstances. If you fail to do so, you may face prosecution or other sanctions (see p27).

Leave extended for an application, appeal or administrative review

Limited leave is automatically extended beyond the date it is due to expire if you make a valid application to extend or vary your leave before this date.[4] Leave extended in this way continues until a decision is made by UKVI. If you are then refused further leave after your original leave expires, your leave is deemed to continue until any in-country appeal rights or rights to administrative review are exhausted. The same conditions attached to your original leave continue to apply during the extension (apart from the time limit).

It is not completely clear whether you are defined as a 'person subject to immigration control' and therefore excluded from most benefits during the time when you are appealing or seeking an administrative review (see p63).

UKVI can take a long time to decide applications, and appeals against refusals to vary or to extend leave can take still longer, so you may have your leave extended in this way for many months, or even for years. Also, if the result of the administrative review is significantly different or additional reasons are given for upholding the decision, you may apply for a further review which, if done in time, extends your leave even further. Your passport or biometric residence permit, if you had one when you applied, may be retained during this time. For these reasons, it can be difficult to show that your leave is ongoing. UKVI may acknowledge a valid application for leave with a letter, but does not always do so. However, it offers to confirm specifically that you have ongoing leave if you request this. There is a helpline for employers, prospective employers and prospective landlords: the number for this service is available from the UKVI website.

Travel and status documents issued to non-UK nationals

Where necessary, leave to enter or leave to remain may have been endorsed on an **immigration status document** (which is simply an A4-sized piece of paper) – eg, because your passport was not available when your leave was granted. Refugee leave and humanitarian protection are never endorsed in a passport issued by the holder's government, because the use of such a passport is considered to be an indication that you are happy to be protected by the government that issued it, which would be incompatible with having asylum in the UK (see Appendix 6, Figure 4).

Refugees are entitled to a **Refugee Convention travel document** (coloured blue), which is similar in format to a passport (see Appendix 6, Figure 11).

A dependant of a refugee or person with humanitarian protection may be granted entry clearance on the basis of refugee family reunion on a standard **European Union form**, if s/he has no passport or cannot obtain one. The previous version, **a GV3 document**, had an endorsement stating: 'visa family reunion – sponsor'. The sponsor referred to is the relative with refugee status who the dependant is joining in the UK. The endorsement does not indicate that a sponsorship undertaking has been given.

People recognised as stateless under the terms of the 1954 United Nations Convention Relating to the Status of Stateless Persons are entitled to a **stateless person's document** (coloured red).

Someone granted indefinite leave but not recognised as a refugee, and someone granted exceptional leave, discretionary leave or humanitarian protection can apply for a **certificate of travel** (coloured black). However, to qualify for such a document, usually you must have applied to your national authorities (if they have a presence in the UK) for a passport or travel document and been formally and unreasonably refused one.

4. People without leave

If you have entered the UK without permission or remained in the UK after your limited leave to enter or remain has expired, you may have committed a criminal offence and could be arrested and detained for removal from the UK. This also applies if you have remained in the UK after you have been refused further leave or had your leave revoked or curtailed and any appeal rights have been exhausted. Any conditions attached to the limited leave that has expired or been revoked or curtailed ceases to apply.

If you are in the UK without leave and come to the attention of the authorities, you are likely to be served with a **notice** informing you that you are liable to be removed from the UK, and explaining why (see Appendix 6, Figure 12). You may also be detained or given temporary admission, temporary release or bail (see p14). If you have any of these types of status, you should have been issued with a notice informing you of this and of any conditions.

If further leave has been refused, a line may be drawn through the previous endorsement of leave in your passport. A decision refusing leave to enter at a port may be endorsed by a crossed-through ink date stamp.

You must be notified of any immigration decision in writing. Sending a notice to your last known address or the address of a representative (eg, a solicitor or other regulated person) might be sufficient, so you may not necessarily be aware of a decision concerning you. Get specialist advice if you are in any doubt.

5. Asylum seekers

People who have applied for refugee or humanitarian protection leave or other forms of international protection are commonly called 'asylum seekers' (see p31).

Until early 2002, asylum seekers were issued with a **standard acknowledgement letter** (SAL). A SAL1 was issued to those claiming asylum at the port of entry and a SAL2 was issued to those who applied for asylum once they were already in the UK. From 2002, UK Visas and Immigration (UKVI) has issued asylum seekers with an **application registration card** (ARC) (see Appendix 6, Figure 8). The ARC may state whether you have any dependants or permission to work.

Asylum seekers who apply at a port of entry and in-country applicants who do not have leave at the time of their application are usually given temporary admission to the UK until their application is decided. If they have been detained, they might have subsequently been granted temporary release or bail. If you have any of these types of status, you should have been issued with a notice informing you of this and of any conditions (see Appendix 6, Figure 13). See p14 for further information.

If you apply for asylum when you have leave to enter or remain for another purpose, your leave might be automatically extended on the same conditions beyond the date it is due to expire until a decision is made by UKVI and, if the application is refused, any appeal rights are exhausted.

6. European Economic Area and Swiss nationals

If you are a European Economic Area (EEA) or Swiss national and have a right to reside in the UK, you have the right to be issued with a **registration certificate** by the Home Office. If you have acquired permanent residence, you have the right to be issued with a **document certifying permanent residence** (see Appendix 6, Figure 6). These documents are in the form of a vignette (sticker) fixed on a card booklet, separate from your passport.

If you are the family member of an EEA or a Swiss national and have a right to reside in the UK, you have the right to be issued with a **residence card** (see Appendix 6, Figure 7). **Note:** this only includes family members of British citizens in limited circumstances (see Chapter 12). If you are the family member of an EEA or a Swiss national and have permanent residency, you have the right to be issued with a permanent residence card. Alternatively, you may have been issued with a family permit entry visa before travelling to the UK. Each of these is usually a vignette (sticker) fixed in your passport.

If you have a right of residence derived from a relationship with an EEA or Swiss national, you have the right to be issued with a **derivative residence card** (see Appendix 6, Figure 7). Again, this is usually a vignette (sticker) fixed in your passport.

Note: the above documents are declaratory. It is not necessary to obtain such a document in order to have the rights recognised by it, and the period of validity should not to be regarded as a grant of permission to reside for that period – ie, the fact that you hold a valid residence card or registration certificate does not necessarily mean that you will continue to have the rights recognised by the Home Office at the time it was issued.

7. Passport issues

Leaving the UK

Embarkation from (leaving) the UK used to be endorsed by a triangular ink stamp in the embarking person's passport (see Appendix 6, Figure 14). This practice was suspended in March 1998, but then reintroduced in 2015.

New or lost passports

If you have been granted leave to enter or remain that has been endorsed in a passport that has expired or been lost before your leave is due to expire, the expiry or loss of the passport does not affect your leave. This is most common for people granted indefinite leave – eg, if you had your leave endorsed in your passport, but this has now expired and your new passport is not endorsed.

In this situation, you can apply for confirmation of your status. This now takes the form of a biometric residence permit card (see p47).

Illegible passport stamps

Problems may arise if an endorsement on a passport is either unclear or illegible, or if the passport of someone requiring leave to enter was not endorsed on her/his last entry.

If your passport has been endorsed illegibly, you may be deemed to have been granted leave to enter for six months with a condition prohibiting employment,[5] or, if you arrived in the UK before 10 July 1998, to have been given indefinite leave to enter the UK.[6] If you required leave to enter the UK, but your passport was not endorsed on entry, you may be considered an illegal entrant.[7] Specialist advice should be obtained.

Notes

2. **British nationals and people with the right of abode**
   1 s39(8) BNA 1981

3. **People with leave to enter or remain**
   2 See UKVI policy guidance ECB9.4, at www.gov.uk/government/publications/entry-clearance-vignettes-ecb09
   3 s3(3)(b) IA 1971
   4 s3C IA 1971

7. **Passport issues**
   5 Sch 2 para 6(1) IA 1971, as amended
   6 Sch 2 para 6(1) IA 1971, prior to amendment and as interpreted by the courts
   7 *Rehal v SSHD* [1989] Imm AR 576

Part 3

Benefits and immigration status

Chapter 7

People subject to immigration control

This chapter covers:
1. Introduction (below)
2. The effect of immigration status on benefits and tax credits (p56)
3. Who is a 'person subject to immigration control' (p57)

You should check this chapter, together with Chapters 8 and 9, if you, your partner and children are not all European Economic Area (EEA) nationals (see p40). If you, your partner and children *are* all EEA nationals, the rules in these three chapters do not apply to you.

1. Introduction

Entitlement to many benefits and tax credits can depend on your immigration status. The immigration status of your partner can also affect how much you are paid. It is also important to know the immigration status of any partner or child included in your claim, because if s/he has leave which is subject to the condition that s/he has no recourse to public funds, her/his right to remain in the UK could be jeopardised if you are paid an additional amount for her/him. This chapter provides an overview of how immigration status affects your benefit and tax credit entitlement and how a benefit claim can affect your partner's or child's right to remain in the UK.

If you are defined as a 'person subject to immigration control', the general rule is that you are excluded from many benefits and tax credits. However, there are limited exceptions. The relevant benefits and tax credits and the exempt groups are covered in Chapter 8, which also covers the rules on how your benefits or tax credits are affected if your partner or child is a 'person subject to immigration control'.

If you applied for asylum in the UK and have been granted refugee leave, humanitarian protection or discretionary leave to be in the UK, additional benefit rules can apply (see Chapter 9).

7

Chapter 7: People subject to immigration control
2. The effect of immigration status on benefits and tax credits

In addition to immigration status restrictions, most benefits also have presence and residence conditions. If your immigration status does not exclude you from a benefit or tax credit, you must still satisfy these. See Part 4 for more details.

2. The effect of immigration status on benefits and tax credits

It is important to know your immigration status, and that of anyone included in your claim, before making a claim for a benefit or tax credit. This is because your immigration status can affect your entitlement to benefits and tax credits. Also, an increased amount for someone included in your claim can affect her/his right to remain in the UK if her/his leave is subject to a condition that s/he has no recourse to public funds.

There are two ways in which your immigration status affects your entitlement to benefits and tax credits.

- Your immigration status may mean that you come within the definition of a 'person subject to immigration control'. In most cases, this means that you are excluded from many benefits and tax credits (although there are exceptions).
- Your immigration status can mean that you satisfy, or are exempt from, the residence requirements for the benefit or tax credit you want to claim.

As the rules are complicated, it is helpful to approach them systematically. If you, or anyone who you could include in your claim, are not a European Economic Area national (see p40), work through the following steps.

- **Step one:** be clear about your immigration status. See Chapter 6 for help in determining on what basis you are in the UK. If you are unsure about your immigration status, or that of anyone included in your claim, get specialist advice from your local law centre, Citizens Advice Bureau or other advice agency that gives immigration advice (see Appendix 2).
- **Step two:** check whether you are defined as a 'person subject to immigration control' (see p57). If you are not, you can claim the benefits you want, provided you meet the other conditions of entitlement, including any rules on residence and presence (see Part 4). Your partner's immigration status may still affect the amount you are entitled to (see Step five).
- **Step three:** check whether being a 'person subject to immigration control' excludes you from the particular benefit or tax credit you want to claim (see p65).
- **Step four:** if the benefit you want to claim is one from which 'people subject to immigration control' are generally excluded, check whether you are in one of the exempt groups. These vary between the different benefits and tax credits

(see p66). Even if you are in an exempt group, you must still satisfy all the other conditions of entitlement, including the residence and presence requirements (see Part 4).

- **Step five:** if you cannot claim the benefit you want, but you have a partner who can (or if you can but have a partner or child who is subject to immigration control), check the rules on partners and children (see p73).
- **Step six:** if you or a member of your family have leave to enter or remain in the UK that is subject to a condition not to have recourse to public funds, check whether any claim for benefits or tax credits could affect your (or her/his) immigration status (see p59).

---

3. **Who is a 'person subject to immigration control'**

Most people, apart from British citizens, are subject to immigration control. However, for benefit and tax credit purposes, the term 'person subject to immigration control' has a specific meaning (see below). It is this meaning that is referred to when the phrase 'person subject to immigration control' is used in this *Handbook*.

In order to establish whether you are a 'person subject to immigration control', you must know:

- whether or not you require leave to enter or remain in the UK;
- if you require leave, whether or not you have it;
- if you have leave, what, if any, conditions are attached to it; *and*
- if you have leave, whether this was granted as a result of someone giving an undertaking to maintain and accommodate you.

For benefit and tax credit purposes, you are a **'person subject to immigration control'** if you are not a European Economic Area (EEA) national (see p40) and you:[1]

- require leave to enter or remain in the UK, but do not have it (see p58); *or*
- have leave to enter or remain in the UK which is subject to the condition that you do not have recourse to public funds (see p59); *or*
- have leave to enter or remain in the UK, given as a result of a maintenance undertaking (see p61); *or*
- have leave to remain in the UK solely because you are appealing against a refusal to vary your previous leave (see p63).

Note:

- An EEA national (including a British national) can never be a 'person subject to immigration control' because the definition only applies to non-EEA nationals. If you are an EEA national, you cannot be refused benefit as a person subject to immigration control, and the rules in this part of this *Handbook* do not apply to you unless you are claiming for a partner or child who is a person subject to immigration control. However, if you are an EEA national, you may still be refused benefit for other reasons, including if you do not satisfy the presence and residence conditions (see Part 4).

- If you are not an EEA national, but you have a right to reside under European Union (EU) law (eg, as a family member of an EEA worker – see p164), you do not require leave to enter or remain.[2] If this applies to you, you cannot be refused benefit on the basis of your immigration status even if, for example, you have been given leave to enter or remain on condition that you do not have recourse to public funds, or as a result of a maintenance undertaking. The conditions attached to any leave you have do not have any effect while you have such a right to reside.[3]

You require leave to enter or remain, but do not have it

If you are not an EEA national and require leave to enter or remain in the UK but do not have it, you are 'a person subject to immigration control'.[4] If you are not an EEA national, you require leave to enter or remain in the UK unless you are:

- a person with the right of abode;
- a person with a right of residence in EU law. This applies if, for example, you are:
  - a family member of an EEA national who has a right to reside in the UK (see p164);[5]
  - a Swiss national with a right to reside. As a result of an agreement between Switzerland and the EU, Swiss nationals, in general, have the same residence rights as EEA nationals and do not require leave to enter or, if they have a right to reside, leave to remain in the UK;[6]
  - a family member of a Swiss national with a right to reside;
  - the primary carer of a British citizen who is in the UK, and it is necessary for you to have a right to reside in the UK so that s/he can continue to reside within the EU.[7] **Note:** although you do not require leave and are therefore not defined as a 'person subject to immigration control', you are still excluded from benefits that require a right to reside, because this particular right to reside does not satisfy the right to reside requirement (see p115). However, you are not excluded from other benefits that do not require a right to reside, such as personal independence payment (PIP) and carer's allowance (CA). If the British citizen is a child, you may also be able to get support under the Children Act 1989 (or Children (Scotland) Act 1995) from your local authority (see p450). If you are a primary carer in this category, you should obtain specialist immigration advice as it may be possible for you to obtain leave to remain that would give you access to benefits.

All other non-EEA nationals require leave to enter or remain in the UK. If you are not an EEA national and not in any of the above groups, you are a person subject to immigration control if you do not have leave to enter or remain. For more information on when leave to enter or remain is granted, see Chapter 3.

Examples of when you require leave to enter or remain but do not have it include if you:

- are an asylum seeker with temporary admission (see p14);
- have overstayed your limited leave to remain – ie, you did not apply for further leave before your period of leave expired. **Note:** if you apply for further leave on the same or a different basis before your current leave expires, your leave is extended from the date it would have expired until your application is decided or withdrawn. In this situation, you are not someone who requires leave but does not have it;[8]
- have entered the UK illegally and since then have not obtained any leave to remain;
- are subject to a deportation order.

Note: there are close links between the benefit authorities and the Home Office UK Visas and Immigration (UKVI). Making a claim for benefit could alert the immigration authorities to your presence and status in the UK. If you are an illegal entrant or an overstayer, or you are unsure of your immigration status, get specialist immigration advice before making a claim for benefits (see Appendix 2).

Your leave has a no recourse to public funds condition

You are a 'person subject to immigration control' if you have leave to enter or remain in the UK which is subject to a condition that you do not have recourse to public funds.[9]

Most people admitted to the UK with time-limited leave given for a particular purpose, such as spouses/civil partners, students or visitors, are given leave to stay on condition that they do not have recourse to public funds. Increasingly, this condition is also being added to those given leave to remain for other reasons, such as family ties, so you should always check whether your leave is subject to this condition.

People granted refugee leave, humanitarian protection (see p32) or, in most cases, discretionary leave (see p36) do not have any condition restricting access to public funds.

Indefinite leave (see p23) is never given with this condition attached. However, if you have been granted indefinite leave as a result of someone else undertaking to maintain and accommodate you, you come under the definition of a 'person subject to immigration control' (see p61).

What are public funds

'Public funds' are defined in the Immigration Rules as:[10]
- attendance allowance;
- CA;
- child benefit;
- child tax credit;
- council tax benefit (now abolished);
- council tax reduction;
- disability living allowance;
- income-related employment and support allowance (ESA);
- homelessness assistance and housing provided under specific provisions;
- housing benefit (HB);
- income support (IS);
- income-based jobseeker's allowance (JSA);
- local welfare assistance (see p443);
- pension credit;
- PIP;
- severe disablement allowance;
- social fund payments;
- universal credit (UC);
- working tax credit.

Only the benefits, tax credits and other assistance listed in the Immigration Rules are public funds. Therefore, if you get any other benefit, or other financial help, you are not in breach of any 'no recourse to public funds' condition attached to your leave.

If you have recourse to public funds when your leave prohibits you, you have breached a condition of your leave. This may affect your right to remain in the UK. You could be liable to be deported, have further leave refused and/or be prosecuted for committing a criminal offence.[11]

If you are subject to a 'no recourse to public funds' condition, you are defined as a 'person subject to immigration control' and (unless you are exempt – see Chapter 8) are not entitled to the above benefits and tax credits.

However, if you come within one of the exceptions, you can claim and receive these benefits as (except for council tax reduction), you are not regarded as having recourse to public funds under the Immigration Rules.[12] If you claim council tax reduction as a result of being exempt, you still count as having recourse to public funds.[13] This is because the council tax reduction regulations are not referred to by the part of the Immigration Rules that disregards claims made as a result of exemptions.[14]

Note: you are regarded as having recourse to public funds if someone else's benefit is increased because of your presence.[15] For example, if the amount of your partner's HB is greater because you are included in her/his claim, this counts as recourse to public funds. You have therefore breached a condition of your leave, which could jeopardise your immigration status (see p25). Get specialist immigration advice before making a claim (see Appendix 2).

Domestic violence

If you were granted leave to enter or remain in the UK as a spouse, civil partner or unmarried partner (including a same-sex partner), but that relationship has broken down because of domestic violence, you may be able to apply for leave to remain under the 'destitution domestic violence' concession (see p35). This leave lasts for three months and is not subject to any condition that you do not have recourse to public funds. During this period of leave, you are not defined as a 'person subject to immigration control' and can, therefore, claim all benefits, subject to the normal conditions of entitlement.[16]

If you apply for indefinite leave (under what is commonly known as the 'domestic violence rule'[17]) before this period of leave expires, your leave is extended while the Home Office determines your application. You continue not to be defined as a 'person subject to immigration control', and continue to be entitled to benefits.

If you do not apply for indefinite leave by the end of the three months, you once again become a 'person subject to immigration control'. If you are claiming any of the benefits listed on p65, your entitlement ceases unless you come into any of the exempt groups listed on p66.

If you were originally granted leave on the basis of your relationship, but in some other way to those referred to above, you should obtain specialist immigration advice, as caselaw developments in this area are pending (see p35).

Your leave is given as a result of a maintenance undertaking

If you are a non-EEA national who has leave to enter or remain in the UK given as a result of a maintenance undertaking, you are a 'person subject to immigration control'.[18]

***

Maintenance undertaking

A '**maintenance undertaking**' means a written undertaking given by another person under the Immigration Rules to be responsible for your maintenance and accommodation.[19]

***

There are specific Home Office forms on which an undertaking can be given. However, no official form need be used, provided the undertaking is sufficiently formal and definite.[20] The document must contain a promise or agreement that the other person will maintain and accommodate you in the future. If it merely contains a statement about her/his present abilities and intentions, it does not amount to an undertaking.[21]

Your leave is considered to be 'as a result of a maintenance undertaking' if this was a factor in granting it. It does not need to have been the only, or even a major, factor.[22] However, if the maintenance undertaking was not relevant to your being granted leave, its existence does not make you a 'person subject to immigration control'.

If it is unclear whether or not your leave was granted as a result of a maintenance undertaking, the onus is on the benefit authority to prove that it was.[23] If your leave has been granted outside the Immigration Rules, the causal connection between the leave and the undertaking cannot be inferred.[24]

If you are in doubt about whether you have leave given as a result of an undertaking, get specialist immigration advice (see Appendix 2).

Consequences for your sponsor if you claim benefits

If you have leave to enter or remain as a result of a maintenance undertaking and you claim benefits, it is possible that the person(s) who signed the undertaking to maintain and accommodate you could be asked to repay any IS, income-based JSA, income-related ESA or UC paid to you. However, in practice, this provision is rarely used because the rules for these benefits exclude from entitlement people with this form of leave for the first five years (unless the person(s) who gave the undertaking has died – see p67).

In certain circumstances, the DWP can recover any IS or UC paid to you from the person who gave the undertaking.[25] Recovery is through the magistrates' court (in Scotland, the sheriff court).

The DWP can also prosecute for failure to maintain if that failure results in the payment of IS, income-based JSA, income-related ESA or UC.[26]

As the DWP can recover benefit or to take court action, if it asks you about an undertaking, you should obtain independent advice (see Appendix 2).

Sponsors

People who have been given leave to enter or remain as the result of a maintenance undertaking are often referred to as '**sponsored people**' and those giving the undertakings as '**sponsors**'. This terminology is used by the benefit authorities, including in their guidance to decision makers. However, the term 'sponsor' is also used in connection with other types of leave and this can lead to confusion and errors in decision making. For example, the word occurs in the Immigration Rules in relation to those seeking leave to enter or remain on the basis of their relationship to their partner (see p26),[27] and people commonly describe themselves as having been 'sponsored' by their partner when they are granted such leave. The Upper Tribunal has provided a helpful discussion of this confusion.[28]

Another common area of confusion is when a family member of someone with refugee leave or humanitarian protection is given leave to enter or remain under the family reunion provisions (see p80). Although the person with refugee leave or humanitarian protection is not required to provide a maintenance undertaking, the confusion arises because the

Home Office policy on family reunion and the entry visa given to the family member uses the word 'sponsor'.

It is important to remember that it is only if you have been given leave to enter or remain *as a result* of an undertaking that you come within this group of people who are defined as 'people subject to immigration control'. However, if you have been given time-limited leave to enter or remain because, for example, you were 'sponsored' by your spouse/civil partner, your leave is subject to a 'no recourse to public funds' condition and you come within the second group of people subject to immigration control (see p59).

In order not to add to any existing confusion, this *Handbook* makes minimal use of the word 'sponsor'.

If you have leave to remain only because you are appealing

If you are a non-EEA national who has leave to enter or remain, but only because your leave has been extended while you appeal against a decision to vary or refuse to vary your leave (see p47), you may be a 'person subject to immigration control'.[29]

If you have time-limited leave (see p44), you can apply to extend your leave or apply for further leave to remain on a different basis. Provided you do this before your existing leave expires, this leave is extended from the date it would have expired until your application is decided by UKVI.[30] You therefore continue to have the same type of leave, subject to the same conditions, until your application is decided.

If your application is refused and you are entitled to appeal against the refusal from within the UK (or seek an administrative review of that refusal), you continue to have the same type of leave during the short time period in which you can do this.[31]

If you appeal from within the UK (or seek an administrative review) within the time limit, your leave is extended until the appeal or review is dealt with.[32] You continue to have the same type of leave, subject to the same conditions, while your appeal (or review) is pending.

However, during the time when your leave is extended because your appeal is pending, you *may* count as a 'person subject to immigration control'.[33]

The reason why this is not completely clear is because the relevant part of the definition of a 'person subject to immigration control' cross-refers to a provision that has now been revoked. Consequently, you only come within that part of the definition if the cross reference is read as a reference to a different, subsequent provision. There is no caselaw on this issue and it may be arguable that no one is is defined as a 'person subject to immigration control' on this basis.

In practice, if this part of the definition does apply, it only makes a difference to your benefit and tax credit entitlement if your original leave did not have a 'no recourse to public funds' condition. Otherwise, you were already a person subject to immigration control and an extension of your leave simply means that you carry on being so.

Example

Banu is an Iranian national who was granted 30 months' discretionary leave in the UK without any public funds condition attached. She is not a 'person subject to immigration control' and so has full access to benefits and tax credits during the period of her leave. Just before her discretionary leave expires, she applies for a further period of discretionary leave. Her application is refused. Banu has a right to appeal against this decision from within the UK, and she does so immediately. Her discretionary leave is extended while the appeal is pending. The benefit authorities may argue that she is now a 'person subject to immigration control' as she has leave only because she is appealing.

Notes

3. **Who is a 'person subject to immigration control'**
   1 s115(9) IAA 1999
   2 s7 IA 1988
   3 Sch 2 para 1(2) I(EEA) Regs
   4 s115(9)(a) IAA 1999
   5 s7 IA 1988; reg 11 I(EEA) Regs
   6 *The Agreement Between the European Community and its Member States, of the one part, and the Swiss Confederation, of the other, on the Free Movement of Persons,* Luxembourg, 21 June 1999, Cmd 5639; reg 2 I(EEA) Regs defines Switzerland as an EEA state; reg 11 provides that no EEA national requires leave to enter the UK.
   7 *Zambrano,* C-34/09 [2011] ECR I-01177; *Dereci and Others,* C-256/11 [2011] ECR I-11315
   8 s3C IA 1971
   9 s115(9)(b) IAA 1999
   10 para 6 IR
   11 s24(1)(b)(ii) IA 1971
   12 para 6B IR
   13 para 6A IR
   14 para 6B IR
   15 para 6A IR
   16 Confirmed in Vol 2, paras 073191-94 DMG
   17 paras 289A-C IR
   18 s115(9)(c) IAA 1999
   19 s115(10) IAA 1999
   20 *R (Begum) v Social Security Commissioner* [2003] EWHC 3380 (Admin); CIS/2474/1999; CIS/2816/2002 and CIS/47/2002
   21 *Ahmed v SSWP* [2005] EWCA Civ 535; CIS/426/2003
   22 CIS/3508/2001
   23 R(PC) 1/09
   24 R(PC) 1/09; *SJ v SSWP (SPC)* [2015] UKUT 505 (AAC)
   25 s106 SSAA 1992
   26 s105 SSAA 1992
   27 para 6 IR
   28 *OO v SSWP (SPC)* [2013] UKUT 335 (AAC)
   29 s115(9)(d) IAA 1999
   30 s3C(2)(a) IA 1971
   31 s3C(2)(b) and (d) IA 1971
   32 s3C(2)(c) and (d) IA 1971
   33 s115(9)(d) IAA 1999 refers to leave continuing while you appeal because of the rule in Sch 4 para 17. Sch 4 para 17 was repealed by NIAA 2002, which also inserted s3C into IA 1971. The reference to Sch 4 para 17 in s115(9)(d), therefore, now arguably must be read as a reference to s3C IA 1971 (see s17(2) IA 1978).

Chapter 8

....

People subject to immigration control and benefits

This chapter covers:
1. Benefits and tax credits affected by immigration status (below)
2. People subject to immigration control who can be entitled (p66)
3. Partners and children who are subject to immigration control (p73)

Before using the information in this chapter, you should establish whether you, your partner or child are a 'person subject to immigration control'. This is explained in Chapter 7.

---

1. Benefits and tax credits affected by immigration status

The general rule is that if you are defined as a 'person subject to immigration control' (see p57), you are excluded from council tax reduction[1] (see p439) and the following benefits and tax credits:[2]

- attendance allowance;
- carer's allowance;
- child benefit;
- child tax credit;
- disability living allowance;
- contributory employment and support allowance (ESA) in youth;[3]
- income-related ESA;
- housing benefit;
- incapacity benefit in youth;[4]
- income support;
- income-based jobseeker's allowance (JSA);
- pension credit;
- personal independence payment;
- severe disablement allowance;
- social fund payments;

8

Chapter 8: People subject to immigration control and benefits
2. People subject to immigration control who can be entitled

- universal credit;
- working tax credit.

However, there are limited exceptions which mean that, despite being a person subject to immigration control, you can claim means-tested benefits (see below), non-means-tested benefits (see p68) and tax credits (see p71).

Even if cannot claim yourself, a family member might be able to claim a benefit that includes an amount for you, or you might be able to make a joint claim (see p73).

A person subject to immigration control is only excluded from the above benefits and tax credits, so you can claim any other benefit. For example, if you have paid sufficient national insurance contributions, you can claim any of the contributory benefits – eg, retirement pension, contribution-based JSA and contributory ESA. You can also claim benefits that depend on previous employment – eg, maternity allowance (MA) or industrial injuries benefits. You may also be able to get help from your local welfare assistance scheme (see p443). **Note:** the government intends to make it a condition of entitlement to contribution-based JSA, contributory ESA, MA and statutory sick, maternity, adoption, paternity and shared parental pay that you be entitled to work in the UK.[5] See CPAG's online service and *Welfare Rights Bulletin* for updates.

2. People subject to immigration control who can be entitled

Although the general rule is that you are excluded from the benefits and tax credits on p65 if you are defined as a 'person subject to immigration control', there are exceptions that mean you can still be entitled. The exceptions vary between the different categories of benefits and tax credits, so being in an exempt group for one category does not necessarily mean you can receive a benefit in a different category.

Note: if your leave prohibits you from having recourse to public funds (see p25), you can still claim any benefit to which you are entitled on the basis of being in an exempt group (but not council tax reduction), even though these benefits (except employment and support allowance (ESA) in youth and incapacity benefit (IB) in youth) are defined as 'public funds'. This is because the Immigration Rules do not regard you as having recourse to public funds, if you are entitled to them because you are in an exempt group (see p59).[6]

Means-tested benefits

If you are in any of the exempt groups below, being a person subject to immigration control does not exclude you from getting:[7]

Chapter 8: People subject to immigration control and benefits
2. People subject to immigration control who can be entitled

8

- income support (IS);
- income-based jobseeker's allowance (JSA);
- income-related ESA;
- pension credit;
- housing benefit;
- universal credit (UC).

Your leave is as a result of an undertaking and you have been resident for five years

You are not excluded from the above means-tested benefits on the basis of being a person subject to immigration control if you have:[8]

- leave to enter or remain given as a result of a maintenance undertaking (see p61); *and*
- been resident in the UK for at least five years since either the date the undertaking was given or the date when you came to the UK, whichever is later.

If you go abroad during the five years, you may still count as resident in the UK during your absence. This depends on the duration and circumstances of your absence (see p95).[9] If your absence abroad is such that you cease to be resident in the UK, you can add together periods of residency either side of the gaps in order to meet the five-year rule.[10]

Your leave is as result of an undertaking and your sponsor has died

You are not excluded from the above means-tested benefits on the basis of being a person subject to immigration control if:[11]

- you have leave to enter or remain given as a result of a maintenance undertaking (see p61); *and*
- the person who gave the undertaking (often referred to as your 'sponsor') has died. If the undertaking was given by more than one person, they must all have died.

Nationals of Turkey and Macedonia

You are not excluded from the above means-tested benefits on the basis of being a person subject to immigration control if you are:[12]

- a national of a country that has ratified either the European Convention on Social and Medical Assistance or the European Social Charter (1961). The only non-European Economic Area (EEA) countries to which this applies are Turkey and Macedonia; *and*
- lawfully present in the UK. You satisfy this if you currently have leave to enter or remain in the UK.

8

Chapter 8: People subject to immigration control and benefits
2. People subject to immigration control who can be entitled

Note:
- You are also not excluded from council tax reduction by your immigration status if you come into this category.[13] However, if your leave is subject to a 'no recourse to public funds' condition and you receive council tax reduction as a result of being in this category, this counts as having recourse to public funds and so breaches the condition of your leave.[14] This is because the council tax reduction regulations are not referred to by the part of the Immigration Rules that disregards claims made as a result of exemptions.[15]
- You must satisfy all the other conditions of entitlement, including the requirement to have a right to reside (see p115).[16] Therefore, if you are an asylum seeker with temporary admission in the UK, although you are 'lawfully present', you are likely to be excluded from benefit or council tax reduction, because having temporary admission does not give you a right to reside.[17]

You applied for asylum before April 2000

You are not excluded from the above means-tested benefits (except UC) on the basis of being a person subject to immigration control if:[18]
- you claimed asylum before 3 April 2000 and you have not had a decision on your asylum application (or appeal if it was against a decision made before 5 February 1996), or you were part of the benefit family of someone who applied for asylum and was receiving a means-tested benefit on 4 February 1996; *and*
- you are covered by the rules on transitional protection. See Chapter 58 of the 2011/12 edition of CPAG's *Welfare Benefits and Tax Credits Handbook* for these.

Non-means-tested benefits

If you are in any of the exempt groups below, being a person subject to immigration control does not exclude you from getting any of the following non-means-tested benefits:[19]
- attendance allowance (AA);
- carer's allowance;
- child benefit;
- disability living allowance (DLA);
- ESA in youth;
- IB for incapacity in youth;
- personal independence payment (PIP);
- severe disablement allowance.

Your leave is as a result of an undertaking

You are not excluded from the above non-means-tested benefits on the basis of being a person subject to immigration control if your leave to enter or remain was given as a result of a maintenance undertaking (see p61).[20]

Chapter 8: People subject to immigration control and benefits
2. People subject to immigration control who can be entitled

8

Note: your entitlement to benefit still depends on your satisfying all the other conditions of entitlement, including those on presence and residence (see Part 4).

You are a family member of a European Economic Area national

You are not excluded from the above non-means-tested benefits on the basis of being a person subject to immigration control if you are a 'family member' of an EEA national.[21]

'**Family member**' is not defined in the regulations and it is therefore arguable that it should be given its ordinary everyday meaning and include, for example, a sister or uncle, as well as a partner.

It is also arguable that no additional conditions should be placed on the EEA national. So, for example, British citizens who have never left the UK should be covered, as should other EEA nationals in the UK who do not have a right to reside.

In practice, decision makers often interpret who is covered in this way, and child benefit guidance states that you are covered if your family member is an EEA or Swiss national or UK national, including if s/he is the child for whom you are claiming child benefit, or your partner or spouse.[22]

However, a much more restrictive view was taken by a commissioner in a case concerning DLA. This held that someone only comes into this exempt group if they are a 'family member' as narrowly defined in European law (see p165) and that EEA nationals are only covered if they are exercising certain European Union (EU) rights – eg, as a 'worker'.[23]

If you are refused benefit because the decision maker has followed this decision and used a more restrictive interpretation of who is a family member of an EEA national, you should challenge the decision on the basis that the case was wrongly decided. In support of your challenge, cite a more recent case in which a Northern Ireland commissioner considered this earlier decision in detail, but rejected its reasoning.[24] However, Northern Irish decisions are not binding on the First-tier Tribunal in Great Britain and so its decision would need to be appealed to the Upper Tribunal, which could then follow the reasoning of the Northern Irish decision. **Note:** the Upper Tribunal has considered both judgments and preferred the reasoning of the earlier, more restrictive, decision.[25] However, this view was not part of the actual decision and is, therefore, not legally binding.

If your leave is subject to the condition that you do not have recourse to public funds, the Home Office does not regard you as having recourse if you are entitled to a benefit because you are in an exempt group (see p59). If you are paid a non-contributory benefit because the benefit authority accepts that you are in an exempt group, but the Home Office takes the view (due to the above caselaw) that you are not, receipt of that benefit could then be regarded as having recourse to public funds and, therefore, a breach of the conditions of your leave. CPAG is not aware of any such cases, but get specialist immigration advice if this could affect you.

8

Chapter 8: People subject to immigration control and benefits
2. People subject to immigration control who can be entitled

Note: 'family members' (as defined in European law) of EEA nationals who have residence rights (eg, as workers) are not excluded from non-means-tested benefits, as they are not defined as 'people subject to immigration control'. This is because they do not require leave to be in the UK, as they have rights under EU residence law (see p58).

Nationals of Algeria, Morocco, San Marino, Tunisia and Turkey

You are not excluded from the non-means-tested benefits listed above on the basis of being a person subject to immigration control if you:[26]

- are a national of Algeria, Morocco, San Marino, Tunisia or Turkey and you are either currently lawfully working (see below) in Great Britain, or you have ceased lawfully working for a reason such as pregnancy, childcare, illness or accident, or because you have reached retirement age;[27] *or*
- you are living with a member of your family (see p265) covered by the above bullet point.

Lawfully working

'**Lawfully working**' has been equated with being an 'insured person' under the EU co-ordination rules (see p264).[28] In broad terms, this means that you must have been insured by paying (or being credited with) national insurance (NI) contributions.[29] It is likely that you will only be accepted as lawfully working if your work does not breach any work restrictions attached to your leave or, if you are an asylum seeker, you have permission to work from UK Visas and Immigration (UKVI).

For further details on the agreements with these countries, see p300.

You are covered by a reciprocal agreement

You are not excluded from claiming AA, DLA, PIP or child benefit (but not the other non-means-tested benefits listed on p68) on the basis of being a person subject to immigration control if you are covered by a reciprocal agreement the UK has with another country.[30] In practice, this is most helpful for child benefit and, in particular, if you are covered by the agreement with former Yugoslavia which applies to Bosnia-Herzegovina, Kosovo, Macedonia, Montenegro and Serbia.[31]

See p291 for more information about reciprocal agreements.

You have been in receipt of a benefit since 1996

You are not excluded from the non-means-tested benefits on p68 on the basis of being a person subject to immigration control if you have received that particular benefit continuously since 4 February 1996 (6 October 1996 for child benefit).[32]

Chapter 8: People subject to immigration control and benefits
2. People subject to immigration control who can be entitled

8

This transitional protection only enables you to continue to receive that benefit. You cannot make a new claim. If you are receiving benefit on this basis, your transitional protection (and therefore your entitlement) ends if:

- your benefit award ends;
- you request a revision or supersession; *or*
- your asylum application (if any) is decided or abandoned.

If you think you may be getting benefit as a result of this transitional protection, it is important that you do not request a revision or supersession, as this will bring your entitlement to an end. However, given that you must have been getting benefit continuously since 1996 and still be a person subject to immigration control, the number of claimants affected will be extremely small.

Tax credits

If you are in any of the exempt groups below, being a person subject to immigration control does not exclude you from getting child tax credit (CTC) or working tax credit (WTC).[33] Some of the exempt groups only apply to one of the tax credits, and some apply to both.

Note: if you are a person subject to immigration control, but your partner is not (or s/he is in one of the groups below), you can make a joint claim for tax credits (see p75).

Your leave is as a result of an undertaking and you have been resident for five years

You are not excluded from CTC or WTC on the basis of being a person subject to immigration control if you have:[34]

- leave to enter or remain given as a result of a maintenance undertaking (see p61); *and*
- been resident in the UK for at least five years since either the date the undertaking was given or the date when you came to the UK, whichever is later.

If you go abroad during the five years, you may still count as resident in the UK during your absence. This depends on the duration and circumstances of your absence (see p95).[35] If your absence abroad is such that you cease to be resident in the UK, you can add together periods of residency either side of the gaps in order to meet the five-year rule.[36]

Your leave is as a result of an undertaking and your sponsor has died

You are not excluded from CTC or WTC on the basis of being a person subject to immigration control if:[37]

- you have leave to enter or remain given as a result of a maintenance undertaking (see p61); *and*

8

Chapter 8: People subject to immigration control and benefits
2. People subject to immigration control who can be entitled

- the person who gave the undertaking (often referred to as your 'sponsor') has died. If the undertaking was given by more than one person, they must all have died.

Nationals of Turkey and Macedonia

You are not excluded from WTC on the basis of being a person subject to immigration control if you are:[38]

- a national of a country that has ratified either the European Convention on Social and Medical Assistance or the European Social Charter (1961). The only non-EEA countries to which this applies are Turkey and Macedonia; *and*
- lawfully present. You satisfy this if you currently have leave to enter or remain in the UK.

Note: you must still satisfy all the other conditions of entitlement, including working a sufficient number of hours.

If you are an asylum seeker with temporary admission in the UK (see p14), you are accepted as 'lawfully present',[39] but you are only entitled to WTC if you satisfy the other conditions of entitlement. In practice, therefore, since you must work a sufficient number of hours and temporary admission usually prohibits you from working, you cannot benefit from this provision unless you have obtained permission to work from UKVI and you work in accordance with this (see p32).

Nationals of Algeria, Morocco, San Marino, Tunisia and Turkey

You are not excluded from CTC on the basis of being a person subject to immigration control if you are a national of Algeria, Morocco, San Marino, Tunisia or Turkey and:[40]

- you are currently lawfully working in the UK (see p70); *or*
- have ceased lawfully working for a reason such as pregnancy, childcare, illness or accident, or because you have reached retirement age.[41]

For further details on the agreements with these countries, see p300.

You are transferring to child tax credit from income support or income-based jobseeker's allowance

You are not excluded from CTC on the basis of being a person subject to immigration control if you:[42]

- claim CTC on or after 6 April 2004; *and*
- immediately before you claimed CTC, you were entitled to an increase in your IS or income-based JSA for a child because either:
  - you are Turkish and lawfully present (see p67); *or*
  - you applied for asylum before 3 April 2000 and are covered by the transitional protection rules (see p68).

Chapter 8: People subject to immigration control and benefits
3. Partners and children who are subject to immigration control

8

This only applies if you are transferring to CTC from an IS or JSA claim that included amounts for a child. It does not apply if you have not been receiving IS or income-based JSA for a child.

Note: as Macedonia only ratified the European Social Charter on 31 March 2005, nationals of Macedonia cannot benefit from this provision (because they could not have established their entitlement to IS or income-based JSA for a child before 6 April 2004).

Social fund payments

You are not excluded from social fund payments on the basis of being a person subject to immigration control if you are in one of the exempt groups for either means-tested benefits (see p66) or non-means-tested benefits (see p68).[43]

You must meet the other conditions of entitlement, including (except for winter fuel payments) being in receipt of a qualifying benefit. What counts as a qualifying benefit varies for different social fund payments but is broadly the means-tested benefits and, in some circumstances, tax credits. See CPAG's *Welfare Benefits and Tax Credits Handbook* for details.

3. Partners and children who are subject to immigration control

Some benefits and tax credits have special rules that apply if your partner or child who lives with you is a 'person subject to immigration control'. These rules vary, so check the rules for the benefit or tax credit you want to claim.

Means-tested benefits

Income support, income-based jobseeker's allowance and income-related employment and support allowance

If your partner is a person subject to immigration control (see p57), s/he is included in your claim for income support (IS), income-based jobseeker's allowance (JSA), including if you are a joint-claim couple, or income-related employment and support allowance (ESA). However, you are only paid a personal allowance at the single person's rate, unless s/he comes into one of the exempt groups that can get the means-tested benefits on p66, in which case you are paid at the couple rate.[44]

In all cases, your partner is still treated as part of your household and part of your claim. Therefore, her/his work, income and capital can all affect your benefit entitlement. Her/his presence also means you cannot claim IS as a lone parent. Similarly, unless your partner receives a qualifying benefit or is severely

8

Chapter 8: People subject to immigration control and benefits
3. Partners and children who are subject to immigration control

sight impaired or blind, her/his presence might mean that you are not entitled to a severe disability premium.

Premiums are payable if either you or your partner satisfy the qualifying conditions and should be paid at the couple rate.

Note: if your partner's leave to enter or remain in the UK is subject to the condition that s/he does not have recourse to public funds, you should be aware that receiving the couple rate of a premium breaches this condition and could affect her/his right to remain in the UK. Obtain specialist immigration advice before making a claim that includes a higher premium because of your partner.

Pension credit

If your partner is a person subject to immigration control (irrespective of whether or not s/he is in one of the exempt groups listed on pp66–68), s/he is treated as not being part of your household.[45] This means that you are paid as a single person and your partner's income and capital do not affect your claim. If you would otherwise be entitled to the additional amount for severe disability, your partner's presence may mean that you are not entitled to it, as the DWP may count her/him as 'normally residing with' you for this purpose.[46] See CPAG's *Welfare Benefits and Tax Credits Handbook* for more details on the additional amount.

Housing benefit

If your partner and/or child for whom you are responsible is a person subject to immigration control, this does not affect the amount you are paid. Your partner is included in your claim and your applicable amount includes the couple rate of the personal allowance and any premiums to which either of you are entitled. Similarly, your child is included in your claim and your applicable amount includes a personal allowance for her/him, together with any premiums for which s/he qualifies.

Note: if your partner's and/or child's leave is subject to a condition that s/he does not have recourse to public funds, you should be aware that your claim for housing benefit could (depending on your circumstances) result in additional public funds being paid as a result of her/his presence. This breaches the 'no recourse to public funds' condition and could affect her/his right to remain in the UK (see p59). Obtain specialist immigration advice before making a claim (see Appendix 2).

Council tax reduction (see p439) is also defined as a public fund, so if your council tax reduction is greater (eg, because you lose a single person's discount) as a result of the presence of someone whose leave is subject to a 'no recourse to public funds' condition, that person's right to remain in the UK could be affected. Obtain specialist immigration advice before making a claim (see Appendix 2).

Chapter 8: People subject to immigration control and benefits
3. Partners and children who are subject to immigration control

8

Universal credit

If your partner is a person subject to immigration control (see p57) and is not in one of the groups who can get universal credit (UC) listed on p66, you must claim UC as a single person.[47] Your award is based on the maximum amount for a single person, but your partner's income and capital are taken into account.[48]

Non-means-tested benefits

Non-means-tested benefits that are either contributory or based on employment are not affected by your or your partner's or child's immigration status. **Note:** the government intends to make it a condition of entitlement to contribution-based JSA, contributory ESA, maternity allowance and statutory sick, maternity, adoption, paternity and shared parental pay that you be entitled to work in the UK.[49] See CPAG's online service and *Welfare Rights Bulletin* for updates.

Only the claimant's immigration status affects entitlement to non-contributory, non-means-tested benefits. Therefore, for **child benefit**, if you are not a person subject to immigration control, or you are but are in one of the exempt groups (see p68), you can claim for any child for whom you are responsible, regardless of the child's immigration status. However, if your child has leave which is subject to a 'no recourse to public funds' condition, a claim for child benefit will result in additional public funds being paid as a result of her/his presence. This could affect her/his right to remain in the UK (see p59). Obtain specialist immigration advice before making a claim.

If your child is not a person subject to immigration control, or s/he is but s/he comes into one of the exempt groups on p68, s/he can claim **disability living allowance**, even if you are a person subject to immigration control.

Tax credits

If your partner is a person subject to immigration control and you are not, or you are but are in one of the exempt groups on p71, your joint claim for tax credits is treated as if your partner were not subject to immigration control. You are therefore entitled to working tax credit (WTC) and child tax credit (CTC).[50] However, unless you or your partner are responsible for a child, or your partner is a national of Macedonia or Turkey and is lawfully present in the UK, your WTC does not include the couple element.[51]

Note: if your partner is a person subject to immigration control because s/he requires leave and does not have it and you make a joint claim for CTC, in practice an award is usually made. This is despite the fact that each partner making a joint claim for CTC is required to have a right to reside (see p117). It appears that HM Revenue and Customs treats the above exception as overriding this. If your joint claim is refused for this reason, argue that it should be treated as a single claim. Get advice if you are in this situation.

If your partner is a person subject to immigration control because s/he requires leave and does not have it and does not have a national insurance (NI) number, you can still make a joint claim as s/he is exempt from the NI number requirement (see p336).

There are no immigration status conditions for children. Any child for whom you are responsible is included in your claim and your CTC and/or WTC includes amounts for her/him, provided you meet all the conditions of entitlement, including, for example, that the child normally lives with you.

If you are not a person subject to immigration control, but your partner is because her/his leave is subject to a 'no recourse to public funds' condition , s/he is *not* regarded as having such recourse by making a joint tax credits claim with you. This means that you and your partner can make the joint claim without it affecting her/his right to remain in the UK. If such a joint claim includes a child whose leave is subject to a 'no recourse to public funds' condition, any tax credits awarded in respect of that child are also not regarded as having had recourse.[52]

However, if your claim for CTC or WTC is not a joint claim as described above (ie, it is a single claim or a joint claim but neither you nor your partner are a person subject to immigration control) and it includes an amount for a child whose leave is subject to a 'no recourse to public funds' condition, this breaches that condition and could affect her/his right to remain in the UK (see p59). Obtain specialist immigration advice before making a claim (see Appendix 2).

Notes

1. Benefits and tax credits affected by immigration status
1 Reg 13 CTRS(PR)E Regs; reg 19 CTR(SPC)S Regs; reg 19 CTR(S) Regs; reg 29 CTRSPR(W) Regs; Sch para 20 CTRS(DS)W Regs
2 s115(1) IAA 1999; reg 3(1) TC(Imm) Regs
3 Reg 11(1)(b) ESA Regs; reg 12(1)(b) ESA Regs 2013
4 Reg 16(1)(b) SS(IB) Regs
5 ss61-63 WRA 2012

2. People subject to immigration control who can be entitled
6 para 6B IR
7 Reg 2(1)-(1A) and Sch Part 1 SS(IA)CA Regs
8 Reg 2(1)-(1A) and Sch Part 1 para 3 SS(IA)CA Regs
9 CPC/1035/2005
10 R(IS) 2/02
11 Reg 2(1)-(1A) and Sch Part 1 para 2 SS(IA)CA Regs
12 Reg 2(1)-(1A) and Sch Part 1 para 4 SS(IA)CA Regs, confirmed in *OD v SSWP (JSA)* [2015] UKUT 438 (AAC)

13 Reg 13(1A) CTRS(PR)E Regs; reg 19(2) CTR(S) Regs; reg 19(2) CTR(SPC)S Regs; reg 29(2) CTRSPR(W) Regs; Sch para 20(2) CTRS(DS)W Regs
14 para 6A IR
15 para 6B IR
16 *Yesiloz v London Borough of Camden* [2009] EWCA Civ 415
17 *Szoma v SSWP* [2005] UKHL 64, reported as R(IS) 2/06 and see *Yesiloz v London Borough of Camden* [2009] EWCA Civ 415
18 Reg 12 SS(IA)CA Regs; reg 12 SS(PFA)MA Regs
19 Reg 2(2), (3) and (4)(b) and Sch Part 2 SS(IA)CA Regs; reg 2(1)(a)(ib) SS(AA) Regs; reg 9(1)(ia) SS(ICA) Regs; reg 16(d)(ii) SS(PIP) Regs; reg 2(1)(a)(ib) SS(DLA) Regs; reg 11(1)(b) and (3) ESA Regs; reg 12(1)(b) and (3) ESA Regs 2013; reg 16(1)(b) and (5) SS(IB) Regs
20 Reg 2 and Sch Part 2 para 4 SS(IA)CA Regs
21 Reg 2 and Sch Part 2 para 1 SS(IA)CA Regs
22 para 10140 CBTM
23 CDLA/708/2007
24 *JFP v DSD (DLA)* [2012] NICom 267
25 *MS v SSWP (DLA)* [2016] UKUT 42 (AAC)
26 Reg 2 and Sch Part II SS(IA)CA Regs
27 *Zoulika Krid v Caisse Nationale d'Assurance Vieillesse des Travailleurs Salariés (CNAVTS)*, C-103/94 [1995] ECR I-00719, para 26
28 *Sema Sürül v Bundesanstalt für Arbeit*, C-262/96 [1999] ECR I-02685
29 *Sürül v Bundesanstalt für Arbeit*, C-262/96 [1999] ECR I-02685, in particular paras 85-86 and 93
30 Reg 2(3) SS(IA)CA Regs
31 FANIII(Y)O
32 Reg 12(10) SS(IA)CA Regs
33 Reg 3(1) TC(Imm) Regs
34 Reg 3(1) TC(Imm) Regs, case 1
35 CPC/1035/2005
36 R(IS) 2/02
37 Reg 3(1) TC(Imm) Regs, case 2
38 Reg 3(1) TC(Imm) Regs, case 4
39 *Szoma v SSWP* [2005] UKHL 64, reported as R(IS) 2/06 and see *Yesiloz v London Borough of Camden* [2009] EWCA Civ 415
40 Reg 3(1) TC(Imm) Regs, case 5
41 *Zoulika Krid v Caisse Nationale d'Assurance Vieillesse des Travailleurs Salariés (CNAVTS)*, C-103/94 [1995] ECR I-00719, para 26
42 Reg 3(1) TC(Imm) Regs, case 4
43 Reg 2 SS(IA)CA Regs

3. Partners and children who are subject to immigration control
44 **IS** Reg 21(3) and Sch 7 para 16A IS Regs
JSA Reg 85(4) and Sch 5 para 13A JSA Regs
ESA Reg 69 and Sch 5 para 10 ESA Regs
45 Reg 5(1)(h) SPC Regs
46 Vol 13, para 78946 DMG
47 Reg 3(3) UC Regs
48 Regs 18(2), 22(3) and 36(3) UC Regs
49 ss61-63 WRA 2012
50 Reg 3(2) TC(Imm) Regs
51 Reg 11(4) and (5) WTC(EMR) Regs
52 para 6B IR. The TC(Imm) Regs are made under s42 TCA 2002.

Chapter 9

. . . .

Asylum seekers and refugees

This chapter covers:
1. Asylum seekers (below)
2. Benefits and tax credits for people granted leave (p79)
3. Integration loans (p82)

This chapter explains some of the specific benefit and tax credit rules that apply to asylum seekers and to those who are granted refugee leave, humanitarian protection or discretionary leave following an asylum application. For more information about these categories of leave, see Chapter 4.

---

1. Asylum seekers

You are referred to as an **'asylum seeker'** while you are waiting for a Home Office decision on your application for refugee status (see p31). If you are a non-European Economic Area (EEA) national seeking asylum in the UK, unless you have leave on some other basis or you do not require it (eg, because you are a family member of an EEA national with a right to reside in the UK as a 'worker' – see p58), you come within the definition of a 'person subject to immigration control'. This is because you are someone who requires leave, but does not have it (see p58). You are therefore excluded from the social security benefits listed on p65, unless you are in one of the exempt groups (see p66).

Remember, even if you are in one of the exempt groups, you must still satisfy all the other conditions of entitlement for the particular benefit or tax credit, including the presence and residence conditions (see Part 4).

If benefit can be paid for you, either because you are not excluded from making a claim or because your partner can include you in her/his claim, this does not affect your asylum application. You can receive any benefit defined as a 'public fund' (see p60) because asylum seekers are not subject to the 'no recourse to public funds' condition (see p59). If you receive public funds, this does not affect the outcome of your asylum application.

If your partner is entitled to benefits and you are included in her/his benefit claim, or you make a joint tax credit claim with her/him, and you do not already have a national insurance (NI) number, you are exempt from the NI number requirement (see p336).

If you are excluded from claiming social security benefits because you are a person subject to immigration control, you may be entitled to alternative forms of state support. If you are destitute, you may be eligible for asylum support from the Home Office (see Chapter 21).

Note: asylum support for essential living needs is taken into account as income when calculating any housing benefit your partner claims. It is not taken into account for universal credit (UC) and, if it is 'income in kind', is disregarded for income support (IS), income-based jobseeker's allowance (JSA) and income-related employment and support allowance (ESA).[1]

However, any IS, income-based JSA, income-related ESA or UC your partner receives is taken into account as income when calculating your asylum support (see p397).

If you are not eligible for asylum support or benefits, ask your local authority for help. If you have children, you may be eligible for support under the Children Act 1989 or Children (Scotland) Act 1995 (see p391). You may be able to get assistance from your local authority under one or more of the community care provisions, particularly if you have additional needs as a result of your age, health or disability (see p389). You may also be entitled to help from your local welfare assistance scheme (see p443). See Chapter 21 for more details.

2. Benefits and tax credits for people granted leave

If, following your asylum application, you are granted leave that is not subject to the condition that you do not have recourse to public funds, you are no longer a 'person subject to immigration control'. For example, if you are granted refugee leave, humanitarian protection or discretionary leave, you are not a person subject to immigration control during that period of leave. However, if you are granted leave that is subject to the condition that you do not have recourse to public funds, you come within the definition of a 'person subject to immigration control' (see p59) and you are excluded from the benefits and tax credits listed on p65, unless you are in an exempt group (see p66).

If your leave means you are not a person subject to immigration control, you are no longer excluded from the benefits listed on p65 and can claim all benefits, provided you meet the usual conditions of entitlement. The following rules may also affect you.

- If you are granted refugee leave, humanitarian protection or discretionary leave, you are exempt from the habitual residence test (see p106).

- If you are granted refugee leave or humanitarian protection, you can be joined by certain family members under family reunion provisions (see p33). The benefit authorities sometimes make mistakes about their benefit rights (see below).
- If you are granted refugee leave, you have leave as a result of joining your family member under the family union provisions, or if you or the family member you are joining have humanitarian protection, the Upper Tribunal has held that you should be exempt from the past presence test for personal independence payment, disability living allowance, attendance allowance and carer's allowance (see p209).
- If you are granted refugee leave, you may be able to claim backdated child benefit, guardian's allowance, child tax credit and working tax credit (WTC – see p81).
- If you are granted refugee leave, you may be entitled to income support (IS) while you study English (see p81).
- If you are granted refugee leave or humanitarian protection, you may be eligible for an integration loan (see p82).

Family reunion

If you have been granted refugee leave or humanitarian protection, certain family members may join you under the family reunion rules (see p33).

A family member who comes to the UK and is given leave under these provisions is not a person subject to immigration control and can claim all benefits, provided s/he meets the usual rules of entitlement.

However, sometimes the benefit authorities decide that your family member is a person subject to immigration control on the basis that her/his Home Office documents describe you as her/his 'sponsor' and they wrongly conclude from this that your family member has been given leave as a result of a maintenance undertaking (see p61). This is incorrect. No undertaking is required from a person with refugee leave or humanitarian protection and your family members who come to the UK under the family reunion provisions are not given leave as a result of an undertaking. DWP guidance states this clearly (although it incorrectly states the family member will have indefinite leave).[2]

If you are a family member with leave in the UK under the family reunion provisions and you are refused benefits or tax credits because the decision maker decides you are a person subject to immigration control, you should challenge the decision, and refer the decison maker to the DWP guidance.

Backdated child benefit and tax credits

If you have been granted refugee leave (not humanitarian protection or discretionary leave), you can claim child benefit, guardian's allowance and tax credits and have them backdated to the date of your asylum application (or 6 April 2003 for tax credits, if this is later).[3] Generally, you are required to reclaim tax credits each year. However, under the special backdating rules for refugees, the claim is treated as having been renewed each April.[4] You are treated as having made your claim on the date you claimed asylum and each subsequent April and, therefore, even if you are not currently entitled to tax credits you can claim for the past period.

You must claim backdated tax credits within one month, and child benefit and guardian's allowance within three months, of receiving the Home Office letter granting you leave as a refugee.[5] If the Home Office letter is sent to a solicitor acting for you, the three- or one-month period starts from the date your solicitor receives it.[6]

The amount of tax credits paid is reduced by the amount of asylum support you received for your essential living needs over the period.[7]

In many cases, this is more than the amount of tax credits and, therefore, cancels out any entitlement over the backdated period. However, if you did not receive asylum support or your tax credit entitlement exceeds the amount of asylum support paid (eg, if you worked sufficient hours to qualify for WTC), you can be entitled to an amount of backdated tax credits.

The amount of child benefit and guardian's allowance paid is not reduced by any asylum support you may have received.

Note: there is no equivalent provision in the universal credit (UC) rules. However, if you came under the UC system part way through the period in which your asylum application or appeal was outstanding (eg, when 'full service' UC was introduced in the area where you live), you can claim tax credits for the previous period. You will need to explain this to HM Revenue and Customs (HMRC) when you make your claim and request that, if your claim cannot be processed through the usual computer-based sytems, it be processed clerically. Get advice if HMRC refuses to accept your claim.

Income support for refugees studying English

Refugees who are studying English are one of the categories of people who are entitled to IS.

If you have been granted refugee leave (not humanitarian protection or discretionary leave), you can claim IS for up to nine months while you are studying if you:[8]

- attend, for more than 15 hours a week, a course for the purpose of learning English so you may obtain employment; *and*

- have been in Great Britain for not more than 12 months on the date the course began.

Note: there is no equivalent rule for UC.

3. **Integration loans**

Integration loans are interest-free loans, made to assist people who have recently been granted either refugee status or humanitarian protection to integrate into UK society.

Note: you may also be entitled to help from local welfare assistance schemes (see p443). Depending on the nature of your local scheme, you may want to apply to this before applying for a repayable integration loan, but be aware that many local authorities do not give cash and some require the assistance to be repaid. You may also want to get advice on charitable and other assistance that may be available in your area before applying for a repayable integration loan.

Who can apply

An application for an integration loan is only considered if you are eligible to apply for one and you make a valid application (see p83). Whether or not you are awarded a loan is at the discretion of the decision maker (see below).

You are eligible to apply for an integration loan if you:[9]
- have been granted, after 11 June 2007, refugee leave, humanitarian protection (see p32), or leave to enter or remain as a dependant of someone with either refugee leave or humanitarian protection;
- are aged 18 or over;
- have not previously had an integration loan; *and*
- are, in the view of the Home Secretary, capable of repaying the loan.

When deciding whether to give you a loan, the decision maker must take into account:[10]
- the length of time since your leave was granted;
- your financial position – ie, your income, assets, liabilities and outgoings;
- your likely ability to repay the loan;
- what you intend to use the loan for; *and*
- the total available budget for loans.

Although the legislation does not specify which intended uses of a loan are more likely to be accepted, the application form provides the following headings for you to set amounts against, and guidance to decision makers confirms that these examples of 'integration needs' can be accepted (if they cannot be met through assistance available from Jobcentre Plus):[11]

- help with housing, including:
  - deposits for rented accommodation;
  - rent payments;
  - house-moving expenses;
  - essential items;
- help with finding work, including:
  - travel expenses to attend interviews;
  - work clothing/equipment;
  - initial childcare costs;
  - subsistence while training;
- help with education, including:
  - the cost of a training programme;
  - requalification/professional qualification.

There is also space on the form for other needs that would assist your integration. However, the guidance states that a loan should normally be refused for:[12]

- non-essential items;
- domestic assistance and respite care;
- mobility items;
- general living expenses (including utility bills);
- council tax payments;
- medical items;
- cars, including driving lessons and a licence, unless this is essential for your employment;
- repayment of debts;
- airfares for dependants to join you in the UK.

It is helpful to read the guidance before making your application, as it covers examples of factors that can be relevant. For example, in addition to how long you have been in the UK, your financial independence can also be relevant – your application may be considered weaker if you have been working and living independently in the UK for a long time before you apply than if you were not working or living independently – eg, if you have been receiving asylum support. The guidance also states that decision makers can take your 'character' into account – eg, a loan will usually be refused if you have been convicted of an offence.

Making a valid application

You should apply for a loan by completing the form on the UK Visas and Immigration (UKVI) website. If fully completed, this ensures your application is valid.[13]

To be valid, the application must be in writing and contain:[14]
- your full name;
- your other names you have used;
- your date of birth;
- your address;
- your telephone number (if you have one);
- your email address (if you have one);
- evidence about your leave to remain and your age;
- your national insurance number;
- details of your (and any dependants') income, assets, liabilities and outgoings;
- confirmation of whether any member of your household has applied for or received an integration loan; *and*
- the amount requested.

Decisions, payment and repayments

After you have applied for a loan, you should be sent a written decision stating:[15]
- whether the application was valid;
- if so, whether a loan will be made;
- if so, the amount, conditions and terms of repayment; *and*
- the deadline for responding to say whether you wish to take the loan.

If you are entitled to a loan, a loan agreement should be attached to the decision letter, which you can sign and return to the decision maker. Usually, you must do this within 14 days of being sent the decision. If you are unhappy with the decision, either because you were refused a loan or offered a smaller amount than you need, you can ask for a reconsideration, which is carried out by a different decision maker. Your request for a reconsideration must be received within 14 days of the date on the decision letter.[16] There is no right to an independent appeal.

If UKVI decides that you are entitled to an integration loan, it passes your details to the DWP, which then pays the loan and manages your repayments.

Integration loans are recovered through direct deductions from benefits in the same way as for other third-party debts.[17] The rate of recovery and the start date of deductions should be notified to you. See CPAG's *Welfare Benefits and Tax Credits Handbook* for further details about deductions from benefit.

If direct deductions from your benefit are not possible (eg, because you do not receive a relevant benefit), you should be notified when repayments will begin, and the method, amount and frequency of these.

If your circumstances change, you can ask the DWP to revise the terms of recovery. These should be notified to you in writing.[18]

Notes

1. Asylum seekers
1 **IS** Sch 9 para 21 IS Regs
JSA Sch 7 para 22 JSA Regs
ESA Sch 8 para 22 ESA Regs
HB Sch 5 para 23 HB Regs
UC Reg 66 UC Regs

2. Benefits and tax credits for people granted leave
2 Vol 2, para 070709 DMG
3 **CB/GA** Reg 6(2)(d) CB&GA(Admin) Regs
TC Regs 3(4)-(9) and 4 TC(Imm) Regs
4 Reg 3(6)(b) TC(Imm) Regs
5 **CB/GA** Reg 6(2)(d) CB&GA(Admin) Regs
TC Reg 3(5) TC(Imm) Regs
6 *Tkachuk v SSWP* [2007] EWCA Civ 515; CIS/3797/2003
7 Reg 3(9) TC(Imm) Regs
8 Reg 4ZA(3)(b) and Sch 1B para 18 IS Regs

3. Integration loans
9 Reg 4 ILRFO Regs
10 Reg 6 ILRFO Regs
11 *Integration Loans Policy Guidance*, available at www.gov.uk/government/ uploads/system/uploads/ attachment_data/file/257390/ integration-loans-policyguidance.pdf
12 *Integration Loans Policy Guidance*, available at www.gov.uk/government/ uploads/system/uploads/ attachment_data/file/257390/ integration-loans-policyguidance.pdf, para 9.3
13 www.gov.uk/refugee-integration-loan
14 Reg 5 and Sch ILRFO Regs
15 Reg 8(1) ILRFO Regs
16 *Integration Loans Policy Guidance*, available at www.gov.uk/government/ uploads/system/uploads/ attachment_data/file/257390/ integration-loans-policyguidance.pdf, Part 12
17 Reg 9(1) and (3) ILRFO Regs; Sch 9 para 1 SS(C&P) Regs; Sch 6 para 12 UC,PIP,JSA&ESA(C&P) Regs
18 Reg 10 ILRFO Regs

Part 4

Benefits and residence rules

Chapter 10

· ·

Residence and presence rules: overview

This chapter covers:
1. Introduction (p90)
2. Presence (p91)
3. Past presence (p92)
4. Living in for three months (p92)
5. Residence (p95)
6. Ordinary residence (p96)
7. Habitual residence (p100)
8. The right to reside (p101)

This chapter describes the different residence and presence conditions that apply when you make a claim for benefits and tax credits in the UK. The two most significant conditions are the habitual residence test and the right to reside requirement, which are covered in more detail in Chapter 11. The groups of people who have a right to reside are covered in Chapter 12. The residence and presence requirements for individual benefits and tax credits are covered in Chapter 13.

If you are not a European Economic Area (EEA) national (see p40), first check Part 3 to see if your immigration status means you are excluded from benefits as a 'person subject to immigration control'. If you are not excluded, you must still satisfy the residence and presence conditions described in this chapter.

If you live with a partner or child who is not an EEA national, you should check whether her/his immigration status affects your benefits. If her/his immigration leave is subject to a 'no recourse to public funds' condition, check whether your claim will affect her/his right to stay in the UK (see p73).

If you, or a member of your family included in your claim, go abroad (either temporarily or to stay), see Part 5 for the way this affects your benefits and tax credits.

1. **Introduction**

There are residence and presence conditions for the following benefits and tax credits:
- attendance allowance;
- carer's allowance;
- child benefit;
- child tax credit;
- disability living allowance;
- contributory employment and support allowance (ESA) in youth;
- income-related ESA;
- guardian's allowance;
- housing benefit (residence conditions only, except during an absence from your home);
- incapacity benefit (IB) for incapacity in youth;
- income support;
- income-based jobseeker's allowance (JSA);
- pension credit;
- personal independence payment;
- Category D retirement pension;
- severe disablement allowance;
- social fund payments;
- universal credit;
- working tax credit.

There are presence conditions for the following benefits:
- bereavement payment;
- contributory ESA;
- IB;
- industrial injuries benefit;
- contribution-based JSA;
- maternity allowance;
- retirement pensions;
- severe disablement allowance.

Council tax reduction also has residence conditions (see p439).

There are no residence or presence requirements for statutory sick pay, statutory maternity pay, statutory adoption pay, statutory paternity pay or statutory shared parental pay paid by your employer.

The residence and presence conditions vary between the different benefits and tax credits. If you satisfy the rules for one, it does not necessarily mean you will satisfy the rules for another.

The way in which the different residence and presence conditions affect your entitlement to benefit is set out in the UK benefits and tax credits legislation. Depending on the benefit or tax credit, you may be required to satisfy tests for:

- presence;
- past presence;
- 'living in' for three months;
- residence;
- ordinary residence;
- habitual residence;
- the right to reside.

However, the way the requirements work can be modified by the following.

- The European Union (EU) rules on the co-ordination of social security systems. If these rules apply to you (see p264), they can help you get benefits or tax credits in the UK – eg, by exempting you from certain past presence requirements or by enabling you to count periods of residence (or employment or national insurance contributions) in another European Economic Area (EEA) state to satisfy the conditions of entitlement (see p281). They can also allow you to 'export' certain benefits to other EEA states. **Note:** the EU co-ordination rules are different from the residence rights provided under EU law, which can enable you to satisfy the right to reside requirement. In general, you do not need to know if you are covered by the co-ordination rules to know if you have a right to reside under EU law. The EU co-ordination rules are covered in Chapter 16, and the main ways they can assist with the residence and presence tests are highlighted for each benefit in Chapter 13.

- International agreements, including reciprocal agreements. Reciprocal agreements exist between the UK and some other EEA and non-EEA countries which can help you to qualify for benefits and tax credits if you have recently come to the UK or while you are abroad. They operate in similar ways to the EU co-ordination rules and, in general, apply only when the EU co-ordination rules cannot assist you. There are also some international agreements between EU and non-EU countries, which can also have similar effects (see Chapter 17).

Note: you must also check where you are required to satisfy a particular residence or presence test. This varies for different benefits and tax credits, and can be Great Britain, the UK or the common travel area – ie, the UK, Ireland, the Channel Islands and the Isle of Man.

2. **Presence**

Most benefits and tax credits have rules about presence and absence. You usually must be present in Great Britain at the time you make your claim and continue to be present. There are specific rules that allow you to be treated as present during some temporary absences (see p228) and the European Union co-ordination rules can also mean that the presence requirement does not apply if you are staying or living in another European Economic Area state (see p40). All these exceptions to the requirement to be present vary between the different benefits and tax credits and are covered in Chapters 14 and 15.

To satisfy the presence requirement, you must show that you are physically present in Great Britain. If a benefits authority wants to disqualify you from benefit because you were absent from Great Britain, it must show you were absent throughout that day.[1] This means that, on the day you leave Great Britain and the day you arrive in Great Britain, you count as present.

3. **Past presence**

The following benefits have a past presence requirement:
* attendance allowance;
* carer's allowance;
* disability living allowance;
* employment and support allowance in youth;
* incapacity benefit in youth;
* personal independence payment;
* severe disablement allowance.

In addition to being present at the time you make your claim for the above benefits, you must also have been present for a period of time before you become entitled. The requirement depends on the benefit you are claiming.

If you are covered by the European Union co-ordination rules (see p264), depending on the benefit, these can assist either by exempting you from the past presence requirement or by enabling you to count periods of time in another European Economic Area state.

For more details of the past presence test, including exemptions, for each benefit, see Chapter 13.

4. **Living in for three months**

There is a requirement to have been living, for the past three months, in:
* the common travel area (the UK, Ireland, Channel Islands and the Isle of Man) in order to satisfy the habitual residence test for income-based jobseeker's allowance (JSA) (see p93); or
* the UK for child benefit and child tax credit (CTC) (see p94).

The phrase 'living in' is not defined in the regulations and should, therefore, be given its ordinary, everyday meaning.

You may satisfy this condition even if you have had one or more temporary absences during the three months.[2] Factors such as the reasons for your absence, the intended and actual length of your absence and whether you maintained your accommodation in the common travel area/UK while you were gone are all relevant when deciding whether you ceased 'living in' the common travel area/UK. See p228 for more information about temporary absences. Note, also, for child benefit and CTC only, if you return to the UK after a specific temporary absence, you are exempt from the requirment to have been living in the UK for the past three months (see p94).

If you are covered by the European Union (EU) co-ordination rules (see p264) and have moved to the UK from another European Economic Area (EEA) state, you may be able to use periods of residence in that other EEA state to satisfy this condition by applying the aggregation principle (see p281). This is confirmed in guidance to child benefit and CTC decision makers.[3] However, this guidance is arguably overly restrictive in suggesting that this only applies if your residence would satisfy an entitlement condition to a family benefit in the other state, which would only be the case in Croatia, Cyprus, Denmark and Hungary.

Income-based jobseeker's allowance

To satisfy the habitual residence test (see p104) for income-based JSA, you must have been living in the common travel area for the past three months (in addition to having a right to reside and being habitually resident 'in fact').[4] This requirement does not apply if:

- you are in one of the groups that are exempt from the habitual residence test (see p106);
- any time during the last three months you have worked abroad and paid Class 1 or 2 national insurance (NI) contributions, or been posted abroad as a Crown servant or while a member of HM forces. **Note:**the government has announced that this also applies to family members of HM forces, but at the time of writing the law had not been amended;[5]
- your claim began before 1 January 2014.[6]

If you are covered by the EU co-ordination rules (see p264), it may be possible to argue that this requirement is unlawful.

In the *Swaddling* case, the European Court of Justice (ECJ) held that someone covered by the co-ordination rules cannot be deemed not to be habitually resident in a state merely because the period of actual residence is too short.[7] See p114 for more details.

There is also a separate argument that the requirement is contrary to the principle of equal treatment (see p280). JSA is a benefit intended to facilitate access to the labour market.[8] The ECJ has held that it is legitimate for a state to grant such a benefit to someone only after s/he has established a real link with the labour market of that state.[9] However, requiring a single condition to be satisfied without allowing any other method of establishing a real link to the national labour market has been held to be unlawful.[10] Arguably, the income-based JSA requirement to have been living in the common travel area for three months is such an unlawful condition. This argument is supported by the Advocate General's opinion that a three-month residence requirement for EEA jobseekers to be entitled to a German benefit was unlawful.[11] However, the Court of Justice of the European Union did not address this question in its judgment, as it had already been held that the German benefit was not a benefit designed to facilitate access to the labour market.[12] The argument, in relation to income-based JSA, is currently being considered by the Northern Ireland Commissioners.[13] See CPAG's online service and *Welfare Rights Bulletin* for updates.

Note: you cannot make an 'advance claim' for income-based JSA for a future date when you will have been living in the common travel area for three months because the rules prevent your claim from being treated as made on a future date if you do not satisfy the habitual residence test.[14]

Child benefit and child tax credit

To be treated as present in Great Britain for child benefit, and present in the UK for CTC, you must have been living in the UK for three months, ending on the first day of your entitlement.[15] This requirement does not apply if you:[16]

- are an EEA national who is a 'worker' in the UK (see p140), including if you have retained that status (see p146);
- are an EEA national who is a self-employed person in the UK (see p153), including if you have retained that status (see p157);
- are a Croatian national working in accordance with your worker authorisation document (see p127);
- are a non-EEA national who would be classed as a worker or self-employed person if you were an EEA national;
- are a family member, other than an extended family member (see p165), of someone in any of the above four groups;
- are a refugee;
- have been granted humanitarian protection;
- have been granted leave to remain in the UK under the 'destitution domestic violence' concession, pending an application for indefinite leave to remain under the 'domestic violence rule' (see p35);
- have leave granted outside the Immigration Rules with no restriction on accessing public funds;
- have leave under the displaced persons provisions;

- have been deported or otherwise legally removed from another country to the UK;[17]
- are returning to the UK after a period working abroad and, other than for last three months of your absence, you were paying UK Class 1 or Class 2 NI contributions;
- are returning to the UK after an absence of less than 52 weeks and either:
  - before departing the UK you were ordinarily resident for three months; *or*
  - you were covered by the rules that treat you as present during a temporary absence for eight or 12 weeks during payment of child benefit (see p243) or CTC (see p255).

Note: the child benefit regulations exclude the UK from the definition of EEA state.[18]

If you are not covered by one of the above exemptions, you must satisfy the requirement to have been living in the UK for three months. However, see p92 for ways that you may be able to include time spent outside the UK.

5. **Residence**

The requirement to be simply 'resident', rather than 'ordinarily resident' or 'habitually resident', is only a condition for Category D retirement pension. However, it is a necessary part of being ordinarily resident (see p96) or habitually resident (see p100).

Residence is more than a physical presence in a country and you can be resident without being present – eg, if you are abroad for a short holiday. Similarly, you can be present without being resident.

To be resident in a country, you must be seen to be making your home there for the time being; it need not be your only home, nor a permanent one.[19] You can remain resident during a temporary absence, depending on the duration and circumstances of your absence.[20] Your intentions to return, your accommodation, and where your family and your personal belongings are can all be relevant. It is possible to be resident in two countries at once.[21]

Children

The only benefits that can be claimed by a child under 16 that have residence requirements are disability living allowance (DLA), housing benefit (HB) and child benefit. For DLA and HB, the claimant must be habitually resident (unless, for DLA, s/he claimed before 8 April 2013, in which case s/he must be ordinarily resident until her/his award is terminated, revised or superseded, from which point s/he must be habitually resident). For child benefit, the claimant must be ordinarily resident and have a right to reside.

Although children are covered by the same rules as for adults, in order to decide whether or not they satisfy the residence requirement,[22] in practice, a child's ordinary or habitual residence is usually decided by looking at the residence of her/his parent(s) or person(s) with parental responsibility (in Scotland, parental rights and responsibilities) for her/him. A child who lives with that person usually has the same ordinary or habitual residence as her/him, so a child who joins a parent (or person with parental responsibility) may become ordinarily and habitually resident almost immediately.[23] If there is only one person with parental responsibility, the child has the same ordinary and habitual residence as her/him.[24]

However, the Upper Tribunal recently held that a non-EEA national child was not ordinarily resident because he had overstayed his immigration leave and was therefore not lawfully resident, despite the child living with his mother who was both lawfully and ordinarily resident (see p99).[25]

Whether or not a child has a right to reside is determined in the same way as it is for an adult. So if a child under 16 is claiming child benefit, s/he (but not the child s/he is responsible for) must have a right to reside. If a child under 16 is claiming HB, s/he must have a right to reside in order to satisfy the habitual residence test.

6. **Ordinary residence**

The following benefits and tax credits have a requirement to be ordinarily resident:
- child benefit;
- child tax credit (CTC);
- employment and support allowance in youth;
- incapacity benefit in youth;
- Category D retirement pension;
- severe disablement allowance;
- social fund funeral payments and winter fuel payments;
- working tax credit (WTC);
- (if claimed before 8 April 2013 until the award is terminated, revised or superseded) attendance allowance (AA), carer's allowance (CA) and disability living allowance (DLA).

There are some limited exceptions to the requirement to be ordinarily resident and, if you are covered by the European Union (EU) co-ordination rules, these may assist you in satisfying the requirement. The exceptions and assistance provided by the co-ordination rules vary between the different benefits and tax credits and are covered in Chapter 13.

In practice, claims are rarely refused on the basis of ordinary residence.

You cannot be ordinarily resident without being resident (see p95).

The term 'ordinary residence' is not defined in the legislation, but caselaw has confirmed:

- the words should have their natural and ordinary meaning;[26]
- you are ordinarily resident in a country if you have a home there that you have adopted for a settled purpose and where you live for the time being (whether for a short or long duration);[27]
- ordinary residence can start on arrival (see below);
- a person in the UK for a temporary purpose can be ordinarily resident in the UK (see below);
- in general, your residence must be voluntary for you to be ordinarily resident (see p98);
- ordinary residence can continue during absences abroad, but leaving to settle abroad usually ends ordinary residence (see p98);
- although rare, it is possible for a person to be ordinarily resident in more than one place or country;[28]
- a person who lives in the UK but has no fixed abode can be ordinarily resident;[29]
- ordinary residence is different from the concept of 'domicile'.[30]

Ordinary residence on arrival

Ordinary residence can begin immediately on arrival in Great Britain.[31] In a family law case, a man who separated from his wife in one country (where he had lived and worked for three years) and went to live at his parents' house in another was found to become immediately ordinarily resident there. The Court of Appeal found that, where there is evidence that a person intends to make a place her/his home for an indefinite period, s/he is ordinarily resident when s/he arrives there.[32] In another case, a court decided that a woman returning from Australia after some months there had never lost her ordinary residence in England. However, if she had, she would have become ordinarily resident again when the boat embarked from Australia.[33] In a case involving students, they had to show that they were ordinarily resident within a few weeks of first arriving in the UK, and it was not argued that they could not be ordinarily resident because they had only just come to Great Britain.[34]

Ordinary residence while here for a temporary purpose

To be ordinarily resident in Great Britain, you do not have to intend, or be able, to live here permanently. The purpose can be for a limited period. In one case, Lord Scarman said that, 'Education, business or profession, employment, health, family, or merely love of the place spring to mind as common reasons for a choice of regular abode.'[35] If you are solely in the UK for business purposes, you can still be ordinarily resident here.[36] You may have several different reasons for a single stay – eg, to visit relatives, get medical advice, attend religious ceremonies and sort out personal affairs.[37]

The reason must be a settled one. This does not mean that the reason has to be long-standing,[38] but there must be evidence of it. Although in some cases concerning ordinary residence, the courts have looked back to see whether a person had been ordinarily resident months or years beforehand,[39] there is no minimum period of residence required before you are ordinarily resident. If, for example, you have arrived in the UK and started work, the benefit authorities should consider how long you are likely to reside in the UK. If you intend to live here for the time being, they should accept your intention as sufficient, unless it is clearly unlikely that you are going to be able to stay. The benefit authorities should not make a deep examination of your long-term intentions.[40] The type of accommodation you occupy may be relevant.[41] If you have made regular visits to the UK, this may be relevant.[42]

Involuntary residence

Ordinary residence generally requires that you have 'voluntarily adopted' to live somewhere with a settled purpose.[43] Therefore, a person who is held in a place against her/his will is not usually ordinarily resident there. It can be arguable that if you were taken out of the UK against your will (eg, as a child or for a forced marriage), you should be ordinarily resident on your return. However, if you are in the UK because of circumstances that limit or remove your choice, this does not necessarily prevent you from being ordinarily resident here.

In practice, the question of determining ordinary residence if you lack the capacity to 'voluntarily adopt' your place of residence rarely arises when determining entitlement to benefits and tax credits. However, it is far more common when trying to determine local authority responsibility for providing support, and so the principles established in that caselaw can be relevant. Depending on the facts, if you lack capacity you can be held to be ordinarily resident where the person who makes decisions on your behalf resides, if that is where you are based, or alternatively, where your residence is sufficiently settled (omitting the criteria for it to be 'voluntarily adopted').[44]

Deportation to the UK does not prevent you from becoming ordinarily resident here.[45] The issue is whether your residence is part of your settled purpose. If you have decided to live in the UK, it does not matter if the reason for your decision is because you were deported here. For the purposes of tax credits and child benefit, you are treated as ordinarily resident if you are in the UK as a result of deportation or having been otherwise legally removed from another country.[46]

Absence from the UK

If you are ordinarily resident, you may lose this status if you go abroad. This depends on:

- why you go abroad;
- how long you stay abroad;
- what connections you keep with the UK – eg, accommodation, furniture and other possessions.[47]

If you decide to move abroad for the foreseeable future, you normally stop being ordinarily resident in the UK on the day you leave.[48] There can be exceptions, which depend on your circumstances, including if your plans are clearly impractical and you return to the UK very quickly.

If your absence abroad is part of your normal pattern of life, your ordinary residence may not be affected.[49] This can apply if you are out of the UK for half, or even most, of the year – eg, if you spend each summer in the UK and the winter abroad, you may still be ordinarily resident in the UK.[50]

If your absence abroad is extraordinary or temporary and you intend to return to the UK, your ordinary residence may not be affected.[51]

In one case, a British woman who spent 15 months in Germany with her husband over a period of three years kept her ordinary residence in the UK; she had always intended to return here.[52]

However, if you are away from the UK for a long time and do not keep strong connections with Great Britain, you may lose your ordinary residence, even if you intend to return. In one case, a citizen of the UK and colonies lived in the UK for over four years and then returned to Kenya for two years and five months because her business here failed and there was a business opportunity in Kenya. She intended to make enough money to support herself on her return to the UK. Her parents and parents-in-law remained in the UK. She was found to have lost her ordinary residence during her absence.[53]

In deciding whether an absence affects your ordinary residence, the decision maker must consider all your circumstances. Every absence is unique and distinct, and you should provide full details of all your circumstances including:

- why you wish to go abroad;
- how long you intend to be abroad; *and*
- what you intend to do while you are abroad.

Each of these considerations needs to be taken into account, and it is your responsibility to demonstrate that your absence is to be a temporary one.[54]

Note: in addition to affecting your ordinary residence, an absence may also affect your benefit entitlement if it means you cease to satisfy other residence or presence requirements for the benefit or tax credit you are claiming (see p227), or if it means you cease to be treated as a couple (see p230).

Legal residence

Whether or not residence must be legal or lawful to count as ordinary residence arguably depends on the context. However, caselaw suggests that if the context entails entitlement to a state benefit, the residence must be lawful.[55] This approach was applied recently to exclude from DLA a non-European Economic Area (EEA) national child who had overstayed his immigration leave in the UK, on the basis that he was not ordinarily resident.[56] This reasoning is problematic if you are a non-EEA national claimant defined as a 'person subject to immigration control' because you require leave and do not have it (see p58), but you are not excluded on this basis because you are in an exempt group. See p68 for the exempt groups for non-contributory benefits and p71 for tax credits. However, as ordinary residence is no longer a requirement for DLA or AA, CA or personal independence payment claimed since 8 April 2013 (see p208), this case only potentially affects entitlement to child benefit, CTC and WTC.

Note: if you are entitled to tax credits because you are making a joint claim with a partner who is not excluded by her/his immigration status, HM Revenue and Customs appears to treat the provision that allows the immigration status of one partner to be ignored in a joint claim as overriding the right to reside requirement for CTC (see p75). Arguably, it should also override the requirement to be ordinarily resident.

7. **Habitual residence**

The following benefits and tax credits have a habitual residence requirement:
- attendance allowance (AA);
- carer's allowance (CA);
- disability living allowance (DLA);
- income-related employment and support allowance;
- housing benefit;
- income support;
- income-based jobseeker's allowance;
- pension credit;
- personal independence payment;
- universal credit.

You must satisfy (or be exempt from) the habitual residence test to get the above benefits (see p106). See Chapter 11 for details of the way the test works.
Note:
- You are also excluded from council tax reduction if you do not satisfy (and are not exempt from) the habitual residence test (see p441).[57]
- You may be entitled to a winter fuel payment from the social fund if, instead of being ordinarily resident in Great Britain, you are habitually resident in a non-excluded other European Economic Area country or Switzerland (see p217).

- If your claim for AA, DLA or CA began before 8 April 2013, you must be ordinarily, rather than habitually, resident until your award is revised or superseded.[58]

8. **The right to reside**

The following benefits and tax credits have a right to reside requirement:
- child benefit;
- child tax credit (CTC);
- income-related employment and support allowance;
- housing benefit;
- income support;
- income-based jobseeker's allowance;
- pension credit;
- universal credit.

The right to reside requirement for all the above benefits, other than child benefit and CTC, is part of the habitual residence test. For all the benefits and tax credits listed above, you must satisfy the right to reside requirement, unless, for the means-tested benefits only, you are in group that is exempt from the habitual residence test (see p106).

You are also excluded from council tax reduction if you do not satisfy the right to reside requirement (see p441).[59]

See Chapter 11 for details of the way the test works for each benefit and tax credit and Chapter 12 for who has a right to reside.

Notes

2. **Presence**
   1 R(S) 1/66

4. **Living in for three months**
   2 Confirmed in para 072996 DMG
   3 para 02035 TCTM; para 10025 CBTM
   4 Reg 85A(2) JSA Regs
   5 Reg 85A(2A) JSA Regs; 'Changes to jobseeker's allowance to benefit armed forces families', announced 1 November 2015 on www.gov.uk
   6 Reg 3 JSA(HR)A Regs
   7 Swaddling v Chief Adjudication Officer, C-90/97 [1999] ECR I-01075
   8 Collins v SSWP, C-138/02 [2004] ECR I-02703, para 63
   9 Vatsouras and Koupatantze v Arbeitsgemeinschaft Nürnberg, C-23/08 [2009] ECR I-04585, para 38 and caselaw cited
   10 Prete v Office National de L'Emploi, C-367/11 [2012] para 34 and caselaw cited
   11 Vestische Arbeit Jobcenter Kreis Recklinghausen v García-Nieto C-299/14 AG Opinion (4 June 2015)
   12 Vestische Arbeit Jobcenter Kreis Recklinghausen v García-Nieto, C-299/14 [2016] not yet reported; Jobcenter Berlin Neukölln v Alimanovic, C-67/14 [2015] not yet reported
   13 AEM v DSD (JSA), C11/14-15 (JSA)
   14 Reg 13(9) SS(C&P) Regs
   15 **CB** Reg 23(5) CB Regs
      CTC Reg 3(6) TC(R) Regs
   16 **CB** Reg 23(6) CB Regs
      CTC Reg 3(7) TC(R) Regs
   17 **CB** Reg 23(3) CB Regs
      CTC Reg 3(3) TC(R) Regs
   18 Reg 1(3) CB Regs

5. **Residence**
   19 R(IS) 6/96, para 19; R(P) 2/67
   20 CPC/1035/2005
   21 R(IS) 9/99, para 10
   22 Re A (A Minor) (Abduction: Child's Objections) [1994] 2 FLR 126: on habitual residence, but also applies to ordinary residence

   23 Re M (Minors) (Residence Order: Jurisdiction) [1993] 1 FLR 495
   24 Re J (A Minor) (Abduction: Custody Rights) [1990] 2 AC 562 at p578
   25 MS v SSWP (DLA) [2016] UKUT 42 (AAC)

6. **Ordinary residence**
   26 Levene v Inland Revenue Commissioners [1928] AC 217; R(M) 1/85
   27 R v Barnet London Borough Council ex parte Shah [1983] 2 AC 309
   28 IRC v Lysaght [1928] AC 234; R(P) 1/01; CIS/1691/2004; GC v HMRC (TC) [2014] UKUT 251 (AAC)
   29 Levene v Inland Revenue Commissioners [1928] AC 217
   30 R v Barnet London Borough Council ex parte Shah [1983] 2 AC 309, Lord Scarman at p345E-H
   31 R(F) 1/62
   32 Macrae v Macrae [1949] 2 All ER 34. The countries were Scotland and England, which are separate for family law purposes. In R(IS) 6/96, para 27 the commissioner doubted the correctness of Macrae because he considered it used a test very close to the 'real home' test rejected in Shah. He does not seem to have heard any argument about this; Macrae was cited in Shah and was not one of the cases mentioned there as wrong: pp342-43.
   33 Lewis v Lewis [1956] 1 All ER 375
   34 R v Barnet London Borough Council ex parte Shah [1982] QB 688 at p717E
   35 R v Barnet London Borough Council ex parte Shah [1983] 2 AC 309, Lord Scarman at p344C-D
   36 Inland Revenue Commissioners v Lysaght [1928] AC 234; AA v SSWP (IS) [2013] UKUT 406 (AAC)
   37 Levene v Inland Revenue Commissioners [1928] AC 217, HL; GC v HMRC (TC) [2014] UKUT 251 (AAC)
   38 Macrae v Macrae [1949] 2 All ER 34
   39 R v Barnet London Borough Council ex parte Shah [1983] 2 AC 309
   40 R v Barnet London Borough Council ex parte Shah [1983] 2 AC 309, Lord Scarman at p344G

41 R(F) 1/82; R(F) 1/62; R(P) 1/62; R(P) 4/
54
42 *GC v HMRC (TC)* [2014] UKUT 251 (AAC)
43 *R v Barnet London Borough Council ex
parte Shah* [1983] 2 AC 309
44 *R Waltham Forest LBC ex parte Vale*,
unreported 11 February 1985; but see
also *R (Cornwall Council) SSH and Another*
[2015] UKSC 46
45 *Gout v Cimitian* [1922] 1 AC 105
46 **TC** Reg 3(3) TC(R) Regs
CB Reg 23(3) CB Regs
47 R(F) 1/62; R(M) 1/85
48 *Hopkins v Hopkins* [1951]; *R v Hussain*
[1971] 56 Crim App R 165; *R v IAT ex
parte Ng* [1986] Imm AR 23 (QBD)
49 *R v Barnet London Borough Council ex
parte Shah* [1983] 2 AC 309
50 *Levene v Inland Revenue Commissioners*
[1928] AC 217; *Inland Revenue
Commissioners v Lysaght* [1928] AC 234;
AA v SSWP (IS) [2013] UKUT 406 (AAC)
51 *R v Barnet LBC ex parte Shah* [1983] 2 AC
309, Lord Scarman at p342D
52 *Stransky v Stransky* [1954] 3 WLR 123,
[1954] 2 All ER 536
53 *Haria* [1986] Imm AR 165
54 *Chief Adjudication Officer v Ahmed and
Others*, 16 March 1994 (CA), reported
as R(S) 1/96
55 *R v Barnet London Borough Council ex
parte Shah* [1983] 2 AC 309, Lord
Scarman – comments obiter; *Mark v
Mark* [2005] UKHL 42, para 36
56 *MS v SSWP (DLA)* [2016] UKUT 42 (AAC)

7. Habitual residence
57 Reg 12 CTRS(PR)E Regs; reg 16
CTR(SPC)S Regs; reg 16 CTR(S) Regs;
reg 28 CTRSPR(W) Regs; Sch para 19
CTRS(DS)W Regs
58 Reg 1(2),(3) and (4) SS(DLA,AA&CA)(A)
Regs

8. The right to reside
59 Reg 12 CTRS(PR)E Regs; reg 16
CTR(SPC)S Regs; reg 16 CTR(S) Regs;
reg 28 CTRSPR(W) Regs; Sch para 19
CTRS(DS)W Regs

Chapter 11

· ·

Habitual residence and the right to reside

This chapter covers:
1. The habitual residence test (below)
2. 'Habitual residence in fact' (p110)
3. The right to reside (p115)

This chapter explains the way in which the habitual residence test and the right to reside requirement apply to the various benefits and tax credits. For information on who has a right to reside, see Chapter 12.

1. **The habitual residence test**

The habitual residence test applies to the following benefits:
- attendance allowance (AA);
- carer's allowance (CA);
- disability living allowance (DLA);
- income-related employment and support allowance (ESA);
- housing benefit (HB);
- income support (IS);
- income-based jobseeker's allowance (JSA);
- pension credit (PC);
- personal independence payment (PIP);
- universal credit (UC).

To be entitled to one of the above benefits, you must be habitually resident in the 'common travel area' (ie, the UK, Ireland, the Channel Islands and the Isle of Man) or be exempt from the test (see p106).

Unless you are exempt (see p106), to satisfy the habitual residence test for **means-tested benefits** you must:

- be 'habitually resident in fact' (see p110); *and*
- have a right to reside that is not excluded for the benefit you want to claim (see p115); *and*
- (for income-based JSA only) have been living in the common travel area for the past three months (see p92).

Some groups of people are exempt from the habitual residence test for means-tested benefits (see p106). If you are in one of these groups, you are treated as satisfying the test.

To satisfy the habitual residence test for **AA, DLA, PIP and CA**, you must be 'habitually resident in fact' (see p110).

Note: if your claim for AA, DLA or CA began before 8 April 2013, the previous requirement to be ordinarily, rather than habitually, resident continues to apply until your award is revised or superseded.[1]

Note also:

- You are also excluded from council tax reduction (see p439) if you do not satisfy (and are not exempt from) the habitual residence test.[2]
- You may be entitled to a winter fuel payment from the social fund if, instead of being ordinarily resident in Great Britain, you are habitually resident in a non-excluded European Economic Area (EEA) country or Switzerland (see p217).

The habitual residence test for means-tested benefits

If you are exempt (see p106), your residence need not be examined further. Provided you meet the other conditions of entitlement, you are eligible for benefit. However, in practice, the DWP or local authority does not always consider whether you are exempt. The administration of the test, either by sending you one or more paper forms to complete or by asking you for an interview, tends to follow the same format regardless of whether you are in an exempt group or not. In general, the decision maker first considers your right to reside. If you satisfy this requirement and you are claiming income-based JSA, s/he then considers whether you have been living here for the past three months and then (for all means-tested benefits) whether you are 'habitually resident in fact'.

Therefore, if you come into one of the exempt groups, make this clear to the DWP or local authority, particularly if you might not otherwise be accepted as satisfying the habitual residence test – eg, because you have only recently arrived in the common travel area.

The DWP sometimes develops policies for varying the usual procedures for specific groups. For example, at the time of writing, internal guidance states that if, when you make your new claim, you can provide evidence that you have come to the UK under the 'gateway protection programme' or 'vulnerable person relocation scheme', or you have been granted leave as a refugee in the last eight weeks, you are subject to a shorter habitual residence test (because you are clearly exempt) and your claim is fast-tracked.[3]

Who is exempt from the habitual residence test

You are exempt from the habitual residence test for **means-tested benefits** if you:[4]

- are an EEA national and are a 'worker' (see p140), including if you retain this status (see p146);
- are an EEA national and are a self-employed person (see p153), including if you retain this status (see p157);
- are the family member (see p164), other than an extended family member, of someone in either of the above two groups;
- are an EEA national with a permanent right of residence that you acquired in less than five years (the main groups cover certain former workers or self-employed people who have retired or are permanently incapacitated, and their family members – see p190);
- are a refugee. If you are a family member of a refugee, see p107;
- have humanitarian protection;
- have discretionary leave (see p36), leave granted under the 'destitution domestic violence' concession (see p35) or temporary protection granted under the displaced persons' provisions;
- have been deported, expelled or otherwise legally removed from another country to the UK and you are not a 'person subject to immigration control' (see p57);
- (for income-related ESA only) are being transferred from an award of IS which was transitionally protected from the requirement to have a right to reside (see p118);
- (for HB only) receive IS, income-related ESA or PC;[5]
- (for HB only) receive income-based JSA and either:
  - you have a right to reside other than one that is excluded for HB (see p116); *or*
  - you have been receiving both HB and income-based JSA since 31 March 2014. Your exemption on this basis ends when either you cease to be entitled to that income-based JSA or you make a new claim for HB.[6]

If you are not in one of the above groups, you must show that you have established 'habitual residence in fact' (see p110) in the common travel area and that you have a sufficient right to reside to claim the means-tested benefit you want (see p115). For income-based JSA only, you must also show that you have been living in the common travel area for the past three months (see p92).

The above exemptions do not apply to **AA, DLA, PIP and CA**. For these benefits, you must show that you have established 'habitual residence in fact' (see p110) in the common travel area, unless you:

- are abroad in your capacity as a serving member of the forces; *or*
- are living with someone who is abroad as a serving member of the forces and s/he is your spouse, civil partner, son, stepson, daughter, stepdaughter, father, stepfather, father-in-law, mother, stepmother or mother-in-law.

If this applies to you, you are treated as being habitually resident (as well as treated as present).[7]

Family members of refugees

If you are the family member of a refugee and have leave on the basis that you joined her/him under the family reunion provisions (see p33), your leave does not bring you into any of the groups that are exempt from the habitual residence test. This means you are not entitled to any of the means-tested benefits until you have established your habitual residence, and for income-based JSA, until you have been living in the common travel area for three months.

Note: if you live with your partner and claim UC, both of you must satisfy, or be exempt from, the habitual residence test. If only your partner does so, s/he must make a single claim. Her/his award is based on the maximum amount for a single person, but your income and capital are taken into account (see p201).[8]

If you have leave as a family member of a refugee or someone with humanitarian protection, this exclusion is arguably unlawful discrimination. In relation to the past presence test for DLA, the Upper Tribunal held that the requirement was unlawful, not only for a claimant with leave as a refugee but also for a claimant with leave as a family member of a refugee and the DWP accepts that the argument also applies if you, or the family member you are joining, have humanitarian protection (see p209).[9]

Who does the habitual residence test apply to

The habitual residence test applies to the benefit claimant.

For means-tested benefits, other than income-based JSA claimed as a joint-claim couple and UC, this means that it does not matter if your partner does not satisfy or is not exempt from the test; you are still paid as a couple. You and your partner should therefore consider which one of you is most likely to satisfy, or be exempt from, the habitual residence test. For joint-claim JSA or UC couples, the rules are different (see below).

Joint-claim jobseeker's allowance

If you are a member of a 'joint-claim couple' for income-based JSA (see CPAG's *Welfare Benefits and Tax Credits Handbook* for what this means) and either you or your partner do not satisfy, or you are not exempt from, the habitual residence test, a special rule applies. The partner who is habitually resident can claim income-based JSA for both of you without the other partner being required to be a claimant as part of the joint claim – ie, you do not need to make a joint claim.[10] You are paid as a couple.

Couples claiming universal credit

If you live with your partner and claim UC, you are generally required to make a joint claim, and you and your partner must each satisfy the habitual residence test. However, if only one of you satisfies, or is exempt from, the habitual residence test, you cannot make a joint claim for UC. Instead the person who satisfies, or is exempt from, the habitual residence test can claim UC as a single person.[11]

If you satisfy, or are exempt from, the habitual residence test, but your partner does not, the following special rules apply to the calculation of your UC.
* The maximum amount of UC is that for a single person.[12]
* Only you have to accept a claimant commitment and comply with the conditionality requirements.[13]
* Your partner's capital is included in the amount of capital taken into account.[14]
* Your partner's income is included in the amount of income taken into account when calculating how much should be deducted from the maximum amount of UC.[15]

If you fail the habitual residence test

The way in which your failure to satisfy, or be exempt from, the habitual residence test affects your benefit is slightly different for each benefit, but the outcome is the same: if you are not habitually resident in the common travel area, you are not entitled to be paid IS, income-based JSA, income-related ESA, PC, HB, UC, AA, DLA, PIP and CA. The precise way in which this is achieved is as follows.
* For IS, income-based JSA, income-related ESA and HB, you are classed as a 'person from abroad'. This means for IS, income-based JSA and income-related ESA, you have an applicable amount of nil,[16] and for HB you are treated as not liable for rent.[17]
* For PC and UC, you are treated as not present in Great Britain.[18]
* For AA, DLA, PIP and CA, you have failed to meet the prescribed residence requirements.[19]

Have you failed the habitual residence test?

1. If you are refused benefit because you have failed the habitual residence test, consider challenging this decision. See CPAG's *Welfare Benefits and Tax Credits Handbook* for information on how to do so. You may want to contact a local advice agency for help with this.
2. While challenging the decision, make another claim. If this is refused, also challenge this decision and make another claim, and so on. This is because when the decision

refusing your initial claim is looked at again, the decision maker (or First-tier Tribunal) cannot take account of circumstances that did not exist at the time the original decision was made.[20] So, if the decision maker (or First-tier Tribunal) considers that you were not habitually resident at the time benefit was originally refused, but you are now (because you have been resident for an appreciable period of time or, for income-based JSA, you have been living here for three months), s/he cannot take this into account when looking again at the original decision. However, if by the date of the decision on your second or subsequent claim, you had completed an appreciable period of residence (or, for income-based JSA, you had been living here for three months), s/he can take this into account.

The benefit authority may say that you cannot make another claim while your appeal (or request to have the first decision looked at again) is pending. This is is not the case.[21] It may help to refer to the fact that when amending regulations were introduced, the Secretary of State said in his report that 'it needs to be emphasised that neither the fact that a person's claim for benefit has been disallowed on the grounds that the habitual residence test has not been satisfied, nor the fact that there is an outstanding appeal against that decision, prevents that individual from making a fresh claim for benefit.'[22]

3. Check whether you come into one of the exempt groups (see p106).

4. If you are not in one of the exempt groups, establish which part of the test the decision maker says you have failed.

5.Remember that the local authority must make its own decision on HB and not just follow a DWP decision that you are not habitually resident. Similarly, if the DWP decides you are entitled to income-based JSA on the basis of your right to reside as a jobseeker, the local authority must determine whether you have *another*, non-excluded, right to reside (see p116), which would mean you were exempt from the habitual residence test for HB (see p106).

6. If the decision maker considers you do not have a right to reside, check Chapter 12 for the factors relevant to demonstrating your right to reside.

7. If you have claimed income-based JSA and the decision maker considers that you have not lived in the common travel area for the past three months, see p92.

8. If the decision maker considers you not to be habitually resident in fact, see p110.

9. Remember that the habitual residence test applies to the claimant, so (unless you are claiming UC) even if you have been found not to be habitually resident, your partner may satisfy the test and should make the claim. This applies even if you have claimed income-based JSA as a 'joint-claim couple' (see p107). You can still challenge the refusal of your claim while your partner makes a new claim.

10. Although the onus of proof is on the benefit authorities to establish that you are *not* habitually resident, produce as much evidence as possible to show that you *are*. See Chapter 20 for more information on evidence.

2. 'Habitual residence in fact'

There is no definition of habitual residence in the regulations. However, there is a considerable amount of caselaw on the meaning of 'habitual residence' and, from this, certain principles have emerged. To count as 'habitually resident in fact':

- you must be resident in the common travel area (see below);
- your residence must be voluntary (see below);
- you must have a settled intention to make the common travel area your home for the time being (see p111);
- in most cases, you must have resided in the common travel area for an 'appreciable period of time' (see p112). **Note:** this is not a fixed period and there are some exceptions.

Of the above four factors, most disputes about whether a person who has claimed a relevant benefit is habitually resident in fact concern the latter two.

The decision about whether or not you are habitually resident is a factual question and must be made on the 'balance of probabilities'. If the probabilities in favour of each answer are exactly equal, the decision should be that you *are* habitually resident. This is because the benefits authority must show that you are *not* habitually resident. However, it is preferable to examine the facts further rather than rely on the 'balance of probabilities'.[23]

You should therefore always provide as much evidence as you can about all your circumstances that are relevant to your habitual residence. See Chapter 20 for more information about providing evidence.

Residence

You cannot be habitually resident in the common travel area unless you are resident in the common travel area. It is not enough merely to intend to reside here in the future.[24] For information on residence, see p95.

Voluntary residence

You cannot be habitually resident in fact in the common travel area unless your residence is voluntary.[25] This factor, in practice, is rarely a barrier to your being found habitually resident in fact. However, it can also be relevant if you are returning to live in the common travel area after having been taken or kept away against your will (see p113). **Note:** if you have been deported, expelled or otherwise legally removed from another country to the UK and you are not a 'person subject to immigration control' (see p57), you are exempt from the habitual residence test for means-tested benefits (see p106).

Settled intention

For your residence to become habitual, you must have a settled intention to reside in the common travel area. This is not determined just by your declaring your intention, but depends on the evidence about all the factors that are relevant to it.[26]

Your settled intention to reside in the common travel area does not need to be permanent; it is enough that you intend to make the common travel area your home for the time being.

***

Do you have a settled intention?

The following factors are relevant when determining whether or not you have a settled intention.

1. Your reasons for coming to the common travel area. If there is one or more clear reason why you have moved here (such as a family breakdown, a desire to study here or an offer of employment), this helps to show your settled intention.

2. The steps you took to prepare for coming to the common travel area – eg, the plans you made beforehand about where you would live, enquiries about work, making arrangements for your children to attend school, contacting people you know and settling your affairs in the country you were leaving, such as closing bank accounts, disposing of property and ending a tenancy.

3. The strength of your ties to the common travel area compared with your ties to other places (this is sometimes called your 'centre of interests') – eg, whether you have family or friends living in the common travel area, whether you have registered with a doctor or joined any clubs or associations here, whether your children are in school here, whether you have begun a course of study, or whether you have spent money here (such as a deposit on a rented property). Similarly, if you have these sort of ties abroad, this may indicate a less strong settled intention.

4. The viability of your residence in the common travel area (see p112).

***

As with the requirement to be resident (see p95), you must be seen to be making a home here, but it need not be your only home or a permanent one.[27] Therefore, a long-standing intention to move abroad (eg, when debts are paid) does not prevent someone from being habitually resident.[28]

Events after you claim benefit or receive a decision may confirm that your intention was always to reside in the UK – eg, if you are refused benefit because the DWP does not accept that you have a settled intention to stay in the UK, the fact that you are still here by the time of the appeal hearing may help show that you always intended to reside here.[29]

There is a close connection between 'settled intention' and 'appreciable period' (see p112): the stronger your settled intention, the shorter the period you need to reside in order to count as 'habitually resident in fact'.[30]

Viability of your residence

The viability of your continued residence, although a relevant factor, is not an additional requirement. This means that the question of whether you could survive in the common travel area without claiming the benefits to which the habitual residence test applies is not a separate question that must be answered positively in order for you to count as habitually resident in fact.[31] The viability of your residence is simply one factor that can be taken into account when considering your settled intention to reside in the common travel area.[32]

This means that you can be accepted as habitually resident in fact even though you have very few or no resources.

Appreciable period

In most cases, you do not count as habitually resident in fact until you have resided in the common travel area for an 'an appreciable period of time'.[33]

However, your appreciable period is reduced or may not apply at all if you are:
- a returning resident in certain circumstances (see p113); *and/or*
- covered by the European Union (EU) co-ordination rules (see p114).

There is no fixed period of time that amounts to an appreciable period and it depends on your circumstances.[34] Benefit authorities must not set a standard period of time for which all claimants must be resident before they can become habitually resident, and any such policy should be challenged by judicial review. There is extensive caselaw on what constitutes an appreciable period of residence. Periods of between one and three months are frequently cited,[35] but too much weight should not be put on any one decision, nor should any general rule about a specific time period be derived from it.[36]

Your appreciable period can include visits to prepare for settled residence made before that residence is taken up.[37]

The stronger your settled intention to make your home in the common travel area for the time being, the shorter your period of actual residence need be before you can be accepted as habitually resident in fact (and vice versa).[38]

Advance claims

You can make an advance claim of carer's allowance, disability living allowance (DLA) or personal independence payment (PIP) if in the next three months (six months for attendance allowance) you will (in addition to satisfying all the other conditions of entitlement) have been resident for an appreciable period and therefore satisfy the requirement to be 'habitually resident in fact'.[39] However, in practice, this is only relevant if you are exempt from, or can satisfy, the past presence test (see p208).

You cannot make an advance claim for income-based jobseeker's allowance (JSA), income-related employment and support allowance (ESA), income support, pension credit (PC) or housing benefit for a future date when you will have been resident for an appreciable period because the rules prevent your claim from being treated as made on a future date if you do not satisfy the habitual residence test.[40]

This exclusion does not apply to universal credit, but the provision for advance claims is, in any case, very limited. Advance claims can be accepted if the DWP considers you will be entitled within the next month and you are in a group accepted by the DWP (note that DWP guidance states this is limited to prisoners[41]).[42]

Returning residents

If you were living in the common travel area in the past and you return here, you may count as habitually resident in fact either immediately on your return or after a much shorter period of residence than would otherwise be the case.[43]

Are you a returning resident?

If you are a returning resident, you should consider the following issues.[44]

1. Were you habitually resident when you were previously here?

2. If so, did you cease to be habitually resident when you went abroad either immediately on departure or while you were abroad?

3. If you ceased to be habitually resident while you were abroad, when did you resume habitual residence in the common travel area? This may involve deciding when you resumed residence, and then when that residence became habitual.

If you never stopped being habitually resident in fact, you continue to be habitually resident on your return. This could apply if you only went abroad for a short period – eg, for a holiday. Similarly, it can apply if your absence abroad was only ever intended to be for a temporary period. For example, in one case, a man was held not to have ceased to be habitually resident on his return from a two-year Voluntary Service Overseas placement, during which time he had given up his tenancy in the UK and put his possessions in storage.[45] It may also apply if your absence abroad was involuntary. Guidance to decision makers states that people who leave, or remain away from, the UK because of a forced marriage are not considered to have lost their habitual residence as they were abroad through no fault of their own. They are therefore considered habitually resident from the date of their claim.[46]

If you have ceased to count as habitually resident in fact while outside the common travel area, whether or not you need to complete a further period of residence here on your return before you can resume your habitual residence depends on the following.[47]

- The circumstances in which your earlier habitual residence was lost. If you went abroad for a temporary or conditional reason and/or you stayed away longer because of circumstances beyond your control, you may be more likely to be found habitually resident immediately on your return.

- The links between you and the UK while abroad. This could include retaining property, bank accounts and membership of organisations, maintaining contact with family and friends and making visits back to the common travel area (their frequency, length and purpose are all relevant).
- The circumstances of your return to the UK. Evidence of your settled intention is relevant (see p111).

Applying the above factors in two cases that were heard jointly, a commissioner found both claimants to be habitually resident on the day of their return.[48]

Even if you are not able to resume your previous habitual residence immediately on your return, you may still be able to argue that your previous habitual residence here is a factor that reduces the period of time that counts as an appreciable period of actual residence.

If you are covered by the European Union co-ordination rules

If you are covered by the EU co-ordination rules (seep264), the period of time you must be resident before you can be found to be habitually resident in fact can be shorter than otherwise might be required, and can be outweighed by other factors that show you are habitually resident. The co-ordination rules can only assist you to be found habitually resident in fact if you are claiming a 'special non-contributory benefit' (see p270) – ie:

- JSA;
- income-related ESA;
- PC;
- DLA mobility component.

Note: PIP mobility component has not yet been listed as a 'special non-contributory benefit', but the DWP treat it as such.[49]

The co-ordination rules state that you are entitled to 'special non-contributory benefits' in the member state in which you are 'resident'[50] and define 'residence' as the place where you 'habitually reside'.[51] See p272 for the factors that should be considered when deciding where you habitually reside for the purpose of the co-ordination rules.

The European Court of Justice (ECJ) has held that when assessing where someone habitually resides, her/his length of residence in the member state cannot be regarded as an intrinsic element of the concept of residence. The case concerned a British national who lived in the UK until he was 23 and then moved to France, where he worked for 14 years until he was made redundant. He returned to the UK and was refused benefit on the basis of not having completed an appreciable period of actual residence. The ECJ found that the claimant, who was covered by the EU co-ordination rules and was claiming a special non-contributory benefit, could not be deemed not to be habitually resident merely because the period of residence completed was too short.[52] Although the case concerned a returning resident, subsequent caselaw confirms that the principle applies to any claimant covered by the EU co-ordination rules.[53] So, while 'duration and continuity of presence' is one of the factors that should be considered when determining where you habitually reside, it is only one factor and can be outweighed by others. Therefore, you cannot be denied income-based JSA, income-related ESA, PC and DLA mobility component solely because you have not completed an 'appreciable period' of actual residence in the common travel area.

3. The right to reside

The right to reside requirement applies to:
- child benefit;
- child tax credit (CTC);
- income-related employment and support allowance (ESA);
- housing benefit (HB);
- income support (IS);
- income-based jobseeker's allowance (JSA);
- pension credit (PC);
- universal credit (UC).

Note: you are also excluded from council tax reduction (see p439) if you do not have a right to reside.[54]

The way the test works varies between the different benefits.

For **means-tested benefits**, the right to reside requirement forms part of the habitual residence test (see p104). Therefore, if you are exempt from the habitual residence test, you do not need to demonstrate your right to reside (see p106). If you are not exempt from the habitual residence test, in addition to being 'habitually resident in fact' (see p110), and, for income-based JSA, having lived in the common travel area for the past three months (see p92), you must satisfy the right to reside requirement.

For **child benefit** and CTC, the right to reside requirement is part of the presence test. This also requires you to be ordinarily resident (see p96) in the UK and to have lived in the UK for the past three months (see p92).

Note: if you have been claiming benefits in the UK since 30 April 2004, you may have transitional protection from the right to reside requirement and therefore not need a right to reside (see p118).

If you do not have transitional protection and, for means-tested benefits, you are not exempt from the habitual residence test, you must have a right to reside that is sufficient for the benefit or tax credit you wish to claim. The regulations for each benefit or tax credit specifically exclude certain types of right to reside. However, you are only excluded if this is your only right to reside. If you have any other non-excluded right to reside, you satisfy the requirement for that benefit.

Means-tested benefits

To satisfy the right to reside requirement within the habitual residence test for IS, income-based JSA, income-related ESA, PC, HB, and UC, you must have a right to reside in the common travel area, other than as:[55]

- a European Economic Area (EEA) national with an initial right of residence during your first three months in the UK (see p132);
- a family member of the above;
- the 'primary carer' of a British citizen who is dependent on you and would have to leave the European Union (EU) if you were required to leave (see p181). **Note:** this exclusion is arguably unlawful and although legal challenges have not yet been successful, future ones may be.[56] See CPAG's online service and *Welfare Rights Bulletin* for updates;
- (except for income-based JSA) an EEA jobseeker (see p133);
- (except for income-based JSA) a family member of an EEA jobseeker.

Jobseekers

If your only right to reside is as an EEA jobseeker, you do not satisfy the right to reside test for any of the means-tested benefits *except* for income-based JSA. If you have been receiving both HB and income-based JSA since 31 March 2014, you are exempt from the habitual residence test for HB (see p106) and, therefore, can continue to receive HB, even though you would not be entitled if you were to make a new claim.

If your only right to reside is as an EEA jobseeker, you are excluded from UC. In practice, this is relevant if:

- you live in a UC 'full service area'. If you live in area where 'gateway' conditions apply, you are excluded from UC in any case because these currently include the requirement to be British (see p201); *or*
- you start living with a partner who is already receiving UC. As you do not satisfy the right to reside requirement, you cannot make a joint claim and be paid as a couple. Instead, your partner claims UC as a single person. S/he is paid a maximum amount for a single person, but your income and capital are taken into account.[57]

Note: the Court of Appeal recently rejected an argument that income-related ESA is a benefit designed to facilitate access to the labour market, and therefore should be available to someone whose only right to reside is as a jobseeker.[58] However, permission to appeal against this decision is being sought. See CPAG's online service and *Welfare Rights Bulletin* for updates.

Child benefit and child tax credit

For child benefit and CTC, if you do not have a right to reside you are treated as not present in the UK and therefore not entitled to the benefit or tax credit.[59]

Any right of residence in the UK enables you to satisfy the requirement for child benefit and CTC *except* a right to reside as the primary carer of a British citizen who is dependent on you and who would have to leave the EU if you were required to leave (see p181).[60] This exclusion is arguably unlawful and although legal challenges have not yet been successful, future ones may be.[61] See CPAG's online service and *Welfare Rights Bulletin* for updates.

Note:

- If you are not entitled to child benefit for a child living with you because you do not have a non-excluded right to reside, someone else who contributes to the cost of that child may be able to claim child benefit instead. To be entitled, that person must contribute at least the amount of child benefit that would be payable for the child.[62] See CPAG's *Welfare Benefits and Tax Credits Handbook* for further details.
- The Court of Justice of the European Union (CJEU) recently dismissed an application from the European Commission to declare the right to reside test for child benefit and CTC unlawful, finding that it did not impose a condition that cannot be imposed under the co-ordination rules, it was not directly discriminatory and, although it was indirectly discriminatory, this was justified (see p280).[63] The Court of Appeal in Northern Ireland has held that the right to reside requirement for child benefit is not unlawful, thereby overturning the decision of the Northern Ireland Chief Commissioner that the right to reside test was either directly or indirectly discriminatory.[64]

Who does the right to reside test apply to

The right to reside test only applies to the claimant.

For means-tested benefits, other than income-based JSA claimed as a joint-claim couple and UC, if your partner does not have a right to reside, you can still include her/him in your claim and you are still paid as a couple. For joint-claim JSA and UC couples, the rules are different (see p107).

If you make a joint claim for CTC, both you and your partner must have a right to reside (see p219). If your partner does not have a right to reside, you may be able to make a single claim.

The right to reside requirement does not apply to a child for whom you are claiming CTC, child benefit, HB or UC.

Transitional protection: when you do not need a right to reside

If you have been receiving benefit since before 1 May 2004, you should check whether you have transitional protection from the requirement to have a right to reside. The rules vary depending on the benefit you are claiming.

Means-tested benefits

The right to reside requirement was introduced as part of the habitual residence test for means-tested benefits on 1 May 2004. If you have been receiving a means-tested benefit continuously since 30 April 2004, you do not need a right to reside in order to continue to receive that benefit. Furthermore, you do not need a right to reside for a new claim for a different means-tested benefit, provided the periods of entitlement have been continuous since 30 April 2004. The relevant benefits are:[65]

- council tax benefit (until it was abolished from 1 April 2013);
- income-related ESA (only from 31 October 2011 – see below);
- HB;
- IS;
- income-based JSA;
- PC.

The rules on transitional protection did not apply to income-related ESA when ESA was introduced, and it was only added to the list from 31 October 2011. In addition, you can make a new claim for income-related ESA without needing a right to reside if it is linked by a gap of less than 12 weeks to a previous award of income-related ESA that was part of a continuous period of entitlement to the above benefits going back to 30 April 2004.

Example
Astrid is Swedish and came to the UK in March 2004 with her baby. She claimed IS as a lone parent while living with friends. In 2006, she moved into a bedsit and claimed HB. In 2008 her partner, who was working part time, moved in, so Astrid stopped claiming IS, but she continued to get HB as they had a low income. In 2010 Astrid's partner moved out, but as Astrid now had another baby, she once again claimed IS. In 2012 Astrid became very ill, moved in with some friends, stopped claiming HB and claimed income-related ESA instead of IS. Today Astrid makes a claim for HB as she has just moved into a rented flat.
Astrid does not need to satisfy the right to reside requirement for any of these benefit claims because she has been in receipt of one or more of the relevant benefits for every day since 30 April 2004.

Most people who were entitled to IS on the grounds of disability or incapacity for work have now been reassessed for transfer to income-related ESA. However, if your award has not yet been reassessed and you have been receiving transitionally protected IS (ie, you have continuously received this and/or another means-tested benefit since 30 April 2004), when your IS award is converted to income-related ESA you are exempt from the habitual residence test at the date of transfer.[66] As these cases are now so rare, you may need to explain this to the decision maker.

For transitional protection to apply, you must have been the claimant throughout the whole period of continuous entitlement, rather than a partner, child or parent of the claimant.[67]

The benefit authorities rarely check, or even ask, whether you are transitionally protected from the need to have a right to reside. So, if you have been receiving one or more of the above benefits since 30 April 2004, you should always make this clear when you make your claim, and provide evidence.

Child benefit and child tax credit

The right to reside test only applies to child benefit and CTC if you make a new claim for one of these benefits on or after 1 May 2004.[68]

If you are still receiving the same award of **child benefit** that began before 1 May 2004, you do not need a right to reside.

If you have been claiming **CTC** since before 1 May 2004, you also do not need a right to reside to continue to receive it. Although the tax credit rules treat you as making a new claim each year when you respond to your annual declaration (or when you receive a notice saying you will be treated as having made a declaration), this renewal claim does not require a right to reside.[69]

Notes

1. The habitual residence test

1 Reg 1(2), (3) and (4) SS(DLA,AA&CA)(A) Regs
2 Sch para 21 CTRS(DS)E Regs; reg 12 CTRS(PR)E Regs; reg 16 CTR(SPC)S Regs; reg 16 CTR(S) Regs; reg 28 CTRSPR(W) Regs; Sch para 19 CTRS(DS)W Regs
3 DWP email to CPAG confirming internal guidance, 6 May 2016
4 **IS** Reg 21AA(4) IS Regs
JSA Reg 85A(4) JSA Regs
ESA Reg 70(4) ESA Regs
PC Reg 2(4) SPC Regs
HB Reg 10(3B) HB Regs; reg 10(4A) HB(SPC) Regs
UC Reg 9(4) UC Regs
5 *LB Hillingdon v MJ and Another (HB)* [2009] UKUT 151 (AAC)
6 Reg 3 HB(HR)A Regs
7 **AA** Reg 2(2)&(3A) SS(AA) Regs
DLA Reg 2(2)&(3A) SS(DLA) Regs
PIP Regs 19 and 20 SS(PIP) Regs
CA Reg 9(3) SS(ICA) Regs
8 Regs 3(3), 18(2), 22(3) and 36(3) UC Regs
9 *MM and IS v SSWP (DLA)* [2016] UKUT 149 (AAC)
10 Reg 3E(1) and (2)(d) JSA Regs
11 Reg 3(3) UC Regs
12 Regs 3(3) and 36(3) UC Regs
13 ss3 and 4(1)(e) WRA 2012; reg 3(3) UC Regs
14 Regs 3(3) and 18(2) UC Regs
15 Regs 3(3) and 22(3) UC Regs
16 **IS** Regs 21 and 21AA and Sch 7 para 17 IS Regs
JSA Regs 85 and 85A and Sch 5 para 14 JSA Regs
ESA Regs 69 and 70 and Sch 5 para 11 ESA Regs
17 Reg 10(1) HB Regs; reg 10(1) HB(SPC) Regs
18 **PC** Reg 2 SPC Regs
UC Reg 9 UC Regs

19 **AA** s64(1) SSCBA 1992; reg 2(1) SS(AA) Regs
DLA s71(6) SSCBA 1992; reg 2(1) SS(DLA) Regs
PIP s77(3) WRA 2012; reg 16 SS(PIP) Regs
CA s70(4) SSCBA 1992; reg 9(1) SS(ICA) Regs
20 Reg 3(9) SS&CS(DA) Regs; reg(5)(2) UC,PIP,JSA&ESA(DA) Regs; s12(8)(b) SSA 1998
21 s8(2) SSA 1998
22 Statement by the Secretary of State for Work and Pensions given as part of Cm 7073, para 20, available at www.gov.uk/government/uploads/system/uploads/attachment_data/file/243307/7073.pdf

2. 'Habitual residence in fact'

23 R(IS) 6/96, para 15
24 CIS/15927/1996
25 *R v Barnet London Borough Council ex parte Shah* [1983] 2 AC 309 at 342; *Cameron v Cameron* [1996] SLT 306; R(IS) 9/99
26 *Nessa v Chief Adjudication Officer* [1999] UKHL 41
27 R(IS) 6/96, para 19
28 *M v M (Abduction: England and Scotland)* [1997] 2 FLR 263
29 R(IS) 2/00, para 30
30 CJSA/1223/2006; R(IS) 7/06; CIS/1304/97 and CJSA/5394/98, paras 29-31
31 CIS/4474/2003, paras 15-16
32 R(IS) 2/00, para 28, followed in CIS/1459/1996 and CIS/16097/1996
33 *Nessa v Chief Adjudication Officer* [1999] UKHL 41, reported in R(IS) 2/00
34 *Nessa v Chief Adjudication Officer* [1999] UKHL 41, reported in R(IS) 2/00; *Cameron v Cameron* [1996] SLT 306
35 CIS/4474/2003; R(IS) 7/06
36 CIS/1972/2003; CIS/2559/2005
37 *Nessa v Chief Adjudication Officer* [1999] UKHL 41, reported in R(IS) 2/00, para 26
38 CJSA/1223/2006; R(IS) 7/06; CIS/1304/97 and CJSA/5394/98, paras 29-31

39 **AA** s65(6) SSCBA 1992
   CA Reg 13 SS(C&P) Regs
   DLA Reg 13A(1) SS(C&P) Regs
   PIP Reg 33(1) UC,PIP,JSA&ESA(C&P)
   Regs
40 **IS/JSA/ESA** Reg 13(9) SS(C&P) Regs
   PC Reg 13D(4) SS(C&P) Regs
   HB Reg 83(10) HB Regs; reg 64(11)
   HB(SPC) Regs
41 para A2048 ADM
42 Reg 32 UC,PIP,JSA&ESA(C&P) Regs
43 *Nessa v Chief Adjudication Officer* [1999]
   UKHL 41, reported in R(IS)2/00
44 CIS/1304/1997 and CJSA/5394/1998,
   para 11
45 *KS v SSWP (SPC)* [2010] UKUT 156 (AAC)
46 HB/CTB Circular A22/2010, paras 11-12
47 CIS/1304/97 and CJSA/5394/98, paras
   34-38
48 CIS/1304/97 and CJSA/5394/98, paras
   40-41
49 Ch C2 para C2097 ADM
50 Art 70(4) EU Reg 883/04
51 Art 1(j) EU Reg 883/04
52 *Swaddling v Chief Adjudication Officer,* C-
   90/97 [1999] ECR I-01075
53 R(IS) 3/00

3. **The right to reside**
54 Sch para 21 CTRS(DS)E Regs; reg 12
   CTRS(PR)E Regs; reg 16 CTR(SPC)S
   Regs; reg 16 CTR(S) Regs; reg 28
   CTRSPR(W) Regs; Sch para 19
   CTRS(DS)W Regs
55 **IS** Reg 21AA(3) IS Regs
   JSA Reg 85A(3) JSA Regs
   ESA Reg 70(3) ESA Regs
   PC Reg 2(3) SPC Regs
   HB Reg 10(3A) HB Regs; reg 10(4)
   HB(SPC) Regs
   UC Reg 9(3) UC Regs
56 *Sanneh and Others v SSWP* [2015] EWCA
   Civ 49. Permission to appeal to the
   Supreme Court in the joined case of *HC*
   was granted on 7 March 2016 – file
   reference: *R (on the application of HC) v
   SSWP* UKSC 2015/0215
57 Regs 3(3), 18(2), 22(3) and 36(3) UC
   Regs
58 *Alhashem v SSWP* [2016] EWCA Civ 395
59 **CB** s146 SSCBA 1992; reg 23(4) CB
   Regs
   TC s3(3) TCA 2002; reg 3(5) TC(R) Regs
60 **CB** Reg 23(4) CB Regs
   TC Reg 3(5) TC(R) Regs

61 *Sanneh and Others v SSWP* [2015] EWCA
   Civ 49. Permission to appeal to the
   Supreme Court in the joined case of *HC*
   was granted on 7 March 2016 – file
   reference: *R (on the application of HC) v
   SSWP* UKSC 2015/0215.
62 s143(1)(b) SSCBA 1992
63 *European Commission v UK,* C-308/14
   [2016] ECR, not yet reported
64 *Commissioners for HMRC v Aiga
   Spiridonova,* 13/115948
65 Reg 6(1) SS(HR)A Regs, preserved by reg
   11(2) SS(PA)A Regs
66 Reg 70(4)(l) ESA Regs; reg 10A
   ESA(TP)(EA) Regs
67 CIS/1096/2007
68 **CB** Reg 23(4) CB Regs
   CTC Reg 3(5)(a) TC(R) Regs
69 Reg 3(5)(a) TC(R) Regs

Chapter 12

. . . .

Who has a right to reside

This chapter covers:

1. Introduction (below)
2. Non-European Economic Area nationals (p123)
3. British, Irish and Commonwealth citizens (p123)
4. European Economic Area nationals (p124)
5. Croatian, A2 and A8 nationals (p127)
6. Initial right of residence (p132)
7. Jobseekers (p133)
8. Workers (p140)
9. Retaining worker status (p146)
10. Self-employed people (p153)
11. Retaining self-employed status (p157)
12. Self-sufficient people and students (p159)
13. Family members of European Economic Area nationals (p164)
14. Derivative residence rights (p175)
15. Permanent right to reside (p184)

This chapter explains who has a right to reside. For information on the benefits and tax credits that require a right to reside, details of how the requirement operates for each and the types of residency rights that are specifically excluded, see p115.

The right to reside requirement is only one of the residence and presence conditions that must be satisfied for each individual benefit and tax credit. See Chapter 13 for more information.

---

1. **Introduction**

Whether or not you have a right to reside depends on the nationality, immigration status and other particular circumstances of you, your family members and certain people for whom you care. You may have a right of residence under UK law or one that comes directly from European Union law, or both. You may have more than one right of residence, or you may not have any.

Any residence right is sufficient to satisfy the right to reside requirement, unless it is specifically excluded for the benefit or tax credit you want to claim.

The residence rights of some people are more complicated than others. In general, if you are a European Economic Area (EEA) national (see p124), or a family member or primary carer of an EEA national, your residence rights are more complex. Consequently, the majority of this chapter focuses on these groups. See the checklist on p126.

Note: the phrases 'right to reside' and 'right of residence' have the same meaning and are used interchangeably in this *Handbook*.

2. Non-European Economic Area nationals

If you are a non-European Economic Area (EEA) national, you have a right to reside if:
* you have been granted leave to enter or remain under UK immigration law. You have a right to reside during your period of leave. Any form of leave gives you a right to reside – eg, indefinite leave, refugee leave, humanitarian protection, discretionary leave or limited leave granted under the Immigration Rules, such as as a spouse or visitor. However, if you have leave which is subject to a condition that you do not have recourse to public funds, or indefinite leave granted as the result of a maintenance undertaking, you are defined as a 'person subject to immigration control' (see p57), and unless you are in an exempt group, you are excluded from benefits on this basis (see Part 3); *or*
* you are someone who does not need leave to enter or remain under UK immigration law because you have a right to reside under European law. The most common examples are if you are the family member (see p164) or primary carer (see p175) of an EEA national who has a right to reside and who confers her/his residence rights on you.

3. British, Irish and Commonwealth citizens

British citizens have an automatic right of residence in the UK. However, this right is under UK law and British citizens do not usually have residence rights in the UK under European Union law if they have not lived with a right to reside in another European Economic Area (EEA) country before returning to the UK. Therefore, unless otherwise stated, all references in this chapter to EEA nationals should be read as *not* including British citizens.

British citizens do not automatically confer residence rights on their family members. If you are not a British citizen but you are a family member of a British citizen, or if you are a dual British/other EEA state citizen, see p168.

If you are the primary carer of a British citizen, see p181.

Commonwealth citizens with the right of abode also have a right of residence in the UK (see p15).

Irish citizens

If you are an Irish citizen you have a right to reside in Ireland, which is part of the common travel area – ie, Ireland, Channel Islands, Isle of Man and the UK. You therefore satisfy the right to reside requirement for means-tested benefits, as these require you to have a right to reside in the common travel area.

If you are the family member of an Irish citizen in the UK, your residence rights as a family member require the Irish citizen to have a relevant right to reside in the same way as family members of other EEA nationals (see p164).

4. European Economic Area nationals

In practice, the right to reside requirement mainly affects nationals from the European Economic Area (EEA). The residence rights of EEA nationals, their family members and carers can be complex, as both European Union (EU) law and UK law must be considered, and both are subject to a considerable amount of interpretation through caselaw.

Legal sources of European Economic Area residence rights

The right of residence of EEA nationals and their family members derives from the EU treaties, in particular the **Treaty of the Functioning of the European Union** (TFEU), or the EEA Agreement which provides similar (although not always equivalent) rights for Norway, Iceland and Liechtenstein. The most relevant provisions of the TFEU include the following.

- Discrimination on nationality grounds is prohibited wherever the provisions of the Treaty apply.[1]
- Every person holding a nationality of an EU state is an EU citizen and has certain rights that stem from this.[2]
- EU nationals have the right to move and reside freely within the territory of the EU states.

However, the right to move and reside freely within the EU is subject to the limitations and conditions set out in the TFEU and in other legislation that gives effect to it.[3] This means that those covered by the TFEU must satisfy certain conditions to have a right of residence. The most important secondary legislation that sets out residence rights and the conditions that must be satisfied is **EU Directive 2004/38**. This brings together most rights of residence under EU law into one piece of legislation and replaces many earlier directives and regulations, which previously set out EU residence rights. Directive 2004/38 has been in force since 30 April 2006 and was extended from 1 March 2009 to cover nationals of Norway, Iceland and Liechtenstein.[4] **Note:** while the EU Directive is the most important source of residence rights for EEA nationals and their family members, it is not the only one – eg, some derivative rights of residence (see p175) stem from other EU legislation.

Swiss nationals and their family members are covered by a separate agreement, which provides similar rights.[5]

The Immigration (European Economic Area) Regulations 2006, referred to in this *Handbook* as the **'EEA Regulations'**, apply to all EEA nationals (except British citizens – see p123) and Swiss nationals.[6] These give similar rights of residence to those contained in the Directive. Where they conflict with, or do not completely incorporate, EU Directive 2004/38, you can rely on whichever is more favourable to you.

Who can have European Economic Area residence rights

You may have EEA residence rights if you are:
- an EEA national (other than a British citizen, except in limited circumstances – see below) or a Swiss national; *or*
- a family member of an EEA national (other than a British citizen, except in limited circumstances – see below) or Swiss national who has a right to reside. You can have these rights whether or not you are an EEA national;
- someone who was previously in the above group; *or*
- the primary carer of certain EEA nationals (including British citizens).

In all cases, whether or not you have EEA residence rights also depends on other factors.

For a list of **EEA member states**, see p40. However, note that, unless otherwise stated, references to EEA nationals in this chapter should be read as *not* including **British citizens**.[7] This is because British citizens have different rights in the UK compared to other EEA nationals. If you are a British citizen, you always have a right to reside in the UK under UK law. However, most British citizens do not have residence rights in the UK under EU law.[8] This means that family members and primary carers of British citizens do not have the same rights as family members and primary carers of other EEA nationals. If you are the family member of a British citizen, see p168. If you are the primary carer of a British citizen, see p175.

In general, **Swiss nationals** have the same residence rights as EEA nationals, so unless otherwise stated, references to EEA nationals include Swiss nationals.

Croatian, A2 and A8 nationals can have their residence rights affected by additional restrictions. These countries are listed on p127. The restrictions are summarised on p128 and noted in the sections of this chapter where they are relevant.

Checklist

As EEA residence rights can be complex and affected by many different factors, it can be helpful to work through the following checklist of the main residence rights.

- **Step one:** are you an EEA national with a right to reside based on your current or previous employment, self-employment, jobseeking or self-sufficiency (including being self-sufficient while a student)? You have a right to reside if you:
  - are a 'qualified person' (see below); *or*
  - have a permanent right of residence (see p184). This is usually after five years of 'legal residence', but in limited circumstances can be acquired before five years.
- **Step two:** are you a 'family member' (see p164) of someone covered in Step one? You have a right to reside, even if you are not an EEA national yourself. In limited circumstances, you may have a right to reside if you were the family member of someone in Step one but s/he has now died, left the UK or your marriage or civil partnership has been terminated (see p171).
- **Step three:** do you have a 'derivative right to reside' – ie, through someone else's right to reside, but not as her/his family member? Certain primary carers and children have a 'derivative right to reside'. See p175 for more details.

Qualified person

You are a **'qualified person'** if you are a:[9]

- jobseeker (see p133);
- worker (see p140), including if you have retained this status (see p146);
- self-employed person (see p153), including if you have retained this status (see p157); *or*
- self-sufficient person, including a self-sufficient student (see p159).

Note:

- The term 'qualified person' appears in the EEA Regulations, but is not used in the EU Directive, although the same groups of people are covered.[10]
- You can have more than one right to reside at a time – eg, you may be a self-employed person and also the family member of someone with a permanent right of residence.[11]
- If you are an EEA national or family member of an EEA national, you also have an initial right of residence for the first three months that you are in the UK. However, if this is your only right to reside, it does not entitle you to means-tested benefits (see p132). It can count towards the five years of 'legal residence' required to acquire a permanent right of residence (see p184).
- If you are a Croatian, A2 or A8 national, a 'family member' (see p165) of a Croatian, A2 or A8 national, or if you have a derivative right to reside (see

p175) as the child or primary carer of a Croatian, A2 or A8 national, see below for the additional restrictions that can affect your right to reside.

5. **Croatian, A2 and A8 nationals**

Croatia, A2 and A8 states

Croatia joined the European Union (EU) on 1 July 2013.
Restrictions are currently in force until 30 June 2018.
The A2 states are: Bulgaria and Romania.
These states joined the EU on 1 January 2007.
Restrictions applied until 31 December 2013.
The A8 states are: Czech Republic, Estonia, Hungary, Latvia, Lithuania, Poland, Slovakia and Slovenia.
These states joined the EU on 1 May 2004.
Restrictions applied until 30 April 2009 (although this date is the subject of an appeal – see below).

The treaties under which the above 'accession' states joined the EU allowed existing member states to restrict accession national's access to their labour markets, and their residence rights as workers and jobseekers. These restrictions can only be imposed for a maximum of five years from the date the states joined the EU, but can be extended for a further two years if certain conditions are met. The UK government imposed the restrictions for five years and then extended them for A2 and A8 nationals for an additional two years. However, this extension of restrictions for A8 nationals from 1 May 2009 to 30 April 2011 has now been held to be unlawful.[12] This means that A8 nationals were *not* subject to restrictions during this two-year period. However, the DWP has been granted permission to appeal against this decision.[13] Guidance has been issued to decision makers advising that they not decide any claims in which this two-year period is relevant, pending the outcome of the appeal, and that they invite the First-tier Tribunal to do the same.[14]

Most **Croatian nationals** have certain restrictions on their residence rights as jobseekers, workers or people who retain worker status. These restrictions have applied since 1 July 2013 and apply until 30 June 2018, but they may be extended for a further two years.

Although the restrictions on A2 and A8 nationals have now ended, you need to know what the restrictions were and how they operated if your current or future residence rights are affected by the residence rights you or your family member had in the past – eg, when establishing permanent residence.

While in force, the restrictions apply unless you are in one of the exempt groups.

If you are a **Croatian national** and are not exempt, you must obtain an 'accession worker authorisation document' (in most cases, an accession worker registration certificate, specifying the employer you can work for) before taking up employment, and then work in accordance with it.[15] See p129 for details.

If you are an **A2 national** who was subject to restrictions, you were required to obtain an accession worker authorisation document (in most cases, an accession worker card specifying the employer you could work for) before taking up employment, and then have worked in accordance with it.[16] See p129.

If you are an **A8 national** who was subject to restrictions, you had to work for an 'authorised employer' (see p131).[17]

Broadly speaking, this meant you had to register each job you took with the Worker Registration Scheme (but see p131 for the precise meaning as it can affect your residence rights).

Restrictions on residence rights

If you are a Croatian national, unless you are in one of the groups listed on p129, you are subject to worker authorisation (see above) and your residence rights are restricted until 30 June 2018 as follows.[18]
- You do not have a right to reside as a jobseeker.
- You are only defined as a 'worker' if you have an accession worker authorisation document and are working in accordance with it.
- You cannot retain your worker status when you stop work in the ways other workers can (see p146).

If you are an A2 national who was subject to restrictions (see p129 for exemptions), your residence rights were restricted between 1 January 2007 and 31 December 2013 in the same way as Croatian nationals.[19]

If you are an A8 national who was subject to restrictions (see p130 for exemptions), your residence rights were restricted between 1 May 2004 and the date the restrictions ended (now held to be 30 April 2009, rather than 30 April 2011, but this is subject to appeal – see p127) as follows.[20]
- You did not have a right to reside as a jobseeker.
- You were only defined as a 'worker' if you were working for an 'authorised employer' (see p131).
- You could not retain your worker status when you stopped work in the ways other workers could (see p146). However, if you lost your job within the first month of employment, you could retain your status in those ways, but only until the end of the month.

The restrictions do not affect other residence rights you may have as a European Economic Area (EEA) national – eg, as a self-employed or self-sufficient person.[21]

The restrictions also do not affect the application of other provisions of EU law, including the co-ordination rules in Chapter 16. These apply to Croatian, A2 and A8 nationals in the same way as they do to other EEA nationals.

Croatian and A2 nationals not subject to worker authorisation

If you are a Croatian national, you are subject to worker authorisation and have additional restrictions on your residence rights, unless you are in one of the groups listed below.

If you are an A2 national, you were subject to worker authorisation until 31 December 2013 and had additional restrictions on your residence rights (see p128), unless you were in one of the groups listed below. **Note:** these restrictions for A2 nationals ended on 31 December 2013.

You are not subject to worker authorisation, and your residence rights are not restricted, if you:[22]
- have (or had on 30 June 2013 (Croatian) or 31 December 2006 (A2)) leave to enter or remain with no restriction on employment;
- were 'legally working' (see p131) in the UK for 12 months without breaks of more than 30 days (in total), up to and including 31 December 2006 (A2) or 30 June 2013 (Croatian);
- have 'legally worked' for 12 months (beginning before or after 31 December 2006 (A2) or 30 June 2013 (Croatian)), disregarding any breaks of less than 30 days (in total);
- are a posted worker – ie, you are working in the UK providing services on behalf of an employer who is not established in the UK;
- are a member of a diplomatic mission (or the family member of such a person) or a person otherwise entitled to diplomatic immunity;
- have dual nationality with the UK or another (non-A2/Croatian) EEA state;
- are the spouse/civil partner (or, Croatian only, unmarried or same-sex partner) of a UK national or of a person settled (ie, with indefinite leave to enter or remain – see p23[23]) in the UK;
- are the spouse/civil partner (or, Croatian only, unmarried or same-sex partner) or child under 18 of a person with leave to enter or remain in the UK that allows employment;
- have a permanent right of residence (see p184);
- are a student with a registration certificate that states that you cannot work more than 20 hours a week (unless it is part of vocational training or during vacations) and you comply with this. If the certificate confirms you can work during the four months after the course ends, the exemption continues for this period;
- are a family member of an EEA national who has a right to reside, unless the EEA national is an A2 (or, if you are Croatian, a Croatian) national subject to

worker authorisation (or, A2 only, the only reason s/he is not an A2 national subject to worker authorisation is because s/he is covered by the group below);
- are a family member of an A2 (or, if you are Croatian, a Croatian) national subject to worker authorisation who has a right to reside (for an A2 national only, as a worker, student, self-employed or self-sufficient person). If you are a Croatian national (or an A2 national relying on an A2 worker), you are a 'family member' if you are the descendant and either under 21 or dependent, the spouse/civil partner, or (Croatians only) the unmarried or same-sex partner;
- are a 'highly skilled person' – ie, you:[24]
    - met the points-based criteria in the Immigration Rules for entering the UK on this basis; *or*
    - have a qualification at degree level or higher in the UK, or Higher National Diploma in Scotland and, within 12 months of this award, you apply for a registration certificate confirming your unconditional access to the labour market.

A8 nationals who were not required to register

If you are an A8 national, during the period of restrictions (see p127) you were defined as 'requiring registration', any work you did had to be for an 'an authorised employer' (see p131) and your residence rights were restricted (see p128), unless you:[25]
- had leave to enter or remain on 30 April 2004 which had no restriction on employment;
- were 'legally working' (see p131) in the UK for 12 months, without breaks of more than 30 days (in total), up to and including 30 April 2004;
- had 'legally worked' for 12 months (beginning before or after 30 April 2004), disregarding any breaks of less than 30 days (in total);
- were the spouse/civil partner or child under 18 of a person with leave to enter or remain in the UK that allowed employment;
- had dual nationality with the UK and another (non-A2/A8) EEA state or Switzerland;
- were a family member of another EEA or Swiss national who had a right to reside under the EEA Regulations (other than an A2/A8 national subject to registration/authorisation if her/his only right to reside was for the first three months in the UK);
- were the member of a diplomatic mission (or the family member of such a person) or a person otherwise entitled to diplomatic immunity;
- were a posted worker – ie, you were working in the UK providing services on behalf of an employer who was not established in the UK.

Legally working

The phrase 'legally working' is relevant for determining whether you completed your 12 months of legal work in order to be exempt from restrictions (see p130 for A8 nationals and p129 for Croatian and A2 nationals), and for whether you are, or were, a 'worker' at any a particular time. It has a specific meaning and only refers to employment, not self-employment. Although there are no additional restrictions placed on self-employment, periods of self-employment do not count as 'legally working' for the purpose of exempting you from restrictions.

If you are a Croatian national (or an A2 national before 1 January 2014), you are/were 'legally working' if:[26]

- you are/were working in accordance with your worker authorisation document; *or*
- you are/were working during a period when you are/were in one of the exempt groups on p129 (other than posted workers); *or*
- the work was done before 1 July 2013 (for Croatian nationals) or before 1 January 2007 (for A2 nationals), either in accordance with any leave you had under the Immigration Act 1971 or when you did not require leave. The Court of Appeal has held that this does not apply to work done with permission from the Home Office while you were an asylum seeker.[27]

If you are an A8 national, you were 'legally working' before the restrictions ended (now held to be 30 April 2009, rather than 30 April 2011, but this is subject to appeal – see p127) if:[28]

- you were working for an authorised employer (see below); *or*
- you were working during a period when you were in one of the exempt groups listed above (other than if you were the spouse/civil partner or child of a person whose leave to enter or remain in the UK allowed employment); *or*
- the work was done before 1 May 2004 either in accordance with any leave you had under the Immigration Act 1971 or when you did not require leave. The Court of Appeal has held that this does not apply to work done with permission from the Home Office while you were an asylum seeker.[29]

Authorised employer

If you were an A8 national subject to restrictions, you were defined as working for an 'authorised employer' if you:[30]

– were within the first month of employment; *or*
– applied for a worker's registration certificate under the Worker Registration Scheme within the first month of work, but did not yet have a certificate or refusal; *or*
– had a valid worker's registration certificate issued under the Worker Registration Scheme for that employer; *or*
– had been 'legally working' for that employer since 30 April 2004; *or*

– began work at an agricultural camp between 1 May 2004 and 31 December 2004, and before 1 May 2004 you had been issued with leave under the Immigration Act 1971 as a seasonal worker at such a camp.

If you only applied for a registration certificate after the first month of work, you only count as working for an authorised employer from the date it was issued. It does not apply retrospectively.[31]

If you are a Croatian national and your employment ends, you stop legally working, stop being a 'worker' and, unless you are in an exempt group, you cannot retain your worker status. However, if you are still under a contract of employment, you continue to be legally working and a worker – eg, if you are on maternity leave, holiday leave, sick leave or compassionate leave (including if the leave is unpaid).[32]

The same applied to A2 nationals between 1 January 2007 and 31 December 2013 and A8 nationals between 1 May 2004 and the end of restrictions (currently subject to appeal – see p127).

6. **Initial right of residence**

All European Economic Area (EEA) nationals have a right to enter any member state.[33] If you are an EEA national, you also have an initial right of residence in any member state for the first three months of your stay, provided you hold a valid identity card or passport.[34] You have this initial right of residence whether or not you are working or seeking work, but it is subject to your not becoming an unreasonable burden on the social assistance system of the UK.[35]

You also have a right of residence if you are not an EEA national, but are a family member of an EEA national who has this initial right of residence for three months.[36] For details of who counts as your family member, see p164.

Note: you can have one or more right of residence (eg, as the family member of a worker and/or as a jobseeker) in addition to your initial right of residence – ie, you do not have to wait for the three months to end before you have another right of residence.

If your *only* right of residence is on the basis of your (or your family member's) initial three-month right of residence, the benefit rules exclude you from entitlement to **income support, income-based jobseeker's allowance (JSA), income-related employment and support allowance, pension credit, housing benefit and universal credit.** However, if you have a right of residence on another basis during your initial three months in the UK, you can satisfy the right to reside requirement, provided it is not a residence right that is excluded for the means-tested benefit you want to claim (see p116).

Note: the requirement for you to have been living in the common travel area for the past three months for income-based JSA is a separate part of the habitual residence test (see p92) and unrelated to this initial right of residence.

If your *only* right of residence is on the basis of your (or your family member's) initial three-month right of residence, the **child benefit and child tax credit** (CTC) rules do not exclude you from entitlement. Therefore, you satisfy the right to reside requirement for child benefit and CTC, but only for the first three months of your residence in the UK, unless you have some other right of residence. **Note:** unless you are exempt, you must still have been living in the UK for the past three months (see p92).

Note: you can count a period during which this is your only right of residence as part of the continuous five-year period of 'legal residence' required to acquire permanent residence (see p184).

7. Jobseekers

If you are a European Economic Area (EEA) national looking for work in the UK, you may have a right to reside as a 'jobseeker' (see below). You may also have a right to reside if you are the family member (see p164) of a jobseeker. However, both these residence rights only satisfy the right to reside requirement for certain benefits (see p139). Furthermore, because of the way the benefit authorities apply the EEA Regulations (see p124), you may have difficulty claiming these benefits over the longer term solely on the basis of your right to reside as a jobseeker. You should therefore always check whether you have a right of residence on some other basis.

Note:
* If you have previously been a 'worker' (see p140) and are now looking for work, in addition to having a right to reside as a jobseeker, you may also have a right of residence as someone who retains worker status (see p146). This satisfies the right to reside requirement for all benefits.
* Periods when you have a right to reside as a jobseeker count towards the five years required to acquire permanent residence (see p184), which, once acquired, satisfies the right to reside requirement for all benefits.

Who has a right to reside as a jobseeker

If you are an EEA national, you have a right to reside as a jobseeker if:[37]
* you are in the UK and you can provide evidence that you are seeking employment and have a 'genuine chance of being engaged';
* you entered the UK in order to seek employment, or (EEA Regulations only – see p134) you are present in the UK seeking employment immediately after having a right to reside as a worker (except if you retained worker status while

involuntarily unemployed – see p147), a student, a self-employed or self-sufficient person; *and*

- (EEA Regulations only[38]) either you have not already had a right to reside as a jobseeker for 91 days or, if you have, the evidence you provide to show that you are seeking employment and have a genuine chance of being engaged is 'compelling' (see p135).

If you *previously* had a right to reside as a jobseeker for 91 days since 31 December 2013, or you retained worker status while involuntarily unemployed (see p147) for at least six months, in order to have a right to reside as a jobseeker the EEA Regulations require that (unless since having either residence right you have been absent from the UK continuously for at least 12 months):[39]

- you must have since had an absence from the UK. **Note:** at the time of writing, the benefit authorities were not enforcing this requirement and have not done so since it was included in the regulations, but it could be applied at any time; *and*
- the evidence that you are seeking employment and have a genuine chance of being engaged must be 'compelling' (see p135) from the start of this current period of residence as a jobseeker.

Only periods since 31 December 2013 count towards any of the time periods referred to here.[40]

Note: if you are refused benefit because of a requirement that is in the EEA Regulations only, you should challenge the decision on the basis that these interpret the category of jobseeker more narrowly than the European Court of Justice.[41] This is particularly relevant to the standard of evidence that you can be required to submit (see p135).

Croatian, A2 and A8 nationals

If you are a Croatian national subject to worker authorisation (see p129), you do *not* have a right to reside as a jobseeker.[42] Similarly if, during the relevant period of restrictions, you were an A2 national who was subject to worker authorisation (see p129) or an A8 national who was required to register your work (see p130), you did not have a right to reside as a jobseeker (see p128).[43]

For how long do you have a right to reside as a jobseeker

There is no time limit on how long you can have a right to reside as a jobseeker. It continues for as long as you can provide evidence that you are continuing to seek work and have a genuine chance of being engaged.[44]

However, the EEA Regulations require that to continue to have a right to reside as a jobseeker for longer than 91 days, you must provide 'compelling' evidence that you are continuing to seek work and have a genuine chance of being engaged. The benefit authority ends your entitlement if it decides you fail this requirement. It is referred to as the 'genuine prospects of work test' (see below).

Evidence requirements

To have a right to reside as a jobseeker, you must be able to provide evidence that you are continuing to seek work and have a genuine chance of being engaged. See below for the type of employment you must be seeking and have a genuine chance of obtaining.

The EEA Regulations, but not European Union (EU) law, require that to continue to have a right to reside as a jobseeker for longer than 91 days you must provide 'compelling' evidence that you are continuing to seek work and have a genuine chance of being engaged. The 91 days comprises any periods when you have had a right to reside as a jobseeker since 31 December 2013. This could be one continuous period or a cumulative total of shorter periods.[45]

However, the requirement for your evidence to be 'compelling' applies from the *start* of your period of residence as a jobseeker if, since 31 December 2013, you:[46]

- previously had a right to reside as a jobseeker for a total of 91 days; *or*
- retained worker status while involuntarily unemployed (see p147) for at least six months and you have since been absent from the UK for a period of less than 12 months. **Note:** at the time of writing, the benefit authorities have not enforced this requirement to have had an absence since it was included in the regulations, but it could be applied at any time.

If you have had an absence from the UK for a continuous period of at least 12 months, on your return you can have 91 days with a right to reside as a jobseeker before your evidence of seeking work and having a genuine chance of being engaged must be 'compelling'.[47]

Genuine prospects of work

'Genuine prospects of work test'
The **'genuine prospects of work test'** is the term used by the benefit authorities, including in their guidance. It refers to the requirement in the EEA Regulations for the evidence that you are continuing to seek work and have a genuine chance of being engaged to be 'compelling' after 91 days as a jobseeker or six months as someone with worker status retained on the basis that you are involuntarily unemployed.
Although the term and the detail of the guidance emphasise the need for evidence that you have a 'genuine chance of being engaged' over the need for evidence that you are continuing to seek work, the EEA Regulations require both.

- If you are subject to the 'genuine prospects of work test', first check whether it should be applied to you, either at this time or at all. If you are claiming income-based jobseeker's allowance (JSA) with a right to reside because of worker status retained on the basis of being involuntarily unemployed (see p147), the test does not apply until you have retained your worker status on this basis for six months. The test should therefore not be applied to you after 91 days, but will be applied after six months. If you are claiming income-based JSA with a right to reside *other than* as either a jobseeker or with worker status retained on the basis of involuntary unemployment, the test does not apply to you at any point.[48] You can continue to receive income-based JSA for as long as your other right of residence continues. However, this is frequently overlooked. If you have another right to reside, make sure that the DWP is aware of this. If the DWP tries to apply the genuine prospects of work test, make it clear that your alternative right of residence means that the test should not be applied to you.

- If your only right to reside is as a jobseeker, the test will be applied to you after 91 days. **Note:** although the EEA Regulations require you to provide compelling evidence after 91 days' *residence* as a jobseeker, in practice, the DWP only counts the period when you were entitled to JSA (income-based or contribution-based).[49] Guidance to decision makers states that certain periods can be disregarded when calculating the 91-day period, including up to 13 weeks when you are treated as being available for work because you have experienced domestic violence, periods of temporary absence when you are treated as being in Great Britain (see p235) and periods of sickness.[50]
- The term 'compelling' is not defined in the legislation and therefore should have its ordinary, everyday meaning. In considering this meaning, the Upper Tribunal held that the requirement to provide 'compelling' evidence means you are required to provide evidence that shows, on the balance of probabilities, that you are seeking employment and have a genuine chance of being engaged. To interpret the phrase as meaning that a higher standard of proof is required would be contrary to EU law.[51] Under EU law, although you must be able to provide evidence that you are continuing to seek work and have a genuine chance of being engaged, there is no requirement for the quality of this evidence to change after a particular period of time.[52] This was recently confirmed by the Upper Tribunal, which also held that in determining whether you have a genuine chance of being engaged a period of six months or more seeking employment without success is a relevant factor, among others. However, the requirement to provide 'compelling' evidence of a genuine chance of being engaged 'cannot raise the bar' of what constitutes a genuine chance of being engaged beyond chances that are founded on something objective and offer real prospects of employment within a reasonable period.[53] For further details on the argument that the compelling evidence requirement in the EEA Regulations is contrary to EU law, see CPAG's website for a document written before the above two Upper Tribunal decisions.[54]

- You should ensure that your evidence of seeking employment and having a genuine chance of being engaged is as strong and extensive as possible. Include details of all your work search activities, any interviews or responses, your qualifications, work history (paid and unpaid, both in and out of the UK), skills and abilities that make you employable. It can also be relevant to include evidence of qualifications and experience you will be obtaining in the near future.[55]
- DWP guidance to decision makers was written before the above two Upper Tribunal decisions. It gives limited examples of what could be accepted as 'compelling' evidence, including evidence that you have been offered a specific job that is due to start in less than three months, or a change of circumstances (such as completing vocational training or relocating to a better labour market area) that has given you genuine prospects of employment resulting in job interviews.[56] Although this guidance is not legally binding and can be disregarded, if it applies to your circumstances you should still refer to it.
- In rare circumstances, if you have an offer of a job that you cannot take up immediately, but which is being held open for you and is due to start in less than three months, you may have a right to reside as a 'worker' rather than as a jobseeker (see p142).[57]
- If your JSA has been stopped because the DWP decided you failed the 'genuine prospects of work test' and you have a partner, s/he may be able to claim JSA for you both.[58] This does not prevent you challenging the DWP's decision.
- If you have been a jobseeker without obtaining work for some time, your evidence must demonstrate that you have a genuine chance of being engaged, despite the long period of unemployment.[59]
- Further Upper Tribunal caselaw on the requirement for 'compelling' evidence is expected. See CPAG's online service and *Welfare Rights Bulletin* for updates.
- For further information on the types of evidence that may be helpful, see p362.

Employment you must seek and have a genuine chance of obtaining

In order to have a right of residence as a jobseeker, you must be looking for and have a genuine chance of obtaining employment that would be sufficient for you to be a 'worker' (see p140) if you obtained it.[60]

If you are only looking for work as a self-employed person, this does not give you a right to reside as a jobseeker. However, if you are taking steps to establish self-employed activity, you may count as a self-employed person and have a right of residence on that basis (see p153).

In most cases, you should be accepted as seeking employment and having a genuine chance of being engaged if you are 'signing on' and satisfy the requirements to be 'actively seeking' and 'available for' work for the purposes of entitlement to JSA, or national insurance (NI) credits, or you satisfy the 'work search' and 'work availability' requirements if you come under the universal credit system.

For an explanation of these requirements, see CPAG's *Welfare Benefits and Tax Credits Handbook*.

However, it has been held that, in rare circumstances, it is possible for someone to satisfy these conditions and not be accepted as having a genuine chance of being engaged.[61]

If the decision maker decides that, despite satisfying the benefit requirements regarding your work seeking and availability, you do not have a genuine chance of being engaged, you can try to argue that your case is not one of the rare cases where this applies. It may help to look in detail at the provisions you have been held to satisfy. For example, to be accepted as actively seeking work for JSA, you must, in any week, take such steps as you can reasonably be expected to take in order to have the best prospects of securing employment.[62] Except in limited situations, if you put any restrictions on your availability for work, you must be able to show that you still have 'reasonable prospects of securing employment'.[63] If you have placed restrictions on your availability and these have been accepted as satisfying this requirement for JSA, it may be arguable that is then irrational to decide that you do not have a 'genuine chance of being engaged'. This argument was discussed at the Upper Tribunal, but it was accepted that it did not apply in any of the cases in question, and so no decision was required.[64]

If you have already been receiving JSA for 91 days, the DWP is likely to require you to provide 'compelling' evidence that you are continuing to seek work and have a genuine chance of being engaged (referred to as the 'genuine prospects of work test' – see p134). However, there is no change to the *type* of work you must be seeking and have a genuine chance of obtaining.

If you do not claim jobseeker's allowance

There is no requirement that you must have claimed or be in receipt of JSA in order to have a right to reside as a jobseeker. The requirements are simply that you are an EEA national who can provide evidence that you are seeking employment and have a genuine chance of being engaged.

The most straightforward way to be accepted as meeting these requirements is if you claim, and are entitled to, contribution-based or income-based JSA on the basis of being available for and actively seeking work or, if you come under the universal credit (UC) system, contribution-based JSA on the basis that you satisfy the work search and work availability requirements, or NI credits on the basis of unemployment.

However, if you are not eligible for JSA or NI credits, or you are still waiting for a decision on your claim, you can argue (eg, to HM Revenue and Customs in respect of a claim for child benefit or child tax credit (CTC)) that you still meet the essential requirements of being a jobseeker.[65]

Benefit entitlement

If you have a right to reside as a jobseeker, this satisfies the right to reside requirement for:
- income-based JSA;
- child benefit; and
- CTC.

Note:
- To satisfy the habitual residence test for income-based JSA, you must still be accepted as 'habitually resident in fact' (see p110) and have been living in the common travel area for the three months prior to your claim (see p92).
- You must have been living in the UK for the three months prior to your claim for child benefit and CTC, unless you are exempt from this requirement (see p94).

If you have a right to reside as a jobseeker, this does *not* satisfy the right to reside requirement for:
- income support (IS);
- income-related employment and support allowance (ESA) (but see below);
- pension credit (PC);
- housing benefit (HB) (but see p140);
- UC.

You must therefore have another right to reside to get one of the above benefits.

Jobseekers have more limited benefit entitlement than most other groups with residence rights under EU law. EU Directive 2004/38 states that the host member state is not obliged to provide entitlement to social assistance to those with a right to reside as a jobseeker.[66] However, the UK is required to give EEA jobseekers who have established real links with the UK labour market equal access to financial benefits that are intended to facilitate access to the UK labour market as British citizens.[67] Therefore, the UK provides entitlement to income-based JSA along with child benefit and CTC.

Income-related employment and support allowance

If your only right to reside is as a jobseeker, the UK rules state that this is not sufficient to obtain income-related ESA.[68] Therefore, you should claim income-based JSA instead, if you can.

The Court of Appeal recently rejected an argument that this exclusion from income-related ESA of those whose only right to reside is as a jobseeker is unlawful. The argument was that, because most claimants (other than those entitled to the support component) are required to engage in work-related activity which is intended to assist them in obtaining a job, income-related ESA is a benefit intended to facilitate access to the UK labour market. The European

Court of Justice held that financial benefits intended to facilitate access to the UK labour market must be made available to EEA jobseekers who have established real links with the UK labour market on an equal basis to British citizens.[69] However, the Court of Appeal held that income-related ESA was not a benefit intended to facilitate access to the UK labour market.[70] Permission to appeal against this decision is being sought. See CPAG's online service and *Welfare Rights Bulletin* for updates.

Housing benefit

If you have a right to reside as a jobseeker, this does not satisfy the right to reside requirement for HB.

However, you are exempt from the habitual residence test for HB (see p106) if you are receiving income-based JSA and either:

- have a right to reside other than one that is excluded for HB (see p116); *or*
- have been receiving both HB and income-based JSA since 31 March 2014. Your exemption on this basis ends when either you cease to be entitled to that income-based JSA or you make a new claim for HB.[71]

8. **Workers**

If you are a European Economic Area (EEA) national working in the UK, you may have a right to reside as a 'worker' (see below). You may also have a right to reside if you are a family member (see p164) of a worker. Once you have established worker status, it is important to be clear when you cease to be a worker (see p145). In limited circumstances, you can retain your worker status after you stop being a worker (see p146).

If you have a right to reside as a worker, as someone who has retained worker status, or as the family member of a worker, your right to reside satisfies the right to reside requirement for all benefits.

Who has a right to reside as a worker

If you are an EEA national and a 'worker', you have a right to reside.[72]

The term 'worker' is not defined in European Union (EU) legislation and the EEA Regulations simply cross-refer to EU law.[73] It should therefore be interpreted in accordance with EU law and the principles established through EU caselaw.

You count as a 'worker' if:

- you are in an employment relationship (see p142); *and*
- the work you do entails activities that are 'genuine and effective' rather than 'marginal and ancillary' (see p143).

The reason why you moved to the UK is irrelevant, provided you meet the above conditions.[74] For example, if your principle intention in coming to the UK was to pursue a course of study, this is not relevant when determining whether you are a worker.[75]

Your motives for seeking employment can be taken into account when determining whether you are pursuing activity as an employed person. However, once it is established that you are, your motives are irrelevant.[76]

Note: if you have been a worker, you do not necessarily lose this status just because you stop working. For more information on when you cease to be a worker see p145, and for the circumstances in which you can retain your worker status, see p146.

Croatian, A2 and A8 workers

If you are a Croatian national subject to worker authorisation, you do *not* have a right to reside as a worker unless you hold an accession worker authorisation document and you are working in accordance with it (see p131).[77]

Similarly, if, during the period of restrictions (1 January 2007 to 31 December 2013), you were an A2 national who was subject to worker authorisation, you did not have a right to reside as a worker unless you held an accession worker authorisation document and worked in accordance with it (see p131).[78]

Before the restrictions ended, if you were an A8 national who was required to register your work, you did not have a right to reside as a worker unless you were working for an 'authorised employer' (see p131).[79] The Upper Tribunal has held that the restrictions on A8 nationals ended on 30 April 2009 and their extension to 30 April 2011 was unlawful (see p127). This means that although you might not have been accepted as having worker status during these two years because you were not working for an 'authorised employer', you can retrospectively be accepted as having had worker status during this period. However, the DWP has been granted permission to appeal against this decision.[80] Guidance has been issued to decision makers advising that they not decide any claims in which this two-year period is relevant, pending the outcome of the appeal, and that they invite the First-tier Tribunal to do the same.[81] See CPAG's online service and *Welfare Rights Bulletin* for updates.

Guidance to decision makers

From March 2014, decision makers are advised to follow a two-tier process when determining whether or not someone is, or was, a worker (or self-employed).[82] Although this guidance is not legally binding, it is helpful to know its content either to offset potential problems before your claim is decided or to challenge an incorrect decision more effectively.

The first tier in deciding whether you are, or were, a worker (or self-employed) is to establish whether your average gross earnings reach a minimum earnings threshold equal to the level at which you start to pay national insurance contributions (called the 'primary earnings threshold'). This is £155 a week (£672 per month) in 2016/17. If your gross earnings were at or above this amount for a continuous period of three months immediately before you claim benefit, you are automatically accepted as a worker (or self-employed).

The second tier applies if you do not satisfy the minimum earnings threshold for the relevant three-month period. If this is the case, the decision maker should, *in all cases,* assess your case and take into account all your circumstances to determine whether your activity was genuine and effective and not marginal and ancillary, and whether you are a worker (or self-employed).[83]

This guidance is clear that if you are not automatically accepted as a worker (or self-employed) under the first tier, the decision maker should then assess all your circumstances in relation to the criteria set out below. You should not be told that you are not a worker (or self-employed) just because you have not met the minimum earnings threshold for three months.

Employment relationship

You count as being in an 'employment relationship' if you:[84]
- provide services;
- receive remuneration in return for those services (see below);
- perform your work under the direction of another person (see below).

The services you provide must entail activities that are 'genuine and effective' as opposed to 'marginal and ancillary' (see p143).

Although, in general, your employment must have begun for you to be a worker, you may be a worker if you have moved to the UK to take up a job offer and it is not possible for you to begin work immediately but the offer is being held open for you.[85]

What counts as remuneration

In order to be a worker, you must receive 'remuneration' in return for the services you provide.

If you do voluntary work and receive payments for expenses, you are not a worker.[86] This is because the payments you receive are not provided in return for the services you perform, but rather to compensate you for the expenses you have incurred in providing them.

You can still count as a worker if the remuneration you receive is in the form of payment in kind rather than, or in addition to, in money.[87]

Working under the direction of another person

To count as a worker, you must perform the services for, and under the direction of, someone else – ie, there must be someone who can tell you how to do the work. If you provide services in return for remuneration and you are not under the direction of another person, you count as a person who is self-employed (see p153) rather than a worker.[88]

If you are taxed as a self-employed person, this fact by itself does not prevent you from being in an employment relationship, although it is a relevant factor in determining the question. For example, many people who work in the construction industry and pay tax as sub-contractors under the Construction Industry Scheme clearly provide services in return for payment and while at work are under the direction of another person. They are therefore workers and not self-employed.

It does not matter whether the person or organisation that provides the remuneration is the same as the person or organisation to whom you provide services.[89]

'Cash in hand' and agency work

You count as being in an 'employment relationship' if you provide services in return for renumeration under the direction of another person. This is not affected by the fact that:

- you are paid 'cash in hand'. The concept of 'worker' is an economic status, rather than a legal one.[90] However, you are still required to provide evidence of your employment and this may be harder to do if your work is paid cash in hand. See p360 for more information on providing evidence of your work;
- you did not declare the work to the DWP at the time.[91] This is likely to be most relevant when you are relying on past periods of employment;
- the person or organisation to whom you provide the services is different from the person or organisation that pays you for these – eg, if you are 'employed' by an employment agency.[92] However, the activities entailed in your provision of services must still be accepted as genuine and effective rather than marginal and ancillary (see below and, in particular p145, regarding the regularity of the work). There is nothing inherent in working for an agency that would exclude this and it depends on the facts of each case.[93]

Example
Nora is a Hungarian national working as a nurse 'employed' by an employment agency. The payment she receives is via the agency, but the services are provided to a private care home. The care home has a contractual relationship with the agency, rather than with Nora, and pays the agency. Nora still counts as a worker in EU law because she is providing services and doing so in return for remuneration, even though there is a separation between the care home where she provides the services and the agency that pays her.

'Genuine and effective', not 'marginal and ancillary'

Even if you are in an employment relationship, you only have a right to reside as a worker if the services you provide entail activities that are 'genuine and effective' as opposed to those that are on such a small scale as to be regarded as 'marginal and ancillary'.[94]

The assessment of whether or not your employment is 'genuine and effective' must assess, as a whole, all the circumstances of your case.[95] See p141 for details of the guidance issued to decision makers. Relevant factors that must be considered include:

- the number of hours you work;
- the duration of your employment;
- the level of earnings;
- whether the work is regular or erratic;
- other employment rights;
- whether the work is not for the economic benefit of the employer or is just a small part of a larger relationship between the parties.

Number of hours worked

The number of hours you work in a given period is a relevant factor in determining whether your work is genuine and effective. There is no minimum number of hours you must work. Provided the other factors indicate that the work is genuine and effective, even work for a very small number of hours is capable of counting as genuine and effective.

In one case, the European Court of Justice held that, following an overall assessment of the employment relationship in question, the possibility could not be ruled out that someone who worked 5.5 hours a week could be a worker.[96] However, in most circumstances, you must work for more than 5.5 hours a week for your activity to be accepted as genuine and effective. Working as an au pair for 13 hours a week for £35 per week plus board and lodging for a period of 5.5 weeks was held in one case to result in worker status.[97]

The duration of employment

The duration of the employment is a relevant factor to consider when deciding whether or not your work is genuine and effective. However, it is not conclusive, so if your work only lasts a short time, this fact by itself cannot exclude you from being a worker.[98]

Provided the other factors indicate that the work you do is genuine and effective, even very short periods of work can still be sufficient to mean that you have the status of being a worker while doing this work. In one case, the Court of Appeal found that someone was a worker during work which was, and was always known to be, of two weeks' duration.[99] Although a short duration of employment may still not be a barrier to being a worker, even if it was known to be such from the outset,[100] work that is curtailed prematurely may be more likely to be held to be genuine and effective.[101]

Level of earnings

If the level of earnings from your employment is very low, this may be a factor that indicates that your work is not genuine and effective. However, low earnings cannot, by themselves, prevent you from being found to be a worker. Even if the level of your earnings is so low that they do not meet your needs and you supplement them by claiming means-tested benefits, this does not prevent you from being a worker.[102]

Note: your earnings can include non-monetary payments in kind (see p142).

Irregular or erratic work

If you are in an employment relationship in which you are only occasionally called upon to work, this may indicate that the work is not genuine and effective. However, the decision maker must always look at all your circumstances. There is nothing inherent in an 'on-call' or 'zero-hour' contract that prevents you from being a worker; it depends on the work that you do.[103] Similarly, there is nothing inherent in doing temporary work for an agency that prevents you from being a worker. If the work is regular, rather than intermittent, and for a prolonged period or with a high likelihood of further work being obtained, you may be a worker.[104]

Other employment rights

Other contractual issues, such as the fact that you have a right to paid holidays or payment in the event of sickness, or that you are a member of a trade union recognised by your employer, are factors that may indicate that the employment is genuine and effective.[105]

Work not for an economic purpose or part of a wider relationship

Work may count as 'marginal' or 'ancillary' if it is done as part of some other relationship which is more significant, such as if a lodger performs a small task for her/his landlord as part of the terms of her/his tenancy.[106]

Work does not count as 'genuine and effective' if its main purpose is not for the economic benefit of the employer – eg, if the work is a means of rehabilitation to enable people with health problems to reintegrate into the labour market. Similarly, fostering children or caring for a person with disabilities have been held not to be economic activities and receipt of a fostering allowance or carer's allowance does not amount to remuneration in a commercial sense.[107]

Ceasing to be a worker

You only cease to be a worker when the employment relationship (see p142) ends. While you are still under a contract of employment, you continue to be a worker. Consequently, you are still a worker if you are a woman on maternity leave (including unpaid maternity leave), or if you are on holiday leave or sick leave (including if it is unpaid).[108]

If you *have* ceased to be a worker, you may retain your worker status in certain circumstances (see p146).

Benefit entitlement

If you are a worker, you have a right to reside for as long as you continue to be a worker. See below for the circumstances in which you can retain your worker status after you have ceased to be a worker.

If you have a right to reside as a worker, or as a family member (see p164) of a worker, this satisfies the right to reside requirement for all benefits that have such a requirement (see p115). You also come within one of the groups exempt from the habitual residence test for means-tested benefits (see p106). You therefore do not need to be 'habitually resident in fact' nor to have lived in the common travel area for the three months prior to your claim for income-based jobseeker's allowance. You also come into one of the groups exempt from the requirement to have been living in the UK for the past three months for child benefit and child tax credit (see p92).

Note: to claim benefit on the basis of being a worker, or the family member of a worker, you must provide evidence of this (see p360).

9. Retaining worker status

You can retain the status of 'worker', even though you are no longer working if:[109]
- you are involuntarily unemployed and registered as a jobseeker (see p147);
- you are undertaking vocational training (see p149);
- you are temporarily unable to work because of an illness or accident (see p150);
- you are unable to work because you are in the late stages of pregnancy or have just given birth (see p151).[110]

Before arguing that you have retained your worker status, check whether you have ceased to be a worker (see p145). For example, if you are off work on unpaid sick leave but you can return to your job when you are better, you are still a worker, and so you do not need to argue that you have retained your worker status.

In addition to the four groups listed above, it may also be possible to argue that you can retain your worker status in other circumstances. The Court of Justice of the European Union has held that European Union (EU) Directive 2004/38 does not list exhaustively the circumstances in which a worker who is not longer in an employment relationship can continue to have the rights of a worker.[111]

Croatian, A2 and A8 nationals

If you are a Croatian national subject to worker authorisation (see p128), you cannot retain your worker status in the ways described in this section. Similarly, if during the periods of restrictions you were an A2 national subject to worker authorisation (see p128), or an A8 national who was required to register (see p128), you could not retain your worker status in the ways described in this section. However, if you were an A8 national required to register and you stopped working during the first month of employment, you could retain your worker status in the ways described in this section for the remainder of that month.[112]

The Upper Tribunal has held that the restrictions on A8 nationals ended on 30 April 2009, since their extension to 30 April 2011 was held to be unlawful (see p127). This means that although you might not previously have been accepted as retaining your worker status during these two years because you were subject to restrictions, you can retrospectively be accepted as having retained your worker status during that period. However, the DWP has been granted permission to appeal against this decision.[113] Guidance has been issued to decsion makers advising that they not decide any claims in which this two-year period is relevant, pending the outcome of the appeal, and it invites the First-tier Tribunal to do the same.[114] See CPAG's online service and *Welfare Rights Bulletin* for updates.

You are involuntarily unemployed and registered as a jobseeker

Note: the European Economic Area (EEA) Regulations impose additional requirements for you to be able to retain your worker status beyond those required under EU Directive 2004/38. Therefore, if you are refused benefit on the basis that you do not satisfy the additional requirements of the EEA Regulations, you should challenge the decision on the basis that these are not requirements under EU law.

Under **EU Directive 2004/38**, you retain your status as a worker if you:[115]
- are recorded as involuntarily unemployed (see below); *and*
- have registered yourself as a jobseeker with the relevant employment office (see p148).

In addition to the above, under the **EEA Regulations** you must also:[116]
- provide evidence that you are seeking employment and have a genuine chance of being engaged; *and*
- either:
  - have entered the UK in order to seek employment; *or*
  - be present in the UK seeking employment immediately after having a right to reside as a worker (except if you retained your worker status on this basis), a student, or a self-employed or self-sufficient person.

Note: the EEA Regulations impose an additional requirement that, if you retain your worker status beyond six months, the evidence referred to above must be 'compelling' (see p148).

Involuntary unemployment

You are 'involuntarily unemployed' if you are seeking and are available to take up a job. This depends on your remaining in the labour market. The circumstances in which you left your last job, including whether you left voluntarily, are relevant in determining whether you remained in the labour market. However, they are just one factor and your actions and circumstances, both at the time of leaving work and since then, should also be taken into account.[117]

Example

Karl is German. He was working at food processing factory for seven months. The shift times have changed recently, which means that when he is on late shifts he now has to catch three buses to get home from work. He finds this commute exhausting and asks his employer if he can just do the early shift when the bus connections are better. His employer says that all employees must work both early and late shifts, so Karl hands in his notice. Even while working his notice, Karl looks for other alternative work closer to home. He does not find any, but once his job ends he spends more time contacting potential employers. Karl counts as involuntarily unemployed, despite the fact that he left his previous employment voluntarily.

Registering as a jobseeker

You must register as a jobseeker with the 'relevant employment office'. In the UK, this is Jobcentre Plus.

The best way to register as a jobseeker is to claim jobseeker's allowance (JSA) and/or universal credit (UC) if you come under the UC system, and keep signing on to confirm that you are available for and actively seeking work, or that you satisfy the work search and work availability requirements. If you are not entitled to benefit, contact the jobcentre and claim national insurance credits on the basis of unemployment. You do not need to receive JSA or UC in order to be registered as a jobseeker.

You may also satisfy the requirement to register as a jobseeker if you claim a different benefit, such as income support (IS), and you declare to the jobcentre in the course of making your claim that you are looking for work – eg, by stating this on your claim form or on your habitual residence questionnaire.[118] You should provide evidence of your work search. **Note:** this way of registering as a jobseeker is only relevant to retaining your worker status and claiming benefit on the basis of having a right to reside as a worker. It does not enable you to claim benefits, such as IS, if your only right to reside is as a jobseeker.

For how long can you retain worker status

The length of time you can retain your worker status while involuntarily unemployed depends on whether or not you have already been employed in the UK for more than a year.

Under EU Directive 2004/38, if you were employed for more than a year, you can retain your worker status on this basis indefinitely.[119] This has been held to mean that your retention of worker status is open-ended in the absence of an event indicating that you have entirely withdrawn from the labour market. Receipt of maternity allowance by a woman who remained registered with employment agencies has been held not to be such an event.[120]

In order to be employed for more than a year, you need not have been in one continuous job. Also, small gaps between jobs (such as around two weeks) do not necessarily mean that you were not employed for more than a year.[121]

In order to retain your worker status while involuntarily unemployed under the EEA Regulations, you must provide evidence that you are seeking employment and have a genuine chance of being engaged. If you were employed for more than a year, the EEA Regulations require that after a continuous period of six months of retaining worker status on this basis, this evidence must be 'compelling'.[122] The benefit authorities refer to this requirement as the 'genuine prospects of work test' (see p135). **Note:** there is no requirement to provide 'compelling' evidence under EU Directive 2004/38.

If you were employed for less than a year, the EEA Regulations limit the period during which you can retain your worker status while involuntarily unemployed to a maximum of six months.[123] The EU Directive allows you to retain worker status for no less than six months.[124]

Once you have retained worker status on this basis, before you can then have a right to reside as a jobseeker, the EEA Regulations require:

- you to have a period of absence from the UK. **Note:** at the time time of writing, the benefit authorities were not enforcing this requirement; *and*
- (unless your absence was for at least 12 continuous months) your evidence of seeking employment and having a genuine chance of being engaged to be 'compelling' from the start of your period of residence as a jobseeker (see p135).[125]

You have started vocational training

You retain your worker status if you have either:

- started vocational training related to your previous employment; *or*
- started vocational training and you are 'involuntarily unemployed' (see p147). This applies if you have to retrain in order to find work that is reasonably equivalent to your former employment.[126]

In general, you should be able to argue that any training or study that can assist you in obtaining employment counts as vocational training. This can include a course leading to a qualification for a particular profession, trade or employment or a course that provides the necessary training or skills.[127] A course can be vocational for you even if it is not vocational for someone else – eg, a photography course if you want to work as a photographer.

Training related to previous employment

If you are not involuntarily unemployed, your vocational training must be related to your previous employment for you to retain your worker status. For this to apply, there must be a relationship between the purpose of the studies and your previous occupational activity.[128] The decision maker must take account of all your previous occupational activity in the UK, not just your most recent employment.[129] If you consider that the course you are pursuing is related to any of your previous employment in the UK, explain this relationship in detail to the decision maker and provide evidence.

You are temporarily unable to work because of an illness or accident

You can retain your worker status if you are temporarily unable to work as a result of an illness or accident.[130]

As a result of an illness or accident

To retain your worker status on this basis, your inability to work must be as a result of an illness or accident. The test of your inability to work is unrelated to any test in the benefits system – eg, you do not need to show you have 'limited capability for work' or that you are 'incapable of work'. Instead, the test is whether you can be fairly described as unable to do the work you were doing or, if it follows a period in which you were seeking work, the sort of work you were seeking.[131] You do not need to have claimed a benefit payable on grounds of illness or disability, such as employment and support allowance (ESA), or any benefit at all, to retain your right to reside as a worker on this basis. However, you must provide evidence of your inability to work, such as a medical certificate from your GP.

Your inability to work must be caused by an illness or accident which *you* have. You cannot retain your worker status if, for example, you are unable to work because you are looking after a child who is ill.[132]

Temporary inability to work

Your inability to work must be temporary. This simply means not permanent.[133] It is your inability to work that must be temporary not your health condition, so you can retain your worker status on the basis of a permanent illness or effect of an accident if this fluctuates and causes temporary periods when you are unable to work.[134]

You are considered temporarily unable to work if, taking into account all the available evidence, there is a realistic prospect of your being able to work again and re-enter the labour market.[135]

You are pregnant or have recently given birth

If you have established worker status and you are now not working because you are pregnant or have recently given birth, you may still count as a worker or you may be able to retain your worker status.

You do not cease to be a worker while you are still under a contract of employment (see p145). You are therefore still a worker while on maternity leave, whether or not it is paid. **Note:** this also applies to Croatian nationals from 1 July 2013, and, including during the period of restrictions, A2 and A8 nationals who have established worker status.[136]

If you have ceased to be a worker, you may retain your worker status if you have a pregnancy-related illness that prevents you from working on the basis that you are temporarily unable to work because of an illness or accident (see p150).[137] You can also retain your worker status on this basis if you have another illness, unrelated to your pregnancy, that results in your being temporarily unable to work. **Note:** pregnancy itself does not mean you are temporarily unable to work because of an illness or accident.[138]

The physical constraints of pregnancy

You retain your worker status if you stop work, or stop seeking work if you retained your worker status while involuntarily unemployed (see p147), because of the physical constraints of the late stages of pregnancy and the aftermath of childbirth, provided you start work again (or seeking work and thereby retain your worker status while involuntarily unemployed) within a reasonable period after the birth of your child.[139] The Upper Tribunal has held that, in most cases, a 'reasonable period' is 52 weeks, although this may differ if your circumstances are unusual.[140] Decision makers are advised of this in a guidance memo that states they should not follow the main DWP guidance that 15 weeks after the date of birth be used as a 'yardstick' in determining a 'reasonable period'.[141]

You start your 'reasonable period', and therefore the period during which you retain your worker status, on this basis, in most cases from 11 weeks before your due date. However, exceptionally, it could be earlier if the physical constraints of your pregnancy require you to cease work (or seeking work with retained worker status) sooner, and you are able to provide evidence of this – eg, if you have a multiple pregnancy or if you can no longer carry out particular requirements of your work.[142]

If you intend to work again within a 'reasonable period', you should always make this clear to the decision maker. You should still be accepted as retaining worker status on this basis unless you state you have absolutely no intention of returning to work under any circumstances.[143]

If the basis on which you retain your worker status changes

You can retain your worker status if you are in one of the groups on p146 and continue to do so if you move into another category.[144]

Example

Nikolas is Greek. He worked for 13 months in a hotel. The hotel was losing money and Nikolas was made redundant. He claimed income-based JSA. Five months later, Nikolas became depressed and was unable to carry on looking for work, so he claimed income-related ESA. Nikolas was entitled to ESA because he had retained his right to reside as a worker – initially, as someone who was involuntarily unemployed and who had registered as a jobseeker, and then because of his temporary inability to work as a result of his illness.

There is no limit to the number of times you can change the basis on which you retain worker status. However, if you lose worker status, you cannot regain it without undertaking further employment that is sufficient to give you worker status.

Gaps

If you cease to be a worker and do not retain your worker status, you cannot regain your worker status again. To be a worker in the future, you must acquire that status afresh. However, if there is just a gap between your having worker status and your being covered by one of the groups that can retain worker status on p146, you may not have lost the status of worker. Whether a gap prevents you from retaining worker status depends on all your circumstances, including the length of the gap.

A gap between your employment ending and your registering as a jobseeker does not necessarily mean that you lose your worker status. Its significance depends on whether the length of the gap and the reasons for it indicate that you have left the labour market.[145] If the delay is for more than a few days, all your circumstances (including the reasons for the gap and what you did during that time) should be considered to establish whether there are reasonable grounds for the delay, so that it is not considered an 'undue delay'. The longer the gap, the more compelling the reasons must be.[146]

Arguably, you should be able to retain your worker status if there is a gap between your ceasing work and your being temporarily unable to work because of illness or an accident, since there is no requirement for the illness or accident to be the reason for your ceasing work. You do not need to have been receiving any benefit while you were temporarily unable to work, so if there was a delay before you claimed benefit, this does not necessarily mean there was a gap between your being a worker and retaining your worker status on the basis of your temporary inability to work.

Example

Rita is a Portuguese national who came to the UK a year ago and began full-time work in a restaurant. After eight months she was injured in a cycling accident and so left her job. She did not claim any benefits as she lived with her partner who supported her. She has just separated from him and has made a claim for income-related ESA, as she is still unable to work because of her injuries. Rita provides the DWP with a medical certificate that confirms her inability to work since the date of her accident. She satisfies the right to reside requirement for income-related ESA as she retains her worker status because she is temporarily unable to work as a result of her accident. There is no gap between her retaining her worker status on this basis and her last day of employment.

You can also retain your worker status during a short gap between two different bases on which you can retain worker status. Whether the gap is relevant also depends on your circumstances, the bases you are switching between, the length of the gap and your actions during it.

Benefit entitlement

If you retain your worker status, this satisfies the right to reside requirement for all benefits that have such a requirement (see p115).

If you are the family member (see p164) of someone who retains her/his worker status, your residence rights are the same as if you were the family member of someone who is a worker, and therefore you satisfy the right to reside requirement for all the benefits that have it.

If you retain worker status (or you are the family member of someone who does), you also come within one of the groups that are exempt from the habitual residence test for means-tested benefits (see p106). You therefore do not need to be 'habitually resident in fact' nor to have lived in the common travel area for three months before your claim for income-based JSA. You also come within one of the groups exempt from the requirement to have been living in the UK for the past three months for child benefit and child tax credit (see p92).

10. **Self-employed people**

If you are a European Economic Area (EEA) national undertaking self-employed activity in the UK, you may have a right to reside as a 'self-employed person' (see p154). You may also have a right to reside if you are a family member (see p164) of a self-employed person. Once you have established your status as a self-employed person, it is important to be clear when you cease to be self-employed (see p156). In limited circumstances, you can retain your status as a self-employed person even after you cease self-employed activity (see p157).

If you have a right to reside as a self-employed person, as someone who has retained status as a self-employed person, or as a family member of a self-employed person, your right to reside satisfies the right to reside requirement for all benefits.

Who has a right to reside as a self-employed person

If you are an EEA national and a 'self-employed person', you have a right to reside.[147]

The term 'self-employed person' is not defined in European Union (EU) legislation and the EEA Regulations simply cross-refer to EU law.[148] It should therefore be interpreted in accordance with EU law and the principles established through EU caselaw.

You count as a self-employed person if you:[149]

- provide services;
- receive remuneration in return for those services (see p142);
- do not perform your work under the direction of another person (see p142); *and*
- the work you do entails activities that are 'genuine and effective', rather than 'marginal and ancillary' (see p143).

The meanings of the above conditions are the same as they are for workers. The main difference between the definition of a self-employed person and a worker is that the work a self-employed person does is not done under the direction of another person.

Whether or not you satisfy these requirements depends on all your circumstances. For example, in one case, the Upper Tribunal held that someone selling the *Big Issue* was self-employed, as the activities involved were 'genuine and effective'.[150] A subsequent case held that someone selling the *Big Issue* was not self-employed, as his activities were not genuine and effective. However, this decision was largely due to insufficient evidence for the whole period and arguably did not give adequate consideration to all the relevant circumstances.[151]

Fostering children, or caring for a person with disabilities, has been held not to be self-employment because it is not an economic activity and the fostering allowance or carer's allowance received does not amount to remuneration in a commercial sense.[152]

From March 2014, decision makers are advised to follow a two-tier process when determining whether or not you are self-employed (or a worker).[153] Although this guidance is not legally binding, it is helpful to know its content either to offset potential problems before your claim is decided or to challenge an incorrect decision more effectively (see p141).

Croatian, A2 and A8 nationals

If you are a Croatian national, there are no additional restrictions that apply to you if you are a self-employed person. Your residence rights as a self-employed person are exactly the same as for nationals of any other EEA country.

Similarly, if you are an A2 or an A8 national, no additional restrictions applied if you were a self-employed person during the relevant period of restrictions. Your residence rights as a self-employed person were exactly the same as for nationals of any other EEA country.

For further details of the other restrictions that apply to Croatian nationals and that previously applied to A2 and A8 nationals, see p127.

What is self-employment

Whether you have become self-employed or you have ceased to be self-employed can be harder to determine than whether you have become a worker or you have ceased to be a worker. Unlike a person who is working, a person who is self-employed does not have a contract of employment that can be regarded as starting and ending on a particular date. It is possible that you may count as self-employed when you are setting yourself up to work as a self-employed person. Similarly, you may continue to count as self-employed, despite the fact that you have no work coming in for the time being.

Becoming self-employed

You count as self-employed when you establish yourself in order to pursue activity as a self-employed person.[154] You must have more than merely an intention to pursue self-employed activity, and you must provide evidence of the steps you have taken or the ways in which you have set yourself up as self-employed.[155] Exactly what steps you must take depends on the nature of your self-employed activity and on your particular circumstances. It helps if you have registered with HM Revenue and Customs (HMRC) as self-employed. However, if you have not registered, this does not necessarily mean you are not self-employed.[156]

Relevant steps include:

- advertising your services;
- researching opportunities to find work;
- setting up your accounts;
- registering with HMRC as self-employed for purposes of national insurance contributions and taxes;
- obtaining equipment required for the work you intend to do;
- setting up a website for your business.

The above steps are only examples of the sort of steps that can contribute to your having established yourself in order to pursue self-employed activity. You do not have to take any of these particular steps, but the more you have done, the more likely it is that you will be accepted as having a right to reside as a self-employed person.

Note: if you are told that you do not have residence rights as a self-employed person until you have been earning money on the basis of your self-employed activity for three months, this is incorrect. It is likely to be based on an incorrect interpretation of decision makers' guidance (see p141).

Ceasing to be self-employed

If you have stopped all self-employed activity and do not intend to resume that activity, it is clear that you have ceased to be a self-employed person. However, not all situations are as clear as this, and if you stop working, you do not necessarily cease to be self-employed. If you are in a temporary lull, you can continue to be self-employed. Whether you continue to be a self-employed person during a period when you have little or no work depends on your particular circumstances and the evidence you provide.[157]

Factors that are relevant in determining whether or not you have ceased self-employment include:[158]

- the amount of work you have coming in;
- steps you are taking to find new work;
- whether you are continuing to market your services;
- whether you are developing your business in new directions;
- whether you are maintaining your accounts;
- your motives and intentions.

Which factors are relevant depend on the nature of your self-employment and all your circumstances. However, the more factors that show you are still undertaking self-employed activity, the stronger your argument that you have not ceased to be a self-employed person. See below for the benefit implications of arguing that you have not ceased to be self-employed.

If you have ceased to be self-employed, you may be able to retain your self-employed status in certain circumstances (see p157).

Pregnancy

If you are working on a self-employed basis and you become pregnant, you continue to count as self-employed during your maternity period when you do no self-employed work, provided you intend to resume your self-employment at the end of your maternity period.[159]

Benefit entitlement

If you are a self-employed person, you have a right to reside for as long as you continue to be a self-employed person. See p157 for when you can retain your status as a self-employed person after you have ceased to be self-employed.

If you have a right to reside as a self-employed person, or as a family member (see p164) of a self-employed person, this satisfies the right to reside requirement for all benefits that have such a requirement (see p115). You also come within one of the groups exempt from the habitual residence test for means-tested benefits (see p106). You therefore do not need to be 'habitually resident in fact' nor to have lived in the common travel area for the three months prior to your claim for income-based jobseeker's allowance (JSA). You also come within one of the groups exempt from the requirement to have been living in the UK for the past three months for child benefit and child tax credit (see p92).

If you are not currently working, but you have not ceased to be self-employed (see p156), you may be entitled to income-based JSA based on your right to reside as a self-employed person, if you are seeking employment and satisfy the other conditions for JSA.[160] This is particularly significant if you are a Croatian national subject to restrictions and therefore with no right to reside as a jobseeker (see p128). It is also relevant if you want to claim housing benefit, as you will then have a non-excluded right to reside, as well as be in receipt of income-based JSA, and so will be in an exempt group (see p106).

See p360 for information on providing evidence of self-employment.

11. Retaining self-employed status

You can retain the status of a self-employed person, even though you are no longer working, if you are temporarily unable to work because of an illness or accident (see p158).[161] However, before arguing that you have retained your status as a self-employed person, check whether you have ceased to be a self-employed person, as you may still count as self-employed if you are just in a temporary period with little or no work (see p155).

If you have ceased your self-employment because of pregnancy or childbirth, see p158.

The Court of Appeal has held that you do not retain your self-employed status if you are involuntarily unemployed and registered as a jobseeker. The Court also took the view (although it was not the issue being appealed) that you do not retain self-employed status if you are doing vocational training.[162] **Note:** questions about the residence rights of a European Economic Area (EEA) national who ceased self-employment and registered as a jobseeker have been referred to the Court of Justice of the European Union.[163] See CPAG's online service and *Welfare Rights Bulletin* for updates.

Croatian, A2 and A8 nationals

If you are a Croatian national, you can retain your status as a self-employed person in exactly the same circumstances as nationals of any other EEA country. There are no additional restrictions that apply.

Similarly, if you are an A2 or an A8 national, no additional restrictions applied if you were retaining your status as a self-employed person during the relevant period of restrictions. The circumstances in which you could retain your status as a self-employed person were exactly the same as for nationals of any other EEA country.

For further details of the other restrictions that apply to Croatian nationals, and that previously applied to A2 and A8 nationals, see p127.

You are temporarily unable to work because of an illness or accident

If you have established self-employed status, you can retain this status if you have ceased to be self-employed and are temporarily unable to work because of an illness or accident.[164] The circumstances in which this applies are the same as those for retaining 'worker' status on this basis (see p150).

You are pregnant or have recently given birth

If you have established your status as a self-employed person and you are now not working because of pregnancy or childbirth, you may still count as a self-employed person or you may be able to retain your status as a self-employed person.

You remain a self-employed person if you intend to resume your self-employment after your maternity period.[165]

If you have ceased to be a self-employed person (see p156), you may retain this status if you have an illness, whether or not it is pregnancy related, that means you are temporarily unable to work because of an illness or accident (see above). **Note:** pregnancy in itself does not mean you are temporarily unable to work because of an illness or accident.'[166]

Benefit entitlement

If you retain your status as a self-employed person, this satisfies the right to reside requirement for all benefits that have such a requirement.

If you are the family member (see p165) of someone who retains her/his status as a self-employed person, your residence rights are the same as if you were the family member of someone who is a self-employed person and, therefore, you satisfy the right to reside requirement for all benefits to which this applies.

If you retain your status as a self-employed person (or you are a family member of someone who does), you also come into one of the groups exempt from the habitual residence test for means-tested benefits (see p106). You therefore do not need to be 'habitually resident in fact' or to have lived in the common travel area for the three months prior to your claim for income-based jobseeker's allowance. You also come within one of the groups exempt from the requirement to have been living in the UK for the past three months for child benefit and child tax credit (see p92).

12. **Self-sufficient people and students**

You have a right of residence as a self-sufficient person if you are a European Economic Area (EEA) national and you, and any family members who do not have an independent right to reside, have:[167]
- sufficient resources (see p160) not to become a burden on the social assistance system of the UK during your period of residence (see p161); *and*
- comprehensive sickness insurance cover in the UK (see p161).

You have a right to reside as a student if you are an EEA national and:[168]
- you are enrolled as a student in a government-accredited college;
- you provide an assurance that you have sufficient resources (see p160) for yourself, and any family members who do not have an independent right to reside, not to become a burden on the UK social assistance system during your period of residence (see p161);
- you, and any family members who do not have an independent right to reside, have comprehensive sickness insurance cover in the UK (see p161).

The requirements to have a right to reside as a student are very similar to the requirements to have a right to reside as a self-sufficient person. For this reason, those who have a right to reside as a student are referred to as 'self-sufficient students' in this section. The specific differences that apply to students are on p162.

You can also have a right to reside if you are a family member of a self-sufficient person. **Note:** the definition of 'family member' of a student is narrower than that which applies to family members of other EEA nationals (see p163).

Periods when you have a right to reside as a self-sufficient person or student, or family member of either, count as periods of 'residing legally' for the purposes of acquiring permanent residence after five years (see p184). This is the most common way in which periods of residence as a self-sufficient person or student can enable you to access benefits and tax credits, because during your period of self-sufficiency, your resources can exclude you from means-tested benefits. However, this is not always the case. In addition, your resources would have to be a lot greater to exclude you from child tax credit (CTC) and would never exclude you from child benefit.

Croatian, A2 and A8 nationals

If you are a Croatian national, there are no additional restrictions that apply to you if you are a self-sufficient person or a self-sufficient student. Your residence rights as a self-sufficient person are the same as for nationals of any other EEA country.

Similarly, if you are an A2 or an A8 national, no additional restrictions applied if you were a self-sufficient person or a self-sufficient student during the relevant period of restrictions. Your residence rights as a self-sufficient person or self-sufficient student were, and are, the same as for nationals of any other EEA country.

Note: certain students are exempt from the additional restrictions that apply to Croatian nationals and that applied to A2 nationals for the seven years up to 1 January 2014. You are/were not subject to worker authorisation if you are a student with a registration certificate which states that you cannot work more than 20 hours a week (unless it is part of vocational training or during vacations) and you comply with this. If the certificate confirms that you can work during the four months after the course ends, the exemption continues for this period (see p129).

If this applies to you and you work no more than 20 hours a week, you may have a right to reside as a 'worker' (see p140). In addition, working while in the group counts as 'legally working' and, therefore, after a year of 'legally working' (see p131), you permanently cease to be subject to worker authorisation.

If you are a Croatian national (or an A2 or an A8 national during the relevant periods of restrictions) employed in the UK but without a right to reside as a worker because your work is not in accordance with your worker authorisation document (or, if you are an A8 national, for an 'authorised employer'), you do not have a right to reside as a self-sufficient person on the basis of these earnings.[169]

For further details of other restrictions that apply to Croatian nationals and that previously applied to A2 and A8 nationals, see p127.

Sufficient resources

Your resources must be 'sufficient' to avoid you, and any family members who do not have an independent right to reside, becoming a burden on the social assistance system of the UK (see p161).The UK government cannot set a fixed amount to be regarded as 'sufficient resources' and must take account of your personal situation.[170]

You have 'sufficient resources' for the purpose of being either a self-sufficient person or a self-sufficient student if they:[171]

- are more than the maximum level you (and your family) can have to be eligible for 'social assistance' (see p161); *or*
- do not exceed that level, but the decision maker considers that you have sufficient resources, taking into account your (and your family's) personal situation.[172]

The 'maximum level' is the equivalent of your means-tested benefit applicable amount, including any premiums. Your resources also include your accommodation, so if your resources are more than your applicable amount plus your rent, they should be considered to be sufficient. You may also be self-sufficient if your resources are more than your applicable amount and you are provided with free and stable accommodation by friends or family.[173]

You do not need to own the resources that make you self-sufficient. It is enough if you have access to them – eg, if you are supported by someone else.[174]

The source of the resources does not matter.[175] However, you cannot rely on your earnings from your employment in the UK to give you self-sufficient status.[176] In most circumstances, this does not matter as your employment means you are a 'worker'. It is relevant if, for example, you do not have worker status because you do not satisfy the additional conditions imposed on you as a Croatian, A2 or A8 national (see p127). You can however rely on the earnings of your non-EEA national spouse/civil partner.[177]

Not a burden on the social assistance system

You count as self-sufficient if you have sufficient resources 'not to become a burden on the social assistance system of the UK during your period of residence'.

'Burden' has been held to be an 'unreasonable burden'.[178]

The 'social assistance system of the UK' includes all means-tested benefits.[179] In its guidance, the DWP does not include CTC, but lists all the means-tested benefits.[180]

You cannot automatically be regarded as not self-sufficient just because you make a claim for a means-tested benefit. While such a claim could indicate that you do not have sufficient resources to avoid becoming an unreasonable burden on the social assistance system of the UK, the decision maker must carry out an assessment of the specific burden that granting a benefit would make on the system as a whole. This assessment must take all your circumstances into account, including the likely duration of your claim.[181] It is done at the point you make your claim for benefit on the basis of your right to reside as a self-sufficient person so, for example, you do not need to have had sufficient resources at the start of your period of residence. However, from the point the assessment is carried out, you must show sufficient resources for your intended period of residence, including for five years if permanent residence is sought.[182]

Comprehensive sickness insurance

To have a right of residence as a self-sufficient person, in addition to having sufficient resources (see p160), you must also have comprehensive sickness insurance cover in the UK.

This requirement is satisfied if you have private health insurance.[183] It is also satisfied if the UK can be reimbursed by another EEA state for any NHS costs you incur while in the UK.[184] This usually applies if you are covered by the European Union co-ordination rules (see p264) and another state continues to be your 'competent state' (see p271) – eg, if you are:

- resident in the UK but you are working or self-employed in another EEA member state;
- resident in the UK, you receive a pension from another EEA member state, you do not also receive a pension from the UK, and you are not working or self-employed in the UK (see p274);[185]
- living temporarily in the UK (eg, you are a student on a course in the UK) and are entitled to health treatment in another EEA state because you are insured there.[186]

In these circumstances, you can get a European health insurance card. However, this does not, in itself, confirm that you have comprehensive sickness insurance cover in the UK. As with other residence documents (see p353), having the card only confirms your rights at the date it was issued; it does not mean you retain those rights if your circumstances change – eg, if the UK becomes your competent state.

Access to NHS treatment where the UK bears this cost has been held not to satisfy the requirement to have comprehensive sickness insurance cover in the UK.[187]

Depending on your circumstances, you may be able to argue that it is disproportionate to insist on this requirement being met if it is the only barrier to your having a right to reside as a self-sufficient person.[188]

If you have difficulty satisfying the requirement to have comprehensive sickness insurance cover, get specialist advice, as this is an area in which caselaw is developing.

Self-sufficient students

You have a right to reside as a student if you are an EEA national and:[189]

- you are enrolled as a student in a government-accredited establishment for the principal purpose of following a course of study (including vocational training); *and*
- you provide an assurance that you have sufficient resources for yourself, and any family members (see p163) who do not have an independent right of residence, not to become a burden on the UK social assistance system during your period of residence (see p163); *and*
- you, and any family members who do not have an independent right of residence, have comprehensive sickness insurance (see p161).

The conditions for having a right of residence as a student are therefore very similar to the conditions for having a right of residence as a self-sufficient person. The only differences are as follows.

- To have the right to reside as a student, you must be enrolled on a course of study.

- The requirement to have sufficient resources is met by providing an assurance, either by means of a declaration or some other equivalent means that you choose, that you have 'sufficient resources'.
- The definition of family member is different (see below).

The assessment of what counts as 'sufficient resources' is the same as for a self-sufficient person (see p160). This requirement is satisfied by providing an assurance of these resources, but it is not clear what practical difference this makes. Although you may be more easily accepted as having a right to reside if you provide an assurance of your resources at the start of your studies, this does not prevent you from losing your right of residence if your circumstances change. However, such a loss is never automatic and always depends on your circumstances.[190] Furthermore, if the need for you to claim benefits is only likely to be temporary, depending on the length of your course, it may be easier to argue that any benefit claim does not amount to an unreasonable burden on the social assistance system of the UK (see p161).

Family members

Family member of a student
You are the **'family member'** of a student (once s/he has been in the UK for three months) if you are:[191]
– her/his spouse or civil partner; *or*
– her/his dependent child (regardless of your age); *or*
– the dependent child (regardless of your age) of the student's spouse or civil partner.

The above definition of family member is narrower than that which generally applies (see p165), and only applies if the student does not have another right to reside that can confer a right of residence on you.

If you are the parent of a student who has been in the UK for at least three months, or a parent of her/his spouse or civil partner, you may be able to be treated as a family member on the basis of being an extended family member if you have the relevant documentation (see p167).[192]

This means that when assessing whether you have sufficient resources, you do not need to take account of anyone who does not come within this narrower definition of family member after you have lived in the UK for three months – eg, your resources do not need to be sufficient for your non-dependent children under 21 or dependent parent living in the UK.

Benefit entitlement

If you have a right to reside as a self-sufficient person, a family member (see p164) of a self-sufficient person, or as a student or family member of a student (see above), this satisfies the right to reside requirement for all benefits that have such a requirement (see p115).

Note: it cannot automatically be decided that you are not self-sufficient just because you have claimed a means-tested benefit (see p161).

However, the most common way in which periods of residence as a self-sufficient person or student (or family member of a self-sufficient person or student) can assist you to access benefits and tax credits that require a right to reside is when such periods are used towards the five years of residence required for permanent residency (see p184). This is because during your period of self-sufficiency, your resources often exclude you from means-tested benefits.

---

13. Family members of European Economic Area nationals

You have a right to reside if you are a 'family member' (see p165) of a European Economic Area (EEA) national who has:[193]

- a right to reside as a 'qualified person' – ie, a:[194]
  - jobseeker (see p133);
  - worker (see p140), including if s/he has retained this status (see p146);
  - self-employed person (see p153), including if s/he has retained this status (see p157);
  - self-sufficient person, including a self-sufficient student (see p159); *or*
- a permanent right of residence (see p184); *or*
- an initial right to reside (see p132).

You have this right to reside as a family member, whether or not you are an EEA national yourself.

You have a right to reside for as long as the EEA national has one of the residence rights listed above, and for as long as you remain her/his family member. In general, if s/he ceases to have a relevant right to reside or if you cease to be her/his family member, your right to reside ends. However, there are some limited circumstances in which you can continue to have residence rights as a former family member of an EEA national with a right to reside (see p171).

British citizens only give residence rights to their family members in limited circumstances (see p168).

The type of right to reside you have depends on the type of right to reside your family member has. For more information and the consequences of this for entitlement to benefits and tax credits with a right to reside requirement, see p174.

Croatian, A2 and A8 nationals

If you are a Croatian national and a family member of an EEA national with one of the residence rights listed on p164, you have a right to reside in the same way as a family member of any other EEA national. In addition, this may mean that you come into one of the groups not subject to worker authorisation and that you do not have additional restrictions on your residence rights (see p129).

Similarly, if you are an A2 or an A8 national and during the period of restrictions you were the family member of an EEA national with one of the residence rights listed above, you had a right to reside in the same way as a family member of an other EEA national. In addition, being such a family member could have meant you were exempt from these restrictions (see p129 for A2 nationals and p130 for A8 nationals).

For further details of the other restrictions that apply to Croatian nationals and that previously applied to A2 and A8 nationals, see p127.

Who is a family member

To have a right to reside as a family member of an EEA national who has a relevant right to reside (see p164), you must come within the definition of 'family member'.

Family member
You are a **'family member'** of the EEA national if you are her/his:[195]
– spouse or civil partner;
– child, grandchild or great-grandchild (or child, grandchild or great-grandchild of her/his spouse/civil partner) and you are under 21;
– child, grandchild or great-grandchild (or child, grandchild or great-grandchild of her/his spouse/civil partner) and you are dependent on her/him;
– parent, grandparent or great-grandparent (or parent, grandparent or great-grandparent of her/his spouse/civil partner) and you are dependent on her/him.

If you are not covered by the above definition of 'family member', you can be treated as a family member and have residence rights on that basis if:
● you are an 'extended family member' (see p167); *and*
● you have been issued with an EEA family permit, a registration certificate or a residence card (see p353). If you do not have this documentation, or it is no longer valid, you are not treated as a family member.[196]

Note: a narrower definition applies to family members of students who have been in the UK for at least three months (see p163).

Spouses and civil partners

Spouses and civil partners are family members. If you are not married to, or in a civil partnership with, your partner, see p167.

You remain a spouse or civil partner if you have separated, including while you are in the process of getting divorced or dissolving a civil partnership. It is only once you are legally divorced (in the UK when the *decree nisi* is given) or the civil partnership has been legally terminated that you cease to count as the spouse or civil partner of the other person.[197]

Even when your marriage or civil partnership has been terminated (or if your spouse/civil partner dies or leaves the UK), you may still continue to have a right to reside (see p171).

Aged under 21

You count as a family member of a person if you are her/his child (or grandchild or great-grandchild), or a child of her/his spouse/civil partner, and you are aged under 21.

You do not need to show that you are dependent on the person in order to count as her/his family member. Therefore, you do not need to live with her/him or show you are receiving support from her/him, and it is irrelevant whether you do or not.[198]

Example

Greta is a Lithuanian national aged 18. She is eight months pregnant and lives in rented accommodation. She has claimed income support (IS) and housing benefit (HB). Her father is also Lithuanian and is working full time in the UK. Greta has been estranged from her father since she got pregnant. Despite this, she is still defined as his family member, as she is his daughter and is under 21. Greta therefore has a right to reside as the family member of a worker, and this enables her to be entitled to IS and HB.

For information on providing evidence of your age, see p359.

Dependent

To count as a family member of someone, you may need to be dependent on that person – eg, if you are her/his parent or grandparent, or child aged 21 or over.

'Dependence' is not defined in the legislation, but caselaw has established a number of principles.[199]

There are only three things you must show in order to establish that you are dependent on a person.
- You receive support from her/him.
- The support you receive is 'material'. If the person is providing you with financial help, paying your bills, buying you food or providing your

meals, providing you with accommodation or is providing you with care because you are ill or disabled, this should all count as material support.
- The support contributes to the 'basic necessities of life'.

It is irrelevant if there are alternative sources of support, including potential employment, available to you, either in your country of origin or in the UK.[200]

If you only became dependent on the EEA national in the UK, this does not prevent you from being classed as a family member. It is sufficient that you are dependent at the point when your claim for benefit is decided.[201] **Note:** this does not apply if you are an extended family member on the basis of dependency, for which you must already have been dependent in the country from which you have come (see p168).[202]

Receipt of benefit does not preclude you being dependent on someone else, and your dependency should be considered independently of any benefit you claim. A decision maker should not make the 'circular' decision that you are not entitled because awarding you a benefit that depends on your residence rights as a dependent family member causes you to cease to be dependent. Whether you are dependent while receiving a benefit depends on whether or not your evidence shows the three things listed above.[203]

Extended family members

If you do not come within the definition of 'family member' on p165, but you have a relative in the UK who is an EEA national with a relevant right to reside (see p164), you can be treated as a family member, and therefore have residence rights on that basis, if you:
- are an 'extended family member' (see below); *and*
- have been issued with an EEA family permit, a registration certificate or a residence card (see p353).[204] If you do not have this documentation, or it is no longer valid, you are not treated as a family member.[205]

Extended family member

You are an **'extended family member'** of an EEA national if you are her/his:[206]
– partner and you are in a durable relationship with her/him; *or*
– relative and would satisfy the requirements of the Immigration Rules for indefinite leave as her/his dependent relative if s/he were present and settled in the UK; *or*
– relative (or a relative of her/his spouse or civil partner) and:
  – you have serious health problems that require her/his care (or the care of her/his spouse or civil partner); *or*
  – you previously were dependent on the EEA national, or were a member of her/his household, in a country other than the UK and you are accompanying her/him to the UK, wish to join her/him in the UK, or you have joined her/him in the UK, and you continue to be dependent on her/him or to be a member of her/his household.

The term 'dependent' is not defined in legislation and its meaning is the same as that for a family member (see p166). However, if you are relying on being dependent on (or a member of the household of) the EEA national to come within the definition of an 'extended family member', you must have previously been dependent on her/him (or a member of her/his household) in the country from which you have come.[207] It is not necessary for your previous connection to have been in the same capacity as it is now – eg, you may have been part of the EEA national's household before coming to the UK and then be dependent on her/him once you arrive in the UK.[208]

If you are the extended family member of a self-sufficient student (see p162), there are further limitations on when you can be treated as a family member. These depend on the basis on which the EEA family permit, registration certificate or residence card was issued to you.[209] **Note:** European Union (EU) Directive 2004/38 treats a student's parent (or her/his spouse or civil partner) who has been in the UK for at least three months as an 'extended family member'.[210]

Family members of a British citizen

British citizens do not automatically give residence rights to their family members. This is because most British citizens living in Britain do not generally have a right of residence under EU law, so they cannot confer an EU right of residence on their family members. EU Directive 2004/38 applies to people who 'move to or reside in' an EEA country 'other than that of which they are a national'.[211] The UK rules achieve a similar effect by setting out the residence rights of EEA nationals and their family members, but defining an EEA national 'as a national of an EEA state who is not also a British citizen'.[212]

However, there are circumstances in which a British citizen can have a right of residence under EU law. If you are that person's family member, s/he can then confer a right of residence on you.

The main ways in which s/he can do this are if:

- the British citizen has resided with a right to reside (eg, as a worker) in another EEA state. On her/his return to the UK, s/he has the same rights as other EEA nationals and can confer rights on you (see p169);
- the British citizen is self-employed and carries out some of her/his business activities in another EEA state (see p170);
- s/he is a dual British/other EEA state citizen in limited circumstances (see p170).

In addition, you may have a right to reside in the following circumstances.

- If you are the primary carer of a British citizen who would not be able to continue live anywhere in the EEA if you were required to leave the UK, you may have a 'derivative right to reside' on this basis (see p181). **Note:** having a derivative right to reside is different from having a right to reside as a family member (see p175).

- If you are a non-EEA national joining your family member who is British, and you have been given leave by the Home Office (eg, as a spouse or civil partner), you have a right to reside during that period of leave. However, this is under domestic immigration law and not under EU law. See Part 2 for more information on immigration law. If your leave is subject to a condition that you do not have recourse to public funds, you are defined as a 'person subject to immigration control' (see p59) and excluded from all the benefits listed on p65, unless you are in an exempt group (see p66).

The British citizen has resided in another state

If you are a family member (see p165) of a British citizen, you have a right to reside on the basis of EU law as her/his family member if s/he has resided with a right to reside as a worker, self-employed person, self-sufficient person or self-sufficient student in another EEA state and has now returned to the UK.[213] The residence of the British citizen in the other EEA state must have been 'genuine' residence which is more than mere physical presence.[214]

The EEA Regulations contain these rights, but interpret them more restrictively than the European Court of Justice (ECJ) has done.[215] If your benefit is refused because the decision maker follows the more restrictive interpretation of the EEA Regulations, you should challenge the decision if the more generous interpretation by the ECJ would give you a right to reside.

- If you are the spouse or civil partner of a British citizen, the EEA Regulations state that you must have lived together in the other EEA state. This conflicts with an ECJ decision, which held that you can have residence rights as a family member if you became a family member either before or after entering the member state.[216]
- The EEA Regulations only treat a British national as an EEA national if s/he was a worker or self-employed person in the other EEA state.[217] Arguably, a British citizen should also be treated as an EEA national if s/he has resided in another EEA state with a right to reside as a self-sufficient person or self-sufficient student.
- The EEA Regulations require the British citizen to have transferred her/his 'centre of life' to the other EEA state. The factors relevant to whether her/his centre of life has been transferred include the period of residence in the other EEA state as a worker or self-employed person, the location of her/his principle residence and degree of integration in that country.[218] The condition to have transferred your centre of life is not required under the EEA Regulations if, on 1 January 2014, you had (and continue to have) a permanent right to reside or a residence document confirming your right to reside (or an outstanding application for such a document, or you were appealing against its refusal).[219] This requirement for the British citizen to have transferred her/his centre of life is not a condition under EU law.

• The EEA Regulations only give you a right to reside as a family member of a British citizen who has returned to the UK if s/he currently has a right to reside under these regulations. However, the ECJ has decided that it was not necessary for someone who had been a worker in another EEA state and then returned to her/his own state to carry out an economic activity in order for her/his family member to have a right of residence.[220]

The British citizen lives in UK and carries out activities in another state

If you are the family member (see p165) of a British citizen who is employed or self-employed in the UK and whose business involves her/him undertaking some activities in another EEA state, you may have a right of residence, depending on your circumstances. This right is not covered in the EEA Regulations or the EU Directive, but is confirmed by the ECJ as coming directly from the Treaty on the Functioning of Europe. One case concerned the spouse, who was a non-EEA national, of a British citizen who provided services to recipients in other member states from a business established in the UK.[221] A separate judgment held that a non-EEA national family member of a Dutch national residing in Holland, but who regularly travelled to another member state as a worker, must have a right to reside.[222]

The British citizen also has citizenship of another state

The ECJ has held that a dual British/other EEA state citizen does not have rights under EU law if s/he has never moved between member states, but has lived all her/his life in the UK. Therefore, s/he cannot confer any rights on her/his family members.[223]

Following this judgment, the EEA Regulations were amended so that the definition of 'EEA national' that applies throughout these requires that you are not also a British national.[224] Limited transitional protection was given to family members of dual nationals who had acquired residence rights before 16 October 2012, when family members of someone who had both British and another EEA nationality had the same rights as family members of other EEA nationals.[225] If you had already acquired such a right before this date, it continues in limited circumstances.[226] See p1604 of the 2013/14 edition of the *Welfare Benefits and Tax Credits Handbook* for details.

If you are a family member of a dual British/other EEA state citizen who has resided with a right of residence as a 'worker', self-employed person, or self-sufficient person or self-sufficient student in another member state (other than the one of which s/he is a national), when s/he returns to the UK s/he may have residence rights and be able to confer these on you in the same way as if s/he were a British citizen (see p169).[227]

It is arguable that the amendment to the EEA Regulations goes wider than the ECJ judgment, even taking account of the rules immediately above, because the judgment was specific to someone who had lived all her life in the UK. Clarity on the rights of dual British/other EEA citizens who have moved between member states before acquiring dual citizenship, and their family members, should be provided by the Court of Justice of the European Union in a case that is pending.[228] See CPAG's online service and *Welfare Rights Bulletin* for updates.

Former family members

In general, if you are the family member of an EEA national who confers a right to reside on you, your right to reside ceases if s/he:
- stops being your family member (see p165); *or*
- ceases to have a relevant right to reside.

However, there are some exceptions which mean that you can retain your right to reside in certain circumstances. Whether or not these apply to you depends on the type of right to reside your family member has. **Note:** several of these circumstances may mean that you have other residence rights that could be easier to prove or may apply instead (see p173).

When you may retain your right to reside

You may retain your right to reside if the EEA national who confers this right on you dies or leaves the UK, or if your marriage or civil partnership to her/him is terminated. These rights are in EU Directive 2004/38, but they are not exactly reproduced in the EEA Regulations (see below). The decision maker is more likely to accept that you retain your right to reside if you satisfy the requirements of the EEA Regulations, so you should check these first. If you cannot satisfy these, check whether you satisfy the requirements of the EU Directive (see p172). Provided you satisfy the requirements, you can rely on rights under either the EEA Regulations or the EU Directive.

There are several differences in the specific wording of the provisions in the EEA Regulations and the EU Directive that could affect you. The two most significant differences are the following.
- Under the EEA Regulations, you can count periods of residence spent as a former family member who retains her/his right of residence towards the five years of residence required to acquire permanent residence (see p184).
- Under the EU Directive, if you are an EEA national, you retain your right to reside if your relevant family member dies or leaves the UK, or if your marriage or civil partnership to her/him is terminated, *without* needing to satisfy any other conditions. These rights are not reproduced in the EEA Regulations.

European Economic Area Regulations

You retain your right to reside under the EEA Regulations if you are a family member of a 'qualified person' (see p126) or a person with a permanent right to reside (see p184) and:[229]

- that person dies and you are:
  - not an EEA national, but if you were, you would be a worker, or a self-employed or self-sufficient person (or you are the family member of such a non-EEA national) and you resided in the UK with a right to reside under the EEA Regulations for at least a year immediately before s/he died; *or*
  - the child or grandchild of the qualified person (or her/his spouse or civil partner) and you were in education immediately before the death and you remain in education; *or*
  - a parent with custody of a child in the previous bullet point; *or*
- that person leaves the UK and you are:
  - the child or grandchild of the qualified person (or her/his spouse or civil partner) and you were in education immediately before s/he left the UK and you remain in education; *or*
  - a parent with custody of a child in the previous bullet point; *or*
- your marriage or civil partnership to that person is terminated, and you are not an EEA national, but if you were, you would be a worker or a self-employed or self-sufficient person (or you are the family member of such a non-EEA national), and you were residing in the UK with a right to reside under the EEA Regulations at the date of the termination and:
  - the marriage/civil partnership had, prior to the termination, lasted for at least three years with you both residing in the UK for at least one of those years; *or*
  - you have custody of the qualified person's child; *or*
  - you have a right of access to the qualified person's child which a court has said must take place in the UK; *or*
  - your continued right of residence in the UK is warranted by particularly difficult circumstances, such as your (or another family member's) being subject to domestic violence during the period of the marriage/civil partnership.

You have a right to reside on this basis for as long as the conditions apply to you,[230] until you can acquire a permanent right of residence (see p184).[231] For details on using periods with this residence right to acquire permanent residency, see p171.

European Union Directive 2004/38

The rules under the EU Directive treat you differently depending on whether you are an EEA national (see p125) or not.

You should retain your right to reside under EU Directive 2004/38 if you are a family member of an EEA national who has a right to reside as a worker, self-employed or self-sufficient person, or as a self-sufficient student and:

- the EEA national dies and you:[232]
  - are an EEA national; *or*

- have lived in the UK as her/his family member for at least a year before her/his death and you are a non-EEA national; *or*
- the EEA national leaves the UK and you are:[233]
  - an EEA national; *or*
  - the child, grandchild of great-grandchild of the EEA national and in education; *or*
  - the parent with custody of a child in education; *or*
- your marriage or civil partnership to the EEA national is terminated and:[234]
  - you are an EEA national; *or*
  - prior to the initiation of termination proceedings, the marriage/civil partnership had lasted for at least three years with you both residing in the UK for at least one of these. Your rights are not retained in this way if your spouse or civil partner left the UK before the termination proceedings began;[235] *or*
  - you have custody of the EEA national's child; *or*
  - you have a right of access to the EEA national's child, which a court has said must take place in the UK; *or*
  - your continued right of residence in the UK is warranted by particularly difficult circumstances, such as your being subject to domestic violence during the period of the marriage/civil partnership. Your rights are not retained in this way if your spouse or civil partner left the UK before the termination proceedings began.[236]

Periods when you have retained your right to reside as a former family member are not on their own sufficient to enable you to acquire a permanent right of residence after five years, because you are also required to show that you are a worker, or a self-employed or a self-sufficient person, or you are the family member of such a person.[237]

Other residence rights

If you are covered by any of the circumstances that enable you to retain your right to reside as a family member, under either the EEA Regulations or the EU Directive, or if your circumstances are similar but you do not fit within these rules, check whether similar rights could apply to you. The main ones that might apply are the following.

- If you have had a right to reside in the UK as the family member of an EEA national who has conferred a right to reside on you for five years, you may have a permanent right to reside (see p184).
- If you were the family member of an EEA national who has died and s/he was a worker or a self-employed person, you may have a permanent right to reside (see p190).
- If you are the child of a worker and you are in education, or you are the primary carer of such a child, you may have a 'derivative right to reside' (see

p175). **Note:** whereas periods during which you had a derivative right to reside do *not* count towards the five years needed to acquire permanent residence, time spent as a former family member who has retained her/his right to reside under the EEA Regulations *do* count towards the five years (see p184).

Benefit entitlement

Whether your right to reside as the family member of an EEA national satisfies the right to reside requirement depends on:
- the type of right to reside the EEA national has; *and*
- the benefit you want to claim.

Your right to reside is the equivalent of the EEA national's right to reside if s/he has:
- a right to reside as a 'qualified person' – ie, a:[238]
  - jobseeker (see p133);
  - worker (see p140), including if s/he has retained this status (see p146);
  - self-employed person (see p153), including if s/he has retained this status (see p157);
  - self-sufficient person, including a self-sufficient student (see p159);
- an initial right to reside (see p132).

This means the following.
- If you are the family member of a worker or self-employed person, you have the same residence rights as if you were a worker or a self-employed person yourself. Not only does this satisfy the right to reside requirement for all benefits that have such a requirement (see p115), but you also come within one of the groups exempt from the habitual residence test for means-tested benefits (see p106). You therefore do not need to be 'habitually resident in fact' nor have lived in the common travel area for the three months prior to your claim for income-based jobseeker's allowance (JSA).
- If you are the family member of a self-sufficient person or self-sufficient student, you have the same residence rights as if you were a self-sufficient person or student. This satisfies the right to reside requirement for all benefits that have such a requirement (see p115).
- If your only right to reside is as the family member of an EEA national who has a right to reside as a jobseeker, you have the same residence rights as if you were a jobseeker yourself. If this is your only right to reside, this does not enable you to satisfy the right to reside requirement for IS, income-related employment and support allowance (ESA), pension credit (PC), HB and universal credit (UC) (see p115).
- If you are the family member of an EEA national who has an initial right of residence for three months, you have an equivalent right to reside. If this is

your only right to reside, this does not enable you to satisfy the right to reside requirement for IS, income-based JSA, income-related ESA, PC, HB and UC (see p115).

If you are the family member of an EEA national who has a permanent right of residence, your right to reside satisfies the right to reside requirement for all benefits that have such a requirement (see p115). However, you only have a permanent right to reside yourself (and are exempt from the habitual residence test – see p106) if you are the family member of an EEA national who acquired this permanent residency in less than five years (see p190).

If you have a right to reside as a former family member (see p171), your right to reside satisfies the right to reside requirement for all benefits that have such a requirement (see p115).

Note: to claim benefit on the basis of being a family member, you must provide evidence of this (see p355).

14. **Derivative residence rights**

You may be able to derive a right to reside from someone with a right to reside without being her/his family member. These rights are not listed in European Union (EU) Directive 2004/38, but are based on other provisions of EU law as interpreted by caselaw. The European Economic Area (EEA) Regulations list these rights as 'derivative rights of residence'. However, they interpret them more narrowly in some respects and impose some additional conditions. If these mean you do not have a right to reside, you can rely on the rights confirmed by the caselaw.

Note:
- You cannot count periods when you have a derivative right to reside towards the five years of residence required for permanent residency (see p184).
- Some of the circumstances below are similar to those that enable you to retain a right to reside if you are a former family member of an EEA national who conferred a right to reside on you and who has now died or left the UK, or your marriage or civil partnership to her/him has been terminated (see p171). Check whether these circumstances apply because, in some cases, you can count periods with a right to reside as a former family member towards the five years required for permanent residence.
- If you do not fit into any of the groups below, but your circumstances are similar, it may be arguable that you have a right to reside (see p182).

Who has a derivative right to reside

You have a derivative right to reside if you are not an 'exempt person' (see p176) and you are:[239]

- the child of an EEA national who was a 'worker' in the UK (see p140) while you were living in the UK, and you are currently in education (see p177);[240] or
- the primary carer of a child in the above bullet point and the child would be unable to continue her/his education if you were required to leave (see p179);[241] or
- the primary carer of a self-sufficient child who is an EEA national, who would be unable to remain here if you were required to leave (see p180);[242] or
- a dependent child of a primary carer in either the second or third bullet points above, and s/he would be prevented from residing in the UK if you were required to leave and you do not have leave to enter or remain in the UK (see p180); or
- the primary carer of a British citizen residing in the UK who would be unable to reside in the UK or another EEA state if you were required to leave (see p181).[243] **Note:** this right to reside does not satisfy the right to reside requirement for any of the benefits that have this requirement.

Who is exempt

The EEA Regulations exclude you from having a derivative right to reside if you are an 'exempt person'.[244]

You are an 'exempt person' if you have a right to reside:[245]

- under any other provision of the EEA Regulations;
- as a British citizen or as a Commonwealth citizen with a right of abode;
- as a person with indefinite leave; or
- under provisions that exempt certain people from the requirement to have leave – eg, specified aircrew and diplomats.

If you are refused benefit on the basis that you do not have a derivative right to reside because you are an exempt person, but your other right to reside (eg, as a jobseeker) does not enable you to claim benefit, you should challenge the decision on the basis that you are not excluded under EU law, and refer to the EU caselaw in which your right to reside is confirmed.

Croatian, A2 and A8 nationals

The rules about derivative residence rights apply to Croatian nationals in exactly the same way as for other EEA nationals, and they applied in exactly the same way to A2 or A8 nationals during the period when other restrictions applied. However, if you are deriving your right to reside from being a worker's child in education, the primary carer of such a child, or a child of such a primary carer, the restrictions that apply (or applied) to workers could affect you, because they affect who can have 'worker' status.

If a Croatian national is subject to restrictions (see p128), the work s/he does only gives her/him worker status if it is done in accordance with her/his worker authorisation document. Similarly, if an A2 national subject to restrictions worked between 1 January 2007 and 31 December 2013, that work only gave her/him worker status if it was done in accordance with her/his worker authorisation document. If you are the child of a Croatian or A2 national and you are in education, or you are the primary carer of such a child, the work done by the parent must have been done in accordance a worker authorisation document for it to enable you to have a derivative right to reside.[246]

The situation for A8 nationals is slightly different. If an A8 national was subject to restrictions (see p128), the work that s/he did between 1 May 2004 and the date the restrictions ended (now held to be 30 April 2009 rather than 30 April 2011, but this is subject to appeal – see p127) only gave her/him worker status if it was done for an 'authorised employer' (see p128). Therefore, if you are the child of an A8 national and you are in education, or you are the primary carer of such a child, the work done by the parent must have been for an authorised employer for you to have a derivative right to reside. This includes a period when the parent had a valid worker's registration certificate for her/his employer, but s/he did not complete 12 months of working for an 'authorised employer'.[247] It also includes a period in which the parent was in her/his first month of employment, since the first month of any employment, even if it was never registered, counted as working for an 'authorised employer', provided s/he satisfied the requirements of being a worker, including that the work was accepted as 'genuine and effective' (see p140).[248]

For further details of other restrictions that apply to Croatian nationals and that previously applied to A2 and A8 nationals, see p127.

Worker's child in education

A child (see p178) has a right to reside if:

- s/he was living in the UK at a time when one of her/his parents (or the parent's spouse or civil partner) had a right to reside in the UK as a worker (see p178); *and*
- s/he is now in education (see p178).

The purpose of this right of residence is to enable a child to take up her/his right to be educated in the member state where her/his (step-)parent is employed if s/he is also living in that state.[249] For this right to education to be effective, the child must have a right of residence.[250] The right continues for as long as s/he is a child in education.

The nationality of the child does not affect this right of residence. However, the child's parent (or step-parent) who had the right to reside as a worker must have been an EEA national when s/he was a worker.

It is the child's parent, or the child's parent's spouse or civil partner, who must have been an EEA worker. The child does not have this type of right to reside if the EEA worker is:

- her/his grandparent;[251] *or*
- her/his parent's partner who is not in a formal legal relationship with the parent.[252]

Who is a 'child in education'

To have a derivative right to reside as the child of a worker in education, the child must generally need to be aged from around five and be under the age of 'majority'.

The lower age is determined by the need to be 'in education'. This excludes nursery education.[253] A child's rights begin when s/he enters compulsory education around the age of five and excludes preschool.[254] The DWP conceded in one case that the child's rights begin if s/he has started school in reception class, but has not yet turned five.[255]

Differences in Scotland may affect when residence rights begin. Although there is no reception class in Scotland, it may still be arguable that a child can be 'in education' when s/he is approaching age five. Furthermore, with the Scottish Curriculum for Excellence starting at the age of three, it maybe arguable that a child in Scotland can be in education well before the age of five.

Residence rights apply until at least the age of majority, and may apply beyond then if someone is still in education, as the principle of equal treatment requires someone to be able to continue her/his studies in order to complete her/his education successfully.[256]

The child must have been in the UK while one of her/his parents (or her/his spouse/civil partner) was employed as a worker in the UK. The parent (or her/his spouse/civil partner) does not need to have been a worker when the child entered education or at any time since then.[257]

Under the EEA Regulations, the child must have been in education at a time when her/his parent was in the UK.[258] However, the Court of Justice of the European Union (CJEU) has recently held that this is not an additional requirement and that the residence rights of the child are not affected by a parent who had been a worker in the UK, but who left the UK before the child begins attending school.[259] This is consistent with earlier European caselaw that has repeatedly held that all that is required is for the child who is in education to have lived in the member state during a period when one of her/his parents was exercising rights as migrant worker in that state.[260]

Who is a 'worker'

The EEA Regulations state that, for this purpose, 'worker' does not include a jobseeker or someone who retains her/his worker status (see p146). It may be arguable that the latter exclusion is wrong. Caselaw consistently confirms that a child has a right to reside if s/he is now in education and was in the member state during a time when one of her/his parents was exercising rights of residence in that state as a 'worker' or a 'migrant worker'.[261] It appears from the wording of EU

Directive 2004/38 that a person who retains her/his status as a worker does reside in a country as a 'migrant worker', as s/he has equivalent rights to 'workers', provided s/he continues to satisfy the conditions of retaining worker status. Furthermore, the family members of someone who has retained her/his status as a worker have equivalent rights of residence to family members of workers.

Absence of the child from the UK

A child may lose her/his right to reside as a worker's child in education if s/he leaves the UK but then returns. However, this depends on all the circumstances. The DWP takes the view that if a child leaves the UK, other than for a temporary reason, s/he may lose her/his right to education (and her/his associated right to reside) when s/he returns. DWP guidance suggests that, while a substantial period of habitual residence in another EEA state means that the right to education, and hence to reside, is lost, 'an absence that can properly be regarded as temporary will not have that effect'.[262] However, it may be arguable that what matters is whether the child's studies undertaken on her/his return are a continuation of her/his earlier education. The European Court of Justice held that a worker's child in education continued to have his rights, despite an absence in which the child went back to his state of origin, because he returned to continue his studies which he could not pursue in his own state.[263]

Primary carer of a worker's child in education

You have a derivative right to reside under the EEA Regulations if you:[264]
- are the 'primary carer' (see p180) of a child of a worker who is in education; *and*
- the child would be unable to continue to be educated in the UK if you were required to leave.

The basis of this right of residence builds on the residence rights of the child, which are necessary in order to be educated in the state where her/his parent is employed.[265] It is assumed that the child needs an adult to look after her/him and, consequently, her/his primary carer must also have a right of residence.[266] Your rights as the primary carer continue until the child reaches at least the age of majority, and beyond if s/he continues to need your presence and care in order to pursue and complete her/his education.[267]

You can have a right to reside as the primary carer of a worker's child in education if you were that worker or if the worker was someone else.

There is no need for the child or you, as her/his primary carer, to be self-sufficient in order to have residence rights.[268]

The nationality of you or the child does not affect this right of residence.[269] However, the child's parent who had the right to reside as a worker must be an EEA national.

Who is a primary carer

Primary carer

The EEA Regulations define you as a **'primary carer'** of another person if you are her/his direct relative or legal guardian, and either you:[270]

– have primary responsibility for that person's care; *or*

– share equally the responsibility for that person's care with one other person who is not an 'exempt person' (see p176).

Note: if you share care equally, whether or not the child would be unable to continue her/his education or remain in the UK, or the British citizen would be unable to reside in the EEA, is considered on the basis of both carers being required to leave the UK, unless the person with whom care is shared had already acquired a derivative right to reside before assuming equal care responsibility.[271]

You are not regarded as someone's primary carer solely on the basis of a financial contribution you make towards her/his care.[272]

If you do not come within the above definition of 'primary carer', you may be able to argue that you have rights based on EU caselaw (see p175) – eg, if you are the primary carer of someone who is dependent on you, but you are not her/his direct relative or legal guardian.

Primary carer of a child who is self-sufficient

You have a derivative right to reside under the EEA Regulations if:[273]

- you are the 'primary carer' (see above) of a child under 18 who is residing in the UK as a self-sufficient person (see p159); *and*
- the child would be unable to remain in the UK if you were required to leave.

The basis of this right of residence is to make effective the rights of the child, as it is assumed that s/he needs an adult to look after her/him and so her/his primary carer must also have a right of residence.[274]

Your nationality does not affect this right of residence. However, the child must be an EEA national to have a right to reside as a self-sufficient person.

Child of a primary carer

You have a derivative right to reside under the EEA Regulations if:[275]

- you are the child under 18 of a 'primary carer' of either:
  - a worker's child in education (see p177); *or*
  - a child under 18 who is residing in the UK as a self-sufficient person (see above); *and*
- you do not have leave to enter; *and*

- were you required to leave, it would prevent the primary carer from residing in the UK.

The basis of this right of residence is to make effective the rights of the primary carer and the other child for whom s/he is caring. Your nationality does not affect this right of residence.

Example

Veronika is Czech. She is aged 16, has learning difficulties and is eight months pregnant. She has stopped attending school. Veronika's mother last worked in the UK in 2013. She has a right to reside as the primary carer of Patrik, Veronika's younger brother who is eight years old and in school. Veronika has a derivative right to reside because her mother has to look after her, and if Veronika had to leave the UK, so too would her mother. Therefore, Veronika can claim income support (IS) on the basis of her pregnancy and satisfies the right to reside requirement. When Veronika's baby is born, she will be able to claim child benefit and child tax credit, and continue to get IS as a lone parent.

Primary carer of a British citizen

You have a derivative right to reside under the EEA Regulations if you:[276]
- are the 'primary carer' (see p180) of a British citizen who is residing in the UK; and
- the British citizen would be unable to reside in the UK or another EEA state if you were required to leave.

This right of residence is based on the rights provided by Article 20 of the Treaty on the Functioning of the European Union (TFEU) for every person holding the nationality of an EU member state to be a citizen of the EU, and for every EU citizen to have the right to move and reside freely within the EU. If an EU citizen is dependent on another to make her/his right effective, her/his primary carer must be given a right of residence.[277]

The British citizen, therefore, must be dependent on the primary carer – eg, because s/he is a child or has health problems that require another person's care.

The key question for this right of residence is whether the British citizen would be required to leave the territory of the EU (or, under the EEA Regulations, the EEA) if you were required to leave the UK. This is a question of fact, determined by taking into account all the circumstances.[278] However, this is difficult to satisfy if you are an EEA national and, therefore, in most cases, this residence right only applies to non-EEA nationals.

Having a right to reside on the basis of being the primary carer of a British citizen does not enable you to be entitled to any benefit that requires you to have a right to reside (see p115). Since 8 November 2012, it is listed as an excluded right of residence in each of the benefit and tax credit regulations. This exclusion applies whether you have a derivative right to reside under the EEA Regulations or on the basis of Article 20 of the TFEU. **Note:** this exclusion is arguably unlawful and although legal challenges have not yet been successful, future ones may be.[279] See CPAG's online service and *Welfare Rights Bulletin* for updates.

However, although this right of residence does not entitle you to benefits that require a right to reside, it can mean that you are not defined as a 'person subject to immigration control' (see p58). This means you may be able to claim attendance allowance, disability living allowance (DLA), personal independence payment and carer's allowance, provided you meet all the other presence and residence requirements (see p208). You may also be entitled to working tax credit, since you have a right to work in addition to your right to reside.

Note: if this is your only right of residence and you need to claim benefits that require a right to reside, you should obtain immigration advice, as it may be possible for you to apply for immigration leave on the basis of your right to family life (see p34). If this leave is granted without the condition that you have 'no recourse to public funds', you are not excluded from benefits, as you are not defined as a 'person subject to immigration control' (see p57) and you have a non-excluded right to reside (see p123).

Other derivative rights

It is arguable that you may have a right to reside if your circumstances do not exactly fit the criteria for the derivative rights on p175, but they are similar and the legal principles underlying derivative residence rights could be applied. For example, you may be able to argue that you have a right to reside in the following situations.

- You are the child of a self-employed person in education or the primary carer of such a child. The question of whether a primary carer has a right of residence was referred to the CJEU in two joined cases.[280] Although the CJEU stated that the provision that gives a right to education in the state where the child's parent has been a worker[281] cannot apply to the child of a self-employed person,[282] it did not consider other possible bases for such a right. It did not need to do so because the UK government conceded at the hearing that, in each case, the person had a right of residence on another basis. Consequently, when the cases were referred back to the Upper Tribunal, the judge confirmed that the question of whether the primary carer of a (former) self-employed person's child in education has a right of residence remained to be determined in a future case.[283] However, when the same judge did consider the issue, he held that the reasoning of the CJEU's judgment made it impossible to find that the primary carer of a self-employed person's child in education has a right to reside.[284] Further caselaw is pending.[285] See CPAG's online service and *Welfare Rights Bulletin* for updates.

- You are the primary carer of a worker's child who is under school age. Such a child has a clear right to reside as the family member of a worker and, depending on the facts, it may be arguable that you need a right to reside to make the child's right effective.
- You are the primary carer of a child who has a permanent right to reside. The same principles that apply to give other primary carers residence rights arguably apply if the child has permanent residence – ie, to make effective the rights of the child.

There may be other circumstances in which you need a right to reside to make someone else's residence rights effective. The strength of your argument always depends on your circumstances and those of the other relevant people, but you may be able to apply some of the principles on which derivative rights are based.

Benefit entitlement

If you have a derivative right to reside (other than on the basis of being the primary carer of a British citizen), this satisfies the right to reside requirement for any of the benefits or tax credits to which that requirement applies (see p115).

If your right to reside is as a result of your being the primary carer of a British citizen, this is specifically excluded for each of the benefits and tax credits that have a right to reside requirement. This exclusion applies whether you have a derivative right to reside under the EEA Regulations or on the basis of Article 20 of the TFEU. **Note:** this exclusion is arguably unlawful and although legal challenges have not yet been successful, future challenges may be.[286] See CPAG's online service and *Welfare Rights Bulletin* for updates.

Note: the period of time when you have a derivative right to reside does not count towards the five years of residence required for acquiring permanent residence (see p184). This means that, unless you have another right to reside, when you cease to satisfy the conditions for your derivative right to reside, your residence rights end together with your entitlement to any benefits that have a right to reside requirement.

Example

Rosa is an Italian national who came to the UK in 2008 with her son Roberto. She worked for five months, but left her job because Roberto began to have night-time seizures and was awarded DLA. Rosa then claimed IS as Roberto's carer for a couple of years. Her health deteriorated and so she switched to claiming income-related employment and support allowance (ESA). Roberto is just completing his A levels at school. When he leaves school, Rosa will cease to have a right to reside, as it was based on being the primary carer of a worker's child in education, and her entitlement to income-related ESA and housing benefit will end (even though she has had a derivative right to reside for over five years).

Note: to claim benefit on the basis of having a derivative right to reside, you must provide evidence of this (see Chapter 20).

15. **Permanent right to reside**

You can acquire a permanent right of residence after periods of residing with a right to reside in the UK. In most cases, you must have resided with a right to reside for a continuous period of five years, disregarding certain gaps (see below). However, in limited circumstances you can acquire a permanent right of residence after having resided for a shorter period of time (see p190).

Once you have a permanent right of residence, you do not need to satisfy any other conditions[287] (eg, you do not also need to be a worker) and this right of residence satisfies the right to reside requirement for all the benefits that have such a requirement.

Once acquired, you only lose your permanent right of residence if you are absent from the UK for more than two consecutive years.[288]

Acquiring permanent residence after five years

You acquire a permanent right to reside if you have 'resided legally' (see below) for a continuous period of five years (see p188).[289]

You can acquire a permanent right of residence whether you are a European Economic Area (EEA) national or non-EEA national, provided you satisfy the criteria. However, if you are a non-EEA national, there are fewer ways in which you count as having resided legally (see p186). If you are a Croatian, A2 or A8 national, you can only count periods of residence in the UK before you became an EEA national in limited circumstances (see p187).

Guidance for decision makers on acquiring permanent residence after five years was produced in summer 2015 and it can be helpful to refer the decison maker to this if it supports your circumstances.[290] As guidance, it is not legally binding.

Note: in limited circumstances, you can acquire a right of residence in less than five years (see p190).

Legally resided

The European Union (EU) Directive requires you to have 'resided legally', and the EEA Regulations require you to have resided 'in accordance with these regulations', for a continuous period of five years in the UK.[291] In most cases, this makes no difference, and so the phrase 'resided legally' is used in this section and any difference between the EEA Regulations and EU Directive are noted where they are significant.

You always count as residing legally during periods when you have a right to reside as a:[292]
- worker (see p140), including if you have retained this status (see p146);
- self-employed person (see p153), including if you have retained this status (see p157);
- self-sufficient person, including a self-sufficient student (see p159);
- family member (see p165) of any of the above; *or*
- (EEA Regulations only) jobseeker, or family member of a jobseeker, since 30 April 2006 (see below).

Periods when you resided with another residence right can be more complicated.

The right of permanent residence was only introduced on 30 April 2006 when both the EU Directive 2004/38 and the EEA Regulations came into force. However, you can still count periods when you had a right of residence before 30 April 2006 towards the required five years, if the residence was on the basis of one or more of those listed above (other than the last bullet). (These periods must be taken into account because each of the residence rights was provided under earlier EU[293] and UK[294] legislation.)

If you completed five years' legal residence before 30 April 2006 and then had a gap of less than two years when you were either out of the UK or residing in the UK but not counted as 'residing legally', this does not affect your acquisition of permanent residency.[295]

Jobseekers

You can count periods when you had a right to reside as a jobseeker (see p133) or a family member of a jobseeker from 30 April 2006 towards your five years of residing in accordance with the **EEA Regulations**.[296] You cannot count periods before this date, as jobseekers were not given a right to reside under earlier regulations. Therefore, if you need to rely on periods when you were seeking work before 30 April 2006, always check whether you had another residence right at that time – eg, if you retained worker status.

Guidance to decision makers confirms that if you have been awarded income-based jobseeker's allowance (JSA) on the basis of your right to reside as a jobseeker for a continuous period of five years, this is sufficient for you to acquire permanent residence.[297] It further states that if your JSA is disallowed, the continuity of your legal residence is broken.[298] This is not necessarily correct, as you can have a right to reside as a jobseeker without receiving JSA (see p138). The guidance also confirms that a period when your income-based JSA is not paid due to a sanction does not affect your continuity of residence as a jobseeker.[299]

You cannot count periods when your only right of residence was as a jobseeker, or as a family member of a jobseeker, towards the five years required to give you permanent residence under the **EU Directive**, as it does not count as 'residing legally'.[300] However, this is rarely a problem in practice since you can count such periods under the EEA Regulations.

Initial right of residence

You can count periods after 30 April 2006 when you had an initial right of residence for the first three months after your arrival in the UK (see p132), or as the family member of someone with an initial right of residence, towards your five years of residing in accordance with the EEA Regulations.[301] You can also count such periods towards the five years required to give you permanent residency under the EU Directive.[302]

There was no initial right of residence under earlier regulations or earlier EU legislation, so it is not relevant to periods before 30 April 2006.

Family members

If you are the family member (see p165) of a person who has acquired permanent residency after residing legally in the UK for five years, you have a right to reside for as long as you remain her/his family member.[303] Under the EEA Regulations, you can also use periods as a family member of a person with a permanent right of residence to count towards your five years of residing in accordance with those regulations, and so acquire a permanent right of residence yourself.[304] This is in addition to any other periods listed in this section (pp184–88) that you can count, some of which are specific to family members.

Note: if you are the family member of a person who has acquired permanent residency in less than five years, you may have permanent residency yourself (see p190).

Former family members

You can count periods since 30 April 2006 when you had a right to reside as a former family member under the EEA Regulations (see p171) towards your five years of residing in accordance with the EEA Regulations. This only applies to periods since 30 April 2006, as this right of residence was not provided under earlier regulations. If you are a non-EEA national, you must have a right to reside as a former family member at the end of your five-year period to acquire a permanent right to reside under the EEA Regulations.[305]

If you have been a former family member under the EU Directive (see p172) for five years, this is not sufficient to enable you to acquire permanent residency under that Directive because you are also required to show that you are a worker, or a self-employed or self-sufficient person, or that you are the family member of such a person.[306]

Non-European Economic Area nationals

Periods when you are in the UK with leave to enter or remain do not count as periods of 'residing legally'. They do not count under the EEA Regulations as they are not periods in which you resided in accordance with those regulations and the European Court of Justice has held that they do not count towards the five years required to acquire permanent residency under the EU Directive.[307]

If you are a non-EEA national, you cannot have a right of residence as a worker, self-employed person, person who retains either of these statuses, a self-sufficient person or a self-sufficient student. However, you can have a right of residence as the family member of an EEA national who is in one of these groups.

In practice, therefore, the only ways for you to acquire a permanent right of residence after five years of residing legally is by either:

- residing for a five-year period as the family member of an EEA national who is legally residing; or
- retaining the right as a former family member on the basis of either the death of your spouse or civil partner or the termination of your marriage or civil partnership (see p172).[308]

Note: in limited circumstances, you can also acquire a right of permanent residence in less than five years if you are the family member of an EEA national who has acquired a permanent right of residence in less than five years (see p190).

Croatian, A2 and A8 nationals

If you are a Croatian, A2 or A8 national, you can acquire permanent residency after five years of residing legally in the same way as any other EEA national. However, if:

- you are relying on periods when you were subject to additional restrictions on your residence rights, these may affect whether you had a right to reside as a jobseeker or a worker, or retained worker status (see p127). **Note:** the Upper Tribunal has held that the restrictions on A8 nationals ended on 30 April 2009 and their extension to 30 April 2011 was unlawful. This means that, although you might not have been accepted as having, or retaining, worker status during these two years due to the restrictions, retrospectively these restrictions do not apply. If you would otherwise have had, or retained, worker status during this two-year period, it counts as residing legally. However, the DWP has been granted permission to appeal against this decision.[309] Guidance has been issued to decision makers advising that they not decide any claims in which this two-year period is relevant, pending the outcome of the appeal, and that they invite the First-tier Tribunal to do the same.[310] See CPAG's online service and *Welfare Rights Bulletin* for updates;
- you are relying on periods when you were living in the UK before your country joined the EU, you do not count as residing legally just on the basis that you had leave to enter or remain in the UK (see above). However, you count as residing legally if:[311]
  - you had leave to enter or remain in the UK; and

– you would have had a right of residence as a worker, self-employed person, person who retains one of those statuses, a self-sufficient person or self-sufficient student, except for the fact that you were not an EU national at the time.

Derivative right to reside

Periods when you have resided with a derivative right to reside (see p175) do not count as periods of residing legally, and so you cannot count them towards your five years for the purposes of acquiring permanent residency under either the EEA Regulations or the EU Directive.[312]

Continuity of residence

You acquire permanent residency when you have been 'residing legally' (see above) for a continuous period of five years.[313] However, the continuity of your residence is not affected by certain absences (see below). It is also arguable that the continuity of your residence is not affected by certain gaps during the five years when you were in the UK, but did not count as 'residing legally' (see p189).

Absence from the UK

When calculating whether you have five years' continuous residence, temporary absences from the UK do not affect the continuity of your residence if:[314]

• they are not more than a total of six months a year;
• they comprise one absence of up to 12 consecutive months for important reasons, such as pregnancy and childbirth, serious illness, study or vocational training, or a posting abroad. These are just examples. If you have one absence of up to 12 months for a similar important reason, it should also not affect the continuity of your residence;[315] *or*
• they are for compulsory military service.

If you have one or more of the above temporary absences from the UK, you can count the time spent abroad as part of your five continuous years.[316] However, you are likely to need to make this argument to the benefit authority, as guidance to decision makers only refers to earlier caselaw that held that time spent abroad during a temporary absence does *not* count towards your five continuous years.[317] Remember that the guidance is not legally binding and that the approach of the more recent caselaw, each heard by a two-judge panel rather than a single commissioner, should be followed.

> **Example**
> Botond is a Hungarian national. In June 2011 he came to the UK and began working as a self-employed carpenter. His business was declining, so he ceased self-employment in August 2015 and returned to Hungary. Botond was then offered employment in the UK, which he returned to take up in January 2016. However, his new (British) partner became

very sick and so, last month, he left work to care for her and claimed income support (IS) as her carer. Botond satisfies the right to reside right requirement for IS as he has legally resided in the UK for a continuous period of five years (including the five months he was in Hungary).

Your continuity of residence is broken if you are removed from the UK under the EEA Regulations.[318]

Gaps

Between periods when you are residing legally you may have one or more temporary periods when you remain in the UK, but you are not counted as 'residing legally'. You may be able to argue that the continuity of your residence is not affected by such a gap, on the grounds that if the continuity of your residence is not affected by your being abroad for certain specified periods, it should also not be affected for equivalent periods when you remain in the UK but do not count as residing legally.[319] Although this argument was rejected by the Court of Appeal,[320] it is arguable that the judgment did not adequately consider all the arguments and relevant caselaw.[321] Future cases may succeed.

Guidance to decision makers states that you can have a cumulative gap of up to 30 days in any 12-month period between periods of residence on different bases – eg, a gap between having a right to reside as a self-employed person and then as a worker. However, it goes on to state that a gap between two periods of the same type of residence (eg, as a jobseeker) breaks the continuity of residence.[322] The guidance gives no legal basis for either assertion and, as guidance, it is not legally binding.

If the gap was spent in prison, however, this interrupts the continuity of your residence and you cannot count the time spent in prison towards your five years.[323] The Court of Justice of the European Union (CJEU) found that taking time spent in prison into account when calculating the five years is contrary to the EU Directive's aim of strengthening social cohesion. This aim was a key factor behind establishing the right of permanent residency and was also the reason why permanent residency was made dependent, not just on the duration, but also on the qualitative elements of residence relating to the level of integration in the member state. Receiving a prison sentence shows the person's non-compliance with the values of that state.[324]

This reasoning suggests that other gaps in your five-year period should be treated differently, particularly if they do not call into question your level of integration in the UK – eg, periods when you temporarily ceased to be a worker or self-employed because you were caring for someone. **Note:** if you stopped work to care for someone, you may be able to argue that you retained your worker status, as the CJEU has held that the ways in which you can retain worker status listed in the Directive are not exhaustive (see p146).[325]

Acquiring permanent residence in less than five years

In certain circumstances, you can acquire a permanent right of residence in less than five years. You have a permanent right to reside if you:[326]

- are a worker (see p140) or self-employed person (see p153) and you:
  - have reached retirement age, or (workers only) taken early retirement, and you either:
    - have a spouse or civil partner who is a UK national (or who lost that nationality by marrying you); *or*
    - have worked in the UK for the preceding year and resided in the UK continuously (see p191) for more than three years; *or*
  - stopped your activity as a worker or self-employed person in the UK because of a permanent incapacity (see below) and:
    - you have a spouse or civil partner who is a UK national (or who lost that nationality by marrying you); *or*
    - you have resided in the UK continuously (see p191) for more than two years; *or*
    - the incapacity was as a result of an accident at work or occupational disease that resulted in benefit entitlement – eg, industrial injuries disablement benefit; *or*
  - have worked and resided in the UK continuously (see p191) for three years and you then work in another member state and return to the UK at least once a week; *or*
- are the family member (see p192) of a worker or self-employed person in any of the above groups and you 'reside with' her/him (see p192 for what this means); *or*
- are the family member of a worker or self-employed person who died while still working and who did not acquire a permanent right of residence under one of the above groups and:
  - s/he had resided (see p191) in the UK for two years; *or*
  - the death resulted from an accident at work or an occupational disease; *or*
  - you lost your UK nationality as a result of marrying her/him.

. . . .

Permanent incapacity

'**Permanent incapacity**' is the opposite of temporary incapacity.[327]

If your incapacity is not permanent, you may be able to retain your worker or self-employed status on the basis that you are temporarily unable to work due to illness or accident (see p150).

. . . .

What can be treated as a period of work

If the basis on which you acquire a permanent right to reside in less than five years requires you to have worked for a period of time, in addition to the periods when

you are actually working, the following are treated as periods of activity as a worker or self-employed person:[328]
- periods when you were not working for reasons not of your making;
- periods when you were not working because of an illness or accident;
- (workers only) periods of involuntary unemployment (see p147) recorded by the relevant employment office – ie, Jobcentre Plus.

If you are a Croatian, A2 or A8 national, additional restrictions that apply or applied to your residence rights can affect whether you can count periods as periods of work (see p127).[329]

Note: if you retire or become permanently incapable of work while you are in one of the above situations, since you are treated as in a period of activity as a worker or self-employed person, provided you satisfy the other requirements, you should be able to acquire permanent residence on that basis. This approach was followed by the Court of Appeal when determining the date a Portuguese national who had been off work sick became permanently incapable of work. The Court upheld the decision that he had become permanently incapable as soon as he stopped work. Because this was before he had resided in the UK for two years, this meant he failed to acquire permanent residence. However, had he become permanently incapable of work after residing in the UK for two years, it was accepted that he would then have had a permanent right to reside, even though the permanent incapacity would have been preceded by temporary incapacity rather than actual employment.[330]

Residing in the UK

Some of the ways in which you can acquire permanent residence in less than five years require you to have resided in the UK continuously for specified periods. Whether or not you satisfy this may be affected by the way the phrase 'resided in the UK continuously' is interpreted. This can be affected by the fact that acquiring permanent residency in less than five years is the exception to the general rule. Of particular relevance are:
- how the period of continuous residence is calculated. It is arguable that certain absences should not affect your continuity of residence in the same way as for acquiring permanent residence after five years (see p188); *and*
- the quality of residence required. The Upper Tribunal has held that actual residence is sufficient,[331] and that earlier caselaw that interpreted 'reside' as 'legally reside' should not be followed.[332] The sufficiency of actual residence is consistent with ensuring that the provision under EU Directive 2004/38 is not more restrictive than under the previous legal provisions.[333] However, this Upper Tribunal decision is currently being appealed.[334] Guidance has been issued to decision makers advising that they not decide any claims in which the quality of residence is relevant, pending the appeal, and that they invite the First-tier Tribunal to do the same.[335]

Family members

You acquire permanent residence in less than five years if you are living in the UK and are the family member (see p165) of someone who has acquired a permanent right to reside under the first bullet point on p190. You do not have to live with the person; it is sufficient that you are living in the UK now.[336] You do not have to have lived in the UK for the same period as the person of whom you are a family member, and you do not need to have been her/his family member throughout this time.[337]

Loss of permanent right to reside

Once you have acquired a permanent right to reside, whether because of residing legally in the UK for at least five years or under the rules that enable you to acquire permanent residence in less than five years, you can only lose this right if you are absent from the UK for more than two consecutive years.[338]

Benefit entitlement

If you have a permanent right to reside, this satisfies the right to reside requirement for all the benefits that have this requirement (see p115).

If you acquired a permanent right to reside under the rules that enable you to do so in less than five years, you are exempt from the habitual residence test for means-tested benefits (see p106). You therefore do not need to be 'habitually resident in fact' nor, for income-based JSA, to have lived in the common travel area for the three months prior to your claim.

Note: to claim benefit on the basis of your permanent residence, you must provide evidence of this. It may help you to refer to decision maker's guidance on evidence, if this supports your situation.[339] You should always provide as much documentary evidence that you satisfy the conditions for permanent residence as you can. However, if you are unable, for example, to prove you worked for a relevant period, the decision maker should use additional records available to her/him – eg, national insurance contribution records.[340] This is covered in more detail on p349. For more information on evidence, see Chapter 20.

Notes

4. European Economic Area nationals
1 Art 18 TFEU
2 Art 20 TFEU
3 Arts 20 and 21 TFEU
4 EEA Joint Committee Decision No.158/ 2007
5 *Agreement between the European Community and its Member States, of the one part, and the Swiss Confederation, of the other, on the free movement of persons,* Cmd 5639, 21 June 1999 (in force on 1 June 2002)
6 Reg 2(1) I(EEA) Regs
7 This approach is taken in the I(EEA) Regs – see reg 2(1), definition of 'EEA national', I(EEA) Regs
8 Art 3(1) EU Dir 2004/38
9 Regs 6 and 14(1) I(EEA) Regs
10 Arts 7 and 14 EU Dir 2004/38
11 *SSWP v JB (JSA)* [2011] UKUT 96 (AAC)

5. Croatian, A2 and A8 nationals
12 *TG v SSWP (PC)* [2015] UKUT 50 (AAC)
13 *SSWP v Gubedladze,* Court of Appeal hearing due in February 2017
14 DMG Memo 2/16, ADM Memo 4/16
15 Reg 8 AC(IWA) Regs
16 Reg 9 A(IWA) Regs
17 Reg 7 A(IWR) Regs
18 Regs 4 and 5 AC(IWA) Regs
19 Reg 6 A(IWA) Regs; reg 7B I(EEA) Regs
20 Reg 5 A(IWR) Regs; reg 7A I(EEA) Regs
21 CIS/1042/2008; *SSWP v JB* [2011] UKUT 96 (AAC)
22 Reg 2 AC(IWA) Regs; reg 2 A(IWA) Regs
23 s33(2A) IA 1971
24 Reg 3 AC(IWA) Regs; reg 4 A(IWA) Regs
25 Reg 2 A(IWR) Regs
26 Reg 2(5) AC(IWA) Regs; reg 2(12) A(IWA) Regs
27 *Miskovic and Another v SSWP* [2011] EWCA Civ 16
28 Reg 2(7) A(IWR) Regs
29 *Miskovic and Another v SSWP* [2011] EWCA Civ 16
30 Reg 7 A(IWR) Regs
31 *SSWP v ZA* [2009] UKUT 294 (AAC); *Szpak v SSWP* [2013] EWCA Civ 46
32 *BS v SSWP* [2009] UKUT 16 (AAC)

6. Initial right of residence
33 Reg 11 I(EEA) Regs
34 Reg 13(1) I(EEA) Regs; Art 6(1) EU Dir 2004/38
35 Reg 13(3) I(EEA) Regs; Art 14(1) EU Dir 2004/38
36 Reg 13(2) I(EEA) Regs; Art 6(2) EU Dir 2004/38

7. Jobseekers
37 Art 45 TFEU; Art 14 EU Dir 2004/38; reg 6 I(EEA) Regs
38 Reg 6(7) and (8) I(EEA) Regs
39 Reg 6(7)-(11) I(EEA) Regs
40 Sch 3 para 1 I(EEA)A Regs 2013; reg 4 I(EEA)A Regs 2014; reg 4 I(EEA)A(No.3) Regs
41 Art 45 TFEU; *The Queen v Immigration Appeal Tribunal, ex parte Gustaff Desiderius Antonissen,* C-292/89 [1991] ECR I-00745
42 Reg 5 AC(IWA) Regs
43 **A2** Reg 6 A(IWA) Regs
    A8 Regs 4(2) and (4) and 5(2) A(IWR) Regs
44 *The Queen v Immigration Appeal Tribunal, ex parte Gustaff Desiderius Antonissen,* C-292/89 [1991] ECR I-00745, para 21; confirmed in *SSWP v MB (JSA) (and linked cases)* [2016] UKUT 372 (AAC) para 49
45 Reg 6(7) and (8) I(EEA) Regs; Sch 3 para 1 I(EEA)A Regs 2013; reg 4 I(EEA)A Regs 2014; reg 4 I(EEA)A(No.3) Regs
46 Reg 6(4) and (8)-(11) I(EEA) Regs; Sch 3 para 1 I(EEA)A Regs 2013; reg 4 I(EEA)A Regs 2014; reg 4 I(EEA)A(No.3) Regs
47 Reg 6(9) I(EEA) Regs
48 Confirmed in para 073080 DMG
49 para 073107 DMG
50 para 073108 DMG; DMG Memo 18/15
51 *KS v Secretary of State* [2016] UKUT 269 (AAC) and ECJ caselaw cited
52 *The Queen v Immigration Appeal Tribunal, ex parte Gustaff Desiderius Antonissen,* C-292/89 [1991] ECR I-00745, para 21
53 *SSWP v MB (JSA) (and linked cases)* [2016] UKUT 372 (AAC), paras 49-60, especially paras 49 and 57

54 www.cpag.org.uk/genuine-prospects-
of-work
55 *SSWP v MB (JSA)* (and linked cases)
[2016] UKUT 372 (AAC), para 47
56 para 073099 DMG
57 *SSWP v RR (IS)* [2013] UKUT 21 (AAC)
58 Confirmed in Vol 2, para 073122 DMG
59 *SSWP v MB (JSA)* (and linked cases)
[2016] UKUT 372 (AAC)
60 CH/3314/2005
61 R(IS) 8/08, para 6; *SSWP v MB (JSA)* (and
linked cases) [2016] UKUT 372 (AAC) in
particular para 32-33; CIS 1951/2008,
para 21
62 s7 JSA 1995
63 Reg 8 JSA Regs
64 *SSWP v MB (JSA)* (and linked cases)
[2016] UKUT 372 (AAC), paras 63-79
65 *The Queen v Immigration Appeal
Tribunal, ex parte Gustaff Desiderius
Antonissen*, C-292/89 [1991] ECR I-
00745, para 21; R(IS) 8/08, para 5
66 Art 24(2) EU Dir 2004/38; see also
Jobcentre Berlin Neukölln v Alimanovic, C-
67/14 [2015] ECR, not yet
reported; *Vestische Arbeit Jobcenter Kreis
Recklinghausen v García-Nieto*, C-299/14
[2016] ECR, not yet reported
67 *Athanasios Vatsouras and Josif
Koupatantze v Arbeitsgemeinschaft
Nürnberg*, C-23/08 [2009] ECR I-04585,
paras 40 and 45
68 Reg 70(3)(b) and (d) ESA Regs
69 *Athanasios Vatsouras and Josif
Koupatantze
v Arbeitsgemeinschaft Nürnberg*, C-23/08
[2009] ECR I-04585, para 40
70 *Alhashem v SSWP* [2016] EWCA Civ 395
71 Reg 3 HB(HR)A Regs

8. Workers
72 Reg 6(1)(b) I(EEA) Regs; Art 7(1)(a) EU
Dir 2004/38
73 Reg 4(1)(a) I(EEA) Regs
74 *Levin v Staatssecretaris van Justitie*, C-53/
81 [1982] ECR I-1035
75 *LN v Styrelsen for Videregående
Uddannelser og Uddannelsesstøtte*, C-46/
12 [2013] ECR, not yet reported
76 *MDB (Italy) v SSHD* [2012] EWCA Civ
1015, paras 61-65
77 Reg 5 AC(IWA) Regs
78 Reg 6 A(IWA) Regs
79 Reg 5(2) A(IWR) Regs
80 *SSWP v Gubedladze*, Court of Appeal
hearing due in February 2017
81 DMG Memo 2/16, ADM Memo 4/16

82 paras 073031-58 DMG; HB A3/2014;
HMRC, 'Child Benefit and Child Tax
Credit: right to reside establishing
whether an EEA national is/was a worker
or a self-employed person under EU
law', February 2014
83 para 073040 DMG; para C1489 ADM;
HB A3/2014 para 15; HMRC, 'Child
Benefit and Child Tax Credit: right to
reside establishing whether an EEA
national is/was a worker or a self-
employed person under EU law',
February 2014, para 7
84 *Raulinv Minister van Onderwijs en
Wetenschappen*, C-357/89 [1992] ECR I-
1027, para 10
85 *SSWP v RR (IS)* [2013] UKUT 21 (AAC)
86 CIS/868/2008; CIS/1837/2006; see also
VW v SSWP (PC) [2014] UKUT 573 (AAC)
87 *Steymann v Staatssecretaris van Justitie*,
C-196/87 [1988] ECR 06159; R(IS) 12/
98
88 *Jany v Staatssecretaris van Justitie*, C-268/
99 [2001] ECR I-08615, para 34
89 *SSWP v KP (JSA)* [2011] UKUT 241 (AAC);
SSWP v MM (IS) [2015] UKUT 128
(AAC), paras 31 and 36
90 *Bettray v Staatssecretaris van Justitie*, C-
344/87 [1989] ECR 1621, para 16; *JA v
SSWP (ESA)* [2012] UKUT 122 (AAC)
91 *Barry v London Borough of Southwark*
[2008] EWCA Civ 1440, para 45; *NE v
SSWP* [2009] UKUT 38 (AAC), para 4
92 *Bettray v Staatssecretaris van Justitie*, C-
344/87 [1989] ECR 1621; *SSWP v KP
(JSA)* [2011] UKUT 241 (AAC)
93 *NE v SSWP* [2009] UKUT 38 (AAC), para
9; *SSWP v MM (IS)* [2015] UKUT 128
(AAC), paras 31 and 36
94 *Levin v Staatssecretaris van Justitie*, C-53/
81 [1982] ECR 1035, para 17
95 *Ninni-Orasche v Bundesminister für
Wissenschaft, Verkehr und Kunst*, C-413/
01 [2003] ECR I-13187, para 27
96 *Genc v Land Berlin*, C-14/09 [2010] ECR
I-00931
97 R(IS) 12/98
98 *Ninni-Orasche v Bundesminister für
Wissenschaft, Verkehr und Kunst*, C-413/
01 [2003] ECR I-13187, para 27
99 *Barry v London Borough of Southwark*
[2008] EWCA Civ 1440
100 *Ninni-Orasche v Bundesminister für
Wissenschaft, Verkehr und Kunst*, C-413/
01 [2003] ECR I-13187, para 19
101 In *NE v SSWP* [2009] UKUT 38 (AAC),
para 9; R(IS) 12/98

102 *Vatsouras and Koupantze v Arbeitsgemeinschaft (ARGE) Nürnberg 900* [2009] C-22/08 and C-23/08 [2009] ECR I-04585, paras 27 and 28

103 *Raulin v Minister van Onderwijs en Wetenschappen,* C-357/89 [1992] ECR I-1027

104 *NE v SSWP* [2009] UKUT 38 (AAC); CIS/1793/2007; *SSWP v MM(IS)* [2015] UKUT 128 (AAC)

105 *Genc v Land Berlin,* C-14/09 [2010] ECR I-00931

106 *Barry v London Borough of Southwark* [2008] EWCA Civ 1440, para 20

107 *SSWP v SY (IS)* [2012] UKUT 233 (AAC); *JR v SSWP (IS)* [2014] UKUT 0154 (AAC); *JR v Leeds City Council (HB)* [2014] UKUT 154 (AAC)

108 *BS v SSWP* [2009] UKUT 16 (AAC); CIS/4237/2007

9. Retaining worker status

109 Art 7(3) EU Dir 2004/38; reg 6(2), (2A) and (5)-(8) I(EEA) Regs

110 *Jessy Saint Prix v SSWP,* C-507/12 [2014] ECR, not yet reported

111 *Jessy Saint Prix v SSWP,* C-507/12 [2014] ECR, not yet reported, para 38

112 Reg 5(4) A(IWR) Regs; reg 7A(4) I(EEA) Regs

113 *SSWP v Gubedladze,* Court of Appeal hearing due in February 2017

114 DMG Memo 2/16, ADM Memo 4/16

115 Art 7(3)(b) and (c) EU Dir 2004/38

116 Reg 6(2)(b) and (ba), (5) and (6) I(EEA) Regs

117 CH/3314/2005, para 11; confirmed in *SSWP v EM (IS)* [2009] UKUT 146 (AAC), para 10; *SSWP v MK* [2013] UKUT 163 (AAC), paras 44-47

118 *SSWP v Elmi* [2011] EWCA Civ 1403; paras 072826-27 DMG

119 Art 7(3)(b) EU Dir 2004/38

120 *SSWP v MM (IS)* [2015] UKUT 128 (AAC), paras 53-58

121 *SSWP v MM (IS)* [2015] UKUT 128 (AAC), paras 45-46

122 Reg 6(2)(b) and (5)-(8) I(EEA) Regs

123 Reg 6(2)(ba), (2A), (5) and (6) I(EEA) Regs

124 Art 7(3)(c) EU Dir 2004/38

125 Reg 6(4) and (8)-(11) I(EEA) Regs

126 *SSWP v EM (IS)* [2009] UKUT 146 (AAC), para 10

127 *Steven Malcolm Brown v Secretary of State for Scotland,* C-197/86 [1988] ECR I-03205

128 *Lair v Universität Hannover,* C-39/86 [1988] ECR I-03161, para 37

129 *Raulin v Minister van Onderwijs en Wetenschappen,* C-357/89 [1992] ECR I-01027, paras 18 and 19

130 Art 7(3)(a) EU Dir 2004/38; reg 6(2)(a) I(EEA) Regs

131 CIS/4304/2007, para 35

132 CIS/3182/2005

133 *SSHD v FB* [2010] UKUT 447 (IAC), para 23

134 CIS/3890/2005

135 *De Brito v SSHD* [2012] EWCA Civ 709; *Konodyba v Royal Borough of Kensington and Chelsea* [2012] EWCA Civ 982; *Samin v Westminster CC* [2012] EWCA Civ 1468 (this part of the decision was not in dispute in the further appeal to the Supreme Court)

136 CIS/4237/2007

137 CIS/731/2007

138 CIS/4010/2006

139 *Jessy Saint Prix v SSWP,* C-507/12 [2014] ECR, not yet reported; *SSWP v SFF and Others* [2015] UKUT 502 (AAC)

140 *SSWP v SFF and Others* [2015] UKUT 502 (AAC), para 35

141 DMG Memo 5/16 paras 7-8, correcting Vol 2, para 073215 DMG

142 *SSWP v SFF and Others* [2015] UKUT 502 (AAC), para 26; *Weldemichael and Another v SSHD* [2015] UKUT 540 (IAC), paras 22-23

143 *SSWP v SFF and Others* [2015] UKUT 502 (AAC), paras 24 and 25

144 CIS/4304/2007, para 34; *SSWP v IR* [2009] UKUT 11 (AAC); *SSWP v SFF and Others* [2015] UKUT 502 (AAC), para 40

145 CIS/1934/2006; *SSWP v IR (IS)* [2009] UKUT 11 (AAC)

146 *SSWP v MK* [2013] UKUT 163 (AAC); *VP v SSWP (JSA)* [2014] UKUT 32 (AAC), paras 56-61; *SSWP v MM (IS)* [2015] UKUT 128 (AAC), paras 47-52

10. Self-employed people

147 Reg 6(1)(c) I(EEA) Regs; Art 7(1)(a) EU Dir 2004/38

148 Reg 4(1)(b) I(EEA) Regs

149 *Aldona Malgorzata Jany and Others v Staatssecretaris van Justitie,* C-268/99 [2001] ECR I-08615

150 *Bristol City Council v FV (HB)* [2011] UKUT 494 (AAC)

151 *HMRC v IT (CTC)* [2016] UKUT 252 (AAC), paras 25-28

152 *SSWP v SY (IS)* [2012] UKUT 233 (AAC);
JR v SSWP (IS) [2014] UKUT 154 (AAC);
JR v Leeds City Council (HB) [2014] UKUT
154 (AAC)
153 paras 073031-58 DMG; HB A3/2014;
HMRC, 'Child Benefit and Child Tax
Credit: right to reside establishing
whether an EEA national is/was a worker
or a self-employed person under EU law,
February 2014
154 Reg 4(1)(b) I(EEA) Regs; R(IS) 6/00
155 R(IS) 6/00, para 31
156 *TG v SSWP* [2009] UKUT 58 (AAC), para
5
157 *SSWP v JS (IS)* [2010] UKUT 240 (AAC),
paras 5 and 8; *RJ v SSWP(JSA)* [2011]
UKUT 477 (AAC), paras 9 and 17
158 *SSWP v JS (IS)* [2010] UKUT 240 (AAC),
para 5
159 CIS/1042/2008
160 *SSWP v JB (JSA)* [2011] UKUT 96 (AAC)

11. Retaining self-employed status
161 Art 7(3)(a) EU Dir 2004/38; reg 6(3)
I(EEA) Regs
162 *R (Tilianu) v SSWP* [2010] EWCA Civ
1397
163 *Gusa v Minister for Social Protection*
[2016] IECA 237
164 Art 7(3)(a) EU Dir 2004/38; reg 6(3)
I(EEA) Regs
165 CIS/1042/2008
166 CIS/4010/2006

12. Self-sufficient people and students
167 Art 7(1) EU Dir 2004/38; regs 4(1)(c),
6(1) and 14(1) I(EEA) Regs
168 Art 7(1) EU Dir 2004/38; regs 4(1)(d),
6(1) and 14(1) I(EEA) Regs
169 *VP v SSWP (JSA)* [2014] UKUT 32 (AAC),
paras 88-97
170 Art 8(4) EU Dir 2004/38
171 Reg 4(4) I(EEA) Regs
172 With effect from 2 June 2011
173 *SG v Tameside MBC (HB)* [2010] UKUT
243 (AAC)
174 *Zhu and Chen v SSHD*, C-200/02 [2004]
ECR I-09925
175 *Commission of the European Communities
v Kingdom Belgium*, C-408/03 [2006]
ECR I-02647; *Zhu and Chen v SSHD*, C-
200/02 [2004] ECR I-09925
176 *VP v SSWP (JSA)* [2014] UKUT 32 (AAC),
paras 88-97
177 *Singh and Others v Minister of Justice and
Equality* C-218/14 [2015] ECR, not yet
reported

178 *Pensionsversicherungsanstalt v Brey*, C-
140/12 [2013] ECR, not yet reported,
paras 54-57
179 CH/1400/2006; *SG v Tameside MBC
(HB)* [2010] UKUT 243 (AAC);
Pensionsversicherungsanstalt v Brey, C-
140/12 [2013] ECR, not yet reported
180 para 073244 DMG
181 *Pensionsversicherungsanstalt v Brey*, C-
140/12 [2013] ECR, not yet reported,
paras 64 and 75-78
182 *VP v SSWP (JSA)* [2014] UKUT 32 (AAC),
paras 77, 84 and 94
183 *W (China) and Another v SSHD* [2006]
EWCA Civ 1494
184 *SG v Tameside MBC (HB)* [2010] UKUT
243 (AAC); *VP v SSWP (JSA)* [2014] UKUT
32 (AAC); *SSWP v HH (SPC)* [2015] UKUT
583 (AAC); para 073246 DMG
185 *SSWP v HH (SPC)* [2015] UKUT 583
(AAC); para 073246 DMG
186 Arts 1(j) and (k) and 19 EU Reg 883/
2004; *I v Health Services Executive*, C-
255/13 [2014] ECR, not yet reported,
para 59
187 *FK (Kenya) v SSHD* [2010] EWCA Civ
1302; *VP v SSWP (JSA)* [2014] UKUT 32
(AAC); *SSWP v LL (SPC)* [2014] UKUT
136 (AAC); *Ahmad v SSHD* [2014] EWCA
Civ 988
188 *Baumbast and R v SSHD*, C-413/99
[2002] ECR I-07091; *KS v SSWP* [2016]
UKUT 269 (AAC), para 6
189 Art 7(1) EU Dir 2004/38; regs 4(1)(d),
6(1) and 14(1) I(EEA) Regs
190 *Rudy Grzelczyk v Centre Public d'aide
Sociale d'Ottignies-Louvain-la-Neuve*, C-
184/09 [2001] ECR I-06193
191 Art 7(4) EU Dir 2004/38; reg 7(2) I(EEA)
Regs
192 Art 7(4) EU Dir 2004/38

13. Family members of European Economic Area nationals
193 Arts 6(2) and 7(1)(d) and (2) EU Dir
2004/38; *Clauder*, C-E-4/11 [2011]
EFTACR 216, para 43; regs 13(2)
and 14(2) I(EEA) Regs
194 Regs 6 and 14(1) I(EEA) Regs. The same
groups are covered in Arts 7 and 14 EU
Dir 2004/38, although the term
'qualified person' is not used.
195 Art 2(2) EU Dir 2004/38; reg 7(1) I(EEA)
Regs
196 Reg 7(3) I(EEA) Regs; CPC/3588/2006;
SS v SSWP (ESA) [2011] UKUT 8 (AAC);
SSWP v LZ (SPC) [2014] UKUT 0147
(AAC)

197 *Aissatou Diatta v Land Berlin*, C-267/83 [1985] ECR I-00567
198 CF/1863/2007
199 CIS/2100/2007, which considers the findings of *Centre Public d'Aide Sociale de Courcelles v Lebon*, 316/85 [1987] ECR I-02811, *Zhu and Chen v SSHD*, C-200/02 [2004] ECR I-09925 and *Jia v Migrationsverket*, C-1/05 [2007] ECR I-00001; *SSWP v MB (JSA)* (and linked cases) [2016] UKUT 372 (AAC), paras 132-39
200 *Flora May Reyes v Migrationsverket* C-423/12 [2014] ECR, not yet reported; *Centre Publique d'Aide Social de Courcelles vLebon* C-316/85 [1987] ECR 02811; *ECO v Lim (EEA dependency)* [2013] UKUT 437 (IAC)
201 *Pedro v SSWP* [2009] EWCA Civ 1358. Arguably, this remains good law despite the assumptions made in *Flora May Reyes v Migrationsverket*, C-423/12 [2014] ECR, not yet reported.
202 *SSHD v Rahman and Others*, C-83/11 [2012] ECR, not yet reported; *Oboh and Others v SSHD* [2013] EWCA Civ 1525; *AA (Algeria) v SSHD* [2014] EWCA Civ 1741
203 *Centre Publique d'Aide Social de Courcelles v Lebon*, C-316/85 [1987] ECR I-02811, para 20; *SSWP v MB (JSA)* (and linked cases) [2016] UKUT 372 (AAC), paras 132-39
204 Reg 7(3) I(EEA) Regs
205 CPC/3588/2006; *SS v SSWP(ESA)* [2011] UKUT 8 (AAC); *SSWP v LZ (SPC)* [2014] UKUT 147 (AAC)
206 Reg 7(3) and 8 I(EEA) Regs; the same groups are covered in Art 3 EU Dir 2004/38, but the term is not used.
207 *SSHD v Rahman and Others*, C-83/11 [2012] ECR, not yet reported; *Oboh and Others v SSHD* [2013] EWCA Civ 1525; *Soares v SSHD* [2013] EWCA Civ 575; *AA (Algeria) v SSHD* [2014] EWCA Civ 1741
208 *Dauhoo (EEA Regs – Reg 8(2)) v SSHD* [2012] UKUT 79 (IAC)
209 Reg 7(4) I(EEA) Regs
210 Art 7(4) EU Dir 2004/38
211 Art 3(1) EU Dir 2004/38
212 Reg 2(1) I(EEA) Regs
213 Art 7(2) EU Dir 2004/38
214 *O and B v Minister voor Immigratie, Integratie en Asiel*, C-456/12 [2014] ECR, not yet reported; *VW v SSWP(PC)* [2014] UKUT 573 (AAC)
215 Reg 9 I(EEA) Regs
216 *Metock and Others v Minister for Justice, Equality and Law Reform*, C-127/08 [2008] ECR I-06241
217 Reg 9(2) I(EEA) Regs
218 Reg 9(2) and (3) I(EEA) Regs
219 Sch 3 para 2 I(EEA)A 2013 Regs
220 *Minister voor Vreemdelingenzaken en Integratie v Eind*, C-291/05 [2007] ECR I-10719, para 45. The case relates to an earlier EU Regulation, but the same reasoning applies to Art 7(2) EU Dir 2004/38.
221 *Mary Carpenter v SSHD*, C-60/00 [2002] ECR I-06279, para 46
222 *S and G v Minister voor Immigratie, Integratie en Asiel*, C-457/12 [2014] ECR, not yet reported
223 *McCarthy v SSHD*, C-434-09 [2011] ECR I-03375
224 Reg 2(1) I(EEA) Regs
225 *AA v SSWP* [2009] UKUT 249 (AAC); *HG v SSWP (SPC)* [2011] UKUT 382 (AAC)
226 Sch 3 I(EEA)A Regs 2012
227 Reg 9 I(EEA) Regs
228 *Lounes v SSHD* [2016] EWHC 436 (Admin) (8 March 2016)
229 Regs 10 and 14(3) I(EEA) Regs
230 Reg 14(3) I(EEA) Regs
231 Reg 10(8) I(EEA) Regs
232 Art 12 EU Dir 2004/38
233 Art 12 EU Dir 2004/38
234 Art 13 EU Dir 2004/38
235 *Singh and Others v Minister of Justice and Equality*, C-218-14 [2015] ECR, not yet reported
236 *SSHD v NA*, C-115/15 [2016] ECR, not yet reported
237 Arts 12, 13 and 18 EU Dir 2004/38
238 Regs 6 and 14(1) I(EEA) Regs. The same groups are covered in Arts 7 and 14 EU Dir 2004/38, although the term 'qualified person' is not used.

14. Derivative residence rights

239 Reg 15A I(EEA) Regs
240 See also *London Borough of Harrow v Nimco Hassan Ibrahim and SSHD*, C-310/08 [2010] ECR I-01065; *Maria Teixeira v London Borough of Lambeth and SSHD*, C-480/08 [2010] ECR I-01107; *GBC Echternach and A Moritz v Minister van Onderwijs en Wetenschappen*, joined cases 389/87 and 390/87 [1989] ECR 00723; *Baumbast and R v SSHD*, C-413/99 [2002] ECR I-07091

241 See also *London Borough of Harrow v Nimco Hassan Ibrahim and SSHD*, C-310/08 [2010] ECR I-01065; *Maria Teixeira v London Borough of Lambeth and SSHD*, C-480/08 [2010] ECR I-01107; *GBC Echternach and A Moritz v Minister van Onderwijs en Wetenschappen*, joined cases 389/87 and 390/87 [1989] ECR 00723; *Baumbast and R v SSHD*, C-413/99 [2002] ECR I-07091

242 See also *Zhu and Chen v SSHD*, C-200/02 [2004] ECR I-09925

243 See also *Zambrano v ONEm*, C-34/09 [2011] ECR I-01177; *Dereci and Others v Bundesministerium für Inneres*, C-256/11 [2011] ECR I-11315

244 Reg 15A(1) I(EEA) Regs

245 Reg 15A(6)(c) I(EEA) Regs

246 *HMRC v IT (CTC)* [2016] UKUT 252 (AAC)

247 *SSWP v JS (IS)* [2010] UKUT 347

248 *DJ v SSWP* [2013] UKUT 113 (AAC)

249 Art 10 EU Reg 492/2011 (before 1 June 2012, Art 12 EC Reg 1612/68 was in identical terms)

250 *Baumbast and R v SSHD*, C-413/99 [2002] ECR I-07091

251 *JS v SSWP (ESA)* [2016] UKUT 314 (AAC)

252 *Baumbast and R v SSHD*, C-413/99 [2002] ECR I-07091, para 57; *IP v SSWP (IS)* [2015] UKUT 691 (AAC)

253 Reg 15A(6)(a) I(EEA) Regs; CIS/3960/2007

254 *SSWP v IM (IS)* [2011] UKUT 231 (AAC), paras 17 and 28

255 *Shabani v SSHD* [2013] UKUT 315 (IAC)

256 *Landesamt für Ausbildungsförderung Nordrhein-Westfalen v Lubor Gaal*, C-7/94 [1995] ECR I-1031, paras 24 and 25

257 *Teixeira v LB Lambeth and SSHD*, C-480/08 [2010] ECR I-01107, para 74

258 Reg 15A(3)(c) I(EEA) Regs

259 *SSHD v NA*, C-115/15 [2016] ECR, not yet reported

260 *Teixeira v LB Lambeth and SSHD*, C-480/08 [2010] ECR I-01107, para 74; *Baumbast and R v SSHD*, C-413/99 [2002] ECR I-07091, para 63

261 *London Borough of Harrow v Nimco Hassan Ibrahim and SSHD*, C-310/08 [2010] ECR I-01065; *Maria Teixeira v London Borough of Lambeth and SSHD*, C-480/08 [2010] ECR I-01107; *Baumbast and R v SSHD*, C-413/99 [2002] ECR I-07091; *SSWP v Czop and SSWP v Punakova* joined cases, C-147/11 and C-148/11 [2012] ECR, not yet reported; *Landesamt für Ausbildungsförderung Nordrhein-Westfalen v Lubor Gaal*, C-7/94 [1995] ECR I-1031

262 para 073401 DMG

263 *Echternach and Moritz v Netherlands Minister for Education and Science*, joined cases 389/87 and 390/87 [1989] ECR 00723, paras 18-23

264 Reg 15A(1) and (4) I(EEA) Regs

265 Art 10 EU Reg 492/2011 (before 1 June 2012, Art 12 EC Reg 1612/68 was in identical terms)

266 *Baumbast and R v SSHD*, C-413/99 [2002] ECR I-07091

267 *Teixeira v LB Lambeth and SSHD*, C-480/08 [2010] ECR I-01107, paras 84-86

268 *Teixeira v LB Lambeth and SSHD*, C-480/08 [2010] ECR I-01107, para 3

269 See for example, *SSWP v RR (IS)* [2013] UKUT 21 (AAC)

270 Reg 15A(7) I(EEA) Regs

271 Reg 15A(7A) and (7B) I(EEA) Regs

272 Reg 15A(8) I(EEA) Regs

273 Reg 15A(1) and (2) I(EEA) Regs

274 *Zhu and Chen v SSHD*, C-200/02 [2004] ECR I-09925; see also *SSHD v NA*, C-115/15 [2016] ECR, not yet reported

275 Reg 15A(1) and (2) I(EEA) Regs

276 Reg 15A(1) and (4A) I(EEA) Regs

277 *Zambrano v ONEm*, C-34/09 [2011] ECR I-01177; *Dereci and Others v Bundesministerium für Inneres*, C-256/11 [2011] ECR I-11315

278 *Harrison and AB v SSHD* [2012] EWCA Civ 1736; *O and S v Maahanmuuttovirasto and Maahanmuuttovirasto v L*, joined cases C-356/11 and C-357/11 [2012] ECR, not yet reported.

279 *Sanneh and Others v SSWP* [2015] EWCA Civ 49. Permission to appeal to the Supreme Court in the joined case of *HC* was granted on 7 March 2016 – file reference: *R (on the application of HC) v SSWP* UKSC 2015/0215

280 *SSWP v Lucja Czop and Margita Punakova*, joined cases C-147/11 and C-148/11 [2012] ECR, not yet reported

281 Art 12 EC Reg 1612/68 replaced, in identical terms, by Art 10 EU Reg 492/2011 since 1 June 2012
282 *SSWP v Lucja Czop and Margita Punakova,* joined cases C-147/11 and C-148/11 [2012] ECR, not yet reported, para 33
283 *SSWP v Punakova* [2012] UKUT 352 (AAC) and *SSWP v Czop* [2012] UKUT 351 (AAC)
284 *RM v SSWP (IS)* [2014] UKUT 401 (AAC)
285 *Hrabkova v SSWP* C3/2015/2886, due to be heard in the Court of Appeal 28 February 2017
286 *Sanneh and Others v SSWP* [2015] EWCA Civ 49. Permission to appeal to the Supreme Court in the joined case of *HC* was granted 7 March 2016 – file reference: *R (on the application of HC) v SSWP* UKSC 2015/0215

15. Permanent right to reside
287 Art 16(1) EU Dir 2004/38
288 Art 16(4) EU Dir 2004/38; reg 15(2) I(EEA) Regs
289 Art 16(1) EU Dir 2004/38; reg 15(1) I(EEA) Regs
290 Vol 2, paras 073350-68 and 073414-43 DMG; HB Circular A8/2015
291 Art 16(1) EU Dir 2004/38; reg 15(1)(a) I(EEA) Regs
292 Arts 7 and 16(1) EU Dir 2004/38; regs 6, 14 and 15 EEA Regs; *Tomasz Ziolkowski and Barbara Szeja v Land Berlin,* joined cases C-424/10 and C-425/10 [2011] ECR I-14035
293 *SSWP v Lassal,* C-162/09 [2010] ECR I-09217; *Alarape and Tijani v SSHD,* C-529/11 [2013] ECR, not yet reported
294 Sch 4 para 6 I(EEA) Regs
295 *SSWP v Lassal,* C-162/09 [2010] ECR I-09217; *SSWP v Dias,* C-325/09 [2011] ECR I-06387; Sch 4 para 6(4) I(EEA) Regs
296 Regs 6(1)(a), 7, 14(1) and (2) and 15(1) I(EEA) Regs
297 Vol 2, para 073428 DMG; HB Circular A8/15 para 19
298 Vol 2, para 073440 DMG; HB Circular A8/15 para 27
299 Vol 2, para 073439 DMG; HB Circular A8/15 para 26
300 *Ziolkowski and Szeja,* joined cases C-424/10 and C-425/10 [2011] ECR, I-14035
301 Regs 13 and 15(1) I(EEA) Regs
302 *Ziolkowski and Szeja,* joined cases C-424/10 and C-425/10 [2011] ECR I-14035, para 46
303 Reg 14(2) I(EEA) Regs; *Clauder,* E-4/11 [2011] EFTACR 216, para 43
304 Regs 14(2) and 15(1)(a) and (b) I(EEA) Regs
305 Reg 15(1)(f) I(EEA) Regs
306 Arts 12 and 13 EU Dir 2004/38; *Ziolkowski and Szeja,* joined cases C-424/10 and C-425/10 [2011] ECR I-14035
307 *Ziolkowski and Szeja,* joined cases C-424/10 and C-425/10 [2011] ECR I-14035
308 Art 18 EU Dir 2004/38
309 *SSWP v Gubedladze,* Court of Appeal hearing due in February 2017
310 DMG Memo 2/16, ADM Memo 4/16
311 *Ziolkowski and Szeja,* joined cases C-424/10 and C-425/10 [2011] ECR I-14035; Sch 4, para 6(1) and (3) I(EEA) Regs; *SSWP v LS (IS)* [2012] UKUT 207 (AAC)
312 *Oakfor and Others v SSHD* [2011] EWCA Civ 499; *Alarape and Tijani v SSHD,* C-529/11 [2013] ECR, not yet reported; *Bee and Another v SSHD* [2013] UKUT 83 (IAC); reg 15(1A) I(EEA) Regs
313 Art 16(1) EU Dir 2004/38; reg 15(1) I(EEA) Regs
314 Art 16(3) EU Dir 2004/38; reg 3 I(EEA) Regs
315 *Babajanov v SSHD* [2013] UKUT 513 (IAC)
316 *Idezuna v SSHD* [2011] UKUT 474 (IAC); *Babajanov v SSHD* [2013] UKUT 513 (IAC)
317 Vol 2, paras 073360 and 073417 DMG; HB Circular A8/2015, para 7; CIS/2258/08
318 Reg 3(3) I(EEA) Regs
319 Following *SSWP v Dias,* C-325/09 [2011] ECR I-06387; see also *Saint Prix v SSWP,* C-507/12 [2014] ECR, not yet reported, paras 45 and 46
320 *SSHD v Ojo* [2015] EWCA Civ 1301
321 For example there is no discussion of *Saint Prix v SSWP,* C-507/12 [2014] ECR, not yet reported, paras 45 and 46
322 Vol 2, paras 073433-35 DMG; HB Circular A8/2015, paras 20-22
323 *Nnamdi Onuekwere v SSHD,* C-378/12 [2014] ECR, not yet reported
324 *Nnamdi Onuekwere v SSHD,* C-378/12 [2014] ECR, not yet reported, paras 24-26
325 *Jessy Saint Prix v SSWP,* C-507/12 [2014] ECR, not yet reported, para 38
326 Regs 5 and 15 I(EEA) Regs; Art 17 EU Dir 2004/38

327 *SSHD v FB* [2010] UKUT 447 (IAC), para 23
328 Reg 5(7) I(EEA) Regs; Art 17(1) EU Dir 2004/38
329 Regs 5(7), 6(2), 7A(3) and 7B(3) I(EEA) Regs
330 *De Brito v SSHD* [2012] EWCA Civ 709
331 *TG v SSWP (PC)* [2015] UKUT 50 (AAC)
332 *ID v SSWP (IS)* [2011] UKUT 401 (AAC), paras 17 and 18
333 EC Reg 1251/70; recital 19 preamble to EU Dir 2004/38
334 Listed for Court of Appeal hearing in February 2017
335 DMG Memo 2/16, ADM Memo 4/16
336 *PM (EEA – spouse – 'residing with') Turkey* [2011] UKUT 89 (IAC)
337 Reg 15(1)(d) and (e) I(EEA) Regs and Art 17(3) EU Dir 2004/38; see also *RM (Zimbabwe) v SSHD* [2013] EWCA Civ 775, para 56 – cited in *TG v SSWP (PC)* [2015] UKUT 50 (AAC), para 33; paras 62-64 of the AG's opinion in *Givane*, C-257/00 [2003] ECR I-00345, although the ECJ did not address the issue itself.
338 Reg 15(2) I(EEA) Regs; Art 16(4) EU Dir 2004/38
339 Vol 2, paras 073350-68 and 073414-43 DMG; HB Circular A8/2015
340 Vol 2, paras 073429-32 DMG

Chapter 13

Residence and presence: rules for individual benefits

This chapter covers:
1. Means-tested benefits (below)
2. Bereavement benefits (p205)
3. Child benefit and guardian's allowance (p207)
4. Disability and carers' benefits (p208)
5. Industrial injuries benefits (p212)
6. Contribution-based jobseeker's allowance and contributory employment and support allowance (p213)
7. Maternity allowance (p215)
8. Retirement pensions (p215)
9. Social fund funeral and winter fuel payments (p216)
10. Tax credits (p218)

This chapter explains the residence and presence rules for each benefit. It also covers how you may be assisted by the European Union (EU) co-ordination rules. Further information on the different residence and presence tests is in Chapter 10, further information on the habitual residence and right to reside tests is in Chapter 11, and further information on the EU co-ordination rules is in Chapter 16. This chapter does not explain the rules on being paid while you are abroad. These are covered in Part 5.

1. Means-tested benefits

To be entitled to income support (IS), income-based jobseeker's allowance (JSA), income-related employment and support allowance (ESA), pension credit (PC) and universal credit (UC), you (and your partner for joint-claim JSA or UC) must:
- be present in Great Britain (see p91);[1] *and*
- satisfy the habitual residence test (see p104) or be in a group that is exempt (see p106).[2]

To satisfy the habitual residence test for these benefits, in addition to being 'habitually resident in fact' (see p110), unless you have transitional protection (see p118), you must have a right to reside (see p115) in the common travel area – ie, the UK, Ireland, Channel Islands and the Isle of Man. For income-based JSA only, you must also have been living in the common travel area for the past three months (see p92).

In certain circumstances, the rules treat you as present in Great Britain during a temporary absence, so you can continue to receive these benefits while you are abroad for limited periods (see p233).

For all means-tested benefits, the habitual residence test applies to the claimant. This means that if you live with your partner, for all the benefits except UC and joint-claim JSA, it only applies to you as the claimant.

If you live with a partner and claim UC or joint-claim JSA, in general you must both satisfy the habitual residence test for your joint claim. If you satisfy the habitual residence test but your partner does not, the rules are different for each benefit. For UC, you must claim and are paid as a single person, but your partner's income and capital are taken into account (see p108). For joint-claim JSA, you do not need to make a joint claim and are still paid as a couple (see p107).

If you come under the UC system, unless you are in a 'full service area', you must meet certain 'gateway' conditions. See CPAG's *Welfare Benefits and Tax Credits Handbook* for more details on these. They include satisfying the following additional residence and presence rules. You (and, if you are in an area where couples can claim, your partner) must:[3]

- be a British citizen; *and*
- have resided in the UK throughout the two years before the date of your claim; *and*
- not have left the UK for a continuous period of more than four weeks during the above period.

If you do not satisfy the 'gateway' conditions for UC, you may be able to claim existing means-tested benefits. For further details, see CPAG's *Welfare Benefits and Tax Credits Handbook*.

To be entitled to housing benefit (HB), you must be habitually resident (see p104), including having a right to reside (see p115) in the common travel area, unless you are in a group that is exempt from the habitual residence test (see p106).[4]

There is no requirement to be present in Great Britain for HB. However, you must be liable to make payments in respect of a dwelling in Great Britain, which you occupy as your home.[5] There are rules that treat you as occupying your home, including during a temporary absence from it. These rules vary depending on whether the absence from your home is inside or outside Great Britain (see p230).[6]

If you are claiming income-based JSA, note that looking for work abroad does not count towards satisfying the requirement that you be 'actively seeking employment'.[7]

If your partner is abroad

If you have a partner who is abroad, the effect this has on your benefit depends on whether the separation is permanent or, if temporary, whether you still count as members of the same household.

If you are still regarded as a couple, your partner's absence abroad can affect your benefit in two ways.

- At some point, you will cease to be paid an amount of benefit for your partner.
- Your partner's capital and income can continue to affect your entitlement.

If you separate permanently (ie, you do not intend to resume living with your partner), you no longer count as a couple.[8]

If you and your partner are living apart temporarily, you continue to count as a couple because you are still treated as members of the same household, unless:[9]

- **for IS, income-based JSA, income-related ESA, PC and HB**, you are likely to be separated for more than 52 weeks. However, you still count as a couple if you are unlikely to be separated for 'substantially' longer than 52 weeks and there are exceptional circumstances, such as a stay in hospital, or if you have no control over the length of the absence;
- **for IS, income-based JSA, income-related ESA and PC**, you or your partner are detained in custody or in a high-security psychiatric hospital, or are on temporary release, or are living permanently in a care home;
- **for UC**, you have been separated (or expect to be separated) for more than six months.

Your partner's absence is from *you*, not from the family home, so these rules can apply even if your partner has never lived in your current home and your former household need not have been in this country.[10] However, you must have been living with your partner in the same household before you can be treated as continuing to be members of that household.[11] The length of the absence is calculated from when it started to when it is likely to finish.

Where questions of 'intention' are involved (eg, when deciding whether you or your partner intend to resume living with your family), the intention must be 'unqualified'. This means that it must not depend on a factor over which you have no control – eg, the right of entry to the UK being granted by the Home Office[12] or the offer of a suitable job.[13]

If you still count as a couple, there are rules that allow you to continue to receive an amount of benefit for your partner while s/he is abroad for a limited period, depending on the circumstances. These rules vary between the different means-tested benefits (see Chapter 15).

If you cease to be paid for your partner because these rules do not apply, or at the end of the limited period:

- **for IS, income-based JSA, income-related ESA and HB,** your applicable amount no longer includes an amount for your partner. However, your partner's capital, income and work are still taken into account as s/he is still treated as part of your household;[14]
- **for PC,** you are paid as a single person. Your partner's income and capital are ignored because s/he is no longer treated as part of your household;[15]
- **for UC,** you cease to be entitled as joint claimants and must claim as a single person. Your award is based on the maximum amount for a single person, but your partner's income and capital are taken into account until you have been, or you expect to be, apart for six months (as then you cease to be treated as a couple).[16] **Note:** if your partner's absence abroad means s/he ceases to be habitually resident (including if s/he ceases to have a right to reside) in the common travel area, s/he is treated as no longer present. You can claim as a single person, but your partner's income and capital are taken into account.[17]

If your child is abroad

If you have a child who is abroad, the effect this has on your benefit depends on whether s/he is still treated as being part of your household, despite temporarily living away from you.

S/he ceases to be treated as part of your household if:[18]

- **for IS, JSA, ESA and HB,** s/he is not living with you and:
  - has no intention of resuming living with you; *or*
  - is likely to be absent for more than 52 weeks, unless there are exceptional circumstances, such as being in hospital, or if you have no control over the length of absence and the absence is unlikely to be substantially longer than 52 weeks;
- **for IS, JSA and ESA,** s/he is not living with you and has been abroad for more than:
  - four weeks; *or*
  - eight weeks (26 weeks for ESA) to get medical treatment;
- there are other reasons that are not related to residence or presence, such as being fostered. See CPAG's *Welfare Benefits and Tax Credits Handbook* for more information.

For IS or income-based JSA, once the child ceases to be treated as part of your household, s/he permanently ceases to be included in your applicable amount. If s/he returns to your household, you must claim child tax credit for her/him instead. See p235 for IS and p238 for income-based JSA.

The rules for UC are different. You cease to be responsible for a child if s/he is absent from your household and the absence exceeds, or is expected to exceed, one month, or up to six months in limited circumstances (see p242).[19]

European Union co-ordination rules

If you are covered by the European Union (EU) co-ordination rules, these can assist you to satisfy the habitual residence test for some of the means-tested benefits sooner than might otherwise be the case.

If you are covered by the EU co-ordination rules (see p264) and you are claiming:

- **income-based JSA, income-related ESA or PC**, you cannot be denied benefit solely on the basis that your length of actual residence is too short, because the period of your residence is only one relevant factor in determining whether you are 'habitually resident in fact' and can be outweighed by others (see p114);
- **income-based JSA**, you may be able to argue that it is unlawful to exclude you from benefit until you have been living in the common travel area for three months if you are 'habitually resident in fact' and have a right to reside (see p92).

Reciprocal agreements

Most means-tested benefits are not covered by reciprocal agreements. One exception is the agreement between Great Britain and Northern Ireland which, since 6 April 2016, has covered income-related ESA (as well as contributory ESA).[20] If you moved to Great Britain from Northern Ireland (or vice versa) while claiming ESA before 6 April 2016, the DWP policy was to make an extra-statutory payment to cover any loss of income-related ESA (or contributory ESA) that resulted from having to make a new claim. See p293 for further details.

---

2. **Bereavement benefits**

You do not need to satisfy any residence or presence rules to be entitled to bereavement benefits, with the one exception that only applies to bereavement payment.

If you are absent from Great Britain when you claim bereavement payment, you can only be entitled if:[21]

- your late spouse or civil partner was in Great Britain when s/he died; *or*
- you were in Great Britain on the date of the death of your spouse or civil partner; *or*
- neither of the above two bullets apply, but you returned to Great Britain within four weeks of the death of your late spouse or civil partner; *or*

- your late spouse's/civil partner's national insurance (NI) contribution record is sufficient for you to satisfy the contribution conditions for widowed parent's allowance and bereavement allowance; *or*
- your spouse or civil partner died while abroad in another European Economic Area (EEA) state and the European Union (EU) co-ordination rules apply to you (see p264); *or*
- your spouse or civil partner died while abroad in a state which has a reciprocal agreement with the UK that covers your entitlement to bereavement payment.

According to official guidance, the DWP takes the view that if you and your late spouse or civil partner were outside Great Britain when s/he died and you do not return to Great Britain within four weeks of the death (and none of the last three bullets above apply), you are disqualified from bereavement payment, even if you claim within the necessary time limit when you are back in Great Britain.[22] It is arguable that this approach is incorrect and you should only be disqualified if you are absent from Great Britain when you make your claim (and none of the above bullets apply).

Note: a new benefit, bereavement support payment, will replace the current bereavement benefits for people whose spouse or civil partner dies on or after the date it is introduced (likely to be in April 2017). It will consist of an initial lump sum, followed by regular payments for one year. Entitlement will depend on you being ordinarily resident in Great Britain (or a specified territory) when your spouse or civil partner dies.[23] At the time of writing, no other information about the residence rules for this new benefit were available. See CPAG's online service and *Welfare Rights Bulletin* for updates.

European Union co-ordination rules

If you are covered by the EU co-ordination rules (see p264) and the UK is your 'competent state' (see p271):[24]

- you can, if necessary, rely on NI contributions paid by your late spouse or civil partner in other EEA states to calculate your entitlement to bereavement benefits under the aggregation principle (see p281);
- if your late spouse/civil partner died in another EEA state, s/he can be treated as having died in the UK for the purposes of entitlement to a bereavement payment;
- you can be entitled to a bereavement payment even if you reside in another EEA state.

Reciprocal and other international agreements

If you have lived and worked in a country with which the UK has a reciprocal agreement (see p291), you may be able to count periods of insurance paid in that country towards your bereavement benefit entitlement. Similarly, if you are covered by an international agreement between the EU and another state, you may be able to do the same (see p300).

3. **Child benefit and guardian's allowance**

Child benefit

To be entitled to child benefit, you and your child(ren) must be present in Great Britain (see p91).[25]

You are treated as not present and, therefore, not eligible for child benefit if:[26]

- you are not ordinarily resident in the UK (see p96); *or*
- you do not have a right to reside in the UK (see p115); *or*
- you have not been living in the UK for the three months prior to your claim, unless you are exempt from this requirement (see p92).

Note: you do not need to have a right to reside if you claimed child benefit before 1 May 2004 and you have been receiving it continuously since that date.

You are treated as present if you are:[27]

- a Crown servant posted overseas and:
  - you are, or immediately before your posting abroad you were, ordinarily resident in the UK; *or*
  - immediately before your posting you were in the UK in connection with that posting; *or*
- the partner of a Crown servant posted overseas and in the same country as her/him, or temporarily absent from that country under the same exceptions that enable child benefit to continue during a temporary absence from Great Britain (see p243); *or*
- a person who is in the UK as a result of your being deported or legally removed from another country.

You and/or your child can be treated as present for limited periods during a temporary absence (see p243).

While you are treated as present, you continue to satisfy that condition of entitlement. This means that you can continue to receive child benefit if it is already being paid and you can also make a fresh claim during your, or your child's, absence. If you, or your child, spend longer abroad than the permitted periods (see p243), you (or s/he) cease to satisfy the presence condition and your entitlement to child benefit ends.

Note: if you or your child are treated as present, you must satisfy all the other conditions of entitlement including, if your child is not living with you, contributing to the costs of her/him at least the amount of child benefit that would be payable for her/him.[28]

Note also: the lawfulness of the right to reside test for child benefit is being challenged (see p117).

Guardian's allowance

Entitlement to guardian's allowance depends on entitlement to child benefit, so you must meet the conditions for child benefit set out above. In addition, at least one of the child's parents must:[29]

- have been born in the UK; *or*
- have spent a total of 52 weeks in any two-year period in Great Britain at some time after reaching the age of 16.

In order to satisfy the second condition above, you are treated as being present in Great Britain during any absence abroad which is due to your employment as a serving member of the forces, an airman or airwoman, mariner or continental shelf worker.

European Union co-ordination rules

If you are covered by the European Union (EU) co-ordination rules (see p264), you may be able to:

- use periods of residence in another European Economic Area (EEA) country to satisfy the child benefit requirement to have been 'living in' the UK for the past three months under the aggregation principle. For further information, including on HM Revenue and Customs guidance that suggests this only applies to residence in four EEA countries, see p92;
- use time spent in another EEA state to satisfy the guardian's allowance requirement to have spent 52 weeks in any two-year period in Great Britain (see above). It may also be arguable that this condition should not apply to you if you are covered by the co-ordination rules and have a 'genuine and sufficient link to the UK social security system' (see p211);[30]
- be paid child benefit, and, if applicable, guardian's allowance, for a child resident in another EEA country without her/him needing to satisfy the UK rules on temporary absences. However, you must still satisfy all the other conditions of entitlement, including contributing to the costs of the child an amount at least equal to the amount of child benefit payable for that child.[31] Child benefit and guardian's allowance are classified as 'family benefits' under the EU co-ordination rules. For more details on the payment of these, see p284.

4. Disability and carers' benefits

For attendance allowance (AA), disability living allowance (DLA), personal independence payment (PIP) and carer's allowance (CA), you must:[32]

- be present in Great Britain at the time of your claim;

- have been present in Great Britain for at least 104 weeks in the last 156 weeks (the 'past presence test'). See p92, but see also the exceptions below;
- be habitually resident in the common travel area (see p104) unless your award of AA, DLA or CA began before 8 April 2013, in which case you must be ordinarily resident, rather than habitually resident, until your award is revised or superseded.[33]

If the DLA claimant is a child under 16, her/his residence is generally determined by the residence of the person responsible for her/him (see p95).

For AA, DLA, PIP and CA, you are treated as habitually resident (as well as treated as present) if you:[34]
- are abroad in your capacity as a serving member of the armed forces; *or*
- are living with someone who is abroad as a serving member of the armed forces and s/he is your spouse, civil partner, son, stepson, daughter, stepdaughter, father, stepfather, father-in-law, mother, stepmother or mother-in-law.

For employment and support allowance (ESA) **in youth, incapacity benefit (IB) in youth and severe disablement allowance (SDA)**, you must:[35]
- be present in Great Britain at the time of your claim (see p91);
- have been present in Great Britain for not less than 26 weeks in the last 52 weeks (the 'past presence' test – see p92);
- be ordinarily resident in Great Britain (see p96).

For ESA in youth, IB in youth and SDA, once you satisfy these tests, you do not need to do so again while you are in the same period of limited capability for work or incapacity for work.[36]

Note: in the future, the rules on AA, DLA, PIP and CA may be different in Scotland. See CPAG's online service and *Welfare Rights Bulletin* for updates.

When you can be treated as present

You are treated as being present during certain absences (see p245). Any period when you are treated as present can be counted to satisfy both the presence and the past presence tests.

Exceptions to the past presence test

If you are claiming the DLA care component for a baby under six months old, there is a shorter 13-week past presence test. If covered by this, it continues to apply until your child's first birthday. If your child becomes entitled to DLA aged between six months and 36 months, the past presence test is 26 weeks in the last 156 weeks.

For AA, DLA and PIP, the 104-week (or 26-week or 13-week) past presence test does not apply if you are terminally ill.[37]

The definition of 'terminal illness' is the same as applies for other purposes for these benefits – ie, that you have a progressive disease and your death as a result of that disease can reasonably be expected within six months.[38]

If you are a refugee, or have leave on the basis that you joined your family member who is a refugee under the family reunion provisions (see p33), you should be exempt from the past presence test. This follows a case in which the Upper Tribunal decided that the test in DLA unlawfully discriminated against a refugee child and another child with leave on the basis of being a family member of a refugee mother, and must therefore be disapplied.[39] The argument applies equally to an adult or child with refugee or humanitarian protection leave, or a family member of either with leave as a refugee under the family reunion provisions. The DWP has issued guidance confirming it is not appealing the Upper Tribunal decision and that any cases that had been 'stayed' following earlier guidance should now be decided (DMG Memo 20/16, replacing DMG Memo 15/16, and ADM Memo 21/16, replacing ADM Memo 17/16).

European Union co-ordination rules

If you are covered by the European Union (EU) co-ordination rules (see p264):

- you are not entitled to AA, DLA care component, the daily living component of PIP or CA unless the UK is your 'competent state' (see p271).[40] This might not be the case if you (or your family member who brings you within the co-ordination rules) receive a pension from another member state (see p274);
- you may be able to claim AA, DLA, PIP and CA in the UK more quickly. Check below to see whether the past presence test can be disapplied or whether periods of residence in another European Economic Area (EEA) state can be used to satisfy the test;
- you may be able to make a new claim for AA, DLA care component, the daily living component of PIP or CA if you live in another EEA state (see p211).

The past presence test does not apply to AA, DLA, PIP and CA if:[41]

- you are habitually resident in Great Britain; *and*
- you are covered by the EU co-ordination rules (see p264); *and*
- you can demonstrate 'a genuine and sufficient link to the UK social security system' (see p211).

If you are covered by the EU co-ordination rules (see p264), but are not exempt from the past presence test because you are not accepted as having 'a genuine and sufficient link to the UK social security system', you may be able to count periods of residence in another EEA member state to satisfy the past presence test for these benefits (and also for ESA in youth). This is achieved under the aggregation principle of the co-ordination rules (see p281).[42] **Note:** at the time of writing, a number of Upper Tribunal cases on the operation of the aggregation principle to satisfy the past presence test were due to be heard. See CPAG's online service and *Welfare Rights Bulletin* for updates.

If you are living in another EEA member state, you can make a new claim for AA, DLA care component, the daily living component of PIP or CA without needing to satisfy the habitual residence, presence and past presence requirements if the UK is your 'competent state' (see p271)[43] and:[44]

- you are habitually resident in another EEA state or Switzerland; *and*
- you are covered by the EU co-ordination rules (see p264); *and*
- you can demonstrate a genuine and sufficient link to the UK social security system (see below).

DLA mobility component is listed as, and PIP mobility component is treated by the DWP as, a special non-contributory benefit and is therefore not 'exportable'.[45] You can only be paid these in the state where you are resident.[46] Under the EU co-ordination rules, this means where you 'habitually reside'.[47] The EU co-ordination rules can still assist you to be entitled to the DLA or PIP mobility component sooner than you would otherwise be because, if you are covered by these rules (see p264), you cannot be denied benefit on the basis that you have not been actually resident for an 'appreciable period' of time, and your length of actual residence is only one relevant factor in determining whether you are 'habitually resident in fact' and can be outweighed by other factors (see p114).

Genuine and sufficient link to the UK social security system

The phrase **'genuine and sufficient link to the UK social security system'** is not defined in regulations, but comes from a case decided by the Court of Justice of the European Union (CJEU).[48] The circumstances which applied in that case and which were held to have amounted to a 'genuine and sufficient link to the UK social security system' are therefore relevant, but they are not an exhaustive list. Other factors may be equally or more relevant in your case and may also be affected by the benefit you are claiming.[49] Relevant factors accepted by the CJEU include whether you:[50]

– have worked in the UK;

– have spent a significant part of your life in the UK;

– are receiving a UK contributory benefit;

– are dependent on a family member who has worked in the UK and/or receives a UK contributory benefit. 'Family member' in this context is not limited to the definition that determines who is covered by the co-ordination rules (see p265). In a recent case, a child claiming DLA was held to have a 'genuine and sufficient link to the UK social security system' on the basis that he was dependent on his sister who had worked in the UK for at least five years.[51]

Note: the interpretation of this phrase is still evolving and is affected by developments in caselaw. See CPAG's online service and *Welfare Rights Bulletin* for updates.

5. **Industrial injuries benefits**

Industrial injuries benefits are:
- industrial injuries disablement benefit;
- reduced earnings allowance;
- retirement allowance;
- constant attendance allowance;
- exceptionally severe disablement allowance.

To be entitled to any of these benefits, you must have been:
- in Great Britain when the accident at work happened;[52] *or*
- engaged in Great Britain in the employment that caused the disease (even if you have also been engaged outside Great Britain in that employment);[53] *or*
- paying UK national insurance (NI) contributions, either at Class 1 rate or at Class 2 rate as a volunteer development worker when the accident at work happened or you contracted the disease. Benefit is not payable until you return to Great Britain.[54]

There are exceptions to these rules, which mean you can qualify for benefit in respect of an accident which happens, or a disease which is contracted, outside Great Britain while you are:[55]
- employed as a mariner or airman or airwoman;
- employed as an apprentice pilot on board a ship or vessel;
- on board an aircraft on a test flight starting in Great Britain in the course of your employment.

In these cases, there are also more generous rules for defining when accidents arise 'out of and in the course of' your employment, and for complying with time limits under benefit rules.[56]

Note: in the future, the rules on industrial injuries disablement benefit may be different in Scotland. See CPAG's online service and *Welfare Rights Bulletin* for updates.

European Union co-ordination rules

If you are covered by the European Union (EU) co-ordination rules (see p264), you can, if necessary, rely on periods of employment and NI paid in other

Chapter 13: Residence and presence: rules for individual benefits
6. Contribution-based JSA and contributory ESA

13

European Economic Area (EEA) states in order to qualify for industrial injuries benefits in the UK. This is achieved under the aggregation principle (see p281).

Industrial injuries benefits, except retirement allowance, are classed as 'benefits for accidents at work and occupational diseases' under the EU co-ordination rules (see p268).

If you have an accident while travelling abroad in another member state, this can be deemed to have occurred in the state liable to pay benefits for accidents at work and occupational diseases. If one state determines that you have had an accident or contracted a disease, this should be accepted by the state liable to pay benefit in respect of that accident or disease. These outcomes are achieved under the principle of equal treatment of facts of events (see p281).[57]

If you have worked in two or more EEA states in jobs that gave you a prescribed industrial disease, you get benefit from the member state in which you last did work that, by its nature, is likely to cause that disease and which recognises that disease under its industrial injuries scheme.[58] If you make your claim to the state that does not have responsibility under this rule, your claim and all supporting evidence must be forwarded to the relevant institution in the correct state without delay.[59]

Reciprocal agreements

The UK has reciprocal agreements with several countries that cover industrial injuries benefits. The agreements determine which country is responsible for determining and paying your entitlement, and if and how you can combine injuries or take account of new accidents or diseases. For more information on reciprocal agreements covering industrial injuries benefits, see p297.

6. Contribution-based jobseeker's allowance and contributory employment and support allowance

To be entitled to contribution-based jobseeker's allowance (JSA) or contributory employment and support allowance (ESA), you must be in Great Britain.[60] The rules about when you can be paid during a temporary absence abroad are covered on p235 and p238. There are no residence conditions, unless you are claiming contributory ESA in youth (see p208).

Note: looking for work abroad does not count towards satisfying the JSA requirement that you be 'actively seeking employment'.[61]

See p201 for the residence and presence conditions for income-based JSA and income-related ESA.

13

Chapter 13: Residence and presence: rules for individual benefits
6. Contribution-based JSA and contributory ESA

European Union co-ordination rules

Contribution-based jobseeker's allowance

If you are covered by the European Union (EU) co-ordination rules (see p264) you can, if necessary, rely on the equivalent of national insurance (NI) contributions paid in another European Economic Area (EEA) state to entitle you to contribution-based JSA in the UK. This is achieved under the principle of aggregation. However, an additional condition applies for unemployment benefits that means that, in most cases, you can only aggregate your contributions if your most recent period of paying or being credited with those contributions was in the UK.[62] See p281 for more details.

If you are coming to, or returning to, the UK to look for work and have been insured in another EEA member state, you may be able to continue to receive that other member state's unemployment benefit for up to three months if:[63]

- you were getting that unemployment benefit immediately before coming to the UK;
- you have been registered as available for work for four weeks (or less if the member state's rules allow) in the other member state;
- you claim JSA within seven days after you were last registered in the other member state; *and*
- you meet whichever of the jobseeking requirements apply for the type of contribution-based JSA you are claiming – eg, if you do not come under the universal credit (UC) system, you satisfy the JSA jobseeking conditions or, if you come under the UC system, you accept a claimant commitment and you meet any work-related requirements that have been imposed on you.

The three months can be extended to a maximum of six months if the state from which you are claiming the unemployment benefit agrees.[64]

Contributory employment and support allowance

If you are covered by the EU co-ordination rules (see p264) you can, if necessary, rely on the equivalent of NI contributions paid in another EEA state to entitle you to contributory ESA in the UK. This is achieved under the principle of aggregation (see p281).

If you are covered by the EU co-ordination rules (see p264) and have moved to the UK from another EEA state, you may be able to continue to receive a sickness or invalidity benefit from that other EEA state if it continues to be your competent state for the payment of that benefit (see p271).

Reciprocal and other international agreements

If you have lived and worked in a country with which the UK has a reciprocal agreement (see p291), you may be able to count periods of insurance paid in that country towards your entitlement to contribution-based JSA or contributory

ESA in the UK if the agreement covers you and that benefit. Similarly, if you are covered by another type of international agreement between the EU and another state, you may be able to do the same (see p300).

Although most reciprocal agreements do not cover ESA (see p296), the reciprocal agreement between Northern Ireland and Great Britain was extended to cover contributory ESA (as well as income-related ESA) from 6 April 2016.[65] If you moved from Northern Ireland to Great Britain or vice versa while claiming ESA before this date, the DWP policy was to make extra-statutory payments to cover any loss arising from having to make a new claim. For further details see p293.

7. Maternity allowance

Entitlement to maternity allowance (MA) is based on past employment. There are no residence requirements, but you are disqualified if you are absent from Great Britain.[66] See p249 for the rules allowing you to be paid during a temporary absence.

European Union co-ordination rules

If you are covered by the European Union co-ordination rules (see p264) you can, if necessary, rely on periods of employment in other European Economic Area states in order to qualify for MA in the UK. This is achieved under the principle of aggregation (see p281).

8. Retirement pensions

Retirement pensions, other than a Category D retirement pension, do not have any residence or presence entitlement conditions.[67] They can be paid without time limit, whether or not you are present in Great Britain. However, going abroad can mean you are not paid the annual uprating, can be relevant to decisions on deferring your retirement and can prevent you from 'de-retiring' while you are abroad (see p253).

To be entitled to a Category D retirement pension, you must have been:
- resident in Great Britain for at least 10 years in any continuous period of 20 years ending on or after your 80th birthday; *and*
- ordinarily resident (see p96) in Great Britain on either:
  – your 80th birthday; *or*
  – the date on which you claimed the Category D pension, if later.

13

Chapter 13: Residence and presence: rules for individual benefits
9. Social fund funeral and winter fuel payments

European Union co-ordination rules

If you are covered by the European Union (EU) co-ordination rules (see p264), you can, if necessary, rely on the equivalent of national insurance contributions paid in other European Economic Area (EEA) states to calculate your entitlement to retirement pensions in the UK. Similarly, for a Category D retirement pension, you can count periods of residence in other EEA states to meet the residence requirement. Both of these possibilities are achieved under the aggregation principle (see p281).

Note: your award may be reduced to reflect the proportion of years of contributions paid, or periods of residence completed, in the UK out of the total years of contributions paid or periods of residence completed in all states.[68]

The requirement to be ordinarily resident for a Category D retirement pension may not apply to you if you are covered by the EU co-ordination rules and you can show that you have a 'genuine and sufficient link to the UK social security system' (see p211).[69]

Reciprocal and other international agreements

If you have lived and worked in a country with which the UK has a reciprocal agreement (see p291), you may be able to count periods of residence or insurance paid in that country towards your UK retirement pension entitlement. For further information on reciprocal agreements and retirement pensions, see p297.

Similarly, if you are covered by another international agreement between the EU and another state, you may be able to do the same (see p300).

9. Social fund funeral and winter fuel payments

The only two social fund payments that have residence conditions are funeral expenses payments and winter fuel payments.

Note: in the future, the rules on funeral expenses payments and winter fuel payments, as well as cold weather payments and Sure Start maternity grants, may be different in Scotland. See CPAG's online service and *Welfare Rights Bulletin* for updates.

Funeral expenses payment

To qualify for a funeral expenses payment:
- the deceased must have been ordinarily resident (see p96) in the UK;[70]
- the funeral must take place in the UK. However, it can take place in any European Economic Area (EEA) country if you or your partner are:[71]

Chapter 13: Residence and presence: rules for individual benefits
9. Social fund funeral and winter fuel payments

13

- an EEA national and a 'worker' (see p140), including if you have retained this status (see p146);
- an EEA national and a self-employed person (see p153), including if you have retained this status (see p157);
- a family member of one of the above (see p164);
- an EEA national with a permanent right of residence acquired in less than five years, or you are the family member of such a person (see p190);
- arguably, a person with any other right of residence in the UK under European Union (EU) law (see below).

It is arguable that you can also qualify for a funeral expenses payment if the funeral takes place in an EEA state other than the UK if you have *any* right to reside in the UK under EU law. This is because the EU law on residence rights has developed since the above provisions were introduced and now covers additional groups of EEA nationals and their family members. The above provisions were introduced following a case in which the European Court of Justice held that the rule which required the funeral to be in the UK was unlawfully discriminatory against EU migrant workers.[72] Arguably, the same applies to other groups who now have residence rights under EU law, but who are not listed in the funeral payment regulations – eg, people who have a permanent right of residence following five years of legal residence in the UK. Furthermore, EU Directive 2004/38 contains a general rule that (subject to certain limitations) prohibits discrimination against anyone with a right of residence.[73]

Winter fuel payment

To qualify for a winter fuel payment, you must be ordinarily resident (see p96) in Great Britain on any day in the qualifying week.[74]

The qualifying week
The **'qualifying week'** is the week beginning on the third Monday in September before the winter you want to be paid for.

European Union co-ordination rules

You are not required to be ordinarily resident in Great Britain in order to be entitled to a winter fuel payment if, on any day in the qualifying week, you are:[75]

- covered by the EU co-ordination rules (see p264);
- habitually resident in Switzerland or an EEA country (other than Cyprus, France, Gibraltar, Greece, Malta, Portugal, Spain or the UK); *and*
- can demonstrate a 'genuine and sufficient link to the UK social security system' (see p211).

* * *

Was your application for a winter fuel payment refused before September 2013?
The EU rules were only included within the UK regulations from 16 September 2013. However, they are based on a judgment of the Court of Justice of the European Union, dated 21 July 2011.[76] If you had your winter fuel payment refused because, at the relevant time, you were not ordinarily resident in Great Britain, but you satisfied the above rules, you can request that the decision be revised. The DWP will revise its decision on the grounds of official error if it was made on or after 21 July 2011.[77] If the decision was made before this date, the DWP's position is that it can only be revised if another ground for revision is available.[78] For a discussion of similar issues in relation to previous refusals of disability benefits, see p248.

* * *

10. Tax credits

To be entitled to **child tax credit** (CTC), you (and your partner if you are making a joint claim) must:[79]
* be present in the UK (see p91); *and*
* be ordinarily resident in the UK (see p96); *and*
* have a right to reside in the UK (see p115); *and*
* have been living in the UK for the three months prior to your claim (unless you are in one of the exempt groups – see p92).

To be entitled to **working tax credit** (WTC), you (and your partner if you are making a joint claim) must be:[80]
* present in the UK (see p91); *and*
* ordinarily resident in the UK (see p96).

There are, however, some exceptions.[81]
* There are several groups of people who are exempt from the requirement to have been living in the UK for three months prior to the date you made your CTC claim (see p94).
* You do not need to have a right to reside for CTC if you claimed CTC before 1 May 2004 and you have been receiving it since that date.
* You are treated as ordinarily resident in the UK for CTC and WTC and, for CTC, you are not required to have been living in the UK for the past three months, if you have been deported or otherwise legally removed from another country to the UK.
* You are treated as ordinarily resident in the UK for WTC if you have a right to reside under European Union (EU) Directive 2004/38 (see p124). However, in practice, being accepted as ordinarily resident is rarely a problem.
* You can be treated as present for either eight or 12 weeks during a temporary absence, or while you or your partner are a Crown servant posted overseas (see

p255). While you are treated as present, you continue to satisfy the conditions of entitlement to tax credits. This means that you can continue to receive tax credits that are already in payment and can make a fresh or renewal claim during your absence. If you spend longer abroad than the permitted periods, you cease to satisfy the presence condition and your tax credit entitlement ends.

Note: if you are a self-employed European Economic Area (EEA) national, the definition of 'self-employed' that applies for WTC (ie, that you are carrying out a trade, profession or vocation that is organised and regular, on a commercial basis and with a view to making a profit[82]) is separate from, and does not affect, the meaning of 'self-employed' for the purpose of having a right to reside that satisfies that requirement for CTC (see p153).

Being absent (other than while you are treated as present), ceasing to be ordinarily resident or losing your right to reside are all changes that you must notify to HM Revenue and Customs (HMRC) within one month. Failure to notify may result in your being overpaid and/or being subject to a penalty.

Couples and children

If you are a member of a **couple** and make a joint tax credit claim, you must both satisfy the residence requirements. Your entitlement to tax credits as a couple ends if either you or your partner:
- are abroad for longer than a permitted temporary absence of eight or 12 weeks (see p255);
- (for CTC only) lose the right to reside;
- cease to be ordinarily resident.

The person who continues to satisfy the residence rules can make a fresh claim for CTC and/or WTC as a single person if s/he is entitled on that basis.

If your partner returns to the UK, or becomes ordinarily resident or acquires a right to reside, you must terminate your single person claim and claim again as a couple.

If you or your partner are abroad (even for a permitted temporary absence of less than eight or 12 weeks) and you (or s/he) were the only partner in full-time work, you may lose entitlement to WTC if the requirement to be in full-time work is no longer satisfied.

If at any point HMRC considers that you and your partner have separated and this is likely to be permanent, you cease to be entitled to make a joint claim as a couple and each of you may be entitled to make single claims.[83]

You have a duty to notify HMRC of any of the above changes within one month of their taking place. Failure to notify may result in your being overpaid or being subject to a penalty, as well as missing out on any potential alternative entitlement that you may have as a single person or as a couple.

There are no presence or residence requirements for any **child** in your claim, but you must be responsible for the child. You count as being responsible if the child normally lives with you or, if there are competing claims, you have main responsibility for her/him.[84]

If your partner or child is a non-EEA national, also check the rules in Part 3. In particular, see p75 if:

- your child is a non-EEA national with leave that is subject to a 'no recourse to public funds' condition; *and/or*
- your partner is a non-EEA national who does not have immigration leave to enter or remain in the UK and does not have a right to reside.

European Union co-ordination rules

If you are covered by the EU co-ordination rules (see p264), you may be able to:

- be paid CTC for a partner or child resident in another EEA country;
- use periods of residence in another EEA country to satisfy the requirement for CTC to have been living in the UK for the past three months under the aggregation principle. For further information, including HMRC guidance that suggests this priniciple only applies to residence in four EEA countries, see p92.

CTC is classed as a 'family benefit' under the EU co-ordination rules. For more details on the payment of family benefits, see p284.

WTC is not covered by the EU co-ordination rules. Therefore, if your partner is in another EEA country, although you may be able to make a joint claim for CTC as a couple, your WTC claim is treated as a single claim.[85] In this case, or if you are a single claimant with a child living in another EEA country, your CTC claim is determined in accordance with the EU co-ordination rules, but your WTC claim is determined solely under UK legislation.

If you or your partner are working in another EEA country but live in the UK, and therefore remain present and ordinarily resident in the UK, this work can count for the purposes of your WTC claim.[86]

In any of the circumstances above, your claim(s) is likely to be deemed 'complex' and processed by the 'international team' at HMRC. Detailed guidance for decision makers on how these claims should be administered can be referred to if you experience difficulties.[87]

Notes

1. Means-tested benefits
1 **IS** s124(1) SSCBA 1992
JSA s1(2)(i) JSA 1995
ESA s1(3)(d) WRA 2007
PC s1(2)(a) SPCA 2002
UC s4(1)(c) WRA 2012
2 **IS** Regs 21-21AA IS Regs
JSA Regs 85-85A JSA Regs
ESA Regs 69-70 ESA Regs
PC Reg 2 SPC Regs
UC Reg 9 UC Regs
3 Sch 5 WRA(No.9)O, as applied in UC areas by subsequent commencement orders
4 Reg 10 HB Regs; reg 10 HB(SPC) Regs
5 s130(1)(a) SSCBA 1992
6 Reg 7 HB Regs; reg 7 HB(SPC) Regs
7 *GP v SSWP (JSA)* [2015] UKUT 746 (AAC)
8 **IS** Reg 16(2)(a) IS Regs
JSA Reg 78(2)(a) JSA Regs
ESA Reg 156(3)(a) ESA Regs
PC Reg 5(1)(a)(i) SPC Regs
HB Reg 21(2)(a) HB Regs; reg 21(2)(a) HB(SPC) Regs
UC Reg 3(6) UC Regs
9 **IS** Reg 16(1)-(3) IS Regs
JSA Reg 78(1)-(3) JSA Regs
ESA Reg 156(1)-(4) ESA Regs
PC Reg 5 SPC Regs
HB Reg 21(1) and (2) HB Regs; reg 21(1) and(2) HB(SPC) Regs
UC Reg 3(6) UC Regs
10 CIS/508/1992
11 *Broxtowe Borough Council v CS (HB)* [2014] UKUT 186 (AAC)
12 CIS/508/1992; CIS/13805/1996
13 CIS/484/1993
14 **IS** Regs 4, 16 and 21 and Sch 7 paras 11 and 11A IS Regs
JSA Regs 78 and 85 and Sch 5 paras 10 and 11 JSA Regs
ESA Reg 156 and Sch 5 paras 6 and 7 ESA Regs
HB Reg 21 HB Regs; reg 21 HB(SPC) Regs
15 Regs 3-5 SPC Regs
16 Regs 3(3) and (6), 18(2), 22(3) and 36(3) UC Regs
17 Regs 3(3), 9, 18(2), 22(3) and 36(3) UC Regs

18 **IS** Reg 16 IS Regs
JSA Reg 78 JSA regs
ESA Reg 156 ESA Regs
HB Reg 21 HB Regs; reg 21 HB(SPC) Regs
19 Reg 4(7) UC Regs
20 SS(NIRA) Regs; SS(GBRA)(NI) Regs

2. Bereavement benefits
21 s113 SSCBA 1992; reg 4(1) and (2B) SSB(PA) Regs
22 para 077081 DMG, Example 2
23 s30(1)(c) PA 2014
24 Arts 5, 6, 42 and 43 EU Reg 883/04

3. Child benefit and guardian's allowance
25 s146 SSCBA 1992
26 Reg 23 CB Regs
27 Regs 23, 30 and 31 CB Regs
28 s143(1)(b) SSCBA 1992
29 Reg 9 GA(Gen) Regs
30 *Stewart v SSWP*, C-503/09 [2011] ECR I-06497; *SSWP v JG (IS)* [2013] UKUT 298 (AAC); *SSWP v Garland* [2014] EWCA Civ 1550
31 s143(1)(b) SSCBA 1992; *RK v HMRC (CHB)* [2015] UKUT 357 (AAC)

4. Disability and carers' benefits
32 **AA** Reg 2 SS(AA) Regs
DLA Reg 2 SS(DLA) Regs
PIP Reg 16 SS(PIP) Regs
CA Reg 9 SS(ICA) Regs
33 Reg 1 SS(DLA,AA&CA)(A) Regs
34 **AA** Reg 2(2) and (3A) SS(AA) Regs
DLA Reg 2(2) and (3A) SS(DLA) Regs
PIP Regs 19 and 20 SS(PIP) Regs
CA Reg 9(3) SS(ICA) Regs
35 **ESA** Reg 11 ESA Regs; reg 12 ESA Regs 2013
IB Reg 16 SS(IB) Regs
SDA Reg 3 SS(SDA) Regs
36 **ESA** Reg 11(4) ESA Regs; reg 12(4) ESA Regs 2013
IB Reg 16(6) SS(IB) Regs
SDA Reg 3(3) SS(SDA) Regs
37 **AA** Reg 2(3) SS(AA) Regs
DLA Reg 2(4) SS(DLA) Regs
PIP Reg 21 SS(PIP) Regs

38 **AA** s35(2C) SSA 1975
   DLA s66(2) SSCBA 1992
   PIP s82(4) WRA 2012
39 *MM and IS v SSWP (DLA)* [2016] UKUT
   149 (AAC)
40 ss65(7), 70(4A) and 72(7B) SSCBA
   1992; s84 WRA 2012
41 **AA** Reg 2A SS(AA) Regs
   DLA Reg 2A SS(DLA) Regs
   PIP Reg 22 SS(PIP) Regs
   CA Reg 9A SS(ICA) Regs
42 Art 6 and Annex XI UK entry para 2 EU
   Reg 883/04
43 ss65(7), 70(4A) and 72(7B) SSCBA
   1992; s84 WRA 2012
44 **AA** Reg 2B SS(AA) Regs
   DLA Reg 2B SS(DLA) Regs
   PIP Reg 23 SS(PIP) Regs
   CA Reg 9B SS(ICA) Regs
45 *Bartlett and Others v SSWP*, C-537/09
   [2011] ECR I-03417; para C2097 ADM
46 Art 70 EU Reg 883/04; *Robin Swaddling v
   Adjudication Officer*, C-90/97 [1999] ECR
   I-01075
47 Art 1(j) EU Reg 883/04
48 *Stewart v SSWP*, C-503/09 [2011] ECR I-
   06497
49 *SSWP v JG (IS)* [2013] UKUT 298 (AAC);
   SSWP v Garland [2014] EWCA Civ 1550
50 *Stewart v SSWP*, C-503/09 [2011] ECR I-
   06497
51 *PB v SSWP (DLA)* [2016] UKUT 280 (AAC)

5. Industrial injuries benefits
52 s94(5) SSCBA 1992
53 Reg 14 SS(IIPD) Regs
54 Reg 10C(5) and (6) SSB(PA) Regs
55 Reg 2 SS(II)(AB) Regs 1975; reg 2
   SS(II)(MB) Regs
56 Regs 3, 4, 6 and 8 SS(II)(MB) Regs; regs
   3 and 6 SS(II)(AB) Regs
57 Art 5 EU Reg 883/04
58 Art 38 EU Reg 883/04; Art 36 EU Reg
   987/09; *SSWP v OF (by MF) (II)* [2011]
   UKUT 448 (AAC)
59 Art 36(2) EU Reg 987/09

6. Contribution-based jobseeker's allowance and contributory employment and support allowance
60 **JSA** s1(2)(i) JSA 1995
   ESA ss1(3)(d) and 18(4)(a) WRA 2007
61 *GP v SSWP (JSA)* [2015] UKUT 476 (AAC)
62 Art 61(2) EU Reg 883/04
63 Art 64 EU Reg 883/04
64 Art 64(3) EU Reg 883/04
65 SS(NIRA) Regs; SS(GBRA)NI Regs

7. Maternity allowance
66 s113(1) SSCBA 1992

8. Retirement pensions
67 s113 SSCBA 1992; reg 4(1) SSB(PA)
   Regs
68 Art 52 EU Reg 883/04; for example, see
   Vol2 para 075771 DMG
69 *Stewart v SSWP*, C-503/09 [2011] ECR, I-
   06497; *SSWP v Garland* [2014] EWCA
   Civ 1550, paras 14 and 28

9. Social fund funeral and winter fuel payments
70 Reg 7(5) SFM&FE Regs
71 Reg 7(9) and (10) SFM&FE Regs
72 *John O'Flynn v Adjudication Officer*, C-
   237/94 [1996] ECR I-02617; R(IS) 4/98
73 Art 24 EU Dir 2004/38
74 Reg 2 SFWFP Regs
75 Reg 2 SFWFP Regs
76 *Stewart v SSWP*, C-503/09 [2011] ECR I-
   06497
77 Reg 3(5)(a) SS&CS(DA) Regs; para
   73245 and Vol 2 Part 6 Appendix 1, para
   10 DMG
78 Vol 2 Part 6 Appendix 1, para 11 DMG

10. Tax credits
79 s3(3) TCA 2002; reg 3(1) and (5) TC(R)
   Regs
80 s3(3) TCA 2002; reg 3(1) TC(R) Regs
81 Reg 3 TC(R) Regs
82 Reg 2(1) WTC(EMR) Regs
83 s3(5A) TCA 2002
84 s8(2) TCA 2002; reg 3(1) CTC Regs
85 paras 20090, 20160, 20170 and 20260
   TCCCM
86 para 0288580 TCM; see also *GC v
   CHMRC (TC)* [2014] UKUT 251 (AAC)
87 para 20000 TCCCM

Part 5

Benefits while abroad

Chapter 14

Going abroad

This chapter covers:
1. Introduction (below)
2. How your benefits and tax credits are affected (p227)

This chapter provides an overview of the way your entitlement to benefits and tax credits is affected if you, or a member of your family for whom you claim, go abroad. The specific information about individual benefits and tax credits is in Chapter 15.

1. Introduction

Most benefits and tax credits are affected if you, or your partner or child, go abroad. The rules vary between different benefits and tax credits. Some can always be paid abroad, some can only be paid in certain circumstances and for limited periods, and some benefits have rules affecting the amount that can be paid if you are abroad.

Your entitlement while you, or your partner or child, are abroad depends on any or all of the following factors:
- the benefit or tax credit you are claiming (see Chapter 15);
- the reason for going abroad;
- whether the absence is temporary or permanent;
- the length of time the absence will last;
- the country to which you are, or s/he is, going;
- whether you are covered by the European Union (EU) co-ordination rules;
- whether you are covered by a reciprocal agreement the UK has with the country you, or your partner or child, are going to.

In addition to the above factors, other changes that occur indirectly as a consequence of your being abroad can also affect your entitlement – eg, if your income changes, or you cease to count as being in full-time work for the benefit or tax credit you are claiming. Further details on the way these other changes affect your entitlement are covered in CPAG's *Welfare Benefits and Tax Credits Handbook*.

Before you go abroad

If you are thinking about going abroad, check how your entitlement will be affected well in advance of your departure, as this could affect the decisions you make. It also ensures you have sufficient time to take any necessary action before you leave the UK. You should notify the Jobcentre Plus/local authority/HM Revenue and Customs (HMRC) office that pays your benefit before you leave, providing details of your destination, purpose and expected duration of your absence abroad. If it is possible for you get your UK benefit paid abroad, you should give the relevant benefit authorities as much notice as possible, as they can be very slow in making these arrangements.

To see how going abroad affects your entitlement, check which rules apply (see below) and then check the rules for the specific benefit or tax credit you are claiming (see Chapter 15).

If you might want to claim a benefit from the country you are going to, it is worth checking what the conditions of entitlement are, as you might want to take relevant documents with you – eg, a statement of the national insurance contributions you have paid, which you can obtain from HMRC, or proof of your past employment. **Note:** check whether claiming a benefit in another country could affect your entitlement to benefits paid abroad by the UK – eg, if you claim a benefit in another European Economic Area (EEA) state, this can cause the UK to cease to be your 'competent state' for the purposes of paying a different benefit under the EU co-ordination rules (see p271).

Which rules apply

Your entitlement to UK benefits or tax credits while you, or a family member, are abroad can be affected by three different sets of rules.

- **The UK benefit and tax credit legislation** contains rules about how your absence, or the absence of your family member, affects your entitlement (see p227). You should check these rules first. If your circumstances mean that, under these rules, you can obtain the benefits you want when you or your family member are outside the UK, you do not generally need to check the other rules. However, if you want to be paid a disability or carer's benefit when you go to another EEA state, if you are covered by the EU co-ordination rules, you should check whether they affect your entitlement.
- If you or your family member are going to another EEA state (see p40 for a list of EEA states), even if you have no entitlement under UK legislation, you might be able to receive UK benefits because of the **EU co-ordination rules** (see p231). If these rules apply to you (see p264) and allow you to get benefit outside the UK, they can override any specific UK rules that prevent you getting your benefit outside the UK.

- **Reciprocal agreements** exist between the UK and some other countries and can assist in similar ways to the EU co-ordination rules (see p232). In general, they only apply if the EU co-ordination rules do not assist you (see p291).

---

2. How your benefits and tax credits are affected

UK law

There are different ways in which the UK benefits and tax credits rules can affect your entitlement when you (or your family member) go abroad.

The main ways in which they result in your not receiving benefit (or not being paid for your family member) when you (or s/he) are abroad are as follows.

- During your (or her/his) absence you do not (or s/he does not) meet the requirement to:
  - be present in Great Britain (see below);
  - be ordinarily resident in the UK (see p229);
  - be habitually resident in the common travel area (ie, the UK, Ireland, Channel Isles and the Isle of Man) (see p229); *or*
  - have a right to reside (see p229).
- Your partner's absence abroad can mean you no longer count as a couple (see p230).
- Your child's absence abroad can mean s/he is no longer included in your claim (see p230).
- You stop being covered by the rules that allow you to receive housing costs for a certain period while you are absent from your home (see p230).

All of the above rules have exceptions. In particular, you can be treated as present in certain circumstances, provided (in most cases) your absence is temporary.

The way these different rules affect your entitlement when you go abroad is explained below. For details on how to satisfy the presence and residence rules when you are in the UK, see Part 4.

Presence and absence

Most benefits require you to be present in Great Britain (the UK for tax credits). You can be treated as present and, therefore, continue to be entitled to the benefit or tax credit, during a temporary absence in specified circumstances (see p228). You are disqualified from entitlement to some benefits if you are absent from Great Britain, although there are exemptions for each benefit.

Presence and absence

'**Presence**' means being physically present in Great Britain (the UK for tax credits) and '**absence**' means 'not physically present' in Great Britain. If the DWP, HM Revenue and Customs or a local authority wants to disqualify you from benefit because you were absent from Great Britain, it must show that you were absent throughout that day. This means that, on the day you leave Great Britain and the day you arrive in Great Britain, you count as present.

Temporary absence

Many benefits or tax credits allow you to be treated as present, and therefore entitled to that benefit or tax credit, during a temporary absence in specified circumstances. Your entitlement depends on:

- whether your absence counts as 'temporary' for the benefit or tax credit you are claiming (see below); *and*
- how long (if at all) during your temporary absence the rules for that benefit or tax credit allow you to be treated as present (see Chapter 15).

Temporary absence

For attendance allowance (AA), disability living allowance (DLA), personal independence payment (PIP), tax credits and (for the claimant's, but not the child's, absence) child benefit, you are '**temporarily absent**' from the UK if, at the beginning of the period of absence, it is unlikely to exceed 52 weeks.[1]

For all other benefits, temporary absence is not defined. It is your responsibility to demonstrate that your absence will be temporary, and you should therefore provide full details of why you are going abroad, how long you intend to be away and what you intend to do while you are abroad.[2] However, although your intentions are relevant, they are not decisive.[3] The nature of an absence can also change over time. If your absence is found to be temporary at the beginning of the period, it does not mean that it will always remain temporary. If your circumstances change while you are abroad (eg, you go abroad for one reason and decide to stay for a different purpose), your absence may no longer be regarded as temporary.[4] Although there is no set period for a temporary absence (except for tax credits, child benefit, AA, DLA, and PIP), as a general rule, absences of more than 12 months are not considered to be temporary unless there are exceptional circumstances.[5] If the purpose of your trip abroad is obviously temporary (eg, for a holiday, to visit friends or relatives or for a particular course of medical treatment) and you buy a return ticket, your absence should be viewed as temporary.

If your absence counts as temporary for the benefit or tax credit you are claiming (see above), you are entitled to receive the benefit or tax credit for a specified period. This period varies for each benefit or tax credit and according to your circumstances. Many of the rules that entitle you to benefit during a specified period only do so if certain circumstances apply, but some simply state a maximum period. See Chapter 15 for information on the specific benefit you are claiming.

Note: for many benefits and tax credits, your intended absence still counts as temporary even if it is longer than the maximum period for which the benefit or tax credit is payable.

Example

Mohsen receives PIP. He goes to visit family in Iran and buys a return ticket to come back after seven months. Mohsen is entitled to PIP for the first 13 weeks of his absence (the maximum period in these circumstances – see p245). Although his intended period of absence is longer than this maximum period, it is still a temporary absence.

Ordinary residence

In order to be entitled to some benefits and tax credits, you must be ordinarily resident in Great Britain (the UK for tax credits). See p96 for a list of benefits and tax credits that require you to be ordinarily resident and an explanation of what 'ordinary residence' means. If, by going abroad, you cease to be ordinarily resident, your entitlement to any benefit or tax credit that requires you to be ordinarily resident ends. However, if your absence abroad is temporary and you intend to return to the UK, your ordinary residence is not usually affected.[6] Ceasing to be ordinarily resident will rarely be the reason why your entitlement ends when you go abroad. It is more likely that your entitlement ends simply because you are absent (see p227). If you receive a decision that your entitlement to a benefit or tax credit has ended because you have ceased to be ordinarily resident, ask for the decision to be looked at again and obtain specialist advice.

Habitual residence

In order to be entitled to some benefits, you must be habitually resident in the common travel area (the UK, Ireland, Channel Isles and the Isle of Man) or be exempt from this requirement. See p104 for a list of benefits that require habitual residence, an explanation of what it means to be 'habitually resident' and a list of who is exempt. If, by going abroad, you cease to be habitually resident, your entitlement to any benefit that requires you to be habitually resident ends. However, if your absence abroad is temporary and you intend to return to the UK, your habitual residence is not usually affected.[7] Ceasing to be habitually resident will rarely be the reason why your entitlement ends when you go abroad. It is more likely that your entitlement ends simply because you are absent (see p227) or, for housing benefit (HB), absent from your home (see p230).

Right to reside

In order to be entitled to some benefits and tax credits, you must have a right to reside in either the UK or the common travel area (the UK, Ireland, Channel Isles and the Isle of Man). See p115 for a list of benefits and tax credits that require a right to reside and an explanation of how this requirement operates. If, by going abroad, you lose your right to reside, your entitlement to any benefit or tax credit that requires you to have a right to reside ends. However, an absence does not necessarily mean you lose your right to reside – it depends on your circumstances.

Couples and children living apart

There are UK benefit and tax credit rules on when members of a couple who are living apart continue to count as a couple and when a child living elsewhere is still included in your claim. Although these rules are not only about situations where one member of a couple or a child is living abroad, when this is the case, these rules can affect your benefit.

If your partner goes abroad, this can affect your benefit or tax credit in one or more of the following ways:

- for tax credits and universal credit (UC), you may cease to be entitled to make a joint claim as a couple and may need to make a single claim;
- depending on the circumstances, including the permanence or duration of your partner's absence, at some point you will cease to be paid for your partner;
- even if you are not paid for your partner, in some circumstances her/his income and capital can still affect your claim.

If your child goes abroad, depending on the circumstances, including the duration, s/he can cease to be part of your claim. This can affect your entitlement, as either you cease to be paid for her/him or your entitlement ends altogether.

For further details of the rules about couples and children for means-tested benefits see p203, and for tax credits, see p219.

Absence from your home

If you are temporarily absent from the accommodation you normally occupy as your home, you can be treated as occupying it for a period. These rules apply to HB and to housing costs in income support (IS), income-based jobseeker's allowance (JSA), income-related employment and support allowance (ESA), pension credit and UC. They mean you can continue to receive payments during your temporary absence.

The absence rules are not (except for HB) specific to your being outside Great Britain, but can still affect you if you are absent from your home when abroad. They are only briefly summarised here – for further details, see CPAG's *Welfare Benefits and Tax Credits Handbook*.

A new period of absence starts if you return home, even for a short stay. A stay of at least 24 hours may be enough.[8]

If you are temporarily absent from home, have not rented out your home and intend to return to it, you can continue to be paid housing costs in your **IS**,

income-based JSA, income-related ESA or PC (provided you remain entitled to these benefits). You can be paid for up to:

- **13 weeks** while you are absent, whatever the reason. You must be unlikely to be away for longer than this;[9]
- **52 weeks** if you come into one of a list of specific groups.[10] See CPAG's *Welfare Benefits and Tax Credits Handbook* for more details.

From 28 July 2016 for **HB**, the above 13- or 52-week rule applies if your absence is within Great Britain.[11] However, if you are temporarily absent from home and you are outside Great Britain, the period when you can be treated as occupying your home is different and, in most cases, shorter (see below). If you were already outside Great Britain on 28 July 2016, these new rules do not affect you, and you are covered by the previous rules until you return (unless you were abroad as a member of HM forces, a mariner or as a continental shelf worker, in which case the new rules apply).[12]

If you are temporarily absent from home while abroad, have not rented out your home and intend to return to it, you can continue to be paid HB for up to:[13]

- **four weeks**, if you are absent outside Great Britain and the absence is unlikely to be more than four weeks;
- **eight weeks**, if the absence abroad is in connection with the death of your partner, your (or your partner's) close relative, or a child for whom you (or your partner) is responsible and the decision maker considers it unreasonable for you to return within the first four weeks;
- **26 weeks**, if you come into one of a list of specific groups. These are broadly if you are: a hospital inpatient; undergoing or recovering from medical treatment; absent from home because of domestic violence; a member of HM forces posted overseas; a mariner; or a continental shelf worker.

HB guidance contains a useful table summarising when you can receive HB during different periods of absence, both in Great Britain and abroad.[14]

If you are temporarily absent from your home, you can continue to be paid **UC** housing costs for up to six months while you are absent for any reason. You are no longer treated as occupying your home once your absence has lasted, or is expected to last, longer than six months.[15] The main exception to this is if you are absent because of a fear of domestic violence, in which case you can be treated as occupying your home for up to 12 months.[16]

European Union co-ordination rules

If you are a European Economic Area (EEA) national (including a UK national) or a family member of an EEA national, and you are going to another EEA state, you may be able to benefit from the European Union (EU) co-ordination rules. These can help you to be paid your benefits or tax credits when you go abroad for longer than would be the case under UK law. The EU co-ordination rules can also enable you to be paid benefit for a family member living in another EEA state. See Chapter 15 for information on the individual benefits and tax credits and Chapter 16 for further information on the co-ordination rules.

Reciprocal agreements

The UK has reciprocal agreements with several EEA and non-EEA countries. For a list of these and further information, see p291. In general, a reciprocal agreement only applies if the EU co-ordination rules do not assist you (see p293). They are therefore of most relevance for non-EEA countries, but they can also assist if you are moving to or from Northern Ireland, the Channel Islands or the Isle of Man. In addition, the EU and the Council of Europe have other agreements with some countries that can also affect your entitlement. See Chapter 17 for further information on all the agreements.

Notes

2. **How your benefits and tax credits are affected**
   1 **AA** Reg 2(3C) SS(AA) Regs
     DLA Reg 2(3C) SS(DLA) Regs
     PIP Reg 17(2) SS(PIP) Regs
     CB Reg 24(2) CB Regs
     TC Reg 4(2) TC(R) Regs
   2 *Chief Adjudication Officer v Ahmed and Others*, 16 March 1994, CA, reported as R(S) 1/96
   3 *Chief Adjudication Officer v Ahmed and Others*, 16 March 1994, CA, reported as R(S) 1/96
   4 R(S) 1/85
   5 R(U) 16/62
   6 *R v Barnet London Borough Council ex parte Shah* [1983] 2 AC 309, Lord Scarman at p342D
   7 *KS v SSWP (SPC)* [2010] UKUT 156 (AAC)
   8 *R v Penwith District Council ex parte Burt* [1988] 22 HLR 292 (QBD); para A3/3.460 GM
   9 **IS** Sch 3 para 3(10) IS Regs
     JSA Sch 2 para 3(10) JSA Regs
     ESA Sch 6 para 5(10) ESA Regs
     PC Sch 2 para 4(10) SPC Regs
   10 **IS** Sch 3 para 3(11)-(13) IS Regs
     JSA Sch 2 para 3(11)-(13) JSA Regs
     ESA Sch 6 para 5(11)-(13) ESA Regs
     PC Sch 2 para 4(11)-(13) SPC Regs
   11 Reg 7(13), (16), (17) and (18) HB Regs; reg7(13), (16), (17) and (18) HB(SPC) Regs
   12 Reg 5 The Housing Benefit and State Pension Credit (Temporary Absence) (Amendment) Regulations 2016, No.624
   13 Reg 7(13A)-(13G), (16), (17A)-(17D) and (18) HB Regs; reg 7(13A)-(13G), (16), (17A)-(17D) and (18) HB(SPC) Regs
   14 HB Circular A7/2016
   15 Sch 3 para 9(1) UC Regs
   16 Sch 3 paras 6 and 9(3) UC Regs

Chapter 15

Going abroad: rules for individual benefits

This chapter covers:
1. Means-tested benefits (below)
2. Bereavement benefits (p243)
3. Child benefit and guardian's allowance (p243)
4. Disability and carers' benefits (p245)
5. Incapacity benefit, severe disablement allowance and maternity allowance (p249)
6. Industrial injuries benefits (p250)
7. Contribution-based jobseeker's allowance and contributory employment and support allowance (p251)
8. Retirement pensions (p253)
9. Statutory payments (p254)
10. Tax credits (p255)

This chapter explains the UK benefit and tax credit rules on being paid when either you or your family members are abroad. It also covers the ways in which the European Union (EU) co-ordination rules may affect whether you can be paid benefit. See Chapter 14 for an overview of how the UK benefit rules and the EU co-ordination rules operate, and see Chapters 16 and 17 for more details on the EU co-ordination rules and international agreements.

1. Means-tested benefits

You cannot usually receive means-tested benefits when you are abroad, because the rules for each benefit require you to be present in Great Britain (although the rules are different for housing benefit, as your absence from Great Britain affects whether you can be treated as occupying your home – see p241). However, you can be treated as present in certain circumstances. The rules differ between the different benefits.

Income support

You cannot usually get income support (IS) if you are not in Great Britain.[1] However, IS can be paid while you are temporarily absent from Great Britain in the circumstances listed below, provided you meet the other conditions of entitlement.

If you were entitled to IS immediately before leaving Great Britain and are temporarily absent, your entitlement can continue:[2]

- **indefinitely** if your absence is for NHS treatment at a hospital or other institution outside Great Britain;
- during the first **four weeks** of your absence, if it is unlikely to exceed 52 weeks and:
  - you are in Northern Ireland; *or*
  - you and your partner are both abroad and s/he satisfies the conditions for one of the pensioner premiums, a disability premium or a severe disability premium; *or*
  - you are claiming IS on the grounds of being incapable of work and are abroad for the sole purpose of receiving treatment for that incapacity. The treatment must be carried out by, or under the supervision of, a person qualified to provide medical treatment, physiotherapy or similar treatment; *or*
  - you are incapable of work and:
    - you have been continuously incapable of work for the previous 28 weeks and you are terminally ill or receiving the highest rate of disability living allowance care component, the enhanced rate of the daily living component of personal independence payment or armed forces independence payment; *or*
    - you have been continuously incapable of work for 364 days; *or*
  - you come within one of the groups of people who can claim IS (see CPAG's *Welfare Benefits and Tax Credits Handbook* for these), other than if you are:
    - in 'relevant education'; *or*
    - involved in a trade dispute, or have returned to work for 15 days or less following the dispute; *or*
    - entitled to statutory sick pay; *or*
    - appealing a decision that you are not incapable of work; *or*
    - incapable of work and not covered by one of the groups of people incapable of work listed above;
- during the first **eight weeks** of your absence, if it is unlikely to exceed 52 weeks and is solely in connection with arrangements made for the treatment of a disease or disablement of a child or qualifying young person. The treatment must be carried out by, or under the supervision of, a person qualified to provide medical treatment, physiotherapy or similar treatment, and the child or young person must be someone for whom you count as responsible under

the IS rules. See CPAG's *Welfare Benefits and Tax Credits Handbook* for who counts as a child or young person and when you count as responsible for her/him.

If you are entitled to housing costs in your IS, your temporary absence from your home can mean that you cease to be entitled to receive these (see p230).

If your partner is abroad

If you are the IS claimant and you stay in Great Britain, your IS applicable amount includes an amount for your partner who is abroad for:[3]
- the first **four weeks**; *or*
- the first **eight weeks**, if s/he meets the conditions of the eight-week rule on p234.

If you are the IS claimant and both you and your partner are abroad, your IS includes an amount for your partner for the first eight weeks if both of you meet the conditions of the eight-week rule on p234.[4]

After this four- or eight-week period, your benefit is reduced because your applicable amount is calculated as if you have no partner. However, your partner is still treated as being part of your household and, therefore, her/his work, income and capital affect your IS entitlement, unless you are no longer treated as a couple (see p230).[5]

If your child is abroad

If you were getting an amount in your IS for your child before s/he went abroad, you continue to be paid for her/him for:[6]
- the first **four weeks**; *or*
- the first **eight weeks**, if your child meets the conditions of the eight-week rule above.

After this four- or eight-week period, you cease to be paid IS in respect of your child. When s/he returns to Great Britain, you must claim child tax credit (CTC) for her/him instead.[7]

European Union co-ordination rules

IS is not classified as a 'social security benefit' under the European Union (EU) co-ordination rules (see p268). This means that the co-ordination rules cannot assist you. If you go to another European Economic Area (EEA) state, you can only be paid under the UK rules above.

Income-based jobseeker's allowance

You cannot usually get jobseeker's allowance (JSA) if you are not in Great Britain.[8] However, both income-based JSA and contribution-based JSA can be paid when you are temporarily absent from Great Britain in the circumstances below, provided you meet the other conditions of entitlement.

You can be treated as available for, and actively seeking, work during certain temporary absences abroad. These are similar to, but more limited than, those listed below. See CPAG's *Welfare Benefits and Tax Credits Handbook* for details.[9] Similarly, if you are getting contribution-based JSA and you come under the universal credit (UC) system, you are exempt from the work search requirement and are treated as 'able and willing immediately to take up work' during these absences.[10]

If you are temporarily absent from Great Britain, you are treated as being in Great Britain and can therefore be paid JSA:[11]

- **indefinitely** if you are entitled to JSA immediately before leaving Great Britain and your absence is for NHS treatment at a hospital or other institution outside Great Britain;
- for up to **four weeks** if you are entitled to JSA immediately before leaving Great Britain and:
  - your absence is unlikely to exceed 52 weeks, you continue to satisfy the conditions of entitlement and you are in Northern Ireland; *or*
  - (except if you come under the UC system) your absence is unlikely to exceed 52 weeks, you continue to satisfy the conditions of entitlement and your partner satisfies the conditions for one of the pensioner premiums, a disability premium or a severe disability premium; *or*
  - (except if you come under the UC system) you are in receipt of a specified type of training allowance that means you do not have to satisfy the JSA jobseeking conditions;[12]
- for up to **eight weeks** if you are entitled to JSA immediately before leaving Great Britain and your absence is unlikely to exceed 52 weeks and is solely in connection with arrangements made for the treatment of a disease or disablement of a child or qualifying young person. The treatment must be carried out by, or under the supervision of, a person qualified to provide medical treatment, physiotherapy or similar treatment and you must count as responsible for the child or young person in the same way as for the similar rule on temporary absence for IS (see p234);
- for an absence of up to **seven days** if you are attending a job interview and you notified the employment officer before you left (in writing if required). On your return, you must satisfy the employment officer that you attended the interview as stated;
- for an absence of up to **15 days** for the purpose of training as a member of the reserve forces.

If you are entitled to housing costs in your income-based JSA, your temporary absence from your home can mean that you cease to be entitled to receive these (see p230).

Joint-claim jobseeker's allowance if your partner is abroad

If you are a member of a 'joint-claim couple' (see CPAG's *Welfare Benefits and Tax Credits Handbook* for what this means) and your partner is temporarily absent from Great Britain **on the date you make your claim**, you are paid as a couple for:[13]

- an absence of up to **seven days** if your partner is attending a job interview;
- up to **four weeks** if your partner is:
  - in Northern Ireland and her/his absence is unlikely to exceed 52 weeks; *or*
  - in receipt of a specified type of training allowance that means s/he does not have to satisfy the JSA jobseeking conditions.

After this seven-day/four-week period, your JSA is reduced because your applicable amount is calculated as if you have no partner.[14] However, your partner is still treated as part of your household and, therefore, her/his work, income and capital affects your joint-claim JSA entitlement, unless you are no longer treated as a couple (see p230).[15]

If you are a joint-claim couple and your partner goes abroad **after you claimed JSA**, you continue to be paid as a joint-claim couple:[16]

- for up to **four weeks** if you were entitled to joint-claim JSA immediately before s/he left Great Britain and:
  - her/his absence is unlikely to exceed 52 weeks, you continue to satisfy the conditions of entitlement and your partner satisfies the conditions for one of the pensioner premiums, a disability premium or a severe disability premium; *or*
  - her/his absence is unlikely to exceed 52 weeks, you both continue to satisfy the conditions of entitlement and your partner is in Northern Ireland; *or*
  - your partner is in receipt of a specified type of training allowance that means s/he does not have to satisfy the JSA jobseeking conditions;[17]
- for an absence of up to **seven days** if your partner is attending a job interview and has notified the employment officer before leaving (in writing if required). On her/his return, s/he must satisfy the employment officer at Jobcentre Plus that s/he attended the interview as stated.

Income-based jobseeker's allowance if your partner is abroad

If you are the income-based JSA claimant and you stay in Great Britain, your applicable amount includes an amount for your partner while s/he is abroad for:[18]

- the first **four weeks** of a temporary absence; *or*
- the first **eight weeks** if your partner meets the conditions of the eight-week rule on p235.

If you are the income-based JSA claimant and both you and your partner are abroad, your applicable amount includes an amount for your partner for the first eight weeks if both of you meet the conditions of the eight-week rule on p236.[19]

After this four- or eight-week period, your benefit is reduced because your applicable amount is calculated as if you have no partner. However, your partner is still treated as part of your household and, therefore, her/his work, income and capital affect your income-based JSA entitlement, unless you are no longer treated as a couple (see p230).[20]

Income-based jobseeker's allowance if your child is abroad

If you were getting JSA for your child before s/he went abroad, you can continue to be paid for her/him for:[21]
- the first **four weeks**; or
- the first **eight weeks** if your child meets the conditions of the eight-week rule on p235.

After this four- or eight-week period, you cease to be paid income-based JSA in respect of your child. When s/he returns to Great Britain, you must claim CTC for her/him instead.[22]

European Union co-ordination rules

Income-based JSA is classed as a 'special non-contributory benefit' under the EU co-ordination rules (see p270) and therefore cannot be exported. This means that if you go to another EEA country, the co-ordination rules cannot assist you and you can only be paid income-based JSA abroad under the UK rules explained above.

However, the EU co-ordination rules may enable you to be paid contribution-based JSA for up to three months if you go to another EEA country (see p252).

Income-related employment and support allowance

You cannot usually get employment and support allowance (ESA) if you are not in Great Britain.[23] However, both income-related ESA and contributory ESA can be paid when you are temporarily absent from Great Britain in the circumstances below, provided you meet the other conditions of entitlement.

If you were entitled to ESA immediately before leaving Great Britain and are temporarily absent, you can continue to be entitled:[24]
- **indefinitely** if:
  - your absence is for NHS treatment at a hospital or other institution outside Great Britain; or
  - you are living with your spouse, civil partner, son, daughter, stepson, stepdaughter, father, father-in-law, stepfather, mother, mother-in-law or stepmother who is a serving member of the armed forces;
- for the first **four weeks**, if your absence is unlikely to exceed 52 weeks;
- for the first **26 weeks**, if your absence is unlikely to exceed 52 weeks and is solely in connection with arrangements made for the treatment of:

- your disease or disablement that is directly related to your limited capability for work which began before you left Great Britain; *or*
- the disease or disablement of a dependent child who you are accompanying.

The treatment must be carried out by, or under the supervision of, a person qualified to provide medical treatment, physiotherapy or similar treatment.

If you are due to have a medical examination to assess your limited capability for work when you go abroad, you can ask for this to be carried out in the country you are going to, or to be postponed until you return. If your request is refused and you go abroad and miss your medical, your ESA will be stopped because you failed to attend your medical, unless it is accepted that you had a good cause for not attending. In deciding whether you had good cause, the decision maker must take all your circumstances into account, including the fact that you were outside Great Britain.[25] See CPAG's *Welfare Benefits and Tax Credits Handbook* for further details.

If you are entitled to housing costs in your income-related ESA, your temporary absence from your home can mean that you cease to be entitled to receive these (see p230).

If your partner is abroad

If you are the claimant and you stay in Great Britain, your income-related ESA includes an amount for your partner for:[26]

- the first **four weeks**; *or*
- the first **26 weeks** if s/he is accompanying a child abroad for treatment in line with the 26-week rule above.

If you are the claimant and both you and your partner are abroad, your income-related ESA includes an amount for your partner for the first 26 weeks if both of you are accompanying a child abroad for treatment in line with the 26-week rule above.[27]

After this four- or 26-week period, your benefit is reduced because your applicable amount is calculated as if you have no partner. However, your partner is still treated as part of your household and, therefore, her/his work, income and capital affect your income-related ESA entitlement, unless you are no longer treated as a couple (see p230).[28]

European Union co-ordination rules

Income-related ESA is listed under the co-ordination rules as a 'special non-contributory benefit' (see p270) and is therefore not exportable. This means that if you go to another EEA country, the EU co-ordination rules cannot assist you and you can only be paid income-related ESA abroad under the UK rules explained above.

However, the co-ordination rules may enable you to continue to be paid contributory ESA if you go to live in another EEA country (see p251).

Reciprocal agreements

In most cases, reciprocal agreements have not been updated to include ESA (see p291).

The exceptions are:
- the agreements with Northern Ireland (see below); *and*
- if your award of contributory ESA was converted from an award of incapacity benefit (IB), in which case it is covered by each of the agreements (with the exception of the Isle of Man, Israel and Switzerland) that cover IB (see Appendix 5).[29]

Since 6 April 2016, the reciprocal agreements between Northern Ireland and Great Britain have been replaced and now include ESA (both income-related and contributory).[30] The purpose of these agreements is to ensure you do not lose out if you move from one territory to the other while claiming ESA. If you moved from Great Britain to Northern Ireland or vice versa before this date the DWP policy was to make an extra-statutory payment to make up any loss of income-related (or contributory) ESA that resulted from having to make a new claim.[31] For more information on arrangements between Great Britain and Northern Ireland, see p293.

Pension credit

You cannot usually get pension credit (PC) if you are not in Great Britain.[32] However, PC can be paid when you are temporarily absent from Great Britain in the circumstances below, provided you meet the other conditions of entitlement.

From 28 July 2016, if you were entitled to PC immediately before leaving Great Britain and are temporarily absent, your entitlement can continue:[33]
- for up to **26 weeks**, if your absence is not expected to exceed that and is solely in connection with you, your partner or a child who you are accompanying, receiving medical treatment or medically approved convalescence or care as a result of medical treatment;
- for up to **eight weeks**, if your absence is not expected to exceed that and is in connection with the death of your partner, your child who normally lived with you or a close relative of you, your partner or child who normally lives with you, and the decision maker considers it unreasonable for you to return to Great Britain within four weeks; *or*
- up to **four weeks**, if your absence is not expected to exceed that.

If you were already outside Great Britain on 28 July 2016, the previous, more generous, rules continue to apply until you return.[34]

- the first **eight weeks**; *or*
- the first **12 weeks** of any period of absence, or any extension to that period, which is in connection with:
  - the treatment of an illness or disability of you, your partner, a child for whom you are responsible, or another relative of yours or your partner's; *or*
  - the death of your partner, a child or qualifying young person for whom you or your partner are responsible, or another relative of yours or your partner's.

'**Relative**' means brother, sister, parent, grandparent, great-grandparent or child, grandchild or great-grandchild.[50]

Your child is treated as present during a temporary absence for:[51]

- the first **12 weeks** of any period of absence; *or*
- **any period** during which s/he is absent for the specific purpose of being treated for an illness or disability which began before her/his absence began; *or*
- **any period** when s/he is in Northern Ireland; *or*
- **any period** during which s/he is absent only because s/he is:
  - receiving full-time education at a school or college in another European Economic Area (EEA) state or in Switzerland; *or*
  - engaged in an educational exchange or visit made with the written approval of the school or college s/he normally attends; *or*
  - a child who normally lives with a Crown servant posted overseas who is either in the same country as her/him or is absent from that country for one of the reasons in the two bullet points immediately above.[52]

If a child is born outside Great Britain during the eight- or 12-week period in which you were treated as present in Great Britain, s/he is treated as being in Great Britain for up to 12 weeks from the start of your absence.[53]

While you and your child are present, or treated as present, you satisfy that condition of entitlement. This means that you can continue to receive any child benefit already in payment and can also make a fresh claim during your or her/his absence. **Note:** if you or your child are treated as present, you must satisfy all the other conditions of entitlement including, if your child is not living with you, contributing at least the amount of child benefit that would be payable, to the costs of that child.[54] For information on all the conditions of entitlement for child benefit, see CPAG's *Welfare Benefits and Tax Credits Handbook*.

Guardian's allowance

Entitlement to guardian's allowance depends on entitlement to child benefit, so you can be paid guardian's allowance abroad for the same period as child benefit (see p243).

However, your guardian's allowance is not uprated each year if you have ceased to be ordinarily resident (see p96) in Great Britain on the day before the annual uprating takes place,[55] unless you have gone to another EEA state and you

If you are entitled to housing costs in your PC, your temporary absence from home can mean that you cease to be entitled to receive these (see p230).

If your partner is abroad

If your partner is abroad and you are entitled to PC, either while in Great Britain or abroad because you are covered by the rules p240, your PC only includes an amount for her/him if s/he is also covered by the above rules. After this, s/he is not treated as part of your household, you are paid as a single person and her/his income and capital do not affect your claim.[35] **Note:** the above rules came into force on 28 July 2016. If your partner was already outside Great Britain on this date, the previous, more generous, rules continue to apply until s/he returns.[36] For further information about your partner going abroad, see p230.

European Union co-ordination rules

PC is classed as a 'special non-contributory benefit' under the EU co-ordination rules (see p270) and therefore cannot be exported. This means that if you go abroad, the co-ordination rules cannot assist you. You can only be paid PC abroad under the UK rules above.

Housing benefit

There is no requirement to be present in Great Britain to be entitled to housing benefit (HB). However, you must be liable to make payments in respect of a dwelling in Great Britain, which you occupy as your home.[37] There are rules that treat you as occupying your home, including when you are temporarily absent from it.[38] These vary depending on whether your absence is inside or outside Great Britain (see p230).

If your partner or child is abroad

Whether or not you have amounts included in your HB for your partner or child who is abroad depends on whether s/he is treated as part of your household (see p203 and p204). The amount of HB you are entitled to may also depend on whether s/he is treated as occupying the home (see p230).[39]

Universal credit

You cannot usually be paid UC if you (and your partner if it is a joint claim) are not in Great Britain.[40] However, UC can be paid while you are temporarily absent from Great Britain in the circumstances outlined below, provided you meet the other conditions of entitlement.

If you were entitled to UC immediately before leaving Great Britain and are temporarily absent, you can continue to be entitled for:[41]

- **one month** if your absence is not expected to exceed, and does not exceed, one month; *or*

- **two months** if your absence is in connection with the death of your partner or child, or a close relative of yours (or of your partner or child), and it would be unreasonable for you to return to Great Britain within the first month; *or*
- **six months** if your absence is not expected to exceed, and does not exceed, six months and you are a mariner or continental shelf worker; *or*
- **six months** if your absence is not expected to exceed, and does not exceed, six months and is solely in connection with the medically approved care, convalesence or treatment of you, your partner or child. You are automatically exempt from the work search requirement and are also treated as 'able and willing immediately to take up work' during this period.[42]

If you are entitled to housing costs in your UC, your temporary absence from your home can mean that you cease to be entitled to receive these (see p230).

If your partner is abroad

If you have a joint claim for UC and both you and your partner go abroad, this does not affect your entitlement during the period when one of the situations listed above applies to both of you. After this time, if you both remain abroad, your entitlement ends.

If you stay in Great Britain while your partner is abroad, her/his absence does not affect your entitlement during the one-, two- or six-month period if the circumstances described above apply to her/him. After this time, you cease to be entitled as joint claimants and if you and your partner have been, and expect to be, apart for less than six months, you must claim as a single person. Your award is based on the maximum amount for a single person, but your partner's income and capital are taken into account.[43] Once you have been, or expect to be, apart for six months, you cease to be treated as a couple[44] and your entitlement is then unaffected by your absent partner.

In addition, if your partner's absence abroad means that s/he stops being habitually resident (including if s/he no longer has a right to reside) in the common travel area, s/he is treated as no longer present (see p91). You can claim as a single person, but your partner's income and capital are taken into account (unless you have ceased to be treated as a couple as described above).[45]

If your child is abroad

If your child is abroad, you cease to be entitled for her/him if her/his absence abroad is, or is expected to be, longer than the one, two or six-month periods allowed in the circumstances set out above. The circumstances must apply to your child.[46]

European Union co-ordination rules

The DWP considers that UC is not a 'social security benefit' under the EU co-ordination rules (see p271), and therefore these rules cannot assist you. If you go to another EEA state, you can only be paid under the UK rules above. The DWP's view is, however, likely to be subject to legal challenge. See CPAG's online service and *Welfare Rights Bulletin* for updates.

2. Bereavement benefits

In general, bereavement benefits are payable while you are abroad. However, your benefit is not uprated each year if, on the day before the annual uprating takes place, you have ceased to be 'ordinarily resident' (see p96) in Great Britain, unless you have gone to another European Economic Area (EEA) state and you are covered by the European Union (EU) co-ordination rules (see p264) or you can rely on a reciprocal agreement (see Chapter 17).[47]

If you are absent from Great Britain when you claim a bereavement payment, you are only entitled in limited circumstances. See p205 for further details.

Note: a new benefit, bereavement support payment, will replace the current bereavement benefits for people whose spouse or civil partner dies on or after the date it is introduced, which is likely to be in April 2017 (see p205). At the time of writing, there was no information about any rules affecting payment abroad. See CPAG's online service and *Welfare Rights Bulletin* for updates.

European Union co-ordination rules

Bereavement benefits are classed as 'survivors' benefits' under the EU co-ordination rules (see p268) and are therefore fully exportable. If these rules apply to you (see p264) and you go to stay or live in another EEA state, you can be paid your bereavement benefits without a time limit and they are fully uprated each year.

If the co-ordination rules apply to you and your late spouse/civil partner died in another EEA state, s/he can be treated as having died in the UK for the purpose of your entitlement to a bereavement payment, provided the UK is your 'competent state' (see p271).[48]

3. Child benefit and guardian's allowance

Child benefit

You and your child can be treated as present in Great Britain and, therefore, you can continue to be entitled to child benefit for a limited period during a 'temporary absence' (see p228).

Provided you are 'ordinarily resident' (see p96), you are treated as present during a temporary absence for:[49]

If you are entitled to housing costs in your PC, your temporary absence from home can mean that you cease to be entitled to receive these (see p230).

If your partner is abroad

If your partner is abroad and you are entitled to PC, either while in Great Britain or abroad because you are covered by the rules p240, your PC only includes an amount for her/him if s/he is also covered by the above rules. After this, s/he is not treated as part of your household, you are paid as a single person and her/his income and capital do not affect your claim.[35] **Note:** the above rules came into force on 28 July 2016. If your partner was already outside Great Britain on this date, the previous, more generous, rules continue to apply until s/he returns.[36] For further information about your partner going abroad, see p230.

European Union co-ordination rules

PC is classed as a 'special non-contributory benefit' under the EU co-ordination rules (see p270) and therefore cannot be exported. This means that if you go abroad, the co-ordination rules cannot assist you. You can only be paid PC abroad under the UK rules above.

Housing benefit

There is no requirement to be present in Great Britain to be entitled to housing benefit (HB). However, you must be liable to make payments in respect of a dwelling in Great Britain, which you occupy as your home.[37] There are rules that treat you as occupying your home, including when you are temporarily absent from it.[38] These vary depending on whether your absence is inside or outside Great Britain (see p230).

If your partner or child is abroad

Whether or not you have amounts included in your HB for your partner or child who is abroad depends on whether s/he is treated as part of your household (see p203 and p204). The amount of HB you are entitled to may also depend on whether s/he is treated as occupying the home (see p230).[39]

Universal credit

You cannot usually be paid UC if you (and your partner if it is a joint claim) are not in Great Britain.[40] However, UC can be paid while you are temporarily absent from Great Britain in the circumstances outlined below, provided you meet the other conditions of entitlement.

If you were entitled to UC immediately before leaving Great Britain and are temporarily absent, you can continue to be entitled for:[41]

- **one month** if your absence is not expected to exceed, and does not exceed, one month; *or*

- **two months** if your absence is in connection with the death of your partner or child, or a close relative of yours (or of your partner or child), and it would be unreasonable for you to return to Great Britain within the first month; *or*
- **six months** if your absence is not expected to exceed, and does not exceed, six months and you are a mariner or continental shelf worker; *or*
- **six months** if your absence is not expected to exceed, and does not exceed, six months and is solely in connection with the medically approved care, convalesence or treatment of you, your partner or child. You are automatically exempt from the work search requirement and are also treated as 'able and willing immediately to take up work' during this period.[42]

If you are entitled to housing costs in your UC, your temporary absence from your home can mean that you cease to be entitled to receive these (see p230).

If your partner is abroad

If you have a joint claim for UC and both you and your partner go abroad, this does not affect your entitlement during the period when one of the situations listed above applies to both of you. After this time, if you both remain abroad, your entitlement ends.

If you stay in Great Britain while your partner is abroad, her/his absence does not affect your entitlement during the one-, two- or six-month period if the circumstances described above apply to her/him. After this time, you cease to be entitled as joint claimants and if you and your partner have been, and expect to be, apart for less than six months, you must claim as a single person. Your award is based on the maximum amount for a single person, but your partner's income and capital are taken into account.[43] Once you have been, or expect to be, apart for six months, you cease to be treated as a couple[44] and your entitlement is then unaffected by your absent partner.

In addition, if your partner's absence abroad means that s/he stops being habitually resident (including if s/he no longer has a right to reside) in the common travel area, s/he is treated as no longer present (see p91). You can claim as a single person, but your partner's income and capital are taken into account (unless you have ceased to be treated as a couple as described above).[45]

If your child is abroad

If your child is abroad, you cease to be entitled for her/him if her/his absence abroad is, or is expected to be, longer than the one, two or six-month periods allowed in the circumstances set out above. The circumstances must apply to your child.[46]

European Union co-ordination rules

The DWP considers that UC is not a 'social security benefit' under the EU co-ordination rules (see p271), and therefore these rules cannot assist you. If you go to another EEA state, you can only be paid under the UK rules above. The DWP's view is, however, likely to be subject to legal challenge. See CPAG's online service and *Welfare Rights Bulletin* for updates.

2. **Bereavement benefits**

In general, bereavement benefits are payable while you are abroad. However, your benefit is not uprated each year if, on the day before the annual uprating takes place, you have ceased to be 'ordinarily resident' (see p96) in Great Britain, unless you have gone to another European Economic Area (EEA) state and you are covered by the European Union (EU) co-ordination rules (see p264) or you can rely on a reciprocal agreement (see Chapter 17).[47]

If you are absent from Great Britain when you claim a bereavement payment, you are only entitled in limited circumstances. See p205 for further details.

Note: a new benefit, bereavement support payment, will replace the current bereavement benefits for people whose spouse or civil partner dies on or after the date it is introduced, which is likely to be in April 2017 (see p205). At the time of writing, there was no information about any rules affecting payment abroad. See CPAG's online service and *Welfare Rights Bulletin* for updates.

European Union co-ordination rules

Bereavement benefits are classed as 'survivors' benefits' under the EU co-ordination rules (see p268) and are therefore fully exportable. If these rules apply to you (see p264) and you go to stay or live in another EEA state, you can be paid your bereavement benefits without a time limit and they are fully uprated each year.

If the co-ordination rules apply to you and your late spouse/civil partner died in another EEA state, s/he can be treated as having died in the UK for the purpose of your entitlement to a bereavement payment, provided the UK is your 'competent state' (see p271).[48]

3. **Child benefit and guardian's allowance**

Child benefit

You and your child can be treated as present in Great Britain and, therefore, you can continue to be entitled to child benefit for a limited period during a 'temporary absence' (see p228).

Provided you are 'ordinarily resident' (see p96), you are treated as present during a temporary absence for:[49]

- the first **eight weeks**; *or*
- the first **12 weeks** of any period of absence, or any extension to that period, which is in connection with:
  - the treatment of an illness or disability of you, your partner, a child for whom you are responsible, or another relative of yours or your partner's; *or*
  - the death of your partner, a child or qualifying young person for whom you or your partner are responsible, or another relative of yours or your partner's.

'**Relative**' means brother, sister, parent, grandparent, great-grandparent or child, grandchild or great-grandchild.[50]

Your child is treated as present during a temporary absence for:[51]
- the first **12 weeks** of any period of absence; *or*
- **any period** during which s/he is absent for the specific purpose of being treated for an illness or disability which began before her/his absence began; *or*
- **any period** when s/he is in Northern Ireland; *or*
- **any period** during which s/he is absent only because s/he is:
  - receiving full-time education at a school or college in another European Economic Area (EEA) state or in Switzerland; *or*
  - engaged in an educational exchange or visit made with the written approval of the school or college s/he normally attends; *or*
  - a child who normally lives with a Crown servant posted overseas who is either in the same country as her/him or is absent from that country for one of the reasons in the two bullet points immediately above.[52]

If a child is born outside Great Britain during the eight- or 12-week period in which you were treated as present in Great Britain, s/he is treated as being in Great Britain for up to 12 weeks from the start of your absence.[53]

While you and your child are present, or treated as present, you satisfy that condition of entitlement. This means that you can continue to receive any child benefit already in payment and can also make a fresh claim during your or her/his absence. **Note:** if you or your child are treated as present, you must satisfy all the other conditions of entitlement including, if your child is not living with you, contributing at least the amount of child benefit that would be payable, to the costs of that child.[54] For information on all the conditions of entitlement for child benefit, see CPAG's *Welfare Benefits and Tax Credits Handbook*.

Guardian's allowance

Entitlement to guardian's allowance depends on entitlement to child benefit, so you can be paid guardian's allowance abroad for the same period as child benefit (see p243).

However, your guardian's allowance is not uprated each year if you have ceased to be ordinarily resident (see p96) in Great Britain on the day before the annual uprating takes place,[55] unless you have gone to another EEA state and you are covered by the European Union (EU) co-ordination rules (see below) or you can rely on a reciprocal agreement.

European Union co-ordination rules

Child benefit and guardian's allowance are classed as 'family benefits' under the EU co-ordination rules (see p268). If these rules apply to you (see p264) and the UK is your 'competent state' (see p271):

- you can be paid child benefit and guardian's allowance for a child resident in another EEA country. The child does not have to be in education. However, you must still satisfy all the other conditions of entitlement, including contributing to the costs of the child an amount at least equal to the amount of child benefit payable for her/him;[56] *and/or*
- you can be paid child benefit and guardian's allowance if you are an EEA national and you go to stay or live in another EEA country, and your benefit is uprated in the normal way.

These rules can be complicated in certain circumstances – eg, if there is entitlement to family benefits in more than one state. See p284 for more information on the payment of family benefits under the EU co-ordination rules.

4. **Disability and carers' benefits**

If you go abroad, you can be treated as being present in Great Britain and therefore continue to be entitled to attendance allowance (AA), disability living allowance (DLA), personal independence payment (PIP) or carer's allowance (CA) for a limited period.

Provided you satisfy the residence condition (see below), you are treated as present and can continue to receive AA, DLA, PIP or CA during an absence from Great Britain:[57]

- (for AA, DLA and PIP only) for the first **13 weeks** of a 'temporary absence' (see p228);
- (for AA, DLA and PIP only) for the first **26 weeks** of a 'temporary absence' (see p228), if the absence is solely in connection with medical treatment for your illness or disability that began before you left Great Britain;
- (for CA only) for up to **four weeks** if your absence is, and was when it began, for a temporary purpose and does not exceed four weeks. If you are not accompanied by the disabled person for whom you are caring, you must satisfy the rules that entitle you to CA during a break from caring. See CPAG's *Welfare Benefits and Tax Credits Handbook* for information;
- (for CA only) if your absence is temporary and for the specific purpose of caring for a disabled person who is also absent from Great Britain and who continues

to receive AA, DLA care component paid at the highest or middle rate, the daily living component of PIP, armed forces independence payment or constant attendance allowance;

- if you were already abroad on 8 April 2013 but continued to be entitled to AA or DLA because your absence was temporary and for the specific purpose of being treated for an illness or disability that began before you left Great Britain, and the DWP has agreed you should be treated as present. You continue to be treated as being present in Great Britain until either you return or your award is revised or superseded;[58]
- while you are abroad as an airwoman/man or mariner or continental shelf worker;
- while you are a serving member of the armed forces, or you are living with your spouse, civil partner, son, daughter, stepson, stepdaughter, father, father-in-law, stepfather, mother, mother-in-law or stepmother who is a serving member of the armed forces.

The residence condition

You must be habitually resident (see p100), unless your current award of AA, DLA or CA began before 8 April 2013, in which case, you must be ordinarily resident (see p96) until that award is terminated, revised or superseeded.[59] You are treated as habitually resident if you are covered by the last bullet point above.

If you lose your entitlement to CA, you should still be eligible for a carer premium paid with your income support, income-based jobseeker's allowance, income-related employment and support allowance and housing benefit for a further period of eight weeks, provided you remain entitled to these benefits while you are away.[60] If you lose your entitlement to CA while you are abroad and the disabled person for whom you care is staying in the UK, s/he may be able to claim a severe disability premium during your absence instead. For further information on premiums, see CPAG's *Welfare Benefits and Tax Credits Handbook*.

You can continue to be paid an increase in your CA for your spouse/civil partner or dependent adult while s/he is abroad if:[61]

- you are entitled to CA; *and*
- you are residing with her/him. **Note:** you can be treated as residing together during a temporary absence from each other.[62]

European Union co-ordination rules

If you move to another European Economic Area (EEA) state, you can continue to be paid (or make a new claim for) AA, DLA care component, PIP daily living component and CA without needing to satisfy the usual presence and residence requirements (see p208) if:[63]

- you are habitually resident in another EEA state or Switzerland; *and*
- you are covered by the European Union (EU) co-ordination rules (see p264); *and*
- you can demonstrate a 'genuine and sufficient link to the UK social security system' (see p210).

Note: if you are covered by the EU co-ordination rules, you can continue to be paid for as long as the UK is your 'competent state' (see p271).[64]

The above exemption has only applied since April 2013. Whether or not you could be paid in another EEA state before this date depends on the date your entitlement began, as AA, DLA and CA have been categorised in different ways under the co-ordination rules at different times.

Before 1 June 1992, AA, DLA and CA were classed as 'invalidity benefits' (see p268). If your entitlement began before this date, you can export your benefit without any time limit to any EEA state.

From 1 June 1992, the UK government categorised AA, DLA and CA as 'special non-contributory benefits' (see p270). These are not exportable. However, the European Court of Justice (ECJ) declared that this was wrong and that these benefits (except DLA mobility component) were 'sickness benefits'.[65] This means they *are* exportable and you should continue to receive the benefit for as long as the UK remains your competent state (see p273).[66]

Note: questions have been referred to the Court of Justice of the European Union on whether DLA care component should be classified as an invalidity, rather than a sickness, benefit, and when the UK ceases to be the competent state, under the old co-ordination rules.[67] See CPAG's online service and *Welfare Rights Bulletin* for updates.

DLA mobility component is listed as (and PIP mobility component is treated by the DWP as) a 'special non-contributory benefit' and is not exportable.[68] You can only be paid in the state where you are resident under the co-ordination rules.[69] See p272 for details on where you are considered 'resident'.

The age cut-off for new claims for DLA mobility component or PIP mobility component at age 65 can mean that if you lose entitlement because you go abroad, you cannot re-establish entitlement when you return to the UK if, by then, you are aged 65 or over. The Upper Tribunal held that this rule is not contrary to EU law in a case concerning a man who returned to the UK aged over 65 after living in France for several years.[70] **Note:** if you lose your entitlement to DLA or PIP because you went abroad and you reached the age of 65 before your entitlement ended, you can become entitled again (including, if you were previously entitled, to the mobility component despite being aged 65 or over), provided you make a renewal claim within 12 months of the previous award ending.[71] For further details on DLA and PIP entitlement criteria and the rules on renewal claims, see CPAG's *Welfare Benefits and Tax Credits Handbook*.

If you receive CA while in the UK and the EU co-ordination rules apply to you (see p264), you may be able to continue to be paid an addition for an adult or child if s/he goes to stay or live in another EEA state. These additions count as 'family benefits' under the co-ordination rules (see p284).

Was your benefit stopped because you moved to another European Economic Area state on or after 8 March 2001?

If your AA, DLA care component or CA was stopped solely because you moved to another EEA state on or after 8 March 2001, this decision was wrong.[72]

The DWP can restore your entitlement and pay arrears from 18 October 2007 (or the date your payment was stopped, if this is later).[73] The DWP pays arrears from this date because it was when the ECJ decided these benefits had been wrongly categorised.

To get your entitlement restored and arrears paid for any period between 8 March 2001 and 18 October 2007, you should do the following.

1. If you appealed within the time limit against the decision that stopped your benefit, the First-tier Tribunal should be able to reinstate it from the date it was stopped. If your appeal is waiting to be determined, the DWP can revise the decision and pay your arrears of benefit in full.

2. If you did not appeal, the DWP can only correct its decision and pay arrears from the date your benefit was stopped if that decision was made because of an 'official error'. However, if a mistake in a decision was not known to be a mistake at the time, but is only shown to have been a mistake by a later court decision, it does not count as an official error.[74] It has been decided that it only became clear that AA, DLA care component and CA were exportable benefits under the EU co-ordination rules when the ECJ decided that they had been wrongly categorised (on 18 October 2007).[75] Therefore, if the decision stopping your benefit (solely because it was mistakenly categorised as a special non-contributory benefit and therefore not exportable) was made before 18 October 2007, this decision does not count as an official error. If the decision is revised, your benefit can only be restored from the date of the revision (although the DWP pays arrears outside these rules back to 18 October 2007).

3. You may be able to get around the above difficulty if you can identify another error in the decision to stop your benefit when you moved to another EEA state which can count as an official error, thus enabling the decision to be revised and your entitlement reinstated from the date it was stopped.[76] One fairly common mistake that may count as another error, if made before 10 April 2006, was a decision to stop your AA or DLA care component from the date you went abroad, rather than from the date of the decision.[77]

Reciprocal agreements

Most reciprocal agreements do not cover disability and carers' benefits. However, the agreements with Guernsey, Jersey, the Isle of Man and Northern Ireland have

Chapter 15: Going abroad: rules for individual benefits
5. Incapacity benefit, severe disablement allowance and maternity allowance

15

relevant provisions. From 6 April 2014, new reciprocal arrangements between Great Britain and Northern Ireland that also cover PIP came into force (see p293).

5. **Incapacity benefit, severe disablement allowance and maternity allowance**

If you are temporarily absent from Great Britain, you can continue to be paid incapacity benefit (IB), severe disablement allowance (SDA) and maternity allowance (MA) if:[78]

- you are receiving attendance allowance (AA), disability living allowance (DLA), personal independence payment (PIP) or armed forces independence payment. For when AA, DLA or PIP can be paid abroad, see p245; *or*
- the DWP certifies that you should continue to be paid. You can then receive the benefit for the first 26 weeks of your temporary absence; *or*
- you are the spouse, civil partner, son, stepson, daughter, stepdaughter, father, stepfather, father-in-law, mother, stepmother, or mother-in-law of a serving member of the armed forces and you are abroad only because you are living with her/him.

In addition:
- when you left Great Britain, you must have been continuously incapable of work for six months and have been continuously incapable since your departure; *or*
- your absence from Great Britain must be for the specific purpose of being treated for an incapacity which began before you left Great Britain; *or*
- for IB only, your incapacity for work is the result of a personal injury caused by an accident at work and your absence from Great Britain is for the specific purpose of receiving treatment for that injury. See CPAG's *Welfare Benefits and Tax Credits Handbook* for more information on industrial injuries.

If you are due to have a medical examination, this can be arranged abroad.

Note: most IB and SDA claims have been reassessed for transfer to employment and support allowance (ESA). If you are still receiving IB or SDA, at some future point you will be reassessed for ESA. If your award of IB or SDA is converted to an award of contributory ESA, you do not need to resatisfy the national insurance (NI) contribution conditions. However, if you are getting IB or SDA and lose entitlement because you go abroad for more than 26 weeks, you do not requalify for IB or SDA on your return to Great Britain, and you can only get contributory ESA if you satisfy all the conditions of entitlement, including the NI contribution conditions. Losing entitlement now could therefore result in a loss of potential future benefit.

You can continue to be paid an increase in your IB or SDA for your spouse/civil partner or dependent adult while s/he is abroad if you are residing with her/him.[79] **Note:** you can be treated as residing together during a temporary absence from each other.[80]

European Union co-ordination rules

Long-term IB and SDA are classed as 'invalidity benefits' under the European Union (EU) co-ordination rules (see p268). If these rules apply to you (see p264) and the UK is your 'competent state' (see p271), you can export your IB and SDA if you go to live in another European Economic Area (EEA) state. Provided you continue to satisfy the rules of entitlement, benefit is paid without any time limit and at the same rate as if you were still in the UK, including your annual uprating.

The state from which you claim benefit is the one that determines your degree of invalidity, but any checks and medicals take place in the state in which you live and the reports are then sent to the paying state.[81]

If the co-ordination rules apply to you and you remain in the UK, you may be able to continue to be paid an increase for an adult or child if s/he goes to stay or live in another EEA state. Such increases are classified as 'family benefits'. See p284 for details about when you can receive these for a family member living abroad.

MA is classed as a 'maternity benefit' under the EU co-ordination rules (see p268). If these rules apply to you (see p264) and the UK is your competent state (see p271), you can be paid MA if you go to live or stay in another EEA country.[82] See p283 for more details.

Reciprocal agreements

The UK has reciprocal agreements with several countries that cover incapacity, sickness and maternity benefits. If you are going to one of these countries, the agreement may enable you to continue to be paid benefit, make a new claim for MA or use NI contributions paid, or periods of employment completed, in the UK to qualify for benefit in the country you are going to. For more information on reciprocal agreements covering sickness and invalidity benefits, see p296, and for maternity benefits, see p297.

6. **Industrial injuries benefits**

Industrial injuries benefits are:
- disablement benefit;
- reduced earnings allowance (REA);
- retirement allowance;
- constant attendance allowance;
- exceptionally severe disablement allowance.

Disablement benefit and retirement allowance are not affected if you go abroad.[83]

Constant attendance allowance and exceptionally severe disablement allowance are payable for the first six months of a temporary absence, or a longer period that the DWP may allow.[84]

REA can be paid while you are temporarily absent abroad for the first three months (or longer if the DWP allows) if:[85]

- your absence from Great Britain is not in connection with employment, trade or business; *and*
- your claim was made before you left Great Britain; *and*
- you were entitled to REA before going abroad.

Note: REA has now been abolished. If you break your claim, you may no longer be eligible for benefit.

European Union co-ordination rules

Industrial injuries benefits, with the exception of retirement allowance, are classed as 'benefits for accidents at work and occupational diseases' under the European Union co-ordination rules (see p268) and are therefore fully exportable. If these rules apply to you (see p264) and you go to stay or live in another European Economic Area state, you can be paid without any time limit and they will be fully uprated each year. See p283 for more details.

Reciprocal agreements

The UK has reciprocal agreements with several countries that cover industrial injuries benefits. These can enable you to continue to be paid benefit indefinitely when you go to a relevant country, and contain provisions for determining entitlement when more than one country is involved. For more information on reciprocal agreements covering industrial injuries benefits, see p297.

---

7. Contribution-based jobseeker's allowance and contributory employment and support allowance

You cannot usually get jobseeker's allowance (JSA) or employment and support allowance (ESA) if you are not in Great Britain.[86] However, contribution-based JSA can be paid when you are temporarily absent from Great Britain in the same circumstances as income-based JSA (see p235), and contributory ESA can be paid when you are temporarily absent from Great Britain in the same circumstances as income-related ESA (see p238).

European Union co-ordination rules

Contribution-based jobseeker's allowance

Contribution-based JSA is classed as an unemployment benefit under the European Union (EU) co-ordination rules (see p268). If these rules apply to you (see p264) and the UK is your 'competent state' (see p271), you can continue to be paid contribution-based JSA for up to three months if:[87]

- you satisfied the conditions for contribution-based JSA before you left the UK for at least four weeks, unless the DWP authorised you to go abroad before then; *and*
- you register as unemployed in the European Economic Area (EEA) state you go to within seven days and comply with its procedures.

Contributory employment and support allowance

If the EU co-ordination rules apply to you (see p264) and the UK is your competent state (see p271), you can generally continue to be paid contributory ESA if you go to live in another EEA state.

After the assessment phase, contributory ESA is classed as an 'invalidity benefit' under the co-ordination rules and is therefore fully exportable if you move to another EEA state. During the assessment phase it is classed as a 'sickness benefit', which can be subject to limitations on exportability under the co-ordination rules. **Note:**

- If you have a long-term or permanent disability, it is arguable that contributory ESA during the assessment phase should be regarded as an 'invalidity benefit' (see p268).[88]
- In most cases, this distinction does not matter, as sickness benefits are exportable in similar circumstances to invalidity benefits (see p283).

If the UK continues to pay your contributory ESA while you are resident in another EEA state, the DWP continues to assess your limited capability for work and your limited capability for work-related activity. However, any checks and medicals take place in the state in which you are living, with reports then sent to the DWP.[89]

If you appeal against a decision on your limited capability for work-related activity while abroad, the tribunal should consider the hypothetical work-related activity that applies in the area of the UK where the tribunal hearing is held, unless you object. This area is usually Newcastle if you opt for a paper hearing.[90]

Reciprocal agreements

If the country you are going to has a reciprocal agreement that covers contribution-based JSA (see Appendix 5), check whether you are covered by it. Such agreements can, for example, enable you to be paid contribution-based benefit for a limited period and/or to use periods of employment completed or national insurance contributions paid in Great Britain to entitle you to unemployment benefits in the country you are going to. See p296 for further information.

Most reciprocal agreements do not cover contributory ESA (see p296). The exceptions are:

- the agreement with Northern Ireland, which, since 6 April 2016, covers contributory ESA (as well as income-related ESA);[91] *and*
- if your award of contributory ESA was converted from incapacity benefit (IB), it is covered by each of the agreements (except the Isle of Man, Israel and Switzerland) that cover IB (see Appendix 5).[92]

If you moved from Great Britain to Northern Ireland (or vice versa) while claiming ESA before 6 April 2016, the DWP policy was to make an extra-statutory payment to cover any loss of ESA that resulted from your having to make a new claim (see p293).

8. **Retirement pensions**

All retirement pensions are payable without time limit while you are abroad.[93] However, if you are not ordinarily resident (see p96) in Great Britain:[94]

- on the day before the annual uprating takes place, your benefit is not uprated each year;
- when you claim state pension (ie, if you reach pension age on or after 6 April 2016) that you have deferred, the upratings that occurred while you were abroad are ignored when calculating both the deferral increase and rate payable;
- you cannot stop claiming ('de-retire') your 'old' retirement pension (ie, if you reached pension age before 6 April 2016) in order to accrue a deferral payment,[95]

unless you have gone to another European Economic Area (EEA) state and you are covered by the European Union (EU) co-ordination rules, or you can rely on a reciprocal agreement (see p254).

Although Category D retirement pension is payable if you are abroad, you must meet the residence requirements at the date you make your claim (see p215).

If you live abroad, your retirement pension can be paid either into a bank in the country where you live or a bank or building society in the UK.

You can continue to be paid an increase in your Category A retirement pension for your spouse/civil partner or dependent adult while s/he is abroad if:[96]

- you are entitled to the pension; *and*
- you are residing with her/him. You can be treated as residing together during a temporary absence from each other.[97]

European Union co-ordination rules

Retirement pensions are classed as 'old age benefits' under the EU co-ordination rules (see p268). If these rules apply to you (see p264), the UK is your 'competent state' (see p271) and you go to live in another EEA state:

- you can 'export' your retirement pension without time limit;
- your retirement pension is paid at the same rate as if you were still in the UK, including your annual uprating; *and*
- you can opt to stop claiming your pension ('de-retire') in order to accrue a deferral payment while living in another EEA state.

If the EU co-ordination rules apply and you remain in the UK, you may be able to continue to be paid an increase for an adult or child if s/he goes to stay or live in another EEA state. These increases count as 'family benefits' under the co-ordination rules. See p284 for more details.

Reciprocal agreements

If you are covered by a reciprocal agreement (see p291) that provides for uprating, you can continue to be paid your pension at the same rate as if you were still in the UK. **Note:** the agreements with Canada and New Zealand, and the former agreement with Australia, do not provide for uprating. For further information on reciprocal agreements and retirement pensions, see p297.

9. **Statutory payments**

There are no presence or residence rules for statutory sick pay (SSP), statutory maternity pay (SMP), statutory adoption pay (SAP), statutory paternity pay (SPP) and statutory shared parental pay (SSPP). You remain entitled to these benefits if you go abroad, provided you meet the usual rules of entitlement, including those relating to being an employee.[98]

Although you are generally required to be employed in Great Britain to count as an 'employee', you count as an employee for the purpose of these benefits, even while employed abroad, in certain circumstances, including if:[99]

- your employer is required to pay secondary Class 1 national insurance (NI) contributions for you; *or*
- you are a continental shelf worker or, in certain circumstances, an airwoman/man or mariner; *or*
- you are employed in another European Economic Area (EEA) state and, had you been employed in Great Britain you would be considered an employee, and the UK is the competent state under the European Union (EU) co-ordination rules (see p271).

Your employer is not required to pay you SSP, SMP, SAP, SPP or SSPP if:[100]
- your employer is not required by law to pay employer's Class 1 NI contributions (even if these contributions are, in fact, made) because, at the time they become payable, your employer:
  - is not resident or present in Great Britain; *and*
  - does not have (or is treated as not having) a place of business in Great Britain; *or*
- because of an international treaty or convention, your employer is exempt from the Social Security Acts, or they are not enforceable against your employer.

European Union co-ordination rules

It is arguable that SSP is a 'sickness benefit' and SMP, SAP, SPP and SSPP are 'maternity/paternity benefits' or family benefits under the EU co-ordination rules (see p268).[101] However, given the generosity of the above UK rules, it is unlikely that you will need to rely on the EU co-ordination rules directly.

10. **Tax credits**

You can be treated as being present and, therefore, entitled to child tax credit (CTC) and working tax credit (WTC) for limited periods during a 'temporary absence' (see p228).

You are treated as present for both CTC and WTC during a temporary absence, provided you are ordinarily resident (see p96), for:[102]
- the first **eight weeks**; *or*
- the first **12 weeks** of any period of absence, or any extension to that period, which is in connection with:
  - the treatment of an illness or disability of you, your partner, a child for whom you are responsible, or another relative (see below) of either you or your partner; *or*
  - the death of your partner, a child or qualifying young person for whom you or your partner are responsible, or another relative (see below) of you or your partner.

'**Relative**' means brother, sister, parent, grandparent, grandchild or great-grandparent or child.[103]

You are also treated as present if you are:[104]
- a Crown servant posted overseas and:
  - you are, or immediately before your posting abroad you were, ordinarily resident in the UK; *or*

– immediately before your posting you were in the UK in connection with that posting; *or*
- the partner of a Crown servant posted overseas and in the same country as her/him or temporarily absent from that country under the same exceptions that enable tax credits to continue during a temporary absence from Great Britain.

While you are treated as present in any of the ways above, you continue to satisfy that condition of entitlement. This means that you can continue to receive any tax credits that are already in payment and can make a fresh or renewal claim during your absence.

Your tax credit entitlement ends if:
- you (or your partner if you are making a joint claim) spend longer abroad than the permitted temporary absence periods, as you cease to satisfy the presence condition; *or*
- you (or your partner if you are making a joint claim) cease to be ordinarily resident; *or*
- you are making a joint claim and separate from your partner in circumstances in which the separation is likely to be permanent, as you cease to count as a couple.[105]

If your entitlement to a joint claim as a couple ends, you may be able to make a single claim. See p219 for considerations if you are making a joint claim as a couple.

European Union co-ordination rules

CTC is classed as a 'family benefit' under the European Union (EU) co-ordination rules (see p268). If these rules apply to you (see p264), and the UK is your competent state (see p271) you can be paid CTC:
- for a child resident in another European Economic Area (EEA) state; *and/or*
- if you are an EEA national and you go to stay or live in another EEA state.

See p284 for more details on the payment of family benefits under the EU co-ordination rules.

WTC is not covered by the EU co-ordination rules. Therefore, if your partner is in another EEA country, although you may be able to make a joint claim for CTC as a couple, your WTC claim is treated as a single claim.[106]

If you or your partner are working in another EEA country but live in the UK and therefore remain present and ordinarily resident in the UK, this work can count for the purposes of your WTC claim.[107]

Notes

1. Means-tested benefits
1 s124(1) SSCBA 1992
2 Reg 4 IS Regs
3 Reg 21 and Sch 7 paras 11 and 11A IS Regs
4 Reg 21 and Sch 7 para 11A IS Regs
5 Reg 16 IS Regs
6 Reg 16(5) IS Regs
7 Reg 1(4B) SS(WTCCTC)(CA) Regs
8 s1(2)(i) JSA 1995
9 Regs 14 and 19 JSA Regs
10 Reg 16 JSA Regs 2013
11 s21 and Sch 1 para 11 JSA 1995; reg 50 JSA Regs; reg 41 JSA Regs 2013
12 Regs 50(4) and 170 JSA Regs
13 Regs 50(6B), 86C and 170 and Sch 5A para 7 JSA Regs
14 Sch 5A para 7 JSA Regs
15 Reg 78 JSA Regs
16 Reg 50(3) and (6C) and Sch 5A para 7 JSA Regs
17 Regs 50(4) and 170 JSA Regs
18 Reg 85 and Sch 5 paras 10 and 11 JSA Regs
19 Reg 85 and Sch 5 para 11 JSA Regs
20 Reg 78 JSA Regs
21 Reg 78(5) JSA Regs
22 Reg 1(8B) SS(WTCCTC)(CA) Regs
23 ss1(3)(d) and 18(4)(a) WRA 2007
24 Regs 151-55 ESA Regs; regs 88-92 ESA Regs 2013
25 Reg 24 ESA Regs; reg 20 ESA Regs 2013
26 Reg 156 and Sch 5 paras 6 and 7 ESA Regs
27 Reg 156 and Sch 5 para 7 ESA Regs
28 Reg 156 ESA Regs
29 SS(RA)O
30 SS(NIRA) Regs; SS(GBRA)NI Regs
31 DWP guidance, 'Extra-statutory Payments for Claimants Moving From Northern Ireland to Great Britain', available at www.cpag.org.uk/content/dwp-guidance-extra-statutory-payments-esa
32 s1(2)(a) SPCA 2002
33 Regs 3 and 4 SPC Regs
34 Reg 5 The Housing Benefit and State Pension Credit (Temporary Absence) (Amendment) Regulations 2016, No.624
35 Reg 5 SPC Regs
36 Reg 5 The Housing Benefit and State Pension Credit (Temporary Absence) (Amendment) Regulations 2016, No.624
37 s130(1)(a) SSCBA 1992
38 Reg 7 HB Regs; reg 7 HB(SPC) Regs
39 Regs 7 and 21 HB Regs; regs 7 and 21 HB(SPC) Regs
40 ss3 and 4(1)(c) WRA 2012
41 Reg 11 UC Regs
42 Reg 99(1)-(3) UC Regs
43 Regs 3, 18, 22 and 36 UC Regs
44 Reg 3(6) UC Regs
45 Regs 3(3), 9, 18(2), 22(3) and 36(3) UC Regs
46 Reg 4(7) UC Regs

2. Bereavement benefits
47 Reg 5 SSB(PA) Regs
48 Arts 5, 42 and 43 EU Reg 883/04

3. Child benefit and guardian's allowance
49 Reg 24 CB Regs
50 Reg 24(1) CB Regs
51 Reg 21 CB Regs
52 Reg 32 CB Regs
53 Reg 21(2) CB Regs
54 s143(1)(b) SSCBA 1992
55 Reg 5 SSB(PA) Regs
56 s143(1)(b) SSCBA 1992; *RK v HMRC (CHB)* [2015] UKUT 357 (AAC), reported as [2016] AACR 4

4. Disability and carers' benefits
57 **AA** Reg 2(2), (3B) and (3C) SS(AA) Regs
DLA Reg 2(2), (3B) and (3C) SS(DLA) Regs
PIP Regs 17-20 SS(PIP) Regs
CA Reg 9(2) and (3) SS(ICA) Regs
58 Reg 5 SS(DLA,AA&CA)(A) Regs
59 Reg 1(2), (3) and (4) SS(DLA,AA&CA)(A) Regs
60 **IS** Sch 2 para 14ZA IS Regs
JSA Sch 1 para 17 JSA Regs
ESA Sch 4 para 8 ESA Regs
HB Sch 3 para 17 HB Regs
61 Reg 13 SSB(PA) Regs; Sch 2 para 7 SSB(Dep) Regs
62 Reg 2(4) SSB(PRT) Regs
63 **AA** Reg 2B SS(AA) Regs
DLA Reg 2B SS(DLA) Regs
PIP Reg 23 SS(PIP) Regs
CA Reg 9B SS(ICA) Regs

64 **AA** s65(7) SSCBA 1992
    DLA s72(7B) SSCBA 1992
    PIP s84 WRA 2012
    CA s70(4A) SSCBA 1992
65 *Commission of the European Communities*
    v European Parliament and Council of the
    European Union, C-299/05 [2007] ECR I-
    08695, 18 October 2007
66 ss65(7), 70(4A) and 72(7B) SSCBA
    1992; s84 WRA 2012
67 *SSWP v Tolley* [2015] UKSC 55
68 *Bartlett and Others v SSWP,* C-537/09
    [2011] ECR I-03417
69 Art 70 EU Reg 883/04; *Swaddling v AO,*
    C-90/97 [1999] ECR I-01075
70 *GS v SSWP (DLA)* [2015] UKUT 687
    (AAC)
71 **DLA** Sch 1 paras 3 and 5 SS(DLA) Regs;
    DMG Memo 1/16
    PIP Regs 15 and 26 SS(PIP) Regs
72 *Commission of the European Communities*
    v European Parliament and Council of the
    European Union, C-299/05 [2007] ECR I-
    08695, 18 October 2007
73 Reg 6(35)-(37) SS(C&P) Regs; reg 7(9A)
    SS&CS(DA) Regs
74 Reg 1(3) SS&CS(DA) Regs
75 *CK and JK v SSWP (CA, DLA)* [2013] UKUT
    218 (AAC)
76 *BD v SSWP (DLA)* [2013] UKUT 216
    (AAC), para 15, but note that this part of
    the decision is not binding; see also R(P)
    2/09
77 CIB/736/2004; *BD v SSWP (DLA)* [2013]
    UKUT 216 (AAC), para 14, but note that
    this part of the decision is not binding.

**5. Incapacity benefit, severe disablement
allowance and maternity allowance**
78 Reg 2 SSB(PA) Regs
79 Reg 13 SSB(PA) Regs; reg 14 SS(IB-ID)
    Regs
80 Reg 2(4) SSB(PRT) Regs
81 Arts 5, 46 and 82 EU Reg 883/04; Arts
    27, 46, 49 and 87 EU Reg 987/2009
82 Arts 7 and 21 EU Reg 883/04

6. Industrial injuries benefits
83 Reg 9(3) SSB(PA) Regs
84 Reg 9(4) SSB(PA) Regs
85 Reg 9(5) SSB(PA) Regs

**7. Contribution-based jobseeker's
allowance and contributory
employment and support allowance**
86 s1(2)(i) JSA 1995; ss1(3)(d) and 18(4)(a)
    WRA 2007
87 Art 64 EU Reg 883/04

88 *Stewart v SSWP,* C-503/09 [2011] ECR,
    not yet reported
89 Arts 5, 46 and 82 EU Reg 883/04; Arts
    27, 46, 49 and 87 EU Reg 987/2009
90 *BB v SSWP (ESA)* [2015] UKUT 545 (AAC)
91 SS(NIRA) Regs; SS(GBRA)NI Regs
92 s179(3),(4) and (5) SSAA 1992; SS(RA)O

8. Retirement pensions
93 s113 SSCBA 1992; reg 4(1) SSB(PA)
    Regs
94 Regs 4(3) and 5 SSB(PA) Regs; ss18 and
    20 PA 2014; regs 21-23 State Pension
    Regulations 2015, No.173; for state
    pension, see DMG Memo 6/16
95 Reg 6 SSB(PA) Regs
96 Reg 13 SSB(PA) Regs; reg 10 SSB(Dep)
    Regs
97 Reg 2(4) SSB(PRT) Regs

9. Statutory payments
98 **SSP** Reg 10 SSP(MAPA) Regs
    SMP Reg 2A SMP(PAM) Regs
    SAP/SPP Reg 4 SPPSAP(PAM) Regs
    SSPP Reg 6 SSPP(PAM) Regs
99 Art 6 EU Reg 883/04
    SSP s163(1) SSCBA 1992; reg 16 SSP
    Regs; regs 5-10 SSP(MAPA) Regs
    SMP s171(1) SSCBA 1992; regs 2, 2A,
    5, 7 and 8 SMP(PAM) Regs
    SAP/SPP ss171ZJ(2)-(3) and 171ZS(2)-
    (3) SSCBA 1992; regs 3, 4, 8 and 9
    SPPSAP(PAM) Regs
    SSPP s171ZZ4(2) SSCBA 1992; regs 5,
    6, 7, 9, 10 SSPP(PAM) Regs
100 **SSP** Reg 16(2) SSP Regs
    SMP Reg 3 SMP(PAM) Regs; reg 17(3)
    SMP Regs
    SAP/SPP Reg 2 SPPSAP(PAM) Regs; reg
    32(3) SPPSAP(G) Regs; reg 24(4)
    ASPP(G) Regs
    SSPP Reg 33(5) SSPP Regs; reg 4
    SSPP(PAM) Regs
101 *Caisse nationale des prestations familiales*
    v Hiddal and Bernard, C-216/12 and C-
    217/12 held that a parental leave
    allowance was a family benefit under EU
    Reg 1408/71

10. Tax credits
102 Reg 4 TC(R) Regs
103 Reg 2(1) TC(R) Regs
104 Regs 3, 5 and 6 TC(R) Regs
105 s3(5A) TCA 2002
106 paras 20090, 20160 and 20170 TCCCM
107 para 0288580 TCM; see also *GC v
    CHMRC (TC)* [2014] UKUT 251 (AAC)

Part 6

European co-ordination rules and international agreements

Chapter 16

European Union co-ordination rules

This chapter covers:
1. Introduction (below)
2. Who is covered (p264)
3. Which benefits are covered (p268)
4. Principles of co-ordination (p271)

This chapter describes the way in which the European Union social security co-ordination rules can assist you to satisfy the entitlement conditions for UK benefits and tax credits if you have moved from another European Economic Area (EEA) state to the UK, and to be paid benefits and tax credits when you or a family member go to live in another EEA state.

The residence and presence conditions for the individual benefits that affect your entitlement while you are in Great Britain are covered in Part 4, and the rules that affect your entitlement to benefits and tax credits if you go abroad are covered in Part 5.

If you are not an EEA national, check Part 3 first as your immigration status may exclude you from the benefit or tax credit you want to claim.

1. Introduction

If you are a European Economic Area (EEA) national (see p40), a family member (see p265) of an EEA national or, in some cases, a non-EEA national, you may be able to benefit from the European Union (EU) social security co-ordination rules. These rules and the European caselaw about their application and meaning apply in the UK and throughout the EEA.

Note: there are two main parts of EU law affecting benefit and tax credit entitlement that are covered in this *Handbook*: the residence rights that enable you to satisfy the right to reside requirement, covered in Part 4, and the social security co-ordination rules, which are summarised in this chapter. In general, you do not need to know whether you have a right to reside in order to understand how the co-ordination rules affect you.

The co-ordination rules can help you qualify for benefits in the UK – eg, by enabling you to count periods of residence, insurance and employment in any EEA state to meet the conditions of entitlement. For the ways the co-ordination rules can help you qualify for individual benefits, see Chapter 13. They can also help you to be paid a UK benefit in another EEA state for longer than you would be able to do under UK law alone. See Chapter 15 for the ways the co-ordination rules can help you claim, or continue to receive, individual UK benefits if you or your family member are in another EEA state.

The co-ordination rules

In order to secure and promote freedom of movement, EU law co-ordinates all the social security systems within the EEA. The intention is that people should not lose out on social security protection because they move to another member state. The rules do not seek to harmonise the social security systems of individual states; their sole objective is to co-ordinate the different schemes.

The co-ordination rules contain the following principles.
- **The single state principle.** You can generally only claim benefit from one member state. This is referred to as the 'competent state' (see p271).
- **Equal treatment of people.** Discrimination on the grounds of nationality in terms of access to, or the rate of payment of, the benefits that are covered is prohibited (see p280).
- **Equal treatment of benefits, income, facts and events.** If receipt of a benefit, or a fact or an event, has a legal consequence in one member state, this must be recognised in the same way by other member states (see p281).
- **Aggregation.** Periods of residence, insurance and employment in any EEA state can be used towards entitlement to benefit in another (see p281).
- **Exportability of certain benefits.** The co-ordination rules allow you to continue to be paid certain benefits abroad if you go to another member state. These rules generally mean that you can take benefit abroad for longer than under the UK rules (see p283).
- **Administrative co-operation.** Member states undertake to co-operate in the administration of the co-ordination rules.

The co-ordination rules set out the above general principles. There are exceptions for specific categories of benefits and, in some cases, there are more detailed provisions on how the principle should apply in certain circumstances. It is therefore helpful to understand the sources of the rules and the structure of the main regulation that sets these out (see p263).

The current co-ordination rules succeed and build on, but do not repeal, the previous set of rules. The latter are referred to in this *Handbook* as 'the old co-ordination rules' (see p263).

Sources of the co-ordination rules

Article 48 of the Treaty on the Functioning of the European Union (TFEU) requires the European Parliament and the Council of Ministers to make such rules in the field of social security:

'as are necessary to provide freedom of movement for workers; to this end, they shall make arrangements to secure for employed and self-employed migrant workers and their dependants:

(a) aggregation, for the purpose of acquiring and retaining the right to benefit and of calculating the amount of benefit, of all periods taken into account under the laws of the several countries;

(b) payment of benefits to persons resident in the territories of Member States.'

Under this Article, the following further legislation has been made.

- **EU Regulation 883/2004** sets out the rules for co-ordinating the different social security systems of the various EU states. The structure of this Regulation is as follows.
  - Preamble. This contains numbered 'recitals' that explain the purpose of the Regulation and the principles it contains. These recitals can be used as an aid to interpret the subsequent substantive Articles.
  - General Provisions. Article 1 contains important definitions. Article 2 explains the 'personal scope' of the Regulation (the people to whom it applies – see p264). Article 3 sets out the 'material scope' (the categories of benefits to which the Regulation applies – see p268). Articles 4 to 10 contain the general principles of the Regulation.
  - Determination of the Legislation Applicable. Articles 11 to 16 contain the general rules for working out which is the competent state (see p271).
  - Special Provisions Concerning the Various Categories of Benefits. Articles 17 to 70 contain more specific rules for different categories of benefits and are divided into chapters – one for each category of benefits.
  - Administrative Commission and Advisory Committee. Articles 71 to 75 establish organisations to oversee and implement the working of the Regulation.
  - Miscellaneous Provisions. Articles 76 to 86 contain various miscellaneous rules on practical issues of administration.
  - Transitional and Final Provisions. Articles 87 to 91 provide for the implementation of the Regulation and transitional measures.
  - Annexes. These contain further rules, most of which concern specific rules for individual member states.
- **EU Regulation 987/2009** contains procedures for implementing EU Regulation 883/2004.

Note: EU Regulation 883/2004 is the successor to **Regulation 1408/71**, which (together with its implementing regulation, EU Regulation 574/72) came into force on 1 April 1973 and is referred to in this chapter as the **'old**

co-ordination rules'. The current co-ordination rules build on their predecessor, taking account of developments in European caselaw and national legislation to modernise and simplify the rules. However, the old co-ordination rules have not been repealed and continue to apply to limited groups (see p266). Since the majority of claims are now determined under the current co-ordination rules, this *Handbook* only covers these. For further information on the old co-ordination rules, see the 2012/13 edition of CPAG's *Welfare Benefits and Tax Credits Handbook*.

The other relevant law in the field of EU co-ordination comprises:
- the provisions in the TFEU on freedom of movement for workers and self-employed people, and citizenship. Even if the EU co-ordination rules do not provide for entitlement to benefits, these provisions may;
- the Charter of Fundamental Rights of the European Union;
- judgments of the Court of Justice of the European Union.

Using the co-ordination rules

In order to establish whether you can rely on the co-ordination rules, you must do the following.
- **Step one:** check whether you are covered by the current or the old co-ordination rules (see p266).
- **Step two:** check whether you are within the 'personal scope' of the co-ordination rules (see below).
- **Step three:** check whether the particular benefit you want to claim is covered by the co-ordination rules, and into which category it falls (see p268).
- **Step four:** check which state is the 'competent state' (see p271).
- **Step five:** check the principle you want to apply – eg, exporting benefit or aggregating periods of insurance (see pp280–83).
- **Step six:** check the individual benefit and tax credit rules in Chapter 13 if you want to check entitlement in the UK, and in Chapter 15 if you want to be paid when you or your family are in another EEA state.

2. **Who is covered**

In order to be covered by the co-ordination rules, you must come within the range of people to whom the rules apply. This is known as their '**personal scope**' (see below). In addition, for the co-ordination rules to apply, your situation must involve more than one member state. This generally means that you must have moved between European Economic Area (EEA) states, or you live in one and work in another, or you live in one and are the national of another.[1]

You are within the 'personal scope' of the co-ordination rules if:[2]
- you have been 'subject to the legislation of one or more member states' (see p265) and you are:
  – an EEA national; *or*

    – a refugee; *or*
    – a stateless person; *or*
- you are a family member (see below) or a survivor of someone covered in the above bullet point. **Note:** the old co-ordination rules defined 'survivor' in terms of national legislation, so in the UK it meant a widow, widower or surviving civil partner.[3] However, there is no definition in the current rules, so it might be possible to argue a wider meaning could apply.

Subject to the legislation of a member state

You have been '**subject to the legislation of a member state**' if you have worked in and paid (or should have paid) the equivalent of national insurance (NI) contributions to that state, or you have paid contributions to that state on interest from assets,[4] or you have received any social security (see p268) or special non-contributory benefit (see p270) from that state. You may also be subject to the legislation if you are potentially eligible for any social security benefit or special non-contributory benefit.

'Legislation' is defined as 'in respect of each member state, laws, regulations and other statutory provisions and all other implementing measures relating to the social security branches covered by Article 3(1) of the Regulation.'[5]

The 'social security branches' referred to in this definition include UK benefits which are intended to assist you in the event of one of the risks covered by the co-ordination rules (see p268).[6] Examples include attendance allowance (AA), disability living allowance (DLA), personal independence payment (PIP), carer's allowance (CA), child benefit and child tax credit. None of these depend on your being an employee or self-employed at any time. Potentially, therefore, even if you have never worked, including in some circumstances if you are a child, you can be covered by the co-ordination rules.

If you are covered by the co-ordination rules, next check which state is the 'competent state' (see p271).

Family members

A family member of someone covered by the co-ordination rules can also rely on the rules that cover that person (which can vary depending on the type of benefit claimed).[7] The definition of a family member under the co-ordination rules is different to that which applies in European Union (EU) residence law (see p164). It is also affected by national social security legislation and can therefore vary between member states.

Note: as economically inactive people, including in some circumstances children, are covered under the current co-ordination rules, you may not need to rely on being a family member. If you are both a family member of a person covered by the rules and also covered by the rules yourself, you can rely on either coverage.

Family member

You are a '**member of the family**' of a person covered by the co-ordination rules if you are:[8]

– a person defined or recognised as a member of the family, or designated as a member of the household, by the legislation under which benefits are provided; *or*
– if the legislation under which benefits are provided does not make a distinction between the members of the family and other people to whom it applies, the covered person's spouse or child who is either under the age of majority (18 in England, Wales and Northern Ireland; 16 in Scotland) or older but dependent on the person covered.

If, under the legislation in either bullet above, you are only considered to be a member of the family or member of the household if you are living in the same household as the person, this condition is considered to be satisfied if you are mainly dependent on her/him.

The 'legislation under which benefits are provided' in the above definition should cover the legislation providing for the particular benefit you are claiming. However, it may be arguable that a broader category of social security legislation should apply. Obtain specialist advice if this affects you.

In a case concerning child benefit, the Upper Tribunal found that the relevant legislation was that of child benefit and held that the claimant's niece and nephew living in a different EU state did not count as members of the claimant's family.[9] **Note:** this case concerned the old co-ordination rules, and while the judge commented that the same would apply under the current co-ordination rules, it is arguable that insufficient consideration was given to the possibility of the children being designated as members of the household. Since they were not living in the same household as the claimant, this would have required the Upper Tribunal to have found that they were mainly dependent on her/him.

In a recent case concerning DLA for a child, the Upper Tribunal, following the above case, found that the relevant legislation was that of DLA and held that the claimant's sister did not count as a member of his family under the current co-ordination rules. However, this did not affect the claimant's entitlement, as he was covered by the co-ordination rules himself.[10]

Note: if you are claiming 'sickness benefits' (eg, AA, CA, DLA care component and PIP daily living component), in limited circumstances a slightly different definition of family member can be relevant and rules can apply to determine whether your rights as a family member or any independent rights you have take priority (see p274).

When the old co-ordination rules apply

The current co-ordination rules[11] apply to the vast majority of current benefit claims. However, the old co-ordination rules[12] (see p263) apply to you if:

- you are receiving a benefit because you claimed it before the current rules came into force.[13] This depends on your nationality (see the dates below). However, if you claimed your benefit before the current rules came into force but did not need to rely on co-ordination rules until after that date (eg, when moving between states), the current rules apply.[14] If the old rules apply to you, they continue to do so during a transitional period of up to 10 years, provided your circumstances do not change. This transitional period is intended to protect anyone who might otherwise have lost benefit under the new rules. However, you can ask to be transferred and considered under the new rules if this would be better for you. If so, the new rules take effect from the start of the following month.[15] **Note:** it is possible that the old co-ordination rules applied to you and then, subsequently, the current rules applied, so a decision maker or First-tier Tribunal may need to consider both sets of rules;[16] *or*
- you are a national of a non-EEA state (other than a refugee), you are legally resident in the UK or another member state,[17] and you have been employed or self-employed and subject to the legislation of a member state because you have paid (or should have paid) NI contributions, or you have been a student and subject to the legislation of an EEA state. You continue to be covered by the old co-ordination rules if the UK is one of the member states where you have legally resided. This is because the UK obtained an opt-out, allowing it not to extend the current rules to 'third-country nationals' – ie, nationals of non-EEA states.[18]

Note: for the co-ordination rules to apply, your situation must involve more than one member state. This generally means that you must have moved between EEA states, or you live in one and work in another, or you live in one and are the national of another.[19]

Relevant dates

The current co-ordination rules apply to nationals (and their family members) of:[20]

– the EU member states (and refugees and stateless people) from 1 May 2010;

– Switzerland from 1 April 2012;

– Iceland, Liechtenstein and Norway from 1 June 2012.

As most claims are now determined under the current co-ordination rules, this *Handbook* only covers these. For further information on the old co-ordination rules, see the 2012/13 edition of CPAG's *Welfare Benefits and Tax Credits Handbook*.

3. **Which benefits are covered**

The benefits to which the co-ordination rules apply are referred to as being within the **'material scope'** of the rules.

Individual social security benefits are not directly referred to. Instead, the rules have broad categories of benefits such as for 'old age' or 'maternity'. The rules refer to these categories as benefits designed to cover certain 'risks'. Any social security benefit in a member state designed to provide assistance in the event of a particular risk comes into that particular category of benefit. Each state must then list the benefits it considers to be designed to assist with that risk.[21] However, the categorisation of a benefit can be challenged, as ultimately it depends on its characteristics rather than on how an individual state lists it.

Benefits are also divided into the following types, depending on the conditions of eligibility:

* social security benefits (see below);
* special non-contributory benefits (see p270);
* social and medical assistance (see p271).

Those benefits deemed to be social security benefits have the most rights, and special non-contributory benefits provide fewer rights. Social and medical assistance is not covered by the co-ordination rules.

Social security benefits

Social security benefits are categorised according to the risk against which they are designed to provide financial protection.[22]

Risk	UK benefit
Sickness	Attendance allowance (AA) (but see p269)
	Disability living allowance (DLA) care component (but see p269)
	Personal independence payment (PIP) daily living component
	Carer's allowance (CA) (but see p269)
	Statutory sick pay
	Contributory employment and support allowance (ESA) in the assessment phase (but see p269)
Maternity and paternity	Maternity allowance
	Statutory maternity, adoption, paternity and shared parental pay (but see p269)

Invalidity	AA, DLA care and mobility components and CA if you were in receipt of benefit before 1 June 1992. If you claimed after this date, see the note below
	Long-term incapacity benefit
	Severe disablement allowance
	Contributory ESA after the assessment phase
	Arguably, contributory ESA during the assessment phase (see below)
Old age	State pension
	Category A, B and D retirement pensions
	Additional pension
	Graduated retirement benefit
	Winter fuel payments
	Increments – eg, to pensions
	Increases of retirement pension for an adult
	Age addition in pensions
Pre-retirement	None
Survivors	Bereavement benefits
Death grants	Bereavement payment
Accidents at work and	Industrial injuries disablement benefit
occupational diseases	Constant attendance allowance
	Exceptionally severe disablement allowance
	Reduced earnings allowance
	Retirement allowance
Unemployment	Contribution-based jobseeker's allowance (JSA)
Family benefits	Child benefit
(see p284)	Guardian's allowance
	Child tax credit
	Increases in other benefits for an adult or a child

Note: AA, DLA care component and CA have been categorised as assisting with different risks at different times. Until 1 June 1992, they were categorised as invalidity benefits. They were then categorised as special non-contributory benefits until this was held to be wrong and they were then re-categorised as sickness benefits.[23] The question of whether DLA care component should be categorised as an invalidity benefit has been referred to the Court of Justice of the European Union.[24] For the relevance of the changing categorisations when you want to be paid one of these benefits in another European Economic Area state, see p246.

The mobility component of DLA continues to be listed as a special non-contributory benefit and this has been held to be lawful.[25] The mobility component of PIP is treated by the DWP as a special non-contributory benefit. Therefore, you cannot export either mobility component (see p246).

Note:
- If you have a long-term or permanent disability, it is arguable that contributory ESA during the assessment phase, as well as after, should be regarded as an invalidity benefit.[26] However, in most cases, whether it is classed as an invalidity benefit or a sickness benefit makes no difference to whether you can export contributory ESA (see p283).
- For rules on exporting family benefits, see p284.
- The DWP considers that statutory maternity, adoption, paternity and shared parental pay are treated as pay rather than social security or special non-contributory benefits.[27] However, it is strongly arguable that these benefits should be classed as maternity and paternity benefits or family benefits.[28] In practice, the scope of the UK rules means that it will be rare for you to need to rely on the co-ordination rules directly.
- The DWP considers that universal credit (UC) is neither a social security nor a special non-contributory benefit and so the co-ordination rules do not apply to it.[29] This view is likely to be subject to legal challenge. See CPAG's online service and *Welfare Rights Bulletin* for updates.

Special non-contributory benefits

Special non-contributory benefits are:[30]
- intended to provide supplementary or ancillary cover against the above risks or specific protection for disabled people closely linked to a person's social environment in the state concerned; *and*
- funded solely from general taxation and do not depend on having made contributions as a condition of entitlement; *and*
- listed as such in European Union (EU) Regulation 833/2004 (see below).

The last criterion above requires each member state to list in an annex to EU Regulation 833/2004 the benefits it considers to be 'special non-contributory benefits'. The UK government has only listed the four benefits below.[31] However, it is expected that the mobility component of PIP will also be listed as a special non-contributory benefit and, until then, the DWP is treating it as such.[32] Income-related ESA replaced income support (IS) in the list from 28 June 2012.

Special non-contributory benefits
DLA mobility component
Income-related ESA
Income-based JSA
Pension credit

Special non-contributory benefits can only be paid in the state in which you are 'resident'.[33] See p272 for details of when you count as resident.

Although you cannot 'export' special non-contributory benefits, all the other co-ordination principles apply.[34]

Social and medical assistance

Benefits which are neither 'social security' nor 'special non-contributory' benefits are considered to be social assistance and consequently excluded from the co-ordination rules.

The UK does not specify which benefits it considers to be social assistance, but it has made it clear that it does not consider UC to be either a social security or a special non-contributory benefit.[35] This view is likely to be subject to legal challenge. See CPAG's online service and *Welfare Rights Bulletin* for updates.

It has also been decided that housing benefit[36] and working tax credit[37] are not social security or special non-contributory benefits. It is likely that the government might argue that IS is now also outside the scope of the EU co-ordination rules, since its removal from the list of special non-contributory benefits on 28 June 2012.

4. Principles of co-ordination

The co-ordination rules set out several general principles. There are exceptions to these principles for specific categories of benefits and, in some cases, there are more detailed provisions on how the principle should apply in certain circumstances. The following information provides an overview of the principles, as it is beyond the scope of this *Handbook* to cover all the exceptions and additional provisions in detail. You should therefore get specialist advice about the way the co-ordination rules apply to your particular circumstances.

The single competent state

Under the co-ordination rules, you are generally only able to claim a particular type of benefit from one member state and only liable to pay national insurance (NI) contributions (or their equivalent) to one member state. This is expressed as the general principle that you can be subject to the legislation of a single member state only.[38]

> *The competent state and competent institution*
>
> The '**competent state**' is the state in which the 'competent institution' is situated.[39] It is the state that is responsible for paying your benefit and to which you are liable to pay NI contributions.

The '**competent institution**' is broadly the institution that is responsible for paying your benefit and to which you are liable to pay NI contributions.[40] In the UK this is the DWP and HM Revenue and Customs (HMRC).

The general rule is that the competent state is the one in which you are:[41]
- employed or self-employed;
- resident and from which you receive an unemployment benefit;
- a conscripted member of the armed forces or someone doing compulsory civilian service; *or*
- a civil servant.

If none of the above bullet points apply, the competent state is the state in which you are 'resident' (see below).[42]

Note: there are exceptions for 'sickness benefits' if you (or your family member who brings you within the co-ordination rules) receive a pension from a state other than the one in which you reside (see p274). There are also exceptions for family benefits if you receive a pension (see p284).

You are treated as still employed or self-employed if, as a result of that activity, you are receiving cash benefits (other than for the risks of invalidity, sickness, old age, being a survivor or accidents at work).[43]

If you work simultaneously in two or more member states, you are subject to the legislation of the state of residence if you pursue a substantial part (generally, at least 25 per cent) of your activities there.[44]

If your employer's business is normally in one state but you are sent to another to work and it is anticipated that the posting will last for no more than 24 months, you remain subject to the legislation of the first state. Similarly, if you are self-employed in one state and go to another state to pursue a similar activity as a self-employed person, you remain subject to the legislation of the first state, provided the anticipated duration of your activity in the other state does not exceed 24 months.[45]

Note: you may continue to be subject to the legislation of the member state where you previously lived and were self-employed if, although you move to live in another state, you continue to be self-employed in the previous state.[46]

If you make a claim, declaration or appeal to the competent institution in a state that is not your competent state, it must be forwarded to the competent state without delay andtreated as if it had been submitted to the competent state on the date it was originally submitted.[47] For further information, including if there is a dispute between states over which is your competent state, see p279.

How residence is determined

'Residence' is defined in the co-ordination rules as 'the place where a person habitually resides'.[48] The following information outlines the factors that should be considered when determining where you habitually reside. Although this list of factors is in a rule which explains what should be done if there is a difference of views between two states or institutions about where you are resident, it should also be used where there is no such dispute. Firstly, it should be established by common agreement where your centre of interests lies. This is based on an overall assessment of the relevant facts, including:[49]

- the duration and continuity of presence in the state(s) concerned;
- your personal situation, including:
  - the nature and specific characteristics of any activity pursued, in particular the place where such activity is habitually pursued, the stability of the activity, and the duration of any work contract;
  - your family status and family ties;
  - any unpaid activity, such as voluntary work;
  - if you are a student, the source of your income;
  - your housing situation, in particular how permanent it is;
  - the member state in which you are deemed to reside for tax purposes.

If there is still a dispute about your place of residence, your intentions should be considered, especially the reasons why you moved. This is decisive in establishing your actual place of residence.

If there is a dispute between states over which is your competent state, see p279.

When the UK remains the competent state

If you are subject to the legislation of the UK, either because you last worked in the UK or you are resident in the UK, the UK remains your competent state until:[50]

- you start to work in another European Economic Area (EEA) member state;
- (unless you last worked in the UK) you receive a pension from another EEA member state and request that the UK ceases to be your competent state;[51]
- in some circumstances, you move to another EEA member state and become resident there (see below).

These general rules can be supplemented by other rules which are specific to the category of benefit being paid.[52]

The point at which the UK stops being responsible for paying your benefit if you move to another state is not always clear and most of the caselaw has considered the old co-ordination rules, which differ in some respects from the current ones (see p263).[53] Questions have been referred to the Court of Justice of the European Union (CJEU) about when the UK ceases to be the competent state for the payment of disability living allowance (DLA) under the old co-ordination rules to someone who moves from the UK to another EEA state.[54] However, in general, if you continue to be entitled to a UK benefit when you move to another EEA state, the UK remains the competent state for paying that benefit until either you become employed/self-employed in the other state or, in certain circumstances, you start to receive a benefit from that state.[55]If you were self-employed in the UK and move to live in another EEA state, you may, depending on your circumstances, continue to be self-employed in the UK, in which case the UK remains your competent state.[56]

Sickness benefits

If you are covered by the co-ordination rules, you are only entitled to attendance allowance (AA), DLA care component, the daily living component of personal independence payment (PIP) and carer's allowance (CA) (which are all classed as sickness benefits) if the UK is the competent state for paying cash sickness benefits.[57] The UK must be the competent state to pay *your* sickness benefits. So, for example, for you to receive CA, the UK must be the competent state to pay you that benefit, even if there is a different competent state for paying sickness benefit to the person you care for.[58]

In most cases, the competent state is determined under the general rule explained on p273.

However, this does not apply to cash sickness benefits if you, or your family member (see p265) who brings you within the co-ordination rules, are a 'pensioner' (see below for the meaning) living in a state other than the one that is paying you a 'pension' (see below). In this case, the competent state is the one responsible for meeting the cost of sickness benefits in kind – eg, in the UK, NHS treatment.[59]

Note: although you receive sickness benefits in kind in the state in which you are resident, the cost of these can be borne by another state.

This means that you must establish which state must bear the cost of sickness benefits in kind to work out which state is competent for paying a cash sickness benefit. Various scenarios are set out below. It may also be helpful to refer decision makers to the DWP guidance, *Deciding the Competent State to Pay Cash Sickness Benefits*.[60]

Pension and pensioner

'Pension', for the purpose of the co-ordination rules, includes more than old-age pensions. It includes lump-sum benefits that can be substituted for pensions and reimbursement of contributions, and can include revaluation increases and supplementary allowances.[61] It has been accepted that, under the old co-ordination rules, a pension can include incapacity benefit, employment and support allowance (ESA), DLA and severe disablement allowance.[62] It may be arguable it also includes pension credit (PC) since this is a supplementary allowance.[63] Although the Upper Tribunal recently commented that PC is not a 'pension', as it is a special non-contributory benefit (see p270),[64] the argument was not considered in depth, and the ECJ has held that a benefit can be both a special non-contributory benefit and a supplementary allowance.[65]

'Pensioner' is not defined, but refers to someone receiving a 'pension'.

Who is a family member for sickness benefits in kind

The definition of 'family member' for sickness benefits in kind is slightly different to the general definition (see p265). The difference is highlighted below in italics.

You are a member of the family of a person covered by the co-ordination rules for the purpose of sickness benefits in kind if you are:[66]

- a person defined or recognised as a member of the family, or designated as a member of the household, by the legislation *of the member state in which you reside*; or
- if the legislation under which benefits are provided does not make a distinction between the members of the family and other people to whom it applies, the covered person's spouse or child who is either under the age of majority (18 in England, Wales and Northern Ireland; 16 in Scotland) or older but dependent on the person covered.

If, under the legislation in either bullet above, you are only considered to be a member of the family or member of the household if you are living in the same household as the person, this condition is considered to be satisfied if you are mainly dependent on her/him.

If you have a right to benefits in kind as a family member as well as an independent right to benefits in kind, there are rules which mean that your independent right takes priority unless this is only based on residence.[67] Examples are given below.

Scenarios

There are several possible scenarios (although see p276 for some exceptions).

If you reside in the UK (or another state in which entitlement to sickness benefits in kind is on the basis of residence, rather than insurance or employment) and you (or your family member who brings you within the co-ordination rules) receive a pension from one or more states, but not from the UK (or the other state of residence), although you can receive sickness benefits in kind from the UK (or the other state), the cost of these is borne by one of the other states that pays a pension, to the extent that you would be entitled to receive sickness benefits in kind from that state if you lived there. Therefore, the state that pays your pension, rather than the UK, is responsible for paying your cash sickness benefit.[68]

Example

Emil is a Swedish national and receives a small Swedish old-age state pension. Emil moves to the UK and claims AA. As he receives a pension from another state (Sweden), that state is responsible to the UK for reimbursing the cost of any NHS treatment he has. Consequently, provided Emil would be entitled to sickness benefits in kind (eg, healthcare) if he were resident in Sweden, he is not entitled to AA (but may be able to claim a Swedish cash sickness benefit).

If you receive a pension from two or more states and one of them is the state in which you reside, that state is responsible for the cost of your sickness benefits in kind (and is therefore the competent state for paying cash sickness benefits).[69]

Example

Emil becomes eligible for and claims a Category D retirement pension. He now receives a pension from two or more states, including the one in which he resides (the UK). That state (the UK) is responsible for the cost of his NHS treatment, so Emil can be entitled to AA.

If you reside in the UK (or another state in which entitlement to sickness benefits in kind is on the basis of residence) and you receive a pension from two or more states other than the UK (or other state of residence), the cost of your healthcare in kind is met by the state in which you were subject to pensions legislation for the longest period (or if that is more than one state, the state in which you were last subject to their pensions legislation).[70] That state is therefore the competent state for paying your cash sickness benefits.

Example

Jonas worked 10 years in Germany and 18 years in France and now resides in the UK. He receives pensions from both Germany and France. France is the state responsible for the cost of any NHS treatment he has while he lives in the UK and so France is the competent state for paying cash sickness benefits.

If you are the family member of a person receiving a pension and reside in a different state to her/him, whichever state must meet the cost of the sickness benefits in kind for her/him must also meet the cost of sickness benefits in kind for you (and is therefore the competent state for paying cash sickness benefits).[71]

However, check whether you also have an independent right to benefits in kind and, if so, whether these take priority. See the second exception below.

Example

Reka is a Hungarian national living in the UK. Her husband Roland is a Dutch national. He lives in Ireland and his only income is his Dutch pension. The Netherlands is the state that must meet the cost of the sickness benefits in kind for Roland and, therefore, is also the state that must meet these costs for Reka.

The above rules do not apply in the following cases.
- You (or your family member who is a pensioner) are entitled to benefits under the legislation of a state because that state is the competent one on the basis of

an activity as an employed or self-employed person.[72] **Note:** the DWP guidance suggests that undertaking activity as an employed or self-employed person in the UK is sufficient to mean that the UK becomes the competent state for paying cash sickness benefits.[73]

Example
Sophia is Portuguese and lives in the UK. She receives a small pension from Portugal. Sophia works part time as a self-employed cleaner and claims child benefit and child tax credit (CTC) for her disabled granddaughter who lives with her and receives DLA middle rate care component. Sophia can claim CA, as the UK is the competent state for paying benefits to her on the basis of her self-employment here.

- You are the family member of a pensioner, but you have an independent right to benefits in kind, either under the legislation of a state or under the co-ordination rules. Your independent right takes priority, unless it exists solely because of your residence in that state.[74]

Examples
Krista is Latvian and resides in the UK with her Latvian husband Andris. Krista and Andris both receive a pension from Latvia, but Krista also receives contributory ESA. Krista wants to claim the daily living component of PIP. She can do so because her independent rights take priority over her rights as the family member of Andris. Because Krista receives a 'pension' from the UK as well as one from Latvia, the UK is the state responsible for the cost of her sickness benefits in kind, and is therefore the competent state for paying cash sickness benefits.

Ryan is a 13-year-old Irish national living in the UK with his Irish mother Megan who receives an invalidity pension from Ireland. Ryan wants to claim the care component of DLA. However, because his independent rights are only based on his residence in the UK, the rights he has as the family member of his mother take priority. Therefore, Ireland is the state responsible for the cost of his sickness benefits in kind, and is therefore the competent state for paying cash sickness benefits.

To check the sickness benefits payable by other EEA states, see the European Commission's website: 'Your rights country by country'.

If the rules exclude you
If you are residing in the UK and you receive a decision that the rules for sickness benefits exclude you from entitlement to AA, DLA care component, the daily living component of PIP or CA, or you think these rules might exclude you, check the following.

Are you excluded by the rules for sickness benefits?

1. Are you (or your family member who brings you within the co-ordination rules) receiving a pension from another state? This must be a pension received under the legislation of a member state, so private and occupational pensions should not bring you within the above rules. See p274 for the meaning of 'pension'.

2. Do, or could, you (or your family member who brings you within the co-ordination rules) receive a pension from the UK as well as from another state? If so, the UK is responsible for the cost of your NHS treatment and so is the competent state for paying sickness benefits (see the example of Emil on p275).

3. Although withdrawing your (or your family member's) claim for a pension from the other state could mean the above rules cease to apply you (or her/him), get advice before doing so as it could affect your (or her/his) future pension entitlement.

4. It may be possible to argue that the exclusion from AA, DLA care component or the daily living component of PIP on the basis that the UK is not your competent state does not apply. Depending on your circumstances, the basis of this argument could one of the following.

– If your health condition is permanent or long term, and particularly if you are terminally ill, the exclusion should not apply because it only applies to cash sickness benefits and it was held by the CJEU that a benefit claimed by someone whose disability is permanent or long term should be classed as an invalidity benefit, rather than a sickness benefit.[75] The question of whether DLA care component, when claimed by someone with a permanent or long-term disability, should be classified as an invalidity, rather than a sickness, benefit has recently been referred to the CJEU.[76] **Note:** the Upper Tribunal recently dismissed this argument in relation to AA.[77] However, this was before the question concerning the DLA care component was referred to the CJEU, and the arguably flawed reasoning given in the Upper Tribunal case may mean that further challenges on this basis are possible, particularly if you are terminally ill and/or not over pension age.

– If you are the dependent family member of an EEA worker, the exclusion is prohibited by the principle of equal treatment (see p280) if the refusal of a disability benefit reduces or impedes her/his ability to work or disadvantages her/him in relation to a British worker.[78] **Note:** this discrimination argument was arguably not considered in a recent Upper Tribunal decision which rejected an argument that refusal of AA was disproportionate and discriminatory, but on the basis that the claimant's permanent residence was irrelevant rather than on the basis that the refusal affected the rights of the family member he was dependent on.[79] However, the argument was considered in a subsequent case when it was put in broad terms.[80] The judge dismissed the argument as presented, but left open the possibility that the principle of equal treatment could prohibit the exclusion from sickness benefits for a family member of a worker in particular circumstances. Such an argument may be accepted if there is no equivalent sickness benefit payable by the competent state and exclusion would result in your being deprived of any entitlement at all.[81]

– If you have previously worked and paid taxes in the UK, the co-ordination rules should not deprive you of entitlement to a benefit paid for by taxation. If this would be the result of the co-ordination rules, a state is not prevented from awarding the benefit, even when it is not the competent state for paying it.[82] The Upper Tribunal has considered this line of argument developed through recent European caselaw, but did not find that it applied in that particular case as the person had not contributed through general taxation.[83]

If the decision maker decides the UK is not the competent state

If, when you claim a UK benefit, the decision maker decides the UK is not the competent state to pay that benefit, s/he must forward the claim to the relevant institution in the state that is considered competent without delay, unless there is evidence that state takes a different view (see below). The date of claim is the date the claim was made in the UK.[84]

If there is a difference of views between the institutions of two or more states on which state is the competent state for paying a cash benefit or meeting the cost of a benefit in kind, while the issue is being resolved you can get provisional payments from, and under the legislation of:[85]

- your state of residence, if you are resident in one of the states concerned; *or*
- the state to which you first applied, if you are not resident in any of the states concerned.

These rules on provisional payments apply if forwarding the claim triggers the different view and also if there is evidence of a different view when the claim is received, in which case it should not be forwarded.[86] The legislation only requires there to be a 'difference of views' between the relevant institutions. It says nothing about the form in which the view must be expresssed nor the evidence required to prove it. The Upper Tribunal has considered this issue and noted that although documentary evidence will 'put the matter beyond doubt', it may not be available and oral evidence could, particularly at tribunals, be accepted.[87] A subsequent case accepted the claimant's oral evidence as sufficient to show the difference of view and therefore held that the DWP had to determine the claim and, if the claimant met the other conditions of entitlement, make provisional payments.[88] However, the DWP has been granted permission to appeal this decision to the Court of Appeal.[89]

If no agreement is reached between the states after one month, the matter can be brought before the Administrative Commission by the competent authorities, which will seek to reconcile the dispute within six months.[90]

If it is established that the state that made provisional payments is not the competent state, it is reimbursed.[91]

The DWP has issued guidance on action to be taken once competency has been decided.[92] **Note:** this states that if there is a difference of view on which state is competent to pay benefit with a state that does not have a similar benefit to the one claimed in the UK, provisional payments need not be made.[93] No reference is given for this assertion and it is arguable that provisional payments should still be made.[94]

Although in most cases the issue is which state is competent to make the payment, if there is a difference of views between states concerning the determination of the applicable legislation, you are provisionally subject to the legislation of one state in the following order of priority:[95]

- if you only work in one state, the state where you work;
- if you either work in two or more states and live in one of them, or do not work, the state where you reside;
- in all other cases, of the states in which you work, the state to which you first applied.

Equal treatment of people

If you are covered by the co-ordination rules, you are entitled to the same benefits under the legislation of the 'competent state' (see p271) as a national of that state.[96] Equal treatment is one of the fundamental rights of European Union (EU) law,[97] and the principle of non-discrimination prohibits discrimination based on your nationality. Both direct discrimination and, if it cannot be justified as proportionate and in pursuit of a legitimate aim, indirect discrimination are prohibited.

Direct discrimination arises when one person is treated less favourably than another. Indirect discrimination arises when rules which, although apparently neutral and non-discriminatory, have, in practice, a greater adverse impact on some people than others – eg, non-nationals of the competent state over nationals of the competent state. For example, the right to reside test in UK law appears to apply equally to all EEA nationals. However, British and Irish citizens always have a right to reside in the common travel area and therefore satisfy the test for means-tested benefits, whereas other EEA nationals only satisfy it in certain circumstances. Therefore, the test is indirectly discriminatory. However, the Supreme Court decided in a case concerning PC that this discrimination is justified and, therefore, legal.[98] Similarly, the CJEU recently held that the right to reside test for child benefit and CTC was not directly discriminatory and, although indirectly discriminatory, this was justified.[99] Although a different view was taken by the Northern Ireland Chief Commissioner who found that, for the purposes of child benefit, the right to reside test was either directly or indirectly discriminatory, this was overturned by the Court of Appeal in Northern Ireland.[100]

Equal treatment of facts and events

The co-ordination rules provide for the 'equal treatment of benefits, income, facts or events'.[101] This is sometimes referred to as the 'principle of the assimilation of facts'. This principle is designed to ensure that if the competent state regards the receipt of a particular benefit or income, or the occurrence of certain facts or events, as producing certain legal effects, it should regard the receipt of an equivalent benefit or income from another state, or the occurrence of particular facts or events in another state, as producing the same effect. For example, a person receiving AA is entitled to a disability premium in her/his housing benefit (HB). Therefore, someone receiving a benefit equivalent to AA from another state who claims HB can argue that s/he should get the disability premium in her/his applicable amount. Similarly, if one member state has determined that a person has had an industrial accident, that fact must be accepted, for the purpose of awarding benefit, in another member state.

There are exceptions to the general principle of the assimilation of facts, some of which are set out in the co-ordination rules, and others arise as a result of a conflict between this principle and other principles of the co-ordination rules. An example of the latter is that the assimilation of facts cannot render another member state competent.[102] The competent state should first be determined (see p271) and then that state should assimilate facts for the purposes of its own legislation. Another example of the assimilation principle not being absolute is that it should not interfere with the principle of aggregation (see below).[103] Therefore, the competent state should count periods of insurance in another member state (under the aggregation principle) without needing to address the question of whether they count as periods of insurance for the assimilation principle to apply. If it counts as a period of insurance under the legislation of the state in which it took place, that period can be aggregated.

Aggregation

The principle of aggregation for the purpose of acquiring and calculating entitlement to benefits is a key co-ordinating principle.[104]

'**Aggregation**' means adding together periods of insurance (such as NI contributions in the UK), residence or employment/self-employment completed under the legislation of other member states to satisfy the conditions of entitlement for a benefit. This may be necessary if your entitlement depends on your fulfilling a certain period of residence, employment or insurance. For example, if you want to claim a UK contribution-based benefit such as contributory ESA, but you have not paid sufficient NI contributions, you can rely on contributions you have paid in other EEA states in order to satisfy the UK contribution rules. The competent institution must contact the institutions in the other relevant states to determine the periods completed under their legislation.[105] What constitutes a period of residence, employment or insurance is determined by the legislation of the state in which it took place.[106]

The principle is that you should not lose out if you choose to exercise your right to move within the EEA. If you were to be at a disadvantage should you need to claim benefit, this may deter you from moving.

Example

Sancha is a Portuguese national who has worked for many years in Portugal. She leaves her job in Portugal and moves to the UK. She works for three weeks before being made redundant. Sancha is expecting a baby in two months' time and claims maternity allowance (MA). She is entitled to MA because she can add her periods of employment in Portugal to her period of employment in the UK to satisfy the condition of having worked for 26 out of the last 66 weeks.

Note: the Upper Tribunal is due to hear a number of cases that concern the operation of the aggregation principle to enable the past presence test to be satisfied for disability and carers' benefits. See CPAG's online service and *Welfare Rights Bulletin* for updates.

Unemployment benefits

When determining entitlement to unemployment benefits, the principle of aggregation has an additional condition. Your periods of insurance (if entitlement depends on insurance) or employment/self-employment (if entitlement depends on employment/self-employment) completed in all member states are only aggregated if you were last insured or last worked (whichever is required) under the legislation of the state from which you are claiming benefit.[107]

Example

Tomasz is Polish and after working and being insured in Poland for four years became unemployed, and so moved to the UK to look for work. If he claims contribution-based jobseeker's allowance (JSA), he cannot use his periods of insurance from Poland to satisfy the NI contribution conditions. However, if he takes two weeks' full-time temporary work in the UK and then claims contribution-based JSA, he can then aggregate his periods of insurance in Poland and the NI contributions paid in the UK to be able to qualify for contribution-based JSA.

However, this additional condition does not apply if, during your last period of employment or self-employment, you resided in a state other than your competent state. In this case, if you claim an unemployment benefit in the state in which you reside, you *can* aggregate periods of insurance or employment or self-employment in order to be entitled to that benefit.[108]

Example

Monique was employed and insured in Belgium where she resided for a year. She then got a job in France for 18 months. As this involved mainly working from home, she did this work while residing in the UK with her boyfriend. She has been made redundant and wants to claim contribution-based JSA. She can aggregate the contributions paid in both Belgium and France to qualify for contribution-based JSA.

Exporting benefits

The co-ordination rules allow you to 'export' certain social security benefits to another state if you cease to be resident in the member state in which the entitlement arose.

This means that certain benefits may not be reduced, modified, suspended, withdrawn or confiscated just because you go to live in a different member state.[109] The rules for exporting vary according to the benefit concerned: some are fully exportable, some may be exportable on a temporary basis, and some are not exportable at all.

Check the individual benefit rules in Chapter 15 to see whether that benefit can be exported. If it can, you should contact the office that pays your benefit well in advance so that arrangements can be made to pay you in the other EEA state. The rules covering periodic reassessments still apply so, for example, if you export contributory ESA, the DWP continues to assess your limited capability for work and your limited capability for work-related activity. However, any checks and medicals take place in the state in which you are living, with reports then sent to the DWP.[110]

Under the co-ordination rules, all benefits categorised as social security benefits are exportable. See p268 for a list of the UK benefits covered.

The following benefits are fully exportable and can be exported indefinitely:
- invalidity benefits;
- old age benefits;
- survivors' benefits;
- pensions for accidents at work or occupational diseases;
- death grants.

The following benefits can be exported for a limited period or subject to certain restrictions:
- unemployment benefits;
- sickness, maternity and paternity benefits. However, in most cases, these benefits are exportable in a similar way to the fully exportable benefits.

Special non-contributory benefits (see p270) cannot be exported. They are paid only in the state in which you are 'resident'.[111] See p272 for details of when you count as resident.

Overlapping benefit rules

A general principle of the EU rules on co-ordination is that you should not use one period of compulsory insurance to obtain more than one benefit derived from that period of insurance.[112] In general, you are only insured in one EEA member state for any one period, so you cannot use insurance from that one period to obtain entitlement to benefits of the same kind from more than one member state. Usually, benefits are adjusted to ensure that either only one state (the 'competent state' – see p271) pays the benefit, taking into account periods of insurance in other EEA member states, or the benefit is paid pro rata according to the lengths of the periods of insurance in different member states.

In certain cases, however, you may be paid both the full level of a UK benefit and a proportion of a benefit from another member state, accrued as a result of having paid NI contributions there. EEA states are not allowed to apply provisions preventing the overlapping of their own benefits with those of other member states if it would reduce what you would have received from your years of contributions in the first member state alone.[113]

There are particular overlapping rules on specific categories of benefits – eg, family benefits[114] (see p285), old age and survivors' benefits.[115]

Family benefits

Under the co-ordination rules, family benefits in the UK include child benefit, CTC, guardian's allowance and child dependants' additions in other benefits.

If you are covered by the co-ordination rules, you can export family benefits without any time limit provided there is no change in your competent state.[116] If you export family benefits, they are uprated in the normal way. You can also be paid for family members living in another member state.[117] For the definition of family member, see p265.

Special rules apply if there is entitlement to family benefits from more than one member state in respect of the same person and for the same period. The rules determine which state has priority when these entitlements overlap (see p285).

Family members resident in another state

Generally, you are entitled to receive family benefits from your competent state, determined in the usual way (see p271), even when the family member for whom you are claiming is resident in another state.[118] In this case, the family member is treated as if s/he were resident in the competent state.

- -

Example
Carla is Italian. She is working in the UK. Carla's two children live with their grandmother in Italy. Carla is entitled to child benefit and CTC in respect of her children.

- -

However, if you are receiving a 'pension', the member state that is competent for paying this is the one from which you claim family benefits.[119] See p274 for definition of 'pension'.[120]

- -

Example

Julien is a French national. He receives a small state pension from France and has moved to the UK. Julien's 15-year-old twin daughters remain living in France. Julien also runs a small business in the UK. Normally, because Julien is working in the UK, the UK would be the competent state for paying family benefits. However, because Julien is in receipt of a pension from France, he is only entitled to claim French family benefits.

- -

HMRC guidance for decision makers covers the operation of the co-ordination rules to enable you to be paid for family members living in other member states.[121] It lists workers and self-employed people paying NI contributions in the UK as examples of those eligible to use these rules, and can therefore easily be misunderstood as meaning that the rules only apply to these groups. This mistaken suggestion that the current co-ordination rules are limited in a similar way to the old co-ordination rules (see p263) has appeared in several HMRC appeal submissions and has been confirmed as wrong by the Upper Tribunal.[122]

Priority when family benefits overlap

It is not uncommon for entitlement to family benefits to be provided for under the legislation of more than one member state in respect of the same family member and for the same period. This can arise when two people are entitled to benefit for the same child – eg, if a mother resides in one state and the father in another and both can claim family benefits for their child. It can also arise when the same person has an entitlement from more than one member state – eg, if a parent lives in one state with her/his children, but works in another.

The general principle in the EU co-ordination rules is that equivalent family benefits should not be payable by more than one state in respect of the same family member for the same period. To achieve this, rules set out which member state has 'priority' – ie, must pay the family benefits.

The way these rules operate depends on:
- the basis on which each of the family benefits in question is paid. Different member states have different criteria for entitlement. In some states, family benefits may be payable on the condition that you live there (payable on the basis of 'residence'); in others, the criterion might be that you must work in that particular state (payable on the basis of 'employment or self-employment'); or family benefits may be paid on the basis that you receive a pension (payable on the basis of 'receipt of a pension'). Working out the basis on which a family benefit from another state is paid can be difficult, but the European Commission has online information on the conditions for each state.[123] In the

majority of states, including the UK, family benefits are mostly payable on the basis of residence, rather than employment or receipt of a pension – eg, there are no employment conditions or a requirement to receive a pension in order to obtain child benefit or CTC;
- the member state in which the child lives.

If there is entitlement to a family benefit in respect of the same family member for the same period from more than one state, and the family benefits from each state are payable on a different basis, the member state which has priority (ie, must pay) is the one whose family benefits are payable under the first of the following bases:[124]
- activity as an employed or self-employed person. This can include temporary periods not working for reasons such as sickness, maternity or unemployment, provided you receive either wages or benefits other than a 'pension' (see p274);[125]
- receipt of a pension (see p274);
- residence.

If there is entitlement to a family benefit in respect of the same family member for the same period from more than one state, and the family benefits from each state are payable on the same basis, the member state which has priority (ie, must pay) is as follows.[126]
- If family benefits are based on employment/self-employment in both states, the state with priority is the one where the child resides, if you (or if there is another potential claimant, s/he) work there, otherwise it is the state that pays the highest amount.[127]
- If family benefits are based on receipt of a pension in both states, the state with priority is the one where the child resides if that state also pays the pension, otherwise it is the state where you, or the other potential claimant, have been insured or resided for the longest period.
- If family benefits are based on residence, the state with priority is the one where the child resides.

If there is an entitlement to family benefits from the state that has priority, the entitlement to family benefits from the other state(s) with lower priority is suspended up to the amount provided under the legislation of the former state. If this suspension does not wipe out all entitlement, a supplement is paid to 'top up' the family benefits paid by the priority state.[128] However, this top-up need not be paid for children residing in another state when entitlement to family benefits in both states is based on residence only.[129]

Examples
Marie and her two children moved to the UK from Belgium four months ago when she separated from their father, Arnaud. Marie is looking for work, but has not found a job yet.

She claims child benefit and CTC. However, Arnaud, who is working in Belgium, is still receiving the Belgian family benefit and sending this money to Marie for the children. The Belgian family benefit is payable on the basis of employment and, therefore, has priority over the UK family benefits, since the latter are based on residence. If the UK family benefits are more than the Belgian family benefits, Marie should be paid the difference to top up the Belgian family benefits.

Alicia moved to the UK from Slovakia to take up a job, but was made redundant after four months. Her husband and their two children stayed in Slovakia. Alicia's husband receives Slovakian family benefits, which are payable on the basis of residence. Alicia claims child benefit and CTC. Since these are also payable on the basis of residence, Slovakia has priority since the children live there. The UK does not need to pay a top-up, even though its family benefits are more generous than the Slovakian ones.

Note: if entitlement to a family benefit in one state depends on a claim having been made and no claim has been made, entitlement to the family benefit that has been claimed in another state cannot be suspended.[130] It is therefore not necessary to consider whether family benefits in another member state have priority or are payable at a higher rate if a claim is required for entitlement but no claim has been made.

If family benefits are paid to someone who is not using them to maintain the family member, the member state paying the benefit can make payments to the person who is, in fact, maintaining the family member. This is done at the request of, and through, the relevant institution in the state where the person who is maintaining the family member lives.[131]

There are rules that cover the administration of claims for family benefits where more than one state could potentially be involved.[132] If a claim is submitted to the relevant institution in a state whose legislation is applicable but which does not have priority under the rules above, it should be forwarded to the relevant institution in the state with priority without delay. The date of claim is the date it was made to the first state.[133] If there is a difference of view between the states about which has priority, provisional payments must be made by the state in which the child resides (or where the benefit was first claimed if the child does not reside in any of the relevant states).[134]

HMRC guidance for decision makers covers the operation of these priority rules, provision for topping up family benefits paid by another state that has priority and the administrative procedures.[135]

Notes

2. Who is covered

1 *Petit v Office National de Pensions*, C-153/91 [1992] ECR I-04973
2 Art 2 EU Reg 883/04
3 Art 1(g) EU Reg 1408/71
4 *Ministre de l'Économie et des Finances v Ruyter*, C-623/13 [2015] ECR, not yet reported
5 Art 1(l) EU Reg 883/04
6 Art 3 EU Reg 883/04
7 Art 2 EU Reg 883/04
8 Arts 1(i) and 2 EU Reg 883/04
9 *KT v HMRC (CB)* [2013] UKUT 151 (AAC)
10 *PB v SSWP (DLA)* [2016] UKUT 280 (AAC), paras 8-10
11 EU Reg 883/04
12 EU Reg 1408/71
13 Art 87(8) EU Reg 883/04; Recital (2), Decision H1 of 12 June 2009 of the Administrative Commission for the Co-ordination of Social Security Systems [2010] OJ C-106/13; *SSWP v PW (CA)* [2013] UKUT 296 (AAC)
14 *KG v SSWP (DLA)* [2015] UKUT 146 (AAC)
15 Art 87(8) EU Reg 883/04
16 For example, *SL v SSWP (DLA)* [2014] UKUT 108 (AAC)
17 Art 1 EU Reg 859/2003
18 Recital 18 EU Reg 1231/2010
19 *Petit v Office National de Pensions*, C-153/91 [1992] ECR I-04973
20 The UK's attempt to challenge this extension of the current co-ordination rules failed in relation to:
Switzerland: *UK v Council of the European Union*, C-656/11 [2014], not yet reported;
Iceland, Liechtenstein and Norway: *UK v Council of the European Union*, C-431/11 [2013], not yet reported

3. Which benefits are covered

21 Art 9 EU Reg 883/04
22 Art 3 EU Reg 883/04
23 *Commission of the European Communities v European Parliament and Council of the European Union*, C-299/05 [2007] ECR I-08695
24 *SSWP v Tolley* [2015] UKSC 55. This case relates to the old co-ordination rules.
25 *Bartlett and Others v SSWP*, C-537/09 [2011] ECR I-03417
26 *Stewart v SSWP*, C-503/09 [2011] ECR I-06497
27 para 070153 DMG
28 *Caisse nationale des prestations familiales v Hiddal and Bernard*, C-216/12 and C-217/12 held that a parental leave allowance was a family benefit under EU Reg 1408/71.
29 SSAC, *Universal Credit and Related Regulations Report and Government Response*, December 2012
30 Art 70(1) and (2) and Annex X EU Reg 883/04
31 Annex X EU Reg 883/04
32 Ch C2, para C2097 ADM
33 Art 70 EU Reg 883/04
34 Art 3(3) EU Reg 883/04; *Dano v Jobcenter Leipzig*, C-333/13 [2014] ECR, not yet reported, paras 46-55
35 SSAC, *Universal Credit and Related Regulations Report and Government Response*, December 2012
36 CH/1400/2006, paras 37-40
37 *MR v HMRC (TC)* [2011] UKUT 40 (AAC), para 17

4. Principles of co-ordination

38 Art 11 EU Reg 883/04
39 Art 1(s) EU Reg 883/04
40 Art 1(q) EU Reg 883/04
41 Art 11 EU Reg 883/04
42 Art 11(3)(e) EU Reg 883/04
43 Art 11(2) EU Reg 883/04
44 Art 13 EU Reg 883/04
45 Art 12 EU Reg 883/04
46 *AR v HMRC (CHB)* [2014] UKUT 553 (AAC); *HB v HMRC (CHB)* [2014] UKUT 554 (AAC), paras 37-39
47 Arts 67, 68 and 81 EU Reg 883/04; Arts 2 and 60 EU Reg 987/2009; *SSWP v AK (AA)* [2015] UKUT 110 (AAC)
48 Art 1(j) EU Reg 883/04
49 Art 11 EU Reg 987/2009
50 Arts 11-16 EU Reg 883/04
51 Art 16(2) EU Reg 883/04
52 Title III EU Reg 883/04

53 See for example, *Kuusijärvi v Riksförsäkringsverket*, C-275/96 [1998] ECR I-03419; *AR v HMRC (CHB)* [2014] UKUT 553 (AAC); *HB v HMRC (CHB)* [2014] UKUT 554 (AAC)

54 *SSWP v Tolley* [2015] UKSC 55

55 See for example, *Kuusijärvi v Riksförsäkringsverket*, C-275/96 [1998] ECR I-03419; *AR v HMRC (CHB)* [2014] UKUT 553 (AAC); *HB v HMRC (CHB)* [2014] UKUT 554 (AAC)

56 *AR v HMRC(CHB)* [2014] UKUT 553 (AAC);*HB v HMRC (CHB)* [2014] UKUT 554 (AAC), paras 37-39

57 **AA** s65(7) SSCBA 1992
DLA s72(7B) SSCBA 1992
PIP s84 WRA 2012
CA s70(4A) SSCBA 1992

58 *SSWP v AH* [2016] UKUT 148 (AAC)

59 Art 29 EU Reg 883/04

60 DMG Memo 26/15; ADM Memo 20/15

61 Art 1(w) EU Reg 883/04

62 *JS v SSWP (DLA)* [2012] AACR 7, para 14; *KS v SSWP (DLA)* [2014] UKUT 19 (AAC), para 81; both in relation to EU Reg 1408/71

63 *Perry v Chief Adjudication Officer* [1998]; *EC v SSWP (SPC)* [2010] UKUT 95 (AAC), para 40

64 *IG v SSWP* [2016] UKUT 176 (AAC), para 25

65 *Skalka v Sozialversicherungsanstalt der Gewerblichen Wirtschaft*, C-160/02 [2004] ECR I-5613; *Naranjo v CRAM Nord-Picardie*, C-265/05 [2007] ECR I-347

66 Art 1(i) and (ii), (2) and (3) EU Reg 883/04

67 Art 32(1) EU Reg 883/04

68 Art 25 EU Reg 883/04; *SSWP v AK (AA)* [2015] UKUT 110 (AAC), reported as [2015] AACR 27

69 Art 23 EU Reg 883/04; *SSWP v HR (AA)* [2013] UKUT 66 (AAC); *SL v SSWP (DLA)* [2014] UKUT 108 (AAC)

70 Arts 24(2)(b) and 25 EU Reg 883/04; *Helder and Farrington v College voor Zorgverzekeringen*, C-321/12 [2013] ECR, not yet reported

71 Art 26 EU Reg 883/04

72 Art 31 EU Reg 883/04

73 DMG Memo 26/15, note to para 22; ADM Memo 20/15, note to para 22

74 Art 32(1) EU Reg 883/04

75 *Stewart v SSWP*, C-503/09 [2011] ECR I-06497, especially paras 53-54

76 *SSWP v Tolley* [2015] UKSC 55. This case relates to the old co-ordination rules.

77 *SSWP v AK (AA)* [2015] UKUT 110 (AAC), paras 9-10

78 *INASTI v Hervein and Others*, C-393/99 and C-394/99 [2002] ECR I-02829, para 51; *Leyman v INAMI*, C-3/08 [2009] ECR I-09085, para 45

79 *SSWP v AK (AA)* [2015] UKUT 110 (AAC), paras 11-12

80 *IG v SSWP* [2016] UKUT 176 (AAC), paras 11-12

81 *IG v SSWP* [2016] UKUT 176 (AAC), paras 32 and 40-42 and caselaw cited

82 *Hudzinski and Wawrzyniak v Agentur für Arbeit Wesel – Familienkasse*, joined cases C-611/10 and C-612/10 [2012]

83 *IG v SSWP* [2016] UKUT 176 (AAC), para 32 and caselaw cited

84 Art 81 EU Reg 883/2004; Art 2 EU Reg 987/2009; *SSWP v AK (AA)* [2015] UKUT 110 (AAC), reported as [2015] AACR 27

85 Art 6(2) EU Reg 987/2009; *SSWP v HR (AA)* [2014] UKUT 571 (AAC), reported as [2015] AACR 26

86 *SSWP v AK (AA)* [2015] UKUT 110 (AAC), reported as [2015] AACR 27, paras 29-30

87 *SSWP v HR (AA)* [2014] UKUT 571 (AAC), reported as [2015] AACR 26, paras 16-19

88 *SSWP v FF* [2015] UKUT 488 (AAC)

89 *Feliccia v SSWP*, C3/2016/358

90 Art 6(3) EU Reg 987/2009

91 Arts 6(4)-(5) and 73 EU Reg 987/2009

92 DMG Memo 27/15; ADM Memo 21/15

93 DMG Memo 27/15, note to para 4; ADM Memo 21/15, note to para 4

94 *SSWP v HR (AA)* [2014] UKUT 571 (AAC), reported as [2015] AACR 26, para 18

95 Art 6(1) EU Reg 987/2009

96 Art 4 EU Reg 883/04

97 Art 18 TFEU; Art 24 EU Dir 2004/38; Art 7 EU Reg 492/2011

98 *Patmalniece v SSWP* [2011] UKSC 11

99 *European Commission v UK*, C-308/14 [2016] ECR, not yet reported

100 *Commissioners for HMRC v Aiga Spiridonova*, 13/115948

101 Art 5 EU Reg 883/04

102 Recital 11 EU Reg 883/04

103 Recital 10 EU Reg 883/04

104 Art 6 EU Reg 883/04; see also Annex XI UK entry, para 2, and Art 48 TFEU

105 Art 12 EU Reg 987/09; see *PB v SSWP (DLA)* [2016] UKUT 280 (AAC), para 10, second ground of appeal

106 Art 6 EU Reg 883/04; *Decision H6 of 16
    December 2010 of the Administrative
    Commission for the Co-ordination of Social
    Security Systems* [2011] OJ C-45/04
107 Art 61 EU Reg 883/04
108 Arts 61(2) and 65(2) and (5)(a) EU Reg
    883/04
109 Art 7 EU Reg 883/04
110 Arts 5, 46 and 82 EU Reg 883/04; Arts
    27, 46, 49 and 87 EU Reg 987/2009
111 Art 70 EU Reg 883/04
112 Art 10 EU Reg 883/04
113 *Teresa and Silvana Petroni v Office
    National des Pensions Pour Travailleurs
    Salariés (ONPTS), Bruxelles* 24-75 [1975]
    ECR 01149
114 Art 68 EU Reg 883/04
115 Arts 53-55 EU Reg 883/04
116 Art 67 EU Reg 883/04; *HB v HMRC (CHB)*
    [2014] UKUT 554 (AAC)
117 Art 67 EU Reg 883/04; *HMRC v Ruas*
    [2010] EWCA Civ 291
118 Art 67 EU Reg 883/04; *HMRC v Ruas*
    [2010] EWCA Civ 291
119 Art 67 EU Reg 883/04, second
    sentence; *Würker v Familienkasse
    Nurnberg*, C-32/13 [2014], not yet
    reported
120 Art 1(w) EU Reg 883/04
121 para 2815 TCTM; para 10203 CBTM
122 *BM v HMRC* [2015] UKUT 526 (AAC)
123 http://ec.europa.eu/social
124 Art 68(1)(a) EU Reg 883/04
125 *Decision F1 of 12 June 2009 of the
    Administrative Commission for the Co-
    ordination of Social Security Systems*
    [2010] OJ C-106/04
126 Art 68(1)(b) EU Reg 883/04
127 See also Art 58 EU Reg 987/2009
128 Art 68(2) EU Reg 883/04; see, for
    example, *Slanina v Unabhängiger
    Finanzsenat, Außenstelle Wien*, C-363/08
    [2009] ECR I-11111
129 Art 68(2) EU Reg 883/04
130 *Gudrun Schwemmer v Agentur für Arbeit
    Villingen-Schwenningen – Familienkasse*,
    C-16/09 [2010] ECR I-09717;
    *Bundesagentur für Arbeit – Familienkasse
    Sachsen v Trapkowski*, C-378/14 [2015],
    not yet reported
131 Art 68a EU Reg 883/04
132 Art 68(3) EU Reg 883/04; Arts 6 and 58-
    61 EU Reg 987/2009
133 Art 68(3) EU Reg 883/04; Art 60(2) and
    (3) EU Reg 987/2009
134 Arts 6(2) and 60(4) EU Reg 987/2009
135 paras 10204-13 CBTM; paras 2815-75
    TCTM

Chapter 17

International agreements

This chapter covers:
1. Reciprocal agreements (below)
2. Council of Europe conventions and agreements (p299)
3. European Union co-operation and association agreements (p300)

The rules in this chapter may help you to obtain benefits in the UK, or to export benefits to certain countries. However, if you are moving within the European Economic Area, the European Union co-ordination rules may be more generous. See Chapter 16 for whether these apply to you.

1. Reciprocal agreements

A reciprocal agreement is a bilateral agreement made between the UK and another country. Reciprocal agreements are part of UK law and their purpose is to protect your entitlement to benefits if you move from one country that is a party to an agreement to the other.[1] A reciprocal agreement can help you qualify for certain benefits by allowing periods of residence and contributions paid in each of the two countries to be added together (this is similar to the aggregation principle in the European Union (EU) co-ordination rules – see p281). It can also mean that you are paid more generously when you go abroad than you would be under the UK rules. Furthermore, they often specify that you must receive equal treatment with nationals of the country to which you have moved.

In general, a reciprocal agreement only applies if the EU co-ordination rules do not assist you (see p293). They are therefore of most relevance for non-European Economic Area countries, but they can also assist if you are moving to or from Northern Ireland, the Channel Islands or the Isle of Man.

The scope of the reciprocal agreements differs greatly, not only in terms of the benefits covered and the provisions made, but also in respect of the people covered. It is therefore crucial to check the individual agreement. You can find the agreements in the *Law Related to Social Security* at http://lawvolumes.dwp.gov.uk – go to the 'List of Statutory Instruments' and search under the relevant country to find the number and year of the statutory instrument. However, although this site is more helpful as it is specific to social security, it has not been updated since October 2015, so for amendments since then you also need to check www.legislation.gov.uk.

This section provides an outline of the benefits covered and the general principles relating to the agreements. A list of all the countries and the benefits covered is in Appendix 5.

Note: the following benefits are *not* covered by any of the agreements:

- housing benefit;
- income support;
- income-based jobseeker's allowance (JSA);
- employment and support allowance (ESA) – but see below ;
- pension credit;
- personal independence payment (PIP) – but see below;
- social fund payments;
- universal credit;
- child tax credit;
- working tax credit.

Note: although amendments have been made enabling reciprocal agreements to be extended to ESA and PIP,[2] in general the necessary amendments to the individual agreements have not been made, except:

- from 6 April 2016, the agreement with Northern Ireland covers both ESA and PIP (see p293); *and*
- if your award of contributory ESA was converted from incapacity benefit (IB), it is covered by each of the agreements (with the exception of the Isle of Man, Israel and Switzerland) that cover IB (see Appendix 5).[3]

It may be arguable that the agreement with the states of former Yugoslavia (Bosnia-Herzegovina, Kosovo, Macedonia, Montenegro and Serbia) does not need to be amended to cover ESA and PIP. This is because it contains provision for cover to be extended to amendments, supplements and consolidations of listed legislation, provided the contracting parties agree.[4]

Agreements with non-European Economic Area countries

The UK has reciprocal agreements with some countries outside the European Economic Area (EEA).

Each reciprocal agreement is different in terms of who is covered, which benefits are included and what arrangements are provided.

For a full list of the countries and the benefits covered, see Appendix 5.

Agreements with Northern Ireland, the Channel Islands, the Isle of Man and Gibraltar

The rules relating to most social security and tax credits apply only to Great Britain – ie, England, Wales and Scotland. This does not include Northern Ireland, the Channel Islands, the Isle of Man or Gibraltar, which have their own social security legislation. There are reciprocal agreements between all of these to ensure you do not lose out if you move between them. However, not all benefits and circumstances are covered, so it is essential that you check the provisions of the relevant agreement.

For further information on the Isle of Man and the new state pension, see p297.

New, replacement, reciprocal arrangements between Northern Ireland and Great Britain came into force on 6 April 2016.[5] These mirror, but also update and extend, the previous arrangements, and continue to co-ordinate the social security systems with the aim of creating, in effect, a single system of social security throughout the UK. The purpose of the arrangements is to ensure that when moving between the two territories you are entitled to the same rights and benefits paid at the same rates, and that you do not need to return to the previous territory if you appeal a decision made there.[6] Although some benefits are still not covered (most means-tested benefits, tax credits and all statutory payments), the new arrangements have been extended to include ESA (both contributory and income-related), PIP and the new state pension.

Note: before these new arrangements came into force, the DWP policy on ESA was to make extra-statutory payments to make up any loss of ESA that resulted from having to make a new claim when moving from Northern Ireland to Great Britain or vice versa (see p296).[7]

Gibraltar is a British overseas territory and the only one which is part of the EU. For social security purposes, it is treated as part of the UK in relation to other EU members under the EU co-ordination rules. However, the reciprocal agreement between Gibraltar and Great Britain provides that, except for family benefits, you are treated as having the same rights under the EU co-ordination rules as you would have if the UK and Gibraltar were separate member states.[8]

Agreements with European Economic Area states

The UK has reciprocal agreements with most, but not all, of the EEA member states. For a list of the states with which the UK has social security agreements and the benefits covered by each, see Appendix 5.

In general, reciprocal agreements can be relied on by EEA nationals if the EU co-ordination rules (see Chapter 16) do not apply.[9] This means, in most cases, you cannot qualify for benefits using a reciprocal agreement if you:

- come within the 'personal scope' of the co-ordination rules (see p264);[10] *and*

• acquired your right to benefit on, or after, the date the EU co-ordination provisions applied.[11]

However, reciprocal agreements between EEA states can continue to apply if either:
• you are not covered by the co-ordination rules;[12] *or*
• you are covered by the co-ordination rules, but:
  – the provisions of an agreement are more beneficial to you than the EU co-ordination provisions; *and*
  – your right to benefit from the reciprocal agreement was acquired (eg, because you moved between the relevant member states) before the EU co-ordination provisions applied.[13]

Note: the UK's agreement with Denmark applies in both the Faroes and Greenland, as they are not part of the EU/EEA. Greenland left the EU on 1 February 1985.

People covered by the agreements

Some of the reciprocal agreements cover nationals of the contracting countries, while others apply to 'people going from one member state to another'. This may be particularly significant if you are a non-EEA national who has worked in two or more EEA states but you cannot benefit under the co-ordination rules (see p264). Of the member states that now comprise the EEA (see p40), the agreements with Belgium, Denmark, France, Italy and Luxembourg are confined to nationals only.[14] The convention with the Netherlands covers those who have been subject to the legislation of one or both member states and their family members and survivors.[15]

The reciprocal agreements define who is counted as a national for the purpose of the agreement, where nationality is an issue. In all of these, a UK national is defined as a 'citizen of the United Kingdom and Colonies'.[16]

This category of people disappeared on 1 January 1983 when the British Nationality Act 1981 came into force. On this date, if you previously had citizenship of the UK and Colonies, you might have become:
• a British citizen;
• a British overseas territories citizen (subsequently renamed British dependent territories citizen); *or*
• a British overseas citizen.

You might also have become one of the above after 1 January 1983, including if you were born after this date. The rules on this are beyond the scope of this *Handbook*.

For the purpose of the UK social security 'nationals only' conventions with Belgium, Denmark, France, Italy and Luxembourg, a UK national now includes anyone in one of the categories above.

See p15 for further details of British nationality.

The definition of nationality contained in the agreements with Denmark, Italy and Luxembourg is simply that of a 'Danish' or 'Italian' or 'Luxemburger' national.[17] These agreements confer no rights if you are not a national of one of these states. The agreement with Belgium, however, covers a 'person having Belgian nationality or a native of the Belgian Congo or Ruanda-Urundi'. The agreement with France refers to 'a person having French nationality' and 'any French-protected person belonging to French Togoland or the French Cameroons'.

When these agreements came into force in 1958, the Belgian Congo and Ruanda-Urundi and French Togoland and the French Cameroons were Belgian and French territories respectively. Which Belgian and French nationals are covered by the agreements is a matter for the Belgian and French authorities. If you come from one of these countries (present-day Democratic Republic of Congo, Rwanda, Burundi, Togolese Republic and the Republic of Cameroon), check with the Belgian or French authorities whether you are covered by these agreements.

The agreements give equal treatment to nationals of the contracting countries, stating that a 'national of one contracting party shall be entitled to receive the benefits of the legislation of the other contracting party under the same conditions as if he were a national of the latter contracting party'.[18]

The agreements with Finland, Iceland, Ireland, Portugal, Spain and Sweden are not confined to nationals but give rights to:

- 'people who go from one country to another' (Ireland);
- 'a person subject to the legislation of one contracting party who becomes resident in the territory of the other party' (Portugal);
- 'a national of one contracting party, or a person subject to the legislation of that party, who becomes resident in the territory of the other contracting party' (Spain);
- 'a national of the state and person deriving their rights from such nationals and other people who are, or have been, covered by the legislation of either of the states and people deriving their rights from such a person' (Sweden).

The agreements with Austria and Norway have nationality restrictions that apply to the protocol on benefits in kind (eg, medical treatment), but not to social security contributions and benefits. A national of the UK is defined as anyone who is recognised by the UK government as a UK national, provided s/he is 'ordinarily resident' in the UK.

The agreement with Germany is not restricted to nationals of either agreement member state insofar as social security benefits are concerned. However, a nationality provision applies to the Articles relating to contribution liability.

Even if you are not a national of one of the contracting parties to these agreements, you may still be able to benefit from their provisions.

Benefits covered by the agreements

The following benefits are covered by some of the reciprocal agreements. See Appendix 5 for a full list of which benefits apply to which countries.

Unemployment benefits

The relevant benefit in the UK is contribution-based JSA.

None of the agreements allow you to receive unemployment benefits outside the country in which you have paid your national insurance (NI) contributions. However, some allow NI paid in one country to count towards satisfying the conditions of entitlement in another. This is the case with the UK agreements with Austria, Canada, Cyprus, Finland, Iceland, Isle of Man, Jersey, Guernsey, Malta, New Zealand and Norway, as well as the agreements between Great Britain and Northern Ireland.

Sickness and invalidity benefits

In the UK, the relevant sickness benefit was short-term incapacity benefit (IB) and the relevant invalidity benefit was long-term IB. However, in 2008 IB was abolished for new claims and replaced by ESA, with existing IB claimants being reassessed for possible conversion to ESA. There are now very few remaining claimants of long-term IB, but if you still receive this the agreements continue to apply.

Although amendments have been made to enable reciprocal agreements to be extended to ESA,[19] in general, the necessary amendments to the individual agreements have not been made.[20] There are two exceptions: the reciprocal agreements cover:

- contributory ESA if your award was converted from IB. In such cases, your ESA is covered by each of the agreements (with the exception of the Isle of Man, Israel and Switzerland) that cover invalidity benefits (see Appendix 5);[21]
- both contributory and income-related ESA under the agreement between Great Britain and Northern Ireland (see below).

It may be arguable that the agreement with the states of former Yugoslavia (Bosnia-Herzegovina, Kosovo, Macedonia, Montenegro and Serbia) does not need to be amended in order to cover ESA. This is because it contains provision for the agreement to be extended to amendments, supplements and consolidations of listed legislation, provided the contracting parties agree.[22]

The reciprocal arrangements between Northern Ireland and Great Britain were updated and extended to cover both contributory and income-related ESA on 6 April 2016. The DWP policy before this date was to make extra-statutory payments to cover any loss of ESA that resulted from having to make a new claim when moving from Northern Ireland to Great Britain or vice versa.[23] For further information see p293.

The agreements in relation to 'sickness' or 'invalidity' benefits vary. For example, some enable you to be paid in another country, and some enable contributions paid under one country's scheme to be taken into account to help you satisfy the conditions of entitlement in another. The agreements with Austria, Cyprus, Iceland, Norway and Sweden allow you to continue to receive your invalidity benefit in these countries, subject to medical checks being undertaken in the agreement country. Similarly, you can receive the other country's invalidity benefits in the UK. The agreement with Barbados allows a certificate of permanent incapacity to be issued, permitting you to receive your 'invalidity benefit' without medical checks.

Maternity benefits

In the UK, the relevant maternity benefit is maternity allowance (MA).

If you are entitled to maternity benefits, some of the agreements allow you to receive your benefit in another country. You may be entitled to MA, or continue to be paid MA, when absent from the UK, under the reciprocal agreements with: Barbados, Cyprus, the Isle of Man, Jersey and Guernsey, Switzerland, Turkey and the countries of the former Republic of Yugoslavia (Bosnia-Herzegovina, Croatia, Kosovo, Macedonia, Montenegro, Serbia and Slovenia), and when you have moved from Great Britain to Northern Ireland or vice versa. The circumstances under which you may be able to claim or retain MA differ from agreement to agreement.

Benefits for industrial injuries

The relevant benefits in the UK are industrial injuries disablement benefit (including any constant attendance allowance or exceptionally severe disablement allowance), reduced earnings allowance and retirement allowance.

Most of the agreements include industrial injuries benefits. The arrangements determine which country's legislation applies to new accidents or diseases, depending on where you are insured at the time. Many of the agreements allow you to combine industrial injuries incurred in each country when assessing the degree of your latest injury. Furthermore, if you work in one country and remain insured under the other country's scheme and you have an industrial injury, you can be treated as though the injury arose in the country in which you are insured. Most agreements include arrangements to allow you to receive all three of the UK benefits for industrial injuries indefinitely in the other country.

Retirement pensions and bereavement benefits

All the agreements include retirement pensions and bereavement benefits. In the UK, the relevant benefits are retirement pensions, bereavement allowance and widowed parent's allowance. All the agreements have been amended to include the new state pension from 6 April 2016.[24]

There is a new reciprocal agreement between the Isle of Man and the UK covering arrangements for all retirement pensions.[25] The new state pension does not apply in the Isle of Man, so if you reach retirement age on or after 6 April 2016 and have worked in both the UK and the Isle of Man, you must make two claims under the two different systems.[26]

The provisions of the reciprocal agreements vary. In most cases, the agreements can enable you to receive a retirement pension or bereavement benefit in the agreement country at the same rate as you would be paid in the country where you are insured. This is, however, not the case under the agreements with Canada, New Zealand and (for those still covered by the agreement revoked on 1 March 2001, subject to limited savings provisions[27]) Australia, as they do not permit these benefits to be uprated. If you go to live in one of these countries, your retirement pension (and any other long-term benefit) is 'frozen' at the rate payable either when you left the UK or when you became entitled to your pension abroad.

The agreements with Canada, New Zealand and (for those still covered by the agreement revoked on 1 March 2001, subject to limited savings provisions[28]) Australia, allow you to be treated as having paid NI contributions in the UK during periods when you were resident in that country. From 1 April 2015, periods of habitual residence in another EEA member state or Switzerland count as period of residence in the UK if you:[29]

- are an EEA national (see p40);
- are covered by the EU co-ordination rules (see p264); *and*
- have a 'genuine and sufficient link to the UK social security system' (see p210).

The agreement with Chile is limited and relates to the continuing liability to pay NI contributions to your home country if you go to work in the other country for a period of up to five years.[30]

If you do not qualify for a retirement pension or bereavement benefit from either the UK or the other country, or you qualify for a pension or bereavement benefit from one country but not the other, the agreements with the following countries allow you to be paid basic old age and bereavement benefits on a pro rata basis, with your insurance under both schemes taken into account: Austria, Barbados, Bermuda, Cyprus, Finland, Iceland, Israel, Jamaica, Malta, Mauritius, Norway, the Philippines, Sweden, Switzerland, Turkey, the USA and the countries of the former Republic of Yugoslavia (Bosnia-Herzegovina, Croatia, Kosovo,[31] Macedonia, Montenegro, Serbia and Slovenia).[32]

Family benefits

In the UK, the relevant family benefits are child benefit and guardian's allowance. The provisions concerning these two benefits enable periods of residence and/or presence in the other country to be treated as residence and/or presence in Great Britain. Arguably, these provisions could enable you to to use periods of residence in the other country to satisfy the requirement for child benefit to have been living in the UK for the past three months (see p92). The extent to which reciprocity exists varies, however, according to the particular agreement. For example, residence or contributions paid in Cyprus, Jamaica, Jersey/Guernsey, Isle of Man, Israel, Mauritius and Turkey count towards your satisfying UK residence conditions for guardian's allowance.

If you are a 'person subject to immigration control' (see p57) and you are covered by a reciprocal agreement for child benefit, your immigration status does not exclude you from entitlement to child benefit (see p70). In practice, this is most helpful if you are covered by the agreement with former Yugoslavia which applies to Bosnia-Herzegovina, Kosovo, Macedonia, Montenegro, and Serbia.[33] You must still meet the other conditions of entitlement, including the residence and presence requirements (see p207).

Dependants' benefits

In the UK, a dependant's benefit is an increase to the benefit covered by the agreement. Dependants' increases can be paid if the dependant is in either country to the agreement.

2. **Council of Europe conventions and agreements**

There are numerous European conventions and agreements. These are prepared and negotiated within the Council of Europe. The most well known is perhaps the European Convention on Human Rights. The purpose of these conventions is to address issues of common concern in economic, social, cultural, scientific, legal and administrative matters and in human rights. However, such agreements and conventions are not legally binding in the UK unless or until they are incorporated into UK law, or legislation is enacted to give specific effect to the Treaty obligations in question – eg, the UK Human Rights Act in respect of the European Convention on Human Rights. They are statements of intent of the individual countries that are signatories. The UK is a signatory to a number of these agreements, including two that are significant for social security.

The European Convention on Social and Medical Assistance

The European Convention on Social and Medical Assistance has been in force since 1954. It requires that ratifying states provide assistance in cash and in kind to nationals of other ratifying states, who are lawfully present in their territories and who are without sufficient resources on the same conditions as their own nationals. It also prevents ratifying states repatriating a lawfully present national of other ratifying states simply because s/he is in need of assistance.

All the European Economic Area (EEA) countries (see p40) plus Turkey have signed and ratified this agreement. The rights given are recognised in UK law. However, the European Union (EU) co-ordination rules are more generous than the Convention, so it would not normally need to be relied on by EEA nationals. They mainly assist you if you are a national of Turkey and are defined as a 'person subject to immigration control' (see p57), as the Convention exempts those covered from being excluded from means-tested benefits (see p66) and working tax credit (WTC) (see p71).

You can only benefit from the Convention if you are 'lawfully present' in the UK. If you are a national of Turkey, this means, in practice, you must be within a period in which you have leave to enter or remain in the UK.

Note: you still must satisfy the other conditions of entitlement including, for means-tested benefits, having a right to reside (see p115).[34] Consequently, although the House of Lords held that an asylum seeker with temporary admission is 'lawfully present' and so potentially able to benefit from the Convention,[35] this will rarely assist you, as temporary admission does not give you a right to reside.[36] However, if you are within a period of leave, you do have a right to reside (see p123).

The 1961 European Social Charter

This agreement is similar to the European Convention on Social and Medical Assistance. The ratifying states are all EEA countries (see p40), plus Macedonia and Turkey. The main relevance of this agreement for entitlement to benefits and tax credits is that if you are a national of Macedonia or Turkey and you are lawfully present, as with the Convention (see above), you are not excluded from means-tested benefits or WTC if you are a 'person subject to immigration control'.

It is only this 1961 Charter that gives access to UK social security benefits. If you are a national of a country that has signed a later charter only and are a 'person subject to immigration control', you are not exempt from being excluded from means-tested benefits and WTC.

3. **European Union co-operation and association agreements**

The Treaty on the Functioning of the European Union provides for agreements to be made with countries outside the European Union (EU).[37]

The EU co-operation and association agreements can be divided into those that include a rule on equal treatment and have quite a wide scope and those that do not include an equal treatment rule and whose scope is much narrower (see p301).

Agreements with equal treatment provisions

The agreements that most directly affect benefits in the UK are those with Algeria,[38] Morocco, San Marino, Tunisia and Turkey.[39]

All of these agreements contain provisions specifying that there must be equal treatment for those covered by the agreement in matters of 'social security'.

UK regulations specify that if you are defined as a 'person subject to immigration control' (see p57) but you are covered by one of these agreements (see below), you are exempt from the exclusion from certain non-contributory benefits (see p68) and tax credits (see p71) that would otherwise apply.

However, the EU agreements offer equal treatment to a wider range of benefits. The European Court of Justice (ECJ) found, in one case, the Turkish agreement and, in another, the Algerian agreement, to be inspired by the old EU co-ordination rules and that these rules should be looked to for guidance in interpreting the agreements. The ECJ held that the benefits covered by these agreements were those classed as 'social security benefits' under the co-ordination rules.[40] See p268 for a full list of these benefits.

Who is covered

To benefit from the agreements, you must be within their 'personal scope' – ie, you must be a national of Algeria, Israel, Morocco, Tunisia, San Marino or Turkey and you must be lawfully working in the UK.

Lawfully working
'**Lawfully working**' has been equated with being an 'insured person' under the EU co-ordination rules. In broad terms, this means that you must have been insured by paying, or being credited with, national insurance (NI) contributions.[41] It is likely that you will only be accepted as 'lawfully working' if your work does not breach any work restrictions attached to your leave or, if you are an asylum seeker, you have permission to work from the Home Office.

Other agreements: Israel

The EU also has various agreements with other countries. In general, these do not contain any provisions on the co-ordination of social security schemes, with the exception of the agreement with Israel.[42] This agreement is narrower in scope than those containing an agreement on equal treatment in matters of social security.

The agreement with Israel covers nationals of the EEA and Israel who are legally working in the EEA (for Israelis) or Israel (for EEA nationals) and members of their family who are legally resident.

The agreement covers benefits designed to protect against the risks of old age, invalidity and accidents at work, benefits for survivors and family benefits. The

EU co-ordination rules, which should be used as an aid to interpret this agreement, also cover these, and other, risks (see p268).

However, the agreement does not go as far as either the EU co-ordination rules or the agreements that contain an equal treatment provision (see p280). Rather, it provides that:

- for Israelis, all periods of residence, insurance and employment fulfilled by a person covered by the agreement in different EEA states are totalled for the purpose of working out entitlement to the benefits covered;
- the benefits covered (except non-contributory benefits) can be exported to (for Israelis) Israel or (for EEA nationals) from Israel to the EEA.

Note: Israel also has a reciprocal agreement with the UK.[43] See Appendix 5 for the benefits covered.

Notes

1. Reciprocal agreements

1 s179 SSAA1992
2 s179(3),(4) and (5) SSAA 1992
3 SS(RA)O
4 Art 2 FANIII(Y)O
5 SS(NIRA) Regs; SS(GBRA)NI Regs
6 Explanatory memorandum to SS(NIRA) Regs, para 4.2
7 DWP guidance, 'Extra-statutory Payments for Claimants Moving From Northern Ireland to Great Britain', available at www.cpag.org.uk/content/dwp-guidance-extra-statutory-payments-esa
8 Sch para 2 The Family Allowances, National Insurance and Industrial Injuries (Gibraltar) Order 1974, No.555; see also *SSWP v Garland* [2014] EWCA Civ 1550, para 33
9 Art 8 EU Reg 883/04
10 Art 2 EU Reg 883/04
11 *Walder v Bestuur de Sociale Verzekeringsbank*, C-82/72 [1973] 599; *Jean-Louis Thévenon and Stadt Speyer-Sozialamt v Landesversicherungsanstalt Rheinland-Pfalz*, C-475/93 [1995] ECR I-03813; *Balazs v Casa Judeteana de Pensii Cluj*, C-401/13 [2015] ECR, not yet reported
12 Art 2 EU Reg 1408/71; Art 2 EU Reg 883/04; *Galinsky v Insurance Officer*, C-99/80 [1981] 503; R(P) 1/81
13 *Rönfeldt v Bundesversicherungsanstalt für Angestellte*, C-227/89 [1991] ECR I-323; *Jean-Louis Thévenon and Stadt Speyer-Sozialamt v Landesversicherungsanstalt Rheinland-Pfalz*, C-475/93 [1995]; *Edmund Thelen v Bundesansalt fur Arbeit*, C-75/99 [2000] ECR I-9399
14 Art 3 to each of the relevant reciprocal agreements
15 Art 2 Social Security (Netherlands) Order 2007, No.631
16 Art 1 to each of the relevant reciprocal agreements
17 Art 1 to each of the relevant reciprocal agreements
18 Art 1 to each of the relevant reciprocal agreements

19 s179(3),(4) and (5) SSAA 1992
20 para 070312 DMG
21 SS(RA)O
22 Art 2 FANIII(Y)O
23 DWP guidance, 'Extra-statutory Payments for Claimants Moving From Northern Ireland to Great Britain', available at www.cpag.org.uk/content/dwp-guidance-extra-statutory-payments-esa
24 SS(NIRA) Regs
25 The Social Security (Reciprocal Agreement) (Isle of Man) Order 2016, No 157
26 para 17 DMG Memo 6/16
27 s299 Pensions Act 2004
28 s299 Pensions Act 2004
29 The Social Security (Application of Reciprocal Agreements with Australia, Canada and New Zealand) (EEA States and Switzerland) Regulations 2015, No.349
30 Convention on Social Security between the Government of the UK and the Government of the Republic of Chile, reproduced as Schedule to The Social Security (Contributions) (Republic of Chile) Order 2015, No.828
31 *AP v SSWP (RP)* [2011] UKUT 64 (AAC)
32 FANIII(Y)O
33 FANIII(Y)O

2. **Council of Europe conventions and agreements**
34 *Yesiloz v London Borough of Camden and DWP* [2009] EWCA Civ 415
35 *Szoma v SSWP* [2005] UKHL 64; [2006] 1 All ER 1, reported as R(IS) 2/06
36 R(IS) 3/08

3. **European Union co-operation and association agreements**
37 Art 217 TFEU
38 Euro-Mediterranean Agreement, establishing an Association between the European Community and its Member States, of the one part, and the People's Democratic Republic of Algeria, of the other part, 2005/690/EC, 1 September 2005
39 Decision No.3/80 of the Council of Association, set up under the EEC-Turkey Association Agreement (sometimes referred to as the 'Ankara Agreement')

40 *Sema Sürül v Bundesanstalt für Arbeit*, C-262/96 [1999] ECR I-02685; *Babahenini v Belgian State*, C-113/97 [1998] ECR I-00183; see also CFC/2613/1997
41 *Sema Sürül v Bundesanstalt für Arbeit*, C-262/96 [1999] ECR I-02685, in particular paras 85-86 and 93
42 Euro-Mediterranean Agreement establishing an Association between the European Communities and their Member State, of the one part, and the State of Israel, of the other part, 2000/384/EC, 20 November 1995. In force on 1 June 2000.
43 The National Insurance and Industrial Injuries (Israel) Order 1957, No.1879

Part 7

Claims and getting paid

Chapter 18

Delays

This chapter covers:
1. Dealing with delays (below)
2. Waiting for a decision on a claim (p308)
3. Delays when challenging a decision (p322)
4. Delays getting paid (p328)

1. Dealing with delays

All benefit authorities should act promptly to process your claim, to process any challenge you make to a decision and to issue payments due to you.

Although all benefit claimants can experience delays in the administration of their benefits and tax credits, you are more likely to experience delays if you are, or someone included in your claim is, a migrant.

If you experience a delay, in order to resolve the matter it can be helpful if you:
- can establish the reasons for the delay (see below);
- are clear at which stage the delay occurs (see p308).

The reasons for the delay

There can be many reasons for delays in benefit and tax credit administration. These are broadly due to the need for decision makers to have sufficient information, which can take time to collect, and the volume of work that decision makers have. This chapter focuses on the rules that are most relevant to migrants, but the cause of the delay in your case can also be due to reasons that apply to all benefit claimants.

If you or your family member have moved to or from the UK or are not British, a delay in the administration of your benefit or tax credit can be because of the following.
- The complexity of the rules on immigration status, residence and presence, and the effect of the European Union (EU) co-ordination rules. This complexity often means that all these decisions are made by specialist decision makers within a benefit authority, and these individuals or teams often have a backlog.

- The initial benefit or tax credit claim form may not ask for all the information that the decision maker needs to be clear about the effect of the rules on immigration status, residence, presence and EU co-ordination. The decision maker must therefore write to you or to other agencies requesting further information, and this takes extra time.
- You may have difficulties obtaining and providing evidence which the decision maker has requested – eg, evidence about your immigration status or residence rights. See Chapter 20 for more details on this and what you can do in this situation.
- If you are covered by the EU co-ordination rules, the benefit authorities may need to get information from benefit authorities in other European states and this can take a long time. See Chapter 16 for more information on the EU co-ordination rules.
- There may be a query about whether you need or have, or have applied for, a national insurance (NI) number. See Chapter 19 for more information on NI numbers.

When the delay occurs

What you can do to resolve a delay depends on the benefit you have claimed and also the stage at which the delay occurs. Delays can occur when you have:
- made a claim for benefit and are waiting for a decision on it (see below);
- had a decision on your entitlement and you have challenged that decision (see p322);
- had a decision on your entitlement and you are awaiting payment (see p328).

2. **Waiting for a decision on a claim**

If you have been waiting for a decision on your claim, what you can do depends on which benefit or tax credit you have claimed.

Are you waiting for a decision on your claim?

1. Check that your claim has been received. If it has not, if possible provide the benefit authority with a copy of the claim and/or any evidence that was previously submitted. If the benefit authority states that it has not received your claim and you have no copy, you must submit a new claim and may be able to ask for it to be backdated. See CPAG's *Welfare Benefits and Tax Credits Handbook* for details on the backdating rules for the different benefits and tax credits.

2. If your claim has been received, but not dealt with, you should ask why. See pp309–22 for your options.

3. If the decision maker is not making a decision on your claim because there is a test case pending, see p322.

4. When trying to resolve delays, it is helpful to show the history of your previous contact. Therefore, keep a copy of any letters you send or receive, and take the name and job title of anyone you speak to on the phone and note the date.

5. In all communication, give your national insurance (NI) number (if you have one).

Note: administrative policy guidance is sometimes issued to decision makers on the processes to be followed when determining claims from particular groups of migrants – eg, to fast track certain claims or accept certain standard pieces of evidence. It can be helpful to refer to this guidance to ensure that it is appropriately applied. For an example of such a policy on the habitual residence test, see p105. Although this guidance is often internal, if you contact organisations that work a lot with particular groups (such as recently arrived refugees), they may be able to give you details of current decision-making policies and practices.

Benefits administered by the DWP and HM Revenue and Customs

The rules about making decisions on claims for benefits and tax credits administered by the DWP or HM Revenue and Customs (HMRC) (ie, all benefits except housing benefit (HB) – see p319) do not state explicitly how long it should take to determine a claim and issue a decision.

However, the decision maker has a duty to decide claims for benefit,[1] which must be fulfilled within a reasonable time.[2]

If you think the decision maker has taken longer than a reasonable time in your case, the strength of your argument depends on:

- the volume of other claims waiting for consideration and the number of decision makers available to deal with them;[3]
- the facts of your individual case, including how long you have waited for a decision and the effect on you of your having to wait. For example, if you have no income while you wait for your claim to be decided, this is more serious for you than if the benefit, once awarded, would top up your existing income. Similarly, if you or a dependent family member has a health condition which is exacerbated by the lack of income, this may be relevant.

If there are specific reasons, such as the examples given above, which mean that the delay is making things particularly difficult for you or your family, you can suggest that it is not appropriate for your claim to be dealt with as part of a normal queuing system (whereby claims are determined in the order they are received). Tell the decision maker of any specific reasons why the delay is causing hardship for you.

If a delay continues, you could:

- request a short-term benefit advance (certain benefits only) (see p311);

- request an interim payment of child benefit and guardian's allowance (see p314);
- make a complaint in writing (see p315 and for HB, see p320);
- escalate a complaint to the Parliamentary Ombudsman (see p317);
- obtain legal advice about sending a 'letter before action' for judicial review (see p318);
- check whether you can get provisional payments if the delay is due to a dispute about which is the competent state to pay your benefit or tax credit under the European Union (EU) co-ordination rules (see p279).

You can pursue more than one of these options – eg, you can make a complaint and if this does not resolve the delay, obtain legal advice about sending a letter before action for judicial review.

Note: you cannot get an advance or interim payment of tax credits.

While waiting for your claim to be decided, you may be able to get help from your local welfare assistance scheme (see p443).

Is the delay due to the DWP determining whether you have a right to reside?

If the delay is due to the DWP determining whether you have a right to reside for the purpose of your claim for income support (IS), income-related employment and support allowance (ESA) or (for men aged between pension credit (PC) age and men's retirement age) PC and you have a right to reside as a jobseeker, you may want to claim income-based jobseeker's allowance (JSA). Your income-based JSA claim is likely to be determined more quickly, as it is easier to establish your right to reside as a jobseeker than other residence rights that satisfy the right to reside requirement for the other benefits (see p115). However, as the DWP computer system cannot have two claims open at once, in practice, you must request that you still want your IS (or the other benefit) claim determined, but that it should be done clerically and taken off the computer system to enable the JSA claim to be determined and put into payment. If the IS (or other benefit) is then awarded, it should be paid from the date you first claimed it. The decision to award JSA should then be revised, either because it was based on a mistake about your entitlement to IS (or other benefit) and the decision was more advantageous to you[4] or because you were awarded benefit (JSA) and then awarded another benefit (IS) for a period including the date the first benefit award (JSA) was made.[5] The IS (or other benefit) should then continue. Get advice if you experience difficulty with this.

Official targets

If there are published targets for the time in which a claim should be processed, it can be helpful to refer to these. HMRC states that it will handle all new claims and changes of circumstances for UK claimants within 22 days and international claimants within 92 days.[6]

The DWP does not currently publish target times. However, an indication of how long claims should take to be processed can be found in the DWP business plan. For example, 90 per cent of new JSA claims were processed within 10 days.[7]

If you are a non-UK claimant and are either covered by the co-ordination rules (see p264) or are a European Economic Area national exercising your rights as a 'worker' (see p140) in the UK, you may be able to argue (as part of a judicial review – see p318) that it is unlawful for HMRC to have a policy that aims to take substantially longer to deal with your claim than a UK claimant. The argument is that you should receive equal treatment and/or should not be deterred from exercising your right of free movement between member states as a worker.[8] For more information on equal treatment, see p280.

Short-term benefit advances

If your claim for a benefit administered by the DWP has not been decided, or payment of your benefit is delayed, you may be able to get an advance payment of your future benefit award. This is called a 'short-term benefit advance' and is intended to help you through a period of 'financial need' (see p312) before you receive your first (or increased) payment.

A short-term benefit advance can be paid if you have made a claim for benefit but it is impracticable for it to be determined, or the amount paid or increased, immediately. The power of the decision maker to make a short-term benefit advance is discretionary – ie, s/he does not have to give you a short-term benefit advance, but must take all the circumstances of your case into account when making her/his decision. Given the discretionary nature of the decision making, it can be particularly helpful to be aware of the DWP's guidance on short-term benefit advances. At the time of writing, this guidance was being updated. The guidance referred to in this section is the previous guidance. The new guidance will be available on 'Ask CPAG online'.[9]

Note: the decision maker should always determine your claim and pay any benefit due, if this is possible, before considering a short-term benefit advance.[10] Consequently, requesting a short-term benefit advance can be an effective way of getting your claim processed and put into payment.

The decision maker can only decide to make a short-term advance if:[11]
- you have made a claim for a benefit in respect of which you can be paid a short-term advance (see p312). The only exception to this requirement is if you are not required to make a claim for benefit in order to be entitled, which only applies in very limited circumstances; *and*
- you are in 'financial need' (see p312); *and*
- either:
  - your claim has not been determined, but it appears likely to the decision maker that you will be entitled to the benefit. **Note:** if there is no reason preventing the DWP from determining your claim, the decision maker should just determine the claim rather than consider a short-term benefit advance;[12] *or*

- your claim has been determined and you have been awarded benefit but:
  - you are waiting for your first payment; *or*
  - you have received your first payment, but it was for a shorter period than subsequent payments will be paid for and you are waiting for your next payment; *or*
  - you have had a change of circumstances that increases your entitlement, but your benefit has not yet been increased and paid to you; *or*
  - you are entitled to a payment but it is impracticable to pay all or some of it on the date on which it is due.

You cannot get short-term benefit advance if there is an appeal pending on the benefit in respect of which the advance would otherwise be paid.[13]

You can get a short-term benefit advance of any benefit *except*:[14]

- HB, although if your HB is delayed and you are a private or housing association tenant, you might be able to get a 'payment on account' (see p319);
- attendance allowance;
- disability living allowance;
- personal independence payment;
- child benefit or guardian's allowance, although you might be able to get an interim payment (see p314);
- statutory sick pay, statutory maternity pay, statutory adoption pay, statutory paternity pay or statutory shared parental pay;
- tax credits.

Financial need

'**Financial need**'means that because you have not received your benefit, there is a serious risk of damage to the health or safety of you or a member of your family.[15] Guidance lists examples of 'serious risk' including fleeing domestic violence and being without money for gas/electricity meters.[16]

'**Family**' means your partner and any children for whom you or your partner are responsible – ie, for whom you or your partner could claim child benefit.[17]

A short-term benefit advance is recovered by deductions from subsequent payments of your benefit. You must be notified of your liability to have the advance recovered by deductions, and to repay any amount not recovered in this way.[18] The DWP aims to recover your advance either in one lump sum from your next benefit payment or by taking deductions from your benefits over a period of up to 12 weeks. In exceptional circumstances, including if your personal allowance is reduced, you can request that the repayments be rescheduled to a maximum period of 24 weeks in total.[19] You can appeal against the decision about the repayment from subsequent payments of your benefit, including the rate of the deductions.[20]

There is no right of appeal against a refusal to award a short-term benefit advance.[21] The only legal remedy is judicial review (see p318). However, you can ask for a reconsideration during the telephone call in which you are told of the decision to refuse your request.[22] If possible, provide any additional information to support your application, and if you are aware that the decision was based on any incorrect information, correct this during the call. The decision maker should then reconsider your application based on the revised information. If you wait until after this telephone call, you will be asked to make a new request.[23]

You can also make a complaint to the DWP, including if you were prevented from making your request, and this can be effective in either obtaining a short-term benefit advance or in getting your claim processed.

You can contact your MP to see if s/he can help with either a complaint or to get the decision reconsidered.

If you have difficulty obtaining a short-term benefit advance, see below.

Note: you may be able to get help from your local welfare assistance scheme (see p443) as well as, or instead of, a short-term benefit advance. However, you should not be prevented from requesting a short-term benefit advance just because local welfare assistance is available.

How to apply

You can request a short-term benefit advance in person or writing (by post, fax or email) to your local jobcentre or by telephoning the Jobcentre Plus contact centre. Your application should set out why you meet the criteria. You should give the relevant history of your claim and confirm that you satisfy all the conditions of entitlement, including any areas where there may be a doubt – eg, provide the basis of your right to reside (see Chapter 12) or the reason why you are not a 'person subject to immigration control' (see Chapter 7). Finally, give the reasons why you are in financial need.

The DWP aims to phone you within three hours to tell you what happens next, and again by the next working day either with a decision or to request more information.[24] However, before considering your request, the DWP should always check whether it can simply determine your claim and issue you a payment and, if so, should telephone you to let you know.[25] If you do not have a phone, provide the DWP with the number of a friend or relative. If you cannot do that, the DWP will tell you to ring the benefit enquiry line after a certain time for an update on your request.[26]

Are you having problems getting a short-term advance?

1. Be aware of the DWP's guidance on short-term benefit advances and refer to it when helpful.
2. You may be told to seek help from your local welfare assistance scheme (see p443) or be referred to a foodbank (see p453) instead. If you consider that you meet the criteria for a short-term benefit advance, you should insist on your request being passed to the

decision maker to consider. Decisions on advances are discretionary and must be made by a decision maker, not frontline staff. Although short-term benefit advances were introduced in April 2013, there still appears to be some confusion among DWP staff about how the system operates.

3. The decision maker who considers your case may not be an expert on the benefit rules for migrants. This can be a problem because s/he can only make a short-term benefit advance if it appears to her/him that you are likely to be entitled to benefit. It may therefore assist your application if you set out clearly how you satisfy the relevant immigration, residence and presence conditions.

4. If the reason your claim cannot be processed is because you are waiting to obtain evidence showing that you satisfy all the conditions of entitlement, it may help to explain the cause of the delay, summarise any other evidence that you have already submitted and explain how it is consistent with the evidence you are waiting for to show that you are entitled to benefit. For more information on the evidence required for the immigration and residence tests, see Chapter 20.

5. The decision maker may suggest that you are not entitled to a short-term benefit advance because you do not have an NI number. If this happens, point out that the guidance issued to decision makers states that a short-term benefit advance should still be considered, provided you can prove your identity and are complying with other requests for required evidence. In addition, the DWP should ensure that all action necessary to allocate an NI number is taken promptly.[27] See Chapter 19 for further information on the NI requirement.

6. You may be refused a short-term benefit advance on the grounds that it cannot be repaid within 12 weeks from your ongoing benefit entitlement (eg, because you have other debts that are being recovered in this way) or because the amount of the advance, and therefore the repayments, will be large in relation to your ongoing entitlement. Although the regulations do not require you to be able repay the advance within any particular period, guidance states that the decision maker must consider whether you can repay the advance within 12 weeks (24 weeks if you are fleeing domestic violence).[28] The guidance also states that repayments can be rescheduled to spread them over a period of up to 24 weeks if there has been an exceptional change in your circumstances and you might otherwise be in hardship.[29] If you are unable to repay your advance within 12 weeks, refer to the domestic violence exception if this applies to you. If you are aware of a pending change in your circumstances which will improve your ability to repay, make sure the decision maker is aware of this.

Interim payments of child benefit and guardian's allowance

An interim payment of child benefit or guardian's allowance can be made if it appears to the HMRC that you may be entitled to benefit and:[30]

- you have not claimed correctly and it is impracticable for such a claim to be made immediately; or

- you have claimed correctly and all the conditions of entitlement are satisfied *except* the NI number requirement (see p335) and it is impracticable for that to be satisfied immediately; *or*
- you have claimed correctly, but it is impracticable for the claim to be dealt with immediately; *or*
- you have been awarded benefit, but it is impracticable to pay you immediately, other than by an interim payment.

Note:

- There is no right of appeal against a refusal to award you an interim payment. The only legal remedy is judicial review (see p318). You could contact your MP to see if s/he can help to get the decision reconsidered.
- An interim payment can be deducted from any later payment of the benefit and, if it is more than your actual entitlement, the overpayment can be recovered. You should be notified of this in advance.[31]
- An interim payment cannot be paid if you have an appeal pending.[32]

Making a complaint

Making a complaint when there is an ongoing problem (such as a claim that has not been decided) is different from making a complaint about a situation that you think should not have happened but which is no longer producing a problem – eg, if your claim has been decided, but you are unhappy it took so long. The information in this section is aimed at enabling you to use the complaints process in order to get the situation resolved (ie, to get a decision on your claim), rather than at seeking compensation or highlighting to the DWP/HMRC the hardship it has caused after a delay has been resolved.

When you make a complaint to try to resolve an ongoing delay, it is very important that you highlight in the complaint that the problem persists, that this is therefore an urgent matter and what you want to be done about it – eg, ask for your claim to be determined within X number of days.

The DWP and HMRC have different procedures for complaining.

Complaints about the DWP

If you want to complain about how a particular DWP agency has dealt with your case, you should first contact the office that is dealing with your claim. If you are unsure which office this is, contact numbers and information about the complaints procedure are provided on the DWP website.[33] You can also make a complaint about JSA or universal credit (UC) online via the DWP website.

You should receive a response to your complaint within 15 working days.

If you are still dissatisfied, your complaint is passed to a complaints resolution manager. This is referred to as a 'tier one' complaint. S/he should contact you, usually by phone, to discuss your complaint. It should be dealt with, or you should be told when it will be dealt with, within 15 working days.

If you remain dissatisfied, you can ask for your complaint to be passed to a more senior DWP officer. The DWP refers to this as a 'tier two' complaint. All 'tier two' complaints should receive a written response, or you should be be told when you can expect a response, within 15 days. If you are still not satisfied, you can complain to the Independent Case Examiner (ICE), and you may also have grounds to make a complaint to the Ombudsman (see p317).

The ICE deals with complaints about DWP agencies and its contracted providers.

A complaint can only be made to the ICE if you have already completed the complaints procedure of the particular agency concerned. This usually means that you have had a response to a tier two complaint. A complaint should be made to the ICE no later than six months after the final response from the agency you are complaining about.

The ICE first considers whether or not it can accept the complaint. If it can, it attempts to settle it by suggesting ways in which you and the agency concerned can come to an agreement. If this fails, the ICE prepares a formal report, setting out how the complaint arose and how it believes it should be settled. The ICE considers whether there has been maladministration. It cannot deal with matters of law or cases that are subject to judicial review or other legal procedures, or cases under appeal.

If you are unhappy with the way the ICE dealt with your case, first use the ICE internal complaints process. If you remain unhappy, ask your MP to consider referring your concerns to the Parliamentary and Health Service Ombudsman (see p317).

Complaints about HM Revenue and Customs

If you want to complain about how HMRC has dealt with your claim for tax credits, child benefit or guardian's allowance, first raise the complaint with the office dealing with your case, or the named contact person on the letters you have received, setting out the nature of your complaint – eg, the delay in processing information you have submitted, requesting supplementary information or evidence or in actually determining your claim. Set out the history of your claim and any telephone contact or written correspondence and say what you think HMRC has done wrong. Also include in the complaint any loss that you have incurred, or difficulty you or your family members have had as a result.

If you are not happy with the response to your complaint, you can ask for it to be passed to an HMRC complaints handler. If you are dissatisfied with her/his response, you can ask that your complaint be reviewed by another complaints handler.

HMRC's complaints procedure is set out in its factsheet *Complaints* (C/FS), available on its website.[34]

If you are not happy with HMRC's reply, you can ask the Adjudicator's Office to look into it.

The Adjudicator only investigates a complaint if you have first exhausted the HMRC internal complaints procedure. A complaint should be made within six months of the final correspondence with HMRC.

Complaints can be made about delays, inappropriate staff behaviour, misleading advice or any other form of maladministration. The Adjudicator cannot, however, investigate disputes about matters of law. The Adjudicator can recommend that compensation be paid. HMRC has undertaken to follow the Adjudicator's recommendations in all but exceptional circumstances.

If you are unhappy with the way the Adjudicator dealt with your case, ask your MP to consider referring your concerns to the Parliamentary and Health Service Ombudsman (see below).

For further details on complaints about tax credits, see CPAG's *Tax Credits and Complaints Factsheet*.[35]

Complaining to the Parliamentary Ombudsman

If you have an ongoing delay in getting a decision made on your claim for benefit, a complaint, or the threat of a complaint, to the Parliamentary and Health Service Ombudsman may result in the DWP or HMRC taking action to determine your claim. You can also make a complaint to the Ombudsman after the issue is resolved.

The role of the Ombudsman is to investigate complaints from members of the public who believe they have experienced an injustice because of maladministration by a government department.[36] 'Maladministration' means poor administration and can include avoidable delays, failure to advise about appeal rights, refusal to answer reasonable questions or respond to correspondence, and discourteousness, racist or sexist behaviour.

The Ombudsman does not usually investigate a complaint unless you have first exhausted the internal complaints procedure. However, if the decision maker is not acting on your complaint, or there are unreasonable delays, this delay may also form part of your complaint. The time limit for lodging a complaint with the Ombudsman is 12 months from the date you were notified of the matter complained about. However, a delay in bringing a complaint does not necessarily prevent a complaint being heard if there are good reasons for the delay.

A public body, such as the DWP or HMRC, is required to follow the recommendations of a complaints panel unless there are good reasons not to. If a public body has failed to do so, you may have grounds to complain to the Ombudsman and, in some circumstances, may have grounds for a judicial review.

The Parliamentary and Health Service Ombudsman deals with complaints about all central government departments. This includes the DWP, HMRC, HM Courts and Tribunals Service and any agencies carrying out functions on their behalf. In order to make a complaint, you must write to your MP, who then refers the complaint to the Ombudsman. To find out who your MP is, contact the House of Commons Information Office on 020 7219 4272 or see www.parliament.uk/mps-lords-and-offices/mps. The Ombudsman can only investigate complaints of maladministration and not complaints about entitlement, which should be dealt with by challenging the decision on this. The Ombudsman has powers to look at documents on your claim held by the benefit authority. You may be interviewed to check any facts. The Ombudsman can recommend financial compensation if you have been unfairly treated or experienced a loss as a result of the maladministration.

Judicial review

Judicial review is a process by which you can ask a court to look at an action (or, in the case of delay, inaction) of any public authority that affects you, on the grounds that such (in)action is unlawful. If the High Court (Court of Session in Scotland) accepts that the (in)action is unlawful, it has the power to order the decision maker to determine your benefit claim (or otherwise resolve the issue).

There are many steps that must be taken before the High Court (or Court of Session) gives such a decision. Furthermore, if you do apply for judicial review about a benefit delay, it is strongly advisable only to do so with the help of legal advice. In particular, you risk having to pay the legal costs of the decision maker (which could be thousands of pounds) if your challenge is unsuccessful. In order to protect against this risk, it is necessary to obtain a legal aid certificate before proceedings are issued (and this is another reason to obtain legal advice).

However, in cases of benefit delay, often a 'letter before action', in which your adviser states that judicial review action will commence unless the claim is determined by a certain date, can lead to a claim being decided promptly. If the adviser works for an organisation that does not have a solicitor able to get legal aid in a public law matter, the letter should state that if your claim is not determined by a certain date, the matter will be referred to such a solicitor with a view to starting judicial review action. The letter should be sent to the solicitor for the DWP or HMRC, together with a copy to the manager of the section responsible for dealing with your claim. Although a 'letter before action' is currently only a requirement in England and Wales, its use in Scotland can still assist in resolving delays.

A template for a pre-action letter (for use in England and Wales) is available online.[37] The letter should include all the details required in that template.

Completing a pre-action letter

Under the section entitled 'the issue', you should include the following.

1. Set out the history of your claim for benefit – ie, which benefit you claimed and when, plus the details of all further correspondence and any complaints you have made. It is useful to do this in the form of a chronology in date order.

2. Explain why you believe you are entitled to the benefit claimed. You should address how you meet the conditions of entitlement, including how you meet the rules about immigration status, residence or the EU co-ordination of social security, and the evidence of this that you have submitted.

3. Explain that there is a legal duty to determine claims within a reasonable time (see p309).

4. Explain why you believe the claim has not been determined within a reasonable time in your particular case and/or why a short-term benefit advance should have been made. It is important to explain in as much detail as possible why you believe the DWP or HMRC has all the information needed to determine your claim, or why it should be able to obtain it. Also explain any specific reasons why the delay is causing you difficulties.

Housing benefit

Your HB claim must be determined within 14 days (or as soon as reasonably practicable after that) of your submitting a valid claim and providing all the information and evidence requested and reasonably required by the local authority.[38]

What counts as 'as soon as reasonably practicable' is the same as for benefits administered by the DWP and HMRC (see p309). In addition, the fact that your home may be at risk of repossession if the rent is not paid can often be a relevant factor in determining how long it should take to make a decision.

If you experience a delay in deciding your claim for HB, you can:

- request a 'payment on account' if you are a private or housing association tenant – ie, not a council tenant (see below);
- make a complaint in writing (see p320);
- escalate a complaint to the Local Government Ombudsman (see p321);
- obtain legal advice about sending a 'letter before action' for judicial review (see p321).

You can pursue more than one of these options – eg, you can make a complaint and if this does not resolve the delay, get legal advice about sending a 'letter before action' for judicial review.

Payments on account

The local authority must make a 'payment on account' if:[39]

- you have claimed HB as a private or housing association tenant; *and*
- it is impracticable for the local authority to make a decision on your claim within 14 days of its being made; *and*
- this is not due to your failure (without good cause) to provide the information it has requested.

A payment on account is sometimes called an 'interim payment'.

A payment on account is not discretionary. The local authority *must* pay the amount it considers 'reasonable', based on the information it has about your circumstances. If your actual entitlement is less, the local authority recovers the overpayment, or pays your arrears if your entitlement is greater.[40]

You do not need to ask the local authority to make a payment on account and you do not need to make a separate claim.[41] However, in practice, it is often necessary to write and request a payment on account, and/or make a complaint (see below), and/or write to the solicitor for the local authority and threaten judicial review (see p321) in order to get a payment.

Making a complaint

Making a complaint when there is an ongoing problem (such as an HB claim that has not been decided) is different from making a complaint about a situation that you think should not have happened but which is no longer producing a problem – eg, if your claim has been decided, but you are unhappy it took so long. The information in this section is aimed at enabling you to use the complaints process in order to get the situation resolved (ie, get a decision on your HB claim), rather than at seeking compensation or highlighting to the local authority the hardship it has caused after a delay has been resolved.

When you make a complaint to resolve an ongoing delay, it is very important that you highlight in the complaint that the problem persists, that this is therefore an urgent matter and what you want to be done about it – eg, ask for your claim to be determined within X number of days. In particular, you should include any relevant details of steps your landlord is taking to obtain possession of the property as a consequence of the rent arrears arising from the HB delay.

Local authorities must have an effective complaints procedure, which should be made available to the public. If you are unhappy about the actions of your local authority and wish to make a complaint, you should ask for a copy of its complaints policy. If you are unable to obtain the policy or there is no formal complaints procedure, you should begin by writing to the supervisor of the person dealing with your claim, making it clear why you are dissatisfied. If you do not receive a satisfactory reply, take up the matter with someone more senior in the department and, ultimately, the principal officer. Send a copy of the letter to your ward councillor and to the councillor who chairs the relevant committee responsible for HB (local authority officers are always accountable to the councillors). If this does not produce results, or if the delay is causing you severe hardship, consider a complaint to the Ombudsman (see p321) or obtain legal advice about a judicial review (see p321).

Government departments also monitor local authorities, so you could contact your MP or write to the relevant minister.

If you want to make a complaint about an elected member of a council, you must write to the local authority. In England, the Localism Act requires all local authorities to promote and maintain high standards of conduct by elected members. However, they can choose whether or not to set up standards committees to consider complaints about the conduct of councillors. The practice may therefore vary and you should ask your local authority for its procedure for complaints against members. In Wales and Scotland, elected members of a council are subject to a code of conduct. Complaints about Scottish councillors can be made to the Commissioner for Ethical Standards in Public Life in Scotland who can refer cases to the Standards Commission for Scotland. Complaints about Welsh councillors can be made to the Public Services Ombudsman for Wales.

Complaining to the Ombudsman

If you have tried to sort out your complaint with the local authority but you are not satisfied with the outcome, you can apply to the Local Government Ombudsman (in England), the Scottish Public Services Ombudsman (in Scotland) or the Public Services Ombudsman for Wales (in Wales). The Ombudsman can investigate any cases of maladministration by local authorities, but not matters of entitlement, which are dealt with by the First-tier Tribunal.

You can complain to the Ombudsman either by completing an online form or by telephone. The Ombudsman has powers to look at documents on your claim held by the local authority. You may be interviewed to check any facts. Straightforward cases can be dealt with in about three months. The Ombudsman can recommend financial compensation if you have been unfairly treated or experienced a loss as a result of the maladministration. A complaint may also make the authority review its procedures, which could benefit other claimants.

One outcome of your complaint may be a 'local settlement'. This is where the local authority agrees to take some action that the Ombudsman considers is a satisfactory response to your complaint and the investigation is then discontinued. If you are unhappy with the way in which the Ombudsman has dealt with your complaint, you can use its complaints process and, if you are still unhappy, obtain legal advice as quickly as possible.

Judicial review

Judicial review when there is a delay in making a decision on an HB claim is similar to when there is a delay in deciding a claim for a benefit administered by the DWP or HMRC (see p318). However, as there are different rules for how quickly a HB claim must be decided, any 'letter before action' for judicial review must refer to these. In particular, if you are a private tenant, your letter should note the rules about payments on account (see p319).

The letter should be sent to the solicitor for the local authority, together with a copy to the manager of the HB section responsible for dealing with your claim.

Note: because of the potential consequences, including costs, it is strongly advised that you obtain legal advice, and a legal aid certificate, before initiating judicial review proceedings.

Pending test cases

The general requirement to decide your claim does not apply if there is a appeal pending against a decision of the Upper Tribunal or a court in a 'test case' that deals with issues relevant to your claim. If this applies, the decision maker must consider whether it is possible that the outcome of the test case would mean you would have no entitlement. If so, the decision maker can postpone ('stay') making a decision on your claim (or revision or supersession request) until the test case is decided.[42] This prevents you appealing until a decision is made in the test case.

If the decision on your claim (or request for a revision or supersession) is postponed, once a decision has been made in the test case, the decision maker makes the decision in your case.[43]

If you would be entitled to benefit even if the test case were decided against you, the decision maker can make a decision.[44] This is done on the assumption that the test case has been decided in the way that is most unfavourable to you. However, this does mean that you are at least paid something while you wait for the result of the test case. Then, if the decision in the test case is in your favour, the decision maker revises her/his decision.

If you already have a decision in your favour, the decision maker can suspend payment of your benefit (see p330).

If you have already appealed to the First-tier Tribunal, see p324.

3. Delays when challenging a decision

If you have challenged a decision on your entitlement to a benefit or tax credit, there can be a delay while the:
- decision maker considers whether or not to revise (or review) the decision (see p323);
- decision maker prepares the appeal to send to the First-tier Tribunal (see p324);
- appeal is with the First-tier Tribunal waiting for a hearing date (see p324).

Note: for benefits other than housing benefit (HB), if you want to appeal to the First-tier Tribunal, you must have first applied for a revision or, for tax credits, a review of the decision. The DWP and HM Revenue and Customs (HMRC) call this 'mandatory reconsideration'. In addition:
- for child benefit and guardian's allowance, HMRC has decided not to revise it. It is understood that HMRC's intention is that if it revises the decision, you can appeal against the original decision as revised without having to apply for another revision;[45]
- for tax credits, HMRC has reviewed the decision and given notice of its conclusion;[46]

- for other benefits, the DWP has considered whether or not to revise it. You must have been notified in writing that you must apply for a revision of the decision before you can appeal (see below).[47]

The DWP or HMRC gives or sends you a 'mandatory reconsideration notice', telling you the result of your application for a revision or review. The notice is proof that the DWP or HMRC has accepted and considered your application for a revision or review. You must send a copy of this to the First-tier Tribunal when you appeal. If the DWP or HMRC only provides a mandatory reconsideration notice after a long delay, this may put you at a disadvantage – eg, if it makes it difficult to obtain evidence to support your appeal. This is something the First-tier Tribunal should take into account if you subsequently appeal, so you should explain how you think the delay has affected your chances of winning your appeal.[48]

For DWP decisions only, you do not need to request a revision before you appeal if you were not sent a written notice of the decision that included a statement that you were required to do this.[49]

For further information on challenging decisions, see CPAG's *Welfare Benefits and Tax Credits Handbook*.

Delay in carrying out a revision

When you submit your request for a revision to the DWP, make it clear that you are asking for a revision, include the fact that this is also referred to as a 'mandatory reconsideration', and ask for your request to be sent immediately to the Dispute Resolution Team to be determined. The Dispute Resolution Team should then decide whether the decision will be revised and send you the mandatory reconsideration notice. If the DWP responds to your revision request with a letter telling you that the decision has been looked at again, but not changed, and either inviting you to request a mandatory reconsideration or informing you that your request is being forwarded to the Dispute Resolution Team, you may be able to argue that your right of appeal has arisen. However, to safeguard your appeal rights, you should also continue with the mandatory reconsideration process and resubmit your revision request, explaining what has happened and clearly asking that it be sent immediately to the Dispute Resolution Team.

There is no express time limit in the legislation for how long it should take the decision maker to carry out a revision (or, for tax credits, a review). However, revision requests should be dealt with within a reasonable time. Tax credit reviews should be carried out as soon as is 'reasonably practicable', and HMRC's stated target is 42 days.[50] See p309 for the factors that are relevant when determining what is reasonable. You should ensure that you highlight any specific circumstances of your case that mean it is urgent for you, and therefore not appropriate for your request to be dealt with in the order in which it was received.

If a delay in conducting a revision or review continues, the options for resolving it are the same as those for resolving a delay in determining a claim and include:

- making a written complaint (see p315 for benefits administered by the DWP or HMRC and p320 for HB);
- escalating a complaint to the relevant Ombudsman (see p317 for benefits administered by the DWP or HMRC and p321 for HB);
- obtaining legal advice about sending a 'letter before action' for judicial review (see p318).

Note:

- The decision maker can postpone making a decision on your revision request if there is a 'test case' pending (see p322).
- The DWP stated that it intended to introduce target times for dealing with revision requests on all benefits, starting with employment and support allowance (ESA) in April 2016.[51] Although no targets have yet been published, the ESA Outcomes of Assessments statistics are due to include clearance times for work capability assessement mandatory reconsiderations from July 2016.[52] See CPAG's online service and *Welfare Rights Bulletin* for updates.

Delay while an appeal is prepared

The rules on the time in which the decision maker must send her/his appeal response to the Tribunal, and the possible solutions if there are delays depend on whether or not you were required to request a revision or, for tax credits, a review (a mandatory reconsideration) before appealing.

If your appeal concerns your rights under European Union (EU) law (eg, your right to reside under EU law or the effect of the EU co-ordination rules), see also p331 for a possible argument that some payments should be paid to you while you wait for your appeal to be heard.

Delay preparing your appeal following a mandatory reconsideration

Once you have sent your appeal to HM Courts and Tribunals Service (HMCTS), you may experience a delay in its being progressed. You should first establish what stage the appeal is at. Contact HMCTS and check whether:

- your appeal has been received. You may wish to obtain proof of receipt – eg, by sending the appeal by a type of postal service that requires a signature or using the Royal Mail tracking service. Once it has been received by the Tribunal, it is responsible for ensuring that the case is dealt with 'fairly and justly', which includes 'avoiding delay so far as compatible with proper consideration of the issues';[53]
- your appeal has been sent onto the DWP or HMRC and, if so, on what date;
- the DWP/HMRC has responded (see p325). A copy of this response should be sent to you and/or your representative;

- you have been sent an enquiry form or, if you have returned this, whether it has been received;
- your appeal is ready to be listed for a hearing date.

The decision maker must send her/his response to the appeal to the First-tier Tribunal within 28 days of having received it.[54] If the DWP/HMRC has not sent its response within 28 days, you can apply to the Tribunal to make a direction giving the DWP/HMRC a further short period in which to do so, after which time the appeal is listed and the DWP/HMRC is barred from taking further part in proceedings.[55]

If your situation is particularly urgent, you can ask the Tribunal to shorten the 28-day time limit.[56]

If the DWP/HMRC applies for a direction to extend the 28-day time limit, you should be notified of this in writing and you can then apply for a direction setting this direction aside.[57]

If you apply for a direction, you should clearly explain the consequences for you of a continuing delay and explain why it would be fair and just to determine the case more quickly than would otherwise happen.

If you request that your appeal be dealt with quickly in this way, you must also be as flexible as possible in terms of preparing your case quickly and making yourself, and any representative, available for hearings at short notice.

If the Tribunal refuses to expedite your appeal, and it is arguable that this means your case is not being dealt with fairly and justly, you should get advice on whether there are grounds for judicial review (see p318).

If your appeal is delayed because of a pending 'test case', see p327.

Delay preparing your appeal without a mandatory reconsideration

The information in this section applies if your appeal is about an HB decision or, in very rare cases, a decision that did not correctly notify you that you were required to request a revision before appealing. For more information on when this applies, see CPAG's *Welfare Benefits and Tax Credits Handbook*. In these cases, you send your appeal to the decision maker in the local authority (or DWP or HMRC). If there is a delay in your appeal being processed, first establish what stage the appeal is at. Contact the relevant benefit authority and check whether:

- your appeal has been received; *and*
- the decision maker has written her/his response and sent it to HMCTS. A copy should also be sent to you and/or your representative;
- you have been sent an enquiry form or, if you have returned this, whether it has been received;
- your appeal is ready to be listed for a hearing date.

The decision maker must send her/his response to your appeal to HMCTS as soon as reasonably practicable.[58] You are entitled to have your appeal heard within a reasonable period of time, so the decision maker should prepare the response and send it to the First-tier Tribunal without delay.[59] Following a complaint about an HB appeal, the Ombudsman said that the local authority should forward an appeal within 28 days.[60]

If your appeal has been received but has not been sent to HMCTS, you should request that this be done. You can complain about the delay using the complaints procedure (see p320 for local authorities, and p315 for the DWP and HMRC).

If there are special reasons why your appeal should be dealt with urgently or there has already been significant delay, you can write to the First-tier Tribunal asking it to direct the decision maker to produce the response and/or list the appeal for a hearing.[61] Set out the history of the appeal, what you have done to try to get the matter resolved and the effect of the delay on you and your family as clearly as possible and include all documents that you have about the decision. Bear in mind that the Tribunal expects normal procedures to be followed in the vast majority of cases, but, if necessary, can deal with your appeal differently. This includes admitting the appeal directly if it has not yet been received from the decision maker or by prioritising the hearing date, so it is not listed in the order in which the appeal was received.

How should you ask the First-tier Tribunal to deal with your appeal if it has not been sent by the decision maker?

If you write to the First-tier Tribunal, there is a risk of a misunderstanding. The clerk to the Tribunal (an administrative officer who processes appeals) may be confused if s/he receives documents concerning an appeal which the decision maker has not told the Tribunal about. In order to minimise the chances of confusion, you should do the following.

1. Clearly head your letter 'Application for a Direction under Rule 6 of the Tribunal Procedure Rules' and mark it 'urgent'.

2. Explain at the start of the letter that the papers have not been sent by the decision maker and you would like the case to be referred to a Tribunal judge to give a direction to resolve this problem.

3. Set out the history of when your appeal was submitted and the contact you have made with the benefit authority since then. If possible, enclose a copy of your appeal request and any accompanying documents.

4. Refer to the caselaw that confirms that HMCTS has the power to issue directions in relation to an unnotified appeal.[62]

5. Clearly explain the consequences for you of a continuing delay and explain why it would be fair and just to determine the case more quickly than would otherwise happen.

6. Follow up your letter or fax with a phone call to the Tribunal to establish that it has been received and passed to a judge.

7. See CPAG's website for a sample letter, which you may want to adapt.[63] This does not specify timescales, because what is reasonable depends on the facts of your case and

the consequences of the continued delay. For example, if you are at imminent risk of losing your home as a consequence of HB not being awarded, the timescale should reflect this.

If you request that your appeal be dealt with quickly in this way, you must then be as flexible as possible in terms of preparing your case quickly and making yourself, and any representative, available for hearings at short notice.

If a Tribunal judge refuses to direct the decision maker to submit her/his response to the Tribunal and to expedite the appeal, you should consider whether there are grounds for judicial review against this refusal (see p318). Depending on the particular facts, it may be arguable that a failure to give such directions has resulted in procedural impropriety because the Tribunal has failed to deal with your case fairly and justly as required.[64] You should obtain legal advice before doing this (there is a risk of costs in applying for judicial review) and you should act promptly. As with delays in processing benefit claims, a 'letter before action' for judicial review in such circumstances can often lead to the issue being resolved (in this case, the requested direction being given). In England and Wales, judicial review proceedings against action (or inaction) of the First-tier Tribunal must be started in the Upper Tribunal.[65] In Scotland, you must begin judicial review proceedings against action (or inaction) of the First-tier Tribunal by applying to the Court of Session. If certain conditions are satisfied, your case can then be transferred to the Upper Tribunal.[66]

Appeal delayed because of a pending test case

If you have appealed to the First-tier or Upper Tribunal and there is a 'test case' pending against a decision of the Upper Tribunal or a court that deals with issues raised in your case, the decision maker can serve a notice requiring the Tribunal in your appeal:[67]
- not to make a decision and to refer your case back to her/him; *or*
- to deal with your appeal by either:
  - postponing making a decision (known as 'stay' or, in Scotland 'sist') until the test case is decided; *or*
  - deciding your appeal as if the test case had been decided in the way most unfavourable to you, but only if this is in your interests. If this happens and the test case is eventually decided in your favour, the decision maker must make a new decision superseding the decision of the First-tier Tribunal or Upper Tribunal in the light of the decision in the test case.

If the decision on your appeal has been postponed, once a decision has been made in the test case, the decision is made on your appeal.

If your appeal concerns European law, see p331.

4. **Delays getting paid**

Once you have a positive decision stating that you are entitled to benefit, there may be delays in the DWP, HM Revenue and Customs (HMRC) or local authority implementing the decision and making any payments due.

It is important to check first that there is a decision in place awarding you a specified amount of benefit (see below). If there is, unless payments can be suspended (see p329), payment should be made to you as soon as reasonably practicable.[68]

If benefit is not paid promptly, you have a right to start action in the county court (England and Wales) or sheriff court (Scotland) for payment of the money owed.[69] However, it is extremely rare that this action is required to obtain benefit that has been awarded but not paid.

The decision awarding you benefit

In most cases, it is clear that there has been a decision awarding you a specified amount of benefit. However, in some cases, you may get a decision which does not award benefit but only decides one or more conditions of entitlement. For example, if you appeal to the First-tier Tribunal against the DWP's decision that it cannot pay you income support (IS) because you do not have a right to reside, the Tribunal can allow your appeal if it decides that the DWP was wrong because you do have a right to reside. However, the Tribunal's decision is not a decision awarding you benefit, because it only relates to one condition of entitlement and does not decide whether you meet all the other conditions of entitlement for IS. The question of your entitlement to IS is then passed back to the DWP decision maker, and it is only if s/he decides you meet all the conditions of entitlement that there is a decision awarding you a specified amount of benefit.

If your appeal about one condition of your entitlement is allowed and there is then a delay in a decision being made to award you benefit:

- check whether the decision maker has received notification of the Tribunal's decision;
- if the decision maker has received notification, establish what is the cause of the delay. A long time may have elapsed since your initial claim was made, and so to ensure that you have met the other conditions of entitlement since your date of claim, the decision maker may write asking you to confirm this, often by completing a claim or review form. Any further delays can be reduced if you provide the information or complete and return any forms as soon as you can;
- if you are advised that the decision maker has all the information s/he requires, but there is still a delay in deciding your claim, your options are the same as for someone who experiences a delay in getting a decision on an initial claim

(see p308). You should include in any correspondence the fact that you have already had a significant wait while your appeal was determined.

Note: you only have the right to sue for benefit awarded but not paid once there is a decision actually awarding you a specified amount of benefit.

Suspension of benefit

In certain circumstances, a decision maker can suspend payment of part or all of your benefit or tax credits. In this case, you have no right to the payment (and so cannot take court action as described on p328). See CPAG's *Welfare Benefits and Tax Credits Handbook* for all the circumstances in which benefit can be suspended. **Note:** the tax credit regulations use the term 'postponement' rather than 'suspension' of payment, but as HMRC uses the term 'suspension', this is used for both benefits and tax credits in this section.

There are two situations when payment of benefit or tax credits can be suspended that are most relevant to the way the immigration, residence, presence and European Union (EU) co-ordination rules operate. These are:
- because the decision maker wants more information to decide whether you continue to be entitled to benefit (see below); *and*
- while an appeal against a positive decision is pending (see p330).

Has your benefit been suspended?
1. The decision maker may be willing to continue to pay your benefit, or at least some of it, if you can show that you will experience hardship otherwise. Guidance to decision makers is clear that, in almost all decisions to suspend benefit, consideration must be given to whether hardship would result and whether this would make the suspension unacceptable. In addition, the decision to suspend your benefit can be reconsidered if the decision maker receives additional information.[70]
2. If you receive a letter telling you that your benefit has been suspended, write explaining how the suspension affects you and ask for the suspension decision to be reconsidered.
In addition to hardship, there may be other arguments why your benefit should not be suspended, based on the information below.
3. You cannot appeal to the First-tier Tribunal against the decision to suspend your benefit. The only way to change the decision is to negotiate to get your benefit reinstated or to challenge the decision in the courts by judicial review (see p318).

The decision maker requires further information

You can be required to supply information or evidence if the decision maker needs this to determine whether your award of benefit should be revised or superseded.[71]

If you do not provide the information and evidence, payment of all or part of your benefit can be suspended if:[72]

- a question has arisen about your entitlement or whether a decision should be revised or superseded;[73] *or*
- you apply for a revision or supersession; *or*
- you do not provide certificates, documents, evidence or other information about the facts of your case as required.[74]

If the decision maker wants you to provide information or evidence, s/he must notify you in writing. Within 14 days (one month for child benefit, guardian's allowance and housing benefit (HB); seven days for contribution-based jobseeker's allowance if you come under the universal credit system; or by the date specified, which must not be less than 30 days after the date of the notice, for tax credits) of being sent the request, you must:

- supply the information or evidence.[75] You can be given more time if the decision maker is satisfied that this is necessary; *or*
- satisfy the decision maker that the information does not exist or you cannot obtain it.[76]

If the decision maker has not already done so, your benefit can be suspended if you do not provide the information or evidence within the relevant time limit.[77] Similarly, your tax credits can be suspended/postponed if you do not provide information or evidence by the date requested.[78]

The complexity of the immigration, residence, presence and EU co-ordination rules, together with the additional information and evidence requirements these rules generate, means that the likelihood of your benefit being suspended on the above grounds is increased. For information on some of the practical issues involved in satisfying the information and evidence requirements, see Chapter 20.

If an appeal is pending

Your benefit or tax credit can be suspended if the DWP, HMRC or local authority is appealing (or considering an appeal) against:[79]

- a decision of the First-tier Tribunal, Upper Tribunal or court to award you benefit (or to reinstate benefit); *or*
- a decision of the Upper Tribunal or court about someone else's appeal if the issue could affect your claim. For HB only, the other case must also be about a HB issue.

The DWP, HMRC or local authority must (although for tax credits this is only guidance[80]) give you written notice as soon as reasonably practicable if it intends to:[81]

- request the statement of reasons for the First-tier Tribunal's decision;
- apply for leave to appeal; *or*
- appeal,

whichever is the first that is yet to be done.

The decision maker must then take that action within the usual time limits for doing so (generally within one month in each case). If s/he does not, the suspended benefit must be paid to you.[82] The suspended benefit must also be paid to you if the decision maker withdraws an application for leave to appeal, withdraws the appeal or is refused leave to appeal and it is not possible for her/him to renew the application.

The decision maker still has discretion not to suspend if s/he considers it would result in hardship and s/he should keep her/his decision under review so that the suspension can be lifted if your circumstances, including level of hardship experienced, change.[83] You should therefore write to the relevant benefit authority if the suspension will cause, or is causing, you hardship.

Suspension on this ground is particularly common following appeals to the First-tier Tribunal concerning the right to reside requirement being allowed. This is due to decision makers seeking to appeal to the Upper Tribunal against the decision of the First-tier Tribunal and the large number of ongoing cases about right to reside that are in the higher courts.

If your appeal concerns your rights under EU law (eg, your right to reside or the effect of the EU co-ordination rules), see below.

If your appeal concerns European law

If the issue in your appeal concerns EU law, you may be able to argue that your benefit or tax credit should not be suspended, or that you should receive some form of interim payment. It has been established in European caselaw that national governments cannot automatically refuse requests for interim relief to individuals seeking to exercise their rights under European law. Effective judicial protection requires a national court to be able to grant interim relief necessary to ensure EU rights are respected.[84]

This argument could be used, for example, if the issue in your appeal is whether you have a right to reside in EU law (see Chapter 12) or whether you are entitled to benefit because of the EU co-ordination rules (see Chapter 16).

It may be possible to make this argument:

- if you are waiting for your appeal to be heard by the First-tier Tribunal. You may be able to argue that you should be paid a short-term advance or that you should receive some form of interim payment while waiting for your appeal. You must request a payment outside the benefit rules from the benefit authority, because its decision is that you are not entitled under these rules;
- if action on your appeal has been deferred (known as your appeal having been 'stayed', or, in Scotland, 'sisted') because there is a test case pending (see p327). You may be able to argue either that this should be disapplied or that you should receive some form of interim payment until your appeal can be determined; *or*

- if you have won your First-tier Tribunal appeal and the decision maker suspends payment of your benefit or tax credit because s/he has appealed, or intends to appeal, to the Upper Tribunal. You may be able to argue that your benefit should not be suspended, or that you should receive some form of interim payment pending the further appeal.

If there is a dispute over which state is the competent state under the EU co-ordination rules for paying your benefit or tax credit, see p279.

Note: benefit authorities can lift the suspension on grounds of hardship (see p329).

Notes

2. Waiting for a decision on a claim

1 **WTC/CTC** s3 TCA 2002
   Other benefits s8(1)(a) SSA 1998
2 *SSHD v R (S)* [2007] EWCA Civ 546, para 51
3 *R v Secretary of State for Social Services and Chief Adjudication Officer ex parte Child Poverty Action Group* [1990] 2 QB 540
4 Reg 3(5)(b) SS&CS(DA) Regs
5 Reg 3(7) SS&CS(DA) Regs
6 www.gov.uk/government/publications/hmrcs-business-plan-2014-to-2016/hmrc-business-plan-2014-to-2016
7 *DWP Operations Business Plan 2015-2016*, April 2015
8 Art 4 EU Reg 883/04; Arts 18 and 45 TFEU; Art 24 EU Dir 2004/38; Art 7 EU Reg 492/2011
9 www.cpag.org.uk
10 Short-term benefit advance benefit processing guidance, paras 3 and 5; short-term benefit advance jobcentre guidance, paras 3 and 6; short-term benefit advance contact centre guidance, paras 2 and 6
11 Regs 5 and 6 SS(PAB) Regs
12 Short-term benefit advance benefit processing guidance, paras 3 and 5; short-term benefit advance jobcentre guidance, paras 3 and 6; short-term benefit advance contact centre guidance, paras 2 and 6
13 Reg 4(2) SS(PAB) Regs
14 Reg 3 SS(PAB) Regs
15 Reg 7 SS(PAB) Regs
16 Short-term benefit advance benefit processing guidance, para 23
17 Reg 7 SS(PAB) Regs
18 Reg 8 SS(PAB) Regs
19 Short-term benefit advance benefit processing guidance, paras 173-89
20 Sch 2 para 20A SS&CS(DA) Regs allows a right of appeal against decisions on deductions under reg 10 SS(PAB) Regs
21 Sch 2 para 20A SS&CS(DA) Regs
22 www.gov.uk/short-term-benefit-advance
23 Short-term benefit advance benefit processing guidance, paras 190-93
24 Short-term benefit advance benefit processing guidance, paras 87 and 115; short-term benefit advance jobcentre guidance, para 27; short-term benefit advance contact centre guidance, para 22

25 Short-term benefit advance benefit processing guidance, paras 3, 5 and 87; short-term benefit advance jobcentre guidance, para 27
26 Short-term benefit advance jobcentre guidance, paras 29-31; short-term benefit advance contact centre guidance, para 22
27 Short-term benefit advance benefit processing guidance, paras 64-65; short-term benefit advance jobcentre guidance, paras 21-22; short-term benefit advance contact centre guidance, para 18
28 Short-term benefit advance benefit processing guidance, paras 16, 29, 30 and 31
29 Short-term benefit advance benefit processing guidance, paras 174 and 185
30 Reg 22 CB&GA(Admin) Regs
31 Regs 22(3), 41 and 42 CB&GA(Admin) Regs
32 Reg 22(2) CB&GA(Admin) Regs
33 www.gov.uk/government/organisations/department-for-work-pensions/about/complaints-procedure
34 www.gov.uk/guidance/complain-to-hm-revenue-and-customs
35 www.cpag.org.uk/content/tax-credits-and-complaints
36 s5(1)(a) Parliamentary Commissioner Act 1967
37 www.justice.gov.uk/civil/procrules_fin/contents/protocols/prot_jrv.htm
38 Reg 89 HB Regs; reg 70 HB(SPC) Regs
39 Reg 93(1) HB Regs; reg 74(1) HB(SPC) Regs
40 Reg 93(2) and (3) HB Regs; reg 74(2) and (3) HB(SPC) Regs
41 *R v Haringey London Borough Council ex parte Azad Ayub* [1992] 25 HLR 566 (QBD)
42 **HB** Sch 7 para 16 CSPSSA 2000
Other benefits s25 SSA 1998
43 **HB** Sch 7 para 18(2) CSPSSA 2000
Other benefits s27(2) SSA 1998
44 **HB** Sch 7 para 16(3) and (4) CSPSSA 2000; reg 15 HB&CTB(DA) Regs
CB/GA s25(3) and (4) SSA 1998; reg 22 CB&GA(DA) Regs
UC/PIP/JSA&ESA under UC s25(3) and (4) SSA 1998; reg 53 UC,PIP,JSA&ESA(DA) Regs
Other benefits s25(3) and (4) SSA 1998; reg 21 SS&CS(DA) Regs

3. **Delays when challenging a decision**
45 s12(1), (2) and (3D) SSA 1998; r22(9)(b) TP(FT) Rules; HMRC Form CH24A, *What To Do If You Think Your Child Benefit Or Guardian's Allowance Decision is Wrong*
46 s38(1A) TCA 2002
47 s12(2)(b) and (3A)-(3C) SSA 1998; reg 3ZA SS&CS(DA) Regs; reg 7 UC,PIP,JSA&ESA(DA) Regs; r22(9)(a) TP(FT) Rules
48 *MM v SSWP (PIP)* [2016] UKUT 36 (AAC)
49 Reg 3ZA SS&CS(DA) Regs; reg 7 UC,PIP,JSA&ESA(DA) Regs; r22(9)(a) TP(FT) Rules
50 s21A(2) TCA 2002; David Gauke MP, Exchequer Secretary to the Treasury, Eighth Delegated Legislation Committee, 26 March 2014
51 Lord Freud, House of Lords *Hansard*, written answer given 26 March 2015 to written question HL5873
52 Published on www.gov.uk
53 r2(2)(e) TP(FT) Rules
54 r24(1)(c) TP(FT) Rules
55 rr2, 5, 6 and 8 TP(FT) Rules
56 rr5(3)(a) and 6 TP(FT) Rules
57 r6(5) TP(FT) Rules
58 r24(1A) TP(FT) Rules
59 Art 6 European Convention on Human Rights; s6 HRA 1998; CH/3497/2005; *MB v Wychavon DC* [2013] UKUT 67 (AAC)
60 Complaint 01/C/13400 against Scarborough Borough Council
61 R(H) 1/07; *FH v Manchester City Council(HB)* [2010] UKUT 43 (AAC)
62 R(H) 1/07; *FH v Manchester City Council (HB)* [2010] UKUT 43 (AAC)
63 www.cpag.org.uk/sites/default/files/CPAG-How-to-expedite-social-security-appeal-Aug-13.pdf
64 r2(3)(a) TP(FT) Rules
65 ss15-21 TCEA 2007 and the Direction of the Lord Chief Justice on classes of cases specified under s18(6) TCEA 2007
66 ss20 and 21 TCEA 2007; Act of Sederunt (Transfer of Judicial Review Applications from the Court of Session) 2008, No.357; *Currie, Petitioner* [2009] CSOH 145, [2010] AACR 8; R(IB) 3/09
67 **HB** Sch 7 para 17 CSPSSA 2000
Other benefits s26 SSA 1998

4. Delays getting paid

68 **HB** Reg 91 HB Regs; reg 72 HB(SPC)
Regs **UC/PIP/ESA&JSA under UC** Reg
45 UC,PIP,JSA&ESA (C&P) Regs
WTC/CTC Regs 8 and 9 TC(PC) Regs
Other benefits Reg 20 SS(C&P) Regs

69 *Murdoch v DWP* [2010] EWHC 1988
(QB), paras 75-79; and for HB see *Jones v
Waveney DC* [1999] 33 HLR 3

70 DWP, *Suspension and Termination Guide*,
paras 1350, 2050-52 and 2301-02,
www.gov.uk/government/uploads/
system/uploads/attachment_data/file/
424064/suspension-termination-
guide.pdf

71 **HB** Reg 86(1) HB Regs; reg 67(1)
HB(SPC) Regs
CB/GA Reg 23 CB&GA(Admin) Regs
UC/PIP/JSA&ESA under UC Reg
38(2) UC,PIP,JSA&ESA(C&P) Regs; reg
45 UC,PIP,JSA&ESA(DA) Regs
WTC/CTC s16(3) TCA 2002
Other benefits Reg 32(1) SS(C&P)
Regs; reg 17 SS&CS(DA) Regs

72 **HB** Reg 13 HB&CTB(DA) Regs
CB/GA Reg 19 CB&GA(DA) Regs
UC/PIP/JSA&ESA under UC Reg
45(6) UC,PIP,JSA&ESA(DA) Regs
WTC/CTC Reg 11 TC(PC) Regs
Other benefits Reg 17(2) SS&CS(DA)
Regs

73 **HB** Reg 11(2)(a)(i) HB&CTB(DA) Regs
CB/GA Reg 18(2)(a) CB&GA(DA) Regs
UC/PIP/JSA&ESA under UC Reg
44(2)(a)(i) UC,PIP,JSA&ESA(DA) Regs
WTC/CTC Reg 11(3A) TC(PC) Regs
Other benefits Reg 16(3)(a)
SS&CS(DA) Regs

74 **HB** Reg 86(1) HB Regs; reg 67(1)
HB(SPC) Regs
CB/GA Reg 23 CB&GA(Admin) Regs
UC/PIP/JSA&ESA under UC Reg
38(2) UC,PIP,JSA&ESA(C&P) Regs
WTC/CTC Reg 11(3A) TC(PC) Regs
Other benefits Reg 32(1) SS(C&P)
Regs

75 **HB** Reg 13(4)(a) HB&CTB(DA) Regs
CB/GA Reg 19(2) CB&GA(DA) Regs
UC/PIP/JSA&ESA under UC Reg
45(4)(a) UC,PIP,JSA&ESA(DA) Regs
WTC/CTC Reg 32 TC(CN) Regs
Other benefits Reg 17(4)(a)
SS&CS(DA) Regs

76 **HB** Reg 13(4)(b) HB&CTB(DA) Regs
CB/GA Reg 19(2)(b) CB&GA(DA) Regs
UC/PIP/JSA&ESA under UC Reg
45(4)(b) UC,PIP,JSA&ESA(DA) Regs
WTC/CTC HMRC leaflet, *Tax Credits:
suspension of payments*, WTC/FS9, April
2016
Other benefits Reg 17(4)(b)
SS&CS(DA) Regs

77 **HB** Reg 13(4) HB&CTB(DA) Regs
CB/GA Reg 19(5) CB&GA(DA) Regs
UC/PIP/JSA&ESA under UC Reg
45(6) UC,PIP,JSA&ESA(DA) Regs
Other benefits Reg 17(5) SS&CS(DA)
Regs

78 Reg 11 TC(PC) Regs

79 **HB** Sch 7 para 13(2) CSPSSA 2000; reg
11(2)(b) HB&CTB(DA) Regs
CB/GA Reg 18(3) CB&GA(DA) Regs
WTC/CTC Reg 11 TC(PC) Regs
Other benefits s21(2)(c) and (d) SSA
1998; reg 16(3)(b) SS&CS(DA) Regs;
reg 44(2)(b) and (c)
UC,PIP,JSA&ESA(DA) Regs

80 para 0014360 Step 1 TCM

81 **HB** Reg 11(3) HB&CTB(DA) Regs
CB/GA Reg 18(4) and (5) CB&GA(DA)
Regs
Other benefits Reg 16(4) SS&CS(DA)
Regs; reg 44(5) UC,PIP,JSA&ESA(DA)
Regs

82 **HB** Reg 12(1)(b) HB&CTB(DA) Regs
CB/GA Reg 21 CB&GA(DA) Regs
Other benefits Reg 20(2) and (3)
SS&CS(DA) Regs; reg 46(b) and (c)
UC,PIP,JSA&ESA(DA) Regs

83 DWP, *Suspension and Termination Guide*,
paras 2050-52 and 2354

84 *The Queen v Secretary of State for
Transport ex parte Factortame and
Others*, C-213/89 [1990] ECR I-02433,
para 23; *Unibet (London) Ltd and Unibet
(International) Ltd v Justitiekanslern*, C-
432/05 [2007] ECR I-02271, especially
para 77; see also *obiter* (not binding)
comments in *R (Sanneh) v SSWP and
HMRC* [2013] EWHC 793 (Admin), paras
104-14

Chapter 19

· ·

National insurance numbers

This chapter covers:
1. The national insurance number requirement (below)
2. Obtaining a national insurance number (p337)
3. Common problems (p340)

This chapter covers the rules on the national insurance number requirement for benefits and tax credits and the issues that arise in satisfying this, particularly if you or a member of your family are not British.

---

1. The national insurance number requirement

In general, in order to be entitled to any social security benefit or tax credit, or, in England and Wales, council tax reduction (see p439), you must satisfy the national insurance (NI) number requirement.[1] This means that you and any partner included in your claim must:

- provide an NI number, together with evidence to show that it is the one allocated to you; *or*
- provide evidence or information to enable your NI number to be traced; *or*
- make an application for an NI number, accompanied with sufficient information and evidence for one to be allocated. There is no requirement for an NI number to have been allocated to you.

Certain groups of people are exempt from the requirement (see p336).

Note: the NI number requirement is only one requirement that must be satisfied as part of making a valid claim. For general information on the main requirements, see p345. For detailed information on the requirements for each benefit and tax credit, see CPAG's *Welfare Benefits and Tax Credits Handbook*.

When the requirement applies

The NI requirement applies when you make a claim for benefit. It also applies when someone who will be included in an existing award of benefit joins your family – eg, if your partner joins you from abroad.[2]

The requirement applies to you, and also to your partner if you are claiming means-tested benefits or tax credits as a couple.[3]

This is the case even if, for income support (IS), income-based jobseeker's allowance (JSA), or income-related employment and support allowance (ESA), you are not going to receive any extra benefit for her/him because s/he is a 'person subject to immigration control' for benefit purposes.[4]

The situation is different, however, if your partner is not included in your claim. This is the case if you are claiming pension credit (PC) and your partner is a person subject to immigration control, as s/he is treated as not being part of your household. In this situation, your partner does not need to satisfy the NI requirement. Similarly, you must make a single claim for universal credit (UC) if your partner is defined as a person subject to immigration control and, consequently, your partner does not need to satisfy the NI requirement. (**Note:** your partner's income and capital still affect your claim for UC).

For the definition of 'person subject to immigration control', see p57 and for more information about your entitlement if your partner is a person subject to immigration control, see p73 for means-tested benefits and p75 for tax credits.

See below for when your partner does not have to satisfy the NI number requirement.

Who is exempt

You do not need to satisfy the NI number requirement:
- if you are under 16 and you are claiming disability living allowance;[5]
- for statutory sick pay, statutory maternity pay, statutory paternity pay, statutory shared parental pay, statutory adoption pay or a social fund payment;[6]
- for housing benefit (HB) if you live in a hostel;[7]
- for tax credits if you have a 'reasonable excuse' for failing to satisfy the requirement (see p337).[8]

If a child or qualifying young person is included in your award of IS or income-based JSA, or in your claim for HB or UC, s/he does not need to satisfy the NI number requirement.[9]

If you are the benefit claimant and your partner is included in your claim, your partner does not have to satisfy the NI number requirement if:[10]
- s/he is a 'person subject to immigration control' because s/he requires leave to enter or remain in the UK, but does not have it (see p58); *and*
- s/he has not previously been given an NI number; *and*
- you are claiming IS, income-based JSA, income-related ESA or PC and your partner is not entitled to that benefit her/himself, or you are claiming HB and your partner fails the 'habitual residence test' (see p104). However, in practice, it is difficult to see who could satisfy the first bullet point and not satisfy this.

You may still be asked for information about an NI number application for your partner, even though s/he is exempt. An NI number will then be refused, but this does not prevent you from being entitled to benefits or tax credits or council tax reduction.[11]

Note: the above exemption is not in the UC regulations. This is because if your partner is defined as a person subject to immigration control because s/he requires leave, you are required to claim UC as a single person and your partner is not required to have an NI number.[12]

Tax credits

The NI number requirement for tax credits is as described above, including the exemption for partners who require leave but do not have it. If you live with your partner, you must make a joint claim for tax credits and both of you must satisfy the NI number requirement unless one of you is covered by the exemption.

However, the NI number requirement does not apply if the Tax Credit Office is satisfied that you (and/or your partner if it is a joint claim) have a 'reasonable excuse' for not complying with it.[13] A 'reasonable excuse' is not defined: whether or not the Tax Credit Office is satisfied that you have one is a matter of discretion. Guidance to decision makers stresses that their discretionary decision must be reasonable, which includes being fair and taking into account all relevant considerations, including available evidence.[14] A 'reasonable excuse' could include if you are unable to prove your identity because the Home Office has all your documents and you can show this – eg, with a letter from your solicitor.

If the decision maker decides that you have not made a valid claim because you have not satisfied the NI number requirement and you believe you had a reasonable excuse for not doing so, you can appeal against that decision.[15] You must request a review ('mandatory reconsideration') of the decision first.

2. **Obtaining a national insurance number**

The DWP allocates all national insurance (NI) numbers.

NI numbers are allocated automatically to children shortly before their 16th birthday, provided child benefit is being claimed for them. If child benefit was being claimed for you when you were that age, you should have an NI number. If you are under 20, you were in the UK when you turned 16 and you did not receive an NI number, you can phone the National Insurance Registration Helpline (tel: 0300 200 3500).

If you have been allocated an NI number but do not know what it is, or if you want written confirmation of your NI number, you should complete Form CA5403 (available online[16]) and send it to HM Revenue and Customs (HMRC). If you attend your Jobcentre Plus office with evidence of your identity, a member of staff may be able to tell you what your NI number is.

If you do not have an NI number, see below.

NI number applications may be completed as part of the process of applying for immigration leave and/or a biometric immigration document. Guidance for immigration officers covers procedures for completing an NI number application during an asylum interview, forwarding the application to the DWP if leave is granted, and notifying you of the NI number if one is allocated.[17] If an NI number has been allocated before a biometric immigration document is issued, it may be included on this document.[18]

These procedures are not always followed and do not always result in an NI number being allocated. If you have not been allocated an NI number as part of the process of your immigration application, you should apply for an NI number in the usual way (see below).

Applying for a national insurance number

If you have not been allocated an NI number, you can apply for one by telephoning the NI number application line on 0345 600 0643 or by contacting your local Jobcentre Plus office.

There are a number of reasons why you may need an NI number, including for employment purposes, for a student loan, to open an Individual Savings Account (ISA), or to claim benefits or tax credits.[19]

If you do not have an NI number, you do not need to obtain one before you make your benefit or tax credit claim.

The procedures for accepting and processing applications for NI numbers are often misunderstood and/or not followed. It can therefore be helpful to refer decision makers to guidance on the processes. Although detailed guidance is currently on the government website,[20] at the time of writing it was headed as 'withdrawn on 17 June 2016' as it is no longer in use. Replacement guidance may become publicly available. See CPAG's online service and *Welfare Rights Bulletin* for updates.

If you claim a benefit or tax credit, or you apply for a supersession of an award of benefit (eg, to include your partner), when you (or s/he) do not have an NI number, the DWP, HMRC or local authority should complete Form DCI1 and send it to the NI number centre.[21] This counts as your having made an application for an NI number. It is advisable to state clearly on the form or letter that you wish to apply for an NI number, if you (or a family member for whom you are claiming benefit) do not have one and you make a claim for benefit or notify the benefit authority that your family member has joined you.

When the NI number centre receives Form DCI1, it carries out a number of checks to ensure that you do not already have an NI number. It should then contact you to arrange an interview at your local DWP office if this is required (usually the case for European Economic Area (EEA) nationals), otherwise the application can be done by post (often the case for non-EEA nationals who have leave to enter or remain in the UK). The interview is generally referred to as an 'evidence of identity interview'.

You should be told what documents to take to this interview. It is important to take as many as possible that establish your identity. The www.gov.uk website on applying for a NI number gives a non-exhaustive list of examples of documents that prove your identity that includes:

- passport;
- identity card;
- residence card;
- birth or adoption certificate;
- marriage or civil partnership certificate;
- driving licence.

If you have any of these documents, take them to your interview. If not, take any documents you do have that could help prove your identity. These could include:

- any biometric immigration document;
- current travel document issued by any national government, including the UK;
- any residence document issued to EEA nationals (see p353);
- certificate of registration or naturalisation as a British citizen;
- standard acknowledgement letter issued by the Home Office;
- application registration card issued by the Home Office to an asylum seeker;
- an expired passport, travel document or EEA identity card;
- local authority rent book or card;
- tenancy agreement;
- council tax documents;
- life assurance/insurance policies;
- mortgage repayment documents;
- recent fuel or telephone bills in your name;
- divorce or annulment papers;
- wage slip from a recent employer;
- trade union membership card;
- travel pass with photograph affixed;
- vehicle registration or insurance documents;
- work permit.

These are only some of the documents that you can use to prove your identity. If you have other documents that are not in the above list, these may also help. Photocopies of documents can be relied on to establish your identity, but you should take the originals if you have them. If not, explain why you do not have the original documents. For example, if some of your documents are with the

Home Office, explain this and, if possible, provide proof in the form of a solicitor's letter or some other evidence. The DWP should not ask you to provide documents which you obviously do not possess.

If you are unable to provide any documentary evidence of your identity (eg, because you are homeless or fleeing domestic violence), a holistic approach should be taken and a decision made on the information which you are able to provide.

At the interview, you are asked to complete Form CA5400. The DWP may also ask you to complete a form allowing it to contact third parties to establish your identity.

An NI number might be refused for various reasons – eg, if you:
- have been unable to prove your identity;
- have failed to provide sufficient information;
- provided identity documents that are considered not genuine;
- failed to attend an evidence of identity interview; *or*
- failed to respond to correspondence.

If your application for an NI number is refused, the reason should be recorded and notified to you.

You cannot appeal directly against a decision not to allocate you an NI number.[22] However, you can appeal against any decision refusing benefit because the NI number requirement is not met (see p342).

3. **Common problems**

Migrants often have problems with the national insurance (NI) number requirement because, unlike most British citizens, they are not issued with an NI number when they turn 16. The three most common problems are:
- being told you cannot apply for benefit unless you have an NI number (see below);
- delays in benefit because of the NI number requirement (see p341);
- being refused benefit on the grounds that the NI number requirement is not met (see p342).

Making a claim

If you (or your partner if s/he is included in your claim) do not have an NI number, you may be told by Jobcentre Plus, HM Revenue and Customs or the local authority that you cannot claim a benefit or tax credit. Similarly, you may find it impossible to claim online if you cannot provide an NI number.

You do not need an NI number in order to claim a benefit or tax credit, and you should not be prevented from claiming in this situation. As noted on p335, you can satisfy the NI number requirement by applying for an NI number and accompanying your application with sufficient information and evidence for one to be allocated. Your claim for benefit should be treated as the first stage in your application for an NI number (see p338).

If you are unable to make your claim online because you do not have an NI number, you should be able to claim by telephone or, for all benefits other than universal credit (UC), on a paper claim form. Although the aim is for all UC claims to be made online, a telephone claim may be accepted if the DWP is willing to do so.[23] In practice, the DWP usually arranges for you to provide further information to support your claim by attending a meeting with a 'work coach'. You are likely to be asked to take proof of your identity and other information relevant to your entitlement to this meeting.

Have you been told you cannot apply for benefit because you do not have a national insurance number?

If you have lost entitlement because you were prevented from making a claim for benefit in this situation, there may be grounds to get a new claim backdated. If the rules for the benefit or tax credit you are claiming do not allow backdating at all, or for the full period, or if the arrears do not cover the full amount lost, consider requesting compensation.

Delays

Payment of benefit or tax credits can often be delayed because you (or your partner) need to satisfy the NI number requirement or you are waiting for an NI number to be allocated.

Is your benefit delayed?

1. Check whether you or your partner are exempt from the requirement to have an NI number (see p336).

2. If you or your partner have applied for an NI number, but there is a delay in one being allocated, ask that your claim be determined, as there is no requirement for a number to be allocated (see p335). It is likely that your claim will have to be processed clerically before the NI number has been allocated, but this should not prevent payment.

3. If it is a new claim for benefit, or you are adding a partner to your claim that will result in your award increasing, you may be able to obtain a short-term benefit advance (see p311). A short-term benefit advance can be paid if you do not have a NI number, provided you meet the usual conditions, including that the decision maker considers it likely you will be entitled to the benefit.[24] The guidance on short-term benefit advances states they should be considered if you do not have an NI number, provided you can prove your identity and are complying with other requests for required evidence. This guidance also states that the DWP should ensure that all action necessary to allocate an NI number is

taken promptly.[25] Applying for a short-term benefit advance may therefore be a way of getting your NI number allocated more quickly.

4. If you have made a new claim for child benefit and/or guardian's allowance, you may be able to obtain an interim payment (see p314).

5. If you have made a new claim for housing benefit (HB), you may be able to obtain a 'payment on account' (see p319).

6. If you are adding your partner to your existing claim and s/he does not have an NI number, your benefit may be suspended (see p329). You may be able to argue that payment should not be suspended if it is clear that the NI number requirement is likely to be met and the only factor is a question of time.

For further information on your options if your benefit or tax credit payments are delayed, see Chapter 18.

Benefit is refused

You cannot appeal directly against a decision not to allocate you an NI number. However, you can appeal against any decision refusing benefit or tax credit because the NI number requirement is not met. Except for HB, you must first request a revision or, for tax credits, a review (both are known as a 'mandatory reconsideration'). In the appeal (and revision/review request) you can argue that the NI number requirement was met.[26]

Usually, if benefit is refused because the benefit authority says the NI number requirement is not met, the issue in dispute is whether your application was accompanied by sufficient information or evidence to enable a number to be allocated, even if the benefit authority has not considered this point.[27]

Even if you have been refused an NI number, it is possible to argue successfully that you still satisfy the NI number requirement if your application was accompanied by sufficient information or evidence to enable a number to be allocated. However, the law is unclear about whether you can satisfy the NI number requirement if you have not attended an interview,[28] or if you must have attended an interview and completed and signed Form CA5400.[29] If you have been refused an NI number after failing to attend an interview, the reasons why you failed to attend will be relevant.[30]

Have you been refused tax credits?

If the decision maker decides you have not made a valid claim for tax credits because you or your partner do not satisfy the NI number requirement, you can challenge this decision. The Upper Tribunal has held that you have a right of appeal if the basis of your appeal is that your partner is exempt from the NI number requirement because s/he requires leave to enter or remain in the UK but does not have it (see p336).[31] In a subsequent case, the Upper Tribunal went further and held that there is also a right of appeal if you or your partner had a reasonable excuse for not satisfying the NI number requirement (see p337).[32] Remember that you must request a review (a 'mandatory reconsideration') before you can appeal.

Other remedies

If you are refused an NI number, you can write to your MP and ask her/him to help. Your MP can also complain to the Parliamentary and Health Service Ombudsman on your behalf. See CPAG's *Welfare Benefits and Tax Credits Handbook* for more information.

Problems with NI numbers also raise issues about race discrimination since, in practice, the NI number requirement often prejudices black and minority ethnic communities. You may therefore want to refer to the DWP's Equality and Diversity statement when you contact it.[33] The Equality Advisory and Support Service may be able to advise or, in certain cases, take up the issue (see Appendix 2).

Notes

1. **The national insurance number requirement**
1 s1(1A) and (1B) SSAA 1992; reg 5(4) TC(CN) Regs
2 *Leicester City Council v OA* [2009] UKUT 74 (AAC), paras 27 and 28
3 s1(1A) SSAA 1992; reg 5(4) TC(CN) Regs
4 *SSWP v Wilson* [2006] EWCA Civ 882, reported as R(H) 7/06
5 Reg 1A SS(DLA) Regs
6 s1(4) SSAA 1992 and s122 SSCBA 1992
7 Reg 4(a) HB Regs; reg 4(a) HB(SPC) Regs
8 Reg 5(6) TC(CN) Regs
9 **IS** Reg 2A(a) IS Regs has continued effect in these cases due to the transitional protection in reg 1(3) SS(WTCCTC)(CA) Regs.
JSA Reg 2A(a) JSA Regs has continued effect in these cases due to the transitional protection in reg 1(7) SS(WTCCTC)(CA) Regs.
HB Reg 4(b) HB Regs; reg 4(b) HB(SPC) Regs
UC Reg 5 UC,PIP,JSA&ESA(C&P) Regs

10 **IS** Reg 2A IS Regs
JSA Reg 2A JSA Regs
ESA Reg 2A ESA Regs
PC Reg 1A SPC Regs
HB Reg 4(c) HB Regs; reg 4(c) HB(SPC) Regs
TC Reg 5(8) TC(CN) Regs
Bereavement benefits and retirement pensions Reg 1A(c) SS(WB&RP) Regs
11 Vol 1, paras 02184-6 DMG; Ch A2, para A2153 ADM; para 06110 TCTM
12 Ch A2, para A2154 ADM
13 Reg 5(6) TC(CN) Regs
14 para 06110 TCTM
15 *CI v HMRC (TC)* [2014] UKUT 158 (AAC)

2. **Obtaining a national insurance number**
16 On www.gov.uk
17 'Procedures for issuing a NINO to asylum claimants granted leave to enter or remain in the UK', available on www.gov.uk

18 Reg 15 Immigration (Biometric
Registration) Regulations 2008,
No.3048
19 www.gov.uk/national-insurance/your-
national-insurance-number
20 www.gov.uk/government/publications/
secure-national-insurance-number-
allocation-process-staff-guide
21 CH/4085/2007; HB/CTB Circular A13/
2010, paras 14 and 15; paras 0316020
and 1000371 TCM
22 CH/1231/2004

3. Common problems

23 Reg 8 UC,PIP,JSA&ESA(C&P) Regs; para
A2030 ADM
24 Reg 5 SS(PAB) Regs
25 Short-term benefit advance benefit
processing guidance, paras 64-
65; short-term benefit advance
jobcentre guidance, paras 21-22; short-
term benefit advance contact centre
guidance, para 18
26 CH/1231/2004; CH/4085/2007;
Leicester City Council v OA [2009] UKUT
74 (AAC)
27 CH/1231/2004
28 CH/4085/2007, para 30
29 *Leicester City Council v OA* [2009] UKUT
74 (AAC), para 35
30 CH/4085/2007, para 32
31 *ZM and AB v HMRC (TC)* [2013] UKUT
547 (AAC)
32 *CI v HMRC (TC)* [2014] UKUT 158 (AAC)
33 www.gov.uk/government/
organisations/department-for-work-
pensions/about/equality-and-diversity

Chapter 20

Providing evidence

This chapter covers:
1. General points about evidence (below)
2. Evidence of immigration status (p351)
3. Evidence of residence rights (p353)
4. Types of evidence (p354)

This chapter covers some of the issues that arise when you are required to provide evidence to show that you satisfy the immigration conditions (see Part 3), the residence conditions (see Part 4) or that you are covered by the European Union co-ordination rules (see Chapter 16).

1. General points about evidence

There are some issues and principles that apply to the evidence you may be asked to provide, or that you should provide, when you make a claim for a benefit or tax credit, or when you challenge a decision about your entitlement.

Evidence required when you make your claim

When you claim a benefit or tax credit, you must normally:
- satisfy the national insurance (NI) number requirement (see Chapter 19); *and*
- provide proof of your identity, if required (see below); *and*
- ensure your claim is valid (see p346).

To determine your claim, the decision maker needs evidence that you satisfy all the conditions of entitlement and that you are not covered by any of the exceptions that mean you are not entitled. You can be asked for evidence to show that you satisfy all the conditions of entitlement, including the immigration, residence or presence conditions, or that the European Union (EU) co-ordination rules apply to you.

Proving your identity

You may be asked to produce further documents or evidence that prove your identity. If your partner is included in your claim, even if you do not receive an amount for her/him (eg, because s/he is a 'person subject to immigration control' – see p73), you may also be asked to prove her/his identity. In addition, if your claim includes an amount for your child, you may be asked to prove her/his identity.

There are various documents that you can provide to the benefit authorities as proof of your identity. You should not be required to supply particular documents that it is unreasonable for you to have or obtain, and you should not be refused a benefit or tax credit simply because you can not provide a particular document. For more information on providing evidence to show your entitlement to a benefit or tax credit, see p347.

The www.gov.uk website on applying for an NI number has a non-exhaustive list of examples of documents that prove your identity, and you should provide one or more of these if possible. For these and other documents that could be used to prove your identity, see p338. It can be helpful to provide details of anyone who can confirm what you have stated – eg, your solicitor or other legal representative or official organisation.

Note: if you are claiming universal credit in a 'full service area', you may be required to prove your identity online using the gov.uk/verify system. This uses various private companies to check your identity. You should not be prevented from making your claim just because you do not have the preferred form of proof.[1] At the time of writing, the details of this system were still being developed, but CPAG understands that if you cannot meet online verification via one of the DWP approved partners, you can provide biometric verification in person at a Jobcentre Plus office. See CPAG's online service and *Welfare Rights Bulletin* for updates.

Making a valid claim

To be entitled to a benefit or tax credit, you must make a valid claim. This means you must claim in the correct way and your claim must not be 'defective'. The DWP, HM Revenue and Customs (HMRC) or the local authority should inform you if your claim is defective and must then give you the opportunity to correct the defect.

If your claim is refused because it is not valid, you have a right to challenge that decision. Note: for tax credits this right is provided by caselaw, rather than legislation.[2] The case concerned a claim that was not accepted as valid because it did not satisfy the NI number requirement (see p342), but the principle that there must be a right of appeal (after a mandatory reconsideration) also applies when a claim is not accepted as valid for a different reason. In all cases, if you challenge a decision that your claim is not valid, you should also make a fresh claim.

If your claim is accepted as valid, the decision maker must make a decision on your entitlement.

What counts as a valid claim varies between the individual benefits and tax credits. What you are required to do to make your claim in the correct way is also affected by the method by which you can make your claim – ie, in writing, only on a certain form, online, and/or also by telephone. The rules for each benefit and tax credit are covered in CPAG's *Welfare Benefits and Tax Credits Handbook*.

Evidence that you are entitled

When you claim a benefit or tax credit you must generally show, on the balance of probabilities, that you meet the conditions of entitlement.[3] If you do not meet these under the UK rules, but the EU co-ordination rules (see Chapter 16) enable you to be entitled, you must provide evidence of this.

The inquisitorial nature of benefit adjudication means that decision makers, who know what information and evidence is needed to decide whether you satisfy the conditions of entitlement, must ask you for that information. If you have been asked for information or evidence and fail, to the best of your abilities, to provide it, the decision maker can assume that you do not meet that particular condition of entitlement. However, the decision maker cannot do this if s/he fails to ask the relevant questions and does not give you a reasonable opportunity to provide the necessary information and evidence.[4]

If you have documentary evidence showing that you meet the entitlement conditions, you should always submit it. However, if you cannot do so, as documentary evidence corroborates and reinforces your own evidence given in the process of making your claim or subsequently, your own evidence can be accepted without its being corroborated. Corroborative evidence is not necessary unless there are reasons to doubt your evidence – eg, if it is self-contradictory or inherently improbable.[5]

If you are asked for a particular document that you do not have, ask why this is needed so that you have the opportunity to provide alternatives. If you cannot provide any documentary proof of a particular fact, explain why not (eg, because all your documents are with the Home Office) and, if possible, provide proof of this – eg, a letter from your legal representative. If you consider any requests for information are unreasonable, you can complain. Get advice if you think you have experienced discrimination – eg, from the Equality Advisory and Support Service (see Appendix 3).

Evidence that you are not excluded

If there is an exception to entitlement that excludes you from a benefit or a tax credit to which you would otherwise be entitled (eg, because you are not habitually resident or because you are defined as a 'person subject to immigration control'), the burden of proving that this exception applies to you lies with the benefit authorities.[6]

If you have evidence that an exception does not apply to you, you should always submit this.

If you do not provide evidence that you are not excluded from entitlement when you make your claim, the decision maker must ask you for the information and evidence required for her/him to make a decision. It is an established principle that the process of benefit adjudication is inquisitorial rather than adversarial, and it is the decision maker (or First-tier Tribunal) who knows what information is required to determine whether you are entitled to benefit or whether you are excluded from entitlement, and who must therefore ask for that information.[7]

If some relevant facts are still unknown after all the enquiries have been made, the question of whether an exception applies that excludes you from entitlement should be decided in your favour.[8]

If the decision maker failed to ask all the relevant questions, because it has an inquisitorial role, the First-tier Tribunal must ask you those questions.[9] However, if you have evidence that an exception to entitlement does not apply to you, you should submit this in advance of the hearing where possible.

If you cannot provide the evidence required to determine whether or not you are excluded, but that evidence is available to the benefit authorities, see p349.

Decisions to end your entitlement

If you are receiving benefits or tax credits and the benefit authority terminates your award on the basis that you no longer satisfy the immigration, residence or presence rules, the burden of proof is on the benefit authority to show the evidence on which this decision is based. If the decision maker has not shown this and based her/his decision on the fact that you failed to provide evidence that nothing has changed, you should challenge the decision and include this argument. You should still set out clearly the reasons why you are not excluded from entitlement by the rules.

The same burden of proof also applies to the First-tier Tribunal.

There are a number of recent Upper Tribunal decisions concerning tax credits that confirm that the burden of proof is on HMRC to establish that there are grounds for revising a decision that you are entitled to tax credits, and that the same burden of proof applies to the First-tier Tribunal. This applies if HMRC wants to revise:

- the entitlement decision for the current year. HMRC must show the evidence for its 'reasonable grounds for believing' that the decision is wrong;[10] *and*
- the entitlement decision for a previous year for which the award has already been finalised.[11]

However, if HMRC decides that you have ceased to be entitled during the tax credit renewal period, the onus of proof is on you to show your continued entitlement.[12]

Example

Nardos is an Eritrean national with discretionary leave to remain in the UK, with no restriction on receiving public funds, for two and a half years. She claimed child tax credit (CTC), provided proof of her leave and was awarded CTC. Her leave was due to expire two months ago, but before it did Nardos applied for a further period of discretionary leave. She received an acknowledgement letter from the Home Office, and forwarded a copy of this to the Tax Credit Office, but has not yet had a decision from the Home Office. Her discretionary leave to remain is extended while she waits for the Home Office to determine her application for further leave (see p352).

The Tax Credit Office wrote to Nardos asking her to provide evidence that she was entitled to receive public funds – both now and since the start of her claim. Nardos did not know how she could show this and so did not reply. She then received a decision letter, informing her that, as she has not shown she can receive public funds, HMRC has decided she is a 'person subject to immigration control' (see p57) and not entitled to CTC. Her award was terminated and HMRC has decided to recover the overpaid CTC since the start of her claim.

Nardos can challenge this decision, by requesting a mandatory reconsideration. HMRC has not provided any evidence to show that her entitlement has ended, nor that the original decision awarding her CTC was incorrect. The evidence that Nardos had already given HMRC shows that she has leave to remain in the UK with no restriction on receiving public funds. She therefore does not need to provide any further evidence that she is not excluded by her immigration status because it has not changed. She should explain this in her mandatory reconsideration request and remind HMRC that the Upper Tribunal has confirmed that the onus of proof is on HMRC to show the evidence relied upon in deciding that she is not entitled to CTC and has not been since the start of her claim.

If evidence is not available to you

If your potential exclusion from benefit entitlement depends on evidence that is not available to you, but which is available to the benefit authority, the benefit authority must take the necessary steps to obtain this information. If it fails to do so and consequently it is not known whether or not you are excluded from benefit, the matter must be decided in your favour – ie, that you are not excluded.[13]

This principle was established by the House of Lords in the case of *Kerr*[14] and is significant for migrants. For example, if the decision maker needs evidence of your immigration status that the Home Office has but you do not, s/he must use her/his channels of communication with the Home Office to obtain it.[15]

The principle is also significant if your entitlement depends on someone else's circumstances and the relevant information about these is not available to you, but it could be available to the benefit authority if the decision maker made enquiries or checked records. For example, the decision maker may need evidence of your right to reside which depends on the current or past economic activity of a family member (see p165), but you cannot contact her/him or s/he will not provide you with the information you need. Examples include if your right to reside depends on your being:

- the spouse or civil partner of a European Economic Area (EEA) national from whom you are now separated or the child under 21 of an EEA national, and in either case the EEA national is in the UK with a right to reside:
  - as a worker (see p140);
  - with retained worker status (see p146);
  - as a self-employed person (see p153);
  - with retained self-employed status (see p157);
  - with a permanent right to reside (see p184);
- previously a family member of an EEA national legally resident in the UK for five years and you are trying to prove that you now have a permanent right to reside (see p184);
- the primary carer of a child in education and you need to prove that one of the child's parents had worker status in the UK while child was also in the UK (see p179).

If this applies to you, you should provide the benefit authority with as much information as possible to enable it to trace the evidence that you cannot provide, but which could be available to the decision maker if s/he made enquiries or checked records.

Example

Kristina is a 19-year-old Slovakian national who came to the UK last week. She came to the UK because she is due to give birth next week and wanted the support of her father, Pavol, who has been in the UK for two years. However, Pavol disapproves of Kristina's pregnancy and has said that he never wants to hear from her again. Kristina is sleeping on a friend's sofa and has claimed income support (IS). If Pavol has 'worker' status, Kristina is entitled to IS as his family member – she has a right to reside as the family member of a worker and is also in a group exempt from the habitual residence test.

Kristina has her own birth certificate which names Pavol as her father and confirms his nationality. However, she cannot get evidence of Pavol's worker status from him as he will not speak to her. Kristina has heard that Pavol was made redundant two months ago and is now claiming jobseeker's allowance (JSA). Therefore, if she can provide sufficient information to the DWP for it to be able to trace Pavol's JSA claim, the DWP will be able to obtain details of his previous work from it and assess whether that work gave him worker status and whether he has retained that status while claiming JSA. The DWP holds this information and therefore must take the necessary steps to enable it to be traced. If it fails to do so, Kristina can argue that she cannot be excluded from IS on the basis of not being habitually resident, as this has not been proved by the DWP.

How do you get the benefit authorities to check someone's residence rights?
If your right to reside depends on someone else's residence rights, but you cannot obtain proof of these, you should ask the benefit authorities to carry out the necessary investigations.

1 Although there is a duty on the benefit authorities to take the necessary steps to trace information which is available to them and not you,[16] it is unlikely they will do so without you clearly asking them to. Your request should explain why you are unable to obtain the necessary information and remind them of their duty to trace the information, citing the principles established in the case of *Kerr*.[17]

2. Explain your right to reside in your letter, how this results from your relationship with the other person (eg, as her/his family member or primary carer of her/his child) and what information needs to be obtained – eg, evidence of current employment.

3. Provide as much as possible of the following information on the relevant person's:
– name;
– date of birth;
– NI number;
– last known address;
– last known place of work;
– nationality;
– previous benefit claims – eg, which benefit and when claimed.

4. The benefit authority must then take the necessary steps to trace the information, by checking records of any benefit claims or NI contributions.

Note: guidance confirms that decision makers should use additional records available to them (eg, NI contribution records) to confirm if a claimant has permanent residence.[18]

5. If the benefit authority fails to make the necessary investigations, you cannot be excluded from benefit on the basis of not having a right to reside, as the burden of proof is on the benefit authority to show that you do not have a right to reside (see p347).

6. If the benefit authority refuses to carry out the investigations, including if it tells you it is prohibited from doing so under date protection legislation, you should appeal. Ask the First-tier Tribunal for a direction requiring the decision maker to carry out the necessary investigations. It can make such a direction once your appeal has been made.[19] If you request a direction before your appeal hearing, this avoids the need for the hearing to be adjourned. It can also mean that, once the necessary information has been traced, the decision refusing your claim is revised, you are awarded benefit and your appeal lapses.

2. **Evidence of immigration status**

If you are not a European Economic Area (EEA) national and you are claiming any of the benefits or tax credits listed on p65, the decision maker needs evidence of your immigration status to determine whether you are a 'person subject to immigration control' (see p57).

If you are claiming means-tested benefits or tax credits and your partner lives with you and is not an EEA national, the decision maker also needs evidence of her/his immigration status to determine whether s/he is a 'person subject to immigration control'. See p73 for the rules if your partner is a 'person subject to immigration control'.

It is rare for a decision maker to need evidence of your child's immigration status, as this does not affect whether or not you can be paid for her/him. However, if your child is the claimant (eg, for disability living allowance), the decision maker requires evidence of her/his immigration status to determine whether s/he is a 'person subject to immigration control'.

Note: if your partner or child has leave which is subject to a 'no recourse to public funds' condition, this condition may be breached if s/he is included in your (or someone else's) claim and this could jeopardise her/his immigration status (see p59).

Further information on checking your immigration status is in Chapter 6. If you are unclear about your, or your partner's or child's, immigration status, you should obtain immigration advice (see Appendix 2) before making any claim for benefits or tax credits.

Problems with evidence

Problems can arise if you do not have documentary evidence or if the documents you have are unclear. The general points about evidence all apply (see p345). You should not be refused benefit because you cannot provide a particular document, and you should ask why a document is being requested so you can provide the evidence through another means. If you cannot provide a document (eg, because it is with the Home Office), it can help if you provide a letter confirming this from your legal representative. S/he may also be able to confirm your current immigration status and the significance of any applications you have pending.

If evidence of immigration status is not available to you, but is available to the decision maker (eg, by emailing the Home Office), s/he must take the necessary steps to obtain this (see p349).

Changes in immigration status

If you have time-limited leave to enter or remain, you can apply to extend your leave or apply for further leave to remain on a different basis. Provided you apply before your existing leave expires, this leave is extended until your application is decided by the Home Office.[20] If your original leave was not subject to the condition that you do not have recourse to public funds, you were not a 'person subject to immigration control' and therefore you were entitled to all benefits and tax credits subject to the normal rules of entitlement. When your leave is extended, you must notify the benefit authorities. Otherwise, they may consider you to be someone whose leave has expired and therefore a person subject to immigration control on the basis of being someone who requires leave but does not have it (see p57) and therefore no longer entitled to benefit.

The benefit authorities need evidence that you applied to vary your leave before your existing leave ended. If possible, you should submit documents showing when your leave was due to expire (which the benefit authorities may already have on your file), together with confirmation of the date when your application to vary that leave was submitted – eg, a letter from a legal representative who helped you with the application, or a letter confirming the date your application was received. Although it should not be necessary, in practice it also helps if you submit a covering letter. In this, explain that your previous leave is extended because you applied to vary your leave before your previous leave expired,[21] you therefore continue not to be a person subject to immigration control, and so your benefit or tax credit entitlement also continues. Include the relevant legal references in your letter.

Note: if your application to vary your leave is refused and your leave is extended while your appeal against that refusal is pending, you may count as a person subject to immigration control (see p63).

3. **Evidence of residence rights**

Your residence rights under European Union law can be complex and involve many steps, each requiring certain conditions to be met. It is advisable to set out your residence rights to the decision maker as clearly as possible and, wherever possible, provide evidence of every requirement. If you lack documentary evidence of one requirement, but you have provided evidence of others, it is more likely that the decision maker will accept your uncorroborated evidence on the remaining requirement (unless it is self-contradictory or inherently improbable – see p347).

The actual requirements vary depending on the residence right you are asserting (see Chapter 12). See p354 for some of the most commonly required types of evidence.

Residence documents

The only circumstance when you need a residence document in order to have a right to reside is if you are an 'extended family member'. In this case, you need a relevant residence document in order to be *treated as* a 'family member' of someone who can confer a right of residence on you (see p167).

For any other right to reside, you do not need a residence document because your right to reside depends on the facts of your situation. Documentation can only confirm a residence right you have and cannot give you a right to reside, if either the documentation was issued in error or correctly confirmed your right to reside when issued but your circumstances have now changed.[22]

However, obtaining a residence document can make it easier for you to demonstrate your residence rights rather than having to provide all your evidence every time. For example, once you have acquired a permanent right of residence, it is easier to provide a permanent residence document, together with evidence that you have not lost this right by leaving the UK for more than two years (see p192) than it is, for example, to provide weekly payslips spanning a five-year period.

You can be issued with the following residence documents.

- **A registration certificate** if you are a European Economic Area (EEA) national with a right of residence provided under the EEA Regulations.[23]
- **A residence card** if you are a non-EEA national and you have a right to reside as the family member of an EEA 'qualified person' (see p126) or an EEA national with a permanent right of residence.[24]
- **A derivative residence card** if you have a derivative right to reside (see p175).[25]
- **A document certifying permanent right of residence** if you are an EEA national with a permanent right of residence, or a **permanent residence card** if you are a non-EEA national with a permanent right of residence.[26]
- **A residence permit**, issued to EEA nationals and their family members before 30 April 2006. These were valid for a five-year period. From 30 April 2006, these documents should be treated as if they were the equivalent type of document issued after that date.[27]
- **A family permit** issued for entry to the UK if you are a non-EEA family member of an EEA national and do not have any of the other residence documentation.

Forms and further information, including about application fees, are available on the UK Visas and Immigration website (see Appendix 3).

---

4. **Types of evidence**

Certain types of evidence are of particular significance for migrants and are discussed below. Depending on your circumstances and the benefit or tax credit being claimed, this evidence may be required by all claimants to satisfy the entitlement conditions, or because it affects the amount to which you are entitled. If the evidence is required by all claimants, you should not be required to submit more evidence because you are a migrant than would be required of a British person in the same circumstances.

It can be helpful to check the guidance issued to decision makers on acceptable evidence and refer to this where it supports your situation. Check both the general guidance applicable to all benefits, such as on age, marriage and death,[28] and guidance specific to migrants,[29] including on the right to reside and habitual residence tests.[30] For example, part of the DWP guidance covers evidence relevant to establishing permanent residence.[31]

Evidence from other countries

If your documentary evidence originates in another country and is not in English, it can be helpful to submit an authorised translation. If obtaining a translation will cause any delay, you should ensure that you do not miss any deadlines for submitting evidence. For example, you could take the original document to a local benefit office to take an authorised copy and accompany this with a letter explaining that you are obtaining a translation.

The authenticity of a document issued outside the UK should not automatically be questioned just because it was not issued in the UK. Decision makers are reminded in guidance that certificates of birth, marriage, civil partnerships and deaths issued abroad can all be accepted as evidence of that event, unless there is a reason to doubt their authenticity.[32]

Even if a document originates in a country in which it is relatively easy to obtain fraudulent documents, a decision maker (or First-tier Tribunal) cannot presume that your document is not genuine. The decision maker (or First-tier Tribunal) can conclude that a document is not genuine on the balance of probabilities, but it is rarely necessary to decide whether or not a document is forged as the decison maker (or First-tier Tribunal) should determine the weight given to any single piece of evidence. This weighting is affected by factors such as whether there is any information or evidence of the accuracy of record keeping by the issuing body, whether other evidence corroborates the document issued abroad, and the overall view taken of your credibility.[33]

Evidence of your nationality

The most common acceptable evidence of your nationality is a current passport, a current European Economic Area (EEA) identity card or, if you are a non-EEA national, a current travel document or biometric residence permit. However, if you cannot provide one of these, other official documents should be accepted (see p338). As with all evidence requirements, it helps if you can provide more than one form of evidence of your nationality.

If you are relying on someone else's nationality for your own rights (eg, to argue you have a right to reside as the family member of an EEA worker), you must provide evidence of her/his nationality – eg, to show s/he is an EEA national.

Evidence of your relationship to someone

If your rights are based on being someone's family member or primary carer, you must provide evidence of this relationship. This can enable you to show that you:

- are covered by the European Union (EU) co-ordination rules (see p265);
- are a family member of an EEA national exercising EU Treaty rights and are therefore not a 'person subject to immigration control' (see p58);
- are in a group of people who can claim a benefit despite being a person subject to immigration control (see p66);
- have a right to reside as a family member of an EEA national (see p164) or as the primary carer of someone who can confer residence rights on you (see p175); *or*
- are exempt from the habitual residence test as the family member of an EEA worker or self-employed person (see p106).

For your residence rights to be accepted, you must show that you are a family member or primary carer and that all the other requirements of that right to reside are satisfied.

For example, if you are asserting that you are a family member of a worker, you must show that:

- the person who is working is an EEA national (see p355);
- the work s/he does gives her/him 'worker' status (see p360);
- if s/he has ceased to be a worker, s/he retains worker status (see p146);
- you come within the definition of being her/his 'family member' (see p165).

If you are asserting that you are the primary carer of a worker's child in education, you must show that:

- the adult who worked is the parent of that child;
- the parent who worked is an EEA national (see p355);
- the work the parent did gave her/him 'worker' status (see p360);
- the child was in the UK while the parent had worker status;
- the child is currently in school;
- you are her/his primary carer (see p180).

Non-European Economic Area nationals

If you are a non-EEA national and are the family member of an EEA national who confers residence rights on you, you are not a 'person subject to immigration control' (see p58).

If you entered the UK as the family member of an EEA national who is in the UK exercising her/his Treaty rights (eg, as a worker), you usually have an entry clearance document that states this. You should provide this to the benefit authorities, as it is the most significant documentary evidence required. However, depending on your circumstances, the benefit authorities may also want evidence that your family member is still in the UK exercising her/his Treaty rights.

If you are a non-EEA national and are the primary carer of someone who confers a derivative right to reside on you (see p175), the benefit authorities require evidence of each requirement that must be satisfied for you to have this right to reside.

If your derivative right to reside is based on your being the primary carer of a British citizen, you must show that s/he would be unable to reside anywhere in the EEA if you were required to leave. However, this derivative right to reside only means you are not excluded from benefits by your immigration status as you are not a person subject to immigration control. It does not enable you to be entitled to any benefit that requires you to have a right to reside (see p181).

In contrast, if you are the primary carer of a worker's child in education (see above for the evidence required to show this), you have a right to reside which enables you to claim all benefits that have a right to reside requirement.

Evidence of marriage or civil partnership

If you have been given leave to enter or remain on the basis of being a spouse or civil partner of someone, evidence of that leave is generally accepted as sufficient evidence of your relationship for the purposes of proving your entitlement to a benefit or tax credit.

Spouses and civil partners have far greater rights under EU law than partners who are not married or who are not civil partners. Consequently, it can be important to show that someone is your spouse or civil partner – eg, when s/he can confer residence rights on you. If you need to prove that you are someone's spouse or civil partner, you must show that you are still married or in a civil partnership. If you have separated and are no longer living together or in a relationship, you are still her/his spouse or civil partner until you are finally divorced or the civil partnership is finally dissolved.[34]

A marriage or civil partnership certificate is the best evidence. If the certificate was issued outside the UK by the appropriate registration authority, it should be accepted as valid evidence (see p355).[35]

If you do not have a marriage or civil partnership certificate, other evidence which confirms your marriage or civil partnership can be accepted. Official documents that refer to your marriage or civil partnership, as well as official correspondence confirming you live together, can be evidence to be taken into account.

There is extensive guidance for decision makers on evidence of marriage and civil partnerships, including religious and national variations.[36]

Evidence of parentage

If you have been given leave to enter or remain on the basis of being a parent or child of someone, evidence of that leave is generally accepted as sufficient evidence of your relationship for the purposes of proving your entitlement to a benefit or tax credit.

If you are showing that you are the parent or child of someone who can confer residence rights on you, it is important to show that you meet all the conditions for being defined as a 'family member'.

To be a 'family member' as a child of someone who can confer residence rights on you, you must show:

- s/he is your parent; *and*
- either you are aged under 21 *or* you are dependent on her/him.

To be a 'family member' as a parent of someone who can confer residence rights on you, you must show:

- you are her/his parent; *and*
- you are dependent on her/him.

A birth certificate, or official DNA test results, that name both child and parent should be sufficient evidence. If the document originates from outside the UK, see p355.

If you do not have a birth certificate or official DNA test results, other documents can also be accepted. If you do not have anything decisive, submit the evidence you have to back up your own evidence and ask for the decision maker to decide on the balance of probabilities (see p347).

Example

Nadifa is 18 and a Dutch national. She has health problems and wants to claim income-related employment and support allowance and housing benefit (HB). She came to the UK four years ago with her mother, who is also a Dutch national, having acquired Dutch citizenship after fleeing to the Netherlands as a refugee 15 years ago. Nadifa's mother is a self-employed translator and has extensive evidence of this. However, Nadifa does not have any evidence that she is her mother's daughter. Her mother fled to the Netherlands without any documents. Nadifa therefore submits evidence of her mother's Dutch nationality and self-employment, together with a letter setting out the relevant details of her life history and documents showing that she was given leave to remain in the Netherlands as a dependant on her mother's asylum claim, evidence that she travelled with her mother to the UK four years ago and letters from her GP and dermatologist discussing Nadifa's eczema and the likelihood of its being linked to her mother's eczema.

Note: if you are trying to show that you are someone's father or that someone is your father, until officially declared otherwise, a man is deemed to be a child's father if he was married to the child's mother at the time of the child's birth or his name was registered on the birth certificate.

Evidence of your age

Your age (or someone else's age) can affect whether or not you meet the basic conditions of entitlement to a benefit, and the amount to which you are entitled. Your age (or someone else's age) can also affect your residence rights, whether your immigration status excludes you from benefits and tax credits and/ or whether you are covered by the EU co-ordination rules. In addition, age can affect whether you (or someone else) are defined as a 'family member' or as 'dependent'.

A birth certificate, passport or identity card is usually accepted as proof of your date of birth. Other evidence that can show your date of birth includes school, medical or army records. Guidance to decision makers states that the 'primary' or best evidence of age is a certified copy of an entry which has to be made in a register by law, such as a birth certificate or adoption certificate.[37] If you were born abroad and have a certificate issued by the appropriate registration authority, this should be accepted unless there is reason to doubt its validity (see p355).[38]

See also the other evidence that can be accepted as proof of your identity on p338 and guidance to decision makers on 'secondary' evidence of age.[39]

You may be able to show your date of birth by referring to the accepted birth dates of other relatives, such as siblings.[40] For example, if you are recorded as the eldest child and your sister has been accepted as born in 1995, you must have been born before then.

If you have no record of your date of birth, or there is conflicting evidence, it is possible for an age assessment to be carried out. However, there is no accurate scientific test that can establish a person's age, and such an assessment can be disputed. See p392 for age assessments for unaccompanied asylum-seeking children. Guidance to decision makers covers the possibility of arranging a physical examination of an adult by medical services, but notes that this is generally only reliable five years either way.[41] However, getting your GP to state her/his opinion of your age, together with her/his reasons, can be helpful supporting evidence, particularly if it is clear that the GP has known you for some time and is familiar with your medical conditions.[42]

A common problem is conflicting evidence due to past errors. Your date of birth may have been wrongly recorded in your passport when it was issued – eg, because you gave the wrong date or because of an administrative error. The date in the passport may then have been used in many other official documents and it may be difficult to persuade the benefit authorities that all these dates are wrong. You should explain that all these dates come from one document and give a detailed account about how the wrong date came to be recorded. This explanation counts as evidence, but if you have (or can obtain) other evidence showing that date is not correct, you should submit it.[43]

While each piece of evidence must be considered, the oldest documents may be more reliable, since they were made nearer to the time of the events to which they refer.

Passports and other immigration documents are commonly recorded as '1 January' when your exact date of birth is unclear. However, if you obtain evidence of your exact date of birth later, this can be accepted.

The decision maker, or First-tier Tribunal, should weigh up all the available evidence and determine your age on the balance of probabilities, not by any higher standard.[44]

If there is no documentary evidence, the benefit authorities should accept your own statements, unless they are contradictory or improbable (see p347).

Evidence of work

Evidence of your own or someone else's current or past employment or self-employment can be required in order to prove that you satisfy, or are exempt from, immigration or residence conditions, or that you are covered by the EU co-ordination rules. The exact evidence required depends on what you need to prove, so it is essential that you check the rules for the specific condition you are trying to satisfy or be exempt from.

Examples

Samir is a national of Algeria and is in the UK to study. He has a student visa, which gives him leave to be in the UK for the next two years, subject to the condition that he does not have recourse to public funds. Samir is therefore a 'person subject to immigration control' (see p57). He works 15 hours a week, which is permitted under the conditions of his student visa. Samir wants to claim child benefit and child tax credit (CTC) because his girlfriend's 14-year-old French son has just come to live with him while she goes to Canada for a year. Samir can claim both child benefit and CTC if he can show that he is 'lawfully working', as this shows he is in a group of people who can claim despite being a 'person subject to immigration control' (see p70 for child benefit and p72 for CTC). Samir must provide HM Revenue and Customs (HMRC) with evidence of his employment (eg, a payslip or letter from his employer), together with confirmation that his work is allowed under the conditions of his immigration leave, proof of his Algerian nationality and his student visa.

Dimitra is a Greek national who wants to claim income support (IS) and HB as she is due to have a baby in three weeks. She came to the UK six years ago and got a job after being here a month. She stayed in this job until she was made redundant last month. If Dimitra can show that she had a right to reside as a 'worker' for a continuous period of five years, she will have a permanent right to reside (see p184), which satisfies the right to reside requirement for IS and HB. Dimitra must provide evidence confirming that she was in an employment relationship (see p142) doing 'genuine and effective' work (see p143) for a continuous period of five years.

As with all evidence requirements, there is no definitive list of what counts as acceptable. The evidence of work is considered stronger if it has several ways of showing it relates to you – eg, if it shows your full name, your date of birth, your address and your national insurance (NI) number, rather than just one or two of these.

Evidence of employment includes:

- a contract of employment;
- payslips;
- correspondence from your employer to you – eg, offering you the job or confirming a change in hours;
- a letter from an employer confirming your employment;
- bank statements showing wages being paid in from the employer.

If you are not actually working (eg, because you are on sick leave or maternity leave), you may not have ceased to have a right to reside as a 'worker' (see p145). You need to provide evidence that you are still under a contract of employment, such as a letter from your employer stating this. Alternatively, if you have ceased to be a worker, you may be able to retain your worker status and must provide evidence of the basis of this (see p146) in addition to the evidence of the worker status you had.

Evidence of self-employment includes:

- documents from HMRC confirming your registration as a self-employed person;
- evidence of paying Class 2 NI contributions;
- business accounts;
- samples of marketing;
- documents showing you have purchased the equipment needed to carry out your trade.

If you are seeking to demonstrate that you have a right to reside as a self-employed person, it should be enough to show that you have established yourself in order to undertake activity as a self-employed person (see p155).

If you are not actually working, you may not have ceased to have a right to reside as a self-employed person. You must provide evidence of all the factors that are relevant in your circumstances (see p156).

You may be able to retain your self-employed status (see p157) and need to provide evidence of this in addition to the evidence of your self-employment.

If your right to reside depends on someone else being, or having been, a worker or self-employed, all the above points apply to evidence of their work. However, if you do not have any documentary evidence of this because you cannot contact the person or s/he will not provide you with the evidence, you may be able to argue that the benefit authorities should obtain this evidence (see p349).

Croatian, A2 and A8 nationals

The additional restrictions (see p127) that currently apply to Croatian nationals and which previously applied to A2 nationals (between 1 January 2007 and 1 January 2014) and to A8 nationals (between 1 May 2004 and the date the restrictions ended, now held to be 1 May 2009 rather than 2011 but this is subject to appeal – see p127) mean that 'workers' from these states must supply additional evidence. If you need to show that you have (or had) a right to reside as a 'worker', you must show that, at the time of working, you:

- were exempt from restrictions (see p129 for Croatian and A2 nationals, and p130 for A8 nationals); *or*
- (for Croatian and A2 nationals) worked in accordance with a valid authorisation document (see p128); *or*
- (for A8 nationals) worked for an 'authorised employer' (see p131). **Note:** a registration certificate that was applied for after the first month of work is not retrospective, and so is only evidence that you were working for an authorised employer from the date the certificate was issued.[45] Also, because you were classed as working for an authorised employer for the first month of any employment, you do not need to provide a registration certificate for this first month.

If you are unable to provide your authorisation document or registration certificate because it has been lost or stolen, you should provide the benefit authority with as much information as you can about your employment and when it was authorised or registered, and ask the decision maker to confirm this through her/his contacts with the Home Office. You can also contact the Home Office yourself and ask for a letter confirming the details of your authorisation or registration(s). Your employer at the relevant time may also be able to assist you with evidence confirming your authorisation or registration.

There are no additional restrictions, and therefore no additional evidence requirements, if you (or the person whose right to reside you are relying on) was self-employed.

Evidence of jobseeking

To have a right to reside as a jobseeker, you must be able to provide evidence that you are seeking employment and have a 'genuine chance of being engaged'.

These requirements are similar to the requirements to be 'actively seeking' and 'available for' work for the purposes of being entitled to jobseeker's allowance (JSA) or NI credits, and to the work search and work availability requirements if you come under the universal credit (UC) system. This means that, in most cases, if the decision maker accepts that you have provided evidence to satisfy these requirements for JSA, UC or NI credits on the basis of unemployment, this should also be accepted as satisfying the requirements that enable you to have a right to reside as a jobseeker. For the circumstances when this might not apply, see p137.

Under European law, there is no time limit on how long you can have a right to reside as a jobseeker – it continues for as long as you can provide evidence that you are looking for work and have a genuine chance of being engaged.[46]

However, under UK EEA Regulations, in order to continue to have a right to reside as a jobseeker for longer than 91 days, the evidence you provide of this must be 'compelling'.[47] This requirement is referred to as the 'genuine prospects of work test' (see p134 and below).

To have a right to reside as someone who retains worker status on the basis of being involuntarily unemployed, the EEA Regulations require you to provide evidence that you are seeking employment and have a genuine chance of being engaged (see p147).[48] After six months of retaining your worker status on this basis, the evidence must be 'compelling' (see p135 and below). **Note:** under the EU Directive 2004/38 there is no requirement to provide 'compelling' evidence in order to retain your worker status on the basis of being involuntarily unemployed.[49]

The Upper Tribunal has held that the requirement to provide 'compelling' evidence means that you must provide evidence that shows, on the balance of probabilities, that you are seeking employment and have a genuine chance of being engaged. It would be contrary to EU law if the phrase was interpreted to mean that a higher standard of proof is required.[50] Under EU law, although you must be able to provide evidence that you are continuing to seek work and have a genuine chance of being engaged, the quality of this evidence is not required to change after a particular period of time.[51] The Upper Tribunal has held that if you have been seeking employment without success for at least six months, this is a factor (along with others) that is relevant when determining whether you have a genuine chance of being engaged. However, the requirement for evidence to be 'compelling' after after a certain period 'cannot raise the bar' for what constitutes a genuine chance of being engaged.[52]

You should therefore provide as much evidence as possible to show that, on the balance of probabilities, you are seeking employment and have a genuine chance of being engaged. Evidence that you are seeking employment could include details of all your work search activities, evidence of enquiries made to potential employers, evidence of applications and any interviews together with responses.

The DWP has produced guidance for JSA decision makers on what counts as 'compelling' evidence of a 'genuine chance of being engaged'. This guidance was written before the two Upper Tribunal decisions referred to above and, in any case, as guidance, is not legally binding.

However, if it is useful because it applies in your circumstances, you should still refer to it. The guidance gives limited examples of evidence that can be accepted as 'compelling'. These include:[53]

- reliable evidence that you have an offer of work that will start within three months and which is 'genuine and effective'; *or*

- proof that your circumstances have changed in a way that improves your prospects of obtaining work – eg, you have recently (the guidance suggests in the last two months) completed vocational training or moved to an area where you are more likely to obtain work.

You should not be refused benefit just because your circumstances are not covered by the guidance. Any examples or time periods during which it is suggested your residence rights as a jobseeker can continue (such as the three- or two-month periods referred to above) are not legally binding requirements. Also note that the guidance is written for JSA decision makers and is therefore less relevant if you are claiming child benefit or CTC on the basis of your right to reside as a jobseeker. The Upper Tribunal has noted that the limited way the guidance is framed could result in decision makers failing to ask all the relevant questions and that, if this happens, tribunals may need to ask a broader range of questions.[54]

The requirement for your evidence to be 'compelling' only applies if your only right to reside that entitles you to benefit is as an EEA jobseeker or as someone who has retained worker status on the basis of being involuntarily unemployed. It does not apply if you are claiming income-based JSA (or CTC or child benefit) and you have another right to reside.[55]

Although it is arguable that you should not be required to alter the quality of your evidence after a particular time period, the longer you have been a jobseeker without obtaining work, the more likely it is that the decision maker will try to argue that this shows that you do not, in fact, have a genuine chance of getting work. As described above, the Upper Tribunal has held that a period of unsuccessful work search of six months or more is a relevant factor in determining whether you have a genuine chance of being engaged.[56] However, other factors are also relevant, so to avoid, or to challenge, a decision that you are not entitled to benefit because you do not have a right of residence as a jobseeker, you need evidence to demonstrate that, on the balance of probabilities, you have a genuine chance of being engaged, despite the long period of unemployment. This can include evidence of your:

- work history in the UK;
- work history in other countries;
- qualifications;
- voluntary work (in the UK and abroad);
- having recently completed a course on obtaining work as part of the Work Programme;
- having broadened the type of work you are looking for or the hours of work you are able to do;
- having arranged for adequate childcare to enable you to attend interviews and take up employment;
- improved English language skills.

Note: you must show that you have a genuine chance of being engaged within a reasonable period in the future. So, developments that are due to happen soon, such as completing a course, satisfying security checks or obtaining professional qualifications, can also be relevant.[57]

Notes

1. General points about evidence
1 www.whatdotheyknow.com/request/ 254608/response/638477/attach/2/ FOI%20IR172%20reply.pdf
2 *CI v HMRC (TC)* [2014] UKUT 158 (AAC)
3 *LS v SSWP (SPC)* [2014] UKUT 249 (AAC)
4 *Kerr v Department for Social Development (Northern Ireland)* [2004] UKHL 23, paras 15-17 and 61-63; *SS v HMRC (TC)* [2014] UKUT 383 (AAC), paras 28-30
5 R(I) 2/51, paras 6 and 7; R(SB) 33/85, para 14
6 R(IS) 6/96, para 15; see also *Kerr v Department for Social Development (Northern Ireland)* [2004] UKHL 23, paras 16-17 and 61-69; CIS/1697/2004, paras 18-20; R(PC) 1/09, paras 16-18
7 *R v Medical Appeal Tribunal (North Midland Region) ex parte Hubble* [1958] 2 QB 228; *Kerr v Department for Social Development (Northern Ireland)* [2004] UKHL 23, paras 15-17 and 61-63; R(PC) 1/09, paras 16-20
8 *Kerr v Department for Social Development (Northern Ireland)* [2004] UKHL 23, paras 61-69; R(PC) 1/09, para 19
9 R(IS) 11/99
10 s16(1) TCA 2002; *NI v HMRC (TC)* [2015] UKUT 490 (AAC) see also caselaw listed in para 4; *JR v HMRC (TC)* [2015] UKUT 192 (AAC)
11 s19 TCA 2002; *TS v HMRC (TC)* [2015] UKUT 507 (AAC); *CS v HMRC (TC)* [2015] UKUT 407 (AAC)
12 s14 TCA 2002; *SB v HMRC (TC)* [2014] UKUT 543 (AAC), para 12
13 *Kerr v Department for Social Development(Northern Ireland)* [2004] UKHL 23, paras 61-69; R(PC) 1/09, paras 16-19

14 *Kerr v Department for Social Development (Northern Ireland)* [2004] UKHL 23
15 R(PC) 1/09, paras 16-19
16 *Kerr v Department for Social Development (Northern Ireland)* [2004] UKHL 23, especially para 62
17 *Kerr v Department for Social Development (Northern Ireland)* [2004] UKHL 23, paras 61-69
18 Vol 2, para 073431 DMG
19 rr5, 6 and 15 TP(FT) Rules; *PM v SSWP (IS)* [2014] UKUT 474 (AAC)

2. Evidence of immigration status
20 s3C(2)(a) IA 1971
21 s3C IA 1971

3. Evidence of residence rights
22 *SSWP v Dias*, C-325/09 [2011] ECR I006387; *EM and KN v SSWP* [2009] UKUT 44 (AAC); *MD v SSWP (SPC)* [2016] UKUT 319 (AAC)
23 Reg 16 I(EEA) Regs
24 Reg 17 I(EEA) Regs
25 Reg 18A I(EEA) Regs
26 Reg 18 I(EEA) Regs
27 Reg 31(2) and Sch 4 para 2 I(EEA) Regs

4. Types of evidence
28 For example, Vol 3 Ch 10 DMG
29 For example, Vol 2 DMG or Ch 20 TCCCM
30 For example, Vol 2 Ch 7 DMG
31 Vol 2, paras 073429-32 DMG
32 see for example, Vol 3 Ch 10 DMG
33 *SW v SSWP (SPC)* [2016] UKUT 0163 (AAC), in particular paras 28 and 41
34 *Diatta v Land Berlin*, C-267/83 [1985] ECR 567
35 Vol 3, para 10155 DMG
36 For example, paras 10120-43 DMG

37 paras 10030 and 10064-65 DMG
38 para 10035 DMG; *SW v SSWP (SPC)*
    [2016] UKUT 163 (AAC), in particular
    paras 28 and 41
39 paras 10036 and 10070-73 DMG
40 para 10071, example 10 DMG
41 paras 10098-102 DMG
42 For example, *SW v SSWP (SPC)* [2016]
    UKUT 163 (AAC)
43 For example *SW v SSWP (SPC)* [2016]
    UKUT 163 (AAC)
44 *LS v SSWP (SPC)* [2014] UKUT 249
    (AAC), para 5
45 *SSWP v ZA* [2009] UKUT 294 (AAC);
    Szpak v SSWP [2013] EWCA Civ 46
46 *The Queen v Immigration Appeal Tribunal
    ex parte Gustaff Desiderius Antonissen*, C-
    292/89 [1991] ECR I-00745, para 21
47 Reg 6 I(EEA) Regs
48 Reg 6(2)(b) and (ba) I(EEA) Regs
49 Art 7(3)(b) and (c) EU Dir 2004/38
50 *KS v Secretary of State* [2016] UKUT 269
    (AAC)
51 *The Queen v Immigration Appeal
    Tribunal, ex parte Gustaff Desiderius
    Antonissen*, C-292/89 [1991] ECR I-
    00745, para 21
52 *SSWP v MB (JSA)* (and linked cases)
    [2016] UKUT 372 (AAC), paras 49-60
53 para 073099 DMG
54 *SSWP v MB (JSA)* (and linked cases)
    [2016] UKUT 372 (AAC), paras 29-30
    and 61
55 Confirmed in para 073080 DMG
56 *SSWP v MB (JSA)* (and linked cases)
    [2016] UKUT 372 (AAC), paras 49-60
57 *SSWP v MB (JSA)* (and linked cases)
    [2016] UKUT 372 (AAC), para 47

Part 8

....

Support for asylum seekers

Support for asylum seekers

Chapter 21

Asylum support

This chapter covers:
1. Introduction (below)
2. Support for asylum seekers (p371)
3. Temporary support (p377)
4. Support for failed asylum seekers (p378)
5. Support for people on temporary admission, temporary release or immigration bail (p387)
6. Support from your local authority (p388)

1. Introduction

Types of support for asylum seekers

There are three main types of government support for people who have made an application for asylum in the UK:

- support for the period until a final decision on an asylum application is made. This is known as **section 95 support** (see p371);[1]
- **temporary support** (often called emergency support), available to asylum seekers waiting for a decision on their application for section 95 support. This is known as **section 98 support** (see p377);[2]
- support available to failed asylum seekers and other migrants who meet certain criteria. This is known as **section 4 support** (see p378).[3]

Section 95 support consists of accommodation and cash, or the option of cash only. Temporary support is full board accommodation, and section 4 support is accommodation and a payment card (known as the Azure card) that can be used in selected shops.

Background to the current system of support

Before 5 February 1996, asylum seekers without funds received income support, at the urgent cases rate of 90 per cent, and housing benefit. Those without accommodation and in 'priority need' were entitled to local authority housing under the homelessness legislation. In February 1996, the government decided that providing benefits was a factor that attracted asylum seekers to the UK. Access to state benefits was removed from many asylum seekers, who therefore sought assistance from local authorities under safety-net legislation.

From 6 December 1999, the Immigration and Asylum Act 1999 restricted the ability of asylum seekers and other migrants to access support from local authorities. These restrictions have been extended, so they now apply to the following local authority support:[4]

- s2 of the Chronically Sick and Disabled Persons Act 1970;
- s21 and Schedule 8 of the National Health Service Act 1977;
- ss17, 23C, 24A and 24B of the Children Act 1989;
- s2 of the Local Government Act 2000;
- s1 of the Localism Act 2011;
- Part 1 of the Care Act 2014.

Note: the exclusions do not prevent a local authority from providing support under the above provisions to a child,[5] or if failing to do so would result in a breach of a person's human rights (see p388).[6]

The Immigration and Asylum Act 1999 also retained the general exclusion of asylum seekers and others from most state benefits and other welfare provisions on the basis that they are 'persons subject to immigration control' (see p57).[7] Instead, the current system of support for asylum seekers was introduced.

Until early 2005, failed asylum seekers could only receive 'hard cases support' under s4 of the Immigration and Asylum Act 1999, provided entirely at the Home Office's discretion. On 31 March 2005, regulations were introduced specifying entitlement to support under s4(2) (known as section 4 support) for certain failed asylum seekers and their dependants (see p378).[8] If your asylum application has been refused, accommodation and support may be provided under s4 of the Act, but with strict eligibility criteria.

Note: the Immigration Act 2016 abolishes section 4 support and replaces it with much more restrictive support for failed asylum seekers. At the time of writing, the part of the Act dealing with asylum support is not yet in force, but it is likely to be brought in during 2017.

Home Office agencies

Since the Immigration and Asylum Act 1999 came into force, the role of providing accommodation and support to asylum seekers has passed between several different Home Office agencies. Until April 2006, the support scheme for asylum seekers and failed asylum seekers was administered by the National Asylum Support Service (NASS). In April 2006, NASS ceased to exist and its role was taken over by the Border and Immigration Agency (BIA). On 7 April 2008, the UK Border Agency (UKBA) was formed, taking over the support role of the BIA, as well as the immigration and asylum functions of the Immigration and Nationality Department. The UKBA was abolished on 26 March 2013 and all its functions were returned to the Home Office. Asylum support applications are now dealt with by the UK Visas and Immigration (UKVI) Department in the Home Office. For simplicity, we refer to the 'Home Office' in this *Handbook*.

You may find that advisers and even officials still refer to asylum support as 'NASS' or 'UKBA' support, even though these agencies no longer exist.

Home Office guidance

The Home Office publishes internal guidance for its decision makers on deciding and processing applications for asylum support. This is published on the government's website at www.gov.uk/government/collections/asylum-support-asylum-instructions. The guidance is in the form of policy bulletins and process instructions. It is important to be familiar with the guidance in addition to the law. It is regularly amended, so always check the website for the latest versions.

There are currently two main policy documents: one dealing with section 95 support (*Asylum Support Instructions: policy bulletins*) and the other with section 4 support (*Asylum Support, Section 4 Policy and Process*). There are also several other shorter supplemental policies. The guidance is not legally binding, but is a useful indication as to how applications are likely to be processed by the Home Office – although it is not the law, the Home Office should follow its own written policies. However, if it is not an accurate representation of the law and less favourable than the law if applied to your particular case, you can argue that it should not be followed.

Asylum Help

Asylum Help is a national confidential and impartial advice service for asylum seekers, funded by the Home Office and provided by the charity Migrant Help. It can help you make your application for support and give general advice about the asylum process. For contact details and a list of other organisations that provide advice services to asylum seekers, see Appendix 2.

---

2. Support for asylum seekers

You are entitled to asylum support under s95 of the Immigration and Asylum Act 1999 (known as **section 95 support**) if:[9]
- you are an asylum seeker or a dependant of an asylum seeker; *and*
- you are destitute or likely to become destitute; *and*
- unless you made your application before 8 January 2003, you have made your application for asylum 'as soon as reasonably practicable' after you entered the UK.[10]

See p377 for who is entitled to temporary support. The criteria are similar, but you must be destitute, not simply likely to become destitute.

Who is an asylum seeker for support purposes

For the purposes of asylum support, you are an asylum seeker if:[11]
- you are over 18 years; *and*
- you have made an application for asylum; *and*
- your application has been recorded by the Secretary of State (see below); *and*
- the application has not yet been determined (see below).

Your asylum application may be made either under the 1951 Refugee Convention (see p12) or under Article 3 of the European Convention on Human Rights. If you have made a different type of application, such as under Article 8 of the European Convention on Human Rights or an application for indefinite leave to remain (see p23), and you have not also made an asylum or Article 3 application, you cannot claim section 95 support, but may be eligible for section 4 support (see p378) or support from your local authority (see p387). For further details on asylum applications, see p31.

When an asylum application is recorded

Asylum applications made 'at port' (ie, on entry to the UK) are recorded immediately. If you are already in the Uk and making an 'in-country' asylum application for the first time, it is processed at the Home Office's Asylum Screening Unit (ASU) in Croydon. You must make an appointment to attend the ASU by telephone in advance, unless you have nowhere to live, in which case you can turn up at the ASU and apply on the same day. Your application is normally 'recorded' at your screening interview on the same day.

If your asylum application has been refused, your appeal rights are exhausted and you make a fresh asylum application (ie, a subsequent claim), this is not recorded until the Home Office accepts that it constitutes a fresh application – ie, it is significantly different to the material considered in your first asylum application.[12] While you are waiting for your further representations to be considered, you may be eligible for section 4 support (see p378).

When an asylum application is determined

An asylum application remains undetermined during the time allowed for any appeal to be made and during any appeal lodged within that time (or any appeal accepted out of time) to the First-tier Tribunal (Immigration and Asylum Chamber), or a further appeal. However, an asylum application is not considered undetermined while a judicial review is outstanding.

For support purposes, you continue to be treated as an asylum seeker for 28 days after:[13]

- your application for asylum is granted; *or*
- you are granted leave to remain; *or*
- your asylum appeal is allowed.

Alternatively, you continue to be an asylum seeker for 21 days after your asylum application has been refused by the Home Office or, if there is an appeal, for 21 days after that appeal is finally dismissed.

Families with children

If you have a dependent child when your application for asylum is determined, you continue to be treated as an asylum seeker for support purposes until her/his 18th birthday, provided s/he remains in the UK.[14] Therefore, families with children aged under 18 continue to receive section 95 support, even after their asylum application has been refused.

The asylum support adjudicators (as the appeal tribunal was called at that time) dismissed an appeal by an asylum seeker who had a dependent child with her in the UK, but was not claiming asylum support at the relevant time.[15] This decision relied on the word 'continuing' in s94(5) of the Immigration and Asylum Act 1999 which says, 'he is to be treated (for the purposes of this Part) as continuing to be an asylum-seeker'. This interpretation, however, is challengeable as it can be argued that the word 'continuing' means that someone continues to be an asylum seeker for support purposes, not that there must be some pre-existing support that will be continued. If you are refused support on this basis, you should appeal.

This provision does not apply if your children were born after your asylum application was refused and you had exhausted all your rights of appeal. In this case, you cease to be an asylum seeker for support purposes and are no longer eligible for section 95 support. However, you and your children may be eligible for section 4 support as a failed asylum seeker (see p378) or for support under the Children Act 1989 (see p388).

The Home Office can withdraw section 95 support from failed asylum-seeker families who, in its opinion, have not taken steps to leave the UK voluntarily.[16] This means that you are expected to demonstrate that you are taking steps to arrange your departure from the UK to return home. However, this power was piloted across the UK in 2005, but has not been adopted as general practice. If the Home Office decides to withdraw your support because it says that you are not taking steps to leave the UK with your family, you can appeal against this decision to the First-tier Tribunal (Asylum Support). For more information, see Chapter 24.

Note: once the relevant section of the Immigration Act 2016 is in force (likely to be in 2017), refused asylum-seeker families will no longer be able to continue to receive section 95 support.

Who is a dependant for support purposes

Support is provided to asylum seekers and their dependants, provided they are destitute. You are a 'dependant' of an asylum seeker if you are:[17]

- her/his spouse or civil partner;
- a child aged under 18 years of the asylum seeker or her/his spouse/civil partner and you are dependent on her/him;
- a child aged under 18 years of the close family of the asylum seeker/spouse/civil partner (you do not have to be dependent on her/him);
- a child aged under 18 years and you have lived in the asylum seeker's household for six out of the last 12 months, or since birth;
- now over 18 years old, but you were under 18 and came within one of the above categories when the asylum support application was made or when you entered the UK;
- a close family member, or someone who has lived with the asylum seeker for six out of the last 12 months (or since birth), and you are disabled and in need of care and attention from a member of the household;
- her/his partner and you were living with her/him as an unmarried couple for at least two of the three years before the application for support or before entering the UK.[18] If you are in an unmarried couple and want to be included as a dependant in your partner's existing asylum support, it can be difficult to comply with this condition. You may be caught in a 'catch-22' situation – eg, your relationship may have started at a time when either you or your partner were already on asylum support and you will not have been allowed to join their household. Therefore, you will have never been able to build up two years of having lived together before the application for support;[19]
- someone who has applied to the Home Office to remain in the UK as a dependant on your relative's asylum claim.

Note: being a dependant for support purposes is not always the same as being a dependant on another person's asylum claim. Whether the Home Office allows you to be a dependant on someone else's asylum claim (and whether this would be in your interests) and, therefore, whether you can be a dependant on her/his asylum support claim, is not always simple. The issue of who can be a dependant overall is a complex one and you should obtain specialist advice if this affects you. Further information is in the Asylum Support Appeals Project Factsheet 11, *Getting s95 or s4 Support for Dependants*.[20]

The definition of destitute

You are considered destitute if:[21]

- you do not have adequate accommodation or any means of obtaining it (whether or not you can meet your other essential living needs); *or*

- you have adequate accommodation or the means of obtaining it, but cannot meet your other essential living needs.

When you make an application for support, you are regarded as destitute if there is a likelihood of destitution within 14 days.[22] If you already receive support, you continue to be regarded as destitute if there is a likelihood of destitution within 56 days.[23]

See p397 for what income and assets are taken into account when deciding whether or not you are destitute.

Who is excluded from support

Even if you are eligible for section 95 support, you can be excluded from getting support if:[24]
- you are not excluded from getting social security benefits because of your immigration status (see p66);
- you are not being treated as an asylum seeker or the dependant of an asylum seeker for immigration purposes;
- you apply for support as part of a group and every person is excluded under either of the above.

If you do not have dependent children and you apply for cash-only support and not accommodation (see p408),[25] you can also be excluded if you did not claim asylum 'as soon as reasonably practicable' on entering the UK.[26]

There is no statutory definition of the term 'as soon as reasonably practicable'. When the rule was first introduced, this led to substantial numbers of in-country asylum seekers (ie, people who did not claim asylum at the port of entry, but only after they had entered UK) being refused support, and subsequent judicial review cases in the High Court. The Home Office has since issued a policy stating that any claim made within three days of arrival is treated as having been made 'as soon as reasonably practicable'.[27]

Support should not be withheld if a refusal of support would be in breach of a person's human rights.[28]

Other exclusions

The following people are excluded from section 95 support:[29]
- people with refugee status granted by a European Economic Area (EEA) state and their dependants;[30]
- EEA nationals and their dependants.[31]

Note: a child cannot be excluded from support, nor can someone if the provision of support is necessary to avoid a breach of human rights.[32]

When support can be suspended or discontinued

If you have been granted section 95 support, the Home Office can discontinue or suspend it in certain circumstances.[33] This is a discretionary power, which the Home Office must exercise lawfully. Support can be suspended or discontinued if:

- the Home Office has reason to believe that you or your dependant have committed a serious breach of the rules of the accommodation, if accommodated in 'collective accommodation' – eg, a hostel or shared house.[34] Each accommodation provider is likely to have a set of 'house rules', which everyone must follow – eg, to be respectful of other residents and not to make any noise late at night;
- the Home Office has reason to believe that you or your dependant have committed an act of seriously violent behaviour;[35]
- you or your dependant have committed a criminal offence under Part VI of the Immigration and Asylum Act 1999.[36] This includes making a false claim to get support and failing to report a change of circumstances to the Home Office – eg, a change in your financial resources;
- you fail within five working days to provide the Home Office with information about an application for, or receipt of, support;[37]
- you fail to attend an interview relating to your or your dependant's support and do not have a reasonable excuse;[38]
- you fail within 10 working days to provide information about your dependant's asylum application;[39]
- the Home Office has reason to believe that you or your dependant have concealed financial resources and unduly benefited from asylum support;[40]
- you or your dependant fail to comply with reporting requirements;[41]
- the Home Office has reason to believe that you or your dependant have made, or you attempted to make, a second application for asylum before the first application is determined;[42]
- there are 'reasonable grounds' to suspect that you have abandoned your 'authorised address' (see p411) without first informing the Home Office or without its permission.[43]

Your support may be suspended (ie, for a temporary period) if the Home Office requires time or more information to decide whether to discontinue your support – ie, to terminate it entirely. If it is satisfied that there has been a breach of conditions, it must take into account the extent of the breach when deciding whether or not to continue to provide support. **Note:** even if the grounds for suspension or discontinuation are established, you can still retain your entitlement to support if you can show that you are destitute and require support to avoid a breach of your human rights.

If you apply for support again after it has been discontinued, unless there are exceptional circumstances that justify considering it, the Home Office may refuse to consider your application if there has been no 'material change in circumstances' since the original decision to suspend or discontinue the support.[44] This means a change of any of the circumstances that you must notify to the Home Office (see p403).[45]

If the Home Office decides to consider your application for support in these circumstances, it may still refuse support.[46]

A decision to refuse or discontinue support can be appealed to the First-tier Tribunal (Asylum Support). See Chapter 24 for more details.

3. **Temporary support**

While the Home Office considers your application for section 95 support, it can provide a temporary form of support to you or your dependant(s) under s98 of the Immigration and Asylum Act 1999.[47] This is known as **section 98 support** and is also commonly called 'emergency support' or (if accommodation is also requested) 'interim accommodation'.

Temporary asylum support can be provided if it appears that you *may* be destitute at the time of the application – ie, even if there is some uncertainty.[48] The definition of 'destitution' is the same as for section 95 support (see p397),[49] except that temporary support cannot be provided solely on the basis that you are likely to become destitute within 14 days.[50]

Temporary support may be provided subject to conditions, which must be given in writing. It can only be provided until the Home Office decides whether or not section 95 support is to be provided. If the Home Office refuses section 95 support, temporary support ends at the same time.

There is no right of appeal to the First-tier Tribunal (see p421) against a refusal or withdrawal of temporary support.[51] The only method of challenging such a decision is by judicial review proceedings.

Who is excluded from temporary support

You are excluded from temporary support if:[52]
- you are not excluded from getting social security benefits because of your immigration status (see p66);
- you apply as a dependant, but you are not being treated as a dependant of an asylum seeker for immigration purposes;
- you apply as part of a group and every person in the group is excluded under either of the above provisions.

4. Support for failed asylum seekers

If you are a failed asylum seeker who has reached the end of the appeal process and exhausted all your appeal rights, you are generally not entitled to support from the Home Office; it expects you to return to your country of origin. If you are unable to leave the UK, you may be able to claim support under s4(2) of the Immigration and Asylum Act 1999. This is known as **section 4 support**.

To get section 4 support you must:
- be destitute (see below); *and*
- meet one of the five criteria for support (see p379).[53]

The Home Office can also provide support under s4(1) of the Immigration and Asylum Act 1999 to people who have been temporarily admitted to the UK or who are on bail from immigration detention, regardless of whether they have claimed asylum (see p387).[54]

The definition of destitute

The definition of 'destitute' is the same as for section 95 support (see p374).[55] If you apply for section 4 support within 21 days of your section 95 support ending, the Home Office automatically accepts that you are destitute. However, if you have not recently had support, the Home Office usually insists that the onus is on you to prove that you are now destitute, and requires detailed information on how you have survived and how your situation has now changed to leave you destitute. In these circumstances, the Home Office asks you to provide evidence, such as letters from friends, family and charities, explaining what support they have given you in the past and why that cannot continue. You may have survived from working (legally or illegally) in the past and so may need to explain this to the Home Office, so that it can fully understand your new situation. If this evidence cannot be obtained, tell the Home Office (and the First-tier Tribunal in any appeal) why this is the case – eg, the friendship may have now deteriorated because you have overstayed your welcome.

Note: the test of destitution is as set out in the regulations (see p374). If you have relied on friends and relatives, you may still have been destitute within the meaning of the regulations, even while receiving that help – eg, you may have spent nights sleeping on various friends' floors without a key to gain access, and walking the streets during the day, or have had no money and/or little food. In this situation, you have been destitute under the regulations throughout this period, as you have not had adequate accommodation and/or have been unable to meet your essential living needs. When applying for section 4 support in these circumstances, it is important to give full details about what support has been made available in the past.

Criteria for support

As well as being destitute, to qualify for section 4 support, you must also prove that you are in one of the following situations.
- You are taking all reasonable steps to leave the UK (see below).
- You are unable to leave the UK because a medical condition prevents you from travelling (see p380).
- You are unable to leave the UK because there is no viable route of return (see p381).
- You have applied for judicial review (see p381).
- Section 4 support is necessary to avoid a breach of human rights (see p381).

You are taking all reasonable steps to leave the UK

To qualify for section 4 support, you must be taking all reasonable steps to leave the UK or place yourself in a position in which you are able to leave the UK, including, if relevant, applying for a travel document.[56]

The Home Office runs an 'assisted voluntary return' scheme, through which failed asylum seekers and others without leave to remain in the UK can receive assistance, and in some cases cash, to return home. Until December 2015, the scheme was run through the charity Refugee Action and was called 'Choices'. Signing up for assisted voluntary return with Choices was usually regarded as sufficient to satisfy this requirement. The scheme is now part of the Home Office's voluntary departure service and it is not yet known how it will work in practice, but the emphasis continues to be on expecting you to be proactive in attempting to get travel documents – eg, by visiting your embassy.

After granting support, the Home Office reviews your case every six weeks or so and asks you for documentary proof of what you have done. It is advisable to keep a diary of the steps you take. It is also important to keep copies of all letters and emails, and notes of telephone calls, emails and visits to, for example, the voluntary departure service and your embassy.

If you get support on these grounds, it is likely to be terminated after three months: it is the Home Office's view that a three-month period of support is sufficient for most people to be able to arrange their departure from the UK.[57] Support only continues in exceptional circumstances or if the initial assisted voluntary return application is not successful within three months of its being made (six months for Palestinians). This policy may not be lawful as it does not reflect the test in the regulations, which refers to whether a failed asylum seeker 'is' taking all reasonable steps to leave the UK. So, the question is what steps you are currently taking and not solely what have you done in the past. If you are refused support on this basis, you should appeal to the First-tier Tribunal (Asylum Support). See Chapter 24 for details.

Support is often withdrawn on the grounds that someone has not taken *all* reasonable steps. It could be argued that the Home Office's view on this is often unrealistic, bearing in mind that applicants are destitute, desperate and may speak little English. However, on appeal, the First-tier Tribunal may take the view that, if any reasonable step can be identified that you have not taken, even if you did not previously think of it, you have not satisfied the requirement and will be refused support. Each case should be considered on its own merits.

You are unable to leave the UK because a medical condition prevents you from travelling

To get section 4 support, you must be unable to travel (ie, to make a single journey from the UK to your country of origin) because of 'a physical impediment' or other medical reason.[58] 'Unable' has been interpreted to mean more than 'unreasonable' or 'undesirable', but not 'impossible'.[59]

If you apply for support on this ground, you must submit a completed medical declaration. The form is available from Appendix B of the *Asylum Support, Section 4 Policy and Process*.[60] Arguably, a letter containing the same information on headed paper should be sufficient, but it is advisable to use the form if possible.

The medical declaration must be completed by your GP, consultant or psychiatrist and must state that you are unable to leave the UK because of your medical condition. The Home Office reimburses doctors their fees for completing this form.[61]

When asking the medical professional to complete the declaration, point out the method of travel (eg, by plane) and how many hours it will take to travel to, and wait at, the UK international airport, as well as the number of hours to travel by air to your country of origin and home area. When deciding whether to grant support, the Home Office does not consider your doctor's opinion that you should be allowed to stay in the UK – eg, on compassionate grounds or to finish a course of treatment or to get medical treatment that may be unavailable in your own country. Indeed, if your doctor says this, the Home Office might discount the report, believing that s/he has applied the wrong test.

The Home Office accepts that a woman cannot travel during the period of 'around' six weeks before the expected date of giving birth and six weeks after the birth.[62] You must provide medical documentation (usually Form MATB1 issued by your GP or midwife) to confirm the pregnancy and expected date of birth, or the birth certificate with your application form. The Home Office recognises that a woman may be unable to travel for a longer period if there are particular medical problems with the pregnancy, so you may be eligible for section 4 support earlier in your pregnancy. You can also argue that, according to the NHS, 'the length of a normal pregnancy varies between about 37 and 42 weeks', although the expected delivery date is 'calculated at 40 weeks from the first day of your last period'.[63] However, only 5 per cent of babies are born on their due date. This means that, in practice, a substantial number of babies are born up to three weeks before the expected due date. The First-tier Tribunal has accepted this argument, in combination with evidence of complications in pregnancy, as evidence of the need to provide support earlier than six weeks before the expected date of delivery.

You should also consider providing evidence of how your social circumstances are impacting on your pregnancy. So, for example, if you are experiencing any form of abuse or if you are unable to sleep and eat properly, include this information on the application form.

You are unable to leave the UK because there is no viable route of return

To qualify for section 4 support under this ground, the Secretary of State must have made a declaration that, in her/his opinion, there is no viable route to a particular country.[64]

At the time of writing, there is no country to which this applies. Irrespective of your personal circumstances, therefore, you will not succeed in claiming support under this criterion unless, by the time of your application, the Secretary of State has made a declaration that there is no safe route. The only time the Secretary of State has made such a declaration was in 2005 for a six-month period with regard to Iraq.[65] If your application under this ground is refused, you might be able to argue that this is a breach of your human rights (see p385).

You have applied for judicial review

To get section 4 support under this ground, you must have lodged with the court an application for judicial review to challenge a decision refusing your application for asylum and, in England and Wales, you must have been granted permission to proceed (or leave to proceed in Northern Ireland).[66] Simply lodging a judicial review application at court in Scotland is sufficient.

If you have lodged an application and are waiting for the court to consider whether to grant permission, you are likely to be able to receive support to avoid a breach of your human rights (see p384).

Section 4 support is necessary to avoid a breach of human rights

You qualify for section 4 support if you can show that the provision of accommodation is necessary to avoid a breach of human rights.[67] The courts have said that denying support to asylum seekers whose claims are outstanding, in the context in which they are not allowed to work and would be faced with street homelessness, constitutes 'inhuman and degrading treatment'.[68] This is prohibited under Article 3 of the European Convention on Human Rights.

If you are a failed asylum seeker, you must also show that it is not reasonable for you to leave the UK. You may be able to rely on the fact that:
* you have lodged fresh representations with the Home Office (see p382);
* you have made an 'out-of-time' appeal to the First-tier Tribunal (Immigration and Asylum Chamber) (see p383);

- you have applied for a judicial review challenging a refusal of your fresh representations, or you have sent a letter threatening proceedings (see p384);
- you have an outstanding application to the European Court of Human Rights (see p384);
- you have no safe route of return (see p385);
- there are other human rights arguments (see p385).

You have lodged fresh representations with the Home Office

This is the most usual situation in which a failed asylum seeker is given support to avoid a breach of her/his human rights. You must show that:

- you have made a further application to the Home Office to remain in the UK (see p38). This is usually in the form of 'further submissions' that you want the Home Office to accept as a fresh asylum claim. It can, however, include an application to remain in the UK under Article 8 of the European Convention on Human Rights (see p34); *and*
- this application is still outstanding – eg, the Home Office has not yet decided whether it amounts to a fresh asylum application;*and*
- it would not be reasonable for you to leave the UK at this stage and to be left destitute (while you remain) would be a breach of your human rights (under Article 3).

The High Court has stated that section 4 support should be provided in the above circumstances.[69]

Since 30 March 2015, if you want to make further submissions, you must book an appointment and travel in person to the Further Submissions Unit (FSU) in Liverpool. If you have exceptional reasons why you cannot travel to Liverpool, such as illness, disability or childcare difficulties, you can apply to submit them by post. Previously, only people whose initial claim was made before 5 March 2007 had to travel to Liverpool, as all others could make further submissions at their local reporting centre.

The First-tier Tribunal has granted support on human rights grounds if someone has prepared fresh representations and has an appointment to attend the FSU and submit them on a future date and, in exceptional cases, if further submissions are still being prepared.[70] This is because the applicant has done all that s/he reasonably can to submit the fresh representations. However, the approach of judges varies and some may refuse support unless the representations have been submitted in person.

Even if the representations have been submitted, the Home Office can refuse support if:[71]

- the fresh claim or representations contain no detail whatsoever – eg, if you are still fearful of returning to your country of origin, but do not give any further information or simply state that you will send new information later; *or*

- the evidence or arguments that you have submitted as part of your fresh claim have already been seen and rejected by the Home Office, or rejected on appeal and they do not rely on any change in the law since the previous refusal.

Once the Home Office has looked at any fresh representations, you are informed in writing whether they have been accepted as a new asylum application. If so, a fresh asylum application is recorded. At this point, you become an asylum seeker again and should reapply for section 95 support (see p371). If your representations are not accepted as an asylum application, your section 4 support is withdrawn unless you can prove that you meet one of the other criteria for support.

Note: the Home Office used to have a policy of delaying making a decision on a section 4 support application for at least 15 working days to allow time to consider the further submissions. In 2012, the High Court ruled that this policy was unlawful, because it led to a 'significant risk' that Article 3 of the European Convention on Human Rights would be breached if applicants were left destitute while waiting for a decision.[72] The Home Office amended its policy to comply with the ruling. According to the new instructions:[73]

- the caseworker must make every effort to consider the further submissions at the same time as considering the section 4 application;
- the decision about support should not be delayed because of administrative or other problems in assessing the merits of the further submissions;
- 'as a general rule', caseworkers must make a decision on support applications made on the basis of further submissions within five working days;
- if the application is a higher priority, the caseworker must make 'every reasonable effort' to decide the application within two working days;
- there is a non-exhaustive list of cases requiring extra prioritisation, including people who are street homeless, families with children, people who are disabled, elderly or pregnant, and potential victims of torture and trafficking;
- caseworkers must 'check that the further submissions are not clearly abusive, manifestly unfounded or repetitious'.

You have made an application for leave under Article 8 of the European Convention on Human Rights

You may qualify for section 4 support if you have an outstanding application for leave under Article 8 of the European Convention on Human Rights (see p34), provided it has some merit and is not obviously hopeless or abusive.[74]

You have made an 'out-of-time' appeal to the First-tier Tribunal

If you want to appeal against the refusal of your asylum application but the time for appealing has expired, you must ask the First-tier Tribunal (Immigration and Asylum Chamber) for permission for an 'out-of-time' appeal to proceed. If you have made such an application, the Home Office and the First-tier Tribunal

(Asylum Support) usually grants section 4 support, considering that it would be unreasonable to expect you to leave the UK in the meantime.

If the First-tier Tribunal (Immigration and Asylum Chamber) gives you permission to appeal out of time, you become an asylum seeker again and are eligible for section 95 support (and, at that stage, no longer eligible for section 4 support).

If you appeal within the prescribed time limits, you are still considered to be an asylum seeker and so you may still be eligible for section 95 support (see p371).

You have issued or threatened judicial review proceedings on an asylum matter

If your further submissions are rejected, you can challenge this by judicial review. You are not eligible for support unless you have been granted permission by the High Court.[75] This can take some time. In the meantime, and while you are preparing to take a judicial review, you may be eligible for support to avoid a breach of your human rights.

A judicial review in the High Court on this issue in 2009 held that the criteria may be satisfied 'in a variety of factual circumstances'. The judge declined to define exactly what these would be, but the implication of the judgment is that they would include if your solicitor has sent the required 'pre-action' letter to the Home Office threatening judicial review proceedings or if you have already issued proceedings and are waiting for a decision on whether you can proceed.[76] You must show that your case is not 'entirely without merit'.

You have applied to the European Court of Human Rights

Failed asylum seekers who have exhausted their appeal rights in the UK, but who claim that their removal would lead to a breach of their human rights, can apply to the European Court of Human Rights in Strasbourg for an order preventing their imminent removal (called a Rule 39 order).

If this applies to you and you are waiting for a decision from the European Court and you are destitute, you may be eligible for section 4 support. In a decision in 2011, a judge in the First-tier Tribunal (Asylum Support) gave criteria for deciding when support should be granted.[77] You must show that:

- your application to the European Court 'has some merit'. This includes showing that it contains details and these are specific to your case. The level of detail required depends on the case;
- you exhausted all remedies in the UK before applying to the European Court, including making a fresh application for asylum and challenging any refusal by judicial review. However, there is no need to have applied for a remedy if it was 'bound to fail'. So, for example, if you have been refused legal aid for a judicial review because of existing UK caselaw, you may still satisfy this ground;
- you have 'raised the prospect of imminent risk on return'. This is usually satisfied if you have applied for a Rule 39 order.

Note: this decision is not binding on other judges in the First-tier Tribunal, but is persuasive.

You have no safe route of return

In the case *M Ahmed v Asylum Support Adjudicator and the Secretary of State,* Mr Ahmed argued that there was no safe route for him to return to his home in Iraq and, therefore, he could not leave the UK and so should be given section 4 support to avoid a breach of his human rights.[78] The High Court ruled that he did not have sufficient evidence to establish that the route back to his home was so dangerous that it would be a breach of his human rights to require him to leave the UK. The Secretary of State, however, agreed that there may be cases in which this argument could succeed and the judge agreed that such an argument might succeed if there were sufficient evidence to support it. However, the Home Office (or the First-tier Tribunal) may conclude that the risks of a return journey would have been considered when your asylum application was refused, and so you would have to show that circumstances had since changed. The issue may need to be tested again in the light of the deteriorating situation in Iraq and Syria.

Other human rights arguments

Many cases depend on their own particular facts. The First-tier Tribunal has granted support on human rights grounds when a medical condition would make travel risky or harmful, but which was not so bad as to mean someone was 'unable to travel'. It has also granted support to a mentally ill person on the basis that he should remain on support while still in the UK.[79]

In one case, the First-tier Tribunal decided that a failed asylum seeker could not be expected to leave the UK while on probation and subjected to reporting requirements and medical tests because of drug offences. Leaving the UK would have meant that he could not comply with the probation order made by the court and support was required to prevent his destitution.

Who is excluded from support

Certain people are excluded from section 4 support. They are the same people who are excluded from section 95 support (see p375).

When support can be suspended or discontinued

The Home Office has no power to suspend section 4 support. This may have been an oversight in drafting the regulations or it may have been thought that, as the nature of the support is in theory temporary, it can simply be terminated.

The Home Office may discontinue your support if it believes that you are no longer eligible – eg, because you are not taking all reasonable steps to leave the UK, your further representations for asylum have been refused or an application for judicial review has failed.

The Home Office's policy is to review section 4 support:[80]
- six weeks after it is granted on the basis that you are taking all reasonable steps to leave the UK, and every six weeks thereafter;

- six weeks after the birth of a baby if you have received support on the basis of late pregnancy or birth of a baby (the Home Office accepts that a woman cannot travel six weeks before or six weeks after giving birth); *or*
- at the end of the period estimated by the Home Office medical adviser or your doctor as the period within which you should recover sufficiently from an illness or disability that has prevented you from travelling earlier.

Before discontinuing support on the basis that you are not taking all reasonable steps to leave the UK or you no longer have a medical impediment to travel, the Home Office should send you a review letter, asking you to provide evidence that you are still eligible. If you do not provide a satisfactory response justifying why it should continue, the Home Office then sends a further letter terminating support. In all other cases where you no longer qualify (eg, because your further submissions have been rejected), Home Office policy is simply to terminate support without first sending a review letter. You can appeal against the decision. See Chapter 24 for details.

If you have breached the conditions of support

Section 4 support can be granted subject to certain conditions. The conditions must be given to you in writing and must involve:[81]
- specified standards of behaviour; *or*
- a reporting requirement; *or*
- a requirement:
  - to reside at an authorised address; *or*
  - if absent from an authorised address without the Home Office's permission, to ensure that the absence is for no more than seven consecutive days and nights or for no more than a total of 14 days and nights in any six-month period; *or*
- specified steps to facilitate your departure from the UK.

The Home Office usually writes to you about an alleged breach of conditions before terminating your support. If support is terminated, either with or without prior warning, you should appeal immediately to the First-tier Tribunal, as the time limit for doing so is very short (see p425). Once you have lodged the appeal, your support should continue until the date of your appeal.

The best interests of children

The Home Office has a duty to ensure that all its decisions take into account the need to safeguard and promote the welfare of children.[82] It has a policy of not discontinuing section 4 support to families, which attempts to reflect this. [83]

If the breach of conditions is a minor one, it may not be appropriate to discontinue support. In any event, the Home Office should liaise with the local authority so that social services can carry out a child in need assessment, with a view to taking over the support. The policy is unclear on what should happen if the local authority refuses to provide support because it has emerged that you and your family are not, in fact, destitute – eg, if you have been concealing funds. In this situation, if funds are still available to you, the local authority may also not have a duty to support you under the Children Act as the children in the family would not be 'in need' (see p388).

5. **Support for people on temporary admission, temporary release or immigration bail**

If you are on temporary admission or temporary release, or you have been released from immigration detention on bail, or you are currently in detention and intend to seek bail, you can apply for accommodation and support from the Home Office under s4(1) of the Immigration and Asylum Act 1999 (see p405).[84] You do not need to be an asylum seeker or a failed asylum seeker to apply for this type of **section 4 support**.[85]

Unlike support for failed asylum seekers under s4(2), there are no regulations setting out the criteria for support.

If you have been given temporary admission or are on temporary release, you will have been given Form IS96, and will probably be required to report to an immigration officer. It is a different status from being on immigration bail. See p14 for more details. Whether or not you can receive support is at the Home Office's discretion. In April 2013, it issued its policy on how applications are decided.[86]

- This type of support is not provided to asylum seekers or to failed asylum seekers.
- Support may be provided to unaccompanied asylum-seeking children who have reached the age of 18, but whose asylum application was determined before their 18th birthday. This is because they do not come within the definition of an asylum seeker or failed asylum seeker. You must show that you are destitute, that you meet the conditions for section 4 support and that you are not eligible for support from your local authority.
- Applications are only considered from people in other immigration categories (eg, overstayers who have never made a claim for asylum) 'in truly exceptional circumstances'. You must show that you are destitute and that support is required to avoid a breach of human rights. This generally means that it is not reasonable for you to leave the country – eg, because you are waiting for travel documents, you are too ill to travel or you have an outstanding application for leave to remain. The guidance states that support should not be provided

solely because you have an outstanding application for leave to remain under Article 8 of the European Convention on Human Rights or based on long residence. However, as it is now accepted that section 4(2) support can be granted on the basis of an outstanding Article 8 application (see p383), it is also possible to obtain section 4(1) support on this basis, depending on the facts.

The First-tier Tribunal has granted support to the following destitute people on temporary admission who had never claimed asylum:[87]

- a 21-year-old man who arrived in the UK aged 15 claiming he was a British citizen. He had been waiting for seven years for the Home Office to decide his case;[88]
- a man with severe mental health problems who had been certified by his doctor as unable to travel and who had applied for leave to remain outside the Immigration Rules;[89]
- a 43-year-old homeless man who had applied for voluntary return and was waiting for a travel document so that he could return to India;[90]
- a separated father, who was involved in bringing up his British citizen child;
- a homeless man who had been in the UK for 23 years, and was waiting for his human rights immigration appeal.

You can also apply for section 4 support if you are currently detained and need to be able to demonstrate to the judge who will hear your bail application that you will have accommodation if you were to be released.[91] Alternatively, you may already have been released on bail to a particular address and your host can no longer let you stay.

Whether you are on temporary admission or bail, there is nothing in the law to say that you should be destitute. However, the Home Office policy refers to the destitution test (see p378).[92] You may wish to argue that there is no requirement to be destitute (eg, if you have received compensation for having been unlawfully detained), but as providing support under s4(1) is discretionary, you may not be successful. If you are refused support, you can appeal to the First-tier Tribunal. You can appeal even if you are still in detention at the time. See Chapter 24 for details.

6. **Support from your local authority**

You may be eligible for support from your local authority if you have care needs or if there is a child in your family. Failed asylum seekers with children generally do not need to apply for local authority support as they remain on asylum support.

Note: this is a complex area of law and beyond the scope of this *Handbook*. What follows is a brief description of the support available for asylum seekers and failed asylum seekers under the Care Act 2014 and the Children Act 1989. If you believe that you may be entitled to support from your local authority, get expert advice from a community care adviser.

Local authority support is not listed as a 'public fund' in the Immigration Rules. Therefore, if you have been granted leave to enter or remain subject to the condition that you do not have 'recourse to public funds' (see p25), receiving community care support does not breach this condition.

Who is excluded from support

You are not eligible for local authority support if you come into an excluded group, unless to exclude you would be a breach of human rights (see below). You are excluded if:[93]

* you have, or you are the dependant of someone who has, been granted refugee status by another European Economic Area (EEA) state;
* you are, or you are the dependant of someone who is, an EEA national;
* you are, or you are the dependant of someone who is, a failed asylum seeker who has not complied with removal directions;
* you are not an asylum seeker and you are in the UK unlawfully – ie, in breach of immigration laws;
* you are a failed asylum seeker with children, you are treated as an asylum seeker for support purposes, and the Secretary of State has stated that you have failed, without reasonable excuse, to take reasonable steps to leave, or place yourself in a position to leave, the UK. **Note:** this exclusion is rarely used.

The above exclusions do not apply to children, or where support is necessary to avoid a breach of human rights.[94] There are various situations in which support may be necessary to avoid a breach. In particular, failed asylum seekers and other migrants who are unlawfully in the UK, but who have made a fresh application for asylum or for permission to remain in the UK on human rights grounds, may be able to argue that a local authority should provide support in order to avoid a breach of their human rights while their further submissions are outstanding. However, the submissions must not be 'manifestly unfounded', or merely repeat grounds you have previously made.[95]

Adults with care needs

If you do not have children but have care needs (eg, because of an illness or disability), you may qualify for support, including accommodation, from your local authority social services department (in Scotland, social work department).[96] This is called 'community care' or 'social care' support.

The fact that you are receiving, or may be eligible for, section 95 support from the Home Office must be ignored by the local authority when deciding whether or not to provide community care support and at what level.[97] So, if you qualify for community care support, this takes precedence over section 95 support and therefore you are supported by the local authority, not the Home Office.

The courts have considered where the dividing line is between the two types of support (and therefore which you receive) several times, most recently in the Supreme Court.[98] In this case, it was decided that there should be a need for care to be provided in the home in order to be eligible for local authority support. So, someone with a physical disability who needs help with tasks in the home would be more likely to qualify for local authority support than a person who is mentally ill, whose care could take place outside the home.

The legislation covering community care support changed in 2015.[99] Different rules apply depending on where you are in the UK.

- In England, from April 2015, support is provided under the Care Act 2014, which replaces most of the previous legislation covering community care. Local authorities can provide support, including accommodation in a care home or other premises, to adults whom they assess as having a need for care and support.[100] There are national eligibility criteria setting out the minimum thresholds for support to be provided. Your care needs must arise from, or be related to, a physical or mental impairment or illness, and as a result you must be unable to achieve at least two specified 'outcomes', as a consequence of which there is likely to be a significant impact on your wellbeing.[101] The outcomes are:
  - managing and maintaining nutrition;
  - maintaining personal hygiene;
  - managing toilet needs;
  - being appropriately clothed;
  - being able to make use of your home safely;
  - maintaining a habitable home environment;
  - developing and maintaining family or other personal relationships;
  - accessing and engaging in work, training, education or volunteering;
  - making use of necessary facilities or services in the local community, including public transport and recreational facilities or services;
  - carrying out any caring responsibilities you have for a child.
- In Wales, in April 2016, similar provisions to those in England came into force under the Social Services and Well-being (Wales) Act 2014.
- In Scotland, local authorities have a general duty to promote social welfare by making available advice, guidance and assistance to 'persons in need'.[102]

Note: if you are a 'person subject to immigration control' (see p57), which includes asylum seekers and failed asylum seekers on temporary admission, your care needs must not arise solely from being destitute or from the anticipated effects of being destitute.[103] In other words, you cannot get community care support if the only reason you need looking after is because you are destitute. There must be some additional reason why you need to be looked after. This test has become known as the 'destitution plus' test.

Support for children

Local authorities have a duty to safeguard and promote the welfare of children who are 'in need' in the area.[104] If you are destitute and have children, you may therefore be eligible for accommodation or support from your local authority under the Children Act 1989 (in Scotland, the Children (Scotland) Act 1995). A child who is destitute is generally considered to be 'in need', but a child can also be in need if s/he is disabled, or if s/he is unlikely to achieve or maintain areasonable standard of health or development without the provision ofservices by a local authority.[105]

Although the duty is to support the child, it extends to supporting parents or other family members if this is in the child's best interests.[106]

If you request accommodation under the Children Act for yourself and your children, some local authorities may suggest that a breach of human rights can be avoided by providing accommodation for the child only and not you, the parent. This is often unlawful. If this happens, you should obtain expert advice from a community care adviser or lawyer, as it may be possible to challenge the local authority's decision by judicial review.

Asylum seekers

If you are eligible for section 95 support (see p371), you and your dependants are excluded from help under the Children Act 1989 or Children (Scotland) Act 1995.[107] However, if you or your children cannot claim section 95 support (eg, because you have breached the conditions of support), you may be eligible for local authority support. **Note:** you cannot be entitled to section 95 support if you are aged under 18. Therefore, if you are an unaccompanied asylum seeker under 18, you are not excluded from Children Act support (see p392). When you turn 18, the local authority may have a duty to continue to provide you with support.[108]

Failed asylum seekers

The parents of a child (although not the child her/himself) who are failed asylum seekers unlawfully in the UK are excluded from local authority support, unless support is necessary to avoid a breach of human rights. Support may be necessary to avoid a breach if you are destitute and you have an arguable application for leave to remain on human rights grounds which is outstanding.[109]

The fact that you may be eligible for section 4 support (see p378) does not exclude you from claiming Children Act support (unlike section 95 support – see above).[110] This is because section 4 is a 'residual power' and any duty to support under the Children Act should come first.[111] Despite this, some local authorities still refuse support on this basis. If this happens, you should get expert advice, as it may be possible to challenge the local authority's refusal by judicial review.

Unaccompanied asylum-seeking children

Local authorities are responsible for supporting children under the age of 18 years who arrive in the UK alone and claim asylum (often referred to as 'unaccompanied minors').

Unaccompanied asylum-seeker children are dispersed around the country, rather than assisted in the areas in which the UK ports and airports are situated.[112] The local authority in the new area should then make arrangements for suitable accommodation, which can include foster care.

If you have already been supported by a local authority as an unaccompanied minor, it may continue to have a duty to provide you with support when you turn 18 under the Children (Leaving Care) Act 2000.[113] This allows for a needs assessment and potential support up to the age of 21, or 24 if you continue in education.

There may be a dispute about your age. If you claim asylum as an unaccompanied minor, the Home Office should refer you to social services for support unless it strongly believes that you are over 18 years old. If the social services department (in Scotland, social work department) has any doubt about your age, it can carry out an age assessment.[114] Get specialist advice if your age has been disputed: refugee organisations, such as the Refugee Council, can assist you (see Appendix 2).

Notes

1. **Introduction**
   1 s95 IAA 1999
   2 s98 IAA 1999
   3 s4 IAA 1999
   4 Sch 3 para 1 NIAA 2002
   5 Sch 3 para 2 NIAA 2002
   6 Sch 3 para 3 NIAA 2002
   7 s115(9) IAA 1999
   8 IA(PAFAS) Regs; see also www.gov.uk/
     immigration-operational-guidance/
     asylum-policy

2. **Support for asylum seekers**
   9 ss94(1) and 95(1) and Sch 9 paras 1-3
     IAA 1999; regs 2(1) and 3 AS Regs
   10 s55 NIAA 2002
   11 ss94(1) and 95(1) and Sch 9 para
     1(1)(2) IAA 1999; reg 3(1) AS Regs
   12 para 353 IR
   13 s94(3) IAA 1999; regs 2 and 2A AS Regs
   14 s95(4) IAA 1999
   15 ASA/02/02/1877
   16 s9 AI(TC)A 2004
   17 s94(1) IAA 1999; reg 2 (4) AS Regs;
     Home Office guidance, Asylum Support
     (Asylum Instructions), *Dependants on an
     Asylum Support Application*, available at
     www.gov.uk/government/collections/
     asylum-support-asylum-instructions
   18 Reg 2(4)(f) and (6)(a) and (b) AS Regs
   19 *R (Chen) v SSHD* [2012] EWHC 2531
   20 www.asaproject.org/wp-content/
     uploads/2013/03/Factsheet-11-
     Getting-s95-or-s4-support-for-
     dependants.pdf
   21 s95(3) IAA 1999
   22 Reg 7 AS Regs
   23 Reg 7(b) AS Regs
   24 s95(2) IAA 1999; reg 4 AS Regs
   25 *R (Limbuela and Others (Shelter
     intervener)) v SSHD* [2005] UKHL 66
   26 s55 NIAA 2002
   27 Home Office guidance, Asylum Support
     (Asylum Instructions), *Asylum Support:
     policy bulletins*, Ch 5, available at
     www.gov.uk/government/collections/
     asylum-support-asylum-instructions
   28 s55 IAA 1999
   29 Sch 3 NIAA 2002
   30 Sch 3 para 4 NIAA 2002

   31 Sch 3 para 5 NIAA 2002
   32 Sch 3 paras 2 and 3 NIAA 2002
   33 Reg 20(1) AS Regs provides that support
     'may' be suspended or discontinued.
   34 Reg 20(1)(a) AS Regs
   35 Reg 20(1)(b) AS Regs
   36 Reg 20(1)(c) AS Regs
   37 Reg 20(1)(e) AS Regs
   38 Reg 20(1)(f) AS Regs
   39 Reg 20(1)(g) AS Regs
   40 Reg 20(1)(h) AS Regs
   41 Reg 20(1)(i) AS Regs
   42 Reg 20(1)(j) AS Regs
   43 Reg 20(1)(d) AS Regs
   44 Reg 21(1) AS Regs; Home Office
     guidance, Asylum Support (Asylum
     Instructions), *Asylum Support
     Instructions: policy bulletins*, 84, available
     at www.gov.uk/government/
     collections/asylum-support-asylum-
     instructions
   45 Reg 21(1)(c) and (2) AS Regs, with
     reference to reg 15 AS Regs
   46 Reg 21(3) AS Regs

3. **Temporary support**
   47 s98 IAA 1999
   48 s98(1) IAA 1999; Home Office
     guidance, Asylum Support (Asylum
     Instructions), *Asylum Support
     Instructions: policy bulletins*, para 1.1,
     available at www.gov.uk/government/
     collections/asylum-support-asylum-
     instructions
   49 s98(3) IAA 1999, applying s95(11)
   50 As compared with the position relating
     to asylum support under s95(1) IAA
     1999.
   51 This is because s103 IAA 1999, which
     deals with appeals, does not refer to s98
     support.
   52 Reg 4(8)(9) AS Regs

4. **Support for failed asylum seekers**
   53 Reg 3(1)(a) IA(PAFAS) Regs
   54 s4(1)(a) IAA 1999
   55 These are listed in reg 3(2)(a-e)
     IA(PAFAS) Regs
   56 Reg 3(1)(b) and (2)(a) IA(PAFAS) Regs;
     ASA/06/03/12859

57 Home Office guidance, Asylum Support (Asylum Instructions), *Asylum Support, Section 4 Policy and Process*, para 4.2.1, available at www.gov.uk/government/collections/asylum-support-asylum-instructions
58 Reg 3(1)(b) and (2)(b) IA(POAFAS) Regs
59 *R (SSHD) v ASA and Osman, Yillah, Ahmad and Musemwa (interested parties)* [2006] EWHC 1248
60 Home Office guidance, Asylum Support (Asylum Instructions), *Asylum Support, Section 4 Policy and Process*, para 1.11.2, available at www.gov.uk/government/collections/asylum-support-asylum-instructions
61 Home Office guidance, Asylum Support (Asylum Instructions), *Asylum Support, Section 4 Policy and Process*, para 1.11.2, available at www.gov.uk/government/collections/asylum-support-asylum-instructions
62 Home Office guidance, Asylum Support (Asylum Instructions), *Asylum Support, Section 4 Policy and Process*, para 1.11.3, available at www.gov.uk/government/collections/asylum-support-asylum-instructions
63 See www.nhs.uk, 'Your pregnancy and baby guide'
64 Reg 3(1)(b) and (2)(c) IA(PAFAS) Regs
65 *R (Rasul) v ASA* [2006] EWHC 435; ASA/06/03/12859
66 Reg 3(1)(b) and (2)(d) IA(PAFAS) Regs
67 Regs 3(1)(b) and (2)(e) IA(PAFAS) Regs
68 *R (Limbuela and Others (Shelter intervener)) v SSHD* [2005] UKHL 66
69 *R (Nigatu) v SSHD* [2004] EWHC 1806 (Admin), para 20
70 See, for example, AS/14/06/31490, 11 June 2014
71 Reg 3(2)(e) IA(PAFAS) Regs
72 *R (MK and AH) v SSHD* [2012] EWHC 1896
73 Home Office guidance, Asylum Support (Asylum Instructions), *Section 4 Review: instruction*, para 11.1, available at www.gov.uk/government/collections/asylum-support-asylum-instructions
74 *R (Malumba) v First-tier Tribunal (Asylum Support)*, unreported. The Home Office conceded in the 2015 judicial review that 'provision of s4 may in any particular case be necessary to avoid a breach of a person's Article 8 rights'; AS/14/11/32141, 10 August 2015
75 Reg 3(2)(d) IA(PAFAS) Regs
76 *R (NS) v First-tier Tribunal* [2009] EWHC 3819 (Admin)
77 AS/11/06/26857, 18 August 2011
78 *M Ahmed v Asylum Support Adjudicator and the Secretary of State* [2008] EWHC 2282 (Admin), judgment given 2 October 2008
79 *Khan*
80 Home Office guidance, Asylum Support (Asylum Instructions), *Asylum Support, Section 4 Policy and Process* and *Section 4 Review: instruction*, available at www.gov.uk/government/collections/asylum-support-asylum-instructions
81 Reg 6 IA(PAFAS) Regs
82 s55 Borders, Citizenship and Immigration Act 2009
83 Home Office guidance, Asylum Support (Asylum Instructions), *Section 4 Review: instruction* para 10.2, available at www.gov.uk/government/collections/asylum-support-asylum-instructions

5. Support for people on temporary admission, temporary release or immigration bail

84 Support provided under section 4(1)(a) and (b) is essentially the same: section 4(1)(a) refers to those on temporary admission and section 4(1)(b) to those who have been in detention and are on temporary release.
85 Home Office guidance, Asylum Support (Asylum Instructions), *Asylum Support, Section 4 Policy and Process*, para 5.7.3, available at www.gov.uk/government/collections/asylum-support-asylum-instructions
86 Home Office guidance, Asylum Support (Asylum Instructions), *Asylum Support, Section 4 Policy and Process*, para 1.1.3, available at www.gov.uk/government/collections/asylum-support-asylum-instructions
87 s4(1)(a) IAA 1999
88 AS/11/09/27448, 30 September 2011
89 AS/11/11/76787, 22 November 2011
90 AS/11/12/27777, 12 January 2012
91 s4(1)(c) IAA 1999
92 Home Office guidance, Asylum Support (Asylum Instructions), *Asylum Support, Section 4 Policy and Process*, para 5.7.3, available at www.gov.uk/government/collections/asylum-support-asylum-instructions

6. Support from your local authority

93 Sch 3 NIAA 2002
94 Sch 3 para 2 NIAA 2002
95 *R (AW) v Croydon London Borough
Council* [2005] EWHC 2950; *Birmingham
City Council v Clue* [2010] EWCA Civ 460
96 CA 2014
97 *R (Westminster) v NASS* [2002] UKHL 38;
*R (AW) v Croydon London Borough
Council* [2005] EWHC 2950
98 *SL v Westminster* [2013] UKSC 27
99 CA 2014
100 ss8,18 and 19 CA 2014
101 Reg 2 Care and Support (Eligibility
Criteria) Regulations 2015, No.313
102 Support is provided under s12 of the
Social Work (Scotland) Act 1968.
103 **E** s21 CA 2014
W s21(1A) NAA 1948
S s12(2A) Social Work (Scotland) Act
1968
104 s17 CA 1989; s22 C(S)A 1995
105 s17(10) CA 1989
106 s17(3) CA 1989; s22(3) C(S)A 1995
107 s122(5) IAA 1999
108 Home Office guidance, Asylum Support
(Asylum Instructions), *Transition at Age
18: instruction,* available at
www.gov.uk/government/collections/
asylum-support-asylum-instructions;
s20 CA 1989; Children (Leaving Care)
Act 2000
109 *Birmingham City Council v Clue* [2010]
EWCA Civ 460
110 *Birmingham City Council v Clue* [2010]
EWCA Civ 460
111 *R (VC and K) v Newcastle CC* [2011]
EWHC 2673 (Admin)
112 s69 IA 2016
113 *R (SO) v London Borough of Barking and
Dagenham* [2010] EWCA Civ 1101;
Home Office guidance, Asylum Support
(Asylum Instructions), *Transition at Age
18: instruction,* available at
www.gov.uk/government/collections/
asylum-support-asylum-instructions
114 *R (C) v London Borough of Merton* [2005]
EWHC 1753 (Admin)

Chapter 22

Applying for asylum support

This chapter covers:
1. Applying for section 95 support (below)
2. Making a decision on your application (p397)
3. Applying for section 4 support (p404)

1. Applying for section 95 support

If you are either an asylum seeker or a dependant of an asylum seeker for support purposes, you can apply for section 95 support from the Home Office.[1] The application can be for you alone, or for yourself and your dependants.[2] See p404 for how to apply for section 4 support if you are a failed asylum seeker who has reached the end of the appeal process, or if you have been temporarily admitted to the UK or are on immigration bail.

You can apply for accommodation and cash support or, if you have somewhere to live, just for the cash support to meet your 'essential needs' (known as '**subsistence-only support**'). Most people apply for both.

You must apply for support on Form ASF1, available from the Asylum Help service at Migrant Help (see p371) and from www.gov.uk/asylum-support/how-to-claim.[3] Even if the application is for both yourself and your dependants, you only need to complete one form. If you wish to obtain support as a dependant of a person who is already being supported by the Home Office, you do not need to complete the application form again – the Home Office will consider providing additional support for you if notified of your existence in writing.[4] However, it is advisable to complete a separate application form, as you then appear to have the right of appeal against any subsequent refusal, which may not be so clear if an asylum seeker simply notifies the Home Office that s/he has been joined by a dependant.[5]

Migrant Help can help you complete Form ASF1 and submit it to the Home Office. It is strongly advised to get assistance from Migrant Help or a local advice agency if you can. You must complete the form in full and in English.[6] There are detailed notes accompanying it, which give further information about the application procedure and guidance on how to complete the form.

The form asks for details of the stage your asylum application has reached, the kind of support you need, your current accommodation, any other kind of support you receive (including support from friends or relatives, details of cash, savings, investments or other property you own, any employment you have and state benefits you receive, both for yourself and your dependants), and details of any disabilities or special needs you have. You must send documents to confirm the information you give. It is a criminal offence to make false representations in order to obtain asylum support (it is believed that the Home Office has not carried out any prosecutions).[7]

Form ASF1 can be downloaded, printed and filled in by hand, or completed and saved to a computer. With either method, it then must be emailed, faxed or posted to the Home Office, although in future it may be possible to submit it via the Home Office website. If you need to use the post, it must be sent via Migrant Help. At the time of writing, Migrant Help's address for this purpose is PO Box 471, Dover CT16 9FN.

The methods of, and addresses for, communicating with the Home Office frequently change, and if it is unclear from the website how to submit the form, it is advisable to contact a specialist agency for advice.

The Home Office may ask you for further information on any of the details contained in the application form.[8]

2. **Making a decision on your application**

Deciding whether you are destitute

If you apply for section 95 support for yourself, the Home Office must be satisfied that you are 'destitute'. If you apply for support for yourself and your dependants, it decides whether the group as a whole is destitute.[9]

'Destitute' includes if you are 'likely to become destitute within 14 days'.[10] You are destitute if either:[11]

- you do not have 'adequate accommodation' (see p399), or any means of getting adequate accommodation; or
- you cannot meet your essential living needs (see p401), even if you have adequate accommodation.

It is an either/or test, so you are 'destitute' and therefore eligible for both accommodation and cash support, if you are without adequate accommodation or without the means to feed yourself.

The Home Office must follow rules that set out what is and what is not relevant in deciding these questions. These apply when you make an application for support and at any stage if there is a question of whether support should continue.

When considering whether you are destitute, the Home Office must take into account any of the following that are available to you or to any of your dependants:[12]
- any income you have, or which you may reasonably be expected to have;
- any other support that is available, or which may reasonably be expected to be available, to you;
- any of the following assets that are available to you, or which might reasonably be expected to be available to you:
  - cash;
  - savings;
  - investments;
  - land;
  - vehicles;
  - goods for trade or business.

This might include support from friends and relatives in the UK (or abroad, depending on the facts) or from voluntary sector organisations. Any income your partner receives (eg, from wages or social security benefits) may be taken into account when assessing whether you are destitute, but only if her/his income is actually available, or might reasonably be expected to be available, to meet your essential living needs.[13]

Land may include property, such as a house and other outbuildings. Investments include business investments, income bonds, life assurance policies, pension schemes, stocks and shares, and unit trusts (but not jewellery[14]). Your land, assets and investments could be in the UK or abroad and must all be disclosed on Form ASF1.

Although jewellery is excluded, you should disclose any items of jewellery or watches belonging to you or your dependants that are worth over £1,000 at the current market value in your application for support, and inform the Home Office immediately if any of these items are subsequently sold and for how much.[15] The money you receive as a result of the sale may be taken into account.

The Home Office examines any visa application you may have made to come to the UK and compares it with the information on Form ASF1. For example, you may have come to the UK on a student or visitor's visa and then claimed asylum. Therefore, it is important to explain how your situation has changed and why you are now destitute.

The Home Office may provide you with support on a limited basis to allow you time to sell items of property – eg, six months if it is a house. The Home Office treats the money received from the sale as cash or savings and takes it into account when deciding whether or not to provide support. If you do not consider it reasonable that you should have to sell your property, give your reasons for this when you send in your application form.[16]

When deciding whether you are destitute, the Home Office must ignore any:

- assets you or your dependants have that are not listed above;[17]
- Home Office support which you are already being provided with.[18]

Note: since 2015 the Home Office has been refusing many more applications for section 95 support, finding applicants 'not destitute'. In the Home Office's view, these people have assets or access to assets. You are therefore strongly advised to obtain specialist help with completing Form ASF1. You may need to appeal against the Home Office's decision and your chances of winning the appeal depend on the information you initially submitted.

Adequate accommodation

If you are applying for support but you have some form of accommodation, the Home Office must decide whether or not this is 'adequate'. The Home Office must take into account whether:[19]

- it is 'reasonable' for you to continue to occupy the accommodation;
- you can afford to pay for the accommodation;
- you can gain entry to the accommodation;
- if the accommodation is a houseboat, a caravan or some other moveable structure that can be lived in, whether there is somewhere you can place it and have permission to live in it;
- you can live in the accommodation with your dependants;
- you or your dependants are likely to experience harassment, threats or violence if you continue to live in the accommodation.

Accommodation may be considered inadequate, for example, if you are staying with a friend and sleeping on her/his floor, or if you cannot gain entry to it during the day, or if it is unsuitable for you because of your health needs or a physical disability.

Note: even if the accommodation is adequate, you are still destitute if you cannot meet your essential living needs.

If you have told the Home Office that you want to stay in your current accommodation and only want financial assistance, the factors listed above are not taken into account when deciding whether you are destitute, except for the question of whether you can afford the accommodation.[20]

Note: if you have sufficient savings to be able to rent accommodation for yourself, since 1 February 2016 in England you must obtain permission from the Home Office for the 'right to rent'.[21] Landlords can only grant tenancies or rent rooms to those with a right to rent. At the request of the landlord, the Home Office checks that you are still a current asylum seeker and is likely to grant permission within 48 hours.

Is it reasonable for you to continue to occupy the accommodation?

The Home Office must consider whether it is 'reasonable' for you to continue to occupy the accommodation.[22] In considering this, it may take into account the general housing circumstances in the district[23] of the local government housing authority in which the accommodation is situated.[24] So if your accommodation is worse or more overcrowded than other accommodation generally found in the area in which you live, it may not be reasonable for you to continue to live there.

Can you afford to pay for the accommodation?

The Home Office must consider whether you can afford to pay for your existing accommodation.[25] It must take into account:[26]

- any income or assets (see p397), other than from Home Office support or temporary support, available to you or any of your dependants, or which might be expected to be available;
- the costs of living in the accommodation;
- your other reasonable living expenses.

Do you have access to the accommodation?

Circumstances in which you would be considered not to have access to your accommodation include if you have been illegally evicted from the accommodation, or squatters have unlawfully moved in.

Is there harassment, threats or violence?

The Home Office must consider whether it is 'probable' that your continued occupation of the accommodation will lead to domestic violence against you or any of your dependants.[27] The domestic violence must be:[28]

- from a person who is, or who has been, a 'close family member'; *and*
- in the form of either actual violence, or threats of violence that are likely to be carried out.

There is no definition of 'close family member'. Depending on the circumstances, it may cover a married or unmarried partner and ex-partner, those to whom you have a blood relationship, in-laws, relatives of your partner and others who live (or have lived) in your household. **Note:** the family member does not have to live with you.[29] You may fear that because your address is known to her/him, your continued occupation of that accommodation is likely to lead to domestic violence.

Although the asylum support rules only specifically refer to *domestic* violence, it is arguable that other forms of violence or threats which you have received from anyone not normally associated with you are also relevant when deciding whether your current accommodation is adequate. This may be in the form of racial harassment or attacks,[30] sexual abuse or harassment, and harassment because of your religion or for other reasons.

Your essential living needs

When deciding whether you can meet your essential living needs, certain items are not treated as essential.[31] When deciding whether you are destitute, your inability to provide any of the following items for yourself is not relevant:[32]

- the cost of sending or receiving faxes, photocopying or buying or using computer facilities;
- travelling expenses;
- toys and entertainment expenses.

If you are granted support, the cost of travelling to your new accommodation is paid for by the Home Office.

If you have another need that is not referred to in these rules, it does not necessarily mean that it is an 'essential living need'.[33] The Home Office must decide whether the need is essential, taking into account your individual circumstances. Once you are in receipt of support, it is possible to apply for additional support if your needs are 'exceptional' (see p412).

Clothing

When deciding whether you can meet your essential living needs in terms of clothing, the Home Office cannot take into account your personal preferences.[34] However, it can take into account your individual circumstances when deciding whether you can meet your clothing requirements, including:[35]

- whether you can afford to provide clothes for yourself that are suitable for the different weather conditions in the UK;
- whether you have sufficient changes of clothes required for cleanliness; *and*
- whether you have clothes that are suitable for any particular health or other individual needs that you have.

Decisions and temporary support

The Home Office may decide not to consider your application if you have not completed the form properly or accurately, or if you have not co-operated with enquiries.[36] This is known as a 'section 57 decision'. There is no right of appeal against this, so it is therefore important to answer all further questions from the Home Office (known as 'further inquiry requests') as best you can and within the time limit given to you. The only remedy against a section 57 decision is judicial review.

While you are waiting for a decision on your application, if you appear destitute, you should be provided with temporary (section 98) support (see p377).[37] You can also apply for temporary support before you have completed Form ASF1.

In practice, obtaining temporary support has become more difficult recently, as the Home Office has sought to save costs and has set up an Accommodation Gatekeeping Team, which examines all temporary support applications. If you apply for asylum on arrival or shortly afterwards at the Asylum Screening Unit in Croydon and are street homeless, you should be given initial accommodation (usually, a full-board hostel). If you need to apply for support at a later stage and also need to apply for temporary support, it is probably quickest to apply via Migrant Help, although it is also possible to apply via other voluntary sector organisations.

There is no application form for temporary support, but there is an initial accommodation referral form, which Migrant Help will complete on your behalf, if it is helping you.

If the Home Office refuses you temporary support, it emails its reasons to Migrant Help. There is no right of appeal; the only method of challenging a decision is by judicial review proceedings.

If the Home Office decides to provide you with support, it informs you in writing that your application has been accepted and about the package of support you will receive. If your application is refused, you receive a letter explaining why, and informing you of your right of appeal, together with an appeal form.[38]

Conditions attached to the support

The Home Office may provide you with support, subject to certain conditions – eg that the accommodation is not sub-let, that noise is kept to a reasonable level in the interests of neighbours or that you must live at the address the Home Office has provided and inform it of any changes in your circumstances.[39] The conditions must be in writing[40] and given to the person who is being supported.[41]

Even if you have only asked the Home Office for financial support and not accommodation (eg, because a friend has offered to let you stay with her/him), you must inform it of your address for support purposes, and this becomes your authorised address. You must tell the Home Office if you need to leave this address, and you are not allowed to leave the address for more than 14 days.

The Home Office may take into account any previous breach of conditions when deciding whether or not to provide you with support, whether to continue to provide support, and in deciding the level or kind of support to be provided.[42]

Dispersal

The Home Office's general policy is to provide support and accommodation outside London.[43] Under this 'dispersal' policy, most people who are entitled to support are provided with accommodation outside London and the south east of England, unless they can show a strong reason for staying where they currently live. For example, if you are receiving treatment from Freedom from Torture, which is based in London, Birmingham, Manchester, Newcastle and Glasgow, the Home Office takes this into account. It also delays dispersal if your child is about to take her/his GCSEs or A levels. There is detailed guidance on how someone who is pregnant or who has a serious medical condition should be dispersed.[44] It is generally very difficult to succeed in arguing against being dispersed away from London and the South East or against being moved away from the area in which you already live (see p411).

Health benefits

If your application for support is accepted, the Home Office should also issue you with a certificate (HC2), enabling you to get free NHS prescriptions, dental treatment, sight tests and wigs. You may also be able to get vouchers towards the cost of glasses and contact lenses. The HC2 certificate itself tells you how to use it and what you can use it for. If you have already paid for any of the above items or for travel to and from hospital for NHS treatment, you may be able to claim the money back.

Change of circumstances

If you are provided with support, you must notify the Home Office of certain relevant changes in your circumstances.[45] These are if you (or any of your dependants):[46]
- are joined in the UK by a dependant;
- receive or obtain access to any money or savings, investments, land, cars or other vehicles, or goods for the purposes of trade or other business, which you have not previously declared;
- become employed or unemployed;
- change your name;
- get married or divorced;
- begin living with another person as if you were married to her/him, or if you separate from a spouse or from a person with whom you have been living as if you were married;
- become pregnant or have a child;
- leave school;
- begin to share your accommodation with another person;
- move to a different address or otherwise leave your accommodation;
- go into hospital;
- go into to prison or some other form of custody;
- leave the UK;
- die.

If there is a relevant change of circumstances, a decision may be made to change the nature or level of the existing support, or to provide or withdraw support for different individuals.

Note: unless you have a reasonable excuse, it is a criminal offence not to notify the Home Office of a change in circumstances.[47]

Eviction from accommodation

The usual law on security of tenure does not apply to Home Office accommodation.[48] Tenancies or licences created when Home Office support is provided can come to an end when asylum support is terminated – ie, if:[49]
- your support is suspended or discontinued (see p376) because:
  - there has been a breach of the conditions or a criminal offence;
  - you have concealed financial resources;
  - you have been absent from the address without permission;
  - you have ceased to reside at the address;
- your application for asylum has been determined;
- you are no longer destitute;
- you move to be supported in other accommodation.

In any of the above circumstances, any tenancy or licence is terminated at the end of the period (minimum of seven days) specified in a 'notice to quit' given to you.[50]

Further applications for support

If you are refused support, in most cases you can make a further application at any time and this must be considered by the Home Office. The exception to this is if your support is suspended or terminated because you breach its conditions.[51] In this case, the Home Office has the discretion not to accept a new application from you unless there has been a 'material change of circumstances' (see p377)[52] or if there are 'exceptional circumstances'. **Note:** the Home Office has discretion and so a change of circumstances is not always necessary.

3. Applying for section 4 support

The procedure for applying for section 4 support is very similar to applying for section 95 support (see p396). There is the same requirement to be destitute and the definition of destitution is the same.[53] You use the same Form ASF1, which can be obtained from Migrant Help or online from the government website (www.gov.uk/asylum-support/how-to-claim). There are additional sections at the end of Form ASF1 that you should complete to show the grounds on which you are eligible for section 4 support.

It is crucial to submit all the necessary information and documentation with your application form. If you supply insufficient or ambiguous information, your application will be rejected or the Home Office will write to you requesting more information, which delays support being provided. There is no interim or emergency support available.

The Home Office previously had a target of making a decision on a section 4 application within two days. In October 2009, this target was removed for people applying for support on the basis that they had submitted a fresh asylum claim. Home Office caseworkers were instructed to delay considering an application for section 4 support for 15 working days in order to first make a decision on the fresh asylum claim/further submissions. In 2012, the High Court found this blanket instruction to be unlawful because it involved a significant risk of human rights being breached.[54] The Home Office then revised its policy instruction to comply with this judgment. The policy is now to make all decisions on applications for section 4 support based on further submissions within five working days and, for priority applicants, within two working days.[55]

However, you may still experience significant administrative delays in decision making. Although the Home Office should provide support as soon as your eligibility is established, there are routine delays. Home Office policy is to give accommodation providers up to nine days in which to provide accommodation, but this often takes longer.

Section 4 support if you have temporary admission or are on temporary release

There is no particular form for applying for section 4 support if you have temporary admission or are on temporary release, so you should use Form ASF1. Make it clear on the form that you are applying for support under s4(1)(a) or (b) and the basis of your application, taking into account the Home Office's policy.[56] **Note:** the policy does not accurately reflect the law in stating that section 4(1)(a) and (b) support cannot be granted to someone who has an outstanding 'Article 8 application'.

Section 4 support if you are applying for bail from immigration detention

If you are detained under the Immigration Acts (or were detained and still on immigration bail) and want to apply for support (under section 4(1)(c)) and an address for bail (see p387), the application form is a very simple four-page form. This is because the destitution test and other detailed section 4 criteria do not apply. Although there is no statutory basis for the destitution test, the Home Office still considers whether you are destitute.[57] You should therefore be ready to provide information on your assets and income, even though you are not required to complete Form ASF1.

How your application is dealt with

Most section 4 applications are dealt with by a centralised team in Leeds, including if your original asylum application was before March 2007. Applications for section 4(1)(c) support from immigration detainees and those on immigration bail are made to a different part of the Home Office in Liverpool (known as the Complex Casework Directorate, Case Assurance and Audit Unit, or Older Live Cases Unit), and some more complex cases are also sent there. Applications to Leeds can be made by email, fax or post.

When the Home Office has decided that you should receive support and has made the necessary arrangements with an accommodation provider, you are notified of the travel arrangements to the dispersal area (see p411).

Notes

1. Applying for section 95 support
1 Reg 3(1) AS Regs
2 Reg 3(2) AS Regs
3 Reg 3(3) AS Regs
4 Reg 3(6) AS Regs
5 See wording of s103 IAA 1999
6 Reg 3(3) AS Regs. See also Form ASF1 on the www.gov.uk website.
7 ss105-07 IAA 1999
8 Reg 3(5) AS Regs

2. Making a decision on your application
9 s95(4) IAA 1999; reg 5(1) AS Regs
10 Reg 7 AS Regs
11 s95(3) IAA 1999
12 s95(5) and (7) IAA 1999; reg 6(4)-(5) AS Regs
13 R (SSHD) v Asylum Support Adjudicator and (1) Berkadle (2) Perera [2001] EWHC 811
14 Reg 6(6) AS Regs; Form ASF1 guidance notes, 'Cash, savings and assets'
15 Form ASF1 guidance notes, 'Jewellery'
16 Form ASF1 guidance notes, section 10
17 Reg 6(6) AS Regs
18 Reg 6(3) AS Regs
19 s95(5)(a) IAA 1999; reg 8(1)(a)-(b) and (3) AS Regs
20 Reg 8 (2) AS Regs
21 IA 2014
22 Reg 8(3)(a) AS Regs
23 Reg 8(6)(b) AS Regs. 'District' for these purposes has the same meaning as in s217(3) Housing Act 1996.
24 Reg 8(4) AS Regs
25 Reg 8(3)(b) AS Regs
26 Reg 8(5)(a)-(c) AS Regs
27 Reg 8(3)(g) AS Regs
28 Reg 8(3)(g) and (6)(a) AS Regs; Home Office guidance, Asylum Support (Asylum Instructions), Asylum Support Instructions: policy bulletins, Ch 23, available at www.gov.uk/government/collections/asylum-support-asylum-instructions
29 Although Form ASF1 guidance notes ask for information about people who 'normally stay with you as members of your family'.
30 See Home Office guidance, Asylum Support (Asylum Instructions), Asylum Support Instructions: policy bulletins, 81, available at www.gov.uk/government/collections/asylum-support-asylum-instructions
31 s95(7)-(8) IAA 1999
32 Reg 9(3)(4) AS Regs
33 Reg 9(6) AS Regs
34 s95(7)(b) IAA 1999; reg 9(1)(2) AS Regs
35 Reg 9(2) AS Regs
36 s57 NIAA 2002; reg 3(5A-5B) AS Regs; see also Home Office guidance, Asylum Support (Asylum Instructions), Asylum Support Instructions: policy bulletins, Ch 10, available at www.gov.uk/government/collections/asylum-support-asylum-instructions
37 s98 IAA 1999
38 Form ASF1 guidance notes, 'What Happens Next?'
39 s95(9) IAA 1999; regs 19 and 20 AS Regs
40 s95(10) IAA 1999

41 s95(11) IAA 1999
42 Reg 19 AS Regs
43 Home Office guidance, Asylum Support
(Asylum Instructions), *Asylum
Accommodation Requests Policy,* available
at www.gov.uk/government/
collections/asylum-support-asylum-
instructions
44 Home Office guidance, Asylum Support
(Asylum Instructions), *Healthcare Needs
and Pregnancy Dispersal Policy,* available
at www.gov.uk/government/
collections/asylum-support-asylum-
instructions
45 Reg 15(1) AS Regs
46 Reg 15(2) AS Regs
47 s105(1)(c) IAA 1999
48 They are 'excluded tenancies' under s3A
(7A) Protection from Eviction Act 1977.
49 Reg 22(2) AS Regs
50 Reg 22(1) AS Regs
51 Reg 21(1) AS Regs
52 Regs 15 and 21(2) AS Regs

3. Applying for section 4 support
53 Regs 2 and 3(1)(a) IA(POAFAS)
54 *MK and AH (Refugee Action Intervening)
v SSHD* [2012] EWHC 1896 (Admin)
55 Home Office guidance, Asylum Support
(Asylum Instructions), *Asylum Support,
Section 4 Policy and Process,* Ch 1.15,
available at www.gov.uk/government/
collections/asylum-support-asylum-
instructions
56 Home Office guidance, Asylum Support
(Asylum Instructions), *Asylum Support,
Section 4 Policy and Process,* para 1.1.3,
available at www.gov.uk/government/
collections/asylum-support-asylum-
instructions
57 Home Office guidance, Asylum Support
(Asylum Instructions), *Asylum Support,
Section 4 Policy and Process,* para 5.7.3,
available at www.gov.uk/government/
collections/asylum-support-asylum-
instructions

Chapter 23

Payment and accommodation

This chapter covers:
1. Section 95 support (below)
2. Section 4 support (p413)
3. Recovery of support (p416)

---

1. Section 95 support

Section 95 asylum support includes:[1]
- accommodation and 'subsistence' (cash) to cover your and your dependants' essential living needs;
- subsistence-only support for your essential living needs if you already have accommodation;
- expenses, other than legal expenses, in connection with your asylum application;
- if your circumstances are exceptional, any other form of support that the Home Office thinks is necessary.[2]

Note: the Home Office can disregard any preference you or your dependants have as to how the support is provided or arranged.[3]

When deciding what support to give you, the Home Office takes into account any income, support or assets (see p397) that you or your dependants have, or which might reasonably be available to you.[4]

Support for your essential living needs

If the Home Office decides you need support for your essential living needs, the general rule is that you are provided with cash on a weekly basis.[5]

Amount of support

Since 10 August 2015, the amount of support, regardless of age, is £36.95.[6]

There are additional payments of:[7]
- £3 a week for pregnant women;
- £5 a week for babies under one;
- £3 a week for children between the ages of one and three.

You collect your financial support on a weekly basis from your local post office using your application registration card. If it is necessary, and as a temporary measure, you may be issued with emergency support tokens, which are delivered to your address.

Legal challenge to the rates of asylum support

Before August 2015, different amounts were paid to adults and children, and to couples and single people. In the past, the rates were based on the equivalent of 70 per cent of the applicable amount of income support (IS), without any premiums, to which an adult would otherwise be entitled if s/he qualified for IS and had no other income (see CPAG'S *Welfare Benefits and Tax Credits Handbook* for more details). Initially, the rates were increased in April every year, but from April 2011 the rates were frozen, meaning a cut in real terms over several years.

In 2013, the charity Refugee Action brought a judicial review challenge against the Home Secretary's decision to freeze the rate of asylum support. This was upheld by the High Court in April 2014,[8] which ruled that the Home Secretary had acted irrationally and failed to take all relevant factors into account, in accordance with her duties under the European Union Reception Directive and the Immigration and Asylum Act 1999 to provide for asylum seekers' essential living needs.[9] Following the judgment, the Home Secretary reconsidered the level of support, but decided it should remain unchanged. In April 2015, the rate for single asylum seekers over 18 was increased by by 33 pence and then, from August 2015, the rates were cut to the above amounts. This is a significant reduction in the rate previously paid for children in families (£52.96 per week).

Exceptional payments

The Home Office can provide additional support if the normal rate of support is not enough to meet your essential living needs and you can show that your particular circumstances are 'exceptional'.[10] The Home Office's ability to provide exceptional payments was a key part of its case in the Refugee Action judicial review (see above), and so you should apply for exceptional payments if you need to. For instance, the High Court found that it was unreasonable to refuse a separated father help with the travel costs he incurred in visiting his young child because the Home Office was unable to provide him with accommodation closer than 130 miles.[11] The court suggested that reasonable travel costs should enable him to visit his son at least fortnightly. At the time of writing, the Home Office is in the process of drafting the application form for exceptional payments (Form ASF2) and guidance.

If your application is refused, the only remedy is judicial review proceedings.

Maternity payments

You may be eligible for a one-off maternity payment of £300.[12] You must apply in writing between one month before the expected birth and two weeks after, enclosing evidence – eg, a birth certificate, Form MAT B1 from your GP or some other original formal evidence. A payment can also be made if you are a supported parent or a parent applying for support and you have a child under three months old who was born outside the UK. It is important to make this application in time. If it is made late, it is likely to be refused. The Home Office policy bulletin that allows maternity payments does not say whether or not it is possible to make a late claim, but it may be worth trying if you can give good reasons for the delay.[13]

Backdating support

There is often a delay between applying for support and getting paid. This can be serious if you are without support in the meantime. With social security benefits, regulations normally stipulate the start date of the particular benefit. This is not the case with asylum support as there are no rules in the legislation identifying the date from when support must be provided. It is, therefore, unclear whether you are entitled to support from, for example, the date the Home Office receives your application or the date it makes a decision.

In the absence of legislation stating otherwise, it is arguable that support should be payable from the date the Home Office receives a full and valid claim – ie, an application that shows that you are destitute and eligible for support. This should be the case, no matter what delays are caused by the Home Office or the appeal procedure.

However, in practice, the Home Office usually only awards support from the date it makes its decision.

In its policy, the Home Office recognises that awards of asylum support can be backdated if payments have been missed and the applicant has not caused it.[14] This relates to missed payments of support after a favourable decision on eligibility has already been made, not to Home Office delays in processing an initial application for support and before a favourable decision has been made.

Contributions to support

When deciding what level of support to give you as a destitute asylum seeker, the Home Office must take into account any income, support and assets that are available (or might reasonably be expected to be available) to you (see p397).[15] However, if you have income and/or assets, it can decide that you should make a contribution to the cost of your support rather than reducing the level of support provided.[16] If this is the case, you are notified of the amount and you must make payments directly to the Home Office.[17] If you are required to make a contribution, the Home Office may also make it a condition of your support that you pay your contributions promptly.[18] In practice, however, we are not aware of any such contributions ever having been required.

Accommodation

The majority of applications for asylum and asylum support are made in the south east of England. However, the Home Office has a strict policy of **'dispersal'**.[19] This means that, apart from a few exceptions, the accommodation and support it provides are outside London and south east England.

The Home Office does not own and provide accommodation itself. It makes arrangements with private contractors, which provide the accommodation throughout the UK.[20] These arrangements, which include transport, are a crucial part of the dispersal scheme.

When deciding the location and nature of the accommodation you are given, the Home Office must consider:[21]

- the fact that you are only being provided with accommodation on a temporary basis until your application for asylum has been dealt with (including any period during which you are appealing);
- the fact that it is desirable to provide accommodation for asylum seekers in areas where there is a good supply of accommodation – eg, outside London, given that there is an acute shortage of accommodation in the London area.[22]

The Home Office does not take into account your preferences on:

- the area in which you would like the accommodation to be located;[23]
- the nature of the accommodation to be provided;[24]
- the nature and standard of the fixtures and fittings in the accommodation.[25]

However, the Home Office may still take into account your individual circumstances if they relate to your accommodation needs.[26] These include:[27]

- your ethnic group and/or religion. Ethnicity is taken into account, although it does not usually prevent dispersal since the Home Office considers asylum dispersal accommodation to be located in areas where there is either an already established ethnic minority community or where one can be sustained.[28] Your freedom to practice your religion is also taken into account and, if you can demonstrate that you should be allocated accommodation in an area because it is the only place you can worship, this may be accepted. However, if others of the same religion have been dispersed, the Home Office is likely to consider it possible that you can practise your religion with others in the dispersal area;
- any special dietary needs you or your dependants may have;
- your or your dependants' medical or psychological condition, any disabilities you have and any treatment you are receiving for these.

The Home Office should delay dispersal on medical grounds, pending further medical advice if:[29]

- you are HIV positive or have tuberculosis;
- you have severe mental health problems;

- you are pregnant and four weeks from your expected due date, or you have experienced complications, or you have medical advice against travel, or you are a new mother whose baby is less than four weeks old. You are not expected to travel for longer than four hours to your dispersal accommodation at any point during your pregnancy;
- you are receiving ongoing treatment which is only available in the area where you currently live or which would be hard to replicate elsewhere;
- you are booked to receive invasive surgery within a month, or you are recovering from an operation, or surgery has been booked to take place in more than a month's time but any delay would have an adverse impact on your health;
- delaying dispersal is necessary to arrange continuity of care – eg, if you are undergoing kidney dialysis;
- an infectious and notifiable disease is present or suspected;
- you have been referred to or admitted to secondary care services due to acute need.

The list is not exhaustive, so the Home Office may consider delaying dispersal in other circumstances.

If you are receiving treatment from Freedom from Torture, the Home Office should give 'careful consideration' to any need to be accommodated where you can continue to receive treatment.[30]

Note: the Home Office must apply the above criteria when deciding how and where support should be provided, even though a private contractor makes the actual arrangements.

Expenses in connection with your asylum application

The Home Office may meet some of the expenses connected to your asylum application.[31] These do not include 'legal' expenses – eg, the costs of paying your lawyer to prepare your case and represent you.

Eligible expenses include the cost of preparing and copying documents and travelling to Home Office interviews,[32] and may include the cost of:
- sending letters and faxes in order to obtain further evidence;
- medical reports and expert reports on your country of origin;
- your travel expenses (or those of your witnesses) to attend your appeal;
- medical or other examinations in connection with your application.

Note: you may also be able to apply for exceptional payments (see p409).

In practice, the difficulties and bureaucratic nature of dealing with the Home Office often make the process of claiming overwhelming and uneconomic. In addition, the Home Office is aware that funding from the Legal Aid Agency is available to pay for assessments and reports to support your asylum application.

Although not paid as asylum support, the cost of your fares incurred in travelling to comply with any immigration reporting requirements can be reclaimed from the Home Office if you live more than three miles from the reporting centre.[33] You must claim these at the reporting centre. It is only possible to claim the travel costs for attending your next reporting date (ie, in advance), not the costs already incurred. Some reporting centres are very strict in applying the wording of the guidance. This says that the test is a three-mile 'radius', interpreted as the straight-line distance between the reporting centre and your accommodation, not whether the distance that you must travel is over three miles. The Home Office has, however, been pressed to interpret the guidance more sensibly.

Services

If you are receiving asylum support, the Home Office may provide the following services:[34]
- education, including English language lessons;
- sporting or other developmental activities.

The Home Office has the power to provide these services, but it is not under a duty to do so. In addition, the services may only be provided in order to 'maintain good order' among supported asylum seekers.[35] This does not mean that 'good order' must have broken down before these services are provided. However, the Home Office must, at least, be able to anticipate that 'good order' is less likely to be maintained without the stimulation of education, language lessons and developmental activities, and general access to, and integration into, the wider community.

Note: at the time of writing, the Home Office is not providing these services.

---

2. **Section 4 support**

Section 4 support is provided as a package of accommodation and a pre-paid payment card which can be used to obtain food and goods in certain shops. The payment card is called an 'Azure card' (it is blue). The card is held by the failed asylum seeker and credited on a weekly basis with the support due.

Unlike section 95 support, there are no specific provisions to reduce the value of any support provided under section 4, to require you to make contributions, or to recover the value of support if it has been provided to someone who is not entitled to it.

The value of the payment card

The financial element of section 4 support is not fixed in the legislation, but is decided by the Secretary of State for the Home Department. When the regulations were made in 2005, the value of the vouchers was set at £35 per individual – ie, for each adult and child. This amount has only been increased once since 2005 – in early 2010, it was raised to £35.39 for each member of the household.

It is possible to carry your balance over from one week to the next – eg, in order to save for more expensive items. However, if too much balance is accrued, the Home Office may query whether you are destitute.

Additional support

There has been criticism of the low level of financial support provided under section 4 and, in order to comply with a European Directive, the government introduced additional section 4 support in 2007.[36] This additional support can be claimed by failed asylum seekers (and/or their dependants) in certain prescribed circumstances. **Note:** this additional support is not provided automatically. You must make an application to the Home Office, using the form *Application for Provision of Services or Facilities for Section 4 Service Users*. The application form includes useful guidance.[37]

You can claim additional support:[38]

- for the costs of travel to receive healthcare treatment where a 'qualifying journey' is necessary. A **'qualifying journey'** is a single journey of at least three miles, or of any distance if:
  - you or your child are unable, or virtually unable, to walk up to three miles because of a physical impediment or for some other reason;
  - you have at least one dependant aged under five years;
- for the costs of travel to register a birth;
- to obtain a child's full birth certificate;
- for telephone calls and letters (ie, stationery and postage) about medical treatment or care and to communicate with:
  - the Home Office;
  - a 'qualified person' – ie, a solicitor, barrister or authorised immigration adviser;
  - a court or tribunal;
  - a voluntary sector partner;
  - a Citizens Advice Bureau;
  - a local authority;
  - an immigration officer;
  - the Secretary of State;
- if you are pregnant (up to £3 a week);
- if have a child under one year (up to £5 a week);
- if have a child between one and five years (up to £3 a week);
- for clothing for a child under 16 years old (up to £5 a week);
- for exceptional specific needs. The Home Office must be satisfied that there is an exceptional need (which may not be met by the above) for travel, telephone

calls, stationery and postage, or essential living needs. This could include travel to your embassy.

There is also a one-off additional payment for pregnant women and new mothers similar to the maternity payment that can be made with section 95 support – see p409). The amount is £250 (£500 if twins) and it is provided as a credit on your payment card. You should apply on the application form, with a MAT B1 certificate or birth certificate. You must apply between eight weeks before the expected due date and six weeks after the birth.

Many failed asylum seekers and others in receipt of section 4 support are required to sign in at an immigration reporting centre at regular intervals and may be able to reclaim their travel costs (see p14).

Accommodation

If you have friends or family who can provide you with accommodation, but who cannot support you, the Home Office cannot provide you with the financial element of section 4 support unless you occupy Home Office accommodation.[39] You must therefore take up the offer of Home Office accommodation in order to receive payment card credits.

This situation can cause severe hardship and can seem absurd. You may have friends who can provide you with accommodation, companionship and social, psychological and moral support which may be crucial to you and, in this case, it would be substantially less expensive for the government simply to provide you with the payment card without accommodation. You may therefore be left with the stark choice of living with your friends but remaining destitute (with the risk that your friends may then refuse to accommodate you), or being dispersed – possibly far from your friends to a place where you know no one and, if you are a single person, where you may have to share a room with strangers.

The Home Office has split adults (ie, over 18 years old) from their families in this way when they have had separate asylum applications. It is therefore important that you obtain advice from your immigration lawyer on the inclusion of a family member in the asylum claim of another as a dependant.

In one case, the High Court found that a refusal to provide support to a refused asylum seeker in a way that allowed him to continue to live with his British partner and child did not breach their right to family life under Article 8 of the European Convention on Human Rights, but the Home Office stated that it would make 'every effort' to house the applicant within a 'reasonable walking distance' of close family members.[40] If you are dispersed to accommodation that is a long distance from your family, you may still be able to challenge the dispersal by judicial review.

3. **Recovery of support**

There are four circumstances in which you may be required to repay your asylum support. These only apply to section 95 support. You do not have to repay any section 4 support you have received.

The Home Office may require you to repay your support if:

- you had assets at the time of your application for support that you can now convert into money (see below);[41]
- you have been overpaid support as a result of an error (see below);[42]
- you have misrepresented or failed to disclose a 'material fact' (see below);
- it transpires that you were not destitute.[43]

In addition, the Home Office may try to recover any support provided to you from a person who has sponsored your stay in the UK (see p417).[44]

The Home Office can recover the support through deductions from your existing asylum support[45] or through the civil courts as though it were a debt.[46]

You have convertible assets

Apart from any overpayments, the Home Office can require you to repay the value of any section 95 support if, at the time of your application for support, you had assets (eg, savings, investments, property or shares) either in the UK or elsewhere that you could not convert into money that is available to you, but you now can (even if you have not done so).[47]

The Home Office cannot require you to repay more than either:[48]

- the total monetary value of all the support provided to you up to the date that it asks you to make a repayment; *or, if it is a lesser amount,*
- the total monetary value of the assets which you had at the time of the application for support and which you have since been able to convert into money.

You were overpaid support

The Home Office may require you to repay any section 95 that has been provided to you as a result of an 'error' by the Home Office.[49] Unlike recovery of overpayments of most social security benefits, you do not need to have been responsible for the overpayment in any way.

The Home Office may recover the support from you whether or not you are still being supported.[50] It cannot recover more than the total monetary value of the support provided to you as a result of its mistake.[51]

You have misrepresented or failed to disclose a material fact

If the Home Office believes that you have received support as a result of misrepresenting or failing to disclose a material fact, it may apply to a county court (or, in Scotland, the sheriff court) for an order to require you (or the person who made the misrepresentation, or who was responsible for the failure to disclose) to repay the section 95 support.[52] This means that recovery is possible from people other than you and your dependants. The total amount that the court can order to be repaid is the monetary value of the support paid as a result of the misrepresentation or failure to disclose, which would not have been provided had there not been that misrepresentation or failure to disclose.[53]

Recovery from a sponsor

Support may be recovered from a sponsor of someone who receives asylum support.[54] A **'sponsor'** is a person who has given a written undertaking under the Immigration Rules to be responsible for the maintenance and accommodation of someone seeking to enter or remain in the UK (see p26).[55] This form of recovery is intended to deal with the situation in which someone obtains admission to the UK under a sponsorship agreement in a non-asylum capacity and then applies for asylum and becomes entitled to asylum support during the process. The sponsor is only liable to make payments for the period during which the undertaking was in effect.[56] S/he should not, therefore, be liable for payments for any period of leave given subsequent to the original leave for which the undertaking was given, unless a further undertaking was also given. The sponsor is not liable for payments during any period of residence without leave.

In order to recover asylum support, the Home Office must apply to a magistrates' court (the sheriff court in Scotland) for an order. The court may order the sponsor to make weekly payments to the Home Office of an amount which the court thinks is appropriate, taking into account all the circumstances of the case and, in particular, the sponsor's own income.[57] The weekly sum must not be more than the weekly value of the support being provided to the asylum seeker.[58] The court can order that payments be made to cover any period before the time the Home Office applied to the court. If it does so, it must take into account the sponsor's income during the period concerned, rather than her/his current income.[59] The order can be enforced in the same way as a maintenance order.[60]

Notes

1. Section 95 support

1 s96(1) IAA 1999
2 s96(2) IAA 1999
3 s97(7) IAA 1999
4 Reg 12(3) AS Regs
5 Reg 10(1)(2) AS Regs
6 Reg 2(2) Asylum Support (Amendment No.3) Regulations 2015, No.1501
7 Reg 10A AS Regs, introduced by The Asylum Support (Amendment) Regulations 2003, No.241; see also Home Office guidance, Asylum Support (Asylum Instructions), *Asylum Support Instructions: policy bulletins*, para 25.5, available at www.gov.uk/government/ collections/asylum-support-asylum-instructions
8 *R (Refugee Action) v SSHD* [2014] EWHC 1033 (Admin)
9 *R (Refugee Action) v SSHD* [2014] EWHC 1033 (Admin)
10 s96(2) IAA 1999
11 *R (MG) v SSHD* [2015] EWHC 3142 (Admin)
12 Home Office guidance, Asylum Support (Asylum Instructions), *Asylum Support Instructions: policy bulletins*, para 25.2, available at www.gov.uk/government/ collections/asylum-support-asylum-instructions
13 Home Office guidance, Asylum Support (Asylum Instructions), *Asylum Support Instructions: policy bulletins*, para 25.2 available at www.gov.uk/government/ collections/asylum-support-asylum-instructions
14 Home Office guidance, Asylum Support (Asylum Instructions), *Asylum Support Instructions: policy bulletins*, para 15.2
15 Reg 12(3) AS Regs
16 Reg 16(2) AS Regs
17 Reg 16(3) AS Regs
18 Reg 16(4) AS Regs. Conditions may generally be imposed under s95(9)-(12) IAA 1999

19 Home Office guidance, Asylum Support (Asylum Instructions), *Dispersal: Accommodation Requests Policy*, available at www.gov.uk/government/collections/ asylum-support-asylum-instructions
20 ss94(2) and 99-100 IAA 1999
21 s97(1)(a) IAA 1999
22 IAA 1999, Explanatory Notes, para 303
23 s97(2)(a) IAA 1999
24 Reg 13(2)(a) AS Regs
25 Reg 13(2)(b) AS Regs
26 Reg 13(2) AS Regs
27 Home Office guidance, Asylum Support (Asylum Instructions), *Asylum Accommodation Requests Policy*, available at www.gov.uk/government/ collections/asylum-support-asylum-instructions
28 Home Office guidance, Asylum Support (Asylum Instructions), *Asylum Accommodation Requests Policy*, available at www.gov.uk/government/ collections/asylum-support-asylum-instructions
29 Home Office guidance, Asylum Support (Asylum Instructions), *Asylum Accommodation Requests Policy*, available at www.gov.uk/government/ collections/asylum-support-asylum-instructions
30 Home Office guidance, Asylum Support (Asylum Instructions), *Asylum Accommodation Requests Policy*, Ch 3, available at www.gov.uk/government/ collections/asylum-support-asylum-instructions
31 s96(1)(c) IAA 1999
32 Expressly included in IAA 1999, Explanatory Notes, para 300
33 Home Office, *Enforcement Instructions and Guidance*, Ch 22, para 22a.3.3, available at www.gov.uk/government/ collections/enforcement-instructions-and-guidance
34 Sch 8 para 4 IAA 1999; reg 14 AS Regs
35 Reg 14(1) AS Regs

2. Section 4 support

36 The Immigration and Asylum (Provision of Services or Facilities) Regulations 2007, No.3627; Home Office guidance, Asylum Support (Asylum Instructions), *Asylum Support, Section 4 Policy and Process*, Ch 10, available at www.gov.uk/government/collections/asylum-support-asylum-instructions

37 www.gov.uk/government/uploads/system/uploads/attachment_data/file/309984/section_4_service_users_2014.pdf

38 Home Office guidance, Asylum Support (Asylum Instructions), *Asylum Support,Section 4 Policy and Process*, Ch 10, available at www.gov.uk/government/collections/asylum-support-asylum-instructions

39 *R (Kiana and Musgrove) v SSHD* [2010] EWHC 1002 (Admin); *MK v SSHD* [2011] All ER(D) 158 (CA); s4(1) and (2) IAA 1999

40 *R (Kiana and Musgrove) v Secretary of State for the Home Department* [2010] EWHC 1002 (Admin)

3. Recovery of support

41 Reg 17 AS Regs
42 s114 IAA 1999
43 Reg 17A AS Regs
44 s113 IAA 1999
45 Regs 17(4) and 18 AS Regs
46 s114(3) and Sch 8 para 11(2)(a) IAA 1999
47 Sch 8 para 11 IAA 1999; reg 17(1) AS Regs. Note that it is unclear whether the Home Office can require a person who is no longer being supported to repay the value of the support. There is no equivalent wording in para 11 or reg 17 to that effect in s114(2) IAA 1999, which expressly refers to both those who are, and those who have ceased to be, supported persons for the purposes of recovery as result of Home Office errors.
48 Reg 17(2)(3)(5) AS Regs
49 s114(1) IAA 1999; Home Office guidance, Asylum Support (Asylum Instructions), *Asylum Support Instructions: policy bulletins*, Ch 15, available at www.gov.uk/government/collections/asylum-support-asylum-instructions
50 s114(2) IAA 1999
51 s114(2) IAA 1999
52 s112 IAA 1999
53 s112(2)(3) IAA 1999
54 s113 IAA 1999
55 s113(1)(a) IAA 1999
56 s113(1)(b) IAA 1999
57 s113(3) IAA 1999
58 s113(4) IAA 1999
59 s113(5) IAA 1999
60 s113(6) IAA 1999

Appeals

This chapter covers:
1. Introduction (below)
2. The right to appeal (p421)
3. How to appeal (p421)
4. Decisions the First-tier Tribunal can make (p430)

1. Introduction

If your application for either section 95 support or section 4 support is refused by the Home Office or, in some circumstances, if your support is discontinued, you can appeal to the First-tier Tribunal (Asylum Support), which is based in East London.

A decision of the First-tier Tribunal (Asylum Support) cannot be appealed to the Upper Tribunal and can only be legally challenged by judicial review, except in limited circumstances when the First-tier Tribunal can 'set aside' some of its own decisions (see p432).

The Tribunal Procedure (First-tier Tribunal) (Social Entitlement Chamber) Rules 2008 (referred to as the 'tribunal rules' in this chapter) contain the rules for appeals in the Social Entitlement Chamber.[1] Most of these are common to all tribunals in the Social Entitlement Chamber, but a few refer solely to the First-tier Tribunal (Asylum Support).

In all asylum support appeals, a single judge considers the appeal and makes the decisions. Tribunal judges have no power to make an order relating to the parties' costs, so even if you lose your appeal you cannot be ordered to pay any legal costs to the Home Office or to the First-tier Tribunal.

Note: in this chapter, we refer to the First-tier Tribunal (Asylum Support) as the First-tier Tribunal.

2. **The right to appeal**

The circumstances in which you have the right to appeal to the First-tier Tribunal are limited. You can only appeal if you have been refused support by the Home Office or your support has been stopped – ie:[2]
- you have applied for section 95 or section 4 support and it has been refused; *or*
- your section 95 support has been stopped for a reason other than because you have ceased to be an asylum seeker (unless the Home Office has made a mistake and you are still an asylum seeker);[3] *or*
- your section 4 support is stopped for any reason.

Further information is in the Asylum Support Appeals Project Factsheet 3, *Appealing to the Asylum Support Tribunal.*

Any other Home Office decision about your support (such as the level of support or the place of dispersal) or *any* decision about temporary support can only be challenged by judicial review. In addition, it is not possible to appeal a decision refusing you support if the reason for the refusal is that:
- you failed to provide complete or accurate information in connection with your application;[4] *or*
- you failed to co-operate with enquiries made in respect of the support application;[5] *or*
- you did not make your application for asylum as soon as reasonably possible.[6]

These decisions must be challenged by judicial review, although the Home Office reconsiders an application if missing information is later provided.

Note: if you are appealing a discontinuation of your section 4 support and you appeal within the time limits (or a late appeal is accepted) while you are still living in the section 4 accommodation, your support should continue until the day of the appeal.[7]

3. **How to appeal**

Notice of appeal

If the Home Office refuses your application for support or terminates your support, it gives you a written decision with its reasons. It also informs you in the decision letter whether you have a right of appeal and, if so, provides an appeal form. You can also get an appeal form from the First-tier Tribunal website at http://hmctsformfinder.justice.gov.uk.

The Home Office does not always get this right. So if you want to appeal, but the Home Office says you do not have the right to appeal, you should get legal advice immediately.

You must use the prescibed form if you want to appeal.[8] It must be completed in English (or in Welsh).[9] This is known as the **'notice of appeal'**. See Asylum

Support Appeals Project Factsheet 4, *Filling in the Appeal Notice*, for more information.

You must state the grounds for your appeal on the form (ie, why you disagree with the Home Office's decision) and include a copy of the decision you are appealing against. If your notice of appeal does not include all the necessary information and/or is not accompanied by the written Home Office decision, the First-tier Tribunal sends it back to you and any later attempt to appeal may not be within the time limit.

If you have any further information or evidence which relates to your application for support or your appeal, you should (if possible) send copies of the relevant documents to the First-Tier Tribunal with the notice of appeal.[10] However, do not delay submitting your appeal in order to obtain any further evidence – this can be faxed or emailed to the First-tier Tribunal later. It is very important that you provide the First-tier Tribunal with any evidence that proves you are entitled to support. For example, if the Home Office does not accept that you are destitute, you may want to provide letters from someone who has been providing you with support, but who cannot continue to do so, or from a voluntary agency who knows your situation.

Once you have completed the appeal form, you[11] (or your representative – see p423[12]) must sign it.

Deciding whether to have a hearing

The notice of appeal form asks whether you want to attend, or be represented at, an oral hearing or whether you are content for the appeal to be decided on the papers submitted to the First-Tier Tribunal. An appeal can be decided on the papers without a hearing if both sides agree and the First-tier Tribunal believes it can make a decision without a hearing.[13] Even if you ask for a paper appeal without an oral hearing, the First-Tier Tribunal may still hold an oral hearing if there are issues to be explored that are raised, but not explained, in the papers (see p426). It is usually advisable to attend the hearing in person. The First-tier Tribunal judge is likely to understand your appeal much better if you are present to explain your situation.

If you choose to have an oral hearing, the Home Office sends you tickets to travel to the hearing.

If your partner is a British national or has leave to remain and is in receipt of state benefits, it is usually important for her/him to attend the appeal in order to be able to give full details of her/his benefits (with documentary evidence) and to explain why s/he cannot support you. However, unless you specifically request it and the Tribunal directs the Home Office to comply with your request, you are only sent travel tickets for yourself.

If you might find it difficult to travel to the hearing (eg, because of medical problems, pregnancy or lack of childcare), you can request on the appeal form for it to be heard by videolink. If the Tribunal approves, you attend the hearing from a court in your local area, with a video line linking you to the Tribunal in London, where the interpreter, Home Office representative and judge attend.

In the notice of appeal you must also state whether you will need an interpreter at the hearing and, if so, in what language and dialect. If you have any difficulties with the English language, you should ask for an interpreter. If required, an interpreter is supplied by HM Courts and Tribunals Service.

Time limits

Your notice of appeal must be received by the First-Tier Tribunal within three working days of the day on which you received the notice of the decision on your asylum support application.[14] If you receive the Home Office's decision letter more than two days after the date it was written, it is advisable to state in your appeal the date on which you received it to show that you are not (or not fully) responsible for any delay. You can submit it to the First-tier Tribunal by email or fax – the details are on the appeal form.

If you do not appeal in time, ask the First-Tier Tribunal in the notice of appeal to extend the time limit.[15] You should explain why you could not appeal earlier – eg, if you were ill and incapable of dealing with your affairs at the time you received the notice, or you needed advice. The First-tier Tribunal usually treats applications for an extension of time favourably, provided a sufficient explanation is given for the delay. Judges recognise that the time limit to appeal is very short, and an extension of a two or three days (or longer) is often granted, especially for destitute people who may not speak English and may be relying for advice on an advice agency that is only open during certain hours. The judge must consider your application fairly and justly,[16] including why you (or your representative) could not comply with the time limit.

If the First-tier Tribunal refuses to extend the time limit, your only alternative is to seek a judicial review of the decision on your asylum application and/or of the decision of the First-tier Tribunal to refuse to give you more time.[17] Alternatively, it may be possible to reapply for support.

Representatives

You may be represented throughout the appeal procedure by a representative of your choice. S/he does not have to be legally qualified.[18] If you are represented, the name and address of your representative must be given in writing to the First-tier Tribunal.[19] This can be done by including the details in the appeal notice. If your representative is unable to attend the hearing with you, you should tick 'no' when asked this question on the form. An adviser should *not* state that s/he is your representative if s/he is simply helping you to complete and submit the appeal form and perhaps acting as a mail box for you. In these circumstances, s/he should write on the form that this is the limit of her/his involvement.

It is generally understood that 'representation' implies an ongoing responsibility for the prompt conduct of all stages of the appeal including:
- securing and preparing all available relevant evidence and submitting it to the First-tier Tribunal;

- dealing with all correspondence with the First-tier Tribunal and the Home Office;
- responding in writing to the directions given by the First-tier Tribunal;
- advising you on each of these steps and at every stage;
- representing you or arranging for a legal adviser to represent you at the First-tier Tribunal;
- advising you on the outcome of the appeal and on any steps to be taken – eg, to secure support if the appeal has been successful or any further challenge (eg, by judicial review) if the appeal was unsuccessful.

If you state that you have a representative, the First-tier Tribunal must give her/his details to the Home Office. Any documents that the Home Office is required to serve must be served on the representative (and need not be served on you).[20] Anyone else who accompanies you to the appeal hearing cannot assist in presenting your case without the First-tier Tribunal's approval.[21]

Advice through legal aid may be available in asylum support cases if you are at risk of homelessness, but only to prepare your case, not to represent you in a First-tier Tribunal hearing.[22]

The Asylum Support Appeals Project (ASAP) attends the First-tier Tribunal, Monday to Friday, to provide free representation and advice to as many people as possible (see Appendix 2). This service is provided by ASAP staff and volunteer solicitors and barristers. You can ask ASAP to represent you when you arrive at the Tribunal on the day. Alternatively, and preferably, you can ask your representative (if you have one) to refer your case to ASAP in advance. If you do not have a representative, you can make the referral yourself. If your named representative on the notice of appeal form is a firm of solicitors (and not an advice agency), the First-tier Tribunal may not allow ASAP to represent you, unless you or your solicitor refer the case to ASAP in advance of the hearing.

Response from the Home Office

On the same day as the First-tier Tribunal receives your notice of appeal or, if not reasonably practicable, as soon as possible on the next day, it must fax a copy to the Home Office, together with any supporting documents that you sent with it.[23]

By the third day after your notice of appeal is received by the First-tier Tribunal, the Home Office must send to the Tribunal:[24]

- a statement saying whether or not the Home Office opposes the appeal;
- a copy of the decision letter refusing or withdrawing support;
- any other evidence that the Home Office took into account when refusing you support;
- any other grounds and reasons for the decision that have not been included in the decision letter;
- copies of all documents the Home Office has that are relevant to the case.

At the same time, the Home Office must provide you (or your representative) with a copy of all the above information and documents.[25]

This is commonly referred to as the Tribunal 'bundle'. It is important that you receive a copy of the bundle before the hearing so that you are aware of all the evidence in the appeal. If you or your representative have not received the bundle on time, you should alert the Tribunal and/or contact the Home Office.

The appeal timetable

The tribunal rules set out a timetable for appeals to the First-tier Tribunal, a summary of which is set out below.[26]

Day	Event
Day one	Notice of decision is received by you.
Day four (latest)	Notice of appeal must be received by the First-tier Tribunal. Delivery of a notice of appeal at any time up to midnight on the relevant day is sufficient. If not lodged in time, you must apply for an extension of time (see p423).
Day four or day five	First-tier Tribunal faxes notice of appeal to the Home Office.
Day seven (latest)	Home Office sends its response and documentation to the First-tier Tribunal by fax/hand, and to you by first-class post or by hand.
Day seven or thereafter 'with the minimum of delay'	First-tier Tribunal judge decides whether to hold an oral hearing and: – if no oral hearing is to be held, determines the appeal and sends a notice of the decision and a statement of reasons for the decision to you and the Home Office; *or* – fixes the hearing date for the oral hearing, giving both parties one to five days' notice. It is likely that, at the same time, directions are given (see p427). If the judge believes the appeal should be 'struck out' (eg, if the First-tier Tribunal does not have jurisdiction – see p430), s/he must give you an opportunity to make representations. It is likely that a hearing date is arranged to consider striking out, and the full hearing follows immediately if the appeal is not struck out.
Day nine or thereafter 'with the minimum of delay'	Oral hearing held. The First-tier Tribunal judge notifies the decision to you and the Home Office at the end of the hearing or, if not present, sends a decision notice.
Within three days after an oral hearing	First-tier Tribunal judge sends a statement of reasons for the decision to you and the Home Office.

Appeals to the First-tier Tribunal should be processed with the minimum of delay.[27] Taking into account the above time limits, the First-tier Tribunal usually holds an oral hearing within two weeks of receiving your notice of appeal.

Notices or documents can be sent to the First-tier Tribunal by post, fax or email or given by hand. If you choose to send documents by fax or email, do not also send them by post.[28]

If a time limit expires on a non-working day (Saturday, Sunday and bank holidays), it is treated as expiring on the next working day.[29]

The hearing

Paper hearings

After it receives the Home Office's response, the First-tier Tribunal judge must consider all the documents and decide whether it is necessary to hold an oral hearing, or whether the appeal can be determined simply by considering the papers. The First-tier Tribunal can only decide the appeal without a hearing if both parties agree, but it can decide that an oral hearing is necessary even if you ask for a paper appeal.

You may have stated on the notice of appeal form that you did not want an oral hearing, but may not have been aware of all of the information or evidence relied on by the Home Office until afterwards – eg, new papers might subsequently be disclosed to you by the Home Office or the First-tier Tribunal. If, having seen any new material, you change your mind and decide that you want an oral hearing in order to make direct representations to the First-tier Tribunal, you should notify the Tribunal as soon as possible by fax, email or telephone. The judge must then take this into account when deciding whether to grant an oral hearing. If you want to make written representations to the First-tier Tribunal about this further evidence, you should do so as soon as possible.

The decision

In all cases, the First-tier Tribunal must make a decision with minimum delay.[30] If no oral hearing is required, the First-tier Tribunal judge proceeds to decide the appeal. S/he must send a copy of the decision notice, together with the written statement of reasons for the decision, to both parties on the same day as the appeal is decided.[31]

Oral hearings

Hearing date

If an oral hearing is necessary, the First-tier Tribunal must promptly inform the parties of the time and date. It is likely that the hearing will take place within two weeks or so of the First-tier Tribunal receiving your notice of appeal.

Tribunal directions

When sending out the notice of a hearing date, the First-tier Tribunal usually also sends 'directions' (a 'directions notice') to both you and the Home Office – eg, to produce further evidence.[32] This is information and evidence which a judge at the Tribunal (not necessarily the same judge who will hear your appeal) has considered on looking through the papers will be useful for both sides to produce in order to make a fair decision on the appeal. It may include evidence of your destitution, medical evidence or copies of a previous asylum determination. If possible, these documents should be sent to the First-tier Tribunal and the Home Office before the hearing. The directions notice tells you to send the information by midday on the day before the hearing. Even if you cannot meet this deadline, you should still send the documents and take them to the appeal hearing. It is important to comply with any directions, because if you do not, the First-tier Tribunal may not have all the evidence needed to make a decision on your appeal. However, if you cannot provide the documents, you should still go to your appeal.

If an agency or solicitor has helped you to complete the appeal form, the directions may be sent to her/him, so it is important to keep in close and regular contact to check that they have been received and whether your adviser/solicitor can help you respond.

You should also note what further information the Home Office has been directed to provide and make sure you see its response. The Home Office does not always respond in time to the directions notice and may only produce the information at the hearing, if at all.

Further evidence

If you decide that you want to submit more evidence in support of your appeal which you did not send with your notice of appeal, you may still send it to the First-tier Tribunal to be considered. In particular, you may wish to rely on evidence which shows a change in your circumstances after the date of the Home Office decision or which has only now come into your possession. You should send this evidence to the First-tier Tribunal judge before the date s/he will determine the appeal. Do this immediately and by fax or email if possible, especially if no oral hearing is to be held, as the First-tier Tribunal will determine the appeal very quickly. This further evidence may overlap with what the First-tier Tribunal has asked you to provide in the directions notice.

You should also send a copy of this further evidence to the Home Office.[33] Although the tribunal rules no longer require you to do so, the First-tier Tribunal judge will want to ensure that the Home Office has seen the further evidence. There is even the (very unlikely) risk that the judge will refuse to allow evidence that is provided late and which has not been seen by the Home Office.[34]

In any event, you should take copies of all the appeal papers, including your evidence and the Home Office's documents and any new evidence, to the appeal hearing as you may need to refer to them. At the start of the hearing, you should also ensure that none of the papers have gone astray and that the judge has all your evidence.

The Home Office can also send further evidence to the First-tier Tribunal before the appeal is determined. It is likely that the Home Office and/or the First-tier Tribunal will send copies to you (or your representative) or, if there is not sufficient time, provide you with copies at the hearing. In any event, you must be provided with copies of any documents on which the Home Office intends to rely at the hearing and you must have time to consider them.

Travel to the hearing

You are sent tickets for your travel to and from the First-tier Tribunal. If you live too far away to travel on the day and arrive on time for your hearing, overnight accommodation is arranged and paid for by the Home Office. If tickets are not sent, a travel warrant can be requested from the Home Office travel bureau.[35] If your tickets have not arrived in time for you to travel, inform the Tribunal urgently and your appeal will be relisted. If you decide to travel anyway and purchase your own ticket, it is unlikely that the Home Office will agree to refund it. If there are good reasons why the Home Office should also provide tickets for dependants or witnesses, ask the Tribunal to direct the Home Office to do this.

The hearing

In principle, oral hearings before the First-tier Tribunal take place in public, but it is extremely rare for members of the public to attend.[36] The First-tier Tribunal judge can decide that a hearing, or part of it, should be in private and can exclude anyone who is likely to cause a disruption or defeat the purpose of the hearing. In practice, judges politely check who is in the hearing room in order to ensure that there is no one present who may intimidate you or otherwise hinder a fair hearing. If, for any reason, you think that someone should be excluded, tell the First-tier Tribunal either before or at the start of the hearing.

As there are no rules setting out the procedure which must be adopted at the oral hearing, this is decided by the First-tier Tribunal judge.[37] S/he should explain the procedure to you at the outset. There are no strict rules on evidence, and so hearsay and letters from third parties can be considered. You can provide oral evidence and call any witnesses to give oral evidence in support of your case. The Home Office is usually represented by a 'presenting officer', who sets out its case and asks you questions. Sometimes the Home Office is unrepresented at the hearing. You or your representative must also have the opportunity of directly addressing the First-tier Tribunal about the decision it should make and commenting on all of the evidence, documentary or oral. If witnesses are called, they may be required to give their evidence under oath or affirmation.[38]

If either you or the Home Office attend the hearing with further evidence which has not previously been provided, the other party must be given the opportunity to photocopy and look at it in order to comment on it before the hearing proceeds. The judge often checks at the beginning of the hearing whether anything further needs to be photocopied.

If possible, take notes of what is said at the hearing. It is usual for the judge to make her/his own written record. If you later want to challenge the decision by judicial review, you can request a copy of this.

If you do not arrive at the hearing in time, it may go ahead without you (or in the absence of a Home Office representative) if the judge:[39]

- is satisfied that you/the Home Office have been notified of the hearing or that reasonable steps have been taken to notify you/the Home Office of the hearing; *and*
- considers that it is in the interests of justice to proceed.

The judge waiting usually waits 30 minutes from the listed start time before starting the appeal without you.

The decision

At the end of the hearing, the judge must tell you and the Home Office representative the decision that has been reached.[40] The judge may retire for a period in order to consider the decision before telling you the outcome.

The judge must provide both parties with a 'decision notice' (ie, without reasons) at the end of the hearing.[41] This simply states whether the appeal has been allowed, dismissed or remitted (see p430). The notice is also sent on the same day to any party (ie, you or the Home Office) who was not present at the hearing of the appeal. In addition, whether or not you were at the hearing, the judge must send a 'statement of reasons' for her/his decision to both parties within three working days of the hearing.[42]

Withdrawing an appeal

If, at any stage before the hearing, you decide you do not wish to carry on with your appeal, you can give written notice of withdrawal.[43] If the withdrawal is made on the day of the hearing, the judge's consent is required. The tribunal rules imply that if either party withdraws from the case in writing before the day of the appeal, the consent of a judge is not required and therefore no reasons need be given.

If the Home Office withdraws, this can be unfair on you because, unless it immediately substitutes its negative decision with a positive one awarding you support, you still need your appeal to go ahead.

If the Home Office withdraws from an appeal when you are not yet receiving support, you should refer it to its policy on withdrawals.[44] Under this, if the Home Office serves a notice of withdrawal before 12 noon on the day before the hearing, it should immediately make a fresh decision, which must be posted or faxed to you or your representative. If this decision is again negative (but for a different reason than the first), you need to appeal immediately again. This will have caused a delay in your getting support (assuming you win your eventual appeal). Make sure you compare the two decisions and if there is no substantial difference, draw this to the judge's attention.

Under the withdrawal policy, if the Home Office withdraws after 12 noon on the day before the hearing, it must apply to do so at the hearing itself. The judge only consents to the withdrawal if:

- the Home Office confirms in writing that the decision under appeal is being withdrawn and you are to be granted support immediately; *or*
- the Home Office serves you with a copy of a fresh refusal or discontinuation decision letter, and you or your representative agree that the hearing can proceed on the basis of this new decision; *or*
- both parties agree to adjourn the proceedings (for no longer than 14 days) and the Home Office confirms in writing that you will be provided with support in the meantime.

In practice, the First-tier Tribunal allows the Home Office to withdraw from appeals at any time before the day of the hearing (as opposed to only up to midday) without providing reasons and it is very difficult to prevent this. If you are not immediately provided with a new decision letter, whether positive or negative, refer the Home Office to its policy and consider judicial review if there continues to be a delay.

Striking out an appeal

The First-tier Tribunal can decide that your appeal cannot continue, even before a hearing takes place. This is called 'striking out' your appeal. The First-tier Tribunal must strike out your appeal if it does not have jurisdiction to decide the matter – eg, it cannot consider an appeal about how much money the Home Office should pay you each week in asylum support.[45] The First-tier Tribunal may also strike out your appeal without a hearing if it considers your case has no reasonable prospect of success.[46]

In either case, before striking out your appeal, the First-tier Tribunal must give you the opportunity to make representations. It may direct you to make these in writing by a certain deadline, following which a decision is made by the judge 'on the papers'. Alternatively, the Tribunal may fix a date for you and the Home Office to attend to make any representations and, if the appeal is not struck out, the appeal then proceeds to a full hearing on the same day.

---

4. **Decisions the First-tier Tribunal can make**

When deciding the appeal, the First-tier Tribunal judge can:[47]
- substitute her/his own decision for the decision made by the Home Office and thus allow the appeal, meaning you are entitled to support; *or*

- dismiss the appeal, so that the decision of the Home Office stands; *or*
- require the Home Office to reconsider the matter. The First-tier Tribunal calls this 'remitting' the appeal (see below).

The effect of remitting a decision is to set aside the decision of the Home Office. This requires the Home Office to reconsider and come to a new decision on whether you should be provided with support. This puts you back into the position you were in before the decision was made. So if you had been receiving support and the Home Office's decision to withdraw your support is remitted by the First-tier Tribunal, the Home Office must immediately reinstate the support until it comes to a new decision. If you were previously without support and are appealing the Home Office's decision to refuse your application, a First-tier Tribunal decision to remit that refusal decision leaves you in your previous position of being without support, at least until the Home Office comes to a new decision.[48]

Cases come before the First-tier Tribunal in which people are not sure of their immigration status or it has changed since an appeal has been lodged. It may become apparent at the hearing that you have applied for the wrong form of support – eg, the Tribunal may find that you are eligible for section 95 support as an asylum seeker, although you have applied for section 4 support as a failed asylum seeker or vice versa. Previously, the practice would have been for the Tribunal to dismiss your appeal, suggesting that you reapply on the correct form. However, in 2011, the Home Office introduced a combined application form for both kinds of support (Form ASF1 – see p396). Since then, most judges have been willing to grant section 95 support if eligibility is established, even if the wrong type was applied for. This fits with the First-tier Tribunal's power to substitute its decision for the decision appealed against.[49]

First-tier Tribunal judges decide issues of fact on a balance of probabilities. This simply means deciding which facts in your case are more likely than not to be true. In appeals against a *refusal* of an application for support, it is up to you to prove, on a balance of probabilities, that you are entitled to support and meet the relevant criteria. If you are appealing a decision to *withdraw* support, it is up to the Home Office to establish, on the balance of probabilities, that the support should be terminated.

The Tribunal can take into account any change of circumstances that took place between the date on which the decision of the Home Office was made and the date of the appeal.[50]

A decision on an appeal by the First-tier Tribunal is legally binding and, if the appeal is allowed, the Home Office is obliged to provide support on that day.

If your appeal is successful, you may be left with a difficult choice. The Home Office offers 'emergency' accommodation situated in a hostel in south east London while you wait to be allocated 'dispersal' accommodation elsewhere in the UK.[51] This emergency accommodation can be requested from the Home

Office representative at the hearing or, if the Home Office did not attend your hearing, you can ask the Tribunal clerk to put you in contact with the representative on duty that day. The accommodation is offered on condition that you stay there on the night of your appeal. If you are then allocated accommodation in a different part of the UK to where you were previously living, the Home Office does not provide travel costs to allow you to go back and collect any belongings.

Alternatively, after the hearing, you can return to the town in which you were living, using the return ticket provided by the Home Office. The Home Office should then contact you directly, or through your advice agency, to arrange your accommodation. This usually takes several days to arrange, in some cases even longer, during which time you may be left homeless. You are given travel tickets to get to your new accommodation. This option is therefore more appropriate if you need to collect belongings and you have somewhere to stay and the ability to feed yourself in the short term.

This arrangement is clearly particularly unsatisfactory if you are street homeless but have left belongings (eg, medication) in the town where you were sleeping. If there is any delay by the Home Office in providing support immediately after a successful appeal, it is acting unlawfully and should be challenged in judicial review proceedings.

If your appeal was heard by video link, the Home Office can provide emergency accommodation at your nearest initial accommodation centre. You should request this at the end of the hearing.

After the hearing

There is no right of appeal against the decision of the First-tier Tribunal. If you are dissatisfied with the decision, in limited circumstances you can ask the Tribunal to set it aside (see below).[52] Otherwise, the only way of challenging the decision is by judicial review.

Setting aside a decision

The First-tier Tribunal can only set aside its own decision and make a new decision (or set aside and remake part of a decision) if:[53]

- it was a decision 'disposing of the proceedings' – ie, a final decision or a decision to strike out the appeal and:
  - a document relating to the proceedings was not sent or was not received at an appropriate time by either party or her/his representative; *or*
  - a document relating to the proceedings was not sent to the First-tier Tribunal at an appropriate time; *or*
  - a party or representative was not present at a hearing; *or*
  - there has been some other procedural irregularity in the proceedings; *and*
- the First-tier Tribunal considers that it is in the interests of justice to do so.

You cannot, therefore, ask the First-tier Tribunal to set aside a decision simply because you do not agree with it. Remember that, even if one of these conditions does apply, the First-tier Tribunal may still decide that it is not in the interests of justice to set aside the decision. For example, even if you did not receive a relevant document at the appropriate time, it may still consider that this did not make any difference to the decision that was eventually made, and so it is not in the interests of justice to set it aside.

If you wish to apply to set aside a decision, your application must be in writing and received by the First-tier Tribunal no later than one month after the date on which it sent the decision to you.[54]

Judicial review

A judicial review is when a judge in the High Court considers the lawfulness of a decision of a public body, including a decision of the First-tier Tribunal. There must be an error in law for an application for judicial review to succeed – it is not enough that you do not agree with the decision the judge made (unless you can clearly show that no reasonable tribunal could have come to that decision). To be successful in judicial review proceedings, you will need help from a solicitor.

An application for judicial review must be made promptly and, in any event, within three months of the decision complained of. It must be in writing, laying out the facts and legal arguments, and be accompanied by copies of all relevant documents.

You must get the permission of a High Court judge to take judicial review proceedings. A judge looks at the papers you send to establish whether there is an arguable point of law and, if not, refuses you permission to proceed. In any event, a judge has a discretion to refuse you permission (or to reject your case at the full hearing) if s/he does not think an order should be made. If you think judicial review might be appropriate in your case, you should immediately get legal advice. Legal aid is available for this.

Decision to remit

If the First-tier Tribunal decides to remit the matter (see p430) and the Home Office then makes a new decision refusing you support, you may appeal again to the First-tier Tribunal against the new decision.

Making a new application for support

Following an unsuccessful appeal, the Home Office cannot consider any further application for support from you, unless it is satisfied that there has been a 'material change of circumstances' between the time of the appeal and the new application.[55] However, if you are destitute and believe that your application or appeal may now be successful, you should reapply. The Home Office and Tribunal will want to see evidence that your situation has changed since the last decision. If you decide to reapply for support after a dismissed appeal, make sure your application deals with the points raised in the 'statement of reasons', including by providing information or evidence that the judge considered to be lacking and, hence, why s/he dismissed your appeal.

Notes

1. Introduction
1 TP(FT) Rules

2. The right to appeal
2 s103(1)-(3) IAA 1999
3 s103(2) IAA 1999. Note that the legislation provides a right of appeal where a decision is made to stop providing support 'before that support would otherwise have come to an end'. The wording is ambiguous, but the intention is to allow a right of appeal in any case where support is terminated before the asylum seeker has ceased to be an asylum seeker for support purposes. See IAA 1999, Explanatory Notes, para 317.
4 s57 NIAA 2002
5 s57 NIAA 2002
6 s55 NIAA 2002
7 Home Office guidance, Asylum Support (Asylum Instructions), *Asylum Support Instructions: policy bulletins*, para 6.6, available at www.gov.uk/government/collections/asylum-support-asylum-instructions

3. How to appeal
8 Practice Direction, 'Social Entitlement Chamber, First-tier Tribunal Asylum Support Cases', 30 October 2008
9 r22(3) TP(FT) Rules
10 The standard appeal form itself indicates this.
11 r22(3) TP(FT) Rules
12 r11(5) TP(FT) Rules
13 r27(1) TP(FT) Rules
14 rr12 and 22(2)(a) TP(FT) Rules
15 rr5(3)(a) and 22(6) TP(FT) Rules
16 r2 TP(FT) Rules

17 Note that, in judicial review proceedings, the court may refuse to interfere with the decision you wish to challenge if you have failed to exercise a right of appeal.
18 r11(1) TP(FT) Rules. Note also that asylum support law is not immigration law, and so an adviser does not have to be registered with the Office of the Immigration Services Commissioner.
19 r11(2) TP(FT) Rules
20 r11(6a) TP(FT) Rules
21 r11(7) TP(FT) Rules
22 Sch 1 Part 1, para 31 Legal Aid, Sentencing and Punishment of Offenders Act 2012
23 r22(7)(a) TP(FT) Rules
24 r24(2) and (4) TP(FT) Rules
25 r24(5) TP(FT) Rules
26 rr22(2)(a) and (7)(a), 24(1)(a), 29, 33 and 34 TP(FT) Rules
27 s104(3) IAA 1999 requires the appeal regulations to provide for this.
28 r13(1) TP(FT) Rules
29 r12(2) and (3) TP(FT) Rules
30 s104(3) IAA 1999
31 s103(4) IAA 1999; r34(1)(b) TP(FT) Rules
32 r15 TP(FT) Rules
33 This used to be the case under r8(1)(2) ASA(P) Rules
34 r15(2)(b)(1) TP(FT) Rules
35 s103(9) IAA 1999
36 r30(1) TP(FT) Rules
37 TP(FT) Rules
38 r15(3) TP(FT) Rules
39 r31 TP(FT) Rules
40 r33 TP(FT) Rules
41 r33(2)(a) TP(FT) Rules
42 s103(4) IAA 1999; r34(1)(a) TP(FT) Rules
43 r17(1) TP(FT) Rules

44 Home Office guidance, Asylum Support
(Asylum Instructions), *Asylum Support
Instructions: policy bulletins*, para 6.5,
available at www.gov.uk/government/
collections/asylum-support-asylum-
instructions
45 r8(2) TP(FT) Rules
46 r8(3) TP(FT) Rules

4. Decisions the First-tier Tribunal can make

47 s103(3) IAA 1999
48 In an application for section 95 support
you could, in theory, receive temporary
support under s98 IAA 1999 until a new
decision is made.
49 s103(3)(b) IAA 1999
50 r10(2) ASA(P) Rules
51 Home Office guidance, Asylum Support
(Asylum Instructions), *Asylum Support,
Section 4 Policy and Process*, para 1.18.1,
available at www.gov.uk/government/
collections/asylum-support-asylum-
instructions
52 Some other tribunals have the power to
review their own decisions under r40
TP(FT) Rules, but the First-tier Tribunal is
expressly excluded from doing so by
r40(1). If an application is made to the
First-tier Tribunal to review one of its
own decisions, it can instead treat the
application as a request for the decision
to be set aside: r41 TP(FT) Rules
53 r37(1) TP(FT) Rules
54 r37(3) TP(FT) Rules
55 s103(6) IAA 1999

Part 9

Other sources of help

Chapter 25

• •

Other sources of help

This chapter covers:
1. Council tax reduction (below)
2. Local welfare assistance schemes (p443)
3. Healthy Start food and vitamins (p444)
4. Education benefits (p447)
5. Free milk for children (p449)
6. Community care support from the local authority (p449)
7. Support under the Children Act 1989 (p450)
8. NHS healthcare (p451)
9. Other financial help (p453)

This *Handbook* is primarily concerned with migrants' entitlement to social security benefits, tax credits and asylum support. However, you may also be entitled to other financial help.

---

1. **Council tax reduction**

If you need help to pay council tax, you might be able to get a reduction under your local authority's council tax reduction scheme. **Note:** a council tax reduction is *not* a social security benefit or a tax credit, and how the scheme operates depends on where you live.[1]

- In England and Wales, local authorities may devise their own local schemes, which must meet minimum requirements. In Wales, if a local authority does not set up its own scheme, a default scheme applies. Check with your local authority whether it has its own local scheme or whether the default scheme applies.
- In Scotland, there is a national scheme, administered by local authorities.

The regulations for all the schemes are in CPAG's *Housing Benefit and Council Tax Reduction Legislation* and a short overview is also provided in CPAG's *Welfare Benefits and Tax Credits Handbook*.

The regulations on the minimum requirements, the default schemes in England and Wales and the national scheme in Scotland contain immigration and residence rules. To be entitled to council tax reduction, you must:

- not be defined as a 'person subject to immigration control' (see below); *and*
- be habitually resident in, including having a right to reside in, the common travel area (see p441), unless you are in an exempt group.

There are also rules that exclude you from council tax reduction if you are absent from the property. However the first 13 weeks of a temporary absence are disregarded if that absence is not intended to be longer or is due to your being in residential accommodation. In limited circumstances, up to 52 weeks of temporary absence can be disregarded.[2]

People subject to immigration control

Unless you are exempt, you are not entitled to council tax reduction if you are defined as a 'person subject to immigration control' (see p57).[3]

You are not excluded from council tax reduction on the basis of being a person subject to immigration control if you are:[4]

- a national of a country that has ratified either the European Convention on Social and Medical Assistance or the European Social Charter (1961). The only non-European Economic Area (EEA) countries to which this applies are Turkey and Macedonia; *and*
- lawfully present in the UK. You satisfy this if you currently have leave to enter or remain in the UK. However, see below if your leave is subject to a 'no recourse to public funds' condition.

Note: you must satisfy all the other conditions of entitlement for council tax reduction, including the requirement to have a right to reside (see below). Therefore, if you are an asylum seeker with temporary admission in the UK, although you are 'lawfully present', you are likely to be excluded from council tax reduction, as having temporary admission does not give you a right to reside.[5]

Public funds

Council tax reduction is defined as a public fund in the Immigration Rules.[6]

If your leave to enter or remain in the UK is subject to a 'no recourse to public funds' condition, you are defined as a 'person subject to immigration control' (see p59) and (unless you come within the exception above) you are not entitled to council tax reduction.

However, if you come within the above exemption and are therefore entitled to council tax reduction, this is still regarded as having recourse to public funds. It breaches one of the conditions of your leave and could affect your right to remain in the UK (see p22).[7]

If your leave is subject to a 'no recourse to public funds' condition, you should also avoid being included in someone else's claim because if s/he receives a larger council tax reduction because of your presence, this also breaches your 'no recourse to public funds' condition and could affect your right to remain in the UK (see p22).[8]

Note: although council tax reduction is defined as a 'public fund', a discount in your council tax liability is not. If you get a discount (eg, because you live alone), this does not breach any condition not to have recourse to public funds.

National insurance number requirement

If you apply for council tax reduction in England and Wales, you and anyone included in your application must satisfy a national insurance (NI) number requirement that is similar to the requirement for benefits (see p335).[9] However, this does not apply to:[10]

* a child or young person; *or*
* a person who:
  – is defined as a 'person subject to immigration control' because s/he requires leave but does not have it (see p58); *and*
  – has not previously had an NI number; *and*
  – is not habitually resident. **Note:** this is always likely to apply if you satisfy the first point, as you do not have a right to reside.

Asylum support

In Wales and Scotland only, asylum support counts as income for council tax reduction purposes, except if you are defined as a 'pensioner'.[11] In England, some local authorities also treat asylum support as income, so you should check your local scheme.

Residence requirements

To be entitled to council tax reduction, you must be habitually resident and have a right to reside (see p443) in the 'common travel area' (ie, the UK, Ireland, Channel Islands and the Isle of Man), unless you are exempt from the habitual residence test.[12]

You are exempt from the habitual residence test for council tax reduction if you:[13]

* are an EEA national and a 'worker' (see p140), including if you retain this status (see p146);
* are an EEA national and a 'self-employed person' (see p153), including if you retain this status (see p157);
* are the family member (see p164) (other than an 'extended family member', except in Scotland) of someone in either of the above two groups;
* are an EEA national with a permanent right of residence acquired in less than five years (the main people affected are certain former workers or self-

employed people who have retired or are permanently incapacitated, and their family members – see p190);
- are a refugee;
- have humanitarian protection;
- have discretionary leave (see p36), leave granted under the 'destitution domestic violence concession' (see p35) or temporary protection granted under the displaced persons' provisions;
- have been deported, expelled or otherwise legally removed from another country to the UK and you are not a 'person subject to immigration control' (see p57);
- (England and Wales only) are a Crown servant or member of HM Forces posted overseas and immediately prior to your posting you were habitually resident in the UK;
- receive income support or income-related employment and support allowance;
- receive income-based jobseeker's allowance (JSA) and (except in Scotland) either:
  - you have a right to reside other than one that is excluded (see p443); or
  - you were receiving both income-based JSA and council tax reduction on 31 March 2015. Your exemption on this basis ends when you cease to be entitled to income-based JSA or you make a new application for council tax reduction.[14]

If you are *not* in one of the above exempt groups, to be entitled to council tax reduction you must be accepted as 'habitually resident in fact' (see p110) and have a right to reside (see p443).

Note: receipt of pension credit does not exempt you from the habitual residence test.

If you are not accepted as 'habitually resident in fact' and/or you do not have a non-excluded right to reside (see p443), you are 'treated as not being in Great Britain' and not entitled to council tax reduction.

In Scotland, provided you are not someone who is 'treated as not being in Great Britain', you can be treated as being present in Great Britain when you are abroad in your capacity as (or accompanying your partner in her/his capacity as) an aircraft worker, mariner, continental shelf worker, Crown servant or member of HM Forces.[15] You can also be treated as being present in Great Britain during certain temporary absences for up to one, two or six months.[16]

Note: a local authority cannot require you to have resided in that local authority area for a set period of time before you can be entitled to council tax reduction.[17]

Right to reside

To satisfy the right to reside requirement within the habitual residence test for council tax reduction, you must have a right to reside in the common travel area, other than as:[18]

- an EEA national with an initial right of residence during your first three months in the UK (see p132);
- a family member of the above;
- (except Scotland) an EEA jobseeker (see p133);
- (except Scotland) a family member of an EEA jobseeker;
- (except Scotland) the 'primary carer' of a British citizen who is dependent on you and would have to leave the European Union if you were required to leave (see p181).

For information on who has a right to reside, see Chapter 12.

---

2. Local welfare assistance schemes

Help may be available under local welfare assistance schemes set up by your local authority (in England) or by the devolved governments (in Wales and Scotland). The DWP may refer to this as 'local welfare provision'.

Depending on your circumstances and whether you live in Wales or, if you live in England or Scotland, which local authority you live in, you may qualify if you need help – eg:

- with immediate short-term needs in a crisis – eg, if you do not have sufficient resources, or you need help with expenses in an emergency or as a result of a disaster, such as a fire or flood in your home;
- to establish yourself in the community following a stay in institutional or residential accommodation, or to help you remain in the community;
- to set up a home in the community as part of a planned resettlement programme;
- to ease exceptional pressure on your family;
- to enable you to care for a prisoner or young offender on temporary release;
- with certain travel expenses – eg, to visit someone in hospital, to attend a funeral, to ease a domestic crisis, to visit a child living with her/his other parent or to move to suitable accommodation.

In Wales, the Discretionary Assistance Fund for Wales offers non-repayable emergency assistance payments and individual assistance payments.

In Scotland, the Scottish Welfare Fund is a national scheme administered in accordance with the Scottish government's national guidance, but with local authorities having some discretion. You can apply for community care grants and crisis grants, and can be entitled if you are, or are about to be, resident in the local authority's area, if you are homeless or stranded in the area, or if there are other exceptional circumstances.[19] The guidance excludes you from the scheme if you are an asylum seeker, despite there being no such exclusion in legislation.[20]

In England, the local scheme is entirely at your local authority's discretion. Check with your local authority to find out what help is available, whether you qualify and how to apply. However, it is arguable that a local authority cannot require you to have resided in that local authority area for a set period of time before you can be entitled to local welfare assistance. This argument is based on a High Court case in which it was held to be unlawful for a local authority to require you to have resided in its area for a set period of time before you can be entitled to council tax reduction (see p441).

See www.cpag.org.uk/lwas for details of the different schemes.

Public funds

From 6 April 2016, local welfare assistance scheme payments are defined as a 'public fund' under the Immigration Rules.[21] If you have leave to enter or remain in the UK which is subject to a condition that you do not have recourse to public funds (see p25), you will have breached this condition if you receive a payment from one of these schemes on or after this date. Get immigration advice before you make a claim. The guidance on the Scottish Welfare Fund excludes 'expenses to meet the needs of people who have no recourse to public funds'.[22] Obtain advice if this affects you.

3. **Healthy Start food and vitamins**

If you qualify for Healthy Start food and vitamins, you get free vitamins as well as vouchers that can be used to buy specified types of food.

Note: in the future, the rules on Healthy Start food and vitamins may be different in Scotland. See CPAG's online service and *Welfare Rights Bulletin* for updates.

Healthy Start food

If you qualify for Healthy Start food (see p445), you:[23]
- get fixed-value vouchers (worth £3.10 each at the time of writing) that can be exchanged for 'Healthy Start food' at registered food outlets; *or*
- you are paid an amount equal to the value of the vouchers to which you are entitled, if there is no registered food outlet within a reasonable distance of your home.

Healthy Start food

'**Healthy Start food**' means liquid cow's milk and cow's milk-based infant formula, fresh or frozen fruit and vegetables including loose, pre-packed, whole, sliced, chopped or mixed fruit or vegetables (but not fruit or vegetables to which fat, salt, sugar, flavouring or any other ingredients have been added).[24]

Who can claim Healthy Start food

You qualify for Healthy Start food vouchers:[25]

- if you are pregnant and have been for more than 10 weeks, and you are:
  - 18 or over and are entitled to (or are a member of the family of someone who is entitled to) a 'qualifying benefit' (see p446); *or*
  - under 18 (whether or not you are entitled to a qualifying benefit), unless you are defined as a 'person subject to immigration control' (see p57); *or*
- if you are a mother who has 'parental responsibility' for a child and:
  - you are 18 or over and either your child is under one or it is less than a year since her/his expected date of birth. This means you can continue to qualify for vouchers for a period after your child is one – ie, if s/he was born prematurely. You must be entitled to (or be a member of the family of someone who is entitled to) a qualifying benefit other than income-related employment and support allowance (ESA); *or*
  - it is less than four months since your baby's expected date of birth and you have not yet notified Healthy Start that s/he was born. You must have been getting a qualifying benefit before your baby was born. This allows your entitlement to vouchers to continue until you notify the birth. Once you do, you can then qualify under the rule above (if you are 18 or over). **Note:** as long as you provided the notification within the four-month period, you can also get extra vouchers for your child from her/his date of birth.

  If you qualify for vouchers for more than one child under this rule (eg, you have twins), you get a voucher for each. If you do not have parental responsibility but would otherwise qualify for vouchers, your child qualifies instead of you;
- for a child under four who is a member of your family. You or a member of the family must be entitled to a qualifying benefit (see p446) other than income-related ESA.

In practical terms, this means that each week you get one voucher for each of your children aged between one and four, two vouchers for each child under one (or within one year of her/his expected date of birth), plus one voucher if you are pregnant.

Definitions

The **'qualifying benefits'** are income support, income-based jobseeker's allowance and income-related ESA (in some cases). Child tax credit (CTC) is also a qualifying benefit (provided that gross income for CTC purposes does not exceed £16,190 and there is no entitlement to working tax credit (WTC), other than during the four-week WTC 'run-on' period).[26] **Note:** at the time of writing, the Healthy Start Issuing Unit operates a discretionary scheme for people getting universal credit (UC) and who are on a low income. Regulations setting out the entitlement criteria if you receive UC are expected in autumn 2016. See CPAG's online service and *Welfare Rights Bulletin* for updates.

'Parental responsibility' means parental responsibility as defined in s3(1) of the Children Act 1989 (in England or Wales) or s1(1) of the Children (Scotland) Act 1995 (in Scotland).[27]

'Family' means a person and her/his partner and any child or qualifying young person who is a member of her/his household and for whom s/he or her/his partner counts as responsible.[28] So for example, if you are not entitled to a qualifying benefit, but are included in your mother's or father's claim for one of these, you can qualify for Healthy Start food vouchers.

Claims

You must make an initial claim for Healthy Start food vouchers in writing, and must provide specified information and evidence.[29] You can:

- complete the form in the Healthy Start leaflet (HS01), available from midwives, health visitors, maternity clinics and some doctors' surgeries or from 0345 607 6823;
- download a form or complete it online and print it off at www.healthystart.nhs.uk;
- email yourself a form from www.healthystart.nhs.uk/healthy-start-vouchers/how-to-apply;
- if you receive UC, contact the Healthy Start Issuing Unit for details of the discretionary scheme. Either email helpdesk@tiu.org.uk or telephone 0345 607 6823.

The form must be countersigned by a health professional (eg, a midwife or health visitor) who certifies when your baby is due (if you are pregnant) and that you have been given appropriate advice about healthy eating and breastfeeding. If you are under 16, your claim must also be signed by your parent or carer. Send the completed form to: Healthy Start Issuing Unit, Freepost RRTR-SYAE-JKCR, PO Box 1067, Warrington WA55 1EG.

If you are getting Healthy Start food vouchers while you are pregnant and then inform Healthy Start of your baby's birth by telephone while s/he is under four months old, you can get extra vouchers for her/him from her/his date of birth.[30] You may need to make a claim for CTC for her/him (or add her/him to your existing claim) to ensure that you continue to get the vouchers.

If you do not get vouchers to which you think you are entitled, or have any other problems with these, contact the Healthy Start helpline on 0345 607 6823.

Healthy Start vitamins

If you qualify for Healthy Start food vouchers, you also qualify for Healthy Start vitamins.[31]

The Scottish government has announced that, from spring 2017, all pregnant women in Scotland will receive vitamins regardless of their age or income.[32] Some health boards in Scotland have already started doing this.

Mothers and pregnant women are entitled to 56 vitamin tablets, and children under four to 10 millilitres of vitamin drops, every eight weeks. Ask your local health professional what the local arrangements are for getting your free vitamins.

You do not have to make a separate claim for Healthy Start vitamins; you are sent Healthy Start vitamin coupons with your Healthy Start food vouchers. However, you must show evidence to the vitamin supplier that you are entitled (ie, the letter to which your most recent Healthy Start vouchers were attached) and, if requested, proof of your child's age.[33]

4. **Education benefits**

Financial help is available from your local authority if you are in school or are a student, or if you have a child in school or college.

Free school lunches

School children are entitled to free school lunches if their families receive:[34]
- income support (IS), income-based jobseeker's allowance or income-related employment and support allowance (ESA);
- child tax credit (CTC) and have annual taxable income of £16,190 (in England) or £16,105 (in Scotland or Wales), or less. This does not apply if the family is entitled to working tax credit (WTC) unless:
  - this is during the four-week 'WTC run-on' period. See CPAG's *Welfare Benefits and Tax Credits Handbook* for when this applies; *or*
  - in Scotland only, the WTC award is based on annual taxable income of £6,420 or less – ie, the family gets maximum WTC;
- universal credit (UC). **Note:** the government has indicated that it will introduce an earnings threshold for 'passported benefits', including free school meals, under UC in the future. At the time of writing, this was due to apply in England, but it was not clear if it would apply in the same way in Scotland and Wales. See CPAG's online service and *Welfare Rights Bulletin* for updates;[35]
- in England and Wales only, guarantee credit of pension credit (PC). PC claimants in Scotland may qualify if they receive CTC, as on p447.

Also entitled are:

- 16–18-year-olds receiving the above benefits or tax credits in their own right;[36]
- asylum seekers in receipt of asylum support (see p371);[37]
- in Scotland, a child attending pre-school nursery (or similar) who is entitled under any of the six bullet points above, or if her/his family receives PC, incapacity benefit or severe disablement allowance, or if since the age of two the child is being, or has been, looked after by a local authority or is the subject of a kinship care or guardianship order.[38]

Note: in England and Scotland, free school lunches are provided to all children during the first three years of primary school. In Wales, free school breakfasts are provided to all children in primary schools maintained by the local authority.[39]

School transport and school clothes

Local authorities must provide free transport to school for pupils aged five to 16 if it is considered necessary to enable that pupil to get to the 'nearest suitable school'. This applies if s/he lives more than a set distance from that school. However, if there is no safe walking route, a pupil must be given free transport no matter how far away s/he lives from the nearest suitable school. Free school transport must also be be provided to pupils with special educational needs and to those whose parents are on a low income – ie, if they receive a benefit that would qualify them for free school lunches or the maximum rate of WTC.

Local authorities can give grants for school uniforms and other school clothes. Each authority determines its own eligibility rules. Some school governing bodies or parents' associations also provide help with school clothing.

Education maintenance allowance and 16 to 19 bursaries

Education maintenance allowance is a means-tested payment for young people aged 16 to 19 from Wales and Scotland who stay on in further education. Payments are made directly to the young person and are conditional on regular course attendance. The young person receives a weekly allowance during term time. The amount depends on the household income. For further details, see www.emascotland.com or www.studentfinancewales.co.uk.

The 16 to 19 bursaries are payments for young people aged 16 to 19 who stay on in further education or training in England. These are available through the school, college or training provider. Certain vulnerable young people (eg, young people in care, care leavers, young people who get IS or UC, or who get ESA and either disability living allowance or personal independence payment) can get the maximum bursary. Discretionary bursaries are available to those in financial difficulty. You should apply as close to the start of the academic year as possible, or as soon as you become in financial need if this is later. See www.gov.uk/1619-bursary-fund for further information.

Neither payment counts as income for any benefits or tax credits the parent may be getting. They are also not affected by any income the young person has from part-time work.

Note: if you are a student, to find out what help is available to finance your studies contact your local authority or college or university, or see www.gov.uk/student-finance. Also see CPAG's *Student Support and Benefits Handbook* and *Benefits for Students in Scotland Handbook*.

5. Free milk for children

Children under five are entitled to 189–200 millilitres of free milk on each day they are looked after for two hours or more:[40]

- by a registered childminder or daycare provider; *or*
- in a school, playcentre or workplace nursery which is exempt from registration; *or*
- in local authority daycare.

Children under one are allowed fresh or dried milk.

In Wales, children in key stage one are entitled to free milk.

6. Community care support from the local authority

If you have care needs, you may be able to get support, including accommodation, from your local authority or NHS primary care trust under community care legislation.

This is a complex area of law and beyond the scope of this *Handbook*, but see p388 for a brief description of the support available for asylum seekers and failed asylum seekers under the Care Act 2014.

There are restrictions and exclusions that affect all groups of migrants, but there are also exceptions to these rules which mean you may still be able to get support.

Note: community care support is not listed as a 'public fund' in the Immigration Rules. Therefore, if you have leave to enter or remain in the UK which is subject to a 'no recourse to public funds' condition, receiving community care support does not breach this condition. For more information on public funds, see p60.

Community care law is complex, and community care support is often misunderstood and poorly administered by local authorities and other providers. You are strongly recommended to obtain specialist advice before applying to your local authority for support and, in all cases, if you want to challenge a refusal of support.

Adults with care and support needs

Local authorities can provide support, including accommodation, to adults who have a need for care and support. However, if you are defined as a 'person subject to immigration control' (see p57), you are excluded if your need for care and support is solely as a result of being destitute or the physical effects, or anticipated physical effects, of being destitute.[41] This means that, even if you are destitute, there must be another reason for your needing the care and support – eg, because of your age, disability, or physical or mental health problem. This test has become known as the **'destitution plus'** test.

There are other exclusions that may also mean you cannot access support. For a summary of the exclusions that affect migrants, see p389.

For a summary of local authority support available to adults, see p388.

Other types of support

There are a number of other types of community care support that may be available from local authority social services departments or from NHS primary care trusts. The type of support available depends on your individual circumstances. The support available may be just services, but could include accommodation – eg, if you have been detained, admitted or transferred to hospital under various sections of the Mental Health Act 1983, you are now no longer detained and you leave hospital, the clinical commissioning group, primary care trust or local health board and the local social services department have joint duties to provide you with aftercare services, which can include accommodation. A summary of the different community care provisions is in the *Disability Rights Handbook*, published annually by Disability Rights UK. The legislation under which these types of support can be provided is complex and frequently miunderstood. You are strongly advised to obtain expert advice from a community care adviser.

7. **Support under the Children Act 1989**

Local authorities have a duty to safeguard and promote the welfare of children who are 'in need' in their area.[42] If you are destitute and have children, you may be eligible for accommodation or support from your local authority under the Children Act 1989 (in Scotland, the Children (Scotland) Act 1995). A child who is destitute is generally considered to be 'in need', but a child can also be in need if s/he is disabled, or if s/he is unlikely to achieve or maintain a reasonable standard of health or development without the provision of services by a local authority.[43] Although the duty is to support the child, it extends to supporting parents or other family members if this is in the child's best interests.[44]

Some people are excluded from Children Act support, including some groups of adult migrants, but there are also exceptions. Children are always eligible for support under the Children Act regardless of immigration status.[45]

The provision of support can be complex, and is often misunderstood and poorly administered by local authorities. You are strongly recommended to obtain specialist advice before applying to your local authority for support and, in all cases, if you want to challenge a refusal of support or if the local authority tells you it can only accommodate your child, and not you as well.

This *Handbook* does not cover support available under the Children Act. However, for limited further information about the rules affecting this support for asylum seekers and failed asylum seekers, see p391.

8. **NHS healthcare**

The UK's NHS is a residence-based healthcare system. However, not all healthcare is provided free of charge to everyone, and the charges can be considerable.

The legislation setting out the rules for NHS charges is different in England, Wales and Scotland. The legislation and policies implementing it are currently-changing rapidly and you are strongly recommended to obtain expert advice in advance of obtaining services, or if you have been told that you will be charged for your healthcare. The following information gives a broad overview, with some references for further information.

At the time of writing, there is a charge for hospital healthcare services, unless the specific service is exempt or you are exempt or accepted as ordinarily resident in the UK.

NHS services are not listed in the definition of 'public funds' in the Immigration Rules (see p25). If you have leave to enter or remain in the UK which is subject to a 'no recourse to public funds' condition, you have not breached this condition if you receive NHS services. However, if you have an outstanding debt for NHS treatment, you will normally be refused certain types of immigration leave,[46] and if you use deception to access NHS treatment without entitlement, your application for leave is automatically refused.[47] The NHS should follow guidance before contacting the Home Office about outstanding debts.[48]

Services exempt from charges

Health services that are currently exempt from charges, regardless of immigration or residence status, are broadly:[49]

- accident and emergency services, but not any provided after you have been admitted as an inpatient or at a follow-up outpatient appointment;

- services not provided in a hospital and not provided by staff employed to work in, or under the direction of, a hospital;
- services for diagnosing and treating specified conditions, including food poisoning, HIV, measles, malaria, tuberculosis, viral hepatitis and whooping cough;[50]
- services for diagnosing and treating sexually transmitted infections;
- services for treating conditions caused by torture, female genital mutilation, domestic violence or sexual violence, provided you have not travelled to the UK for the purpose of seeking that treatment;
- in England only, family planning services (this does not include maternity services or services providing terminations of pregnancies).

Note: there are currently no residence-related charges for primary healthcare, including services delivered through GP practices, NHS walk-in centres, dentists, pharmacists and optometrists. However, some of these services have other charges (eg, for dental care or prescriptions), and these have different exemption criteria.

Who is exempt from charges

You are charged for NHS hospital services, unless you are in an exempt group or you are accepted as 'ordinarily resident' in the UK.

Groups of people who are exempt from charges vary between England, Wales and Scotland, and you should therefore check the details, in both regulations[51] and guidance[52] for the relevant country in which you intend to access the services.

The meaning of 'ordinarily resident' for this purpose is currently evolving, and it is therefore useful to refer to current government guidance. **Note:** you may be of any nationality, including British, and not be 'ordinarily resident' in the UK.

Further information

The rules on health services charges are changing rapidly, so remember to check the current legislation and guidance.

Maternity Action has produced two factsheets on the NHS charging rules – in England, and in Wales, Scotland and Northern Ireland. These are available on its website, together with other resources, including details of its Maternity Care Access Advice line.[53]

9. **Other financial help**

Other financial help is available, to which you may be entitled, especially if you are on a low income, have children, are an older person, or have an illness, disability or other special needs.

See the *Disability Rights Handbook*, published by Disability Rights UK, for help if you have needs resulting from disability, health problems or caring responsibilities.

Food banks

If you are experiencing severe financial hardship (eg, caused by debt or benefit delays), you may be able to get vouchers for food which can be redeemed at a food bank. Vouchers are available from frontline care professionals, such as doctors, health visitors, social workers and advice workers. Jobcentre Plus staff may also give out vouchers. Further information and contact details for many food banks can be found at www.trusselltrust.org or by contacting your local authority.

You may be able to get help with food or meals through local community groups that are part of the FareShare network. Further information is available at www.fareshare.org.uk.

Repairs, home improvements and energy efficiency

Your local authority may be able to provide you with a grant to help with the cost of improving your home. The main types of grant available are:
* home improvement grants; *and*
* disabled facilities grants.

You may also be able to get:
* assistance from a home improvement agency (a local not-for-profit organisation) to repair, improve, maintain or adapt your home – sometimes called 'care and repair' or 'staying put' schemes – or with small repairs, safety checks and odd jobs from a handyperson service. For information see, in England, www.foundations.uk.com, in Wales, www.careandrepair.org.uk and in Scotland, www.careandrepairscotland.co.uk;
* a grant for help with insulation and other energy efficiency measures in your home. Help with fuel bills may also be available. Different schemes operate in England, Wales and Scotland. For further information, contact the Energy Saving Advice Service on 0300 123 1234 (calls charged at standard national rates) (in Scotland, Home Energy Scotland on 0808 808 2282) or at www.energysavingtrust.org.uk. For more details, see CPAG's *Fuel Rights Handbook*.

Special funds for sick or disabled people

A range of help is available for people with an illness or disability to assist with things like paying for care services in their own home, equipment, holidays, furniture and transport needs, and for people with haemophilia or HIV contracted via haemophilia treatment. Grants are also available for practical support to help people do their jobs – eg, to pay for specialist equipment and travel. For more information, see the *Disability Rights Handbook*, published by Disability Rights UK.

Payments for former members of the armed forces

If you are a former member of the UK armed forces, or your spouse or civil partner died while in service, you may be able to claim under the one of the various schemes administered by the Ministry of Defence. The benefits and lump-sum payments include pensions, disablement benefits and compensation payments. Your entitlement depends on your circumstances, including the dates of service and, where relevant, the degree and effect of any disablement or ill health and the final salary. Further details are available from Veterans UK (www.gov.uk/government/organisations/veterans-uk).

Charities

There are many charities that provide various types of help to people in need. Your local authority social services department or local advice centre may know of appropriate charities that could assist you, or you can consult publications, such as *A Guide to Grants for Individuals in Need* and the *Charities Digest*, in your local library. The organisation turn2us has a website (www.turn2us.org.uk) with an A–Z of charities that can provide financial help. In many cases, applications for support can be made directly from the website. Information on grants available for individuals can also be found on the website www.grantsforindividuals.org.uk.

Notes

1. Council tax reduction

1 **E** CTRS(PR)E Regs
W CTRS(DS)W Regs; CTRSPR(W) Regs
S CTR(S) Regs; CTR(SPC)S Regs

2 **E** Sch 1 para 5 CTRS(PR)E Regs
W Reg 26 CTRSPR(W) Regs; Sch para 17 CTRS(DS)W Regs
S Reg 15 CTR(SPC)S Regs; reg 15 CTR(S) Regs

3 **E** Reg 13 CTRS(PR)E Regs
W Reg 29 CTRSPR(W) Regs; Sch para 20 CTRS(DS)W Regs
S Reg 19 CTR(SPC)S Regs; reg 19 CTR(S) Regs

4 **E** Reg 13(1A) CTRS(PR)E Regs
W Reg 29(2) CTRSPR(W) Regs; Sch para 20(2) CTRS(DS)W Regs
S Reg 19(2) CTR(SPC)S Regs; reg 19(2) CTR(S) Regs

5 *Szoma v SSWP* [2005] UKHL 64, reported as R(IS) 2/06 and see *Yesiloz v London Borough of Camden* [2009] EWCA Civ 415

6 para 6 IR

7 para 6A IR. Council tax reduction is not included in the regulations that are referred to in para 6B IR, which disregards claims made as a result of exemptions.

8 para 6A IR

9 **E** Sch 8 para 7 CTRS(PR)E Regs
W Sch 13 para 5 CTRSPR(W) Regs; Sch para 111 CTRS(DS)W Regs

10 **E** Sch 8 para 7(3) CTRS(PR)E Regs
W Sch 13 para 5(3) CTRSPR(W) Regs; Sch para 111(3) CTRS(DS)W Regs

11 **S** Reg 39(11) CTR(S) Regs
W Sch 6 para 17(10) CTRSPR(W) Regs; Sch para 51(10) CTRS(DS)W Regs

12 **E** Reg 12 CTRS(PR)E Regs
W Reg 28 CTRSPR(W) Regs; Sch para 19 CTRS(DS)W Regs
S Reg 16 CTR(SPC)S Regs; reg 16 CTR(S) Regs

13 **E** Reg 12 CTRS(PR)E Regs
W Reg 28 CTRSPR(W) Regs; Sch para 19 CTRS(DS)W Regs
S Reg 16 CTR(SPC)S Regs; reg 16 CTR(S) Regs

14 **E** Reg 3 The Council Tax Reduction Schemes (Prescribed Requirements) (England) (Amendment) (No.2) Regulations 2014, No.3312
W Reg 31 The Council Tax Reduction Schemes (Prescribed Requirements and Default Scheme) (Wales) (Amendment) Regulations 2015, No.44

15 Reg 17 CTR(SPC)S Regs; reg 17 CTR(S) Regs

16 Reg 18 CTR(SPC)S Regs; reg 18 CTR(S) Regs

17 *R (Winder and Others) v Sandwell MBC* [2014] EWHC 2617 (Admin)

18 **E** Reg 12 CTRS(PR)E Regs
W Reg 28 CTRSPR(W) Regs; Sch para 19 CTRS(DS)W Regs
S Reg 16 CTR(SPC)S Regs; reg 16 CTR(S) Regs

2. Local welfare assistance schemes

19 Reg 4 The Welfare Funds (Scotland) Regulations 2016, No.107; *Scottish Welfare Fund: statutory guidance*, April 2016, paras 4.2-4.9

20 *Scottish Welfare Fund: statutory guidance*, April 2016, para 6.7

21 para 6 IR

22 *Scottish Welfare Fund: statutory guidance*, April 2016, Annex A para 19; see also para 6.6

3. Healthy Start food and vitamins

23 Regs 5(2) and 8 HSS&WF(A) Regs

24 Regs 2(1) and 5(1) and Sch 3 HSS&WF(A) Regs; HSS(DHSF)(W) Regs

25 Reg 3 HSS&WF(A) Regs

26 Reg 3 HSS&WFA(A) Regs

27 Reg 2(1) HSS&WF(A) Regs

28 Reg 2(1) HSS&WF(A) Regs

29 Reg 4 and Sch 2 HSS&WF(A) Regs

30 Reg 4(2) HSS&WF(A) Regs

31 Reg 3 HSS&WF(A) Regs

32 Announcement on www.gov.scot, 1 June 2016

33 Reg 8A HSS&WF(A) Regs

4. Education benefits

34 **E** s512ZB Education Act 1996; The
Education (Free School Lunches)
(Prescribed Tax Credits) (England)
Order 2003, No.383
W s512ZB Education Act 1996; The
Education (Free School Lunches)
(Prescribed Tax Credits) (Wales) Order
2003, No.879 (W.110)
S s53(3) Education (Scotland) Act 1980;
The Education (School Lunches)
(Scotland) Regulations 2009, No.178

35 House of Commons, *Hansard*, 1
December 2014, written answer
216015

36 For CTC, the legislation only provides for
this in Scotland.

37 Provided under Part VI of IAA 1999

38 The Education (School Lunches)
(Scotland) Regulations 2015, No.269

39 s88 School Standards and Organisation
(Wales) Act 2013

5. Free milk for children

40 Reg 18 WF Regs

6. Community care support from the local authority

41 **E** s21 CA 2014
W s21(1A) NAA 1948
S s12(2A) Social Work (Scotland) Act
1968

7. Support under the Children Act 1989

42 s17 CA 1989; s22 C(S)A 1995

43 s17(10) CA 1989

44 s17(3) CA 1989; s22(3) C(S)A 1995

45 Sch 3 para 2(1)(b) NIAA 2002

8. NHS healthcare

46 paras 320(22) and V3.14 Appendix V
and Appendix FM IR

47 para 320(11) IR

48 Department of Health guidance,
*Overseas Chargeable Patients, NHS Debt
and Immigration Rules: guidance on
administration and data sharing*

49 **E** Reg 9 National Health Service
(Charges to Overseas Visitors)
Regulations 2015, No.238
W Reg 3 The National Health Service
(Charges to Overseas Visitors)
Regulations 1989, No.306
S Reg 3 The National Health Service
(Charges to Overseas Visitors)
(Scotland) Regulations 1989, No.364

50 **E** Sch 1 National Health Service
(Charges to Overseas Visitors)
Regulations 2015, No.238
W Sch 1 The National Health Service
(Charges to Overseas Visitors)
Regulations 1989, No.306
S Sch 1 The National Health Service
(Charges to Overseas Visitors)
(Scotland) Regulations 1989, No.364

51 **E** National Health Service (Charges to
Overseas Visitors) Regulations 2015,
No.238
W The National Health Service (Charges
to Overseas Visitors) Regulations 1989,
No.306
S The National Health Service (Charges
to Overseas Visitors) (Scotland)
Regulations 1989, No.364

52 **E** Department of Health guidance,
*Guidance on Implementing the Overseas
Visitor Hospital Charging Regulations
2015*
W www. gov.wales/docs/dhss/
publications/
091209overseasguidanceversion6en.pdf
S www.gov.scot/topics/health/services/
overseas-visitors

53 www.maternityaction.org.uk

Appendices

Appendix 1

Glossary of terms

A2 national. A national of the European Union member states Romania and Bulgaria.

A8 national. A national of the European Union member states Czech Republic, Estonia, Hungary, Latvia, Lithuania, Poland, Slovakia and Slovenia.

Absent. Not physically in the UK; the alternative to present.

Accession states. The newer members of the European Union: Croatia, the A2 states and the A8 states.

Administrative removal. A legal mechanism used to remove foreign nationals who have entered the UK illegally, including by deception, or to remove those who have breached the conditions of their leave, including overstaying.

Applicable amount. The maximum amount of benefit set by the government, taking account of certain factors such as age and whether someone is single or part of a couple.

Application registration card. The form of identification for those who have claimed asylum, replacing the standard acknowledgement letter.

Association agreement. A treaty signed between the European Union and a country outside the European Union, giving reciprocal rights and obligations.

Asylum. Leave to enter or remain in the UK as a refugee, given under the Refugee Convention or Article 3 of the European Convention on Human Rights (including protection under the Refugee Qualification Directive).

Asylum seeker. A person who has applied for asylum and whose application has yet to be decided, or whose appeal against a refusal of an asylum application remains outstanding.

Asylum support. Support provided by the Home Office to various categories of asylum seekers and failed asylum seekers. In the past, this was provided by a section of the Home Office called the National Asylum Support Service (NASS). This was abolished in 2007, but the term 'NASS support' continues to be used.

Azure card. A credit card-type card given to failed asylum seekers in receipt of section 4 asylum support. It is credited by the Home Office and then used by the holder to make purchases at designated shops.

Certificate of entitlement. A certificate of entitlement to the right of abode demonstrates that a person has the right of abode – ie, the right to travel freely to and from the UK. British citizens have the right of abode and can demonstrate this by producing their passports. A few Commonwealth nationals also have the right of abode and can obtain a certificate of entitlement, endorsed in their own national passport, to demonstrate this.

Common travel area. The UK, Ireland, Isle of Man and the Channel Islands.

Commonwealth countries. Antigua and Barbuda, Australia, Bahamas, Bangladesh, Barbados, Belize, Botswana, Brunei Darussalam, Cameroon, Canada, Cyprus, Dominica, Fiji Islands, Gambia, Ghana, Grenada, Guyana, India, Jamaica, Kenya, Kiribati, Lesotho, Malawi, Malaysia, Maldives, Malta, Mauritius, Mozambique, Namibia, Nauru, New Zealand, Nigeria, Pakistan, Papua New Guinea, Samoa, Seychelles, Sierra Leone, Singapore, Solomon Islands, South Africa, Sri Lanka, St Kitts and Nevis, St Lucia, St Vincent and the Grenadines, Swaziland, Tanzania, Tonga, Trinidad and Tobago, Tuvalu, Uganda, Vanuatu, Zambia.

Competent state. The European Economic Area country responsible for paying your benefit and to which you are liable to pay national insurance contributions.

Court of Justice of the European Union. The European Union institution that ensures that European Union law is observed by member states. It sits in Luxembourg. Previously known as the **European Court of Justice**.

Deportation. A legal mechanism used to remove a foreign national on the recommendation of a criminal court following her/his conviction for a criminal offence, or if the Home Secretary has decided that a person's presence in the UK is 'not conducive to the public good'. If an order has been signed to deport a foreign national, s/he may not return unless and until the order has been revoked.

Derivative right to reside. The term given to certain residence rights that are derived from someone else.

Destitute. For asylum support purposes, someone who does not have access to adequate accommodation or who cannot meet her/his essential living needs.

Destitution domestic violence concession. A provision under which people who have leave on the basis of a relationship, but which has broken down as a result of domestic violence, can be granted three months' leave in which to apply for indefinite leave to remain.

Discretionary leave. Permission to enter or remain in the UK given to a person outside the Immigration Rules or to someone who is refused asylum but who cannot be removed under another Article of the European Convention on Human Rights or for other humanitarian reasons.

Enforcement. A term used to refer to any of the different ways in which a person can be forced to leave the UK for immigration reasons – ie, having been refused entry at a port, having been declared an illegal entrant, or having been notified that s/he is someone who is liable for administrative removal, or who is being deported.

Entry clearance officer. An official at a British post overseas who deals with immigration applications made to that post.

European Community. The European Union was previously known as the European Community and, before that, the European Economic Community. In this *Handbook*, the legislation of all three is referred to as European Union law.

European Convention on Human Rights. An international instrument agreed by the Council of Europe. The rights guaranteed by it have now largely been incorporated into UK law by the Human Rights Act 1998.

European Convention on Social and Medical Assistance. An agreement signed by all the European Economic Area states, plus Turkey, requiring the ratifying states to provide assistance in cash and kind to nationals of other ratifying states who are lawfully present in their territory and who are without sufficient resources on the same conditions as their own nationals.

European Economic Area. Covers all European Union states plus Iceland, Liechtenstein and Norway. European Economic Area nationals have free movement within these and all European Union member states. From 1 June 2002, the right to free movement also applies to Switzerland.

European Social Charter. The 1961 Council of Europe Social Charter, signed by all the European Economic Area countries, plus Macedonia and Turkey.

European Union. Austria, Belgium, Bulgaria, Croatia, Cyprus, Czech Republic, Denmark, Estonia, Finland, France, Germany, Greece, Hungary, Ireland, Italy, Latvia, Lithuania, Luxembourg, Malta, Netherlands, Poland, Portugal, Romania, Slovakia, Slovenia, Spain, Sweden and the UK (including Gibraltar).

European Union/European Economic Area national. The term used in this *Handbook* to describe citizens of European Union member states/European Economic Area countries.

Exceptional leave. A form of leave to remain granted outside the Immigration Rules that has now been replaced with humanitarian protection and discretionary leave for those seeking asylum.

First-tier Tribunal (Asylum Support). The tribunal that decides appeals against the refusal or termination of asylum support. It sits in east London, but hears appeals nationwide (by video link if necessary).

First-tier Tribunal (Immigration and Asylum Chamber). The tribunal that hears and determines appeals against decisions made by the Secretary of State for the Home Department about asylum, immigration and nationality.

First-tier Tribunal (Social Entitlement Chamber). The tribunal that hears and determines appeals against decisions made by the Department for Work and Pensions and local authorities about benefit entitlement.

Habitual residence. The type of residence someone must usually have to get income support, income-based jobseeker's allowance, income-related employment and support allowance, housing benefit, pension credit, universal credit, attendance allowance, disability living allowance, carer's allowance and personal independence payment. The term 'habitually resident' is not defined in the benefit regulations and is determined by looking at all the person's circumstances.

Home Office. The government department responsible for asylum, immigration and nationality issues.

Humanitarian protection. Permission to enter or remain in the UK given to a person who needs to be protected from harm, but whose case does not fit the criteria for refugee status.

Illegal entrant. A person who immigration officials decide has entered the UK in breach of the immigration laws. This could be by deception or clandestinely.

Immigration judge. A person who determines appeals in the First-tier Tribunal (Immigration and Asylum Chamber) or Upper Tribunal (Immigration and Asylum Chamber).

Immigration officer. An official, usually stationed at a British port of entry, who decides whether to grant or refuse leave to enter. Immigration officers also have responsibility for enforcing immigration control.

Immigration Rules. Rules made by the Home Secretary, setting out the requirements for granting or refusing entry clearance, leave to enter and leave to remain to people applying in the different categories.

Indefinite leave. Permission to enter or remain that has no time limit.

Integration loan. An interest-free loan made to assist people who have recently been given refugee status or humanitarian protection integrate into UK society.

Lawfully working. Depending on the context, either working with the permission of the Home Office or, for accession state nationals, working in accordance with any employment restrictions that apply.

Limited leave. Permission to enter or remain that is given for a certain period of time only. Also referred to as 'time-limited leave'.

Maintenance undertaking. A written undertaking given by someone under the Immigration Rules to be responsible for the maintenance and accommodation of another person who is applying to come to or stay in the UK.

Ordinarily resident. A residence requirement for several benefits and tax credits. A person is ordinarily resident where s/he has her/his home that s/he has adopted for a settled purpose and where s/he lives for the time being.

Past presence test. A requirement for some benefits to have been present in Great Britain or the UK for a period of time before the date of claim.

Person from abroad. A social security definition that refers to a person who has failed the habitual residence test for the purposes of income support, income-based jobseeker's allowance, income-related employment and support allowance or housing benefit.

Person subject to immigration control. A person in one of four specific groups of non-European Economic Area nationals who are excluded from entitlement to most social security benefits and whose entitlement to support under the National Assistance Act 1948 is restricted.

Points-based system. The system of controlling migration to the UK from outside the European Union for economic purposes or studies.

Present. Physically in the UK; the alternative to absent.

Public funds. These are defined in the Immigration Rules as: housing provided by local authorities, either for homeless people or allocated from the local authority's housing register; attendance allowance; carer's allowance; child benefit; child tax credit; council tax benefit; council tax reduction; disability living allowance; income-related employment and support allowance; housing benefit; income support; income-based jobseeker's allowance; pension credit; personal independence payment; severe disablement allowance; social fund payments; working tax credit; and universal credit.

Reciprocal agreement. A bilateral agreement made between the UK and another country, with the purpose of protecting benefit entitlement for people moving between the two.

Refugee. A person who satisfies the definition of someone who needs international protection under Article 1A(2) of the 1951 Convention Relating to the Status of Refugees.

Refugee Convention. The 1951 United Nations Convention Relating to the Status of Refugees, a multilateral treaty defining who is a refugee and setting out the rights of people who are granted asylum.

Removal. The final procedure for sending a person refused entry, or who is being treated as an illegal entrant, or who is subject to the administrative removal or deportation process, away from the UK.

Resident. A requirement of a Category D retirement pension and a necessary part of ordinary residence and habitual residence. Residence is more than presence and is usually where you have your home for the time being.

Restricted leave. Leave to remain given outside the Immigration Rules to someone who is excluded from refugee or humanitarian protection leave but who cannot be removed from the UK for human rights reasons. Replaced discretionary leave.

Right of abode. The right to enter, remain, leave and return freely to the UK without needing to obtain leave from the immigration authorities. All British citizens, and some Commonwealth nationals, have the right of abode.

Right to reside. A residence requirement for entitlement to some benefits and tax credits. For child benefit and child tax credit, a person must have a right to reside in the UK, and to satisfy the habitual residence test for means-tested benefits, s/he must have a right to reside in the common travel area. The right to reside depends on someone's nationality, immigration status and whether s/he has rights under European Union law.

Secretary of State for the Home Department (the Home Secretary). The government minister with primary responsibility for decisions made by the Home Office on immigration, asylum and nationality.

Section 4 support. A form of asylum support for destitute asylum seekers whose asylum application has been refused and who fit certain eligibility criteria. Also a discretionary form of support from the Home Office for those on immigration bail and with temporary admission.

Section 95 support. A form of support for people who have made an application for asylum in the UK.

Settlement/settled status. Defined in immigration law as being ordinarily resident in the UK without any restrictions on the time the person is able to remain here. Those with indefinite leave are generally accepted as being settled in the UK.

Sponsor. The person (usually a relative) with whom someone is applying to join or remain with in the UK, and/or a person who is to be responsible for the applicant's maintenance and accommodation in the UK.

Stateless person. Someone who is not considered a national by any country.

Subject to immigration control. Often used to refer to those who need leave to enter or remain in the UK – and this is the definition given in the Asylum and Immigration Act 1996. However, the Immigration and Asylum Act 1999 gives a different, narrower, definition, which is used to exclude people from non-contributory benefits and certain services provided by local authorities' social services departments. This *Handbook* uses the term as it is defined in the 1999 Act.

Temporary admission. A temporary licence given to people to be in the UK while they are waiting for a decision to be made on their immigration status or while they are waiting to be removed from the UK. The alternative to temporary admission is detention.

Third country. Usually used to refer to a country to which the Home Office wishes to send an asylum seeker for her/his application for asylum to be considered, other than the country of which s/he is a national, rather than in the UK.

The United Kingdom. Comprises England, Wales, Scotland and Northern Ireland. The Channel Islands of Jersey and Guernsey, and the Isle of Man, are Crown dependencies and not part of the UK.

UK Visas and Immigration. The Home Office department that deals with immigration control.

Unmarried partners. A term used in the Immigration Rules to refer to couples (heterosexual or same-sex) who have been together for two or more years, who are in a relationship 'akin to marriage' and who cannot marry according to the law – eg, because they are of the same sex or one of them is already married. The Immigration Rules give unmarried partners some rights to enter and remain in the UK if one partner is settled in the UK or has limited leave to enter or remain here.

Upper Tribunal (Immigration and Asylum Chamber). The tribunal that hears and determines appeals against determinations made by the First-tier Tribunal (Immigration and Asylum Chamber) and most immigration-related applications for judicial review.

Upper Tribunal (Social Entitlement Chamber). The tribunal that hears and determines appeals against decisions made by the First-tier Tribunal (Social Entitlement Chamber) about benefit entitlement.

Visa national. A person who must obtain entry clearance before travelling to the UK for most purposes, unless s/he is a person with indefinite leave returning within two years or returning within a period of earlier leave granted for more than six months. For a list of countries covered, see Appendix 1 to the Immigration Rules.

Work permit. A document issued by UK Visas and Immigration to employers, allowing them to employ a named individual in a particular job.

Appendix 2

Information and advice

Immigration and asylum

If you need help with an immigration problem, you should obtain advice from your local law centre, a solicitor specialising in immigration work or one of the agencies listed below.

Note: anyone who gives immigration advice must be professionally regulated. For further details, see p7.

AIRE Centre (Advice on Individual Rights in Europe)
3rd Floor
17 Red Lion Square
London WC1R 4QH
Tel: 020 7831 4276
info@airecentre.org
www.airecentre.org

Promotes awareness of European legal rights and assists people to assert these.

Asylum Aid
Club Union House
253–254 Upper Street
London N1 1RY
Tel: 020 7354 9631
info@asylumaid.org.uk
www.asylumaid.org.uk
Advice line: 020 7354 9264 (Tues 1–4pm)

Law Centres Network
Floor 1, Tavis House
1–6 Tavistock Square
London WC1H 9NA
Tel: 020 3637 1330
info@lawcentres.org.uk
www.lawcentres.org.uk

Does not give advice, but can provide details of your nearest law centre.

Asylum Help

Language	For advice	Support applications
English (or any other language)	0808 800 0630	0808 800 0631
Albanian	0808 800 0620	0808 800 0621
Amharic	0808 800 0622	0808 800 0623
Arabic	0808 800 0624	0808 800 0625
Bengali	0808 800 0626	0808 800 0627
Chinese Mandarin	0808 800 0628	0808 800 0629
Farsi	0808 800 0632	0808 800 0633
French	0808 800 0634	0808 800 0635
Punjabi	0808 800 0636	0808 800 0637
Pushto	0808 800 0638	0808 800 0639
Somali	0808 800 0640	0808 800 0641
Tamil	0808 800 0642	0808 800 0643
Tigrinya	0808 800 0644	0808 800 0645
Urdu	0808 800 0646	0808 800 0647
Vietnamese	0808 800 0648	0808 800 0649

http://asylumhelpuk.org

Provides confidential advice and information for asylum seekers about the asylum process and applying for accommodation and support.

Asylum Support Appeals Project (ASAP)
Studios 11 and 12
Container City Building
48 Trinity Buoy Wharf
London E14 0FN
Tel: 020 3716 0284
Advice line (advisers only): 020 3716 0283 (Mon, Wed and Fri 2pm–4pm)
www.asaproject.org

British Red Cross
44 Moorfields
London EC2Y 9AL
Tel: 0344 871 1111
information@redcross.org.uk
www.redcross.org.uk

Provides support for refugees and vulnerable migrants in specific areas across the UK.

Civil Legal Advice
Tel: 0345 345 4345
www.gov.uk/civil-legal-advice
www.gov.uk/check-legal-aid

A legal aid eligibility checker.

http://find-legal-advice.justice.gov.uk

A directory of legal aid suppliers in England and Wales.

Greater Manchester Immigration Aid Unit
1 Delaunays Road
Crumpsall
Manchester M8 4QS
Tel: 0161 740 7722
http://gmiau.org

Provides free, confidential immigration and asylum legal advice and representation to people in the local community.

Immigration Law Practitioners' Association
Lindsey House
40–42 Charterhouse Street
London EC1M 6JN
Tel: 020 7251 8383
info@ilpa.org.uk
www.ilpa.org.uk

A professional association aiming to promote and improve advice and representation in immigration, nationality and asylum law.

Joint Council for the Welfare of Immigrants
115 Old Street
London EC1V 9RT
Tel: 020 7251 8708
info@jcwi.org.uk
www.jcwi.org.uk

Migrant Help
Charlton House
Dour Street
Dover CT16 1AT
Tel: 01304 203 977
info@migranthelpuk.org
www.migranthelpuk.org

Delivers support and advice services to migrants in the UK.

Migrant Legal Action (formerly Afro-Asian Advisory Service)

53 Addington Square
London SE5 7LB
Tel: 020 7701 0141
www.aaas.org.uk
Advice line: 0845 618 5385 (Mon – Fri 2–5pm).

Provides a specialist legal service, free of charge.

Refugee Action

Victoria Charity Centre
11 Belgrave Road
London SW1V 1RB
Tel: 020 7952 1511
info@refugee-action.org.uk
www.refugee-action.org.uk

The asylum process and your rights

Liverpool: 07917 093 159
Greater Manchester: 0161 831 5465

Asylum support and homelessness

Greater Manchester: 0161 831 5449/5452
London: 020 7952 1599
Bristol: 0117 941 5960
West Midlands: 0121 201 3090

Refugee Council

PO Box 68614
London E15 9DQ
Tel: 020 7346 6700
www.refugeecouncil.org.uk

Scottish Refugee Council

5 Cadogan Square
Glasgow G2 7PH
Tel: 0141 248 9799
info@scottishrefugeecouncil.org.uk
www.scottishrefugeecouncil.org.uk

Welsh Refugee Council
120–122 Broadway
Cardiff CF24 1NJ
Tel: 02920 489 800
info@wrc.wales
www.wrc.wales

Social security

Independent advice and representation
It is often difficult for unsupported individuals to get a positive response from the Department for Work and Pensions, local authority or HM Revenue and Customs (HMRC). It can help if you obtain advice about your entitlement and how you can demonstrate this. If you can get good quality assistance from an adviser who will take on your case, this is even more helpful, particularly if you need to challenge a decision.

If you want advice or help with a benefit problem, the following agencies may be able to assist.

- Citizens Advice Bureaux (CABx) and other local advice centres provide information and advice about benefits and may be able to represent you. You can find out where your local CAB is from the Citizens Advice website at www.citizensadvice.org.uk (England and Wales) or www.citizensadvice.org.uk/Scotland (Scotland).
- Law centres can often help in a similar way to CABx and advice centres. You can find your nearest law centre at www.lawcentres.org.uk.
- Local authority welfare rights workers provide a service in many areas and some arrange advice sessions and take-up campaigns locally.
- Local organisations for particular groups of claimants may offer help – eg, unemployed centres, pensioners' groups and centres for disabled people.
- Claimants' unions give advice in some areas.
- Some social workers help with benefit problems, especially if they are already working with you on another problem.
- Solicitors can give some free legal advice. This does not cover the cost of representation at an appeal hearing, but can cover the cost of preparing written submissions and obtaining evidence, such as medical reports. However, solicitors do not always have a good working knowledge of the benefit rules and you may need to shop around until you find one who does.
- Civil Legal Advice (tel: 0345 345 4345 or www.gov.uk/civil-legal-advice). **Note:** help with welfare benefits is limited to appeals in the Upper Tribunal and the higher courts.

Advice from CPAG

Unfortunately, CPAG is unable to deal with enquiries directly from members of the public, but if you are an adviser you can phone or email for help with advising your client.

Advisers in England, Wales and Northern Ireland can call from 10am to 12pm and from 2pm to 4pm (Monday to Friday) on 020 7812 5231. Email advice is now limited to possible judicial review cases and enquiries that are specifically about child benefit, tax credits or other HMRC-administered benefits. Our email address is advice@cpag.org.uk.

Organisations based in Scotland can contact CPAG in Scotland at Unit 9, Ladywell, 94 Duke Street, Glasgow G4 0UW or email advice@cpagscotland.org.uk. A phone line is open for advisers in Scotland from 10am to 4pm (Monday to Thursday) and from 10am to 12pm (Friday) on 0141 552 0552.

For more information, see www.cpag.org.uk/advisers.

CPAG takes on a small number of test cases each year. We focus on cases that have the potential to improve the lives of families with children in poverty. If you are an adviser and would like to refer a test case to us, please see www.cpag.org.uk/test-case-referrals.

Human rights

Information, advice and support on discrimination and human rights issues, and the relevant law.

Equality Advisory and Support Service

Freepost FPN4431
Tel: 0808 800 0082
Textphone: 0808 800 0084
www.equalityadvisoryservice.com

Appendix 3

Useful addresses

Immigration and asylum

UK Visas and Immigration
Lunar House
40 Wellesley Road
Croydon CR9 2BY
www.gov.uk/government/organisations/uk-visas-and-immigration

UK Visas and Immigration Contact Centre
Tel: 0300 123 2241
Textphone: 0800 389 8289

Asylum Customer Contact Centre
Tel: 0300 123 2235
For asylum applications submitted before 5 March 2007: 0151 213 4288

Assisted voluntary return
18th floor
Lunar House
40 Wellesley Road
Croydon CR9 2BY
Tel: 0300 004 0202
assistedvoluntaryreturn@homeoffice.gsi.gov.uk
www.gov.uk/return-home-voluntarily

Note: contacting the Home Office directly to discuss your assisted voluntary return may have an impact on any outstanding protection or human rights-based claim that you may have made. You may therefore wish to obtain independent advice before doing so.

Enquiries from European citizens
Tel: 0300 123 2253

Employer and Education Helpline
Tel: 0300 123 4699
educatorshelpdesk@homeoffice.gsi.gov.uk

Citizenship and nationality
Tel: 0300 123 2253
nationalityenquiries@homeoffice.gsi.gov.uk
www.gov.uk/contact-ukvi/british-citizenship-and-nationality

Passport Office
PO Box 767
Southport PR8 9PW
0300 222 0000
www.gov.uk/government/organisations/hm-passport-office

Independent Chief Inspector of Borders and Immigration
5th Floor
Globe House
89 Eccleston Square
London SW1V 1PN
chiefinspector@icinspector.gsi.gov.uk
http://icinspector.independent.gov.uk

First-tier Tribunal and Upper Tribunal (Immigration and Asylum Chamber)
PO Box 6987
Leceister LE1 6ZX
Tel: 0300 123 1711
customer.service@hmcts.gsi.gov.uk
www.gov.uk/immigration-asylum-tribunal

Note: these are not the contact details you must use when appealing.

First-tier Tribunal (Asylum Support)
2nd Floor
Anchorage House
2 Clove Crescent
London E14 2BE
Freephone: 0800 681 6509 (to discuss your appeal or the appeal process)
www.gov.uk/appeal-first-tier-asylum-support-tribunal

Office of the Immigration Services Commissioner
5th Floor
21 Bloomsbury Street
London WC1B 3HF
Tel: 0345 000 0046
info@oisc.gov.uk
www.gov.uk/government/organisations/office-of-the-immigration-services-commissioner

Solicitors Regulation Authority

The Cube
199 Wharfside Street
Birmingham B1 1RN
Tel: 0370 606 2555
www.sra.org.uk

Legal Ombudsman

PO Box 6806
Wolverhampton WV1 9WJ
Tel: 0300 555 0333
Minicom: 0300 555 1777
enquiries@legalombudsman.org.uk
www.legalombudsman.org.uk

For complaints about lawyers.

European Commission Representation in the UK

Europe House
32 Smith Square
London SW1P 3EU
Tel: 020 7973 1992
comm-rep-london@ec.europa.eu
http://ec.europa.eu/unitedkingdom

Social security

HM Courts and Tribunals Service

Tribunal areas

Birmingham
Administrative Support Centre
PO Box 14620
Birmingham B16 6FR
Tel: 0300 123 1142
ASCBirmingham@hmcts.gsi.gov.uk

Cardiff
Eastgate House
35–43 Newport Road
Cardiff CF24 0AB
Tel: 0300 123 1142
SSCSA-Cardiff@hmcts.gsi.gov.uk

Glasgow
Wellington House
134–136 Wellington Street
Glasgow G2 2XL
Tel: 0141 354 8400
SSCSA-Glasgow@hmcts.gsi.gov.uk

Leeds
York House
31 York Place
Leeds LS1 2ED
Tel: 0300 123 1142
SSCSA-Leeds@hmcts.gsi.gov.uk

Liverpool
36 Dale Street
Liverpool L2 5UZ
Tel: 0300 123 1142
SSCSA-Liverpool@hmcts.gsi.gov.uk

Newcastle
Manorview House
Newcastle upon Tyne NE1 6PA
Tel: 0300 123 1142
SSCSA-Newcastle@hmcts.gsi.gov.uk

Sutton
Copthall House
9 The Pavement
Grove Road
Sutton SM1 1DA
Tel: 0300 123 1142
SSCSA-Sutton@hmcts.gsi.gov.uk

Direct lodgement of appeals

England and Wales
HMCTS SSCS Appeals Centre
PO Box 1203
Bradford BD1 9WP

Scotland
HMCTS SSCS Appeals Centre
PO Box 27080
Glasgow G2 9HQ

First-Tier Tribunal (Tax)
PO Box 16972
Birmingham B16 6TZ
Tel: 0300 123 1024
taxappeals@hmcts.gsi.gov.uk
www.gov.uk/tax-tribunal

The Upper Tribunal (Administrative Appeals Chamber)

England and Wales
5th Floor
7 Rolls Buildings
Fetter Lane
London EC4A 1NL
Tel: 020 7071 5662
adminappeals@hmcts.gsi.gov.uk
www.gov.uk/administrative-appeals-tribunal

Scotland
George House
126 George Street
Edinburgh EH2 4HH
Tel: 0131 271 4310
utaacmailbox@Scotland.gsi.gov.uk

Northern Ireland
Tribunal Hearing Centre
2nd Floor
Royal Courts of Justice
Chichester Street
Belfast BT1 3JF
Tel: 028 9072 4848

The Upper Tribunal (Tax and Chancery Chamber)

England and Wales

5th floor
7 Rolls Buildings
Fetter Lane
London EC4A 1NL
Tel: 020 7612 9730
uttc@hmcts.gsi.gov.uk
www.gov.uk/tax-upper-tribunal

Scotland

Tax Tribunals for Scotland
George House
126 George Street
Edinburgh EH2 4HH
Tel: 0131 271 4385
taxtribs@scotcourtstribunals.gov.uk
http://taxtribunals.scot

Department for Work and Pensions

Caxton House
Tothill Street
London SW1H 9NA
www.gov.uk/dwp

Government Legal Department

One Kemble Street
London WC2B 4TS

Department for Work and Pensions (Overseas Healthcare)

Room TC001
Tyneview Park
Whitley Road
Newcastle upon Tyne NE98 1BA
Tel: 0191 218 1999

Disability and Carers Service

Attendance Allowance Service Centre

Mail Handling Site A
Wolverhampton WV98 2AD
Tel: 0345 605 6055
Textphone: 0345 604 5312
www.gov.uk/attendance-allowance

Disability Living Allowance Unit
Claimants born on or before 8 April 1948:
Disability Living Allowance DLA65+
Mail Handling Site A
Wolverhampton WV98 2AH
Tel: 0345 605 6055
Textphone: 0345 604 5312
www.gov.uk/dla-disability-living-allowance-benefit

Claimants born after 8 April 1948 who are over 16 years old:
Disability Living Allowance
Mail Handling Site A
Wolverhampton WV98 2AH
Tel: 0345 712 3456
Textphone: 0345 722 4433
www.gov.uk/dla-disability-living-allowance-benefit

Claimants aged under 16 years:
Disability Benefit Centre 4
Post Handling Site B
Wolverhampton WV99 1BY
Tel: 0345 712 3456
Textphone: 0345 722 4433
www.gov.uk/disability-living-allowance-children

Personal Independence Payment Unit
New claims
Post Handling Site B
Wolverhampton WV99 1AH
Claims: 0800 917 2222 (textphone 0800 917 7777)
Helpline: 0345 850 3322 (textphone 0345 601 6677)
www.gov.uk/pip

Carer's Allowance Unit
Mail Handling Site A
Wolverhampton WV98 2AB
Tel: 0345 608 4321
Textphone: 0345 604 5312
cau.customer-services@dwp.gsi.gov.uk
www.gov.uk/carers-allowance

Exporting benefits overseas

Exportability Team
Room B201
Pension, Disability and Carers Service
Warbreck House
Warbreck Hill Road
Blackpool FY2 0YE
Tel: 01253 331 044
www.gov.uk/exportability-team

Jobcentre Plus (income support, jobseeker's allowance, employment and support allowance and incapacity benefit)

New benefit claims

Tel: 0800 055 6688
Tel: 0800 012 1888 (Welsh speakers)
Textphone: 0800 023 4888
www.gov.uk/contact-jobcentre-plus

Enquiries about ongoing claims

Tel: 0345 608 8545
Tel: 0345 600 3018 (Welsh speakers)
Textphone: 0345 608 8551
www.gov.uk/contact-jobcentre-plus

Contacting your local jobcentre via the national enquiry line

Tel: 0345 604 3719
Tel: 0345 604 4248 (Welsh speakers)
Textphone: 0345 608 8551
www.gov.uk/contact-jobcentre-plus

Universal credit

Tel: 0345 600 0723
Tel: 0800 012 1888 (Welsh speakers: to make a claim)
Tel: 0345 600 3018 (Welsh speakers: to report a change)
Textphone: 0345 600 0743
www.gov.uk/universal-credit

The Pension Service

Tel: 0800 731 7898 (new claims)
Textphone: 0800 731 7339
Tel: 0345 606 0265 (to report a change of circumstances)
Textphone: 0345 606 0285
www.gov.uk/contact-pension-service

Winter fuel payments
Winter Fuel Payment Centre
Mail Handling Site A
Wolverhampton WV98 1LR
Tel: 0345 915 1515
Textphone: 0345 606 0285
www.gov.uk/winter-fuel-payment

International Pension Centre
The Pension Service 11
Mail Handling Site A
Wolverhampton WV98 1LW
Tel: 0191 218 7777
Textphone: 0191 218 7280
www.gov.uk/international-pension-centre

HM Revenue and Customs (tax credits)

Tax Credit Office
Preston PR1 4AT
www.gov.uk/child-tax-credit
www.gov.uk/working-tax-credit

Tax Credit Helpline
Tel: 0345 300 3900
Textphone: 0345 300 3909
Intermediaries helpline (HMRC): 0345 300 3946
Intermediaries helpline (Concentrix): 0845 266 8998

HM Revenue and Customs (child benefit and guardian's allowance)

Child benefit
Child Benefit Office
PO Box 1
Newcastle upon Tyne NE88 1AA
Tel: 0300 200 3100
Textphone: 0300 200 3103
Advice line for advisers and intermediaries: 0300 200 3102
www.gov.uk/child-benefit

Guardian's allowance
PO Box 1
Newcastle upon Tyne NE88 1AA
Tel: 0300 200 3101
Textphone: 0300 200 3103
www.gov.uk/guardians-allowance

HM Revenue and Customs (Solicitor's Office)
South West Wing
Bush House
Strand
London WC2B 4RD

HM Revenue and Customs (national insurance)
National Insurance Contributions and Employer Office
HM Revenue and Customs
BX9 1AN
Tel: 0300 200 3500
www.gov.uk/personal-tax/national-insurance

HM Revenue and Customs (Statutory Payments Disputes Team)
Room BP2002
Benton Park View
Newcastle upon Tyne NE98 1ZZ
Tel: 0300 056 0630

NHS Business Services Authority (help with health costs)
Tel: 0300 330 1343 (low income scheme)
Tel: 0300 330 1341 (medical and maternity exemption certificates)
Tel: 0300 330 1347 (NHS tax credit exemption certificates)
www.nhsbsa.nhs.uk/healthcosts

Local Government Ombudsman

England
PO Box 4771
Coventry CV4 0EH
Tel: 0300 061 0614
www.lgo.org.uk

Scottish Public Services Ombudsman
4 Melville Street
Edinburgh EH3 7NS
Tel: 0800 377 7330
www.spso.org.uk

Public Services Ombudsman for Wales
1 Ffordd yr Hen Gae
Pencoed CF35 5LJ
Tel: 0300 790 0203
www.ombudsman-wales.org.uk

The Parliamentary and Health Service Ombudsman
Millbank Tower
30 Millbank
London SW1P 4QP
Tel: 0345 015 4033
phso.enquiries@ombudsman.org.uk
www.ombudsman.org.uk

The Adjudicator
Helen Megarry
The Adjudicator's Office
PO Box 10280
Nottingham NG2 9PF
Tel: 0300 057 1111
www.adjudicatorsoffice.gov.uk

Independent Case Examiner
The Independent Case Examiner
PO Box 209
Bootle L20 7WA
Tel: 0345 606 0777
ice@dwp.gsi.gov.uk
www.gov.uk/government/organisations/independent-case-examiner

Judicial Conduct Investigations Office
81–82 Queens Building
Royal Courts of Justice
Strand
London WC2A 2LL
Tel: 020 7073 4719
www.gov.uk/complain-judge-magistrate-tribunal-coroner

Standards Commission for Scotland
Room T2.21 Scottish Parliament
Edinburgh EH99 1SP
Tel: 0131 348 6666
enquiries@standardscommission.org.uk
www.standardscommissionscotland.org.uk

• •

Commissioner for Ethical Standards in Public Life in Scotland

Thistle House
91 Haymarket Terrace
Edinburgh EH12 5HE
Tel: 0300 011 0550
info@ethicalstandards.org.uk
To make a complaint: investigations@ethicalstandards.org.uk
www.ethicalstandards.org.uk

Appendix 4

Useful publications

Immigration, nationality and asylum

Macdonald's Immigration Law and Practice
(9th edition), I Macdonald and R Toal, LexisNexis Butterworths, 2015

Immigration Law Handbook
(9th edition), M Phelan and J Gillespie, Oxford University Press, 2015

Support for Asylum-seekers and Other Migrants
(3rd edition), S Willman and S Knafler, Legal Action Group, 2009

Best Practice Guide to Asylum and Human Rights Appeals,
M Henderson and A Pickup, ILPA, 2015 (available only from www.ein.org.uk)

Children

Working with Children and Young People Subject to Immigration Control: guidelines for best practice
(2nd edition), H Crawley, ILPA, 2012, www.ilpa.org.uk/pages/publications.html

Children in Need: local authority support for children and families
(2nd edition), I Wise QC and others, Legal Action Group, 2013

Resources Guide for Practitioners Working With Refugee Children
(4th edition), S Gillan, A Harvey and S Myerscough, ILPA, 2014,
www.ilpa.org.uk/pages/publications.html

Working With Migrant Children: community care law for immigration lawyers,
A Hundt and Z Yazdani, ILPA, 2012, www.ilpa.org.uk/pages/publications.html

Separated Children and Legal Aid Provision,
S Valdez, ILPA, 2012, www.ilpa.org.uk/pages/publications.html

Working With Refugee Children: current issues in best practice
(2nd edition), S Bolton and others, ILPA, 2012, www.ilpa.org.uk/pages/publications.html

Social security legislation

The Law Relating to Social Security
All the legislation but without any commentary. Available at http://
lawvolumes.dwp.gov.uk

Social Security Legislation, Volume I: Non-Means-Tested Benefits and Employment and Support Allowance, D Bonner, I Hooker, R Poynter, R White, N Wikely, D Williams and P Wood (Sweet & Maxwell)
Legislation with commentary. 2016/17 edition (September 2016): £110 for the main volume.

Social Security Legislation, Volume II: Income Support, Jobseeker's Allowance, State Pension Credit and the Social Fund, P Wood, R Poynter, N Wikeley and J Mesher (Sweet & Maxwell)
Legislation with commentary. 2016/17 edition (September 2016): £110 for the main volume.

Social Security Legislation, Volume III: Administration, Adjudication and the European Dimension, M Rowland and R White (Sweet & Maxwell)
Legislation with commentary. 2016/17 edition (September 2016): £110 for the main volume.

Social Security Legislation, Volume IV: Tax Credits and HMRC-Administered Social Security Benefits, N Wikeley, D Williams and I Hooker (Sweet & Maxwell)
Legislation with commentary. 2016/17 edition (September 2016): £110 for the main volume.

Social Security Legislation, Volume V: Universal Credit, J Mesher, R Poynter, N Wikely and P Wood (Sweet & Maxwell)
Legislation with commentary. 2016/17 edition (October 2016): £90 for the main volume.

Social Security Legislation – updating supplement to Volumes I – IV (Sweet & Maxwell)
The spring 2016 update to the 2015/16 main volumes: £68.

CPAG's Housing Benefit and Council Tax Reduction Legislation, L Findlay, R Poynter, C George, S Wright, M Williams, S Mitchell and M Brough (CPAG)
Legislation with detailed commentary. 2016/17 (29th edition, winter 2016): £125 including Supplement.

Social security official guidance

Decision Makers' Guide
Available at www.gov.uk/government/collections/decision-makers-guide-staff-guide.

Advice for Decision Making: staff guide
Available at www.gov.uk/government/publications/advice-for-decision-making-staff-guide.

Housing Benefit Guidance Manual
Available at www.gov.uk/government/collections/housing-benefit-claims-processing-and-good-practice-for-local-authority-staff.

Tax Credits Technical Manual
Available at www.gov.uk/hmrc-internal-manuals/tax-credits-manual.

Budgeting Loan Guide
Available at www.gov.uk/government/publications/budgeting-loan-guide-for-decision-makers-reviewing-officers-and-further-reviewing-officers.

Leaflets

The DWP publishes many leaflets available free from your local DWP or Jobcentre Plus office. To order more than 50 leaflets, contact iON, 2nd floor, One City West, Gelderd Road, Leeds LS12 6NJ, email: ion-pass@xerox.com. To order up to 50 copies of a leaflet, fax order form to 0845 850 0479. www.gov.uk/government/collections/dwp-leaflets-and-how-to-order-them. Leaflets on housing benefit are available from your local council.

Periodicals

Welfare Rights Bulletin (CPAG, bi-monthly)
Covers developments in social security law, including Upper Tribunal decisions. The annual subscription is £40 but it is sent automatically to CPAG Rights members (more information at www.cpag.org.uk/membership).

Articles on social security and immigration can also be found in *Legal Action* (Legal Action Group), *Adviser* (Citizens Advice) and the *Journal of Social Security Law* (Sweet & Maxwell).

Other social security publications

Welfare Benefits and Tax Credits Handbook (CPAG)
£61/£15 for claimants (2016/17, April 2016)

Welfare Benefits and Tax Credits Handbook Online (CPAG)
Includes the full text of the *Welfare Benefits and Tax Credits Handbook* updated throughout the year. Annual subscription £70 per user (bulk discounts available). More information at www.shop.cpag.org.uk.

Universal Credit: what you need to know (CPAG)
£15 (3rd edition, autumn 2015)

Winning Your Benefit Appeal: what you need to know (CPAG)
£15 (2nd edition, autumn 2016)

Help with Housing Costs: guide to housing benefit 2016/17 (Shelter/CIH)
£39.99 (July 2016)

Help with Housing Costs: guide to universal credit and council tax rebates 2016/17
(Shelter/CIH)
£39.99 (July 2016)

Disability Rights Handbook 2016/17 (Disability Rights UK)
£33.50 (May 2016)

Tribunal Practice and Procedure (Legal Action Group)
£65 (4th edition, autumn 2016)

For CPAG publications and most other publications, contact:
CPAG, 30 Micawber Street, London N1 7TB, tel: 020 7837 7979, email:
bookorders@cpag.org.uk. Order forms are available at www.shop.cpag.org.uk.
Postage and packing: free for online subscriptions and orders up to £10 in value;
for order value £10.01–£100, add a flat rate charge of £3.99; for order value
£100.01–£400, add £7.49; for order value £400+, add £11.49.

Appendix 5

Reciprocal agreements

Reciprocal agreements with European Economic Area states

State	Retirement pension	Bereavement benefits	Guardian's allowance	'Sickness benefit'	Incapacity benefit	Contribution-based jobseeker's allowance	Maternity allowance	Disablement benefit	Industrial injuries benefits	Child benefit	Attendance allowance and disability living allowance	Carer's allowance
Austria	✓	✓	✓	✓	✓	✓	✓	✓	✓	✓	–	–
Belgium	✓	✓	✓	✓	✓	✓	✓	✓	✓	✓	–	–
Croatia	✓	✓	–	✓	✓	✓	✓	✓	✓	✓	–	–
Cyprus	✓	✓	✓	✓	✓	✓	✓	✓	✓	–	–	–
Denmark	–	✓	✓	✓	✓	✓	✓	✓	✓	✓	✓	–
Finland	✓	✓	–	✓	✓	✓	✓	✓	✓	✓	–	–
France	✓	✓	–	✓	✓	✓	✓	✓	✓	✓	–	–
Germany	–	✓	✓	✓	✓	✓	✓	✓	✓	✓	✓	–
Iceland	✓	✓	✓	✓	✓	✓	–	✓	✓	–	–	–
Ireland	✓	✓	✓	✓	✓*	✓	✓	✓	✓	–	–	–
Italy	✓	✓	✓	✓	✓	✓	✓	✓	✓	✓	–	–
Luxembourg	✓	✓	✓	✓	✓	–	✓	✓	✓	✓	–	–
Malta	✓	✓	✓	✓	✓	✓	–	✓	✓	–	–	–
Netherlands	✓	✓	✓	✓	✓	✓	✓	✓	✓	✓	–	–
Norway	✓	✓	✓	✓	✓	✓	✓	✓	✓	✓	✓	–
Portugal	✓	✓	✓	✓	✓	✓	✓	✓	✓	✓	–	–
Slovenia	✓	✓	–	✓	✓	✓	✓	✓	✓	✓	–	–
Spain	✓	✓	✓	✓	✓	✓	✓	✓	✓	✓	–	–
Sweden	✓	✓	✓	✓	✓	✓	✓	✓	✓	✓	–	–
Northern Ireland*	✓	✓	✓	✓	✓	✓	✓	✓	✓	✓	✓	✓

*Although Northern Ireland is part of the UK, there is an agreement between Great Britain and Northern Ireland. This is because benefits in Northern Ireland and Great Britain are separate and administered under different social security legislation. The reciprocal arrangements between Great Britain and Northern Ireland were replaced and extended to include employment and support allowance (ESA) and personal independence payment from 6 April 2016. For details of the policy before this date if you were claiming ESA and moved between the two territories, and for details of the the current reciprocal arrangements, see p293.

There is an agreement with Gibraltar, which provides that the UK and Gibraltar are treated as separate European Economic Area countries (except for child benefit).

For more information on reciprocal and other agreements, see Chapter 17.

Reciprocal agreements with non-European Economic Area states

State	Retirement pension	Bereavement benefits	Guardian's allowance	'Sickness benefit'	Incapacity benefit and 'converted' employment and support allowance	Contribution-based jobseeker's allowance	Maternity allowance	Disablement benefit	Industrial injuries benefits	Child benefit	Attendance allowance and disability living allowance	Carer's allowance
Barbados	✓	✓	✓	✓	✓	–	✓	✓	✓	✓	–	–
Bermuda	✓	✓	–	–	–	–	–	✓	✓	–	–	–
Bosnia-Herzegovina	✓	✓	–	✓	✓	✓	✓	✓	✓	✓	–	–
Canada	✓	–	–	–	–	✓	–	–	–	✓	–	–
Chile	✓	✓	–	–	–	–	–	–	–	–	–	–
Israel	✓	✓	✓	✓	✓*	–	✓	✓	✓	✓	–	–
Jamaica	✓	✓	✓	–	✓	–	✓	✓	✓	✓	–	–
Kosova	✓	✓	–	✓	✓	–	✓	✓	✓	✓	–	–
Macedonia	✓	✓	–	✓	✓	–	✓	✓	✓	✓	–	–
Mauritius	✓	✓	✓	–	–	–	–	✓	✓	✓	–	–
Montenegro	✓	✓	–	✓	✓	✓	✓	✓	✓	✓	–	–
New Zealand	✓	✓	✓	✓	✓	–	✓	–	–	–	–	–
Philippines	✓	✓	–	–	–	–	–	–	–	✓	–	–
Serbia	✓	✓	–	✓	✓	✓	✓	✓	✓	✓	–	–
Switzerland	✓	✓	✓	✓	✓*	–	✓	✓	✓	✓	–	–
Turkey	✓	✓	✓	✓	✓	–	✓	✓	✓	–	–	–
USA	✓	✓	✓	✓	✓	–	–	–	–	–	–	–
Guernsey	✓	✓	✓	✓	✓	✓	✓	✓	✓	✓	✓	–
Isle of Man	✓	✓	✓	✓	✓*	✓	✓	✓	✓	✓	✓	✓
Jersey	✓	✓	✓	✓	✓	–	✓	✓	✓	✓	✓	–

* Not employment and support allowance on conversion.

You can find the agreements in the *Law Related to Social Security* at http//lawvolumes.dwp.gov.uk by going to the 'List of Statutory Instruments' and searching under the relevant country.

The UK also has other types of agreements with other countries.

For more information on all agreements, see Chapter 17.

The agreement with Chile has only been in force since 1 June 2015.

The agreements with Bosnia-Herzegovina, Croatia, Kosovo, Macedonia, Montenegro and Serbia are in a single agreement with former Yugolsavia, but are treated as separate agreements.

Until 1 March 2001, there was an agreement with Australia. This was then revoked, subject to limited savings provisions in relation to retirement pensions and bereavement benefits.

There is an agreement with Japan, but it only covers liability for contributions.

Appendix 6

Passport stamps and other endorsements

Figure 1: UK passport

Figure 2: Certificates certifying naturalisation and registration as a British citizen

Figure 3: Certificate of entitlement to the right of above

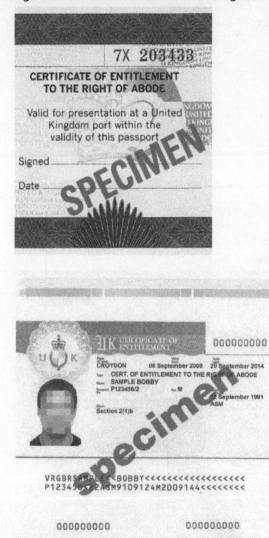

Figure 4: Immigration status document

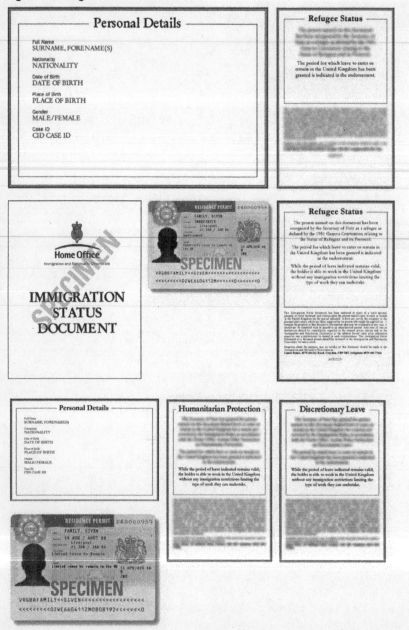

Figure 5: Biometric residence permit

The card's design is set by European Union (EU) regulation. It is a standard credit card size (86mm x 54mm) and will look similar to identity cards issued by other EU countries. The card is made from polycarbonate plastic and contains a chip to make it more secure against forgery and abuse.

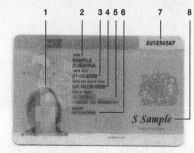

1. Holder's digital image
2. Holder's name
3. Valid until – the date the card expires. This date is at the end of the time the holder is allowed to stay; or five or 10 years if the holder has been given permission to settle in the United Kingdom (known as indefinite leave to remain)
4. Place and date of issue – this is the UK followed by the date the card was issued
5. Type of permit – this is the immigration category the holder is in (for example, STUDENT)
6. Remarks – these are the immigration entitlements for the length of the holder's stay, and may continue on the back of the card
7. ZU1234567 – unique card number
8. Holder's signature

9. Biometric chip
10. Holder's gender
11. Holder's date and place of birth
12. Holder's nationality
13. Remarks – this is a continuation of immigration entitlements for the length of time of the holder's stay (see 6 above)
14. Machine readable zone (MRZ) – this area allows information printed on the card to be read quickly by machine

Figure 6: Registration certificate or document certifying permanent residence

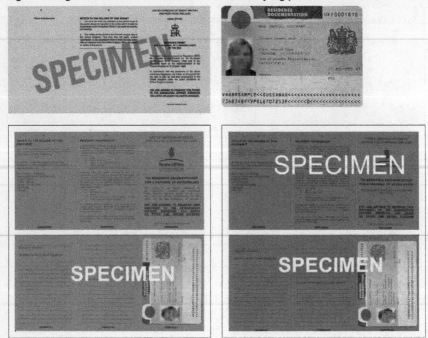

Figure 7: Residence card (including an accession residence card or a derivative residence card) issued by the Home Office to a non-European Economic Area national who is a family member of a national of a European Economic Area country or Switzerland or who has a derivative right of residence

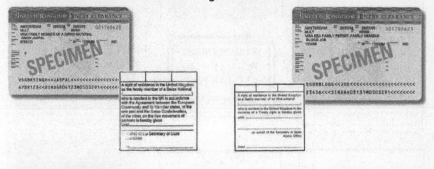

Figure 8: Historic ink stamp endorsements (top left, top middle and bottom left), application registration card (top right and bottom right), visa vignettes (bottom middle and bottom left), and residence permit vignette

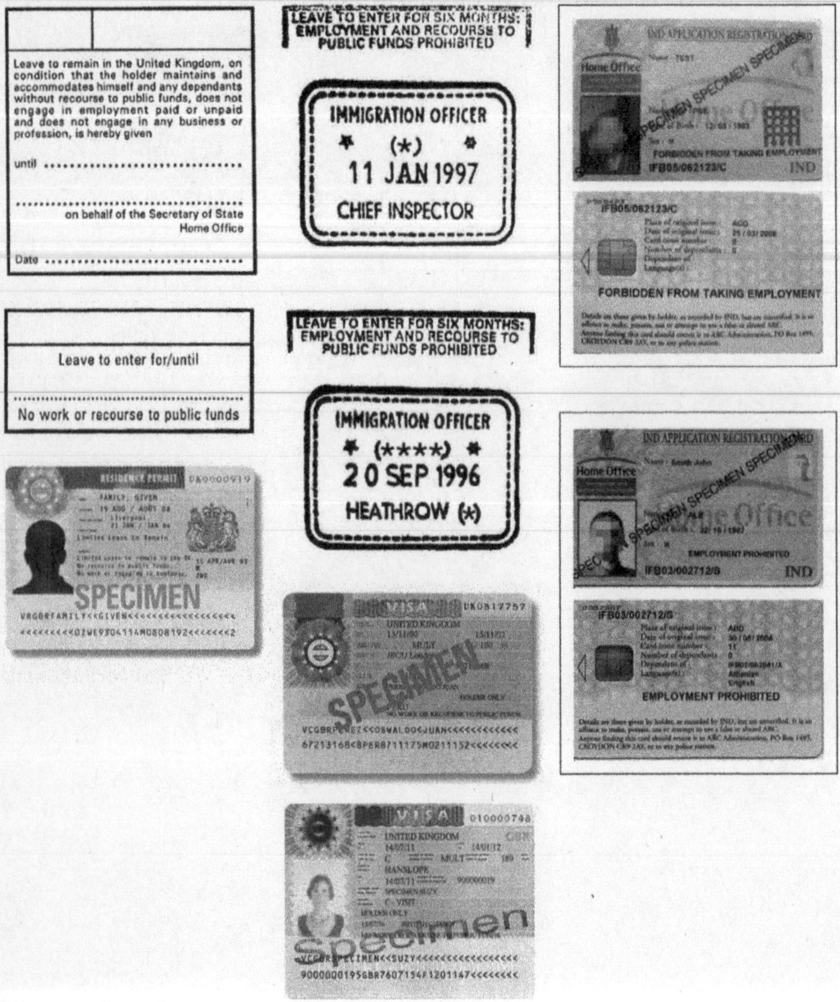

Figure 9: Entry clearance vignette

Figure 10: Date stamp on entry clearance vignette

Figure 11: Refugee Convention travel document

Figure 12: Notice of liability for removal

Port Reference:
Home Office Reference: D1█████████   IS151A

Lunar House
40 Wellesley Road
Croydon
Home Office   CR9 2BY
Tel: 0870 606 7766 Fax:

NOTICE TO A PERSON LIABLE TO REMOVAL
(Illegal entrants and section 10 administrative removal cases)

COH ID: ██████

To: ██████████

I have considered all the information available to me and I am satisfied that you are **either:**

☐   **A)**   A person in respect of whom removal directions may be given in accordance with
             paragraphs 8 to 10A of Schedule 2 to the Immigration Act 1971 as:
             i.   an illegal entrant as defined in section 33(1) of the Immigration Act 1971
             ii. a member of the family of such a person

OR

☒   **B)**   a person in respect of whom removal directions may be given in accordance with section
             10 of the Immigration and Asylum Act 1999 (administrative removal) as:
             i)   a person who has failed to observe a condition of leave to enter or remain, or
                   remains beyond the time limited by the leave;
             ii)   a person who used deception in seeking (whether successfully or not) leave to
                   remain;
             iii) a person whose indefinite leave to enter or remain has been revoked under
                   section 76(3) of the Nationality, Immigration and Asylum Act 2002 (person
                   ceasing to be a refugee).
             iv)   a member of the family of such a person

LIABILITY TO   You are therefore a person who is liable to be detained under paragraph 16(2) of
DETENTION   Schedule 2 to the Immigration Act 1971 pending a decision whether or not to give
                 removal directions and, where relevant, your removal in pursuance of such directions.

Date: ●December 2006   On behalf of the Secretary of State

Important notice for persons detained under the Immigration Act 1971.

You may on request have one person known to you or who is likely to take an interest in your welfare informed at
public expense as soon as practicable of your whereabouts.

IS151A 04/06

Figure 13: Notice of temporary admission

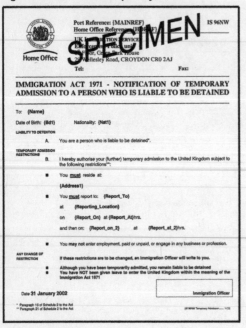

Figure 14: Embarkation stamp (not currently in use)

Appendix 7

Abbreviations used in the notes

AAC	Administrative Appeals Chamber
AACR	Administrative Appeals Chamber Reports
AC	Appeal Cases
Admin	Administrative Court
AG	Advocate General
All ER	All England Law Reports
All ER(D)	All England Law Reports (Digest)
Art(s)	Article(s)
CA	Court of Appeal
Ch	chapter
Civ	Civil Division
CJEU	Court of Justice of the European Union
Crim App R	Criminal Appeal Reports
CSOH	Court of Session, Outer House
Dir	Directive
EC	European Community
ECJ	European Court of Justice
ECR	European Court Reports
EEA	European Economic Area
EFTACR	European Free Trade Association Court Reports
EU	European Union
EWCA	England and Wales Court of Appeal
EWHC	England and Wales High Court
FLR	Family Law Reports
HC	High Court
HL	House of Lords
HLR	Housing Law Reports
IAC	Immigration and Asylum Chamber
Imm AR	Immigration Appeal Reports
NICom	Northern Ireland Commissioner
OJ	Official Journal of the European Union

para(s)	paragraphs(s)
QB	Queen's Bench Reports
QBD	Queen's Bench Division
r(r)	rule(s)
Reg(s)	regulation(s)
s(s)	section(s)
Sch(s)	Schedule(s)
SLT	Scots Law Times
SSAC	Social Security Advisory Committee
SSH	Secretary of State for Health
SSHD	Secretary of State for the Home Department
SSWP	Secretary of State for Work and Pensions
UKAIT	United Kingdom Asylum and Immigration Tribunal
UKHL	United Kingdom House of Lords
UKSC	United Kingdom Supreme Court
UKUT	United Kingdom Upper Tribunal
Vol	volume
WLR	Weekly Law Reports

Acts of Parliament

AI(TC)A 2004	Asylum and Immigration (Treatment of Claimants, etc.) Act 2004
BNA 1981	British Nationality Act 1981
CA 1989	Children Act 1989
CA 2014	Care Act 2014
C(S)A 1995	Children (Scotland) Act 1995
CSPSSA 2000	Child Support, Pensions and Social Security Act 2000
HRA 1998	Human Rights Act 1998
IA 1971	Immigration Act Act 1971
IA 1978	Interpretation Act 1978
IA 1988	Immigration Act 1988
IA 2014	Immigration Act 2014
IA 2016	Immigration Act 2016
IAA 1999	Immigration and Asylum Act 1999
JSA 1995	Jobseekers Act 1995
NAA 1948	National Assistance Act 1948
NIAA 2002	Nationality, Immigration and Asylum Act 2002
PA 2014	Pensions Act 2014
SPCA 2002	State Pension Credit Act 2002
SSA 1975	Social Security Act 1975
SSA 1998	Social Security Act 1998

SSAA 1992	Social Security Administration Act 1992
SSCBA 1992	Social Security Contributions and Benefits Act 1992
TCA 2002	Tax Credits Act 2002
TCEA 2007	Tribunals, Courts and Enforcement Act 2007
WRA 2007	Welfare Reform Act 2007
WRA 2012	Welfare Reform Act 2012

Regulations and other statutory instruments

Each set of regulations has a statutory instrument (SI) number and date. You ask for them by giving their date and number.

A(IWA) Regs	The Accession (Immigration and Worker Authorisation) Regulations 2006 No.3317
A(IWR) Regs	The Accession (Immigration and Worker Registration) Regulations 2004 No.1219
AC(IWA) Regs	The Accession of Croatia (Immigration and Worker Authorisation) Regulations 2013 No.1460
AS Regs	The Asylum Support Regulations 2000 No.704
ASA(P) Rules	The Asylum Support Appeals (Procedure) Rules 2000 No.541
ASPP(G) Regs	The Additional Statutory Paternity Pay (General) Regulations 2010, No.1056
CB Regs	The Child Benefit (General) Regulations 2006 No.223
CB&GA(Admin) Regs	The Child Benefit and Guardian's Allowance (Administration) Regulations 2003 No.492
CB&GA(DA) Regs	The Child Benefit and Guardian's Allowance (Decisions and Appeals) Regulations 2003 No.916
CTC Regs	The Child Tax Credit Regulations 2002 No.2007
CTR(S) Regs	The Council Tax Reduction (Scotland) Regulations 2012 No.303
CTR(SPC)S Regs	The Council Tax Reduction (State Pension Credit) (Scotland) Regulations 2012 No.319
CTRS(DS)E Regs	The Council Tax Reduction Schemes (Default Scheme) (England) Regulations 2012 No.2886
CTRS(DS)W Regs	The Council Tax Reduction Schemes (Default Scheme) (Wales) Regulations 2013 No.3035 (W.303)
CTRS(PR)E Regs	The Council Tax Reduction Schemes (Prescribed Requirements) (England) Regulations 2012 No.2885

CTRSPR(W) Regs	The Council Tax Reduction Schemes and Prescribed Requirements (Wales) Regulations 2013 No.3029 (W.301)
ESA Regs	The Employment and Support Allowance Regulations 2008 No.794
ESA Regs 2013	The Employment and Support Allowance Regulations 2013 No.379
ESA(TP)(EA) Regs	The Employment and Support Allowance (Transitional Provisions, Housing Benefit and Council Tax Benefit) (Existing Awards) (No.2) Regulations 2010 No.1907
FANIII(Y)O	The Family Allowances, National Insurance and Industrial Injuries (Yugoslavia) Order 1958, No.1263
GA(Gen) Regs	The Guardian's Allowance (General) Regulations 2003 No.495
HB Regs	The Housing Benefit Regulations 2006 No.213
HB(HR)A Regs	The Housing Benefit (Habitual Residence) Amendment Regulations 2014 No.539
HB(SPC) Regs	The Housing Benefit (Persons who have attained the qualifying age for state pension credit) Regulations 2006 No.214
HB&CTB(DA) Regs	The Housing Benefit and Council Tax Benefit (Decisions and Appeals) Regulations 2001 No.1002
HSS(DHSF)(W) Regs	The Healthy Start Scheme (Description of Healthy Start Food) (Wales) Regulations 2006 No.3108
HSS&WF(A) Regs	The Healthy Start Scheme and Welfare Food (Amendment) Regulations 2005 No.3262
I(EEA) Regs	The Immigration (European Economic Area) Regulations 2006 No.1003
I(EEA)A Regs 2012	The Immigration (European Economic Area) (Amendment) Regulations 2012 No.1547
I(EEA)A Regs 2013	The Immigration (European Economic Area)(Amendment) (No.2) Regulations 2013 No.3032
I(EEA)A Regs 2014	The Immigration (European Economic Area) (Amendment) Regulations 2014 No.1451
I(EEA)A(No.3) Regs	The Immigration (European Economic Area) (Amendment) (No.3) Regulations 2014 No.2761
IA(PAFAS) Regs	The Immigration and Asylum (Provision of Accommodation to Failed Asylum-Seekers) Regulations 2005 No.930

ILRFO Regs	The Integration Loans for Refugees and Others Regulations 2007 No.1598
IS Regs	The Income Support (General) Regulations 1987 No.1967
JSA Regs	The Jobseeker's Allowance Regulations 1996 No.207
JSA Regs 2013	The Job Seeker's Allowance Regulations 2013 No.378
JSA(HR)A Regs	The Jobseeker's Allowance (Habitual Residence) Amendment Regulations 2013 No.3196
SFM&FE Regs	The Social Fund Maternity and Funeral Expenses (General) Regulations 2005 No.3061
SFWFP Regs	The Social Fund Winter Fuel Payment Regulations 2000 No.729
SMP Regs	The Statutory Maternity Pay (General) Regulations 1986 No.1960
SMP(PAM) Regs	The Statutory Maternity Pay (Persons Abroad and Mariners) Regulations 1987 No.418
SPC Regs	The State Pension Credit Regulations 2002 No.1792
SPPSAP(G) Regs	The Statutory Paternity Pay and Statutory Adoption Pay (General) Regulations 2002 No.2822
SPPSAP(PAM) Regs	The Statutory Paternity Pay and Statutory Adoption Pay (Persons Abroad and Mariners) Regulations 2002 No.2821
SS(AA) Regs	The Social Security (Attendance Allowance) Regulations 1991 No.2740
SS(C&P) Regs	The Social Security (Claims and Payments) Regulations 1987 No.1968
SS(DLA) Regs	The Social Security (Disability Living Allowance) Regulations 1991 No.2890
SS(DLA,AA&CA)(A) Regs	The Social Security (Disability Living Allowance, Attendance Allowance and Carer's Allowance) (Amendment) Regulations 2013 No.389
SS(GBRA)NI Regs	The Social Security (Great Britain Reciprocal Arrangements) Regulations (Northern Ireland) 2016 No.149
SS(HR)A Regs	The Social Security (Habitual Residence) Amendment Regulations 2004 No.1232
SS(IA)CA Regs	The Social Security (Immigration and Asylum) Consequential Amendments Regulations 2000 No.636

SS(IB) Regs	The Social Security (Incapacity Benefit) Regulations 1994 No.2946
SS(IB-ID) Regs	The Social Security (Incapacity Benefit – Increases for Dependants) Regulations 1994 No.2945
SS(ICA) Regs	The Social Security (Invalid Care Allowance) Regulations 1976 No.409
SS(II)(AB) Regs	The Social Security (Industrial Injuries) (Airmen's Benefits) Regulations 1975 No.469
SS(II)(MB) Regs	The Social Security (Industrial Injuries) (Mariners' Benefits) Regulations 1975 No.470
SS(IIPD) Regs	The Social Security (Industrial Injuries) (Prescribed Diseases) Regulations 1985 No.967
SS(NIRA) Regs	The Social Security (Northern Ireland Reciprocal Arrangements) Regulations 2016 No. 287
SS(PAB) Regs	The Social Security (Payments on Account of Benefit) Regulations 2013 No.383
SS(PFA)MA Regs	The Social Security (Persons From Abroad) Miscellaneous Amendments Regulations 1996 No.30
SS(PIP) Regs	The Social Security (Personal Independence Payment) Regulations 2013 No. 377
SS(RA)O	The Social Security (Reciprocal Agreements) Order 2012 No.360
SS(SDA) Regs	The Social Security (Severe Disablement Allowance) Regulations 1984 No.1303
SS(WB&RP) Regs	The Social Security (Widow's Benefit and Retirement Pensions) Regulations 1979 No.642
SS(WTCCTC)(CA) Regs	The Social Security (Working Tax Credit and Child Tax Credit) (Consequential Amendments) Regulations 2003 No.455
SSB(Dep) Regs	The Social Security Benefit (Dependency) Regulations 1977 No.343
SSB(PA) Regs	The Social Security Benefit (Persons Abroad) Regulations 1975 No.563
SSB(PRT) Regs	The Social Security Benefit (Persons Residing Together) Regulations 1977 No.956
SS&CS(DA) Regs	The Social Security and Child Support (Decisions and Appeals) Regulations 1999 No.991
SSP Regs	The Statutory Sick Pay (General) Regulations 1982 No.894

SSP(MAPA) Regs	The Statutory Sick Pay (Mariners, Airmen and Persons Abroad) Regulations 1982 No.1349
SSPP Regs	The Statutory Shared Parental Pay (General) Regulations 2014 No.3051
SSPP(PAM) Regs	The Statutory Shared Parental Pay (Persons Abroad and Mariners) Regulations 2014 No.3134
TC(CN) Regs	The Tax Credits (Claims and Notifications) Regulations 2002 No.2014
TC(Imm) Regs	The Tax Credits (Immigration) Regulations 2003 No.653
TC(PC) Regs	The Tax Credits (Payments by the Board) Regulations 2002 No. 2173
TC(R) Regs	The Tax Credits (Residence) Regulations 2003 No.654
TP(FT) Rules	The Tribunal Procedure (First-tier Tribunal) (Social Entitlement Chamber) Rules 2008 No.2685
UC Regs	The Universal Credit Regulations 2013 No. 376
UC(TP) Regs	The Universal Credit (Transitional Provisions) Regulations 2013 No. 386
UC,PIP,JSA&ESA(C&P) Regs	The Universal Credit, Personal Independence Payment, Jobseeker's Allowance and Employment and Support Allowance (Claims and Payments) Regulations 2013 No.380
UC,PIP,JSA&ESA(DA) Regs	The Universal Credit, Personal Independence Payment, Jobseeker's Allowance and Employment and Support Allowance (Decisions and Appeals) Regulations 2013 No. 381
WF Regs	The Welfare Food Regulations 1996 No.1434
WRA(No.9)O	The Welfare Reform Act 2012 (Commencement No.9 and Transitional and Transitory Provisions and Commencement No.8 and Savings and Transitional Provisions (Amendment)) Order 2013 No.983
WTC(EMR) Regs	The Working Tax Credit (Entitlement and Maximum Rate) Regulations 2002 No. 2005

Other information

ADM	*Advice for Decision Making*
CBTM	*Child Benefit Technical Manual*
DMG	*Decision Makers' Guide*
GM	*Housing Benefit/Council Tax Benefit Guidance Manual*
IDI	Immigration Directorate Instructions
IR	Immigration Rules
TCCCM	Tax credits *Claimant Compliance Manual*
TCM	*Tax Credits Manual*
TCTM	*Tax Credits Technical Manual*

References like CIS/142/1990 and R(IS) 1/07 are to commissioners' decisions. References like *TG v SSWP (PC)* [2015] UKUT 50 (AAC) are references to decisions of the Upper Tribunal. References like ASA/02/02/1877 are references to decisions of the First-tier Tribunal (Asylum Support).

Index

How to use this Index

Entries against the bold headings direct you to the general information on the subject, or where the subject is covered most fully. Sub-entries are listed alphabetically and direct you to specific aspects of the subject. The following abbreviations are used in the index:

AA	Attendance allowance	I-ESA	Income-related employment and support allowance
CA	Carer's allowance		
C-ESA	Contributory employment and support allowance	I-JSA	Income-based jobseeker's allowance
C-JSA	Contribution-based jobseeker's allowance	JSA	Jobseeker's allowance
		MA	Maternity allowance
CTA	Common travel area	NI	National insurance
CTC	Child tax credit	PC	Pension credit
DLA	Disability living allowance	PIP	Personal independence payment
EC	European Community	SAP	Statutory adoption pay
EEA	European Economic Area	SMP	Statutory maternity pay
ESA	Employment and support allowance	SPP	Statutory paternity pay
EU	European Union	SSP	Statutory sick pay
HB	Housing benefit	SSPP	Statutory shared parental pay
IB	Incapacity benefit	UC	Universal credit
IS	Income support	WTC	Working tax credit

A
A2 nationals
  derivative right to reside 176
  evidence of work 362
  family member of an EEA national 165
  jobseekers 134
  legally working 131
  not subject to worker authorisation 129
  permanent right to reside 187
  retaining self-employed status 157
  retaining worker status 146
  right to reside 127
  self-employed 155
  self-sufficient people 159
  subject to worker authorisation 128
  workers 141
A2 states 127
A8 nationals
  authorised employer 128, 131
  derivative right to reside 176
  evidence of work 362
  family member of an EEA national 165
  jobseekers 134
  legally working 131
  not required to register with authorised
    employer 130

  permanent right to reside 187
  retaining self-employed status 157
  retaining worker status 146
  right to reside 127
  self-employed 155
  self-sufficient people 159
  workers 141
A8 states 127
abroad
  benefit abroad 223, 233
    AA 245
    bereavement benefits 243
    C-ESA 251
    C-JSA 251
    CA 245
    child benefit 243
    CTC 255
    DLA 245
    guardian's allowance 244
    HB 241
    I-ESA 238
    I-JSA 235
    IB 249
    industrial injuries benefits 250
    IS 234
    MA 249

PC 240
PIP 245
retirement pensions 253
statutory employment benefits 254
UC 241
WTC 255
child abroad 179, 204, 230
effect of EU law on benefits and tax
credits 231
effect of UK law on benefits and tax
credits 227
indefinite leave 24
ordinary residence 98
partner abroad 203, 230
preparing to go abroad 226
temporary absence abroad 228
absence 227
absence from home 230
child abroad 179, 204, 230
indefinite leave 24
ordinary residence 98
partner abroad 203, 230
temporary absence 228
accession worker document 128, 141
accident
retaining worker status 150, 158
accommodation
asylum seekers 399, 411
dispersal 402
eviction 404
failed asylum seekers 415
overcrowding 27
recourse to public funds 27
section 4 support 415
actively seeking work 137, 362
administrative removal 20
administrative review 19
advance benefit claims 112
advice 7
age
evidence 359
agency workers
EEA workers 143
aggregation
EU co-ordination rules 281
aircrew
leave to enter or remain 22
Algeria
CTC 72
EU agreements 300
non-means-tested benefits 70
appeals 18, 420
asylum support decisions 420
benefit decisions 324
EEA decisions 19
immigration decisions 18
leave to remain extended for an appeal 63

section 4 support 420
section 95 support 420
application registration card 49
armed services
financial help for former members 454
leave to enter or remain 22
single competent state 271
Article 8 leave to remain 34
association agreements 300
Turkish nationals 22
Asylum Help 371
asylum seekers 31, 49, 78
16/17-year-olds leaving care 392
accommodation 411, 415
adequate accommodation 399
appealing against refusal 383
application expenses 412
application refused 38
application registration card 49
applying for asylum 31
bail 14
benefits 78
care needs due to sickness or disability
389
children 392
Children Act support 391
claiming as soon as reasonably
practicable 375
community care 389
definition 31, 372
definition of dependants 374
destitute 377, 378, 397
detention 32
determining an asylum application 372
discretionary leave 36
dispersal 402, 411
duty to report 413
entitlement to benefits and tax credits 370
essential living needs 408
eviction from accommodation 404
failed asylum seekers 378
further submissions to Home Office 382
health benefits 403
humanitarian protection 32
in-country applications 32
leaving the UK 379
means-tested benefits 68
permission to work 32
recording an asylum application 372
standard acknowledgement letter 49
support 369
temporary admission 14
temporary protection 31
travel expenses 412
asylum support 367, 408
accommodation 404, 411
adequate accommodation 399
amount of support 408

appeals 420
application expenses 412
applications 396
assets 416
backdating 410
background to current system 369
change of circumstances 403
children 389, 392
Children Act support 391
claiming asylum as soon as reasonably
     practicable 375
clothing 401
community care support 389
conditions attached 402
contributing to own support costs 410
decisions on asylum support 401
definition of asylum seeker 372
dependants 374
destitute 374, 377, 397
dispersal 402, 411
education costs 413
emergency support 377
essential living needs 401, 408
exceptional payments 409
exclusions 375
families with children 373
further applications 404, 433
health benefits 403
Home Office guidance 371
legal aid 424
local authority support 388
maternity payment 409
misrepresentation 416
organisations providing support 371
overpayments 416
payment 409
recovery from a sponsor 417
repaying support 416
section 4 support 378
section 95 support 371
section 98 support 377
suspension 376
temporary support 377, 401
travel expenses 412
treated as income
     means-tested benefits 79
types of support 369
attendance allowance
abroad 245
EU co-ordination rules 210, 246
habitual residence test 104
person subject to immigration control 68
residence rules 208

available for work 137, 362
azure card 413

B
backdating
asylum support 410
bail 14
applying for support 405
section 4 support 387
benefit claims
applying without an NI number 340
delays 307
ending an award 348
evidence is unavailable 349
exclusions from benefit 347
making a valid claim 346
providing evidence 345
proving entitlement 347
refusal of benefit 342
who may be entitled 66
bereavement allowance
abroad 243
EU co-ordination rules 206
residence rules 205
bereavement benefits
abroad 243
EU co-ordination rules 206, 243, 269
reciprocal agreements 206, 297
residence rules 205
bereavement payment
abroad 243
EU co-ordination rules 206
residence rules 205
biometric residence permits 47
Brexit 3
British citizens
dual British and other EEA state citizens
     170
family members 168
primary carer of British citizen 181
proof of status 44
reciprocal agreements 294
right of abode 16
right to reside 123, 125
British citizenship 15
citizenship at birth 16
British dependent territories citizens
reciprocal agreements 294
British nationals 15
proof of status 43
right of abode 15
British overseas citizens
reciprocal agreements 294
British overseas territories citizens
reciprocal agreements 294

C

care and support needs 389, 449
carer's allowance
  abroad 245
  EU co-ordination rules 210, 246
  habitual residence test 104
  person subject to immigration control 68
  residence rules 208
cash in hand
  EEA workers 143
certificate of patriality 44
certificate of travel 48
challenging a decision
  asylum support appeals 432
  benefits 322
  ending an award of benefit 348
  immigration decisions 18
change of circumstances
  sponsorship 27
Channel Islands
  reciprocal agreements 293
charities 454
child benefit
  abroad 243
  child subject to immigration control 75
  EEA jobseekers 139
  EU co-ordination rules 208, 245
  interim payments 314
  living in UK for three months 94
  person subject to immigration control 68
  reciprocal agreements 298
  refugees 81
  residence rules 207
  right to reside test 115, 117
child tax credit
  abroad 255
  EEA jobseekers 139
  EU co-ordination rules 220, 256
  living in UK for three months 94
  NI numbers 337, 342
  partner subject to immigration control 75
  person subject to immigration control 71
  refugees 81
  residence rules 218
  right to reside test 115, 117
  transfers from IS or I-JSA 72
children
  asylum support 392
  child abroad 179, 204
  Children Act support 391, 450
  discretionary leave 37
  education benefits 447
  family members of EEA nationals 166
  free milk 449
  in education 177
  leave to remain as parent of British child 35

  primary carer of worker's child in education 179
  proof of parentage 355, 357
  residence requirements 95
civil partners
  partner of EEA national 166
  person subject to immigration control benefits 73
  proof of relationship 355, 357
  residence rights when partnership ends 171
  sponsorship 26
civil servants
  single competent state 272
clothing grants
  school clothes 448
co-operation and association agreements 300
common travel area 92, 104
  residence 110
Commonwealth citizens
  freely landed 46
  right of abode 16
  right to reside 123
community care support 389, 449
competent state 271
  determining competent state 272
  disputes over competent state 279
  how long the UK remains competent state 273
  sickness benefits 274
complaints
  benefit delays 309
  HB 320
Council of Europe
  conventions and agreements 299
  Social Charter 300
council tax reduction 439
  habitual residence test 105, 441
  NI number requirement 441
  partner subject to immigration control 74
  person subject to immigration control 440
  recourse to public funds 440
  residence rules 441
  right to reside 443
couples
  partner abroad 203, 230
  proof of relationship 355
criminal offence
  breach of conditions of leave to remain 22
  suspension of section 95 support 376
crisis loans
  local welfare assistance 443
Croatia
  derivative right to reside 176
  evidence of work 362
  family member of an EEA national 165
  jobseekers 134

legally working 131
not subject to worker authorisation 129
permanent right to reside 187
retaining self-employed status 157
retaining worker status 146
right to reside 127
self-employed 155
self-sufficient people 159
subject to worker authorisation 128
workers 141

D
date of birth
providing evidence of age 359
death
right to reside of family members 171
death grants
EU co-ordination rules 269
decisions
benefit decisions 308
delays with benefits 305
appeals 324
challenging a decision 322
HB 319
payment 328, 341
reasons for delay 307
revisions 323
short-term advances 311
suspension of benefits 329
test case pending 322
dental treatment
asylum seekers 403
Department for Work and Pensions
benefit decisions 309
complaints 315
dependants
dependants' benefits, reciprocal
agreements 299
dependent on EEA national 166
deportation 20
derivative right to reside 175, 182
A2 nationals 176
A8 nationals 176
benefit entitlement 183
child of primary carer 180
Croatian nationals 176
permanent right to reside 188
primary carer of a worker's child in
education 179
primary carer of British citizen 181
primary carer of self-sufficient child 180
who has derivative right to reside 175
worker's child in education 177
destitute 453
community care support 449
definition 397
expenses of applying for asylum 412
section 4 support 378

section 95 support 374
temporary asylum support 377
detention 14
asylum seekers 32
section 4 support 387, 405
diplomatic staff
leave to enter and remain 22
single state principle 271
disability
asylum seekers with care needs 389
failed asylum seekers unable to leave UK
380
financial support 454
disability living allowance
abroad 245
EU co-ordination rules 210, 246
habitual residence test 104
person subject to immigration control 68
residence rules 208
special non-contributory benefit 270
Discretionary Assistance Fund for Wales 443
discretionary leave 36
benefits and tax credits 79
children 37
discrimination
EU co-ordination rules 280
dispersal
asylum seekers 402, 411
divorce
right to reside for EEA nationals 166, 171
domestic violence
asylum seekers accommodation 400
leave to remain 35, 61
recourse to public funds 36, 61
dual nationality 170

E
education
benefits 447
child in education 178
education maintenance allowance 448
employment
asylum seekers 32
ceasing to be a worker 145
checks by employers 24
conditions 24
discretionary leave 37
employed in two or more EU member
states 272
evidence of employment record 360
genuine and effective work 143
genuine chance of obtaining 137
lawfully working 70
legally working 131
migrant workers 24
points-based system 28
remuneration 142

sponsorship 28
what counts as employed 142
employment and support allowance in youth
person subject to immigration control 68
residence rules 209
employment and support allowance, contributory
abroad 251
EU co-ordination rules 214, 252
reciprocal agreements 214, 252, 296
residence rules 213
employment and support allowance, income related
abroad 238
child abroad 204
EEA jobseekers 139
EU co-ordination rules 205, 239
habitual residence test 104
partner abroad 203, 239
partner subject to immigration control 73
person subject to immigration control 66
reciprocal agreements 240, 296
residence rules 201
right to reside test 115, 116
special non-contributory benefit 270
English language lessons
asylum seekers 413
entry clearance
applying from outside UK 16
proof of leave to enter or remain 44
proof of limited leave to enter 46
entry clearance officers 13
equal treatment 280, 281
agreements 301
European Convention on Social and Medical Assistance 299
discretionary leave 36
European Court of Human Rights
failed asylum seekers 384
European Economic Area
member states 40
reciprocal agreements 293
benefits covered 296
people covered 294
European Economic Area nationals 40
British nationals 170
checklist of residence rights 126
EU co-ordination rules 261
exclusion from UK 41
family members 165, 265
habitual residence test 106
initial right of residence 132
jobseeker 133
legal basis of residence rights 124
permanent right of residence 184
proof of status 41, 50
qualified person 126
registration certificate 41, 50

removal from UK 41
residence cards 41
right of admission to UK 40
right to reside 115, 124
section 95 support 375
self-employed person 153
worker 140
European Free Trade Association 40
European Union
co-operation and association agreements 300
co-ordination of social security 231, 259
member states 40
reciprocal agreements
benefits covered 296
people covered 294
UK referendum 3
European Union co-ordination of benefits 231, 259
aggregation 281
benefits covered 268
bereavement benefits 206
competent state 271
death grants 269
discrimination 280
equal treatment 280, 281
exporting benefits 283
family benefits 269
family members 265
habitual residence 114
how to use the rules 264
industrial injuries benefits 212, 269
invalidity benefits 269
legislative basis 263
maternity benefits 215, 268
old age benefits 216, 269
old co-ordination rules 263, 266
overlapping benefit rules 284
paternity benefits 268
personal scope of the rules 264
principles 262, 271
sickness benefits 268, 274
single state principle 271
social and medical assistance 271
social security benefits 268
special non-contributory benefits 270
subject to legislation of member state 265
survivors' benefits 243, 269
unemployment benefits 269
who is covered 264
evidence 345
age 359
benefit claims 345
challenging a decision to end a benefit award 348
employment record 360
evidence is unavailable 349
from other countries 355

immigration status 351
jobseeking 135, 362
relationships 355
exceptional leave to enter or remain 38
exporting benefits
EU co-ordination rules 283

F
failed asylum seekers
accommodation 415
additional section 4 support 414
appealing to European Court of Human
Rights 384
appeals 383
applying for section 4 support 404
Children Act support 391
community care support 389
criteria for section 4 support 379
destitution 378
detention 32
fresh applications 38, 382
human rights 381, 385
judicial review 381, 384
no safe route of return 381, 385
pregnancy 415
reasonable steps to leave UK 379
section 4 support 378, 413
sick or disabled 380
family benefits
EU co-ordination rules 269, 284
exporting benefits 284
overlapping benefits 285
reciprocal agreements 298
family life
enjoyment of private and family life 34
family members of EEA nationals 164
benefit entitlement 174
British citizens 168
child abroad 204
Croatian, A2 and A8 nationals 165
EU co-ordination rules 265
evidence of family relationship 355
extended family 167
family benefits 284
family permits 41
former family members 171
initial right of residence 132
non-EEA nationals 186, 356
non-means-tested benefits 69
partner abroad 203
permanent right to reside 186
residence card 50, 354
right of admission to UK 40
right to reside 124, 125, 164
who is a family member 69, 165
family permit 354
family reunion 33
benefits and tax credits 80

fees
appeals 19
applications 17
NHS surcharge 18
fiancé(e)s
sponsorship 26
financial need
benefit delays 312
First-tier Tribunal (Asylum Support)
attending the hearing 422
challenging a decision 432
decision to remit 433
decisions 430
hearing procedure 428
Home Office response 424
how to appeal 421
notice of appeal 421
oral hearings 426
paper hearings 426
representation 423
right to appeal 421
setting aside a decision 432
striking out an appeal 430
time limits 423
timetable for appeals 425
withdrawing the appeal 429
**First-tier Tribunal (Immigration and Asylum
Chamber)** 18
food banks 453
former workers 146
free school lunches 447
freedom of movement
EEA nationals 262
funeral payments
residence rules 216

G
**genuine and sufficient link to UK social
security system** 211
genuine prospects of work test 135
Gibralter
reciprocal agreements 293
guardian's allowance
child abroad 244
EU co-ordination rules 208, 245
interim payments 314
reciprocal agreements 298
residence rules 208

H
habitual residence 100, 104
definition 110
EU co-ordination rules 114
habitual residence in fact 110
habitual residence test 104
benefits affected 100, 104
EEA nationals 106
establishing habitual residence 105, 110

evidence 110
exempt from habitual residence test 106
failing the test 108
length of residence period 112
refused benefit 108
residence 110
returning residents 113
satisfying the test 105
settled intention 111
voluntary residence 110
who is covered by the test 107
health benefits
asylum seekers 403
Healthy Start food and vitamins 444
HM Passport Office 13
HM Revenue and Customs
benefit decisions 309
complaints 316
home improvement grants 453
Home Office
asylum support 370
hours of work
EEA workers 144
household
partner abroad 230
housing benefit
abroad 241
child abroad 204
complaints 320
delays 319
EEA jobseekers 140
habitual residence test 104
partner abroad 203, 241
partner subject to immigration control 74
payments on account 319
person subject to immigration control 66
residence and presence rules 202
right to reside test 115, 116
housing repairs 453
human rights
asylum seekers 31
discretionary leave 36
failed asylum seekers 381, 383, 385
leave to remain for compassionate
reasons 34
restricted leave 37
humanitarian protection 32
benefits and tax credits 79
exclusions 33
family reunion 33
integration loans 82
leave to remain 33
local welfare assistance 82

I
Iceland
residence rights 124

identity
proving identity 345
proving identity for NI number 339
illegal entry 49
administrative removal 20
temporary admission 14
immigration law 11
immigration officers 12
immigration status 13
benefit entitlement 56, 65
checking your status 43
evidence 351
immigration status document 48
in-country applications 32
incapable of work
permanent incapacity 190
temporary incapacity 150
incapacity benefit
abroad 249
EU co-ordination rules 250
reciprocal agreements 296
residence rules 209
income support
abroad 234
child abroad 204, 235
EEA jobseekers 139
EU co-ordination rules 205, 235
habitual residence test 104
partner abroad 203, 235
partner subject to immigration control 73
person subject to immigration control 66
refugees studying English 81
residence rules 201
right to reside test 115, 116
special non-contributory benefit 270
indefinite leave to enter or remain 23
absence abroad 24
entitlement to claim benefits 23
industrial injuries benefits
abroad 250
EU co-ordination rules 251, 269
reciprocal agreements 297
residence conditions 212
initial right of residence 132, 186
integration loans 82
how to apply 83
payment 84
repayments 84
who can apply 82
invalidity benefits
EU co-ordination rules 269
reciprocal agreements 296
Irish citizens
right to reside 124
Isle of Man
reciprocal agreements 293
Israel
EU co-ordination rules 301

J
jobseeker's allowance, contribution-based
abroad 251
EU co-ordination rules 214, 252
reciprocal agreements 214, 252, 296
residence rules 213
jobseeker's allowance, income-based
abroad 235
child abroad 204, 238
EEA jobseekers 139
EU co-ordination rules 205, 238
habitual residence test 104, 107
living in CTA for three months 93
partner abroad 203, 237
partner subject to immigration control 73
person subject to immigration control 66
residence and presence rules 201
right to reside test 115, 116
jobseekers 133
benefit entitlement 116, 139
Croatian, A2 and A8 nationals 134
evidence of jobseeking 135, 362
genuine chance of obtaining work 137
permanent right to reside 185
registering as a jobseeker 148
retaining worker status 147
right to reside 133
time limit on being a jobseeker 134
judicial review 20
asylum support appeals 433
benefit delays 318
failed asylum seekers 381, 384
HB 321

L
leave outside the rules 38
leave to enter or remain 21
applications 17
Article 8 leave to remain 34
conditions of leave 22
discretionary leave to remain 36
domestic violence 35, 61
employment conditions 24
entry clearance 16, 44
exceptional leave 38
exemptions from usual conditions 22
extended to allow appeal 63
extending leave 23
Immigration Rules 21
indefinite leave 23
leave outside the Immigration Rules 38
port of entry applications 46
proof of status 44, 351
recourse to public funds 25, 59
refugees 33
restricted leave 37
right to reside 123
sponsorship 26

stateless people 34
time-limited leave 23
travel documents 48
who needs leave to enter or remain 21, 58
leaving the UK
passport endorsements 50
legal aid
asylum support appeals 424
judicial reviews 433
Liechtenstein
residence rights 124
limited leave to enter or remain 23
domestic violence 36
entry clearance 46
overstayers 49
proof of extension of stay 47
recourse to public funds 25
living in UK or CTA for three months 92
local authorities
asylum seekers 388
community care support 449
support under the Children Act 391
local welfare assistance schemes 443

M
Macedonia
means-tested benefits 67
WTC 72
maintenance undertakings 28, 61
claiming benefits 62
means-tested benefits 67
non-means-tested benefits 68
tax credits 71
**mandatory reconsiderations of benefit
decisions** 322
maternity allowance
abroad 249
EU co-ordination rules 215, 250
reciprocal agreements 297
residence conditions 215
maternity benefits
EU co-ordination rules 268
Healthy Start food 444
Healthy Start vitamins 447
reciprocal agreements 297
maternity payment
asylum seekers 409
failed asylum seekers 415
means-tested benefits
abroad 233
person subject to immigration control 66
reciprocal agreements 205
residence and presence rules 201
medical treatment
discretionary leave 36

Migrant Help 371
migrant workers
  checks by employer 24
  sponsorship under points-based system 28
milk
  free milk 449
Morocco
  CTC 72
  EU agreements 300
  non-means-tested benefits 70
multiple nationalities 15

N
National Asylum Support Service 370
national insurance numbers 335
  applying for a number 338
  claiming benefits without a number 340
  delays 341
  obtaining a number 337
  refusal 342
  requirement 335
    who is exempt 336
  tax credits 337, 342
nationality
  British nationality 15
  evidence of nationality 355
  multiple nationalities 15
  nationality law 11
NHS healthcare 451
  services exempt from charges 451
  who is exempt from charges 452
NHS surcharge fees
  exceptions 18
non-contributory benefits
  EU co-ordination rules 270
non-means tested benefits
  partner subject to immigration control 75
  person subject to immigration control 68
  transitional protection 70
Northern Ireland
  reciprocal agreements 293
Norway
  residence rights 124

O
occupational diseases
  EU co-ordination rules 269
old age benefits
  EU co-ordination rules 269
Ombudsman
  benefit complaints 317
  HB 321
ordinary residence 96, 229
  absence from the UK 98
  access to healthcare 452
  benefits affected 96
  involuntary residence 98

  legal residence 99
  on arrival 97
  temporary purpose 97
overlapping benefits
  EU co-ordination rules 284
overpayments
  asylum support 416
overstayers 49

P
parents
  leave to remain as parent of British child 35
  proof of parentage 355, 357
part-time workers
  EEA workers 144
passports 50
  confirmation of status if passport expires 51
  illegible stamps 51
  proof of immigration status 43
past presence test 92
  exceptions 209
paternity benefits
  EU co-ordination rules 268
payment of benefit
  delays 328
  suspension of payment 329
pension credit
  abroad 240
  child abroad 204
  EEA jobseekers 139
  EU co-ordination rules 205, 241
  habitual residence test 104
  partner abroad 203, 241
  partner subject to immigration control 74
  person subject to immigration control 66
  residence rules 201
  right to reside test 115, 116
  special non-contributory benefit 270
permanent right to reside 184
  after five years 184
  benefit entitlement 192
  continuity of residence 188
  legally resided 184
  loss of permanent right to reside 192
  workers 190
person subject to immigration control 53
  asylum seekers 78
  benefits 65, 66
  children 73
  definition 57
  entry clearance 16
  evidence of status 351
  leave to remain extended for appeal 63
  maintenance undertaking 61
  means-tested benefits 66
  non-means-tested benefits 68

partners 73
recourse to public funds 59
social fund payments 73
sponsored people 62
tax credits 71
temporary admission 387
personal independence payment
abroad 245
EU co-ordination rules 210, 246
habitual residence test 104
person subject to immigration control 68
residence rules 208
points-based system 28
police
powers 13
pregnancy
additional section 4 support 415
asylum seekers 409
Healthy Start food 444
Healthy Start vitamins 447
retaining worker status 151
section 4 support 380
self-employed EEA nationals 156, 158
prescription charges
asylum seekers 403
presence rules 87, 201
benefits affected 90
definition 91, 227
past presence 92
primary carer
child of primary carer 180
of British citizen 181
of self-sufficient child 180
of worker's child in education 179
prison
continuity of residence 189

Q
qualified person
EEA national 126
family members 171

R
reciprocal agreements 232, 291
benefits covered 296
benefits not covered 292
EEA member states 293
means-tested benefits 205
non-EEA countries 292
non-means-tested benefits 70
people covered 294
recourse to public funds 25
accommodation 27
adequate maintenance 26
child with no recourse to public funds
child benefit 75
community care support 449
council tax reduction 440

definition 25, 60
discretionary leave 37
domestic violence 35, 61
leave outside the rules 38
leave under Article 8 35
local welfare assistance schemes 444
NHS healthcare 451
partner with no recourse to public funds
council tax reduction 74
HB 74
IS/I-JSA 74
WTC/CTC 76
person subject to immigration control 59
refugees 32, 78
backdated child benefit and tax credits 81
benefits 79
definition 32
EU co-ordination rules 265
exclusions 33
family members 107
family reunion 33, 80
habitual residence 106
humanitarian protection 32
integration loans 82
leave to remain 33
local welfare assistance 82
past presence test 209
section 95 support 375
studying English 81
tax credits 79
travel documents 48
registration certificate
EEA nationals 41, 50, 354
removal 20
asylum seekers 32
EEA nationals 41
residence
checklist for EEA nationals, family
members or carers 126
continuity of residence 188
definition 95
derivative right to reside 175
EU co-ordination rules 272
evidence of residence rights 353
habitual residence 100
ordinary residence 96
right to reside 101, 122
residence cards 41, 50, 354
residence documents 353
residence permits
EEA nationals 354
leave to remain granted in UK 47
residence rules for benefits 87, 201
AA 208
benefits affected 90
bereavement benefits 205
C-ESA 213
C-JSA 213

CA 208
child benefit 207
council tax reduction 441
CTC 218
DLA 208
guardian's allowance 208
habitual residence 100
HB 201
I-ESA 201
I-JSA 201
IB in youth 209
industrial injuries benefits 212
IS 201
living in UK or CTA for three months 92
MA 215
ordinary residence 96
past presence 92
PC 201
PIP 208
presence 91
retirement pensions 215
right to reside 101
SAP 254
SMP 254
social fund 216
SPP 254
SSP 254
SSPP 254
UC 201
WTC 218
residence tests
habitual residence 100
living in UK or CTA for past three months
92
ordinary residence 96
past presence 92
presence 91
right to reside 101
restricted leave 37
retired people
right of residence 190
retirement pensions
abroad 253
EU co-ordination rules 216, 254, 274
reciprocal agreements 216, 297
residence rules 215
revisions of benefit decisions
delays 323
right of abode 15
evidence of right of abode 43
right of admission
EEA nationals 40
right of residence 122
initial right of residence 132
right to reside 115, 122
A2 nationals 127
A8 nationals 127

benefits with right to reside requirement
101, 115
British citizens 123
checklist for EEA nationals, family
members or carers 126
Croatian nationals 127
derivative right to reside 175
EEA nationals 124, 125
evidence of right to reside 353
family members of British citizens 168
family members of EEA nationals 164
initial right to reside 132
jobseekers 133
non-EEA nationals 123
permanent right to reside 184
registration certificate 50
self-employed EEA nationals 154
self-sufficient people 159
students 159
transitional protection 118
workers 140
right to reside test
benefits covered 115
who is covered by the test 117

S
San Marino
CTC 72
EU agreements 300
non-means-tested benefits 70
savings
asylum support 416
school transport 448
Scottish Welfare Fund 443
seamen
leave to enter or remain 22
section 4 support 378, 413
accommodation 415
additional section 4 support 414
amount of payments 413
appealing to European Court of Human
Rights 384
appeals 420
applications 404
bail 387, 405
breach of conditions 386
children 386
criteria for support 379
decisions 405
destitution 378
disability 380
discontinued 385
exclusions 385
further submissions to Home Office 382
human rights 381, 383, 385
judicial review 381, 384
leaving the UK 379
no safe route of return 381, 385

out of time appeal 383
payment 413
pregnancy 380
review letter 386
sickness 380
suspension 385
temporary admission 387, 405
section 95 support 371, 408
accommodation 411
adequate accommodation 399
amount of support 408
appeals 420
application expenses 412
applications 396
assets 416
backdating support 410
change of circumstances 403
clothing 401
conditions attached 402
contributing to own support costs 410
decisions 401
destitute 374, 397
dispersal 402, 411
essential living needs 401, 408
exceptional payments 409
exclusions 375
further applications 404, 433
health benefits 403
legal aid 424
maternity payment 409
misrepresentation 416
overpayments 416
payment 409
recovery from a sponsor 417
suspension of support 376
temporary support 401
travel expenses 412
who is entitled 371
section 98 support 377, 401
exclusions from support 377
self-employed EEA nationals 153
benefit entitlement 156, 158
Croatian, A2 and A8 nationals 155, 157
deciding what is self-employment 155
evidence of work 360
jobseeker 137
permanent residence 190
retaining self-employed status 157
right to reside 154
self-sufficient EEA nationals 159
benefit entitlement 163
comprehensive sickness insurance 161
Croatian, A2 and A8 nationals 159
primary carer of self-sufficient child 180
sufficient resources 160
separation
right to reside for EEA nationals 166, 171

settled status 23
severe disablement allowance
abroad 249
EU co-ordination rules 250
residence rules 209
short-term advances of benefit 311
applications 313
sickness
comprehensive sickness insurance 161
discretionary leave 36
failed asylum seekers unable to leave UK 380
financial support 454
retaining worker status 150, 158
sickness benefits
competent state 274
EU co-ordination rules 268, 274
exclusion from benefits 277
reciprocal agreements 296
sight tests
asylum seekers 403
single state principle
EU co-ordination rules 271
social and medical assistance
EU co-ordination rules 271
social care support 449
asylum seekers with care needs 389
Social Charter 300
social fund
funeral expenses payments 216
person subject to immigration control 73
residence conditions 216
winter fuel payments 217
special non-contributory benefits 270
sponsorship 26, 62
accommodation 27
asylum seekers 417
change of circumstances 27
claiming benefits 26, 62
employment 28
financial requirements 26
person subject to immigration control 62
undertakings 28
spouses
ending a marriage 171
person subject to immigration control benefits 73
proof of relationship 355, 357
sponsorship 26
spouse of EEA national 166
stamps
checking immigration status 43
standard acknowledgement letter 49
stateless people 34
co-ordination of social security 265
travel documents 48

statutory adoption pay
abroad 254
EU co-ordination rules 255, 270
residence conditions 254
statutory maternity pay
abroad 254
EU co-ordination rules 255, 270
residence conditions 254
statutory paternity pay
abroad 254
EU co-ordination rules 255, 270
residence conditions 254
statutory shared parental pay
abroad 254
EU co-ordination rules 255, 270
residence conditions 254
statutory sick pay
abroad 254
EU co-ordination rules 255
residence conditions 254
students
benefit entitlement 163
comprehensive sickness insurance 161
EEA nationals 159
family members of EEA students 163
no recourse to public funds 59
right to reside 162
survivors' benefits
EU co-ordination rules 269
suspension of benefits 329
Switzerland
exclusion and removal from UK 41
registration certificate 41, 50
residence rights 125
right of admission to UK 40

T
temporary absence abroad 228
EEA nationals 188
indefinite leave 24
ordinary residence 98
temporary admission 14
applying for support 405
asylum seekers 32
section 4 support 387, 405
temporary protection 31
terminal illness
discretionary leave 36
past presence test 209
test case pending 322, 327
time limits
asylum support appeals 423
jobseeking 134
trafficking
discretionary leave for victims 36
travel expenses
asylum applications 412
asylum support appeals 428

exceptional payments for asylum seekers 409
school transport 448
tribunals 13
First-tier Tribunal 18
Tunisia
CTC 72
EU agreements 300
non-means-tested benefits 70
Turkey
CTC 72
EC association agreement 22
EU agreements 300
means-tested benefits 67
non-means-tested benefits 70
WTC 72

U
UK nationals
reciprocal agreements 294
UK Visas and Immigration 12
asylum support 371
unemployment
retaining worker status 146, 147
unemployment benefits
aggregation 282
EU co-ordination rules 269
reciprocal agreements 296
universal credit
abroad 241
child abroad 204, 242
EU co-ordination rules 242
habitual residence test 104, 108
partner abroad 203, 242
partner subject to immigration control 75
person subject to immigration control 66
residence and presence rules 201
right to reside test 115, 116

V
vignettes 44
visas
entry clearance 16
visitors
employment 24
entry clearance 16
leave to enter or remain 21
vocational training
EEA workers 149
voluntary return
asylum seekers 379

W
widowers' benefits
EU co-ordination rules 243
widows' benefits
EU co-ordination rules 243

winter fuel payments
    EU co-ordination rules 217
    residence rules 217
work permits 24
worker authorisation 128
workers 140
    benefit entitlement 146, 153
    ceasing to be a worker 145
    changing basis of worker status 152
    child in education 177
    Croatian, A2 and A8 nationals 141
    deciding who is a worker 141
    employment relationship 142
    evidence of work 360
    gaps in worker status 152
    genuine and effective work 143
    habitual residence 106
    permanent residence 190
    pregnancy 151
    primary carer of worker's child in
        education 179
    remuneration 142
    retaining worker status 146
    right to reside 140
    temporary inability to work 150
    unemployed 147
    vocational training 149
working tax credit
    abroad 255
    EU co-ordination rules 220, 256
    NI numbers 337, 342
    partner subject to immigration control 75
    person subject to immigration control 71
    refugees 81
    residence rules 218
workseekers
    see jobseekers

Y
young people
    family members of EEA nationals 166

Z
zero-hour contract
    EEA workers 145

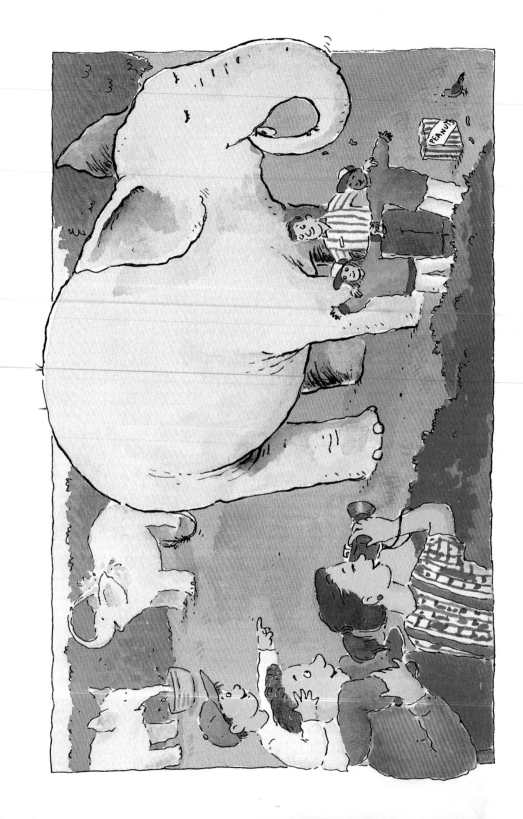

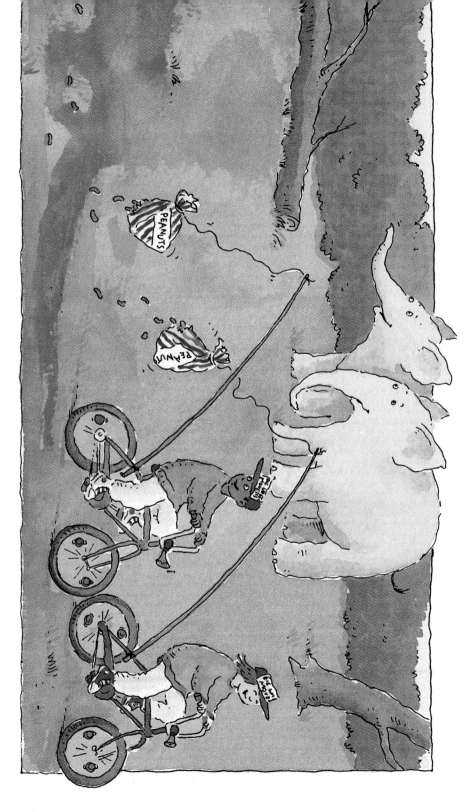

Sure we can! We can move anything!

Can we move it? I'm not sure.

It's very, very big!

It's big...

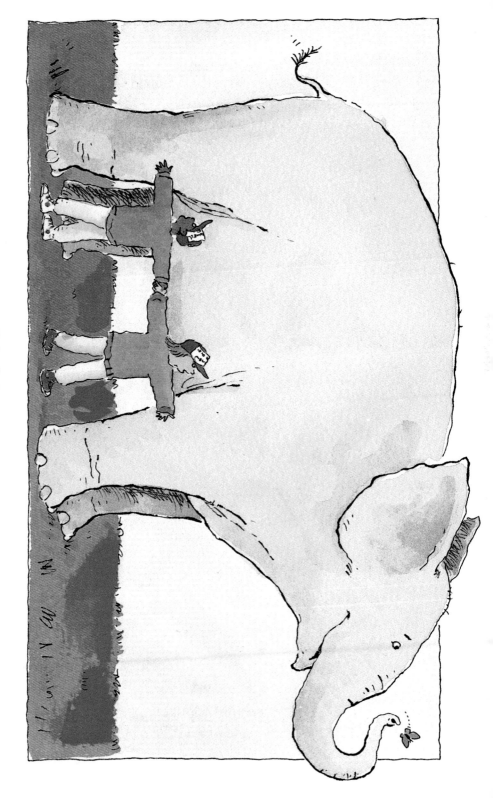

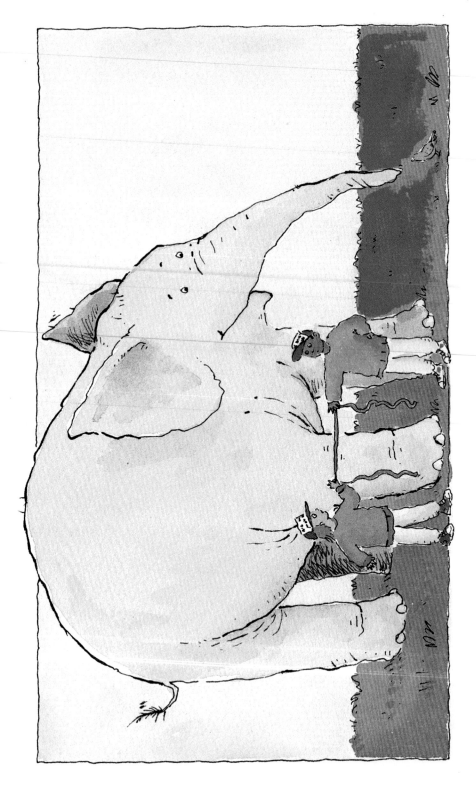

It's wide!

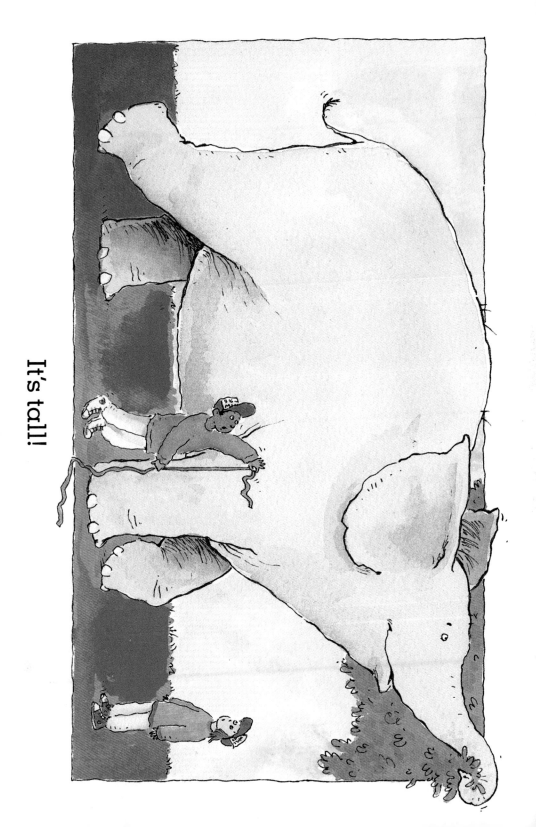

It's tall!

Can we?

Can you move this?

Sure we can! We can move anything!

Can you move this? It's tall.

Sure we can! We can move anything!

Can you move this? It's wide.

Sure we can! We can move anything!

Can you move this? It's big.

THE *13th* DISCIPLE

DEEPAK CHOPRA

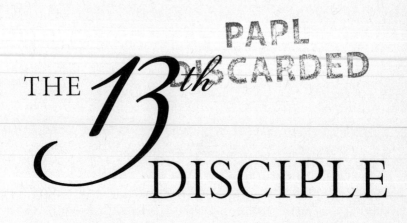

THE 13th DISCIPLE

A SPIRITUAL ADVENTURE

HarperOne

An Imprint of HarperCollinsPublishers

HarperOne

FIRST EDITION

Designed by Ralph Fowler

Library of Congress Cataloging-in-Publication Data is available upon request.

ISBN 978-0-06-224130-6

15 16 17 18 19 RRD(H) 10 9 8 7 6 5 4 3 2 1

CONTENTS

PART ONE

The Mystery School   1

PART TWO

The Invisible Gospel   115

AFTERWORD

The Mystery and You   261

part one

THE
MYSTERY
SCHOOL

CHAPTER *1*

It was a morning without sunrise, frigid and overcast, during the weeks leading up to Christmas. Mare was just heading out to work when her cell phone jingled. Her mother was calling.

"Sister Margaret Thomas just died."

"Who?" The question came out as a garbled mumble. Mare was washing down the last bite of a raspberry Pop-Tart with the dregs of her instant coffee. The last few crystals left dark smears at the bottom of the cup.

Her mother replied impatiently, "Your Aunt Meg, the nun. I'm very upset."

There was silence on the line for a moment. Mare's aunt had been out of the picture for a long time.

"Mare, are you there?" Not waiting for an answer, her mother went on. "The convent won't tell me how she died. They just said she's gone. Gone? Meg was barely fifty. I need you to go out there for me."

"Why can't you go?"

Mare resented her mother for various reasons. One was the fact that she never ran out of demands, most of them trivial and meaningless. Making a demand was like tugging an invisible apron string.

The voice on the phone turned wheedling. "You know I'm afraid of nuns."

"Meg was your sister."

"Don't be silly. It's the other nuns I'm afraid of. They're like scary penguins. Sign something so they can release the body. We're all she has—had." Her mother started crying softly. "Bring my dear sister home. Can you do that?"

Because no one had spoken of Aunt Meg in years, "dear sister" sounded a little insincere. But the job Mare was heading for was temp work, easy to call in sick for.

"I'll do what I can," she said.

Soon she was driving west on the turnpike, half listening to a James Taylor album that came out twenty years ago, about the time her rattling Honda Civic was born. The Great Recession had stalled a career that Mare hadn't actually chosen yet. Like others in her generation, she was drifting, worrying from month to month that she might have to move back in with her parents. That would mean choosing between them. Her mother stayed in the old house after the divorce. Her father relocated to Pittsburgh with his new wife and remembered to call on Christmas and birthdays, usually.

She glanced at herself in the rearview mirror, noticing a scarlet smudge where she'd been careless with her lipstick. *Why did she think nuns would want her to wear makeup?*

Before she ran off to the convent, Aunt Meg used to wear the most stunning shade of lipstick, a dark burgundy red; it contrasted with her pale Irish skin like a drop of wine on a linen tablecloth. There was no question Meg was a looker. She had high cheekbones and that elegant McGeary nose, their proudest feature. She hadn't turned into an old maid for any particular reason. (Meg liked the term "old maid," because it was so outdated and politically incorrect.) Men had vaguely drifted in and out of her life. "I've had my chances, don't you worry," she said tartly.

She even frequented singles bars in the day. "Nasty places," Meg said. "Soul killing."

Nobody remembered her as being especially religious, so it had come as a surprise, and not the pleasant kind, when Aunt Meg suddenly announced, at the ripe age of forty, that she was becoming a nun. She had had enough of her family role as the oldest unmarried sister, being on call to babysit, expected to shop and tend house whenever somebody fell sick, listening to nieces gossiping about their boyfriends before suddenly drawing up short and saying, with embarrassment, "I'm sorry, Aunt Meg. We can talk about something else."

It made the family feel guilty when she announced that she had asked to train as a novice. There was a nagging sense of *What did we do wrong?* Mare's grandmother had died of stomach cancer two years before. If her grandmother had ever held strong religious convictions, months of excruciating pain wiped them away. She didn't ask for Father Riley at the end, but she didn't resist when he showed up at her sickroom. Doped up on morphine, she was barely aware of the wafer and the wine as he lifted her head off the pillow for the Eucharist. Nobody knew whether to be glad that Gran hadn't lived to see the day a McGeary girl took the veil.

Mare's grandfather was adrift in lonely grief after his wife died, retreating into his house and keeping the lights off well past sunset. He mowed the front lawn every Saturday, but the weeds in the backyard grew rank and tall, like a cursed woods guarding a castle of sorrows. When Meg knocked at the door and told him she was entering the convent, he became more animated than he had been in months.

"Don't give yourself away. You're still good-looking, Meg. Lots of men would be proud to have you."

"Don't be such a fool," Meg retorted, blushing. She kissed him on the top of the head. "But thank you."

In the end, she shocked everyone by simply disappearing one night to join a strict Carmelite order that was completely cloistered. She wasn't going to be one of those modern nuns who wore street clothes and picked up some arugula at the supermarket. Once the doors of the convent shut behind her, Meg was never seen again. She left her apartment untouched, the furniture all in place, waiting patiently for a return that would never occur. Her dresses hung neatly in the closet, giving off the forlorn air of things turned useless.

Mare was eighteen when her aunt pulled this vanishing act. "The flight into Egypt," her mother called it, sounding bitter and neglected. "Not one real good-bye."

Being a big family didn't protect them from feeling the hole where Meg once had been. It seemed vaguely sinister that she never wrote or called for ten years. They hadn't heard anything until Mare's mother received the news that Sister Margaret Thomas, the ghost of someone they had known, was gone.

The convent was remote and not listed in the phone book, but GPS knew where to find it. "Turn left in three hundred yards," the voice advised. Mare took the turnoff; after another half mile through some overgrown woodland of pine and birch she slowed down. The convent grounds were protected by a high wrought-iron fence. The road ended at a gate flanked by a deserted sentry box. There was a rusty squawk box for visitors to announce themselves on.

Mare felt the awkwardness of her situation. How do you say you're here for a body? She raised her voice, as if the squawk box might be deaf.

"I'm here for Sister Margaret Thomas. I'm her niece."

No one answered; the box didn't even crackle. A moment passed, and Mare began to think she'd have to turn back. Then with a click the iron gate slowly swung open. She drove through.

In the distance sat a redbrick mansion, drearily Victorian under the gray sky. The old Honda's tires crunched on the gravel. Mare felt increasingly nervous, her mind flashing on Dickens and orphans without enough gruel to eat. The mansion was the real orphan, rescued by the church after it became a stately wreck.

Going up the long driveway to the convent, Mare brought her mind back to what she had to do. The woodland along the way was overgrown, but the grounds skirting the mansion were threadbare, stripped of the fountains and shrubbery that once adorned them. The place was probably built by a ruthless tycoon at a time when such immense piles were "summer cottages," serviced by their own private railway spur.

She parked her car at the end of the driveway and approached the front door. A stern hand-lettered sign hung next to the doorbell: "Silence is observed between vespers and terce. Do not disturb."

Terce? Mare couldn't remember what frighteningly early hour of the morning this meant—it made her shiver to imagine the nuns' bare penitent feet hitting cold stone floors before dawn. She rang the bell. After a reluctant moment she was buzzed in, just as anonymously as at the front gate. Cautiously she entered, allowing her eyes to adjust to the sudden drop in light. She found herself in a grand foyer. On one wall was a niche with a statue of the Virgin. Straight ahead a stout metal grill, divided into four-inch squares, blocked the way. The openings let visitors peer at the inhabitants without getting too close. The effect was a cross between a zoo and a jail.

In this case there was nobody to peer at. Mare took a seat on a rickety visitor's chair with a sagging cane bottom and waited. She began to worry that a nun would swoop down to scold her for dropping out of parochial school after the fifth grade, as if every sister in the area had gotten the guilty news. She gazed at the

sweeping staircase on the other side of the grill. When the place was a rich man's country retreat, those stairs had felt the pumps of satin-gowned debutantes skipping down to meet their beaus, she thought idly.

More time passed. The silence felt eerie and alien. The Carmelite order is unworldly, devoted solely to the rule of "prayer and toil." Mare had found a YouTube video about it. The nuns in the video smiled a lot. They greeted the interviewer from behind a metal screen like the one Mare was sitting at. The brash interviewer asked, "How long have you been behind bars?" The nuns laughed. As far as they were concerned, they were living on the right side of the bars.

Mare glanced at her watch. She had been there less than five minutes. *Let's get this over with,* she thought. It was sad, but trying to recapture Meg as she once was seemed pointless.

At last there was a soft tapping sound as a nun came downstairs— slowly, not swooping—and moved toward the visitor across a wide expanse of marble floor. She couldn't have been more than twenty. Mare had read that convents were having a hard time finding new members and were steadily growing older. Death was thinning the ranks.

"Sorry to keep you waiting," the young nun apologized with a shy smile. She didn't seem like the scolding type. She smelled faintly of laundry soap and Clorox. Her small hands were scrubbed red and raw; she hid them inside the sleeves of her habit when Mare noticed them. Mare resisted the impulse to cross herself.

"I've come about Sister Margaret Thomas," she said. Her nerves made her speak too loudly, creating an echo in the big empty space.

"Ah," said the young nun, who looked Hispanic and spoke with an accent. She had stopped smiling.

"I'm her niece," Mare added.

"I see."

The sister averted her eyes. Her face, encircled by a brown and white cowl, remained friendly, but it was giving nothing away.

Mare cleared her throat. "I don't know your procedures when somebody dies. It was very sudden, a shock."

"What do you mean?" The sister looked genuinely confused.

"You don't know? We got a phone message that Sister Margaret Thomas, my aunt, was gone. I'm here to claim the body. So if there are papers for me to sign, and if you have the number of a local funeral home . . ." Mare's voice trailed off.

Now the sister became alarmed. The faint roses in her soft cheeks suddenly turned pale. "That's not possible. You see—"

Mare cut her off. "You can't keep her and not notify the authorities."

"What? If you'll let me finish." The young nun raised both hands, asking for patience.

But Mare was getting suspicious. "She's not yours to just stick in the ground. How did she die anyway?" Mare tried to sound irate, but a doubt crossed her mind. Maybe the convent had legal possession of anyone who died in the order.

The sister wrung her hands. "Please, stop. Your aunt's not here anymore. She's gone. The whole thing's a misunderstanding."

A light came on in Mare's brain. "My mother assumed that 'gone' meant 'dead.'"

"No. Yesterday Sister Margaret Thomas didn't appear for terce, and her room was empty. We were very worried. We left a message at the only contact number on file. Our interaction with the outside world is minimal. That's the rule we live by. Are you Catholic?"

Mare nodded. She felt ridiculous and started to mumble an apology, but the young nun went on, her accent getting stronger. It took an effort for her not to get emotional.

"Margaret Thomas was our sister. She belonged to Christ, not to her family. But when a sister suddenly doesn't appear for

prayers and her room is deserted, *Dios mio*, we felt obliged to tell someone."

"So she simply left, and you don't know where she went?"

"Exactly. Forgive us. We didn't intend to hurt your heart."

"All right. There's nothing to forgive." Mare wanted to ease the distress of the sister, who seemed very vulnerable in her homespun brown habit and with her raw, red hands. But she was also curious.

"Just one thing. Can I see her room?"

"Oh dear. I'm afraid that won't be possible." Unable to hide her agitation, the sister suddenly turned to leave. She felt bad, but rules are rules. No one was getting past the screen.

Mare called after her. "What about her personal things? If she left any, I want to claim them. You said you didn't want to hurt my heart."

It felt manipulative to throw the young woman's words back at her, but Mare knew her mother wouldn't settle for "She's gone." One vanishing act from Aunt Meg was the limit.

The retreating sister didn't turn around. "Wait here," she muttered.

She scurried upstairs, and the grand foyer returned to silence. After a moment a new nun appeared on the sweeping staircase, which was beginning to look in Mare's eyes like a Hollywood prop fabricated solely for grand entrances. The new nun was older, perhaps seventy, and the habit that concealed her from head to toe like a brown cocoon couldn't disguise her arthritic gait. She looked unsteady as she dealt with the heavy cardboard box she was carrying in her hands. Padding across the marble floor toward the screen, the old nun nodded at an opening off to one side. It was just large enough to allow the cardboard box to slide through.

"That's all there is, I'm afraid," said the old nun. She was panting slightly, her upper lip moist from exertion. Like the young sis-

ter, she didn't introduce herself. Her eyes had remained downcast when Mare tried to look into them. Unlike the young sister, she gave off no waves of sympathy.

Mare mumbled a thank-you, but the old nun had already turned away.

It was time to vacate the eeriness. Mare lifted the box, which was bound in layers of packing tape. Although less than a foot square, the parcel felt as if it contained lead weights. There was a white envelope taped to the top in place of a label.

After she returned to the gray light outside and drew a breath of sharp winter air, Mare's head started to clear. Each step she took toward her car made her feel a little less hazy, as if she was waking up from a narcotic medieval spell. Her hand was on the handle of the car door, now frosted with flakes of snow, before she realized all the questions she had failed to ask.

She'd learned nothing about her aunt's last days in the convent. Had she left the cloister sick or well? Was she disgruntled? Were there signs of mental disturbance? Mare had read about old monks breaking decades of silence, only to reveal that they were insane, driven into hopeless psychosis by their fixation on God.

Suddenly she felt an ache in her wrists from toting the heavy parcel. Getting in the car, she dumped it beside her on the passenger seat. Snow was falling thick enough to blanket the windshield, turning the interior into a twilit cave. She turned on the windshield wipers and checked the radio for weather warnings. The morning forecast said a blizzard would arrive late in the day. Now it was barely two o'clock. The storm had swept in early.

Bald snow tires gave Mare a reason to rush back to the turnpike, but she sat there, gazing blankly at the hypnotic swipe of the windshield wipers. Then the parcel caught her eye, like an object of wonder. The right to open it really belonged to her grandfather, since Meg was his daughter and he was next of kin. But

Mare now saw that the envelope taped to the top wasn't blank. A message was scrawled in a fine spidery hand.

For You

Who was "you"? None of the sisters thought it meant them, or they would have opened the package. If Mare hadn't shown up, the box might have remained sealed and silent forever. Did Aunt Meg anticipate that "you" was certain to arrive? Mare reached over and tore away the envelope, which was affixed to the parcel with a scrap of Scotch tape. There was no one to tell her not to snoop.

There was a crisply folded note inside. Carefully she opened it, reading what was written in the same spidery hand.

Hello, Mare,

This is from the thirteenth disciple. Follow where it leads.

Yours in Christ,
Meg

CHAPTER *2*

Of all the ways to change the world, Frank Weston would never have picked bringing back miracles. First, he wasn't superstitious, and in his mind a miracle was just a superstition that enough gullible people believed in. Second, and more important, he was a reporter, and journalism is a career dependent on facts. (There's an old saying in journalism: "If your mother tells you she loves you, get a second source.") A miracle was the opposite of a fact.

But then the possibility of miracles entered his life through a side door: death.

One day a woman stood in front of Frank's desk.

"Excuse me," she asked. "Are you the obituaries man?"

Frank spoke without looking up from the copy he was editing.

"Down the hallway, second door on the right. Only he's not in. He's out on a story."

His lean, rangy body was sprawled in the battered lounge chair he'd dragged into the newsroom from his shambolic bachelor apartment. His face was hidden under the scooped visor of a baseball cap.

The woman wasn't to be put off. "Can you help me then? It's urgent."

Frank was on a tight deadline, so he had no intention of helping her, or anyone. But he knew he should at least look up before blowing the woman off.

"Mare?" he said, suddenly surprised.

He almost hadn't recognize her. She was swaddled up for winter. She'd pulled a woolen cap down over her forehead against the cold and wrapped a gray muffler high on her chin. Her eyes were hidden behind oversized sunglasses. But Frank remembered those eyes. He could still picture them—it didn't matter how many years had passed.

"You look like a double agent in all that gear, but it has to be you."

Mare took off the sunglasses, confused. Her eyes blinked in the harsh newsroom lighting. She clearly didn't remember him.

"This is awkward," said Frank, taking off the baseball cap so she could get a better look. "It's Frank, from college. Brendan's roommate?"

He had stirred a memory. "Oh, God. Brendan. We were freshmen. I only looked him up because our parish priest told me I should."

"Really? You made quite an impression. He talked about you all the time. And now I know why."

Being tall and self-confident, Frank had gotten into the habit of saying whatever he thought. He tried to ignore Mare's slight flinch.

"Sorry, I meant it as a compliment."

When she didn't respond, he thought about apologizing again, but decided against it. Instead he said, "What's this about an obituary?"

Her eyes, which were large and brown, betrayed anxiety. "I shouldn't be bothering you."

"No, it's okay. We're just short-staffed at the moment."

A nasty flu had taken out two reporters, and Malcolm, the regular obituaries writer, had rushed out to follow up a lead on a breaking story.

Frank straightened up in his chair. "Do you want to submit an obit? I can pass it on. Malcolm will get to it once he's back in the office. I can't promise it will be today." As he said all this, he kept wishing that Mare would remember him.

She shook her head. "I don't want to put in an obituary. I want to take one out."

"I'm sorry. Someone died by mistake?" He meant to be funny, but she didn't smile.

"No. I just don't think anybody needs to know about my aunt's death."

Frank flipped to a new screen on the iPad he used for writing stories. "If it was a private death notice . . ."

"It was. My mother submitted it this morning." Mare bit her lip nervously. "You have to cancel it."

"Like I said, all I can do is pass on the message."

Mare's face fell, and the corners of her mouth started to tremble. He saw how important this was to her.

"Wait, let me call down," he said.

He got hold of the head typographer, who wasn't thrilled. The obits page was already set. Frank did a little arm twisting. "I owe you one," he said and hung up. He directed a triumphant smile at Mare. "Done."

Her eyes lit up, and Frank watched the tension melt from her body, even though she was wearing a puffy down coat.

"Now maybe you can sit down?" he said.

She wavered, her eyes glancing at the door, but she took a seat on the other battered chair in the cubicle, unwrapping the gray muffler. She removed the stocking cap, and her light brunette hair fell close to her shoulders. "I think I'd better have some water," she said.

He fetched a paper cup of water from the office cooler, surprised at how quick he was to please her. *What did it mean?* He didn't know, but he wanted to find out.

Mare sipped the water and went quiet. Frank figured he had about thirty seconds before she took off again.

"I almost didn't remember your name," he said. "I've never known anyone named Mare." He had to start somewhere besides dying relatives.

"I get that a lot. It's short for Ann Marie," she replied absently, glancing at her watch.

Unless Frank called on his renowned powers of invention, she'd be out of his life again. "I'd like to see you," he blurted out. "When nobody's dead. Or not dead."

She sat back and crumpled the empty paper cup in her hand. She was pondering the situation, the way a hitchhiker wonders whether it's safe to get in a car. She made a calculation in her mind, and it must have come out in his favor.

"I have a secret, and I need to tell somebody. Not a complete stranger, I mean."

So she did remember him, however vaguely. When his roommate had aroused Frank's curiosity, he had wangled a seat behind her in a psych class. There were two hundred students in the room, but Frank must have made an impression.

"You can't trust a stranger," Frank said.

Mare nodded nervously. "But I have to talk to somebody. My family wouldn't understand. They'd probably call the police."

"Sounds ominous."

"No, it's not like a crime or anything."

She looked ready to take back her decision to trust him. Frank kept quiet. He had been a reporter long enough to know he couldn't press her.

She took a deep breath. "My aunt left a cardboard box behind

when she died. It was sealed with packing tape and addressed to me. What I found inside is disturbing."

Her pale hands fiddled with the dangling ends of her muffler. She bit her lip again, an unconscious tic, he figured.

"I'm pretty sure it must be stolen. That's why I don't want to announce her death. Not until I find out."

"What is it?"

"A church. Or maybe a cathedral. I can't tell which."

Mare saw the look on his face and caught herself. "A miniature church, I mean." Her hands made a shape in the air about nine inches around. "It looks old, and it seems to be made of gold."

"Wow."

"It's quite lovely, actually." Mare leaned forward, lowering her voice. "My aunt had no money. But in a way, I wasn't surprised. She was a nun."

"An order of nuns is into stealing?" Frank smiled indulgently.

Mare didn't smile back. "No, she was a Carmelite, but rebellious. She left the order very suddenly, probably under a cloud—at least I think so. We weren't close."

She was on the verge of telling him more, but something stopped her. "Why am I saying this to a reporter?"

"Because I'm the first person you actually know. Sort of know," said Frank.

"Maybe." But Mare wasn't reassured. Just the opposite. Her mental image of Frank was vague, a face in a crowded classroom that only stood out because he wore bright red suspenders. It took cockiness to do that. The last thing she needed right now was a cocky boy pretending to be a responsible adult.

She stood up, holding out a gloved hand. "Never mind. It's not your problem."

Frank didn't take her hand. "You have to go?" It was obvious the scales had swung against his favor.

"I'm late already. Thanks for keeping the death notice out of the paper."

Frank frowned. "I might be out of line, but you could be in real trouble. I don't have to be a reporter, you know. I can just be somebody who's ready to help. And I can keep a secret," he added.

"Really?" A smile crept into Mare's voice, despite her anxiety. The way Frank looked at her wasn't subtle. "Is this about wanting to see me again?"

"Is that so bad?" He made as if to straighten the necktie he wasn't wearing. "I'm presentable."

She took a moment to think about this. "Maybe we could go out for coffee. Now, if you can take a break. I'd be more comfortable someplace else."

Frank followed her eyes across the surrounding cubicles. There were about five reporters in the newsroom, where once there had been twice as many. The firing squad hadn't picked Frank off yet, but anyone could be next. After five-thirty, he and a few co-workers would grab a drink and complain about how they hadn't gotten a raise in two years, even though none of them dared to ask for one.

Frank snapped the cover on his iPad. "Now is perfect," he said, mentally kissing his deadline good-bye.

After throwing on his peacoat and leading Mare outside, Frank saw that it was snowing hard. The city was no stranger to the Arctic vortex, even before it became famous. The wind howled from the northeast, and the new snowfall added a layer of white frosting to the brown old snow piled up at the curb. He took Mare's arm, and they crossed the slippery street to the diner where Frank ate half his meals. For the first time that day, he felt good.

A minute later they were settled in a booth at the back of the diner. Mare scanned the menu silently, and then ordered a Greek yogurt with fruit salad. Frank ordered coffee, black.

When the waitress was gone, Mare smiled, looking directly at Frank. Confessing seemed to have calmed her nerves. Her eyes were like still pools no longer ruffled by the wind. *They are the most beautiful thing about her,* Frank thought, distracted for a moment.

"I'll tell you the whole story," Mare said, "and then I can show you what my aunt gave me. I tucked it in the laundry hamper in my closet. I really hope it's not stolen, but it must be."

"Maybe she was just guarding it," Frank suggested. "The Catholic Church has a lot of treasures."

"Maybe."

Mare lost her smile. But she didn't object when Frank took out a spiral notebook and began taking notes. Her story was as strange as promised. He ordered two refills of coffee before she finished telling it. Halfway through, he had already decided that her aunt was either a saint or a nut who needed to be put on stronger meds. Either way, Frank was pretty certain he could rule out archcriminal.

CHAPTER *3*

Mare's eyes took in her cramped studio apartment. "Sorry for how it looks," she said.

A dangling naked lightbulb was covered with a Japanese paper lantern to soften its glare. The room held a few sticks of Ikea furniture, a tired mustard yellow sofa handed down from better decades, and a framed poster of a scared kitty dangling from a branch (the ubiquitous one that says, "Hang in There"). On the far wall was a closed door. Frank suspected a Murphy bed was lurking behind it, since there was no bed in sight.

Mare followed Frank's glance to the poster. "Not mine. I'd take it down, but it was a gift."

She kept the place tidy, what there was of it. All she could afford was a converted basement in an old triple-decker that started life as an Irish boarding house. Mare's apologies had started at the curb before she and Frank even entered the yard enclosed by a chain-link fence. Withered junipers did nothing to beautify the sagging wreck of a building. Self-consciously, she led the way down a set of creaky stairs off the side of the house. Their shoes punched through the crusted old snow that no one had shoveled from the walk.

She shouldn't have bothered with her apologies. At the moment the only thing on Frank's mind was seeing the miniature church she had hidden in a laundry hamper. Somebody had gone to the expense of gilding it, or even making it out of solid gold. Frank suspected there might be something locked inside that was even more precious to a believer. What do you call the receptacle that holds a saint's bones? A reliquary. It would border on blasphemy, but he wanted to hold the little church up to his ear and shake it. The sacred bones inside, if that's what was hiding there, would rattle, unless they had already crumbled to dust.

As long as he was speculating, what about the incidental mysteries that swirled around Mare? Why had her mother put a death notice in the paper? She had no real evidence her sister was dead, just a cryptic phone message from the convent.

Frank had put this question to Mare on the ride across town. All she did was shake her head and say, "You don't know what she's like. My mother always assumes the worst."

"But your aunt is out there somewhere. You told her that, right?"

"Yes. I told her everything I told you, except about the box."

At every red light, Mare's car had skidded on the icy streets. Frank was a bad passenger; he held a tight grip on the door handle to keep from grabbing the wheel.

"Maybe the wish is father of the deed," he suggested.

Mare gave him a puzzled glance. "What's that supposed to mean?"

Another skid zone was coming up at the next corner, where a big furniture truck was sliding halfway through the yellow light.

"Just keep us alive, okay?" Frank said. "I meant that if your mother resented her sister vanishing like that ten years ago, she might not be thrilled to have her back."

"So she makes her dead?"

"I'm just thinking out loud. Where do you suppose your aunt would go? You should have pumped the nuns for information."

"Says the man who has so much experience pumping nuns for information. Have you ever tried?"

"Point taken."

Other questions were on the tip of Frank's tongue, until he remembered his promise not to act like a reporter. He kept quiet the rest of the way, and so did Mare. He noticed that her knuckles were turning white seizing the steering wheel. One step at a time, he told himself.

Inside her apartment, Mare tossed some shoes aside in the bottom of her closet and brought out a laundry hamper. A dirty sheet was on top, ready to be pulled back like a stage curtain.

"Once you see it, you're kind of complicit, aren't you?" Mare asked.

"In a way, I guess. Assuming we don't turn it over to the police."

"Yes, assuming that."

Frank caught a new note in her voice. She had sounded guilty and furtive, but this was something different. Greed, was it? But that would be understandable. The fantasy of finding buried gold was part of growing up, and now it had pretty much come true for her. How far would she go to keep it? Before revealing the treasure to him, she could still change her mind, and the gold's secret would be safe.

Mare hadn't turned back, though. She stood over the laundry hamper, and with a whisk she lifted the sheet, revealing the reliquary. It looked exactly like a miniature church. If the naked lightbulb hadn't had a paper lantern on it, the gleam of pure gold would have hurt their eyes. The object was the size of a loaf of bread. Even hollow, it would be heavy.

"Who's going to lift it out?" Frank asked.

"I'll let you, if that's okay."

Frank wrapped his hands around the miniature church, and as the object emerged from its hiding place, he could see how beautiful it was, carefully wrought on all sides with etched flourishes, tiny flowers, and a border of summer grass fringing the bottom. The conceit was of a chapel sitting in a meadow. The peaked roof was adorned with gothic steeples at the corners, each one topped with a cross. Delicate enamel medallions were embedded on the four walls, painted with scenes from the life of Jesus.

Frank was too astonished to do anything but make light of it. "As the world's leading art experts would say, 'Wow.'"

They gazed at the treasure. Frank had been raised as a Christmas-Easter churchgoer by his lax Methodist parents (in the vernacular, their kind are called "Chreasters" by the regular congregation), but at that moment he felt what a devout believer must feel: reverence, wonder, awe. *That's the trick of great art,* he thought, and he hadn't the slightest doubt that they were in the presence of great art.

"It must have a home somewhere. Somebody knows it's missing," he murmured, finding it hard not to whisper, as if they were in church. "They would have reported it stolen to the local authorities or the FBI."

He'd read about the thousands of paintings stolen from museums every year and the special agencies that track them down. Not to mention the Nazis and their wholesale looting. They had boosted millions of dollars' worth of artworks from all over Europe to haul back to Hitler's Berlin.

Heavy as it was, the miniature chapel didn't have the weight of a solid object. But Frank was too spellbound to rattle it, even though he still suspected that something precious was locked inside. To true believers, that was the whole point. The gold exterior was just a distraction to dazzle the eyes.

For pilgrims in the Middle Ages, traveling immense distances across Europe in search of relics was a costly and dangerous business. After all the trials and dangers of their journey, when they reached a shrine, they expected to be awed before a holy relic— a piece of the True Cross, the jawbone of John the Baptist, the spear that pierced Jesus's side. There had to be a payoff, and if there weren't enough true relics to go around, well, what better way to convince pilgrims that a dubious relic was authentic than to strike awe with shining gold?

Frank's own sense of awe was quickly yielding to more practical thoughts. "I don't think it's empty," he said. "Did you shake it?"

"No, I couldn't."

"Because it's sacrilege?"

"Isn't it?"

"We need to get inside," Frank declared firmly.

But how? It would draw heavy suspicion to try and get the object X-rayed at a museum laboratory, not to mention the expense. There couldn't be many machines that can see through gold. And what would the faint ghostly image of some old bones really tell them? Frank's impatience grew. He was about to shake the reliquary without her permission when Mare touched his hand.

"I suddenly had the strangest feeling. There's someone sleeping inside it. I can feel it."

"And you don't think we should wake them up?"

"Something like that."

Frank shook his head. "Let's assume for the moment that your idea isn't crazy. We don't know if waking them up is good or bad."

"It wouldn't matter. Not if they are meant to sleep."

Before he could respond, the gate in the chain-link fence clinked, and a shadow passed across the room's only window, which was small and high up, letting in a feeble light from the outside. Someone was approaching. If they burst in, the first thing

they'd see would be a man kneeling on the floor surrounded by five pairs of women's shoes and a woman turning red, her hand clapped over her mouth with embarrassment. It wasn't the time to wake the sleeping or the dead.

"Hurry!" Mare exclaimed.

Frank dropped the reliquary back into the hamper, and she threw the sheet back over it. Was she about to be arrested for having it in her possession?

"Wait, don't talk. Listen," said Frank.

Click, click, click. A woman's light, tapping step. It was unmistakable. The police wouldn't be storming the place in high heels. Frank had no time to wonder what kind of woman wears stilettos in the snow.

A very irritated woman, it turned out. There was a sharp rap at the door. Mare opened it nervously. The intruder on their privacy was tall and in her sixties, her graying hair pulled back tightly from her face, which at that moment wore an impatient grimace.

"I won't ask if you have come into possession of a package," she said. "You'd probably just lie." Her voice was clipped and efficient, the kind of voice that meant business.

Mare couldn't hide her nerves. "Who are you?"

"Miss Marple. Perhaps you've heard of me."

"What?"

"My name is Lilith. That's enough for now. I'd advise you to let me in."

Mare gave a weak nod and stepped aside. Lilith looked around the modest apartment with a critical eye.

"You never know where you'll wind up, do you?" she murmured, addressing no one in particular. For the moment she ignored Frank, who stood in front of the open closet.

"Your Aunt Meg is alive," she said. "But you've probably figured that out already, haven't you?"

"What do you have to do with her?" asked Mare.

Lilith thought for a moment. "I'm a connection, just as she is. That's one way to put it." She plopped herself down on the mustard yellow couch, which gave a tired groan. "When your aunt disappeared from the convent, something precious disappeared with her."

"Then you'd have to ask her about that," Mare replied.

"Don't play coy. The trail leads here and nowhere else."

Mare lowered her head, and Lilith's eyes narrowed.

"That's what I thought," she said before turning her attention to Frank.

"And you are who? The boyfriend?"

"Imagine what you like," he replied.

She shrugged. "No. You're not the boyfriend. She's clearly nervous, but you didn't rush in to help her or even put your arm around her. A boyfriend would have."

"No comment."

"Why can't he just be a friend?" Mare asked.

Lilith smiled knowingly. "Because you did something rash. You invited a strange man into your house. For what reason?"

"None of your business," Frank snapped.

Lilith fixed him with a hard stare. "I'm more likely to figure out your game before this young woman does."

Frank bristled. "There is no game."

"Really? You plan to get the goods and the girl at the same time, or will you have to choose?"

Frank turned red, but before he could deny the accusation, Lilith held up her hand.

"You're right. It's none of my business what you're up to. I'm here about the gold shrine. It holds the key to everything."

Mare had been moving toward the closet, either to guard the treasure or show it to Lilith. Frank couldn't be sure. He shot her a warning glance. If Lilith noticed, she chose to ignore it.

She said, "The trouble is, whoever has the shrine *is* meant to have it. That's the first of the secrets I can tell you." She gave Mare a smile that was almost friendly. "You're the rightful owner, I promise you."

Mare looked so relieved that she would have blurted out everything that had happened since the phone call from the convent, but Frank stopped her. "We're not giving this shrine or whatever it is, just because you deliver a load of mumbo jumbo."

Lilith smirked. "There, that's more like a boyfriend."

Frank changed tack. As a reporter, he'd learned to handle all kinds of difficult people, and his first rule was, you catch more flies with honey than with vinegar.

"Maybe we can work something out," he said.

"We? Who gave you the right to say 'we'?" Mare cried. "I don't really know either of you."

She spoke in a loud, anxious voice, and the other two stared at her. Up to this point she'd played the part of the quiet observer, a shaky fawn caught in a room with two bulls.

"I didn't mean anything," Frank stammered.

"No?" said Mare. She took a deep breath, trying to regain her composure. But her heart was racing. Her body couldn't deny the threat it was feeling.

"You pushed too hard," Lilith said smoothly. "That's what insensitive people do."

She turned to Mare. "And you need to calm down. I'm only here to help."

Lilith brushed stray bits of snow sticking to her high heels. "I appreciate your wariness. We all have to be as sharp-witted as possible from now on. There are invisible forces at work. Do you imagine the gold shrine came to you, or to your Aunt Meg, by accident?"

The atmosphere in the room was still tense, but a subtle shift had taken place. It was now the tenseness of a mystery more than

the tenseness of a threat. Lilith took advantage of this. To Frank she said, "You noticed my shoes when I came in. What do they tell you?"

"They tell me that you were doing something else—maybe eating at a fancy restaurant—before you suddenly got the news that brought you here. No time to change."

"So you're a rationalist," Lilith said approvingly. "You reached for a logical explanation. Someone else might assume I was eccentric or out of touch with reality."

"Are you?" Mare asked. She had wandered over to the corner of the studio that served as a kitchen and was holding a battered teakettle under the faucet.

"That's right," said Lilith. "Make tea. It will calm your nerves." Her tone had become less confrontational. "Your mother is still frantic. I apologize, but we can't let her in on any of this. I hope you understand."

"Outside attention would be unwelcome," said Frank.

"Exactly."

Mare turned on the tap, talking over the knocking sound of old plumbing. "But I don't understand. Do you know where my aunt is?"

"She's here in the city."

"Can I see her?"

"Not yet. After all, you haven't wanted to see her for a long time. No need to rush."

Mare went silent, considering what to say next, when her cell phone rang. She went to her purse, pulled it out, and examined the caller ID.

"My sister Charlotte," she said doubtfully.

"Answer it," Lilith advised. "She'll be suspicious if you avoid her."

Mare took the call, and from across the room Frank could hear the angry buzz of her sister's voice. Questions were being jabbed

at Mare, which she fended off with short replies. But it wasn't the words that mattered. Frank sensed that they were closing in. He had no idea who "they" were, but his antennae were out, picking up signals. Mare was the innocent; that part wasn't in doubt. Lilith was a wild card, and behind her seemed to loom hidden figures, hinted at but invisible so far.

Mare closed her outdated cell phone with a click, cutting short the conversation. She looked worried.

"You won't be able to keep your nosey sister away for long," Lilith warned.

"But that doesn't mean we should trust you, does it?" Frank snapped.

Mare let the "we" slip past without comment this time. Her bewilderment outweighed her doubts about Frank.

He crossed the room and held her hand. "Don't be scared. We're in the strong position here, just remember that," he said quietly.

"Touching," Lilith remarked. "But you're not allies yet, not by a long shot. The only ally anyone has is tucked away in there." She pointed toward the closet, which had so obviously been the place Mare was anxious to conceal. "One of you is dazzled by the gold, because that person has a crass mind. But one of you is sensitive, and that person will pierce to the heart of the mystery."

She saw the dark expression on Frank's face. "We'll get nowhere fighting. I propose we get down to business instead. Are we agreed?" she asked.

Lilith sat back, waiting while tea bags were put into chipped blue-and-white china cups and water poured in. When the tea was brewed, she began talking.

"This all goes back ten years ago. Your Aunt Meg woke up one morning from a bad dream. It was an unusually cold winter, like this one. Her sleep had been restless. She crawled out of bed, trying

to shake off her dream, but she couldn't. It wouldn't let her go. You see, it wasn't a dream at all. It was a vision. She hadn't asked for one. It seems rude of God to interrupt a person's nice, comfortable life with something so inconvenient. But what can you do?"

Frank gave her a disgusted look. "Nobody you can trust hauls in God."

"You sound very bitter," said Lilith calmly. "Did someone hurt you, to make you lose your faith? Or is that something you'd rather keep hidden?"

"None of your damn business!"

Frank threw down his teacup, which missed the table and clattered on the floor. "I don't know who you are. But Mare doesn't deserve to be played by a manipulative bitch."

He turned to Mare for support, but she surprised him.

"I want to hear this out." she said quietly.

"Why? It's garbage."

Mare was firm. "You've gotten yourself worked up. Maybe you should go."

"And leave you with her?" Frank was incredulous. "She'll be on you like a cheap suit."

Mare didn't reply, but got up and walked to the door. Frank grabbed his peacoat and followed, fuming.

"I'll call you tomorrow," Mare said, trying to sound reassuring.

Frank shook his head. "You're going to be sorry. That's all I can say."

He trudged up the rickety stairs, and a moment later his shadow went across the grimy window as he tramped through the snow.

Mare closed the door and returned to where Lilith sat, waiting.

"I need to hear the rest of this," she said. "For my peace of mind."

Lilith shook her head. "No, you need to hear it because God wants the story to come out."

CHAPTER 4

Elsewhere in the city, a man was plotting a supreme act of revenge. To look at him, you'd never credit Galen Blake with violence in his heart. It's true that he wore an outdated badge of the revolution—his round, wire-rimmed glasses, which were known as Trotsky glasses in the Seventies, when Galen went to college.

Little round glasses are associated with Harry Potter now. Galen had vaguely heard of Harry Potter. He preferred fact to fiction, with the exception of science fiction, which Galen consumed in binges, the technical kind of sci-fi where computers and robots rebel against their foolish human masters. He was fifty-six, short, and unassuming. He was a loner, retreating from social contact as predictably as his hairline had retreated after he turned forty.

Loners plan acts of violence for various reasons. Delayed revenge for being bullied on the playground at school. Inner desperation that can't find an outlet. Fantasies of grandiosity. But Galen suffered from none of these. His motive was not clearly formulated in the logical part of his brain. It was swallowed up in the hurt and hate that swirled inside him.

However, the main contenders for Galen's hatred were God and love, the two biggest hoaxes in the world. For a long time he had mistrusted love. He knew early on that this was necessary

if he wanted to survive. Young Galen came home from school one day to find his mother standing in the kitchen surrounded by sheets of chocolate chip cookies, warm and fragrant. She sat him down and silently watched him eat as many cookies as he wanted. She offered no warning that gobbling down so much sugar would make him sick. She waited until he could eat no more before telling him the bad news. They were alone; from now on, there would be no more Daddy, because Galen's father had walked out, abandoning them.

Even at ten Galen knew it wasn't healthy to be the only person in his mother's life. She worried about this too, but worry didn't help. She clung to him until she died; Galen was in his thirties. He came home from the funeral, ripping off his black tie and opening his collar so he could breathe. It was a hot July day. He went into the bathroom to splash cold water on his sweaty face.

He caught a glimpse of himself in the mirror over the sink. *You're lucky,* a voice in his head told him. *No more mother. Father gone. You're free.*

The face in the mirror—pale, pudgy, with circles under the eyes—brightened up. *Free!* Galen loved his mother, but she fretted constantly about his being unmarried. "My son's a confirmed bachelor," she told her friends, who took this as code for "gay." Galen wasn't gay. He was just born to be alone, which other people, including his mother, couldn't comprehend. So losing her was like losing one more person who didn't understand.

These sketchy facts might have helped the police after Galen committed his act of revenge. But what do they really say? His worst secret was that he had no secrets.

No one observed his silent plotting. The plan he had in mind was simple, if extreme. It unfolded on a Wednesday, the day the city art museum was open to the public for free. Galen wandered in, mingling with the crowd, staring blankly at the gallery walls as if they were empty. His mind was solely fixed on the task at hand.

He headed upstairs, turning right, then left, before reaching a small, dimly lit gallery on the second floor. It was filled with people craning to see the old masters, but Galen was interested in only one work, a priceless *Madonna and Child* from fifteenth-century Florence.

He paused to take in the painting, loathing what most viewers adored—the rosy, glowing faces of mother and child, those ideal emblems of love. Galen snarled with disgust. The guard standing in the doorway turned her back for a moment. With a small inconspicuous motion Galen reached into his overcoat and pulled out a can of red spray paint. He stepped forward.

"Hey!" somebody yelled.

Galen sped up until he was directly in front of the masterwork, aiming the nozzle at the smiling, chubby baby Jesus. The visitor who yelled out took a dive for him. Galen only finished spraying a single letter, *L,* before he was tackled and pinned to the floor.

"Crazy bastard," muttered the man who had knocked Galen down. He was a middle-aged tourist from Michigan, burly enough to have probably played college football. At that second it wasn't clear if he swore because he loved art or because the red paint had hit his jacket, which now had a large *L* on it. Galen had missed the canvas entirely.

A loud racket broke out, of running feet, shouting voices, an angry alarm bell. Galen lay quietly in the middle of the erupting chaos, staring at the ceiling. He put up no resistance when the police arrived. At the precinct he was given a form to fill out—name, age, current address, phone number—like waiting at the dentist's office. When offered his legally allowed phone call, Galen said he wanted to talk to a reporter from the local paper.

"I want to report a lie," he said calmly, reciting the word beginning with *L* that he had tried to spray across baby Jesus. "There is no mercy. There is no God. Love is a fiction. People have to wake up."

The desk sergeant was indifferent. "Reporters will be crawling all over this. You don't need to phone them. Call your lawyer," he advised. "Unless you have a shrink."

But Galen insisted. Using the desk phone and the yellow pages, he dialed a number but only reached an answering machine.

"No one's picking up," he told the desk sergeant.

"Too bad. Off you go."

Galen paced his cell, practicing the speech he intended to deliver when he got his moment. An hour passed, then two. He was slumped on the floor in the corner when a guard came by and unlocked the steel door.

"It's your lucky day. No one's pressing charges."

Galen slowly got to his feet. So the whole thing had been a waste, a joke to pile on top of God's other jokes. Behind the scenes, the museum officials had worked it all out. They couldn't afford the bad publicity from prosecuting him. The museum's fortunes depended on big traveling exhibitions. If word got out that their collection was this vulnerable, it would become twice as hard to borrow precious masterworks from other museums. Their insurance would skyrocket. Anyway, the *Madonna and Child* had come through unscathed.

As he was being discharged, Galen caught a young man in jeans and a T-shirt staring at him.

"Are you the guy?" the young man asked. He looked about nineteen.

"Leave me alone," Galen grumbled, scooping up his things, the small change, wallet, and belt collected by the police. The kid grabbed up his parka from the waiting bench and followed him outside.

"I'm sorry you couldn't carry out your mission," he said. "Well, not sorry, exactly. Listen, there's still a story here."

"About what, a loony or a laughingstock?" Galen looked up

and down the street, but there were no cabs. He'd left his car at home that morning.

The kid stuck out his hand. "Name's Malcolm. I'm a reporter. I just want to hear your side of the story."

Galen stared blankly at the proffered hand. He turned up the street, heading for the nearest bus stop, which was two blocks north. Malcolm trailed after him. Galen didn't brush him off. As much as he felt humiliated, he still wanted to talk to someone who'd listen.

"Are you on the crime beat?" he asked.

"No crimes so far. I do obituaries, only your story got priority. We have two guys out with the flu."

Great, Galen thought mockingly. *I'm a notch more interesting than the dead.*

He had been stoked on adrenaline all morning, and he realized that he was starving.

Under his parka the kid reporter looked underfed.

"I'll buy you a burger," Galen offered. He couldn't bear the idea of crawling back home yet.

They crossed over to a fast-food franchise, put in their order, and sat down at a plastic table and chairs away from the freezing draft that blew in every time a customer entered. Galen felt a compulsion to wipe the tabletop clean, but restrained himself.

Malcolm pulled out a mini tape recorder. "You mind?"

Galen shrugged.

The reporter wore a smile, but he wasn't thrilled when he first set eyes on the suspect, who looked like a rumpled English professor, completely harmless. The terrorist angle would have been great for Malcolm's career, but it was quickly fading. He clicked on the machine. The tape whirred quietly between them on the table.

"One, two, three. Okay, we're recording now. So why did you do it?"

"Because everything is a lie," Galen said firmly, using the same tone of voice he'd use to return an overcooked steak: matter of fact and displeased.

"Um, can you be more specific?" Malcolm asked. "Do you belong to a movement or something?"

"No. I belong to the mass of humanity who have been swindled for centuries by the biggest lie ever perpetrated." Galen suddenly felt his rage boiling up. "Belief in God has killed more people in history than all genocides put together. Where is mercy, where is love? It's all a monstrous lie." His eyes were glistening now with the fervor of his words.

A nut job, Malcolm thought to himself. But a hint of the terrorist angle was still breathing, on life support.

"Is there a version of God you think needs defending?"

"No. Weren't you listening? I said it's all a lie. Religion is mass hypnosis, and countless people fall victim to it every day."

"Including you? Something must have happened to you. How did God hurt you personally?"

Galen hesitated. He wasn't all that sure how God had hurt him. The whole thing was a jumble. Iris's mad love, the angel paintings, her certainty that she was on some kind of spiritual mission. It had all glommed together in Galen's mind, a festering mass.

"I don't matter," he said insistently. He searched for words. "If God is love, then all love is tainted. That's the gist. That's the thing nobody sees."

"So your message is 'Down with God'? You weren't trying to improve the painting with a little squirt of red?"

"Don't mock me."

"I guess what I'm saying is, a lot of people hate religion or whatever. Not a lot of people vandalize art."

Galen sat back in the flimsy plastic chair. "You don't give a damn, do you?"

"How I feel isn't the point."

"Right."

They were interrupted by hearing their number called. When Galen started to stand up, Malcolm preempted him. "Let me get this." He trotted off and soon returned with a tray of burgers and drinks. "A bit of goodwill," he said brightly.

But Galen's mood was dark. He felt as if he was slowly deflating inside with a faint whoosh, shrinking into a curled-up ball. For a few minutes the two didn't speak, distracted by their food.

In the silence Malcolm reassessed the story, if there was a story. It wouldn't have legs as a feature, not without charges being pressed. He clicked off the mini recorder and put it away in his pocket.

"Wait. You haven't let me finish," Galen complained.

"I've got enough for now."

Malcolm felt sorry for the nut job slumped in his chair knowing he had botched everything. "Frankly, you'd be better off if this whole thing dies down quickly. Put it behind you," he said.

Wadding up the napkin from his burger, Malcom took a shot at a trash bin in the corner, sinking the paper ball in one clean motion, and then stood up.

"No harm, no foul. Okay?"

When Galen looked away, a pained expression on his face, the reporter shrugged. At least he'd have an anecdote for his buddy Frank back at the paper.

"Can I offer you a lift?"

Galen was too upset to do anything but shake his head. His eyes followed the kid out the door. Any chance to get justice went out into the cold with him.

CHAPTER 5

For every strange event that had unfolded so far, Meg McGeary was the absent element. Was she pulling invisible strings? What gave her the right to? Ten years ago Meg didn't stand out for any reason. She could easily have blended into the bustling holiday shoppers at the local outdoor mall. She was forty then, dressed in suburban style: gray parka with fake-fur trim around the hood, baggy jogging pants, and running shoes. Society was changing, so the absence of a wedding ring wouldn't have made her stick out. One thing did, though. On a particular day in November, she was standing stock-still, her eyes fixed on the distance, as if mesmerized by the front of a Subway sandwich shop and the Nike store next door.

The sun was shining feebly through a patchwork of clouds. Shoppers were feeling flush—the Great Recession hadn't yet burst the bubble—and nobody took notice as they walked around Meg. An alert passerby might have suspected that something was very wrong with a woman glued in place. Maybe she was having some kind of psychotic break that made her go catatonic. For now, though, the crowd parted and swirled around Meg like the sea swirling around a rock jutting out from the beach.

Meg wasn't psychotic, but she wasn't normal either. She was suffering from extreme disorientation—and with good reason. In her mind she was on her way to be crucified. Literally. Before noon, she would be hanging from a tall wooden cross. Roman soldiers were going to drive long iron nails through her hands. She could see the angry mob thirsty for her blood.

The "thing," as she called it, started that morning. Her cat had woken her up from a bad dream by clawing at her chest through the coverlet. Outside, winter darkness had cleared. Meg's bare feet hit the cold floor, searching for a pair of fuzzy slippers. She padded down a hallway to the bathroom and stared at herself in the medicine-cabinet mirror.

A puffy face with frowzy bed hair stared back. Yet she also saw an ancient biblical city in the mirror, as if two films were superimposed in a projector. Suddenly the ancient city came to life. People in robes lined the street, eager for a vicious spectacle. Like actors in a silent movie, they jeered at her without making a sound.

Meg was dimly aware that this was the same dream that had kept her awake all night. She splashed cold water on her face to make it go away, but it didn't. Whether she looked in the mirror, out the bathroom window, or at the white-tiled walls, this other scene played—a hot day, the sun burning down from a clear sky, bystanders straight out of Sunday school illustrations. Meg's feet were snug in her slippers, but the man's feet wore sandals and felt hot. She was certain now, with waking clarity, that it was a man. His breathing was heavy as he gazed around at the mob, fighting against his fear. Meg could feel the pressure in his lungs. Was he carrying something heavy on his back? She suddenly felt an enormous weight.

Meg decided to call Clare, the closest of her two sisters. Back to the bedroom she walked, with nervous steps. The cat lay curled

up by the radiator, opening one eye to watch Meg dig around in her purse for her cell phone. Yet the minute she pushed the button for Clare's work number, she thought, *Bad idea. She's a worrier. This will ruin her day.*

Before Meg could hang up, however, Clare answered. "Hey you," she said, expectantly.

"Hey," Meg mumbled mechanically.

"You sound sleepy."

"I'm not sleepy."

"Well, it's nice to hear your voice. It's been a madhouse with the kids out of school and me working." Clare, who had moved to another city after she got married, was always in motion, building her realty business.

"If anyone can cope, it's you," said Meg. She was stalling, disoriented. The movie became twice as vivid now. The man stumbled to his knees under his crushing burden, then struggled to regain his footing. Meg could feel his back muscles cry out in pain. This wasn't a movie. She was inside him.

Clare's worry radar kicked in. "Sweetie, is something wrong? Why are you really calling?"

Luckily, a flickering gap appeared in the movie just then, which gave Meg an opening to think straight. "I was feeling a little lonely. We never connect the way we used to."

"I know. It's been weeks. I'm sorry."

Her sister's voice, which had anxiously risen a few notes, came back down. Clare was usually good about not losing touch. She was good about a lot of things.

"So maybe you should come for a visit?"

"I'd like that," said Meg.

"You won't mind the kids being underfoot?"

"No, it's all great." Meg desperately wanted the call to end.

"All right, sweetie. Love you."

It was a relief to stop pretending, and the call hadn't been a disaster. But as soon as she hung up, Meg was in pain again, gasping and bent over. She tried taking deep breaths, but it didn't help. The movie in her head relentlessly unspooled. The man had regained his footing and was stumbling forward again, sweating heavily now.

Who else could she call? It was a depressingly short list. Nancy Ann, her other sister, would freak out. She rarely left the house without thinking that she had forgotten to lock the front door or left the gas on. Her mother was totally preoccupied with whatever her husband wanted. Some girlfriends came to mind, coworkers at the bank where Meg was assistant manager, but they'd probably laugh and hang up on her.

Meg began to panic. The four walls were closing in, suffocating her. She had to get back in control. A dose of reality might be the best medicine—inhaling the cold winter air, mixing with people. This idea sounded sane. She hastily threw on some clothes and rushed downstairs, squeezing past a bicycle and some moving boxes piled in the foyer. The smell of bacon frying in one of the apartments made her feel faintly sick, but the sensation of nausea distracted her from the movie. *That must be a good sign, right?* On her way out, Meg remembered to call her assistant and tell her she was taking a sick day.

It wasn't far to the outdoor mall. Meg had gotten into the habit of wandering there after work. She didn't do this out of loneliness. At forty, being single had settled in. It felt like something between a comfortable armchair and a stain on the wallpaper you can't be bothered to fix.

She set a brisk pace. It was hard to keep her balance, though, trying to rush when he was struggling just to put one foot in front of the other. He looked up. A hill loomed in the distance. Two dangling silhouettes were outlined against the sun, already

hanging from crosses. Meg shuddered, trying to get back into present time, and quickened her pace.

Five minutes later she was standing in the central square of the mall. Despite her parka, she was freezing. The wind cut through her, biting with wintry fangs.

Something new was happening in the movie. She could feel the ground sloping upward. He was climbing the hill. Behind him a soldier gave a hard shove. The centurion was anxious to return to barracks and get drunk. A third cross was outlined against the sun. The condemned man searched the waiting mob for a friendly face. One young girl was crying, and when he set eyes on her, she shifted her head scarf to hide her tears. He barely caught a glimpse of her, but all at once Meg felt a wave of relief wash over him. More than relief. A deep sense of peace entered him. It erased his fear, and he stopped struggling against what was to come.

The chants of the mob grew obscene, but the man's sense of peace only deepened. The world and its terrifying images faded like a candle flickering invisibly in the noonday sun.

The procession arrived at its destination. He had only an instant to look back at the girl who felt pity for him. He wanted her to see that he was at peace, but she was gone. He didn't think about the crushing finale of his drama. He only wondered what would become of her.

This is where the movie in Meg's head jammed. The images stopped unspooling. The crosses on the hill vanished. Suddenly she was just herself, standing motionless in a crowd, with no idea of how long she had been frozen in place. Tilting her head back, she no longer saw two suns, only the feeble November sun of the present. There was no lingering fear. It was almost as if nothing had happened. But it had, undeniably. Meg noticed a few peculiar looks from people as they walked around her. Time to move on.

So she did. A few minutes longer, and they'd be calling security to take her away.

Two weeks passed. Meg would have forgotten her road to Calvary if she could have. She did her best. Others noticed no blips in her daily routine at work. She still arrived every morning at seven thirty to open the bank. She still took her place at her big desk near the front and smiled reassuringly when young couples nervously approached her about taking out their first home loan. She was genuinely comfortable in her work, never a boss hater or a cause for the assistants she supervised to even remotely hate her.

If a surveillance camera had tracked her every movement, it would have recorded only one odd occurrence, a minor deviation from her normal routine. One night, after leaving the bank, she stopped at a pharmacy near her apartment building, where she asked for the strongest sleeping aid she could buy without a prescription. When she got home, she watched old reruns of *Friends,* ate a Lean Cuisine Chicken Parmesan, and took two of the pills before going to bed. Better to be in a faint chemical haze in the morning, Meg figured, than to revisit the terrible images of her hallucination.

But the echoes still sounded. She couldn't ignore the faint cries of woe that came from inside her. They almost went away if she distracted herself with work and TV or if she turned up the car radio. But there are only so many ways to escape your inner world. The horrifying images in her vision were actually easier to bear. Meg had seen them every day on the walls of her old Catholic school during the Bible class run by the Sisters of St. Joseph. The problem was that now she had lived those images. Who did that? Only saints and psychotics, so far as Meg knew, and she didn't fit into either category. She struggled to imagine a third possibility.

Anxiety comes equipped with a volume control, and the more Meg ignored the wailing voice inside her, the louder it became, little by little. By the third week, the volume of her anxiety was

so loud, she could barely hear anything else. It was hard to keep her composure when she went to her parents' house for Sunday dinner.

"You're unusually quiet," her mother commented at the table. "You've liked my corned beef and cabbage since the day you were born."

Meg managed to smile, because this was only a slight exaggeration. Her mother said the smell of the dish brought back the green hills of Galway, although she hadn't literally come from Ireland or even visited it. She came from near the railroad tracks in Pittsburgh. Still, corned beef and cabbage was like a light in the window, attracting the McGeary sisters home, no matter where they happened to be. This wasn't really true anymore, ever since Clare had gone off to raise a family and Nancy Ann had gotten married to that handsome Tom Donovan. Nancy Ann was barely eighteen, the same age as her daughter Mare. Time was a thief.

It was just Meg and her parents at the table now. Since she never mentioned a man, her mother had to be content with how well her single daughter was doing at the bank. Her father kept her mother's prying impulses in check, usually with a sharp glance if she strayed anywhere near the word "marriage."

"I think I like your cooking more as I get older," Meg offered. "You haven't lost your touch."

"What kind of touch do spuds take?"

Her mother smiled indulgently at the compliment and passed the potatoes. But really Meg was attempting a mild diversion, in case her inner state looked too obvious. It took all her strength not to tell her parents how worried and disoriented she felt. At any moment she could have a relapse. Worse, the movie in her head could pick up from where it had stalled. This was a possibility she didn't dare think about.

After dinner, Meg walked to the bus stop. Her car was in the shop. She felt relieved nothing had gone amiss. The sky over the

city was unusually clear, the stars giving a bright winter show. Meg glanced up, thinking that stars somehow become sharper when it was cold. This observation would have given her pleasure, but the stars suddenly seemed like the points of a million nails. She felt a wave of panic. The animal contentment of having a full stomach wasn't calming her at all. A liquor store on the corner was still open—impulsively she rushed in.

Cheap vodka would be the fastest anesthesia, she figured, running her eye over the shelves. She wasn't a drinker, but the need was urgent.

At the counter a bored clerk was watching a basketball game in overtime on a small TV. When Meg took off her mittens to count out the money, he glanced at her palms.

"I'd have that looked at if I was you, lady," he said, cautiously taking the bills from her hand.

Meg looked down. Her palms were marked by two spots the size of a nickel, bright red and moist. She was sure they hadn't been there at dinner. Her panic escalated, and she started swaying in place. She had to grip the counter to stay upright.

"Hey, are you okay?"

Unable to reply, she stared ahead with wide, frightened eyes. The clerk started to reach for the phone. Meg shook her head violently.

"Please, no," she managed to whisper.

The clerk was no humanitarian; he was glad to get her out of his store with her bottle and eighty-nine cents change. Meg wouldn't have stuck around for the 911 call anyway. She blindly headed for the bus stop, running to catch the bus waiting there. The driver paid no attention to her as she collapsed onto a seat near the front. Except for two older black ladies at the back, the bus was empty.

Her mind wasn't working. Holding on tight was her only tactic now. Meg looked out the window at the passing dinginess of

the city while the bus's fluorescent lights flickered every time the driver pumped the brakes.

Once she got home, she stopped at the small table by the door where she kept her gloves and keys. If she took her gloves off slowly enough and wished hard enough, the round red spots would be gone. Magical thinking, the last resort, the final rung the mind clings to as it gazes into the black abyss. No magic this time. Meg gazed at the spots, which seemed redder than before, the moistness forming into a rivulet of blood.

But her mind didn't let go of the last rung, and she didn't plunge into blackness. She felt unusually calm, in fact, like a surgeon clinically examining a clean incision made by a scalpel. Once the blade slices open the skin, there's no turning back, and with Meg it was the same. This was the point of no return. She knew what the spots meant. She knew about the stigmata. As a girl—ten, maybe eleven—she had gone through a brief period of religious devotion. She took to reading the lives of the saints in books with glossy, colored illustrations. Already an advanced reader, the suffering of saints mesmerized her.

Now, though, it was happening to her. The things that she couldn't bear to see in her movie were now appearing on her body. Holy wounds. First the oozing blood where nails were driven into the hands. If the wounds kept going, there would be a wreath of bloody points around her forehead, a gash in her side, more blood from her feet. But even this didn't disturb her calmness. Instead, she undressed for bed and looked at herself in the full-length mirror on her closet door. Nothing else had manifested, only the two red spots on her palms. Without bandaging them, she fell into bed, skipping the pills, ignoring the vodka. Instantly, she descended into a deep, dreamless sleep.

CHAPTER 6

Lilith's visit was more than strange. As soon as she was gone, Mare couldn't settle down again. She ran to the window, watching the intruder make her way in high heels back through the snow. It felt as if any chance of seeing her aunt again was slipping away. Mare had to do something.

She rushed to the door, grabbing her coat on the way, and flung it open, only to find Frank standing there.

"I've been waiting in the car. What's going on? You're not running after her, are you?"

"I have to," Mare said, peering over his shoulder to see if she could still catch a glimpse of Lilith.

"Whoa. I don't think that's such a good idea."

"Why not? She's figured out everything, and we know nothing."

Mare was biting her lip hard; the tic had returned. But at the sight of Frank she began to calm down.

He came in, shutting the door behind him. "I couldn't just leave like that. God knows what she's capable of."

"Please, don't freak me out any more than I already am."

Mare began pacing the small open patch in her cramped apartment, running her hands through her hair.

"I'm so stupid. I didn't get her number. I don't even know her last name."

"It's okay. We're both wound up right now," Frank said.

"My mouth feels like cotton." Mare opened the battered fridge in the corner and grabbed some bottled water off the shelf, knocking over the two bottles next to it, which she ignored. "I shouldn't have let her in the door. Now she's filled my head with such strange ideas."

"She was spouting nonsense," Frank said firmly. "You know that, right?"

Mare was walking in circles now, taking big gulps of water. Suddenly the phone rang, and she jumped. It had to be her family again. They weren't about to let this die down.

She looked at Frank. "I'm not going to answer it. What could I tell them?"

They both understood her predicament. Even if you subtracted the Lilith quotient, the mystery of Aunt Meg was squarely on Mare's shoulders.

Frank felt a momentary paralysis. There are moments when one step forward or backward makes all the difference. He wasn't going to sweep Mare into his arms and murmur, "It's all right. I'm here. I have your back." He couldn't promise that. So taking a backward step was the smart choice. He could extricate himself now and return to the newsroom. Thompson, the crusty city editor, would scorch him for blowing off his deadline, but he wouldn't fire him. Mare could get through this on her own, somehow. Having worked it all out, Frank stepped forward anyway.

"Let's sit down and think this through," he said, touching Mare's arm.

She took a deep breath and did what he said, draining the last of the water in one gulp.

He began thinking out loud. "Lilith had her suspicions before

she came here, and now she's sure we have the object. But think back. She said it belongs here."

Mare was bewildered. "What does that mean?"

"I don't know. Maybe we'll find out from your aunt. You really have no idea where she might be?"

Mare shook her head.

"Okay, then it's like the news business. If you lose your best source, you fall back to the next best. I hate to say it, but that means Lilith."

"She might not talk to you, not after what you said."

"Right, but if anybody knows the whole story, she does. That's why she was doling it out bit by bit."

Mare was rolling the crumpled plastic water bottle between her hands. Her panic had passed. She could think as logically as Frank now.

"So Lilith doesn't want to get the shrine for herself."

"No, otherwise she'd have tried to scare you—more than she already did, I mean."

He won a faint smile. Then Mare said, "I get the strongest feeling that the shrine isn't stolen, which means somebody gave it to Aunt Meg. Why? And if she's not dead, why pass it on to me?"

"To draw you in."

Frank was stating the obvious, but only now did it hit them. They stared silently at each other. He racked his brain for what to do next.

"You said there was a note. Let me take a look at it."

She fetched it, and for such a short message, Frank realized, it said a great deal.

Hello, Mare,

This is from the thirteenth disciple. Follow where it leads.

Yours in Christ,
Meg

He began to decipher it. "You see how it begins, so casually? She starts talking as if you two are close, as if she's sure you're the one who will read the note first."

"I see that."

"Then she plants a tease. Who is this thirteenth disciple? Your aunt knows already, but she wants you to find out for yourself. The shrine holds the answer."

"That's brilliant!" Mare exclaimed.

"It's all between the lines. When you get to the end, she says 'Yours in Christ,' which means that leaving the convent had nothing to do with losing her faith. She's reminding you that religion is the focus, not how much the treasure is worth. But she signs off with her old name. She could have used her nun's name, but she wanted you to know that she's family again."

He turned the note over before handing it back to Mare, who was looking at him with admiring eyes.

"That's all I can see," he said.

Mare was thoughtful now. "So Aunt Meg is drawing me in. What happened to her in the convent? Why did she decide to vanish a second time after all these years?"

"I don't know. But Lilith isn't acting on her own. Let's say the two know each other, and maybe Meg is orchestrating everything. She must have a reason for staying in the shadows like that. Your aunt could have just phoned. She could walk in the door right now and tell you what's going on without sending somebody else. Either she's toying with you, which leaves us where we started, or this is a test. 'Follow where it leads.'"

Suddenly Mare became animated. "I have an idea." She went to the closet and brought the golden church out from its hiding place.

"Maybe there's some writing on it we didn't notice before. It could be the clue we're supposed to follow."

She started examining every surface minutely. But except for the etched grass and flowers, the outside surface was perfectly smooth. A dead end.

"We need to get inside," said Frank, following his first hunch. "At least let's shake it."

Mare nodded in agreement. She didn't bring up her premonition that someone, not something, was hidden in the church. If she still thought so, she kept it to herself.

Frank lifted the heavy golden object next to his ear and shook it hard. There was no sound from inside, no rattle of bone, no whisper of ashes.

"Damn it. There has to be something." He was quickly growing frustrated.

Mare's face changed, and she took a deep breath. "Please don't laugh. Maybe we should pray for the answer."

He did laugh, abruptly and sarcastically. "Come on."

Mare didn't back down. "There are only two ways to look at the treasure. Either it's a precious artwork or it's sacred. Aunt Meg didn't leave it to me as my inheritance. It's not the gold that matters to her. I mean, isn't that obvious?"

"All right," said Frank reluctantly. "But you do the praying. I'll sit back and watch."

This wasn't good enough for Mare. "Are we in this together or not?"

"I didn't say I was pulling out." Nor did he say that he had never prayed in his life, unless you count "Now I lay me down to sleep" when he was five.

"Okay. You hold one end, and I'll hold the other. Is that asking too much?"

It would have been under other circumstances. The golden church hadn't lost its spell, however, and something about it was irresistible to Frank. He slipped his fingers under one end while

Mare took hold of the other. They grew quiet; she shut her eyes. He was sure that praying would lead nowhere. It was all on her.

So what was on him? Had he committed to anything? Frank felt a guilty twinge. Mare's face had taken on a childlike innocence. Who was going to rescue her before she was pulled farther down the rabbit hole? Not him. He wasn't gallant enough to rescue anyone, if it came to that. His motives ran more the other way. He was nosey enough to pry deeper into the ongoing weirdness. He'd probably wind up writing a helluva story. All kinds of people would read it and start prying into Mare's business. In the end, she'd hate him.

This gloomy line of thought went nowhere, because the room suddenly turned black. Not dark, but as black as a starless night. Frank looked in Mare's direction. He couldn't see her, but he could sense that she was still there, breathing but invisible. A strong gust of wind ruffled his hair, which was impossible. The wind was cold enough to prick his skin, raising goose bumps. He heard Mare gasp, and Frank reached out into the surrounding darkness, catching her arm. There was no golden church between them, no cramped apartment even. They were standing outside on a chilly night.

"What's happening?" he asked, but the words made no sound, the way words in a dream don't make a sound.

Even if Mare had heard him though, there was no time for her to answer. From behind them Frank caught voices. He whipped around, his right shoulder hitting up against a rough plastered wall. The voices continued, quiet and close by. There were two people, a man and a woman. They spoke in a foreign language. No sense came through, but the woman sounded bewildered and scared. The man sounded older, and his voice was calm, as if he was trying to reassure her.

The blackness obscured everything. Frank jumped when Mare's hand found his and clutched it tight. If he was delusional, she was right there with him.

He tried talking again. "Where are we?"

Mare gave no sign of hearing him, but the impenetrable darkness cleared a bit. The plastered wall that Frank had banged his shoulder against belonged to a house; there were windows high up that cast a faint glimmer of flickering candles or oil lamps. He realized that he wasn't afraid. His heart didn't pound in his chest; his legs weren't rubbery. The whole thing was more trancelike than frightening.

The two people who were talking came closer, then stopped. He could hear the woman breathing raggedly; she was quite agitated. The man said only a few words more, and then he turned to walk away. He was headed in their direction. Frank pulled Mare beside him and pressed his back to the wall. The man's approaching steps were measured, and when he got nearer, Frank could make out the silhouette of someone shorter than himself. He wore sandals that flopped against the cobblestones, and each step made a swishing sound, as if he was dressed in robes. If he was armed, the dim light didn't catch the glint of steel. A minute later, he was right on top of them, two figures pressed against the wall.

Now Frank was afraid. His pulse thudded in his ears, and it took all his willpower to stand there. The man must be used to moving around in the dark. He had to see them. But he gave no sign, not turning his head or changing his gait as he passed in the narrow alley. The flop of sandals began to fade away.

Suddenly the woman ran after him, crying out. She rushed by so close that her skirt brushed Frank's leg; in the dark he made out that she was quite tiny. Her cry was that of a girl, not a woman. The man didn't stop. She cried out again, and a shutter swung open overhead. Someone leaned out, waving an oil lamp to see what the commotion was.

Almost with a click, Frank was back in Mare's apartment, holding on to his end of the golden church. The other end was trembling.

"You saw it too?" he mumbled. Mare could barely hold on to her end, and they lowered the church together to the floor. Mare sank down beside it.

"Oh, my God," she mumbled.

He sat down next to her, taking her hand. It felt very cold and small. Frank wasn't so dazed that his mind wasn't working. He could feel a crack in his skepticism.

"It was your prayer. What else could have triggered something like that? I wouldn't believe it if I hadn't been there."

"Where is there?" Mare asked weakly.

He was at a loss. Between them sat the golden shrine, glowing by the light of the dangling bulb in its paper lantern. The scene was more or less the same as when Frank first walked in. The only thing that had changed was a small sign, white with red lettering, hanging right in front of him. It didn't matter that the sign was invisible, because the lettering was unmistakable: "No Exit." Frank could bet on that.

CHAPTER 7

After the kid reporter left, Galen couldn't finish his burger. The whole place reeked of charred grease and cinders, like a crematorium. All he wanted to do was go home and collapse into bed. He trailed out to the street, where a taxi cab was idling at the curb. The driver nodded, and Galen got in, telling him the address.

They headed over to the other side of town. On the way, Galen rebuked himself. He had lied to the kid. He hadn't told him the real story behind his attack on the *Madonna and Child*. How could he? It was the cause of his rage, but love was tangled into the story like gold thread in a martyr's hair shirt.

Two years before, he had decided to spend a rainy afternoon in the art museum. This wasn't a predictable choice. Museums didn't figure into Galen's short menu of possibilities for a rainy afternoon, which usually included catching up on work, reading back issues from a dusty pile of *Scientific American*s, or rearranging the newest samples in his mineral collection—he specialized in rare earths. Nowhere on the menu was visiting the art museum, because he didn't really like art.

What he liked was strolling through places where he could feel alone in a crowd. He went to shopping malls on Black Friday for the same reason. Being part of a mob scene—an invisible

integer—made him feel armored, protected. It reinforced his splendid isolation. It also happened to be a Wednesday, and the art museum was packed because admission was free. If Galen had known that picking up girls was the goal of a good percentage of the day's male art lovers, he would have stayed at home.

A young woman was standing beside Galen as he gazed at a prized *Madonna and Child* from the Italian Renaissance. The serene expression on the Madonna's face was a depiction of timeless peace.

"Mmm," the woman murmured in appreciation.

Galen paid no notice. He was only staring at the painting to figure out which mineral might have produced a peculiar shade of green. Malachite? It was a good guess, unless the lush grass beneath the Blessed Virgin's feet was tinted with a vegetable dye. He decided this was unlikely. A vegetable dye would have long ago faded to gray.

The young woman's glance darted sideways, although Galen had no idea she was taking him in.

"Lovely," she murmured.

This constituted too much communication. Galen sidled away. Without warning, she plucked at his sleeve.

"I could tell you were enjoying it." She gestured at the painting, but her eyes remained on him. "Tell me what you see."

"Why?"

She smiled. "Because I'm interested."

Galen couldn't help but notice how young and attractive she was. His immediate instinct was to retreat, but he took another look at the painting.

"The mother looks hypnotized. The baby's face looks shriveled, like an old man's."

"Fascinating. Go on."

The young woman fixed him with an adoring smile. This was even more unnerving than plucking at his sleeve.

Galen continued. "There's a disease that shrivels children's faces," he pointed out. "Progeria. It's quite horrible. That baby probably had progeria."

His clinical remark didn't repel her. Quite the opposite—her eyes lit up, and with a laugh she exclaimed, "Brilliant! I knew I should talk to you. My name is Iris, by the way."

Galen stared. An attractive woman no more than thirty, with loosely gathered blonde hair that fell to her shoulders, the kind of hair once referred to as tresses, was admiring him. He peered over his shoulder to see if she had an accomplice—chatting up a middle-aged nonentity like Galen might be their way of having a cruel laugh.

His discomfort made Iris laugh again. "Let's get a drink," she suggested. "We'll take one last look at this marvelous painting that we both love, and then I know the most amazing place where the mixologist is divine."

He'd never met anyone so vibrant. If Galen had been imaginative, he could have compared her tinkling laughter to sleigh bells attached to a troika in a romantic Russian novel. If he had been versed in abnormal psychology, on the other hand, he would have frowned at Iris's unquenchable exuberance. Who assails strangers in public with outbursts of emotion? Borderline personalities? Normal people don't act this way.

Caution should have stopped him. Instead, he allowed Iris to drag him, half-dazed, to a bar. Galen didn't drink, so the allure of exotic cocktails was nil. He sat there with a glass of soda water while Iris did all the work of seducing him. She flattered and cooed. His every remark invited a peal of laughter.

Being a virgin and nervous, he didn't ask Iris back to his place that first night, but she got his number. She had to be the one who called; he never would have. A real date followed, then two. He learned, with awkward, embarrassed slowness, how to kiss. An omission in his adolescence, petting with a girl at the movies, was

remedied. Within a span of two months Iris became his wife. An oyster dies when its shell is cracked open, but Galen was reborn as a flood of love entered his being. His initial fear changed to intoxication. He lay awake at night with Iris cradled on his shoulder, and he never complained that the pressure made pins and needles shoot down his arm.

The way that love turned to violence was just as unexpected as their courtship. Iris's passion began to shift. She didn't grow tired of Galen, but suddenly her exuberance demanded a creative outlet. He came home from work one day to find a pile of art supplies stacked up in the living room.

"What's this?" he asked.

There was a large easel with mechanisms to adapt it to any size canvas, along with myriad jars of acrylics in every possible color, and blank canvases ranging in size from miniature to epic.

"I'm a painter!" Iris exclaimed.

"I didn't know," Galen said cautiously. "You didn't tell me."

"Oh, not before. I just realized it. I'm a painter. I always have been, but my talent was hidden."

As much as he loved her, some part of Galen looked upon his wife as an alien being, beginning with her passion for him. He began to worry that this was her first delusion. Being a painter might be her second. Yet his fears proved unfounded. Iris spread a plastic drop cloth in the middle of the living room and set up a makeshift studio. She threw herself into her first painting, and by the time Galen was ready for bed, she rushed in with a wet canvas.

"Done! What do you think? Isn't it beautiful?" she enthused.

He was afraid to look. But instead of being a garish daub, she had produced a semi-abstract landscape in harmonized colors, which, to his eyes, was amazingly good. It didn't matter that the sky was yellow and the grass blue. The colors worked. They

expressed the same vibrant joy that Iris could find in anything, like life bubbling up from an endless spring.

She pointed to a streak of light that crossed the canvas from a source far in the distance. "That's an angel. Angels are pure light." "Oh," Galen said. Angels were a nontopic for him.

Iris began to paint furiously, barely leaving time for sleep. Galen would wake up after midnight to find that his wife had quietly gotten out of bed to return to her latest canvas. Not that her love for him waned. If anything, it grew warmer. She greeted him when he came home from work wearing a dress, complete with matching pearl necklace and earrings.

When he suggested that she needed to slow down, tears welled up in the corners of her eyes. "I just want to show you my soul," she said. The soul was another nonsubject for Galen. He was mystified as he witnessed her paintings grow more religious. Not conventionally religious, though. She produced shimmering organic shapes—they reminded him of intricate snowflakes under the microscope, only in iridescent colors.

"That's what souls really look like," Iris said, as certain as when she told him what angels looked like.

Galen couldn't tell anyone what was happening at home. It was too dreamlike. Not that he had any colleagues to tell. His days were spent at the university library collecting references for scientific articles. He cobbled together a livelihood as a technical writer and researcher for professors at the university; his nights, however, were spent at a love feast. He had married a force of nature, not merely a lover and artist. What did he have to complain about, and who would believe him if he did?

Inevitably the day arrived when the outer world intruded. Iris wanted him to meet her parents, who lived in Milwaukee. There had been no formal wedding, just a civil ceremony at the registrar's office.

"Don't worry," Iris promised. "They'll love you as much as I do."

Galen knew otherwise. Intruders would break the enchantment that protected their crazy bliss. He was sensible enough to know that they were gripped in a *folie à deux* and, like any mad folly, outside eyes would expose it. Iris went to the airport, while Galen waited at home, sitting forlornly in his armchair. He felt naked and vulnerable.

That his in-laws were nice, pleasant people didn't relieve his anxiety. They stayed two days, and no one commented on the wide age difference between Iris and her husband. The chat was civil, if not warm. Her father, a doctor with a prosperous practice, assumed the role of alpha male. He paid for dinner at an expensive restaurant and told hunting stories.

"We've got pheasant and quail in the freezer back home. I'll send you a batch. It's too much for us."

Galen was content to submit. He tried not to look too hard into the mother's eyes. He expected to find worry there, and his own mother's constant worry still cast a shadow, all these years later.

"What's wrong?" Iris asked after her parents had left in a taxi for the airport. Her father had insisted on a cab, which would cost sixty dollars, his last show of dominance.

"Nothing. They're nice," Galen muttered.

He looked around, but could see no shards of wrecked enchantment littering the floor. Maybe they were protected after all. Iris went back to painting—her parents had been astonished at her hidden talents—and, if anything, her output increased. She was shy about approaching a gallery, so Galen set up a website to show off her work.

"Call it *Divine Messenger*," she said. Within days it got dozens of hits, which turned to hundreds very soon. Her paintings clicked with people with spiritual stirrings.

One day an e-mail arrived in his inbox from Arthur Winstone, M.D. It took a moment for Galen to realize that this was his father-in-law.

Mr. Blake,

I've taken the liberty of writing to you privately. I hope you don't mind that I did a web search to find this address.

During our recent visit, I thought I spied a tremor in my daughter's left hand. It was faint, but I noticed that the shaking increased when Iris became emotional. I must add that her heightened exuberance felt unnatural to me. The Iris her mother and I know doesn't act this way.

I'm not a neurologist, and I don't mean to alarm you. But I strongly urge you to take her to a brain specialist. If my fears are unwarranted, I profoundly apologize. You must believe that I write out of a father's love.

One last thing—please don't share our communication with my daughter. In a good marriage, husband and wife tell each other everything, but at least consider keeping this e-mail a secret.

Respectfully,
Arthur Winstone

Galen was stunned. He read the e-mail twice more. His chest began to ache. This couldn't be happening.

The year that followed was a nightmare that ended only when Iris went into hospice and died. As he was leaving the room where Iris lay, unplugged from the medical monitors, pale and cold as a wax effigy, a voice in Galen's head spoke, having waited like a spoiled child holding its breath until it turns blue. *Fool! Wake up. You knew it couldn't be real.*

Now, sitting in the back of the cab on the way home from the burger joint, Galen shuddered. He was too exhausted to feel

enraged anymore. He had been humiliated by God. He had been deceived in love by the very cruelest deception, that he could ever be loved in the first place. Now the last hope was gone. There would be no revenge to wipe the slate clean.

He suddenly noticed the cabbie's eyes in the rearview mirror.

"You okay back there?"

"What?"

"Sorry. You just looked a little upset."

Galen opened his mouth to tell the driver to mind his own business, but he was suddenly overwhelmed by a sense of complete futility.

He sank back into himself, oblivious of the time until the cab driver said, "We're here."

Galen reached for his wallet.

"That's okay," the cabbie said. "No charge."

Galen was confused. "Why not?"

The driver hadn't stopped looking at him in the rear-view mirror. "Because you've been chosen."

For no reason, this meaningless remark sent a wave of panic through Galen. He grabbed for the door handle, but it was stuck. Or had the cabbie locked him in? Galen wrenched the handle as hard as he could, and the door flew open so fast he almost tumbled into the street.

The cabbie jumped out of the front seat and ran around to help him.

"Leave me alone," Galen gasped.

"I can't do that."

The cabbie was short and dark, with stubbled cheeks, the very image of someone Galen feared. Hysterically, he wondered if the man had a bomb strapped to his chest.

Without looking back, Galen lurched from the icy street to the curb. His house, a wooden row house with peeling white

paint and a sagging stoop, offered refuge. He stumbled as he went, kicking up sprays of snow like a rabbit fleeing a fox.

The cabbie followed a few feet behind. Feeling his shadow, Galen became terrified. He could barely extract his keys from his pants pocket, and when he tried to get a key in the door, the bunch flew out of his hand.

"Let me," the cabbie said, picking them up. He inserted the house key and turned the doorknob. "I'm Jimmy, by the way."

Galen's heart thumped in his chest. "If you want money, here," he exclaimed, thrusting his wallet at the man.

"I just want to talk."

Galen's eyes widened helplessly. The cab driver was blocking the door with his body.

"We've been watching you for a while," he said, smiling. "You're kind of my assignment. Look, it's freezing out here. I can explain everything better inside."

Galen was agitated, but he knew one thing for certain. Jimmy was the last person he'd ever let inside his house.

"I'm going past you," he exclaimed, "and if you lay a finger on me, I'll scream for the police."

Jimmy's smile broadened to a grin. "No offense, but I think the cops have had enough of you for one day."

Galen had his head turned away, so he never saw how Jimmy knocked him out, with a truncheon or the butt of a gun. There was no pain. A veil of darkness gently came down over his eyes; his knees crumpled. There was the sensation of cold as his cheek hit the packed snow on the stoop and a vague sense of Jimmy talking into a cell phone.

"I've got him, but he's so scared, he fainted. He's in no shape to plug in. Please advise."

CHAPTER 8

Only half of Frank's suspicions about Lilith were correct. She was acting on orders, and Meg, who issued them, was hiding in the shadows. But the reason for her secrecy went much deeper than he could have imagined. In his world, sane people don't have visions of the Crucifixion, and if their hands bleed where the nails were driven into Jesus's hands, deception is being practiced.

Meg held the same beliefs ten years ago. When her palms suddenly oozed blood, she turned her back on the phenomenon. As soon as she got off the bus, she rushed inside and went to bed without turning on the lights. She didn't want to see what was happening to her. She wanted no part of it.

But it was a mistake not to bandage her hands before she crawled under the covers. When Meg woke up the next morning, the sheets were lightly smeared red. The stains were bright and fresh. She must have been bleeding all night.

She became very frightened seeing the two round spots on her palms, sticky and shiny in the morning sun. She faced herself in the bedroom mirror and said, "I have the stigmata," testing the word out. It sounded unreal.

After scrubbing the spots with soap, they disappeared, but within minutes the film of blood came back. And it was starting

to drip again. She rummaged for a first-aid kit tucked at the back of the linen closet. Inside the kit was a roll of gauze bandages. Perching on the edge of the bathtub, she thoroughly wrapped up her hands. As far as anyone at the bank would know, she had carelessly burned herself taking a hot pan out of the oven.

The story was accepted without question. Meg's assistant winced and offered sympathy; she was careful to insulate a hot cup of coffee in three paper napkins before handing it to her. Otherwise no one took notice of her bandages. A week passed. Meg hung fire, applying a new dressing every morning. She felt a dull pain that didn't get better or worse.

Morbid curiosity sent her online, which was probably a mistake, because all she found were scary photos of people whose stigmata were worse than hers, much worse. Some had a row of ragged punctures across the forehead or a mark on the side of the body that looked like a gash, an open wound. Some stigmatics didn't bleed, some did. Some had recurrences every year, usually at Easter. Meg quickly turned away.

Two weeks later, without warning, a voice in her head said, *I will send you a blessing.* A gentle, unmistakable voice spoke these words. It was a female voice, yet not hers. The exact moment was etched in Meg's memory. She was alone in her office replacing a batch of documents in the filing cabinet. The sky outside was bright and clear. In the park across the street, work crews were stringing the bare trees with fairy lights for Christmas, and the frozen ground was feathered with snow like eiderdown.

After a short pause, the message in her head was repeated: *I will send you a blessing.*

Meg closed her eyes, willing the voice to explain what it meant. It didn't. So she went back to work, pretending that everything was normal. She moved cautiously, like a tightrope walker without a net. The worst thing would be to tip over.

If there was going to be a blessing, it didn't come that day. When evening fell, Meg started to wonder if she needed to do penance. She fumbled with the fingertips of bandaged hands and pulled out her rosary, tucked in the bottom drawer of her bureau.

How desperate am I? she thought. Maybe she would be praying to the God that sent this affliction in the first place. It was a disturbing possibility. She'd never had a reason to doubt her faith or even examine it. When she was just a speck in her mother's womb, her genes were already marked at the factory: female, green eyes, light brown hair, Irish Catholic. She was made this way before birth. God was a given. God was taken care of.

Reflecting on this, Meg felt a burst of anger. Who was God to force her hand? Who said he could point a cosmic finger and say, "You. You're it." Nobody had the right to play God. Which posed a problem, because no matter how hard she wrestled with it, God had a right to play God. He had just waited a long time before deciding to. She put the rosary back in the drawer, defeated.

Then one day a woman passed a sheaf of papers across her desk. A car loan application. Meg stared at it dully and picked up a pen.

"Your first name is Lilith?" she asked. "I don't see a last name."

"You won't need it."

Meg looked up, eying the customer, a tall woman in her late forties, perhaps fifty, with touches of gray at the temples.

"A last name is mandatory," Meg said, wondering why this was even an issue.

"Not this time. I like my old car. I don't need a new one." The woman had a decisive way of speaking that kept Meg from interrupting. "This is all about you—and that." The woman pointed to Meg's bandaged hands. "You've received a blessing."

Meg drew her hands out of sight under the desk.

"I don't know what you're talking about. I burned myself in the kitchen."

Lilith smiled. "Just unwrap them. You'll see."

Meg glanced down. A minute ago the gauze was beginning to show a slight discoloration from the seeping blood, but now it was snow-white.

"The blessing has been sent," said Lilith. "Don't be frightened. You're not crazy. Go ahead."

Meg looked around the office. A line of customers snaked toward the tellers, and her coworker was sitting with another loan applicant at the desk next to hers.

"Here?" she asked, mortified.

Lilith shrugged. "What do you have to lose? It's not like you're having a good day."

Gingerly Meg unwrapped her right hand. There was no stiffness from dried blood on the gauze. The bandage came off as smooth as a ribbon, and underneath her palm was unblemished. Rapidly she undid the other hand, and it was the same.

"What does this mean?" she stammered.

"It means you have a road to travel. Everyone does, but yours is different. You will walk a blessed path."

Without knowing why, Meg felt tears filling her eyes, blurring her view of her visitor.

"The soul is usually silent," Lilith continued. "It watches and waits. But your soul has called you out." She had showed little expression as she said this, but now she smiled wryly. "The good news is, you've been chosen. The bad news is, you've been chosen."

"I've heard better jokes," Meg mumbled. She wiped her eyes, and her strange visitor came back into focus. "Please excuse me. This is pretty overwhelming."

"That's what I'm here for. To make it easier. No one is ever prepared. But we mustn't let our emotions run away with us, must we?"

Meg started to laugh. Lilith seemed like a tart headmistress, right down to the tight bun she wore her hair in and the vaguely British accent. It was faintly outlandish, but effective. Meg's attention was totally focused; her panic was held in check. Fear was a great ocean wave ready to crash over her if Lilith wasn't holding it back.

Meg's laughter must have had a tinge of hysteria in it, because Lilith reached for her hand across the desk. "Do you need some water? Perhaps you should lie down."

"I'll be all right," Meg said, not at all certain. "I've got employees to look after."

She glanced out the window at the bright winter sky. A wave of calmness came over her, the first she'd felt in weeks. It was like a benediction.

"I'll be all right," she repeated.

Lilith watched her closely; she seemed satisfied.

"Then I'll take my leave." She stood up wearing an ambiguous smile, halfway between amused and knowing. She took back the car loan application, folded it neatly, and stuck it into her purse.

"Will I see you again?" Meg asked, feeling anxiety begin to creep back in.

"I'll be at your door when you get home tonight. We've made a beginning. Good."

"How do you know where I live?" asked Meg.

"How do I know anything?" Lilith replied. "It just comes to me."

After she departed, Meg played at finishing the work day normally. The tightrope walker didn't tip over. She balled up the gauze bandages and threw them into the waste bin in the ladies' room. Her reflection in the mirror was trying hard not to look elated.

She drove home at five, and every block deepened her sense of wonder. *Do things like this really happen?* Meg had read the New

Testament when she was sixteen, to please a boyfriend, a Protestant who was going through some kind of phase. The boyfriend dropped away, and Meg thought the Bible had too. Except that now, driving home, an obscure verse came back to her: "I bear on my body the marks of Jesus." A saint said it, and if Meg wasn't a saint, what was she?

Lilith was waiting on the stoop when she pulled into the driveway. She wore a thick tweed coat against the cold and held her handbag in front of her with both hands, as stiff as a palace guard on watch. Meg approached to unlock the front door. Neither spoke.

Once inside, Meg waited for Lilith's next move. The nearest room was the dining room. Lilith went in and seated herself at the head of the table. She patted the chair closest to her, which Meg obediently took.

"Have you reflected on what I told you?"

"I'm not sure. I can't remember anything except relief."

"Understandable."

Suddenly Meg wondered if the voice that had spoken in her head belonged to Lilith. "If I have you to thank . . ." she started to say.

"No. I'm not in such a position," Lilith said, waving off her gratitude. "I'm not a healer. But some people are. Maybe you, one day. In this instance, the soul spoke through your body. The flesh was willing, but the spirit was weak. I'm rather addicted to aphorisms, forgive me. I'll just keep talking until you're not dazed anymore."

Meg felt like she was breathing air from another world, but her mind had begun to clear already.

"Do you believe your experience was real?" Lilith asked.

"I have to, don't I?" Meg glanced at her hands, checking one more time to make sure they looked unblemished.

"You don't have to accept anything, actually. I didn't, not at first." Lilith paused. "You're going to meet some people. They'll also struggle with being chosen."

"When will I meet them?"

"That I don't know. I do know how many—seven, counting you and me."

Meg felt uneasy. She'd assumed all along, ever since the first morning of her ordeal, that she would face it alone.

"What if they don't want to meet me?"

"I won't let that happen."

Lilith was a cross between an oracle and a drill sergeant, but Meg wasn't afraid to stand up to her. "Who says it's your choice?"

"It has nothing to do with me. Reality is covered by a veil of mystery. You've penetrated the veil. It's a rare experience, and these seven people will have it, once you show them the way."

Meg was incredulous. "Me? I can't show anybody anything."

"That's going to change. When the whole group assembles, the person holding it together will be you."

Lilith saw the doubt lingering in Meg's eyes. She became more insistent. "You don't understand. I'm one of the seven. I need you, more than you can possibly know."

But the blessing Lilith had brought was already fading. Fear warned Meg to retreat into her shell.

Lilith read her mind. "The craving to be normal is powerful. It permits a moment of wonder, and then it drags us back, like an undertow we can't resist."

Meg gave an ironic smile. "As if normal is so great."

"Exactly. When all seven of us are gathered, a flame will spring up. If one member refuses to join, there will only be ashes."

Meg had a troubled cousin, Fran, who went to support groups for her addictions. They probably talked this way at the meetings. But she realized that she had to rethink who Lilith was—not a

headmistress, more like a guide leading climbers up a treacherous peak. *Stay on the path. Don't stray. We're all in this together.*

Lilith veered abruptly in a new direction. "Do you think you can see to infinity?"

"I don't even know what that means."

"Then I'll tell you. Right now, your mind is fenced inside a walled courtyard, which keeps you safely enclosed. Anything that lies beyond the wall is frightening, including miracles."

"And you're saying I've had a miracle."

"Yes, and it scares you to death."

"Maybe that's a reason not to run after any more of them," Meg said.

"The chosen don't run after miracles. It's the other way around. The miracle found you. That's another thing that scares you."

Lilith was used to controlling the conversation. That much was clear to Meg. But was Lilith also trying to control her? *If I'm one of the chosen, what are we chosen for?* Meg wondered.

A string of visits followed. Lilith's appearances were punctual, right at ten after five when Meg came up the driveway from work. She always stood at attention with both hands clutching her purse, waiting for the front door to be opened. There was never anyone else with her, and the group of seven, whoever they were, wasn't mentioned again.

One day Meg had sunk into a dark depression. She was waking up every morning feeling exhausted. Nothing in her life was stable anymore. The bank was the worst. She felt like she was doing a bad impersonation of her old self, and every day it was getting harder to keep up the act.

Lilith tried to reassure her. "The beginning is always the worst. You're totally protected, but you can't see it yet. "

After a while their visits were silent for long stretches. Twilight felt gray and empty. Meg got sick of being encouraged. Her hands had healed completely. She would have tried harder to go back

to her former life, but this was impossible. She kept remembering her own words: "What's so great about normal?"

One afternoon the house was desolately quiet, an echo chamber for the ticking clocks and rumbling refrigerator compressor.

Out of the blue Lilith said, "You resent me, don't you?"

Meg gave a silent shrug, unwilling to deny it.

"I'm just the messenger, you know," Lilith added.

There was no reply.

"Then what is it?"

Meg wanted to get up and walk away, but then she surprised herself by letting loose a wail of rage and self-pity. "I'm the one who had to suffer. I was bleeding! You don't know what it's like for me. You have it easy. You call yourself a messenger. Look around. You delivered a curse."

Like a dying siren, her anger trailed off into a whine. "Sorry," she mumbled.

"Don't apologize. Maybe you're right. But not about me."

Meg heaved a sigh. "I don't know anything about you."

"Maybe it's time you did."

The living room where they sat was being overtaken by the falling night, but Meg didn't reach for the lamp. She sat back, wondering what Lilith's story could possibly be.

When she was twenty, Lilith woke up from a bad dream, sweating and distraught. She was back from college on summer vacation. It was a time she loved, and besides, she almost never had bad dreams, nothing like this one, which was like being trapped in a hallucination.

She had landed far back in time, centuries and centuries ago. She was standing in front of a thick wooden door, the kind one might find in a medieval village. The door was nailed shut with rough oak boards. She realized that she wasn't alone. Several men, their faces tense and hard, stood around while two other men pried the boards loose.

The onlookers exchanged worried glances. When the last nail was pulled out, the boards clattered to the cobblestone pavement.

"What's wrong?" Lilith remembered asking in her dream. But the instant she asked, she knew the answer. Plague. She could smell death, a sickly rotten stench that became stronger when one of the men pushed open the door. Inside was darkness, because all the windows had been sealed too. The Black Death was merciless and swift. A boat carrying the plague might land in port, and within a week a quarter of the population in the town would be corpses littering the street.

The men looked at one another, hesitant about who should go inside to look. All eyes drifted to her. *What?* Lilith thought of herself as an unseen presence, but to them she was part of the scene. *You look. You are the one,* the men were speaking Italian, but Lilith understood every word. Around her, the crowd kept repeating the word *morte* excitedly.

With her first step through the door, she was repelled—the stench pushed her back like a hand over her face. The darkness wasn't absolute. Glimmers of sunlight came in through the boarded-up windows, and after a moment she saw something gleaming and gold.

Her eyes adjusted. The gleam took shape; she could see a small object sitting on the floor. At first it didn't register that the shape was a church or chapel, because her attention was frozen on the bodies. Six corpses lay around the object. They were arranged in a symmetrical pattern, extending outward like spokes of a wheel with the gold object as the hub.

The accursed sight caused the group of men—a search party looking for survivors—to disperse, screaming *Dio ci protegga! Dio ci protegga! God protect us! God protect us!* Below their confused shouting, Lilith could hear the sharp clatter of shoes scurrying over the cobblestones.

Her heart was beating fast. Whoever she was in the dream, the town's fear and dread had seized her completely. But she couldn't help staring at the wheel of bodies, wondering who had arranged them in a sealed and boarded house. Maybe no one. The logical answer was that they had lain down to die, deliberately forming the pattern. Knowing they were doomed, they wanted to send a message.

"And then I woke up," Lilith said when she got to this point in her story.

"Before you understood the message?" Meg asked.

"No. It was just a dream. I wasn't curious about it. I got out of bed, threw open the windows to cool off the room, and went for my morning swim. Our family always rented the same cabin by the lake every summer."

"And nothing happened?"

Lilith gave the first warm smile of their time together. "Everything happened. The golden shrine—that's the proper term—had found me. It always finds the chosen, one way or another.

"I came home from a date that night, a little woozy on wine. This boy and I had been teasing each other all evening, but he didn't get past second base. I remember wishing he had, when suddenly the same gleam I saw in my dream was in my bedroom. My hand had found the light switch, but I hadn't turned it on. But I instantly knew where the gleam came from."

"And it frightened you," Meg said.

"Just like you. I was frozen in place, and suddenly my mind was flooded with the truth. My dream was actually a prophecy. I had stumbled onto a mystery school. That's who the dead bodies belong to, a kind of secret society."

"I don't understand," said Meg.

"You will. The society is still around, and we're part of it, along with the others, once they answer the call."

"A mystery school," Meg said to herself, testing out the words. "Why?"

"Because mysteries need to be revealed, and at the same time they need protecting."

Meg was bewildered, but excited and intrigued too. "You saw six bodies in your dream. Why are there seven of us?"

"Because the seventh member of our mystery school is the teacher, and she is inside the shrine. She chooses us, and through her we come together, six complete strangers who share a path."

"Unless we die together. That was in your dream. Is it part of the prophecy?"

"I worried about that, until I realized that you can't be literal about these things," Lilith replied. "I think we will die unto death. Remember those words. You'll hear them in the convent when you get there."

Convent? Meg was speechless. If the McGeary family tree contained any nuns, she had never heard of it. A feeling of unreality returned, the same way Meg had felt when she was staring at her bleeding palms.

Lilith shook her head. "I know. This feels like someone else's life."

Meg nodded. It was good that Lilith understood, but it wasn't enough. The walls of the room began to close in, smothering her. Lilith had told her she was on a blessed path. Wherever that path was leading, Meg didn't care. She only wanted a way out.

CHAPTER 9

After returning from the dark alley, Frank was slow to get to his feet. His eyes told him that he was back in Mare's apartment, but his body wasn't so sure. The chilly air in the alley lingered on his skin. He was finding it hard to calm the racing thoughts in his head. The whole experience was overwhelming.

Mare looked up from where she sat on the floor, the golden shrine still between them.

"Are you okay?" asked Frank.

"I don't know." Mare's voice was shaky and distant. "I pulled you into this, away from work. But is there any way you can stay?"

"Sure, for a while. I just need to call in." Frank couldn't get a signal on his cell. "Let me step outside."

When his hand was on the doorknob, Mare said, "If I got you in trouble, just go."

"And leave you here? No way."

Suddenly Frank realized something. "You're not scared, are you?"

"No. It just took me a moment to get back. That's not why I want you to stay."

"Then what is it?"

"I want to go back," Mare said. "I have to."

Her eyes were steady, almost hard. He hadn't seen them like that before. He'd marked her down as a beautiful but timid girl, the kind who spent too much time feeling insecure.

"You're killing me here," he moaned. "You don't even know if we *can* go back."

"I'm not asking you to come with me. Unless you want to."

"You mean you'd go back without me? No way. It could be dangerous. What if you don't return this time?" Despite all his skepticism, Frank was talking as if they had traveled through some kind of portal.

"The note said, 'Follow where it leads,'" Mare reminded him. "That's what I'm doing. I can't stop now."

Frank couldn't deny that he was being lured in, first by the golden treasure, then Lilith, and now this. Mare was turning into a completely new woman before his eyes.

"I know what this thing is," she exclaimed, pointing at the shrine. "It's a truth-teller, or an oracle."

Frank balked. "You're stabbing in the dark. Where's the proof?"

"It's in the note. We're being led to the thirteenth disciple. He's at the center of everything that's happened. I know what you're thinking: that's not proof. But we saw him, there in the alley."

"That could have been anybody."

"Does it matter? The one who is sleeping inside the shrine. He trusts us. He's willing to give us these clues."

"Which is also why Lilith couldn't tell us the whole story," Frank chimed in. "It sounds too crazy."

"Until you go there. Now we have. We passed the test."

Frank was barely listening now. What mattered to him was the hope and excitement in Mare's eyes. More than anything, he didn't want her to be disappointed, but he had no control over these strange events.

"You can't believe how frustrated I am," he exclaimed. "We could be jumping off a cliff here." His voice became pleading. "We don't have to go back right this minute, do we?"

"I guess not," Mare replied reluctantly.

"Then let me clear my head first." Frank ran to the door and flung it open. "I've got six missed calls on my cell. Let me try and save my job. But I'm not leaving, I promise."

"I know."

He was bothered by the ambiguous smile she gave him, but what choice did he have except to trust her? They had to trust each other. His voice trailed "Sorry, sorry" behind him as he ran out into the cold. For the moment Mare was alone.

She felt woozy and exhilarated at the same time. A brilliant flash had revealed something totally unexpected. Her interior, she now realized, wasn't a dark domain littered with the debris of the past and the creeping footsteps of hidden demons. It was a chamber of secret magic. Whoever had transported her to another reality had only wanted to wake her up. The sleeper in the golden shrine knew her.

Now she was more eager than ever to go back again. Still sitting beside the miniature golden church, she bent over, putting her face close to it, as if she could peer through its windows. She was a giant Alice, and the little shrine was her looking glass.

Who are you? she silently asked. If there was a truth-teller inside, it would answer. She waited a long moment, her eyes closed. When no reply came, she tried what had worked before—praying. *God, if you're listening, guide me where I need to go.*

Her fingers brushed the gilded roof. It was the lightest of touches, and then she was gone.

The scene hadn't changed—the same dark alley, the same inquisitive neighbor leaning out of an upstairs window waving his oil lamp. The glimmering light revealed nothing, and he pulled

his head back inside. Mare couldn't see anything either, but she caught a sound. The girl, the one who had run after the man in robe and sandals, was crying somewhere down the alley.

Mare followed the sound to a niche where the wall had crumbled. Even though the niche was shadowed in darkness, Mare could somehow see into it. The girl's head was covered; she wore a long clean shift, which was pinned with a silver brooch. This wasn't an impoverished waif.

"Why am I here? What do I have to do with you?" Mare whispered, forgetting that no one could hear her.

The girl stopped crying and looked up, staring straight at Mare. Could she see her standing there? The question was never answered, but a voice in Mare's head said something.

I am the sleeper. You have found me.

When Galen passed out cold on his front stoop, the cab driver Jimmy had no choice but to call Lilith. She'd know what to do.

"Get him inside. We can't let him freeze to death." Lilith sounded impatient about this unexpected glitch in her plans. "He's part of the group, but he'll fight against it if you come right out and tell him. Just act friendly, and see if he warms up to you."

"I don't know," Jimmy said doubtfully. "I think we're way past that. He got really upset."

"What did you do to him?"

"Nothing. He's just strange."

"I know that. I've kept an eye on him for weeks. But everything has to come together now. It's what Meg wants. Do I have to remind you?" said Lilith sternly.

"No."

Jimmy hung up. The house key was already in the lock. Before turning it, he lightly shook Galen's shoulder.

"Come on, buddy," Jimmy coaxed, but Galen didn't respond. He had passed out as much from nervous exhaustion as fright, and now he was fast asleep.

Jimmy had a slim build, but was surprisingly strong. He managed to drag Galen into the house and lift him onto the futon

sofa in the living room without much difficulty. As he softly snored, Jimmy removed Galen's shoes, then took a seat in a sagging La-Z-Boy across the room. The house was small; the musty odor of leftover pizza and dirty dishes piled up in the sink pervaded it. The furniture was old and worn, probably handed down from relatives, but the place was neatly kept. Jimmy's eye fell on the bookshelves that lined one wall. He considered whiling away the time by reading until his charge woke up, but when he examined the shelves, all the titles were scientific. They sounded very technical.

He'd have to sit and wait. Jimmy felt uneasy. He hadn't asked for this assignment; he wasn't even a cabbie. Lilith had devised the ruse to get Galen in a spot where he couldn't run away. As it happened, Jimmy had a cab-driver cousin who was willing to part with his car after his early shift ended.

Jimmy wasn't looking forward to Galen's reaction when he woke up. He'd probably make a racket and threaten to call the police again. Jimmy decided not to think about it. A year ago Lilith had told him that there was a group—she called it a mystery school—that was about to convene. The group was like a fraternal order, but even more secretive. Jimmy didn't see what it had to do with him.

"You're going to be part of it," Lilith told him.

"Not me."

But she sounded so certain, Jimmy became nervous. He asked questions, which Lilith kept avoiding. He only managed to coax some hazy details from her, something about the Middle Ages, when mystery schools were persecuted for heresy. If a pious citizen stumbled upon one, the culprits were rounded up, and the Church came down on them like a ton of bricks. A period of atonement was enforced. It began with torture and ended in death (unless you slipped a healthy bag of gold to the local bishop). But even the most extreme physical torture was insignificant compared with

the fate of your soul. Back then, looking for God outside the church was like stepping into outer space, only instead of leaving the pull of gravity, you left everything that constitutes a normal life. Yet a few people dared to take this perilous step—mystics, misfits, freethinkers, and a sprinkling of crazies and spies. This was Lilith's unsavory sketch of the past.

"So why should I sign on?" Jimmy asked. In his mind's eye he could almost see those refugees from society huddled in a wine cellar or abandoned stone barn, dreading a knock at the door by the Inquisition.

"Because you've been chosen," Lilith replied.

"Like I said," Jimmy repeated, "not me."

But he knew in his heart that his protests sounded feeble. If a mystery school needed misfits, he qualified.

Jimmy's real job was as a hospital orderly. He and Lilith had been allies for a year now, a strange relationship that grew from an even stranger beginning. A young girl, not yet sixteen, was rushed to the hospital after a car struck her as she was walking alone on the side of the highway. She was brought to the ER in a coma; her chart said "Jane Doe," because the girl had no identification.

The damage to her brain was severe, and when she didn't regain consciousness in the first twenty-four hours, the doctors all but gave up on her. No family came forward, and after the second week medical care was minimal, not much more than turning her over to prevent bedsores and changing the IV drip.

Jimmy didn't know the medical details. He only knew that an older woman in a tweed suit appeared at the ICU every day. Lilith, he later learned. She showed up the minute visiting hours began and stayed by the girl's bedside until they were over. No one else came to see her.

Three weeks into her vigil, Jimmy approached the woman. "Is she your daughter?" he asked.

"My niece."

"I'm glad she has somebody. They couldn't locate her parents."

Lilith gave him a penetrating look, as if studying an X-ray. "Actually, she's not my niece. She's a total stranger."

Jimmy was taken aback. "Then you don't belong here."

"Why not? I'm not hurting anyone. Besides, you don't look like the kind to turn me in."

This was true enough. But why did she need to pretend?

"So no one will ask questions," was her answer.

Lilith gazed at the girl in the bed, who appeared to be sleeping. "She won't ever wake up."

Jimmy was startled. "You sound so certain. No one really knows."

"You can't say that unless you've met everyone, can you?"

Lilith didn't reveal her real motive for keeping a vigil, and Jimmy didn't pry. That wasn't his nature. But it was his nature to care. He made a point of regularly checking in on the girl, who lay motionless in her hospital bed like a forgotten mannequin, while beeping monitors signaled that the thread of life wasn't broken. If Lilith happened to be there, she'd acknowledge him with a silent nod. Jimmy, who hadn't graduated from high school and came from an immigrant family, was guarded in her presence. He was content, like the rest of his clan, the Noceras, to remember his place.

Then one day Lilith made a request in the form of an order. "When your shift is over, come directly here. Don't dawdle. You're needed."

"Why? I'm no doctor."

"We don't need a doctor." She shot him a stern look, one he would become very familiar with.

Jimmy felt uneasy. He wasn't prone to premonitions, yet the situation worried him. Was she planning to interfere? In the

absence of any family, would she pull the plug on the girl's life support? He could easily have skipped out. At the end of his shift he had already changed into his street clothes and was halfway out the door, when he turned back and headed for the ICU.

Lilith was seated by the bed. She lifted a finger to her lips. "Don't speak. Watch."

Jimmy was spooked, but he did as he was told. He stood behind Lilith's chair; neither spoke for what seemed like an eternity. Suddenly the girl raised her head and opened her eyes. Her stare was glassy. *Dios mio,* Jimmy thought, repeating what his grandmother used to say whenever she felt in need of divine protection.

The comatose girl took no notice of her visitors; she only heaved a deep sigh before her head fell back on the pillow. Jimmy was certain that she had just died. He'd never been in a hospital room at the exact moment of death. The experience caused him to shiver. Lilith had anticipated this, he realized. That was why she had ordered him here. But how could she know?

Before he could ask, Lilith gave a loud "Ssh." It was unnecessary, though, since Jimmy was frozen in place. The dead girl emitted a faint glow around her head, a beautiful luminous vapor. The glow rose toward the ceiling, separating from her body. It formed into a blue-white shape roughly the size of the girl, vaguely outlining a head at one end and feet at the other. In a moment, it was gone. The glowing form had disappeared through the ceiling, or else it had evaporated. It happened too fast for Jimmy to tell.

"What just happened?" he whispered.

"Good, you saw. I had an intuition you would." Lilith got to her feet. "But if you really belong here, you know what just happened."

This last remark didn't sink in. Jimmy was too disconcerted. "How did you know she was going to die tonight?"

"I was directed, and I obeyed."

Lilith gathered up her things. She moved quickly out of the room in order to avoid the ICU nurses, who would appear in response to the monitors going flatline.

Jimmy followed her down the corridor. "Who gave you your orders?"

"It wasn't a who." Lilith looked impatient, annoyed that he was trailing her. "I don't expect you to understand."

She quickened her step, but Jimmy jumped ahead and blocked the way.

"You got me into this," he protested. "I deserve an explanation."

" 'Deserve' is a little strong," she snapped. She didn't like it when the worm turned. But Jimmy refused to budge.

"Dying is pretty strong too, don't you think?" He was surprised by his own defiance. The first thing he'd learned as a child was to keep his head down. Remaining inconspicuous was the best defense for a spindly Hispanic kid whose relatives didn't want their papers to be inspected.

He couldn't guess at the thoughts running through Lilith's head at that moment. Events had been leading up to the mystery school for a decade. She was used to obeying her inner voice without question, which was how she had found Meg. The same voice told her to visit the anonymous runaway in the coma. Now she hesitated, waiting for some kind of signal. The human race can probably be divided into two camps, those who understand what it means to wait for a message from the soul and those who would scoff at the mere suggestion. Lilith had moved from one camp to the other. It had taken years, and she didn't want to recklessly expose herself.

"What you saw isn't so unusual," she began.

"So this isn't your first?" said Jimmy.

"No. Yours?" Lilith gave him another of her X-ray looks.

He stepped back. "Lady, I don't know who you think I am."

"You're someone with possibilities, only you don't realize it yet."

Her inner voice told Lilith that there was no turning back now. She began to unfold the whole story. Ever since entering the hospital, the girl in the coma hadn't moved, but her spirit was agitated. It had been badly shaken by the car crash. The coma sent it into a panic, knowing that death was around the corner, and so Lilith arrived to smooth the way. She knew she had to lay down a path of light for the spirit to follow, like a white line down the middle of the highway.

As he listened, Jimmy's face held an expression Lilith couldn't read. Was all of this foreign territory to him, or was he a natural? She only knew that he had been chosen as a witness for a reason.

"Let me pass," she said. "There's nothing more I can tell you."

"So you're just going to leave me hanging?" said Jimmy, unsatisfied.

"No. Keep your eyes open. If you see something like this again, I'll know, and I'll come back for you."

Jimmy was bewildered, but he stepped aside.

He suspected that what he'd seen wasn't accidental. In the world of his grandmother, a world filled with beeswax candles for the dead, roadside altars to the Virgin, and brightly colored *santos* painted on tin that were handed down from mother to daughter, there were spirits all around. As a boy, he couldn't envision what they looked like, so he thought of them as ghosts wearing white sheets.

He didn't have to use his imagination now. But he needed to know more. A week passed. Lilith didn't return, so Jimmy took the initiative. Nervously he began sneaking into hospital rooms where a patient was dying. An orderly was too lowly for doctors to notice, too harmless for anyone else to care.

Death keeps to its own timetable, and nothing ever happened. He tried standing outside a room during a code blue, but to no avail. The patients were brought back from the edge or resuscitated if they'd gone over it. And how could he explain his presence

there in the first place? Out of desperation he drove to another hospital, claiming to be a dying patient's cousin. This backfired when some actual family members appeared. There were shrieks and pointed fingers. Jimmy mumbled excuses in broken English and was lucky not to get arrested.

Until then, his existence had been strangely content. He lived alone, surrounded by pictures of his many nieces and nephews, in a shoe-box apartment near a busy four-lane highway. His television was an old black-and-white portable, and he had never owned a microwave. Jimmy's family couldn't understand why he never got married or went back to their home country, Dominica, to find a good prospect among the many girls who would be happy to have him and a visa to America.

"That's for your generation," he'd say. "I was born here."

Behind his back, people saw him as an object of pity. The events of Jimmy's early life had unfolded in unfortunate ways, first by dropping out of school to go to work—a demand his father made because there were six younger children to feed. He lost touch with everyone his own age when he got a job as an orderly, where he put in so many hours of overtime that he came home exhausted and fell asleep watching *telenovelas* and Brazilian soccer. Seeing a spirit depart the body disturbed his strange contentment. For some reason, it also gave him new hope.

But as the weeks passed without a second sighting, his wonder at what he'd witnessed began to fade. Lilith didn't make any contact. Jimmy's mood darkened. Trying to catch someone's dying moment began to feel ghoulish. Then one night, as he was dragging himself from the living room after turning off the TV, Jimmy recalled Lilith's exact words when she summoned him: "Come directly here. Don't dawdle. You're needed."

This gave him a clue. Without quite knowing why, he sent a message to God: *Let me serve when I am needed.*

If he hadn't been so dog-tired, this prayer would have disturbed

Jimmy. It smelled too much of church talk and the humility of the priesthood. He wanted none of that—no amount of his mother's scolding drew him to the cathedral, except when his nieces, whom he loved dearly, were making their First Communion in white satin dresses.

Arriving at work the next morning, he was given no sign that anything unusual was going to happen. His pious words from the night before didn't spark any magic. On his lunch break he bought a bouquet of white carnations and took them upstairs to the children's ward. In one bed lay a ten-year-old girl, her body very thin and wasted. Jimmy had heard her family speaking Spanish in low voices; he felt a bond.

From the doorway he saw that she was asleep. He liked it better that way, actually, as he placed the carnations on the bedside table.

"Don't touch that!"

Jimmy whirled around. One of the interns had walked in; he looked very angry. "What are you doing in here?"

"Cleaning," Jimmy stammered.

"I don't see any cleaning materials. You were fiddling next to the patient. Did you touch her?"

Jimmy was too stunned to deny the accusation. The intern had red hair, and his face was turning florid to match it. Pointing to the ID Jimmy wore on his shirt, he said, "Give me your badge. We'll let security deal with this."

Jimmy unpinned the ID from his green uniform and held it out. He felt doomed. Hadn't his grandmother warned him? "*Mi querido,* listen to me. What you fear the most always comes true."

But the red-haired intern never took Jimmy's badge. Before he could, a strange look came over his face. He suddenly reached for his chest.

He croaked hoarsely, collapsing on the floor as heavily as a sack of flour. A passing nurse sounded the alarm; she told Jimmy to clear out and began running to the nurses' station.

Jimmy didn't clear out, but instead knelt beside the fallen man, lifting his head to help him breathe. The intern's eyes were open, and there was a glimmer of consciousness in them. Saliva bubbled in his mouth. The air in the room felt very still. In the moment before the cardiac crash cart appeared, the intern's eyes went dead, and Jimmy felt a slight stirring close by. There was no glow like before, only the faintest sense that an invisible breeze had brushed past Jimmy's cheek.

It can happen this way too, he thought.

The cardiac team rushed in, pushing Jimmy aside. Unlike everyone else hurrying about anxiously, Jimmy felt calmly detached. The little girl in the bed hadn't woken up, amazingly.

He left the room. Lilith was waiting for him at the end of the corridor.

"You kept your word," he said.

She gave an austere smile. "Welcome to God knows what."

After that they became allies. Lilith began to fill him in about the group he would belong to, the mystery school. She had been waiting ten years, and so had someone named Meg, although her name came up only once. Jimmy was baffled by most of what Lilith told him.

"It's better not to ask too many questions," she advised. "A mystery isn't something you figure out. It's something you disappear into."

"Like a ship vanishing in the fog?" Jimmy wondered.

"Exactly."

It wasn't a complete shock, then, when she told him to follow Galen. It meant that everything was finally coming to a head.

"You're excited, I can tell," Jimmy said.

"Just don't mess this up," she replied.

After half an hour, Galen stopped snoring and emitted a low groan. His eyes opened, adjusting to the dark room. Jimmy flicked on a lamp.

Galen gasped. "You! You knocked me out."

"No, you fainted, and I dragged you inside." Jimmy opened his jacket like a suspect ready to be frisked. "No weapon, see?" He braced himself for another outburst, but it didn't come.

Instead, Galen heaved a sigh of resignation. "Take what you want. I don't care. Just leave me alone."

"I'm afraid you've got this all wrong."

Jimmy stood up and approached the futon sofa. From his jacket pocket he pulled a folded sheet of paper. It was a watercolor that Lilith had told him to bring.

Galen mistook why Jimmy was standing over him. "Don't hit me," he pleaded feebly.

"No one's going to hit you."

Jimmy unfolded the picture and held it in the light, so that Galen could get a good look.

"You recognize this?" he asked. The watercolor was of a golden chapel with four steeples nestled in a flowery meadow.

Galen had no reply. He burst into tears and hung his head in shame.

Lilith wasn't prone to self-doubt, and if it had been up to her, the mystery school would have been complete by now. On her instructions Jimmy had secured a meeting place at the hospital where he worked. When he showed it to Lilith, she didn't disguise her disappointment. The conference room was sterile and airless. It had no windows, only a long table with folding chairs around it and harsh fluorescent lighting.

"It's not exactly a palace," she said.

"But it's not a torture chamber either," Jimmy reminded her.

"True. There were too many of those."

Meg had set two weeks as the deadline, which left only three more days to go. The big question mark was Galen. Everyone else had been lured in, thanks to Lilith, with Meg guiding her over the rough spots.

"Leave Galen to someone else," Meg told her. They communicated twice a day by phone. For reasons of her own, Meg didn't want to meet in person. She preferred to be the invisible spider sitting out of sight away from the web.

"I can handle him," Lilith insisted.

"No, you can't. He's a delicate case. One misstep, and we'll lose him."

So when Jimmy called with the news that Galen had passed out, Lilith became worried. That was two hours ago, and still no word. She decided to go over there herself and was putting on her coat when the phone rang.

"Jimmy? Do we have him?"

But it was Meg instead. "You sound anxious. What's happening?"

"I was just about to go and find out."

"Don't." There was a short pause on the line. "Get everything ready. Act as if the pieces are going to fall into place."

If this was a statement of faith, it was wasted on Lilith. "We risk everything if we sit on our hands."

"It's okay."

"How can you say that?"

Another pause. "We're always being tested. It was hard for me to come back after all this time. You know that. It was even harder to let go of the shrine."

There was no more to say, and the call ended. But Lilith couldn't let go. Her frustration was killing her. Three days short of the goal, and the mystery school could collapse before it had even started. She should have been put in charge, not demoted to carrying out Meg's orders. The mystery school had grown out of her dream, hadn't it? The dream set in the plague years when Lilith saw the six bodies and the golden shrine?

But it was Meg who gave up her life. At first she totally rejected the idea of becoming a nun. Lilith was sent away with a flat refusal. Then two days later, Meg began to have symptoms of a strange heart malady. At first it manifested as a mild soreness in the middle of her chest. She applied ice, then a hot pad. But the soreness only grew worse. Meg didn't dare to see a doctor, not after all she'd gone through. *Another punishment,* she told herself, *that's what it has to be.*

Every night, she went to sleep with images of a bleeding heart in her head, stark visions that sent her back to her childhood. When she was seven, the nuns at school gave each child a picture of Jesus's heart. Meg was shocked. Why did Jesus wear his heart on the outside? Why was it wearing a crown of thorns, and above all why did blood drip from it? The very sight sent her running into a bathroom stall to hide. Her teacher, Sister Evangeline, found her and asked what was wrong.

"Jesus needs an operation," Meg said.

"It's a beautiful thing," Sister Evangeline corrected her. "If you love Jesus, you love his Sacred Heart."

Perhaps Meg wasn't suggestible, like people who are immune to being hypnotized. She didn't think a heart encircled with a crown of thorns could ever be beautiful. The dripping blood would always be horrible. Even at seven, though, she knew not to say such things aloud.

Within a few days, the soreness in Meg's chest grew so severe she started to wish for the stigmata to return. The bloody spots on her palms had caused only a dull ache. Some days she felt jealous of Lilith with her vision of a golden chapel; it sounded much nicer, more like what a loving God would send. Other days she looked on the whole thing as a bout of madness she had to escape. But there appeared to be only one way out, a route she dreaded the most: becoming a religious freak.

Just when the pain became intolerable, stabbing Meg's heart like nails, Lilith appeared in the driveway in her stiff tweeds with her hands crossed over her purse. Just like that, without any warning.

They didn't sit, as before, in the dining room. Meg had barely made it through the workday on heavy doses of aspirin and shots of vodka from a flask hidden in her desk. She collapsed on the living-room sofa while Lilith talked.

She showed no interest in Meg's suffering. "You're stuck on one idea, that what's happening is a curse. I told you it wasn't."

"Then what is it—a test, a penance?"

Lilith shook her head. "It's a message."

"Telling me what?"

"That it's better to suffer on your path than to be happy on no path at all."

Meg bolted upright despite the pain. "That's horrible!" she exclaimed. She was ready for an argument. "A loving God wants me to be in pain? Why, because I'm a sinner? No thanks. I've heard it all before."

"I can't read God's mind," Lilith retorted. "What I do know is that you have a path, once you submit to it."

"I hate that word 'submit,'" Meg grumbled.

"I don't blame you. But there's something beyond the pain. You just have to get there, and I can't help you. No one can."

Meg and Lilith sat in silence, wondering if they'd ever cross the gulf between them. Lilith, as stubborn as she could be, wasn't going to wear Meg down. If the pain couldn't, how could she?

"Just go," Meg said in an exhausted voice. When Lilith didn't move, she laughed bitterly. "Why are you so interested in me? It's abnormal."

"I have my own path. And I get messages I can't ignore. You're not the only one."

Silence followed. They had hit a wall, and there was no going around it. Lilith gathered herself and stood up. "If I leave now, I won't be back."

Meg hesitated. The prospect of Lilith leaving for good suddenly felt threatening.

But Lilith didn't wait for her to decide. "One way or another," she said, "God finds us where we are, and then he gets us where we need to be." She walked over to the mantel, where a pair of brass candlesticks stood. Drawing an imaginary line between

them, she said, "You go from A to B. You do it every day, no matter how many days it takes. You put all your trust in the path that God lays out. It's simple."

Meg's resentment boiled over. "It's not simple! Not when you've got a thousand tiny knives sticking you in the heart." Collapsing back on the sofa, she began to cry.

The sight softened something in Lilith. "Don't abandon us. Don't abandon *me*."

Meg drew a ragged breath, trying to regain control. "You'll get along without me. We both know that."

Lilith shook her head. "I told you already, the whole thing falls apart without you."

Meg started to moan, her face in her hands. "It's not fair!"

"You can only know that if you see what God can't see." Lilith's stiffness had returned, but not harshly. "I regret that your path is so painful, but without you the rest of us will return to darkness."

Meg was speechless. The whole thing sounded so preposterous. A helpless feeling swept over her, and she flashed on how this all began, with a man walking to his crucifixion. His sense of helplessness dwarfed anything she had ever experienced.

From that moment, everything had spread out like ripples from a rock thrown into a pond. As most people do, she had accepted the small glimpses of meaning that came her way. All the big words—love, hope, compassion, grace—were minimized, placed into tiny compartments like pills in a pillbox. One compartment was for the few people she really loved and who loved her back. Another held her hopes, which had always been modest. Some compartments, like the ones that contained compassion and faith, she had barely peeked into. But there was no compartment for grace. Perhaps that was why she felt so afraid.

"You can't depend on me," she moaned. "I'm more in the dark than anyone."

Sensing Meg's despair, Lilith became more fervent. "There is another life, one you've barely dreamed about. You have been postponing it every day of your life. It's as close as breathing, but you don't see it yet. When you do, you'll lead the rest of us."

"The rest don't exist. The only one I know is you."

"The others will be just like me."

Meg forced a small laugh. "I hope that's not a promise."

She let Lilith stay until she regained control. Nothing had been settled, but afterwards Meg stopped fighting so hard, and the worst of her heart pains subsided.

She kept going to work. She still saw her parents every Sunday for dinner. She still wore her stunning shade of burgundy lipstick and listened to her nieces talk about their boyfriends. Never once, though, did she utter a word about what had happened. As far as her family was concerned, she was the same old Meg she'd been her entire life. Which is why her decision to enter the convent at forty took everyone by surprise.

"You can't," her bossy sister, Nancy Ann, protested. "I know a therapist."

"Don't bully her," said Clare, her sympathetic sister. But she was just as worried as everyone else in the family.

Meg refused to explain herself. The turning point had been with Lilith, who said, "You need to be away from everybody for a while. You have to ripen."

"I'm not a banana," Meg joked, but she knew what Lilith meant.

Lilith spelled it out anyway. "Your soul is ready, but you aren't. There's a mismatch, which is probably why you've been having so much pain. Your body is still protesting."

Meg couldn't deny it. The soreness in her heart, though lessened, kept reminding her of her dilemma.

"Walk away. Heal," Lilith urged. "And when you do, we'll be waiting for you. All of us."

Neither of them suspected that once Meg became a nun, there would be ten years of silence between them. Lilith visited a few times at first, waiting at the brass grate that separated the sisters from the world. Meg never appeared. On the third visit she sent down a note: "The patient is still in intensive care."

The nun who delivered it didn't know what the note meant.

"Is Meg all right?" Lilith demanded to know.

The nun gave her a starchy smile. "Sister Margaret Thomas belongs to God. There's no question she's all right."

Lilith almost cringed. The very thing she once told Meg was being thrown back at her. Years ago she had stopped visiting and simply waited. On an ordinary afternoon she was taking a nap when the phone rang. She answered reluctantly, in case one of the kids was in trouble.

"Hello?"

Drowsily she could hear a familiar voice on the other end. The first thing it said erased ten years in an instant.

"Have all of you waited for me?"

Lilith was instantly awake. "We have."

"Then it's time."

CHAPTER *12*

When Jimmy held up the watercolor of the golden shrine, he knew that everything depended on it. It was his ace in the hole if all other forms of persuasion failed. But he was shocked by Galen's sobbing reaction.

"Don't be upset," he said. It would be a disaster if Galen slipped out of reach.

"Thief!" Galen cried, his hands balled into fists.

The accusation was true. On Lilith's orders, Jimmy had snatched the picture from a room at the hospital. He felt guilty, but there was nowhere to go now but forward.

"I know your wife painted it," he said hesitantly. "Now I'm giving it back."

Galen lifted his head, wiping his damp cheeks with the back of a shirt sleeve. "You think that makes it better?"

"No, but I needed you to recognize the picture. It's important."

Galen had a flash of recognition. "I've seen you before, in her hospital room."

Jimmy nodded, holding his breath. No matter what, he couldn't let Galen throw him out of the house.

"So you're stalking me?" Galen said bitterly.

"Sort of, but it's for a good cause."

This brought a short, barking laugh. But at least Galen had stopped crying. The whole situation was grotesque, including the part he had played. Jimmy held the watercolor up again, but Galen couldn't look at it. It brought back memories of Iris, cancer, and death.

He had sleepwalked through the agonizing events as they unfolded. Iris showed a surprising lack of resistance to seeing a neurologist about her headaches. She had kept from Galen how severe they were, just as he kept from her the ominous e-mail her father had sent. A brain scan was taken, and the doctor described what it showed.

"See this shadow here? It's what we call a lesion on the prefrontal cortex."

"A tumor?" Galen said dully. Sitting beside him, Iris kept silent, gripping his hand tightly in hers.

The doctor nodded. "I'm very sorry. I have to tell you, it's aggressive, and it probably came on very suddenly, perhaps four or five months ago."

Just when she came up to me in the museum, Galen thought grimly. He winced. Iris's nails were digging into his palm like needles.

"There should have been early signs, though they're not predictable," the doctor went on. "A quiet person might suddenly become very outgoing and emotional." He pointed to the image illuminated on the wall beside him. "The lesion is on the right side, just here. The effects can be quite mysterious. In very rare cases, musical abilities appear out of the blue or a mania for painting that was never there before."

Iris didn't cry out, but tears started streaking down her cheeks. She hung her head as if ashamed.

"Can you make her better?" Galen asked, his face ashen.

There were no promises. Surgery followed, then radiation. Iris's parents rushed back, and their accepting mood had changed. They now looked upon Galen as an interloper, a stranger who had

taken advantage of their sick little girl. Dr. Winstone as much as accused him of hiding Iris's symptoms.

Galen suffered through everything as numbly as he could. Iris moved to the spare room to sleep. They rarely talked, and when they did, it was an effort for her to show Galen any signs of affection. She pitied them both, as if a malicious magician had fooled them with his illusions, and now the spell was broken.

One morning she didn't appear for breakfast. Galen searched for her in her room, but it was empty. He lifted the phone to call 911 when he glanced out the window. Weak as she was, his wife had stacked up her paintings in the back yard and was setting them on fire. He rushed outside and, over her protests, pulled out all the canvases that hadn't been scorched yet.

"We have to save them. Forget the doctor. You're a genius."

A weird, squeezed laugh came from her. "I'm just sick. Art was my affliction."

Two weeks later, Iris died in hospice care. An orderly made up her empty bed as Galen rummaged through the bedside table for Iris's things. The orderly seemed to be eyeing him.

"Do you mind? I'm the husband," Galen said sharply. The vigilant orderly nodded and left. Now Galen knew it was Jimmy.

Iris's parents couldn't keep Galen from attending the funeral, but he stayed on the periphery, a silent incidental presence. As the first spade of earth was thrown on the coffin, the mocking voice in Galen's head said, *The comedy endeth.* The voice sounded very satisfied. Galen wasn't. He wanted to lash out at someone or something for the cruel trick that fate had played on him. Like a spindly sprout in a parched field, a plan for avenging a terrible wrong started to hatch in his numbed mind.

Galen pressed his head tightly between his hands, as if to squeeze these memories out.

Jimmy tried to say something that might bring him around. "This picture is very significant. Would you like to know why?"

"Absolutely not." Worn out as Galen was, he could still get angry.

Jimmy pressed on anyway. "It shows a precious object, a holy relic. Your wife must have seen it in a vision. You are our link to her."

Galen regarded him with disdain. "Whatever bullshit you're peddling, you've come to the wrong place. I don't have any money. I just want to . . ." He didn't know how to finish his thought.

"You just want to curl up into a little ball of misery? I can't let you do that, and you don't have to. You're a prisoner inside yourself. Iris saw it. That's why she was drawn to you. It's also why I was sent here."

Jimmy's strange response forced Galen to look at him more closely. The smile he wore, which Galen had initially despised, looked different now.

"I don't need your pity," he said.

"It would have to wait in line anyway, behind your self-pity."

Galen was about to drop the f-bomb, as his mother called it when he was a child, but Jimmy suddenly made a move. Getting to his feet, he took two steps toward Galen, who had no time for a defensive cringe. Before he knew it, Jimmy was lifting him up under the arms as if he were a cranky two-year-old scooped up by his mother.

"Good, we have you on your feet. Now take another look. If you know nothing about this picture, I'll leave you in peace. Not that you'll find any."

Was that last bit a taunt? Galen felt uneasy.

"Please, stop looking so afraid," Jimmy pleaded. "I'm bringing you hope."

Galen had been jerked to his feet too quickly. The blood was rushing from his head; he felt dizzy. He squeezed his eyes shut and willed himself not to faint twice in one day.

"We can talk," he whispered. "Just let me sit down again, please."

Jimmy stepped back, and Galen sank down on the couch, putting his head between his knees. After a moment, his dizziness cleared.

"Tell me what you remember," Jimmy coaxed.

Galen looked puzzled. "Nothing important. What she painted was just a symptom of being sick."

Jimmy shook his head. "Being sick was only a small part of it. When someone is dying, a part of them reaches out for the truth. As they go through the door into another world, they look back over their shoulder to give us a hint about the truth."

Galen felt helpless to argue back. "Whatever. You sound sincere. But I'm the one who got kicked in the teeth when she died."

"You're right. I apologize. You didn't ask for any of this."

Galen took the picture from Jimmy with a sigh, doing his best to recreate the scene weeks before Iris's death. He hadn't made much time to visit her in the hospital. The strain between them was part of the reason. The other part was that he had thrown himself into his work with ferocity. His days were spent at the research library with stacks of journals in front of him. He typed drafts of articles on the computer far into the night, too drained and distracted to face reality.

Galen took up smoking and threw back a shot of whiskey at sunset, the hour beloved by the demon of depression. Slowly he started to feel a shift inside. He was pulling away from Iris and everything she'd been to him. It was like standing at the rear door of a train as it crept away from the station. Before long, the station lights would recede into a faint dimness, and then nothing.

His escape plan wasn't perfect, though. Guilt made him drop in at the hospital, usually late in the afternoon, his arrival timed to Iris's dinner so he could excuse himself after a few minutes. At that point Iris was still eating a little, but the cancer wasted her

ruthlessly, sucking out every bit of energy. Galen was relieved whenever he found her asleep, which was often.

On one particular afternoon, however, she was wide awake. Her motorized bed was propped up as far as it could go, and her hair was carefully pulled back and pinned, a few stray wisps framing her pale face. Galen tried to smile, but she had put on a drop of his favorite perfume, and the scent made him feel sick.

"You look nice," he mumbled evasively.

"Do I? I made sure I didn't bring a mirror from home." Iris's voice was clear, and her eyes glistened. Galen looked away. Her eyes had glistened like that when she was in her mania for painting.

"Please, don't be afraid of me," she whispered.

Galen's hand instinctively moved toward the cigarettes in his jacket pocket, until he remembered where he was. Before his mother died, she entered a spell of truth-telling. She held him captive by her bedside atoning for her mistakes, trying to make amends. *If we're into the truth,* he wanted to tell her, *I'm bored and fed up. Eat some Jell-O, watch TV. We can't change the past.* He never let the words out though, biding his time like a patient son.

But he wasn't about to play the same game twice. "The doctor wants you to rest," he mumbled. "I should go."

"In a minute," said Iris, not offended by his rudeness. She gestured toward the metal bedside table, which was just out of her reach. "Can you open that drawer, please? I want to show you something."

Galen opened it and retrieved a sheet of fine-grained paper with deckled edges

"I didn't know you brought any supplies with you," he said.

"I met a nice nurse. She fetched some paper and colors for me. You weren't answering the phone."

"You could have waited," Galen complained.

She read the guilt on his face. "I didn't want you to feel bad, seeing all the art stuff again. And I was in a hurry. I had the

strongest desire to make this picture. Imagine that, after trying to burn everything."

She took the paper from his hands and turned it over, exposing the image hidden from sight in the drawer. "I wanted you to be the first to see it."

She wasn't being cruel. Galen knew this, but his heart began to ache. He dully gazed at the picture. It showed a steepled church in a meadow. There was a golden glow suffusing it. He scowled. The religious thing again. Her disease was showing no mercy.

In a sympathetic voice Iris said, "You don't have to like it. You don't even have to keep it. But somehow it's about you." Seeing that he wanted to protest, she rushed on. "The image came to me in a dream. I was happy in the dream, for once. Sleep is usually such a black hole."

She stopped. Galen showed no reaction. Against his will, he had been drawn into a round of deathbed truth-telling again.

Iris tried to keep up her bright mood, even though a tinge of defeat was creeping in. "This isn't something I can explain or help you through, Galen. I don't understand it myself. All I know from the dream is that you belong here." She pointed to the church, and then her hand fell.

She'd spent her energy; her body gave out, and the disease reclaimed her. The color drained from her face. Gray and empty-eyed, her head lolled on the pillow. The transformation was shockingly fast.

Galen couldn't spare any pity for her. He was too angered by what she'd said: "You belong here." The words made him want to rip the picture from her limp hands and tear it in two. Instead, he turned around and left. The ache in his heart had turned into the cold heaviness of stone.

Now, in his living room, Galen made a futile gesture. "That's all I know."

"I understand. It hurts to go back," Jimmy said.

Galen flared up. "Screw you."

Jimmy sighed. "We're going around in circles here."

Pulling out his cell phone, he walked into the nearby kitchen. Galen heard a mumbled exchange.

When he returned, Jimmy said, "We understand why you're resisting this whole thing. It's too much to take in, and you're exhausted. But you showed us what to do."

"Me?"

" 'You belong here.' If that's the message, a sign—whatever you call it—we're going to trust it." He pointed to the picture. "What your wife saw is real, a gift from God, and now it's in the right hands. I hope you get to see it. A lot of people are depending on you."

"I don't care. God is a lie, a huge criminal fraud. If anybody wants something from me, tell them that." Galen's voice trailed off. He didn't want to think about his failed revenge.

"What if you found out once and for all?" Jimmy asked.

"About what?"

"If Iris saw something real. If God is real. Here's your chance to find out."

"You're insane." But Galen's protest wasn't as angry as before. He could hear the compassion in Jimmy's voice.

"I'm just going on faith here," Jimmy said. "But there are people I trust, the way I'm asking you to trust me. They say that anyone who comes into contact with this object is never the same again."

Galen was poised with a torrent of objections, but Jimmy didn't give him the chance to release them.

"Here." He scribbled the number of the conference room on the back of the picture. "We're meeting at the hospital. You know where it is. The room's in the basement."

Galen stared suspiciously at what Jimmy had written. "Do I get paid?"

"That's not up to me. I'm just the messenger."

Jimmy didn't scold him for having selfish motives. He could see that Galen had to defend himself.

"Just think about it. I'll let myself out."

Without another word Jimmy stepped outside, closing the door behind him. He paused on the stoop to look up. It was snowing now, and by morning his footprints would be erased, as if he'd never been there. He headed back to the cab. The news wouldn't please Lilith; but it was her idea, when Jimmy phoned from the kitchen, to appeal to Galen's curiosity. Jimmy was about to report back when his cell phone rang.

"I think he listened." It was a woman's voice, but not Lilith's.

"Who is this?"

"We haven't met, but we will soon. I'm Meg."

Jimmy was confused. "I don't know any Meg."

"Just as well. I only wanted to thank you."

"Really? How do you know about any of this?"

"It's not easy to explain. But I'll try when we meet."

Before he could ask another question, the line went dead. Jimmy brushed the snowflakes from the driver's-side windshield with his glove. He climbed into the cab, not looking over his shoulder. Somehow he was sure that Galen had come to his front window and was gazing out to make sure he really left.

Jimmy tried not to feel disheartened. He had probably revealed more than he should have. Protecting the mystery of the golden shrine was the group's first priority, Lilith had warned. Galen might show up with the others just to snoop. He might extort money. Whatever happened, it was time to walk away. An invisible force was at work. If a miserable skeptic was destined to join, fate would find a way.

The cab left light tracks in the thin, new snow as it sped away. Galen waited at the window until it turned the corner and was out of sight. Seeing the intruder leave was a relief, but not enough

to remove the tension in his body. He crumpled Iris's watercolor into a ball and threw it into the trash bin under the sink; then he hopped into the shower.

There was no reason to trust the intruder and his fantastic talk. What had talking done but stir up painful memories and play on Galen's emotions? Now he was left with nothing except nagging doubts. Iris believed in her vision. The intruder was right about that—she wanted to send Galen a message he couldn't ignore.

He turned up the hot water until it made red splotches on his shoulders as he stood under the steaming spray. It burned, but his muscles started to relax. Galen drank three beers before he went to bed, idly surfing the Internet to distract himself. Soon he was fit for nothing but crashing into stupefied sleep.

He didn't know the next morning how he happened to find the watercolor, rescued from the trash, lying open on the kitchen counter. Still less did he know why he got in his car on Saturday, three days later, headed for the hospital and the room number Jimmy had scrawled on the back of the picture. Galen's heart was racing as he got closer to his destination.

What am I doing? he thought to himself. Doubt, always his default position, began to tug at him.

But another force intervened. *You're going where you belong,* it said.

The words were meaningless. Galen almost turned back, but he had come this far. Besides, all he could think about was Iris, the love she'd shown to a lost soul, and how impossible it was to let go.

part two

THE
INVISIBLE
GOSPEL

CHAPTER *13*

So it befell that at seven o'clock on Saturday evening, they all arrived. First Mare, who brought Frank, who threatened in the car to walk out if anything weird started to happen.

"Weird would be an anticlimax after what we've gone through," said Mare. A grunt was his only reply. She smiled to herself, suspecting that Frank's resistance was merely token. He had a reporter's nose and couldn't wait to follow up this lead.

The rest of the group was already seated around the table when they walked in. Lilith hadn't placed herself at the head, where everyone expected her to be, but in the closest chair to the right.

"Don't introduce yourselves, and try not to stare," she ordered. "Someone's got the jitters."

She meant Galen, who had sunk into a sullen mood the moment he laid eyes on Lilith. Jimmy had switched work shifts with another orderly that day and only had to take the elevator to the basement.

When the five of them were seated, Lilith nodded, and Mare placed the closed cardboard box she'd walked in with on the table.

"Do you want me to open it?" she asked nervously. This was the first time the golden shrine had left her apartment.

"Not yet."

An awkward silence settled over the group. Galen shifted in his seat. Frank took hold of Mare's hand under the table. Lilith was stone-faced. The only person who looked pleased was Jimmy, because he had carried out his task of gathering the black sheep into the fold.

After fifteen minutes, Galen stood up. "Am I the only one who's choking in here? Is the AC broken or what?"

It was never discovered if he was about to bolt from the group at the last minute, because two critical things occurred simultaneously. From between the cracks in the loosely closed cardboard box a faint golden glow started to emanate, giving off a glimmer like the last live coals buried in the ashes of a winter fire. As if on cue the door opened, and a dignified woman entered the room. She wore a black suit and no makeup. She smelled faintly of lily-of-the-valley perfume. Her eyes went immediately to the box.

"Good," she said. "The sleeper is awake."

Mare was eighteen when she last saw her aunt, and the woman just entering didn't fit her memories. Her aunt's hair was more gray than the light brown Mare remembered. She was also smaller, as if shrunk into herself, with dainty hands. Her eyes had a faraway look in them. *The effect of ten years in the convent?* Mare wondered.

If Mare couldn't yet match her recollections with the woman in front of her, Meg immediately recognized her niece. She came over and whispered in her ear. "You've done very well. I'm proud of you."

Mare didn't know whether to feel reassured or to burst into tears—she had almost convinced herself that she would never see her aunt again. "Why is all this happening?" she whispered back.

But there was no time to talk. The room was in a commotion. Everyone's attention was fixed on the golden light peeking through the cardboard box, which was directly in front of Mare and Frank.

Trying to look unfazed, Frank pushed it toward Meg. "Welcome back, if that makes any sense. This belongs to you." He glanced around the table. "As you can see, it did the job."

"I'm sorry you were kept in the dark," Meg apologized. "I'll try my best to explain why we're here."

Lilith cut her short. "That can wait. Not everyone has seen what's inside. Time for the unveiling."

Meg gave a resigned nod. "I suppose you're right."

With visible uncertainty Mare opened the box and lifted out the shrine. At her touch, its glowing aura grew brighter, filling the room even under the harsh fluorescent lights. The reaction around the table was quiet awe, except from Galen. He shielded his face to keep the light out of his eyes.

"This thing could be radioactive. Have you thought about that?"

"Don't make trouble," said Lilith sharply. "There's nothing to be afraid of."

"And we're just supposed to believe you?" he asked.

Frank was getting annoyed. "You need to cool it. I'm as skeptical as anybody, but this"—he held his palms up to the light—"this isn't a cheap trick."

"Unless proven otherwise," Galen shot back.

Meg intervened. "It's our first meeting, and we have some important decisions to make. Let's not waste time arguing." She paused to let the golden light capture their attention again. "The one thing we can all agree on is that none of us, including me, ever imagined a phenomenon such as this. The only possible reaction is wonder."

"This is the mystery that makes us a mystery school," Lilith added.

Galen had to clamp his jaws tight, but no one contradicted her.

"Right," Lilith continued. "So we find ourselves in unknown territory. Each of us has been chosen, even though we don't know why."

"I have a suggestion," Jimmy interrupted, speaking for the first time. He was probably the most transfixed by the glowing light. "We better be careful what we say around this thing. It could be listening to us, you know."

Lilith's reaction was barely concealed pity.

"Really, I'm serious," he protested.

"I agree," said Meg. "We don't have to watch what we say, but it would be foolish to ignore a simple fact. There's something inside there. We have no idea where it came from or what it knows."

Lilith, after trying to seize control, fell back in her chair.

"You mean a ghost?" Jimmy asked, thinking of the dead spirits who surrounded his grandmother. She attributed good fortune to them when they were appeased. More often it was the reverse. If she couldn't find her prayer book or the roof leaked, his grandmother would get a knowing look on her face and mumble "Uncle Tito" or the name of some other deceased relative.

Meg shook her head. "I'd describe it as a presence. The shrine is hypnotic, but it only exists to get our attention."

"Like I said, it does the job. That still doesn't tell us why we're all here," countered Frank.

Now Mare entered in. "Perhaps the six of us are a test case. We've been given a sign to see what we do with it."

"We're being experimented on?" asked Frank, who looked uneasy at the prospect.

"Bingo," Galen said with a twisted smile. "God needs lab rats, and we're dumb enough to volunteer."

"I'm just trying to figure this out," snapped Frank. "If you've got a better idea, let's hear it. Or are you only here to shut us down?"

"I'm just not ready to swallow bogus miracles," Galen said with quiet defiance. "Let's put all our cards on the table, okay? The rest

of you want this to be a miracle, don't you? Some of you in the worst way. If it turns out you were duped, laugh all you like. But you'll feel like fools."

Because you've been there, Jimmy wanted to say. He had a hard time restraining himself. He knew that Galen was churning inside. He had desperately wanted to believe in Iris's love, and he wouldn't be made a fool of twice.

"Why would anyone dupe us?" asked Frank. "Nobody here is rich, and besides, I work for the paper. I could blow the whistle on this in a heartbeat."

Before Galen could fire a new salvo, Lilith came back to life. "I was the first one who saw the object. It came to me in a dream. A nightmare, really. There was death all around, and somehow this glowing church appeared among the dying. Was it a symbol of life, a promise of heaven? I had no idea. A higher reality was reaching out, just like it's reaching out to us now. Will we welcome it or turn our backs and run? Believe me, I've spent anxious nights over this, but I'll never rest easy if I don't see it through."

She had spoken for everyone, but there was no murmur of agreement. The Lilith they all knew harbored no doubts, much less fear.

Galen stood his ground. "You think this is a test of faith? Then why was I chosen?"

"That may be unanswerable, and not just for you," Meg said. "Whatever is meant to happen, it starts now. This is a new moment. How many of those come along in our lives?"

Her words silenced the room, each person lost in private thoughts. They had spaced themselves widely around the table, like a collection of strangers and not a group. Galen had talked about God needing lab rats. He was being sarcastic, but God lurked in the back of everyone's mind. Was God toying with them? It was like one of those carnival machines where you insert

a quarter and try to lift out a prize with a grappling hook. A cosmic player had dropped the hook and chosen them, six people out of all those on the whole planet, as his prize.

The cosmic player liked diversity. Mare and Frank were the only obvious couple. The youngest too, dressed in faded jeans and running shoes. Jimmy, just off his shift, was dressed in his uniform. Galen had thrown on the same khakis and white shirt he'd been wearing all week. Lilith and Meg, the two oldest, wore suits, which gave off an air of authority.

After a few moments, Frank began to speak. "You say the shrine is alive or has someone inside it, whatever. It isn't holding us here against our will. Let's talk to it and get some answers."

"You're right," said Meg. "Wonder isn't enough, and skepticism can't deny what's before us."

When no one protested, she was encouraged. The nervousness in the room, which had dominated everything so far, began to lessen.

"We must make contact," she continued. "The presence has no name. I think it's a she. The person who gave me the shrine said she was the thirteenth disciple of Jesus."

She spoke in a mild tone, but these words sent a shiver through the group.

"How could she still be alive?" Jimmy whispered, overwhelmed by this new piece of information.

"How could she be dead? That's what a believer would say," Lilith pointed out. "Death, where is thy sting? Grave, where is thy victory?" she quoted.

"At the risk of sounding obtuse," said Frank, "we're here with someone who knew Jesus. Is that what you're saying?"

"I think so," Meg said cautiously. "Lilith and I have been waiting a long time to find the rest of you. We were never sure what we were dealing with."

"I don't like the sound of that," Frank muttered. "You have to tell us what you know."

"All right, but it may not help."

Meg's indecision was genuine. She was at the center of the web that drew them together, but she had taken one leap of faith after another.

"Only recently has the golden shrine been given to me," she began, "and it happened as mysteriously as everything that's happened to you."

The delicate string of events went back to her first month as a nun. At vespers on the day she entered the cloister, she waited in a dark hallway. The double doors in front of her swung open, and she faced the entire company of nuns, their first novice in years. She was in her candidacy, they told her, which would last three months. In no uncertain terms, the nuns made it clear they would be keeping an eye on her. But they were mostly older and benign, and if not benign, lost in their private contemplation, with no inclination to bother her.

Her strategy was to blend in, but make no special friends. This wasn't difficult. Several other nuns ate alone and said little. A sister desiring complete contemplation was held up as a shining example for the rest to emulate. As the new arrival, Meg raised no eyebrows when she missed some prayers and worked in the kitchen without speaking to anyone. Outwardly she was accepted, but it still took her some time to be accepted on the inside. Bouts of absolute panic came and went. She would lie on her back staring at the small window of her claustrophobic cell, furnished with a metal-framed cot and a rickety dresser. She felt like a castaway at sea, lost from rescue.

After Meg's first three weeks, Mother Superior called her in to make sure Sister Margaret Thomas, as Meg was now known, was adjusting. Sitting in the hallway outside the old nun's office,

Meg had made up her mind to leave. It would be humiliating, but there was no alternative.

So when she was asked how she liked her new life, Meg was amazed to hear herself say, "It's everything I'd hoped for."

"You're not lonely?" Mother Superior asked. "It can be a shock. The new ones miss television, I believe. I arrived before television, you see."

"You must have been very young, Reverend Mother," Meg murmured. When the old nun looked puzzled, she repeated the words in a louder voice, suspecting deafness. The infirmity had made conversation with her grandparents practically impossible as they got older.

"Well, I came from a small farming town. Television took a long time to get there." Mother Superior was content to see the smile on Meg's face. If she was growing deaf or not, it cued her to end the interview quickly.

Walking away, Meg was mystified at her impulsive decision to stick it out. But what was done was done. In her second month, she stopped waiting for fingers to point at her accusing her of being a fraud. She felt a quiet awe around the Carmelite sisters and their dedication to a life of prayer. *They are married to God,* she thought, remembering the first time her mother had explained to her what a nun was.

It was a relief not to feel panicked and suffocated, but there was no inner light. The cloistered routine she once feared turned into something worse: a bore. The ripening that Lilith had promised hadn't yet shown signs of starting. Meg was stubborn, but how long could she hang from the tree like last year's withered crab apples?

I didn't come here with any guarantees, she reminded herself. *Wait and see.*

Twice a week, the church sent a priest, Father Aloysius, to perform Mass and hear confession as chaplain to the convent. Meg

openly took Communion, but she dreaded going into the confession. It couldn't be avoided, though, and she got through the ordeal by confessing to minor sins, which became harder and harder to dream up. How many times could she covet Sister Beatrice's diamond rosary, a present from a rich, devout grandmother? The visiting priest was old and crusty; he went through the motions without really listening.

Meg enjoyed working in the garden that summer, yet with the arrival of the first hard frost, her spirits matched the somber light outside. Spying the sliver of a new moon through her grated window, she fought off despair. At her next confession, Father Aloysius slid aside the panel that divided them. He smelled of strong soap and wheezed as he breathed.

Instead of saying, "Bless me, Father, for I have sinned," she blurted out, "I don't belong here."

The old priest hesitated. This deviation from the prescribed ritual caught him off guard.

Before he could find a reply, Meg went on, "I'm not here because I want to be a nun. I'm not even a good Catholic. I had to tell somebody. I need a friend who can keep my secret."

The old man's chronic wheezing grew worse. Was he horrified? Outraged? After a long pause he said, "God understands what it means to have doubts. Is there more?"

"Yes." Meg felt the courage of reaching the point of no return. "I've had some very disturbing experiences."

Behind the screen, Father Aloysius shifted. "What kind of experiences?"

"They felt spiritual, but who can really know?"

"Are they why you came to the convent, to escape?"

She had no choice but to describe her visions and the stigmata. "I felt trapped. I didn't belong with normal people anymore."

Father Aloysius murmured sympathetically. "I hear the distress in your voice."

"I think God found the wrong person."

Meg said these words with bitterness. There followed a longer silence. She wondered if she had just committed blasphemy.

"God never finds the wrong person," Father Aloysius replied finally. "Your secret is safe with me. Here's what you need to do. Don't come to confession next Sunday. Find an excuse to go outside. Meet me in the parking lot."

Before Meg could ask why, he slid the door back in place with a click, leaving her alone in the confessional, anxious thoughts swirling in her head. Outside the chapel, she could hear the other nuns begin to file into the refectory for Sunday dinner. Meg rushed out of the box, hoping that her expression didn't give away her agitation.

She spent the next week in suspense. The weather grew colder, and the walls of her freezing cell seemed to close in on her. In the creeping pace of days, Sunday eventually came. She went to Mass, but averted her eyes when Father Aloysius gave her Communion, afraid that his expression might show contempt for her unbelief.

After Mass, Meg found him in the parking lot leaning up against the old black Lincoln town car that the church had assigned him for the long trip to the convent. A sharp wind ruffled his thin white hair, and he was smoking a cigarette.

"You've gotten us into something, haven't you?"

"Have I?" asked Meg in bewilderment.

"More than you know."

The wind stung the old priest's face. He removed his spectacles and rubbed his rheumy eyes with bony knuckles.

Don't. They'll only get redder, Meg thought.

"I checked you out," he continued. "But before I say anything more, let's get one thing straight. You were right when you said you aren't a good Catholic."

Meg was alarmed. "But I have to stay here. Don't send me away."

"Let me finish." The old priest took a final drag on his cigarette before crushing it out under his shoe. "Nasty things."

He looked sharply at Meg, but he wasn't frowning. "Do you know why you're not a good Catholic?" He gave her a grave smile. "Because you've heard from God on his private line. He pushed the church out of the way. You probably have no idea how many teachings he violated to get through to you."

"It was all his fault," Meg blurted out.

"So to speak. Is God allowed to be a bad Catholic? The bishop's quite strict, you know."

They both laughed. Meg felt a wave of relief, and a deep sigh escaped from her lungs. Without realizing it, she hadn't been breathing.

"I believe in a living gospel," Father Aloysius said. "Which means that the truth is all around us, as alive as we are. For most believers, the gospel lies only on the page. And there it dies. The truth is in an invisible gospel, and whoever it touches, well, there's no predicting what happens then."

"You think it's touched me?" asked Meg.

Instead of answering, he said, "You didn't ask me who I checked you out with."

"I was afraid to. The bishop doesn't exactly approve of me."

"I went over his head. You're not alone. Others may be getting messages from God. They may be as troubled as you are, and it could last for many years. That's why I didn't report you."

"But you asked God about me. What did he say?"

Father Aloysius's thin lips tightened. "Have we gotten to the point where a priest can't keep the secrets of the confessional? I hope not."

He reached into his heavy black cassock, fumbling for his car keys. "Meet me here again next Sunday. Be extra careful. You won't get into trouble if someone saw you speaking with me, but Mother Superior is sharp. Don't let her deafness fool you."

Meg was anxious to learn more, but her new ally had turned away, walking around to the driver's side. His arthritic limbs made him groan as he got behind the wheel. The old Lincoln belched a plume of exhaust fumes as it lumbered down the long driveway. Meg watched until it disappeared around the bend. The wind penetrated her habit, but she wasn't shivering. Standing outside in the biting cold didn't feel like penance anymore.

When she finished this part of her story, Meg paused. "I know you all have reactions to what I've just told you, but we've reached a turning point. Look."

She pointed to the golden chapel. Its glow had grown dimmer, now almost masked under the brightness of the fluorescent lights. As soon as their eyes turned to it, the glow went out.

"Show's over," Galen remarked with thinly disguised relief.

They were all bewildered.

"Did it give up on us?" Jimmy asked.

"Not that. It means we don't need a beacon anymore," said Meg. "The lighthouse has served its purpose. So what's our next move?"

"Maybe there isn't one," said Galen. "Maybe we're just spectators."

"I'm not with our resident skeptic on this one," Frank said, pointing at Galen. "Walking away is not an option."

Mare spoke up. "I believe what Father Aloysius said. Once the truth touches you, no one knows what will happen next. I got here by following the truth. There wasn't any plan. It must be the same for the rest of you."

"Sure, but we can't proceed blindly," Frank protested. "What happened to getting answers?"

He stared glumly at the shrine, whose life was snuffed out. No answers were coming from it.

"Let's go around the table, then," Meg suggested. "Each person can ask one question if they have doubts. I'll do my best to answer. Maybe it will clear the way."

There was a murmur of agreement at this suggestion.

"I'll go first," Lilith volunteered. "How did you get the golden church?"

"Father Aloysius passed it to me just before he died."

"So he was part of a mystery school himself?" said Lilith.

Galen piped up. "That's two questions. Who's next?" He kept his arms folded across his chest, where they'd been from the moment he sat down.

Jimmy raised his hand. "I'll use Lilith's question."

"Yes, Father Aloysius belonged to a mystery school. He followed a very difficult path," said Meg. "As a young man he was tormented by doubts, even after he was ordained. Certain signs came to him, but he was afraid to trust them. He made light of being a bad Catholic when actually it was a great fear of his. Eventually, he was drawn into a mystery school, and by the time I met him, he was its only surviving member."

"Which means that it doesn't take the whole membership," Frank pointed out.

"Is that your question?" Meg asked.

Frank nodded.

"It takes the whole membership to be a school, even when it's down to one. The purpose is always the same, keeping the spark alive."

"I guess I'm next," said Mare. "He told you about an invisible gospel. What is that?"

"It's a body of knowledge that doesn't appear in the Bible," Meg replied. "The knowledge gets transmitted from generation to generation by those who are attuned to it. That's why mystery schools began, to see beyond the written word. In our case, the transmission comes from the purest source, the thirteenth disciple. Our school is named after her."

By now it was hard for the group to keep still. They wanted to question Meg for hours. But she hadn't forgotten Galen.

"What would you like to know?" she asked.

"Nothing. I don't need any answers, not the kind you're selling. When it's time to vote, I'll vote with my feet."

Jimmy couldn't contain himself any longer. "Shame on you, mister. God touched you the deepest. He brought you pure love."

Galen turned red; the others looked mystified.

Weakly Galen muttered, "I just want to get back to reality."

"I hear you," said Jimmy. "But you've already gotten there. This is it."

Galen had lost his defiance, but he still looked doubtful.

"Don't leave," Mare coaxed. "The rest of us will be stranded. The mystery school will collapse before it's even begun."

"Don't plead with him," Frank grumbled. "That's just what he wants."

"Pleading won't work. There is no mystery," Galen retorted. "That's what you people don't seem to get."

But Frank had gotten it right. Galen was enjoying being in the driver's seat. It was a very unfamiliar place, as timid and invisible as he had been all his life. He would push the privilege as far as it would take him. But inside he had a secret wish that would blow his cover. Whatever happened, he wanted to hear or see Iris again.

Meg was good at reading the situation. "It's been a long evening. Let's meet here at the same time next week."

Jimmy was startled. "Didn't you hear what he just said?"

"Yes, but I don't think we need a formal vote anymore. Is everyone willing to come back? If not, raise your hand."

The rest felt uncertain about Galen, but when no one raised a hand, neither did he.

Meg smiled with relief. "Then it's decided."

There was nothing more to say, so they began to file out. At the door, Lilith took Galen aside. "You're walking a fine line, mister. You've had a lot of pain. This could be your way out. Don't throw it away."

Trying not to look cowed, Galen stiffened his back and left without a reply.

Putting on his coat, Frank was apologetic to Mare. "Can we do this later? I have to catch up on the work I missed. There's a morning deadline."

She kissed his cheek. "You go. I'm fine."

"You're sure?" Frank sounded concerned, but it was a mask for guilt. He didn't want to lose Mare, and if they got into a deep discussion now, she'd realize how far apart they were about the mystery school.

"I told you, I'm fine."

Frank nodded and left.

Actually, Mare welcomed the chance to be alone with her aunt. When the room was empty, she said to her, "Should we tell the family you're back?"

"That depends," Meg replied. "Will they consider it good news or not? Don't worry about it right now. It's for me to take care of."

Mare was eager to hear more details of Meg's recent life, but Meg made a show of pushing in the chairs, turning off the lights, and rushing them both out. She made small talk on the way to the parking lot and ignored Mare's stare when she saw the silver Mercedes Meg unlocked.

"You're dissatisfied. I see it," Meg said kindly. By driving away, she'd be leaving Mare empty-handed, so she said, "Father Aloysius left me everything in his will—he came from a rich banking family and outlived all his siblings. I was set up to continue the mystery school where he'd left it."

"And the golden chapel, where did it come from?" Mare asked.

"I don't know. It was a deathbed bequest. He'd never even hinted at it." Meg became pensive. "I hope this is the right thing to do. It could all come crashing down around us."

Mare hesitated. Her aunt had become frail-looking in the convent, and she seemed slightly bewildered to be back in the world.

Her eyes, however, contained mystery. She had seen things few others have seen.

"You've sacrificed ten years of your life for this," said Mare. "I want to see it through for your sake."

Meg stepped into her expensive car with undisguised embarrassment. "It looks ridiculous, doesn't it?" she said. "His family believed in having only the best. But he wasn't like that. He was exceptional in a way the world will never know."

"Will we ever be known?" Mare said.

"I'm not the one to ask. Remember, I'm the expert at hiding my light under a bushel basket."

The remark was offhand, but true enough. After her aunt drove off, Mare walked to her car on the far side of the parking lot. The night was frigid, and she wondered why everything about this story seemed to happen in cold weather. She began to hum to herself, half unconsciously, a favorite Christmas carol.

In the bleak mid-winter
Frosty wind made moan.
Earth stood hard as iron,
Water like a stone.

She stopped there, and a shiver ran through her. The mystery school was reborn, but the world was still hard as iron. The tests that lay ahead would be just as hard. Something inside her was sure of it.

CHAPTER *14*

A week later, the second meeting convened like the first. Everyone except for Mare and Frank again sat spaced around the table like strangers. The golden shrine had been placed in the middle. No one paid it any attention, though, now that its spell was gone. Galen eyed it suspiciously. He hadn't abandoned the possibility that the thing might be radioactive.

"All of you were nervous last week. This week you're tense," Meg observed. "But no one stayed away."

"Curiosity wins over doubt," said Lilith, seated again in the lieutenant's chair to Meg's right.

"For the time being," Frank remarked curtly. "My week was a total waste, nothing but waiting. Aren't we supposed to do something?"

"I'm with him," Jimmy chimed in. "We're not going to sit around like in school, are we?" He dreaded school as much as he resented it when his father forced him to drop out.

Not that anyone cared. They had all gone through strange experiences they couldn't explain, but it didn't draw them closer, perhaps the opposite. They wanted to keep the strangeness private.

Frank and Mare had found excuses not to spend much time together. The first meeting had somehow made them shy

around each other—shy or wary. Frank tried to charm her on the phone.

"I'm calling from God Anonymous. Does anyone in your family have a religious addiction? We can spray for that."

Mare wasn't in a joking mood. "Have you heard from anyone in the group?"

"Not a peep. You sound worried."

Mare moved on to another subject. Frank knew better than to try to be funny again. His own life wasn't going that well. He hadn't slept. It was hard to concentrate at work. He thought he was keeping it together fairly well until his buddy Malcolm, the kid reporter, stopped by Frank's cubicle.

"Want to see something hilarious? Like weird and hilarious?"

It was a jolt when Malcolm held up a photo of Galen, looking slumped and sullen in the police station.

Frank's stomach was tied in knots. "How do you know him?"

"I don't. Do you? You look kind of peculiar."

"He just looks like such a sad sack. Was he arrested?"

"Yep. It happened a while back. I forgot to tell you." Malcolm laughed. "This old dude tried to spray-paint a masterpiece. I bought him a burger, and he told me all about hating God. Something to do with his wife dying."

"And you find that funny?" asked Frank.

Frank's disapproval puzzled his friend. "I thought you'd want a laugh. This guy's a nut case. I'll show you my write-up."

"No rush."

Frank buried his head back in his work. Malcolm walked away with a look of, "What's gotten into you all of a sudden?"

When he picked Mare up for the meeting the following Saturday, Frank was right about her being worried.

"Aunt Meg's been out of touch all week," she said. "She told me she'd handle everything about the family, but then there was no word."

"Maybe she just needs time to adjust. She was in a convent for ten years. Be thankful she's not totally bats," he said.

Mare couldn't be talked out of her anxiety. Even when they entered the meeting room and saw that Meg was there, calm and faintly smiling, Mare was unsettled. When Frank reached for her hand, she drew it away.

Now everyone was venting their frustration. Galen said, "Whatever we do, no more Q and A about the ghost in the box. It's like a quiz show with imaginary answers and no prizes." He rocked back in his chair and waited.

Buddy, if you were five feet closer, I'd kick that chair out from under you, thought Frank. But he kept quiet. Last week's arguing had gotten them nowhere.

No one was happy with Galen, who was determined to keep stirring the pot. If Meg was annoyed, however, she didn't show it.

"I hear what you're saying, Mr. Blake."

"Use my first name. I'm not your boss," Galen growled.

"Indeed." Meg regarded him with an unperturbed smile.

The rest of the group exchanged puzzled looks. Why was Meg kowtowing to an obvious troublemaker? She and Lilith wore the same suits as the week before, but the air of authority had faded. *They could have dropped in from a knitting circle,* Frank thought. *Or a spinsters support group.* Lilith gave him a sharp sideways glance, and Frank suddenly recalled her unnerving ability to read minds when she wanted to.

Meg went on. "We went around in circles last week, but we agreed that the presence in the shrine knows we're here. What else does she know about us? Let's find out."

"What if she knows our dirty little secrets?" Jimmy asked nervously.

"Don't be scared," Galen jibed. "Being a stooge isn't a secret. You jump when Lilith says jump."

Jimmy turned red. "Take that back."

"Why? You carry out her dirty work. I know that for a fact. Try thinking for yourself." Galen enjoyed watching Jimmy squirm. They were both as timid as mice when it came down to it, but at least Galen was top mouse.

Meg ignored them. "I imagine the presence knows us at both our best and our worst. That's what God sees. So if she belongs with God, we can expect no less."

This was the first open declaration about God that anyone had made except for Galen's sarcastic outbursts.

After an uneasy silence, Jimmy said, "I believe in God. Is that a crime here?"

"Stop it," Lilith said sharply. "We need to stick to business."

Galen shot Jimmy a look that said, "I told you so." Jimmy's face began to color again.

Before the spark was fanned into a flame, Mare raised her hand. "I have an idea, and I think it will work."

She had been so quiet that stepping forward came as a surprise. The stares she received made her uncomfortable, but she pressed on. "I propose that each of us touch the object, being open to whatever happens. Let it communicate that way."

She gave Frank a meaningful look. They both knew that something was bound to happen.

"Good suggestion," he said. "Let's find out exactly what the presence wants to tell us."

"I want to go first," Jimmy said eagerly. He had lost confidence during the week. He wanted the room to be filled with a golden glow again. The light made him feel that he belonged in its shimmering aura. There was another thing too. What if a disciple of Jesus really lived in the shrine? It wasn't impossible. He heard stories in the neighborhood, where a ghoul, a *demonio necrofago,* crept into someone's body at night while they slept. When Jimmy was a child, the windows in his bedroom had always been shut after sunset, no matter how sweltering it became in August.

"The first to go will be Galen," Meg announced, to Jimmy's disappointment.

"I'm not touching that thing," Galen protested.

"Then don't," Jimmy said, seeing a chance for himself.

Mare took a deep breath. "I haven't told anyone, but I've touched it before, and I had an experience, so maybe I should go first."

Meg shook her head. "It has to be Galen."

Everyone looked puzzled, but Galen felt her words pierce his heart.

Behind his polished Trotsky glasses, his eyes were exhausted, and if you looked deeper, he felt defeated. No matter how hard he tried, he couldn't push the memory of Iris away. He was tormented by images of her body buried in the ground and the grisly process of decay. A doctor had prescribed sleeping pills and an antidepressant, which sent Galen into a chemical haze. Worse, the pills made the images in his dreams more intense and harder to bear.

After the funeral her father had sent a long note to Galen, basically a kiss-off, declaring that the marriage to his daughter had been a sham. Galen skimmed over the caustic accusations. As immature as he was emotionally, he recognized that Iris's father was using blame to disguise his utter helplessness after she died. But a phrase, one of the few that didn't take aim at Galen, read, "She was a saint, but none of us recognized it."

Tears welled up in his eyes. Galen didn't believe in saints, and he loathed sentimentality. He had shut himself off from feeling anything—this had been his habit long before Iris got sick. He had turned to science to keep from sinking into the swamp of emotions. No one ever told him that tears are a release, after which something better comes. To him, tears were a crack in the dam, and unless you patched the crack, you would be washed away in the flood.

So the group didn't know the courage it took for him to suddenly say, "All right, I'll go first. Just don't blame me when nothing happens."

Jimmy shook his head. "Have some faith, bro."

Lilith said, "If God is God, a little skepticism won't stop him. Have at it, Mr. Blake."

If using his last name was meant as a little jab, Galen ignored it. The golden chapel was within his reach, and he pulled it closer until it sat squarely before him.

"See? I touched it. Nothing happened."

"Great, pass it on," Frank said. Mare wasn't the only one who had experienced the shrine's powers.

"Wait," said Mare, putting her hand on Frank's arm to quiet him. "I know you'll probably hate this word, Galen. But there has to be a communion between you and her."

"What garbage!" he snorted. "Either it works or it doesn't." He was already regretting being put on the spot, and by his own doing. It had been foolish and stupid to volunteer.

"He's losing his nerve," Frank taunted. "Predictable."

Jimmy's fear of confrontation came up. "Nobody should do what they don't want to. Can't he just come along for the ride?"

Frank shrugged. "Sure, let him be ballast in the boat. He's not good for much else."

By now Frank was annoying people as much as Galen. But no one disagreed with Jimmy's point. It wasn't compulsory for any of them to participate.

Galen felt his heart thumping, and it began to grow sore again. Against his will, he gave in. With a cryptic smile he closed his eyes and folded his hands around the shrine. Somewhere in the back of his mind, he framed a wisp of hope that Iris might speak to him. He didn't believe in communion, but who knows? Maybe this could turn into some kind of séance.

Behind his closed eyelids, he became aware of a faint light. At first he didn't notice it, because there is always a residual glow in the eyes—no one is literally in the dark. The glow began to swirl and grow brighter. Within seconds a woman's face was starting to form. Galen's heart skipped a beat; his stomach was in knots.

But as the image became clear, he saw it wasn't Iris. The woman had dark hair and eyes. Galen could hear her speak to him, even though her lips didn't move. *You have been suffering so much. There is no need to. Find a way out. I will show you.*

By rights his heart should have sunk when it wasn't Iris. But the woman, who looked no older than a girl, sounded so sympathetic that Galen was drawn to her. She had such a radiant smile. He wanted to speak to her, but he didn't know how.

What should I do? he thought.

A moment passed in silence that seemed like an eternity. He was afraid to open his eyes, certain that she would disappear.

Kill God.

Galen was too dumbfounded to respond. Had he heard wrong, or was this some weird, spiteful mockery? Without changing her smile, the woman communicated again.

Kill God.

A single word sprang to Galen's mind. *Why?*

It can end your suffering.

With a start his eyes opened on their own, and he squinted at the light as if he'd been asleep for an hour. People were staring at him with expectant looks on their faces.

"Did you see her?" asked Mare, who had an intuition that this would happen when anyone touched the golden shrine.

Galen nodded, still speechless. The woman in his vision hadn't faded away gradually like Marley's ghost or the Cheshire Cat. She was there one minute and gone the next.

Lilith looked askance. "Something's wrong. He could be in shock."

"I'm perfectly all right," Galen tried to say. But nothing came out, and the room started to swim. A veil lowered over his eyes. The next moment, he was lying on the floor, and Jimmy was holding a cup of water to his lips.

"You fainted, man. Good thing there's carpet." Then, with a conspiratorial smile, "This is the second time. Maybe you should stay away from me."

Apparently Galen had slipped slowly off his chair and wound up on the floor. "I'm all right," he mumbled. When he glanced to his left, Mare was there kneeling beside him.

She asked again, with quiet urgency, "You saw her, didn't you?"

Galen waved away the question. "Let me up." He accepted the water and gulped it down before getting to his feet, still unsteady.

"You were brave," said Jimmy, patting him on the shoulder. "So tell us."

Galen waited until they had all taken their seats again. "I got a message. But you're not going to like it."

"Just spit it out," Frank said impatiently. He wasn't entirely buying the little scene Galen had just put on.

"I saw a face. It was a young woman, and she said, 'Kill God.'"

Instantly Frank exploded. "I knew it! This guy's nothing but trouble." He jumped to his feet, pointing his finger at Galen. "Tell them about the crazy stunt you pulled. You got arrested, right? It's time we heard all about it."

"Kill God," Galen repeated, in a firm, steady voice.

A wave of confusion ran through the group. Lilith told everyone to keep calm, but no one could hear her above the building chaos. Frank weighed the idea of punching out the obnoxious little twerp. Mare was downcast, which stirred Jimmy's heart. For a fleeting moment he thought he should be with her, not Frank.

Galen looked on, at first with a dazed expression, as if he didn't really know what he had just said. In fact, two impulses were fighting inside him. One was awe that he had encountered the presence in the shrine, actually seen her and talked with her. The other was triumph—he was back in control of the group, just like at the first meeting. The mixture was intoxicating.

A voice inside him exulted. *You're not weak. You're powerful. Go for it.*

So he did. "I can only tell you what she said to me. You're all believers, at least you pretend to be. Now we have something to believe in together. Let's kill God. I'm ready."

"You should be ashamed of yourself," Lilith scolded.

Galen saw fear and revulsion in the eyes of the others. He felt the rush that comes when you've been deprived of attention all your life. Even bad attention is better than no attention at all. *More!* the voice inside told him. His other feeling, the one of awe before a looming mystery, couldn't compete. Galen was about to open his mouth, ready to crow louder. Yet a flicker of the woman's image returned, and he stopped himself.

In the general outrage, it took a while for anyone to notice that Meg had kept silent. She didn't even look distressed.

"Kill God. Yes, maybe that's a good idea," she murmured.

Frank exploded anew. "What? This guy went on a rampage to manipulate us. He's got an agenda. If you don't believe me, I can give you proof. Another reporter wrote the whole story up. There was a crazy plot, but it fizzled, and Galen weaseled out. Go on, tell them."

Galen fixed him with a cold stare and said nothing. So Frank told the story himself, of the botched act of art terrorism, as he dubbed it. He was so worked up that the incident spilled out in a garbled fashion, but they were all transfixed.

"Now you have it," Frank said. "Vote him out, and be done

with it." He didn't dare look over at Mare. Even this worked up, he knew her eyes would make him feel ashamed of himself.

The first to reply was Lilith. "Those who hate God are sometimes the greatest seekers."

"What? Not this character," Frank exclaimed.

How would you know? thought Galen, without speaking up for himself.

Then Frank felt Mare's hand touching his, and he deflated, slumping back down into his chair.

They waited for Meg to speak. She and Lilith were the only ones who seemed to know the territory. Quietly she said, "If we are a mystery school, we'll be guided in ways we don't understand."

"But isn't God the mystery?" Mare asked. "That's what we're here for."

Meg shook her head. "I never said that. We're here for the truth, and we have to have the courage to go where the trail leads us. If the message is 'Kill God,' I can't change it. I'm sorry."

This was no way to calm the group. Lilith stared at her in amazement.

"There is no reason for me to disbelieve Galen," Meg continued in a steady voice. "We all saw how shaken he was. Unless he's the greatest actor in the world, he wasn't following an agenda."

"His hate isn't acting," Frank protested.

"I don't see hate," Meg said. "I see someone who has suffered a great deal. If he did something extreme and reckless, it was only an expression of pain."

Galen felt exposed, his momentary power grab fading. If he agreed with Meg, the truth would be out. Then what? He'd return to his mouse hole. He wasn't going there without a struggle.

"Nobody at this table has a license to shrink me," he snarled. "You think I'm the only one in the whole world who hates God? Wake up." Now he felt some juice returning. "Why are you

people so afraid of two little words? 'Kill God.' If God can't protect himself from someone like me, he must be pretty pathetic."

"No argument with that," Frank muttered to himself.

Meg didn't budge. "The message wasn't for the whole world. It was for you personally, Galen. If I were you, I'd take it seriously."

He couldn't wriggle out. She was a better player at this game than he was. Galen realized this with a sinking feeling; his sense of defeat began to creep back in. He tried a new ploy.

"It's a trick or some kind of code. No one can kill God. He's already dead," he said.

"What if he's not dead enough?" asked Meg.

Galen looked confused.

"There was something you hated enough to get arrested over. You must have thought God was alive then," she pointed out.

He shifted uncomfortably. "I wasn't myself. I did something stupid."

Meg remained dogged. "You can't escape the fact that you hated God, so there had to be something or someone to hate. Maybe that's who you need to kill."

"All right," Galen sighed. "I hated the God that kids are brainwashed into loving and worshipping. That God is a fraud, a cheat. He doesn't exist." Galen felt himself getting emotional. "That's the real truth, more than saying God is dead. He's a figment of our imagination."

"Which you set out to destroy, so that people wouldn't be fooled anymore," Meg prompted.

"Someone had to stand up. My only mistake was thinking I could lead the charge. I'm too insignificant. I'm a nobody."

Running himself down like this came easily to Galen, once he decided to be perfectly candid.

"Then I'd say the presence you met knows you quite well," said Meg. "She's telling you to finish what you set out to do."

Galen turned his head away, and while his stubborn silence lasted, Meg addressed the others. "Why not destroy a God you hate? No one here is naive. Horrible things happen every day, unspeakable things, while God stands by and does nothing."

No one disagreed with her. Their faces looked anxious and guilty.

"Don't be afraid to attack such a God," Meg assured them. "It's time to kill him if that's what it takes to get at the truth."

Galen wanted to sulk, but something new hit him. "Is that why you left the convent?" he asked. "You saw through the hoax?"

Meg's reply was cryptic. "I left for the opposite reason, but this isn't about me." She looked around the table. "When the disciple gives any of you a message, you become the mind and heart of everyone in the group. We look to you to uncover the next piece of the puzzle."

Her little speech caused a shift. Galen was no longer the fly in the ointment. Hostile as he was, at that moment he was holding the flashlight whose beam could melt the darkness. This wasn't the same as respecting him, but it wasn't outright disgust anymore.

He felt the change and said quietly, "I'll try." He paused. "This is the damnedest thing, isn't it? A wimp leads the pack. I promise to let you down."

For the first time he got smiles from the others, even a tight, begrudging one from Frank.

Meg was pleased. " 'Kill God' means eliminating everything false about God, all the images and myths and childish beliefs we never bother to really think about. Get rid of that God; wipe him out."

She turned to Galen. "That's why you went on your rampage. So keep going."

Suddenly Galen's anxiety returned. He was being led into the unknown. His old wounds would be reopened. At that very

moment he could feel them starting to seep, their black poison oozing out.

Meg saw the pain in his face. "Be brave," she whispered. "Can you destroy forever the God who hurt you?"

The room grew deathly quiet, waiting.

"I don't know," Galen mumbled, all but inaudibly. He wanted to clutch at his heart and close up his wounds again.

"You can. It's only an image," she urged.

But he knew otherwise. An image can't be the source of so much pain. An image can't turn someone's life into a desert devoid of love.

He managed a choked laugh to keep himself from crying. "This is harder than I thought."

"I know. It wouldn't be a mystery school otherwise," said Meg. "It would be kindergarten."

You have to see what I lost, Galen thought. He willed Meg to see Iris in all her beauty. Without hating God, he'd be left with no ties to her, no way to keep her with him, even in a shriveled, pathetic way.

Now it wasn't possible to hold back his tears.

"You fear your own emptiness," said Meg gently. "Everyone does." She gave the group a meaningful look. "Why else would they cling to images so desperately? They don't want to tumble into the void. Who will catch them—God? But no one else can. That's the mystery."

Everyone in the group held their breath. They had been fixated on watching Galen unravel before their eyes, but this was a total surprise. Meg's gaze went from one to another.

"When you destroy everything that is false, whatever remains must be true." She waited to let her words sink in. "Do you all understand?"

There were a few nervous smiles, but no one replied.

"To meet God as a reality, you have to reach the zero point, where there is faith in nothing. It's frightening, but totally necessary. At the zero point every false idea about God has been abandoned. You cry with all your heart, 'Show yourself as you really are. I'm finished with fakes. Either show yourself, or I am lost.'

"When you can say that, God hears you. He knows your search for the truth is serious. If God is truth, he has no choice but to reveal himself to you. That's what Galen has guided us to today."

Galen felt a wave of emotion on hearing this. It was as if a tangled web had been transformed into a luminous path. Iris's love was part of the path, and so was his despair after she was taken from him. Every blow had brought him closer to the zero point. Galen had never had much faith in anything, but even the shreds had been stripped bare.

I'm clean, he thought.

"Scraped to the bone," said Lilith, picking up what he was going through.

Galen didn't spare a thought for how she was able to tune into his mind. He was too grateful to be emptied of the poison that had been eating him alive.

CHAPTER *15*

A week passed, and the next meeting was ready to start. Galen came in late. He looked more rumpled than usual, as if he'd slept in his clothes. Frank didn't wait for him to find a seat.

"You got pretty bashed in last time," he said. "Rough week?"

"Sort of," Galen replied guardedly.

There was silent tension in the room. *Why is it focused on me?* he wondered. For the first time, everyone sat together. To Galen it looked like a jury watching him, the reluctant witness giving suspicious testimony. Meg sat back impartially, her hands folded in her lap. Only Mare seemed to look at him with sympathetic eyes, so he sat next to her, in case he needed an ally.

"What's going on?" Galen asked. "I haven't done anything to you people."

"True, but something was done through you," Meg said. She swept her hand over the group. "What you experienced when you touched the shrine spread to everyone."

"Like a virus," Frank added. "And you're the carrier."

This was totally unfair, but Galen felt a grim kind of satisfaction.

"What are you smiling at?" asked Frank sharply.

"Nothing."

Lilith spoke up. "We can't start until somebody explains things."

When no one else volunteered Mare said, "I can only speak for myself. Right after the last meeting, I was on edge. It felt like I was in danger. When I got home, I kept checking to make sure my door was locked. The slightest sound made me jump, and then—" She was on the brink of revealing something, but couldn't.

Jimmy looked the most agitated. "All week I wasn't myself. I felt, like, empty. When I passed myself in the mirror, it was like looking at a zombie. I can't believe you did this to us, man."

Galen was taken aback. He had experienced the same emptiness, but he thought he was alone.

"You don't have a clue what this is about, do you?" asked Frank with disgust. "He's not going to cop to anything."

Meg turned to Frank, and for such a gentle person, her tone was severe. "And what are you ready to cop to?"

Frank sat back in his chair. "I didn't mean—" he stammered.

Frank was getting close to something important—Meg's antennae were always out. Nothing slipped by her. He looked at Mare for support, but she felt helpless about her own situation.

Every night when she went to bed, Mare couldn't close her eyes without feeling that she was suspended over a bottomless pit. Below her she saw only blackness. By Wednesday, she was so anxious and bleary-eyed that she called Frank. He came over. He sat up in bed holding her until she fell into a fitful sleep. He waited to kiss her cheek until she nodded off. It was the tenderest moment between them so far, but what if coming back this evening only made things worse for her?

After an uncomfortable moment Meg said, "Frank is as afraid to show weakness as Galen. But it's not about who's weak or strong. All of you have had a terrible week. It's to be expected. Remember, when a door is opened, we all walk through it."

"Including you?" asked Mare.

It was the first personal question anyone had put to Meg. She took no offense. "I didn't suffer with the rest of you, no," she admitted. "That's not my role."

"You seem to know everything. So why didn't you protect us?" Jimmy asked.

Lilith replied before Meg could. "Don't be childish. She's not your mommy." Jimmy's face colored red, something that happened too easily.

"It's all right," said Meg. "Galen didn't like his experience; none of you did. But you had to experience the zero point. There was no other way."

"You said that reaching the zero point was positive," Mare reminded her.

"And it will be, I promise. At some level we all want to be protected. We crave love. We cling to life as something precious. The zero point strips those things away. The loss is just the same as losing God."

Meg's presence was reassuring, but at the same time she kept aloof. No one had seen her outside the meetings. She stayed apart from Lilith, despite their old friendship. Even Mare hadn't heard from her, and when Mare left messages on her phone, they weren't returned. On Thursday her mother phoned.

"I heard from my dead sister at last," she began. "Your Aunt Meg ran away because she'd had enough of the convent, plain and simple. She waited long enough, I'll say that."

Mare was cautious. "Did she tell you anything else? Will we see her?"

"No, she's rid of us. There's some trip she has to take right away. She might call when she comes back. Don't hold your breath." Mare's mother sounded irritated rather than distressed.

So Meg's intuition had been correct. The family wasn't greeting her return as good news, and when she excused herself from

visiting them, they didn't insist. They were more comfortable with an empty place at the table.

The mood in the room was darker than it had ever been. "I don't think we're going to make it," Jimmy mumbled.

"The zero point is very bleak," Meg said. "But it's not the end. It's a prelude."

"To what?"

"To being filled with grace."

Jimmy's eyes widened, but Frank was still disgruntled. "What about me? I don't care about God. Why do I deserve to go through hell?"

"I think that's the point I'm making," Meg said. "The disciple pulled the rug out from everyone. Fair is fair."

He let it rest there. Mare wasn't the only one who didn't want to reveal what had happened to them. On Monday Frank was sent on assignment to interview homeless single mothers. Beneath an overpass on the edge of town, he found an encampment. The women looked shattered; their kids were gaunt and forlorn.

The photographer who came along was upset. "I gotta shoot all of this," he said. "Some of these kids need a doctor really bad. That little guy over there, his teeth are falling out. Nobody cares."

"Yeah, it's a crime," Frank muttered. He stood back, not taking the tape recorder out of his pocket.

"So where should we start?" the photographer asked.

"Anywhere. It doesn't matter," Frank replied. He felt strangely detached. The roar of overhead traffic on the interstate jangled his nerves. He wanted to get out of there.

The photographer was furiously snapping candid shots. When Frank didn't move, he said, "Something up with you, man?"

"No, I'm fine." Rousing himself, Frank approached one of the gaunt-eyed mothers, who was huddled inside a filthy blanket with a two-year-old wrapped in her arms. She glared at him

suspiciously—visitors to the camp meant that social services would be following close behind, or the police.

"Why are you hassling us?" she demanded.

"I'm not hassling anybody. I'm just a reporter." She told him to buzz off. Frank shrugged and moved on to the next one.

The photographer kept shooting, but he was growing annoyed. "You have to get them to open up."

"I know my job; you just do yours," Frank snapped. He continued to go through the motions a while longer; they got back in the car and left when a cold drizzle started to come down.

The city editor frowned when he read Frank's copy, which was about as emotional as the transcript of a water-board meeting. "Bighearted, that's you," he said. Frank was sent back twice until his story began to show some empathy. He didn't dare reveal how little he actually cared or how frightened this made him feel.

Frank didn't tell his story to anyone, but Meg seemed to see through him.

"Let me tell you what you've all been feeling," she said. "In the absence of God, there's a hole inside you."

Frank felt himself shrinking inside. So that was what it meant when he looked on those homeless mothers without a shred of pity. The memory sent a chill through him.

Galen objected. "There's another explanation. Feeling empty exposes how alone we are. God has nothing to do with it."

To everyone's surprise, Lilith was almost as doubtful. "I want to believe you, Meg. You say fair is fair. A pretty cruel fairness, if you ask me."

Unlike the others, Lilith wasn't referring to a rough week. No one could have guessed what she'd gone through before they met her. She'd kept faith for almost thirty years. Not a word escaped her lips about the strange dream of the Black Death or the golden light that appeared in her bedroom. Lilith had kept up a good

front—marriage, kids, career, all of it—while inside she was secretly in turmoil. This turmoil never completely left her, even during her happiest moments. Her heart always felt like a cave with a cold wind blowing through it, terrifying.

She was comforted by the fact that her husband didn't have a clue about what she was going through. He worked in the insurance business. He carried a card with a slogan he'd made up: "Insure and be sure." Lilith thought this was feeble, but didn't criticize, just as he never criticized her for being too strict with their two daughters.

One Sunday in front of the television he put the golf tournament he was watching on pause. The girls were off to college now. No one was at home except Lilith.

"I wonder who you are," he said. His tone wasn't accusatory, but bemused. "I don't know you."

She was flabbergasted. "I haven't changed, Herb."

"All right." He clicked the golf back on. "But if you ever want to tell me, I'm here."

Lilith felt unmasked and nearly trembled. She grabbed the remote from his hand and turned the TV off. "What are you saying? Do you want a divorce? Are you going to sleep in the spare bedroom from now on?"

Her husband looked bewildered. "Of course not. I love you."

They kept sleeping in the same bed, but Lilith doubled her armor plating. She wasn't about to lose everything. Her life was going to look ordinary if it killed her. Letting Herb in on her secret was unthinkable, like asking him to fly with her to Neptune.

But hiding out wasn't working well enough. She began a lonely search for the truth. Her only clue was the golden object that had appeared in her bedroom so many years earlier. She started to haunt the university library, poring over books about the plague years. Nothing similar to her dream of the six bodies radiating out in a circle was ever recorded.

What next? The golden object was in the shape of a church. Lilith knew what a reliquary was, so she researched pilgrims in the Middle Ages. She discovered hundreds of accounts, then thousands, and tens of thousands, most of them written in foreign languages. That route proved impossible, like everything else she had tried. Lilith remembered the exact moment when she gave up her search.

She was sitting at a long oak table in the library reading room. Before her tottered a tower of volumes devoted to Paris in the eleventh century. They smelled of dust and wilted scholars who never got married.

I'm lost, Lilith thought.

Then from over her shoulder a creaky voice said, "I didn't know I had competition."

She turned around to find an old man with a white goatee, a polka-dot bow tie, and suspenders.

"I study the period too, you see," he explained. "But I'm not selfish. If you need more books on mystery schools, I'll return mine forthwith. I keep them too long anyway."

"Mystery schools?" Lilith said, baffled.

He pointed to the leather-bound volume at the top of the pile. "I peeked at the title. *Mystery Schools, the Ecclesia, and the Role of Magic.* I hope you don't mind."

Lilith's puzzled expression made him hesitate. "You don't think his thesis is sound? I quite agree. Magic indeed."

With a squinty smile the stranger began to walk away, humming to himself. Lilith wanted to run after him. She had never heard of mystery schools, but the words gave off an electric charge. She'd stumbled on some kind of clue, she was sure of it. She started to bolt from her chair, but immediately something stopped her. Scholars like him would be no help to her. She wouldn't even get over the first hurdle, making them believe in her dream, so strange and so long ago. Yet she wasn't discouraged. Pure instinct

would lead her to the next clue. Being the only road left, it was the one she had to follow.

The remaining clues didn't come quickly. They arrived at long intervals usually by happenstance, like a falling autumn leaf landing in your hair or the shadow of a raven crossing your path. Each clue made her excited; each long lapse until the next clue was given drove her mad with frustration. But Lilith was dogged, and when the haul was finally gathered in her net—a flotsam of overheard remarks, chance encounters, and arcane discoveries— she finally understood. It could only be the thirteenth disciple who was leading her on. No biblical historian believed in such a personage. The two Aramaic sources hidden in the depths of the Vatican library had been completely discredited. Yet Lilith believed, and when she found Meg, she felt vindicated—no, triumphant. Everything was real, if you only knew where to look.

So why would the disciple now throw her into desolation all over again? The others might have a hole inside, but not her. It was unfair, cosmically unfair.

Yet only one thing mattered now. If the group fell apart, things would only get worse. "I apologize for my moment of weakness. The zero point is where we have to start," Lilith affirmed.

Galen spoke wearily. "We've chewed this thing to death." He pointed at the shrine in the middle of the table. "I went first. Who's next? We need a volunteer."

When no one made a move, Meg threw up her hands. "The disciple made you feel uncomfortable for a week, and now you're ready to run away?" No one looked happy.

"So what do you want us to do?" asked Mare.

Meg's answer was unexpected. "We're going to start acting like a real mystery school. Touch the shrine."

"All of us?" Mare asked.

"Yes. Follow my lead." Meg lightly touched the roof of the golden chapel with her fingertips. "She's been awaiting us for

centuries. We have to show her she didn't make a mistake." One by one they followed Meg's example, even Galen. The shrine started to glow again.

It wasn't dead; the presence inside had been listening. The glow pulsated faintly, sending out waves of peace. For all their hands to fit on the shrine, their fingers had to intertwine.

"Our Kumbaya moment. I knew it was coming," Galen joked. But his words were lost as the walls of the room melted away. A breeze ruffled their hair.

"I know where we are!" Mare exclaimed. This seemed improbable, because it was a moonless night. She didn't need moonlight to recognize the man standing in the narrow cobbled alley. He was always there. She said Jesus's name, but as before no sound came out. Mare pointed, and the others looked in his direction, silent presences to an unfolding scene. For Mare it was different this time—she was living the scene with him, from inside his mind.

It was cold for spring, even sheltered by the walls of Jerusalem. Jesus's hands were trembling. He could barely see them in the dark, but he felt their fear. Sunrise would be his death sentence, and even his body knew it. What his hands dreaded were the nails. He could do nothing about that. Maybe he should spend the last few hours before dawn asking his hands for forgiveness, then his heart, his eyes.

Instead, he kept walking through the city's labyrinth of hidden streets and alleys, which wove through Jerusalem like arteries and veins. He asked for peace. He prayed, "Our Father, who art in heaven," but the fear wouldn't leave his body.

Just hours before, his hands and heart obeyed his will. It was possible to remain calm at the Passover *seder* with his disciples. Jesus recited the ritual text but added, "When you eat this bread, you partake of my body. When you drink this wine, you partake of my blood."

The words had just come to him, as if out of God's mouth. The disciples looked bewildered. Every part of the *seder* existed to remind them that they were Jews. The meal brought Moses and Abraham into the room. It made the exodus from Egypt a living memory, even though their ancestors fled from captivity centuries ago. At Passover, with Roman soldiers, clubs in hand, patrolling Jerusalem, the Jews were reminded again that they had no power in their own land except the power of memory. It was the one thing the hated occupiers couldn't seize and control.

How could Jesus say, "This meal is about me"? It was beyond outrageous. If there had been a Pharisee in the room, he would have run back and told the temple priests that they had a danger-ous zealot in their midst.

The disciples were following a miracle rabbi, and such men were inspired by God. (The Pharisee would have condemned them simply for thinking such a thing.) Jesus's words always meant more than they seemed. He was constantly pushing the disciples to grasp his meaning. They rarely succeeded, but at least they could argue about it. To be Jewish is to argue endlessly, and so the room grew full of questions and doubts. This time Jesus didn't give them any answers. He sat silently watching. The flick-ering candles made his shadow quiver on the wall. And then he jumped to his feet.

"There's a spy in this room. He knows who he is, but I won't remain in his presence."

"Master, stay and point him out," Peter cried, his voice rising above the din of the confusion.

"Why, so you can attack him?"

"Shouldn't we?" asked Judas in the calmest of voices. "We'd be carrying out the will of God."

Jesus looked away. "I'm going."

The disciples sprang to their feet, blocking the door so he couldn't leave.

"Please, master, think of us. Stay and teach us," Judas pleaded. "This is a holy night."

When a man contemplating suicide has made up his mind, he goes calmly about the small tasks that attend death. He buys a coil of rope and borrows a stool of the right height. He bars the door with a heavy table and sits down to carefully tie the noose. A kind of fatal courage descends on him. It's the same with traitors. The closer they approach their sin, the more brazen they become.

"Let me leave this place," Jesus insisted.

The disciples moved aside except for Iscariot. He put his face close to the master's so that the others couldn't see him smiling. "You are the son of God. You can't be afraid of one of us."

Without reply Jesus quitted the place. He descended the narrow stairs that led from the cramped upper room to the street and was gone. In his mind he now saw every moment of what lay ahead. The Father had granted him that. Judas would flee the room on a feeble pretext. The disciples would wait in bewilderment until the master returned, and after midnight Jesus would ask them to pray in the garden.

Aimlessly his footsteps had taken him to an alley walled in by tall houses, leaving only a sliver of night sky overhead. The closeness pressed in on him, and he stopped wandering. "Thy will be done" gave him no strength. He rebelled against his sacrifice. *Father, I implore you. If you love me, listen to me now.*

The moment the words escaped him, Jesus's face grew hot despite the chill of the night. He was begging. It was the one thing he had taught his disciples never to do. A Jew never begs from a loving God. The Father knows everything his children need and gives it out of his loving grace.

But Jesus's mind was panicking. *Save me, save me!*

The plea was too late. From the far end of the alley, which was hidden by a winding curve, he spied a glimmer of light approaching. Judas's betrayal must have happened earlier than Jesus

saw, and the rough hands of soldiers would be dragging him away. The miracle rabbi faced his worst fear. It was not the dying, but dying in doubt.

The light came closer, rounding the curve. Strangely, there was no sound of tramping boots. And the light didn't flicker like torches.

"Oh," a woman's voice said. The light stopped moving closer.

"Don't be afraid. I won't hurt you," Jesus said. His heart was racing, the way it always did when a mystery sought him out. He hadn't run into a prostitute, who would have boldly approached a man walking alone at night. There was a hesitation; then the woman moved toward him, and in the light he saw that she was just a girl.

"Let me pass. I'm needed," she said. The girl groped her way, as if there were no light. Jesus was transfixed with amazement. "My father was injured when a brick wall fell," she said. "They couldn't move him for hours. I ran to get medicine for his wounds."

She told all this with a slight nervousness in her voice. Otherwise, she seemed unafraid. "I wish I had a torch to see you by. I carried one, but it went out."

She doesn't know, Jesus thought.

There was light everywhere, and it emanated from her. This was what amazed him.

"You are blessed," he said.

"Thank you, *rebbe*." No one had ever blessed her outside of the temple, which meant this stranger must be a priest.

Jesus hesitated. He knew this light. It was the Shekinah of the scriptures, the light of the soul. For it to shine radiantly from the girl meant something. He waited for God to tell him what to do.

And then he did.

"May I speak with you?" Jesus asked.

"I would, but the medicine—" she replied doubtfully, holding up the packet of herbs that were nestled in the sleeve of her gown.

"Your father is healed."

"What?" The girl felt the chill air creep down the alley, making her shiver.

"Your father doesn't need you, but God does." Jesus didn't wait for her to object. The urgency of the hour was upon him. "I have a teaching for you. Pay attention. The Jews prove that they are God's children by two means. What are they?"

The girl wasn't poor. Her family had hired religious tutors for her brothers, and she was allowed to listen in from the other side of a curtain.

"The word and the temple," she replied. "The word binds God to us. Making sacrifice in the temple binds us to him."

Jesus shook his head. "Is that enough? Words are not eternal, and the temple may fall into ruins."

"Pardon me, *rebbe,* but the word *is* eternal."

Jesus smiled to himself. The Father had led him to the right person. He said, "Yes, the word is eternal, but it can be forgotten among men. I tell you a mystery. There is one thing beyond the word—the light. Death cannot touch it. I am the light. Be sure of it. This truth will lead you to heaven."

The girl was baffled, and she still couldn't see the face of the stranger. He turned to walk away, and at that she felt a sharp pang in her heart. She cried out, but he kept walking. She ran to catch up, but a second pain shot through her chest, and she stumbled.

Overhead a window opened, and someone leaned out, waving an oil lamp.

"Who's down there?" he cried, irritated and sleepy.

By then the stranger had reached the end of the alley and disappeared into the night.

The scene was cut off like a broken movie reel, and their hands sprang away from the shrine. Eyes opened. The group gazed at the golden glow, still faintly pulsating.

"Don't speak," Meg warned. "The thirteenth disciple was a young girl, an innocent. She was entrusted with a mystery. Now the same mystery has been passed on to us."

After a moment the golden glow faded. It took away the disciple's presence. Everyone had felt it.

Galen got in the first word. "We've been asses, all of us."

"Definitely," Jimmy seconded.

Meg smiled. "You couldn't help yourselves." She didn't say how close they'd come to failing. Now the fear in their hearts was losing its grip.

"We have one last thing to discuss," Meg said. "We stepped through time tonight. What was the lesson waiting for us?"

Their answers overlapped.

"Jesus is real."

"We're not crazy."

"The light."

The last was from Lilith, and Meg agreed. "Our only salvation is the light. This coming week, I want you to go into the light on your own." There was a murmur of assent. They could feel the protection that encircled them like enfolding arms.

Mare had a question. "How will we know what to do?"

"It can't be planned in advance," Meg replied. "Give in to the light. That's my best advice."

"I don't mean to be a buzzkill," said Frank, "but giving in led to a pretty horrible week last time."

"Then give in more," said Meg. "The disciple knew absolutely nothing. She was sent into the light blindly, if I can put it that way."

Just like me, Lilith thought to herself. What she had considered a curse was a blessing in disguise.

They dispersed in a mood very different from the way the meeting had begun. Meg stayed behind to lock up. Trusting in

the thirteenth disciple meant that the group trusted her. She knew that, and it made her keep some secrets to herself.

"Everything looks good so far," she said to the empty room. Her charges had passed through an invisible veil.

Who really knew what a mystery school should be? Monks in hooded robes kneeling before the cross. Heavy incense in the air. The shields of Crusaders and their dulled swords lining the walls. There was something to be said for stage props.

A mystery school couldn't be ordinary people in an ugly basement meeting room, with greenish skin from the cheap fluorescent lighting.

But this time it was.

The next week passed neither slowly nor swiftly for Meg. She was barely aware of time anymore. She had grown so used to silence that time was no longer useful. It had withered away like the convent garden in winter, leaving bare sticks where sweet fruit once hung. When she came back into the world, time wasn't waiting on the doorstep to greet her.

She was due at the next meeting of the mystery school, but Meg lingered in the huge sitting room of Father Aloysius's house, a cool, gloomy place he rarely entered when he was alive. The good priest preferred a modest rectory. Carved lions' heads silently growled at her from the corners of heavy Victorian furniture. Some of the gilt-framed pictures on the wall were still draped with cloth, but even years of neglect hadn't been able to dim the trappings of family wealth.

Father Aloysius never mentioned that he was leaving Meg the house, a mansion, really. Toward the end, knowing he had little time left, he defied his doctors by visiting the nuns one last time to bless them. The sisters were shocked by his appearance, how gaunt he looked.

"Now we have to discuss the disciple," he said when he and Meg finally found time alone. Their weekly meetings were held

in the ramshackle toolsheds and boarded-up cottages scattered around the grounds of the convent. On this final visit, they sat side by side in a garden shed on a rickety potting bench, the last relic of the Italian gardeners the estate once employed. Their breath fogged in the cold air. None of the outbuildings had heat, and the cracked windows were never repaired.

"When I'm gone, the disciple will have no one to talk to but you," Father Aloysius said.

Meg looked doubtful. "But I don't really know who she is. Have you actually seen her?"

"Oh, yes. But you already know the most important thing. She's the keeper of the invisible gospel." The old priest gave Meg a sharp look. "This would be a bad moment to lose faith."

"I don't want to," Meg mumbled.

He sighed. "You think you haven't done anything these past ten years? You have. You've allowed the presence of God to come to you. Now his presence is with you. It's in you every moment."

Father Aloysius took a drag on his cigarette. He'd never kicked the habit, but he had lived long enough to see e-cigarettes come along. "An electronic nicotine delivery system. What a thing," he mused with a touch of regret.

Meg felt a wave of emotion. "What will I do without you?" she cried.

"You'll leave this place. That's the first thing. You must continue the disciple's mission, and you can't do it sealed away behind these walls."

Sitting there in the frigid drafty shed with her hands tucked into her sleeves for warmth, Meg watched as Father Aloysius opened a worn leather valise he'd brought with him. From inside he lifted a wrapped object. He unwrapped it carefully to reveal the golden shrine, which she'd never seen before.

"We live in a terrible time for miracles," he said. "They're

endangered, like the bird of paradise. When you get back to your cell, commune with this precious object."

As much as she trusted him, Meg was struck with fear. Being a bad Catholic had never gone this far.

Father Aloysius put his hand, which was sinewy and strong despite his sickness, over hers. "I'm not asking you to practice black magic, my girl."

"I'm not sure I'm ready for white magic," Meg said with a nervous laugh. "This could all be a mistake."

"If God makes mistakes, then there is no God."

Meg shook her head. "That's not good enough, Father."

"It has to be, for now."

The old priest's chest was suddenly wracked with an alarming cough, and before her eyes he turned weak and exhausted. He draped one arm over Meg's shoulders, and she helped him out of the shed. The walk back to his car was painfully slow.

"It doesn't really matter who spies on us now, does it?" he said with a grim smile. "We're both about to disappear."

At the parking lot, he rested for a moment before getting behind the wheel of the battered black town car.

"I don't think about death," he mused. "I wait in quietness. What will come will come."

There was nothing more to say. It would have been a blessing if Meg had witnessed what came next. As he drove down the winding road that led away from the convent, Father Aloysius remembered when he was ten years old, dangling his feet in the cool blue water of the town swimming pool. His best friend, Ray Kelly, pointed to the high diving board silhouetted against the sky.

"Double dare you to jump off it," he said. Neither of them had ever worked up the courage to climb that high. But Aloysius, who got his peculiar first name because a strong-minded devout grandmother had insisted on it, couldn't refuse a dare. He climbed

the ladder, and heads turned as a skinny little boy tiptoed gingerly to the edge of the board. No matter how light his step, the board jiggled under his feet. Peering down, he saw the water, which looked miles away. His fear told him not to jump, but what could he do? His reputation depended on not climbing back down the ladder.

Now he stood at the edge of another leap, having tiptoed toward it for seventy-eight years.

I have no choice, he thought. *It would ruin my reputation if I backed down now.*

Meg waited until dinnertime to retrieve the old valise that contained the miniature golden church. She excused herself from the table, saying she had indigestion, and then hurried through the dark to the rickety garden shed. The valise was hidden under a tarp behind a rusty old mowing machine.

She got back to her cell undetected and shoved the valise under her cot. If she didn't attend evening prayers a medical sister would check up on her.

Returning to the group, Meg mumbled that she felt much better, thank you. All through prayers the only thing she could think of was Father Aloysius's mysterious instruction: "Commune with this precious object." What did that even mean?

The sisters went directly to bed after the last prayer. There was no socializing, because the next round of praying began very early in the morning. Meg sat on the edge of her cot, allowing for a safety margin. It was very unlikely that another sister would tap on her door, but Meg waited until the corridor was completely silent and empty.

Dragging the valise out from under the cot, she was struck by its heaviness. She had been too anxious carrying it in the dark to really notice its weight, but when she opened it and lifted the object, still wrapped in a torn piece of white sheet, it almost slipped from her grasp.

For a split second she panicked at the thought of the clattering sound the object would make if it hit the stone floor. She caught it just in time, sat down quickly, and placed it in her lap. She forced herself to breathe while waiting for her heart to stop racing. Too nervous to turn on her reading lamp so late at night, Meg stared at the object in near darkness. *It must be quite valuable,* she thought, *but if that's the only reason for its existence, Father Aloysius wouldn't have cloaked it in secrecy.*

This thought brought his face to mind, and Meg felt a wave of sorrow. She would never see him again. There was great pain around that. She hadn't wanted to face it all day. A final ending brought fear and grief, even though her old friend was still alive. If she weren't a cloistered nun, she could even telephone him to hear his voice again.

It would have been easy to give in to self-pity sitting there in the dark. Meg resisted, focusing her attention on the miniature church.

What do I do with you now? she thought.

It was a rhetorical question, directed at no one, but Meg had the sense that someone heard it. Not that this was possible rationally, only that her doubt receded a little. She felt understood, much the way Father Aloysius, among all the people in her life, made her feel. But it proved unsafe to bring his face to mind a second time. She found herself crying, and she pulled the golden church close to her and embraced it, using it to hold on to the old priest.

Suddenly she saw a hill in her mind's eye, with three crosses outlined against a stormy sky. To witness three bodies hanging from crosses would be unbearable. She had been there before, and her heart pounded. *Please, not again. I can't.*

Voices buzzed around her, and the image went in and out like a weak television signal. Meg had a faint hope that she could escape, until all at once her cramped cell disappeared, and she was

there. She had returned to the Crucifixion, but she didn't see the bodies, only the young girl running away from them.

The scene jumped ahead. Now the girl was in the city. There were no crowds in the narrow streets she ran through. Passover took the Jews to temple; few went to gawk at the spectacle on Golgotha, the "Place of Skulls."

The girl ran blindly, hardly able to see the way through her tears. Meg hovered near her, so close that the disciple's racing heartbeat felt like her own. The girl fled until she was exhausted; she collapsed in the shade of a twisted olive tree just beyond the city walls. For a while nothing happened. Her ragged breath began to subside. Her fear subsided with it, and she was able to think. Her thoughts came through clearly to Meg.

He was a stranger. Now he's dead. I don't have to do anything.

The girl became aware of a shadow passing over her. She looked up, embarrassed to be caught when her emotions had run away with her.

It was him.

She was so startled that childish words sprang from her lips. "Aren't you supposed to be dead?"

Jesus smiled. "That depends on how you look at it."

The figure Meg saw was short and dark, with a general look she thought of as Mediterranean, not even Jewish. The girl had only seen the stranger at night. His voice was gentle, the same as when he found her in the alley. But he looked shockingly ordinary. To Meg, Jesus could be the Iranian who owns the neighborhood dry cleaner's.

The girl was bewildered. There was no possible way he could have escaped.

"I saw what they did to you," she said.

"To men's eyes, I'm still there," Jesus said. "It will not be finished for a while."

He sat down beside her in the shade of the olive tree, which made dappled shadows on his face.

"The one who speaks to you, who appears to you now, he is the only one you must pay attention to. The men who think they can crucify the light are mistaken."

The girl looked stricken. This man could be a magus who had worked a spell on her. Or demons might have entered her body. Or she had lost her mind. None of these explanations fought for her attention, however. Taking a deep breath, she accepted what she saw.

The stranger sensed her acceptance. "You have heard it said, many are called, but few are chosen. You have been chosen, and through you others will be too."

The girl wanted to protest, but Jesus got up and began to walk away in the direction of the Place of Skulls, which couldn't be seen over the city walls and houses in between.

The night before the girl had run after him. This time, though, she sat still, nearly collapsed on the ground. Meg wanted to reach out and hold her in her arms. She knew how insignificant the disciple felt at that moment. Meg was haunted by the same feeling herself.

Suddenly the disciple's head exploded with doubts. "Tell me what to do!" she cried out in a panic.

Jesus was already too far away to hear. But her mind answered for him: *You will be guided, as he was guided.*

In an instant, the flashback vanished. Meg was sitting on her cot back in her cell enveloped in darkness. She became aware of the heavy little church in her lap, her hands wrapped tightly around it. In a moment she regained her wits and even managed a faint smile. She had managed to commune with it after all. The metallic surface of the object felt warm. She knew what her duty was now, and although it was impossible, the object began to glow faintly, as if it too understood.

CHAPTER *17*

The meeting room in the hospital basement was stuffy at the best of times. Waiting an hour for Meg to appear made it seem stifling.

Frank looked at his watch for the fifth time. "She's not coming, so what do we do?"

It wasn't the simplest question. When they arrived the door was locked. Lilith had an extra key. They got inside, and the golden shrine had been placed where it always sat, in the middle of the table. They were baffled.

Now Galen leaned forward and laid his hand on the chapel's smooth roof.

"What are you doing?" Frank asked. His tone wasn't hostile. Last week's session had melted away any rivalry. The mood was more suspenseful than anything else.

"I want to see if something happens when she's not here," Galen replied. "Maybe the mojo comes from Meg."

"And?"

Galen shrugged. "Nothing."

"I think she's deliberately leaving us on our own," Lilith remarked. "We should start without her."

The group wasn't enthusiastic about her suggestion.

Frank jumped to his feet. "We were instructed to go into the light this week. Did anyone succeed?"

Silence.

"Me neither. Meeting adjourned."

"Wait," Jimmy protested. "We should talk about it some more. This week was a lot better for me. I didn't see a zombie in the mirror."

He got a few weak smiles. No one else spoke up. Mare said what they were all starting to think. "What if she's gone, and she's not coming back?"

"Don't get carried away," Lilith said tartly. "Jimmy's made a start. Who else wants to share their experience?" Silence. She shook her head. "This is quite peculiar," she muttered.

"What about you?" Jimmy asked.

"I'm afraid not."

In fact, Lilith had been dead serious all week in her search for the light. She was more ambitious than anyone else in the group, or just more driven perhaps. The disciple must have planned some extraordinary experiences for her. An illumination? A great epiphany? What would it be?

Lilith mulled this over in the big house where she and Herb lived. He had never questioned her again about things he couldn't understand. Their two grown girls had left home for other cities, to attend graduate school or follow a job opening. They were Herb's daughters, really. They had the same literal mind, which made them feel safe. *Too safe,* Lilith thought. She had been tempted many times to reveal herself to them, especially when they faced a crisis.

When Tracy, the older girl, was in high school, she was seeing a boy who suddenly began to lose weight and feel tired. She got irritated when he canceled two dates in a row. He was never home when she phoned. When they finally connected, the first thing he said was "I have bone cancer."

The news devastated her. Lilith stood in the hallway outside Tracy's bedroom, hearing her cry on the other side of the door. Any mother would have gone in to comfort her, but Lilith was conflicted. She didn't feel anything for the sick boy, who was probably doomed. Malignancies progress with vicious swiftness in someone that young. Lilith turned away from the door and went downstairs.

She sat at the kitchen table, still feeling nothing. These were the years when looking into her heart made her afraid. She had a sudden impulse. She should ask why she didn't feel what normal people felt. She silently put the question out to the void.

A voice in her head replied, *Because you know. Because you can see. I will show you.*

Lilith's heart beat faster. *Show me now. I'm ready.*

But no more came. She was bitterly disappointed. Why was every experience a tease? She got up from the table and went up to her daughter's room.

"Tracy, honey, are you okay? May I come in?"

The door opened, and Lilith went over and sat on the bed hugging the girl and comforting her. It went well, because Lilith had learned long ago that other people can't read who we really are. That night, after making sure Tracy had fallen asleep, Lilith had a dream, the kind she thought of as a "special" dream. She saw the boy, Greg, lying in a hospital bed with tubes sticking out of his body. He was asleep, his face pale and worn. Lilith saw him from a bird's-eye view, as if hovering in the air over his bed.

"I'm here to take you home," she whispered.

He stirred in his sleep and moaned softly without waking up. Then a wisp of light emerged from the top of his head. Lilith felt like his mother, tenderly coaxing him not to be afraid. The wisp of light became a silvery thread, and as it emerged, it grew longer, extending up to the ceiling. The boy in the bed stopped moaning or moving. And there the dream ended.

Tracy came home early from school the next day, her face streaked with tears. Greg had died suddenly in the hospital that night. His heart had stopped. The doctors were mystified, but they were spared from telling him that his cancer had spread so far that it was untreatable.

For days Lilith went around feeling good and bad. Good because she had gone on an errand of mercy. Bad because it was just a dream. The experience refused to go away, urging her on. But it took a long time before she screwed up the courage to visit the hospice unit at the hospital, where she proved to herself that she could actually witness someone's spirit leave the body.

So it was true that she hadn't seen the light that week, but the whole truth was that she had seen it many times before.

Another half hour passed in the meeting room. It was hard for the group to accept defeat.

"It's not our fault," said Frank. "Meg didn't tell us enough."

He glanced over his shoulder in case she had come through the door. "As long as Meg's not here, I have a question for everyone. How into Jesus are we supposed to be? The scene we saw last week, it's not in the Bible as far as I know. Do any of you have a clue where this is coming from?"

"I told you, it could be her mojo," said Galen. He had backslid over the week. "Maybe she's a hypnotist. Don't look at me that way. It's a better explanation than believing we met Jesus."

Lilith shot him a sour look. "Bravo. Our archskeptic wants to burn a witch at the stake."

"I didn't say that," Galen shot back. "Don't put words in my mouth."

Frank shook his head. "The bottom line is none of us saw the light."

"Then you looked in the wrong place."

Heads turned. Meg was standing in the doorway listening. "I'm pleased at your honesty, but you gave up too soon."

She walked in and took her place at the head of the table. "I suspected you wouldn't succeed. For some reason that must be what the disciple intended."

"To keep us in the dark?" asked Mare.

"She wanted you to search as hard as you could in all the ordinary places," Meg replied, "until you realized how elusive the light really is. It's nowhere and everywhere. It shines as brightly in a coal mine as in a cathedral."

Their bafflement made her smile. She had a touch of the theatrical about her. "If I'd followed you around this week, how much looking would I have seen? Frank was at work, and so was Jimmy. Mare and Galen mostly watched TV and worried about not having a job. You four barely made an effort." Turning to Lilith, she said, "But that's not so with you, is it?"

"I told them before you came in, I didn't see anything either," said Lilith reluctantly.

"But you didn't tell the whole truth. I'm sure of it." Meg had a touch of the interrogator in her too.

"I didn't go to the store for lightbulbs, if that's what you mean." Lilith's instincts told her to guard her secret. That's how she had survived. But Meg was waiting to hear something from her.

"There was never a special place to go. The light is the same as the presence. If you feel the presence, you are in the light," Lilith said.

"Indeed." Meg nodded approvingly.

"But that's no help," said Mare. "There was no presence outside this room."

"That's the mystery, when something is everywhere and nowhere," Meg replied.

"More riddles," Galen grumbled.

She ignored him. "Imagine, all of you, that you are a fish. You're not satisfied being an ordinary tuna or halibut. You want to be spiritual. One day you swim to the mouth of a deep cave

where a wise teacher is supposed to dwell. You don't swim inside, in case this is just a trick and there's a shark waiting to devour you. 'Tell me how to find God,' you plead. And from deep inside the cave, a low voice says, *Get wet.*

"'What is this?' you think. You ask again. 'I desperately want to see God. Tell me the real answer.' But the same reply rumbles from the cave: *Get wet.* You swim away discouraged and disappointed. You find other teachers who tell you all kinds of things to do. But in the end you never get wet, and God remains a mystery."

Meg looked around the table. "Who sees what this parable means?"

Jimmy spoke up. "The fish is already wet, only he doesn't know it, because all his life the water was too close."

"Right."

While Jimmy enjoyed the pleasure of getting the answer, Lilith argued back. "Now that we know we're in the light, how do we actually see it?"

"With these."

Meg held up a drugstore shopping bag. Inside were half a dozen pairs of plastic sunglasses. "One each. They're all the same."

Frank picked out a pair with neon-green frames. "I wore el cheapos like these to the beach when I was eight."

"Not exactly like these," said Meg. "Don't analyze. Just wear them tomorrow. Agreed?" She didn't wait for answer. The meeting came to an abrupt end as she got up and departed without a backward glance.

As he walked Mare back to her car in the parking lot, Frank twirled the plastic sunglasses in the air, like a kid with a whirligig. Something about the evening had put him in a manic mood.

"Get your God glasses here," he shouted, imitating a carnival barker. "Don't wait for the last trumpet, folks. It's a downer."

Mare didn't do anything to stop him, but she didn't laugh either. After the night when he held her until she fell asleep,

they should have grown closer. Frank wondered why they didn't. Maybe the mystery school was too much to handle on its own.

His manic spell vanished as quickly as it had appeared. "Are we actually supposed to wear these stupid things?" It was a moonless night, too dark to try them on.

"Why not?" said Mare. "The worst that can happen is nothing."

"I dunno. Maybe the worst is that we get sucked in too deep," Frank said. "You really don't mind going along, no matter what?" Now he was restless and uneasy. Every meeting left him feeling that way.

They found Mare's car. Frank searched for an excuse to keep her from driving away. "We should talk more, about everything. Us and what's happening."

Mare didn't go there. "What's really bothering you?"

"You're kidding. All of us should be bothered. I mean, jumping down the rabbit hole is nothing compared to this."

"Galen's scared too. I could see that tonight," Mare said.

"I'm not scared," Frank bristled. "Maybe, just maybe, he had a point about your aunt's mojo. Our minds are being bent, and someone's doing it."

To his surprise, Mare said, "Let's go to my place. You can stay the night and pick up your car in the morning."

Frank nodded and got in on the passenger side. Ordinarily he would have been thrilled at the invitation. He was drawn to Mare, just as he had been in college. Everything physical about her was perfect in his eyes, and whenever he made her smile, he felt as though he'd scored a small victory. But she sparked his insecurity. Mare was deeper than he was, and Frank didn't think she ever let down her guard, not completely. She spent the meetings looking on, saying little. The weirdness they were going through might not be good for her.

They were way past the stage where he would swoop in with a charm offensive. In a serious tone he said, "I meant it about

getting in too deep. I'm concerned about your welfare." As soon as the words came out, he regretted it. "I sound like your father. Sorry."

But she didn't mind. "I don't worry about getting in too deep. I worry that I'm another Aunt Meg."

He was too surprised to react right away. Despite the winter cold, the roads were clear. Frank wasn't holding tight to the door handle, fighting the urge to grab the wheel the way he had the first time Mare drove to her apartment.

She didn't need a response from him. "My aunt gave her life away. I don't know what happened in the convent, but I know she's a total outsider. I can see it in me too."

"So we're not eloping?"

Mare laughed. "Don't be freaked out, but I plan on sleeping with you tonight."

Frank's heart skipped a beat, but his mind didn't go, *Score!* He even held back. "I get the feeling I'm your lab rat. To make sure you're still normal, not like Meg."

"Maybe." Mare said this in a neutral tone, keeping her eyes on the road. The pavement looked clear, but black ice is nearly invisible.

When they got to her place, events unfolded in a pattern familiar to Frank. He enjoyed undressing a woman and admiring her body, confident that she admired his too. Mare turned off the overhead bulb; she lit a candle so the room wouldn't be dark.

They silently agreed that sex was going to be a reprieve. Thinking about the mystery school was forbidden; thinking at all was forbidden. Frank loved the caressing part of being in bed, and this wasn't his first time or his fiftieth—he could stand apart a little, watching how a woman behaved in bed. He was considerate about giving Mare pleasure. He stayed in her as long as she wanted; he was proud that he had enough control to extend their lovemaking without rushing or stealing his own pleasure first.

What he didn't expect was that she would draw him in so deeply or how she did it. She was a quiet lover. When she made soft sounds, they weren't needy or selfish. She wasn't a little girl or a pliant body submitting to his will. He couldn't figure out what she was. The flesh took over after a certain point, and he surrendered to skin hunger, letting himself be carried away by its sensations. At the moment of climax he was alone, not united with her or anyone or anything. It wasn't the moment to question where this feeling came from.

After the physical rapture passed, always too quickly, they kissed and held each other. Each wanted to postpone the return of ordinary existence—when someone's arm has started to fall asleep from the head resting on it, and sweat feels a little clammy, and the bathroom calls. Frank was a realist, and lovemaking was just an interlude, a kind of midnight vacation. *Would this time be more?* He fell asleep thinking about it.

He woke up alone in bed. Mare was taking a shower, and the broken blinds let in bright sunlight. He had slept a long time. Sitting up, he was surprised to see the neon-green sunglasses lying on her pillow. Curious, Frank held them up. *More mojo or something truly unknown?* He didn't know which was better or worse.

At that moment Mare emerged naked from the bathroom, looking beautiful and ridiculous, because she was wearing a pair of the plastic sunglasses. "Don't laugh at me," she said. "Just put them on."

Frank obeyed. At first the greenish-black lenses blocked out everything. He would rather have gazed at her.

"Do you see?" Mare whispered.

"See what?"

And then he did. The air was filled with glittering gold sparks. At first they were like a shimmering mist. In a few seconds, this changed. Everything in the room started to glow, exactly like the glowing chapel.

"Awesome," Frank murmured.

"Wait. Don't talk," she urged.

Nothing changed. Frank wondered if he had to focus harder. Maybe he didn't know what to do. As soon as these doubts entered his mind, the glow faded, turning back into the misty shower of gold.

"I think we have to relax completely. That's the secret," said Mare, sensing what was happening.

"It's not that easy to relax with a gorgeous naked woman in the room."

"Then look away."

He did, reluctantly. Now he was facing the door, and it started to glow. The effect was warm and embracing, just as it was with the chapel. Then the door was gone, and the next instant the walls. Frank gasped. He was staring at the outside world, and everything gave off a lustrous golden light—the bare trees, the dirty snow, the chain-link fence. He turned his head, and in all directions it was as if the real world had melted away, leaving only the vaguest outlines around things.

Neither of them moved. They were transfixed by the beauty. And there was another thing. The light wasn't shining from things.

Everything was the light, and nothing but.

Jimmy woke up the next morning at his usual hour, just before dawn. The sun was peeking over the horizon when he stepped off the bus at the hospital. There was no time to test what the plastic sunglasses would do, so he had stuffed them in his jacket, along with the candy he passed out to sick kids when the staff wasn't looking.

After ten years at the same job, his routine proceeded automatically. As Jimmy emptied wastebaskets and tidied up rooms, he felt what the patients were feeling. Helplessness and fear were epidemic in the hospital. Patients rarely saw their doctors, and when they did, usually for a few anxious minutes, they were like guilty defendants waiting to be sentenced. They strained to read the doctor's face as he glanced at their chart; they waited for the next word out of his mouth, which could send them home with a smile or plunge them into a dark abyss.

Jimmy felt their distress, and he wanted to do something—but what? He had gravitated toward the children's floor, and over the years he'd become a fixture there. This morning he walked into the largest ward, where excited cries of "Señor Lucky!" greeted him. Quickly he was surrounded by six- and seven-year-olds. One little hand reached into his pocket for candy and came up

with the sunglasses instead. They had bright pink rims with sparkles, and suddenly three kids wanted to put them on at once.

Startled, Jimmy grabbed them from the little girl who had found them.

"No, *querida,* these are just for me."

She started to cry. The noise level in the room rose rapidly, and Jimmy knew a nurse would be running in very soon. Mumbling "Sorry, sorry," he got out of there. He scurried down the corridor, avoiding eye contact with anyone he passed.

He was panting, his heart racing, when he made it into the safety of the men's room. Jimmy didn't know why he was so agitated. He'd reacted as if the sunglasses were cursed. But they couldn't be, not when it was Meg who handed them out. He stared at them with uncertainty for a moment before putting them on.

There was no instant effect, and then the outer door to the washroom creaked open. A doctor entered; he didn't acknowledge Jimmy standing at the sinks. Nervously Jimmy left, obeying his usual instinct to remain invisible.

In his distraction, he didn't remember that he was wearing the sunglasses. Diego, another young orderly, was loitering beside a gurney in the hallway. He smirked and gave Jimmy a thumbs-up. *"La vida loca,* eh man?"

Jimmy reached up, but before he could take off the glasses, a rush of golden light filled the air. He froze in place. The process wasn't gradual, the way it had been for Frank. One minute the hospital corridor was there, the next it vanished, replaced by a shimmering glow. The walls melted away. People were illuminated from the inside, yet only for an instant before they vanished too.

Disoriented, Jimmy staggered forward a few steps.

"Hey, watch it."

Jimmy felt his shoulder graze somebody, but he couldn't see who.

"Sorry," he mumbled, or thought he did. The glowing light absorbed him completely. Sounds were blurred and far away. He barely sensed it when a hand clapped him on the back.

"Orderly, stop daydreaming. I just said I need you."

I can't help it, Jimmy thought. *I'm floating away.* He had the uncanny feeling that his feet were lifting off the ground, and every fiber in his being wanted to break free, rising up and up, wherever the light wanted to carry him, like a feather in the wind.

From a distance he heard fuzzy words, more impatient this time. "You coming or not? This kid is seizing."

An alarm went off inside, and Jimmy tore away the sunglasses. The world took a second to return. One of the residents was rushing past him into a private room. On the floor lay a small boy writhing in convulsions. The doctor knelt beside him, clasping his writhing limbs. The boy was only nine or ten, but it was almost impossible to hold him still.

Looking over his shoulder at Jimmy, the doctor issued a torrent of instructions. "I need a nurse, stat. Tell her to prep an IV. We'll inject Dilantin and phenobarb. I'll also need a tongue depressor, and bring restraints in case we have to tie him to the bed."

Seeing no response from Jimmy, the doctor snapped, "You got all that?"

Jimmy wanted to rush off to do what he was told, but the afterglow of the light filled him; he wondered if he was still floating.

"Damn it," the doctor shouted. "Go!"

Suddenly Jimmy's body was galvanized. He hurried to the nurses' station, and within minutes the boy received an injection. The worst of the seizure passed, and he didn't have to be restrained in bed. In the immediate aftermath, the resident, who was younger than Jimmy, gave him a hard look.

"I know you have a good reputation. You don't need to explain anything, but the next time you don't jump when I say jump, I'm ordering random drug testing. You get my drift?"

Jimmy nodded, putting on his most contrite face. But inside he didn't feel humiliated or guilty. In the middle of the crisis, a brave thought had come to him. *I can heal this boy. Once everybody leaves, that will be the right time.* As if struck by lightning, he instantly knew that he, Jimmy, the lowly orderly, was a great healer, the answer to every sick child's prayers.

It was all he could do not to shout his thanks to God. There was too much activity around the epileptic boy's bed, so Jimmy left. There were many other sick children in the wards. His epiphany told him he could cure them all.

They're getting into trouble. I'm sure of it, Meg thought to herself anxiously. Before she handed out the cheapo sunglasses, she knew that seeing the light with your own eyes was a glorious experience. But that didn't save it from being perilous too. One way or another, each person in the group was stumbling.

"Keep them safe," she murmured.

Even after all this time, she still wasn't quite sure who she was talking to. It could be the disciple or the light or just herself. She lay in bed staring at the ornate ceiling overhead, which was painted like an azure sky with cherubs peeking out from billows of rosy clouds. The bed alone was larger than her cell at the convent.

A beam of morning light found a gap in the heavy velvet draperies. Meg got out of bed and pulled them aside. She was looking directly into the sun, and for a second its dazzle filled the world. But this was only a hint at the golden light that really did fill the world, no, the cosmos.

Meg hadn't told the group what to expect. How could she put it into words? Only Father Aloysius had come close.

"The light is alive. It's intelligent beyond anything our minds can understand. It knows us better than we know ourselves," he

told her. "So going into the light can be very simple or very complicated. It's simple if you surrender. It's complicated if you resist."

They were meeting behind the estate's old dairy barn. Meg
couldn't recollect what year this was, but summer had arrived,
and she smelled new-mown grass in the air.

"I used to hate the idea of surrendering," she admitted.

"Resisting is much easier," he replied. "But you already know
that."

"I suppose." Meg was reluctant to talk about her inner struggles.

"You're very special in many ways," Father Aloysius remarked,
"but not in this. Everyone who glimpses the light is thrown into
confusion. I certainly was."

"You, Father?"

He laughed. "I was the worst, quite giddy and beside myself. I
fancied I was in love with every girl on the street. I came close to
proposing marriage to the housemaid. She was from Brazil, and I
planned to surprise her with two plane tickets to Rio." He smiled
at the memory. "Did I mention that I was eleven?"

He was in an expansive mood. In the warm summer breeze the
priest's white hair was like a dandelion puff against the sun. (This
became Meg's favorite image of him after he died, the one she
recalled whenever she wanted to remember him.)

"You see, the light doesn't care if you are young or old," he
said. "It will undo you whenever it wants. The light exposes
everything you've hidden from the world."

"Then what?" Meg asked with feeling. "You're left to crash on
your own?" She still had days when she was lost, twisting in the
wind. One part of her hated God for leaving her that way.

Father Aloysius sensed what she felt. "Be calm, child. I came to
you, didn't I? Someone always comes. The light never works for
anything but the good. It has no other purpose."

Meg wasn't sure she believed him, but she didn't argue. It was
better to be grateful that he had come at all.

Now the tables were turned. The mystery school would be twisting in the wind unless she came for them. Meg dressed quickly. Ten minutes later she was in a taxi heading for the hospital, where Jimmy would already be hard at work. An impulse told her that he was the one who needed rescuing first.

By now, she was used to surrendering. She surrendered to her visions and to the golden chapel. Nothing mystical felt outlandish anymore. (Most people would be bored if the mystical weren't outlandish.) She didn't second-guess the disciple when she guided Meg to the drugstore for those sunglasses. Meg was told that their magic was temporary. After a day, they would go back to being cheap plastic sunglasses. Then the group would be in free fall.

The taxi left her at the front entrance of the hospital. Inside there was a bustle of people. The line in front of the reception desk was three deep. She passed through the lobby unnoticed and headed for a bank of elevators.

Meg didn't know which floor Jimmy worked on, but she remembered that he stopped every morning in the children's ward to cheer the kids up. He pretended to be Señor Lucky, the pony that the hospital owned so that children could ride on its back. She decided to try there first.

When the elevator doors opened, Meg stepped into a corridor painted in bright primary colors, with rainbows and baby animals at play. A dozen doors stood on either side, but she didn't have to peek into them. At the far end of the corridor was a chair with Jimmy sitting in it. He was slumped, hanging his head.

Meg knew that his stillness was deceptive. She rushed down the hallway, and as she got closer, she saw that Jimmy was clutching the plastic sunglasses in his hands.

"Jimmy, what's happening?"

He didn't look up, for the simple reason that he didn't see her. He had gone into a tailspin, sunk deep into himself, and it was entirely his fault. After his epiphany, he had returned to the big

room where Señor Lucky should have handed out candy instead of running away. The atmosphere was calmer now, but the kids didn't rush to his side. They were a bit wary of him.

Jimmy smiled magnanimously, spreading his arms out the way Jesus did in the illustrated Bible stories his grandmother bought for him when he was little. "Suffer the little children to come unto me." That's all it would take. One touch, and they would be healed, one by one.

"Come on," he urged. But they were too nervous.

Too impatient to wait, he went to the bed of a girl with leukemia. She had a shaved head because of her treatments and slept most of the day, her body wasted and weak. She would be the first. Jimmy placed his palm across her forehead. He sent waves of love into her. Whether it was this or feeling his touch, the girl woke up. She looked at him, and Jimmy held his breath.

"How do you feel, baby?" he whispered.

"I hurt."

"You don't feel better now?" Jimmy asked.

She shook her head. "I hurt everywhere. Why are you bothering me?" She wasn't angry with him, just sleepy and cross. Turning her head away, the girl fell back to sleep, but not before Jimmy saw the expression in her eyes, which was vacant and lost.

Oh, my God. Jimmy felt himself crash to earth. He had made a terrible mistake. He tried to bolt from the room, but his knees buckled, and he barely made it into the corridor. If a chair hadn't been sitting there, he would have collapsed. He felt nauseous; far worse, he was sick at heart. What had come over him? A pang of fear struck his chest. What if someone had walked in on him?

As he slumped there, a woman started speaking to him. As if swimming toward the surface from a great depth, Jimmy managed to look up. He recognized Meg.

She bent down and softly said in his ear, "You're not Jesus Christ. Sorry to disappoint you."

He was relieved and bewildered at the same time. "Then who am I?"

"You're one of us. And a very beautiful soul."

Jimmy managed a grateful smile. Then a fresh spasm of nausea came over him, filling his mouth with its bitterness, and he started to cry.

Meg called an emergency meeting that evening, and one way or another every member was rounded up. She was guided to rescue them, as she had been with Jimmy, but she needed help.

Lilith was likely to be the one who hadn't run amok. Meg called her at home. It took three tries before she answered.

"How are you feeling?" Meg asked. She assumed that Lilith had tried on the sunglasses.

"What?"

"Are you feeling anything unusual?"

"I feel very well," replied Lilith. "Very well indeed." She sounded like herself but mildly confused. "Listen carefully," Meg said in an urgent voice.

"All right."

"You're not God. You're not a saint or an angel or waiting for the rapture. I know you're trying to decide which one applies. None of the above. You are still Lilith. Do you understand?"

Silence at the other end. Then in a quavering voice, sounding more vulnerable than Meg had ever heard her, Lilith said, "If I'm not God, wouldn't God tell me?"

"No, he's busy. I'm telling you instead. You got a blast of reality, that's all. It's wonderful, but you need to come to your senses. We've got to find the others, and quickly."

Luckily, Lilith came down to earth after three cups of black coffee; her years of experience had kept her from becoming delusional.

Mare was fairly stable also. They found her at the bus stop near her house. As the buses rolled up, she stood at the door, her hand

raised in benediction. "Bless you," she said to the passengers getting on and off. "Be at peace."

A few people smiled at her. The rest were used to crazies in the city; this one seemed harmless. Only one man was irritated enough to say, "Get yourself some help, lady."

Mare was surprised to see Meg and Lilith at the curb. "Were you sent here too?" she asked. "Everyone is a child of God. I see it. Why don't they?"

"They've got other things on their mind," said Lilith. "We need to get you home."

"Why? I've found my calling."

"Maybe so," Meg said. "But now is not the time."

"What does that mean?" Lilith asked, looking puzzled. She'd caught the look that passed between them.

"Never mind. Let's get her away from here."

Mare had rushed out into the cold wearing only a light jacket and now she was trembling. Like Jimmy she had the plastic sunglasses clutched tightly in her hand. Meg immediately grasped what they were doing to her niece. The look that passed between them had history.

It went back to the legendary Thanksgiving Massacre, as the Donovan family took to calling it. A distant cousin was being ordained, and Mare's family filled two cars, driving a hundred miles to attend what Mare's grandfather Tom referred to as a going-away party.

"He'll miss the best part of life, I'm telling you," he said.

Mare, who was six, wondered what he meant. Her grandmother told Tom to shush.

Tom, who was "black Irish," loved the I.R.A. cause and resented priests. At the party he made a nuisance of himself. He knew better than to make cutting remarks about the church, so, instead, he made mischief by goading the soon-to-be priest into drinking too much.

"Another nip can't hurt you, or you're not a Donovan," he said. The young man, barely out of his teens, did what he was told. Finally someone intervened and told Father Ronnie, as they had already started calling him, to get some fresh air. He walked out alone, tripped over a tree root in the back yard, and hit his head. The result wasn't terrible, a gash on the forehead and a mild concussion. But the gash bled profusely, the parents exchanged hot words with Tom, and that side of the Donovan family was never welcome in the house again.

The disturbing part wasn't the fight, because Tom never liked his snooty, devout cousins to begin with. The disturbing part occurred on the way home when Mare, sitting in the backseat, started to scream, "Stop the car, stop the car!"

Her outburst was completely out of character. Her mother looked around from the front seat. "What's gotten into you?"

Mare began to cry, and no one could calm her down. "Please, please," she whined.

"Do you have to go?" her father said, looking at her in the rear-view mirror.

"No."

"Then what is it?"

Mare remembered that she was going to blurt out, "We're all going to die." A brutal image had flashed through her mind, showing a railroad crossing and a car twisted into a hideous wreckage. At that moment she heard the bells signaling an approaching train, and the flashing red lights for the gate were only a hundred yards away. She was too frightened to speak, squeezing her eyes shut in terror.

"Look out!" her mother warned.

There was a loud horn blast from the locomotive barreling toward the crossing, instantly followed by a sickening crash.

"Look away!" Tom ordered as he slammed on the brakes and leaped out of the car. Ahead of them a driver had tried to beat

the crossing gate, but he had misjudged by a matter of seconds. It was enough. In the horror and confusion at the scene, no one found time to question Mare about why she had cried out. She felt incredibly guilty, as if she could have saved the people who died. The newspaper said the driver had been drinking heavily at a holiday party.

In the aftermath, her mother remembered how Mare made such a fuss, but Thanksgiving was the next day, and there was the main event to discuss, the big row over the soon-to-be priest. Mare never came up.

Aunt Meg poked at her turkey in silence and then took her niece into the back yard while the table was being cleared. "You notice things, don't you? Things other people don't."

Mare was alarmed. "I try not to."

"Why? It's not a bad thing. Did your mother tell you it was?"

Mare bit her lip. "All right, go back inside," her aunt said. "Brush the snow off your shoes first."

At the age of six, it didn't occur to Mare to wonder about Aunt Meg's motivation. All she got into her head from that traumatic Thanksgiving was a recurring nightmare. The sound of crunching metal woke her up shaking.

The plastic sunglasses reawakened this bad memory, which thankfully fled as soon as Mare started blessing the bus passengers.

Now she heard Meg say, "Come with us. We don't want a blessing overload, do we? It might blow the circuits."

Mare looked confused, but she allowed herself to be led away docilely. When Meg and Lilith got her back home and into bed, she fell asleep instantly.

"On to the next one," said Meg with a touch of grimness.

They found Frank sitting in his car in the newspaper parking lot. He was blasting heavy-metal rock at a deafening volume and didn't hear them approach. Lilith rapped on the driver's-side window. Frank lowered it.

"Why are you here?" he asked. He looked badly shaken.

"To see how you're holding together," Meg replied.

He grimaced. "The glue's not dry yet."

"What happened?"

Frank had made a fool of himself. At Mare's apartment the effect of the sunglasses had been overwhelming, but somewhere in the back of his mind he remembered that he had to go to work. He took off the glasses and stumbled to the bathroom. A cold shower helped. He dressed to leave, but Mare paid no attention, perched on the edge of the mustard yellow sofa with a giant grin on her face.

"I'm going now," he said. "Don't keep those things on too long."

"Uh huh."

The streets were clear, but Frank's driving was shaky, and he stopped by his young reporter buddy Malcolm's place. Malcolm was surprised to see him.

"I need you to drive," said Frank, hoping he sounded normal. Perhaps not. Malcolm gave him a puzzled look and took the wheel.

"You've got that political thing in an hour," he said. "Maybe I'll come with."

"Sure, fine," Frank mumbled. He had no idea what the political thing was. He kept staring out the window at the passing scene. Instead of a grimy city, his eyes drank in a whoosh of colors that was almost musical.

"Heavy night?" Malcolm asked. "You look wasted."

The concern in his voice made Frank try to focus. He shut his eyes and concentrated. Things came into view.

"The political thing is a press conference?" he said doubtfully.

"Yeah. Boy, I'm glad you asked me to drive."

At a hotel downtown, a right-wing candidate running for Congress had scheduled a pointless press conference. He was behind in the polls and wanted to agitate about abortion and gay

marriage. The only media who showed up were Frank, Malcolm, and a college-aged girl from the local-access TV station.

The candidate looked miffed. He was a local fundamentalist minister who was bewildered that his old hot-button issues had turned cold. He took out his sheet of talking points, but before he could speak Frank raised his hand.

"Questions can come later," the candidate's PR assistant said.

Frank stood up anyway. "I just wanted to tell Reverend Prescott something. You're beautiful, man."

The candidate, an imposing figure in his late sixties with snowy hair, scowled. "What did you say?"

Frank felt himself slightly tottering. "I said you're beautiful. Actually, you're totally full of it. You've become a laughingstock. But God doesn't care. He loves you."

Frank started to sit down, but had a second thought. "I love you too."

Malcolm looked around nervously; the local-access girl giggled.

With a sense of dreamy detachment Frank watched the candidate's face turn purplish red. The PR assistant, who knew all the local reporters, grabbed the microphone and shouted into it.

"Get the hell out of here, Frank. I'm calling your boss. I hope your little stunt is worth losing your job over."

"No worries. God loves you too. Creep."

No one heard Frank add this parting remark, because Malcolm was dragging him out of the room. Nothing was said in the car on the way back to the paper. But when he got out, Malcolm was visibly angry.

"Sorry, man," Frank mumbled.

"If you want to commit public suicide, it's okay by me," Malcolm said. "But leave me out of it. I don't want to get hit by the shrapnel."

Frank watched him stalk off, then he turned the music on in his car full blast to clear his head. Time passed; he didn't know

how long. The next thing he was aware of was Lilith rapping on the window.

"Can you turn that down?" she said.

"He's still in shock," Meg guessed. They gave Frank a few minutes. He clicked off the music and stepped out of the car.

"Jesus, what a mess," he moaned. "I'm ruined."

He didn't want to talk about his grim mood. The two women decided to wait in the parking lot while he went inside to learn his fate. Frank was back in two minutes.

"I can't believe it. My editor was ready to kick my ass down the street, but he got a call from the owner of the paper. Turns out he hates this wack-job preacher. I might get a raise." Frank shook his head. "There is a God."

Lilith shrugged. "Give the boy a gold star."

Which left only Galen. They swung by his house, but his car was gone, and no one answered the door.

"The painting he tried to deface," said Lilith. "Maybe he's gone back to kneel in front of it."

"No, that's not like him," Meg replied. "Everyone reacts according to their nature. That's how it works."

Guessing where he might be was impossible, but on the first try Galen answered his cell. He sounded calm. Too calm.

"I haven't tried the sunglasses on yet," he said. "I'm still supposed to, right?"

Meg hesitated. She had no right to reverse the disciple's instructions. "Let me come to you first. Where are you?"

"I'm walking into the planetarium."

"Why?"

"I used to like it as a kid. Seemed like a safe place to trip."

Meg said, "Wait there. Don't do anything."

She rushed Lilith back into the car. "I have a bad feeling about this," she said.

When they got to the planetarium, the ticket seller told them

the next showing was delayed. In the distance Meg saw two uniformed guards entering the auditorium.

"I'm going in there," she whispered to Lilith. "Create a distraction."

Lilith's idea of a distraction was to empty her purse on the floor and then beg the ticket seller to help her find a diamond ring that had fallen out. It was feeble, but good enough for Meg to scurry past the gate. She hurried into the empty auditorium, which was dimly lit. The domed ceiling was devoid of stars. She heard a commotion in the middle of the room and, once her eyes adjusted, Meg spied the two guards. They were prying Galen off some kind of machine. She ran up and saw that he had wrapped himself around the star projector. He was wearing the sunglasses.

"Let there be light," Galen was mumbling. "And there was light."

The burly guards were having a surprisingly hard time pulling him loose. One said, "C'mon, mister, you don't want to be doing this."

When they pulled harder, Galen began to squeal and held on tight. Meg intervened. "I'm his sister. Let me try. He's frightened."

The guards didn't give her permission, but she shoved past them anyway, which got her close enough to snatch the glasses off Galen's head.

"I took him out on a day pass. He's under care," she explained.

The guards looked suspicious. At least Galen had let go of the projector. He slid to the ground, softly murmuring "Wow" over and over.

"Your brother needs better doctors," one guard said. He was older and seemed to be in charge.

"Oh, I agree," said Meg. "I appreciate your understanding. And, of course, if we're allowed to leave, there will be a generous contribution to the planetarium."

"Whatever," the younger guard grumbled. "I'm going to lunch."

Between them, Meg and Lilith dragged Galen away. He pawed at Meg's purse, where she had stowed his sunglasses.

"Mine," he babbled. "Mine, mine, mine."

But they managed to keep him from getting at them.

"All gone," he moaned softly. His head lolled to one side, and he fell asleep.

CHAPTER *19*

When the emergency meeting convened that evening, the group looked like five cats scooped out of the river and wrung out. But there were no visible signs of derangement. Meg took a careful look around.

"Everyone is all right?"

"We're safely back in our cages," Lilith said drily. "I'm using a metaphor."

"Maybe," Frank grunted. He was still badly shaken, and he suspected the others were too. But no one wanted to exchange notes, not until things settled down.

Meg picked up Lilith's drift. "It's not a physical cage you're trapped in. The bars are mental. They block out the light. Deep down that's how you want it to be, because living normally means everything if you plan to survive. The disciple has shown you a way out, an escape route."

"So we can enjoy living abnormal lives?" Frank asked. He pulled his plastic sunglasses out. "Help like this I don't need, thank you very much."

Despite his protest, Meg sensed that none of them regretted a moment of their time outside the cage.

She said, "I had a great teacher, and one day he gave me a piece of advice. 'Don't judge anyone for who they appear to be. Get a sense of their soul. One kind of soul is masked from view, and it gives off no light. Another kind of soul sometimes peeks out from behind the mask, giving off a flickering light. The rarest kind of soul hides from nothing; it's out in full view. That's you.'"

"Beautiful," Mare murmured.

"You think so? I didn't. I felt exposed and guilty," Meg said.

"Guilty for what?"

"For being a fraud. If you don't have a clue who you really are, your whole life's a fraud, isn't it?" She gave each person around the table an astute glance. "Now you don't have an excuse anymore."

They grew quiet, and then Lilith stood up. "I want to apologize. I've been seeing the rest of you as ordinary people. The sight was extremely disappointing, let me assure you."

"Thank you, Missus God," Galen muttered under his breath.

"I'm not deaf," said Lilith. "You've all done such a good job hiding your light that you fooled me. No longer, and so I apologize."

She said none of this with a smile. If anything she looked angry as she sat back down. *All those wasted years,* the voice in her head began to say, but she turned her attention away, refusing to listen.

Jimmy held up his sunglasses. "These things freaked me out. I'm with Frank. Just take them back."

"No need," said Meg. "They were just an invitation. God's not going to push himself on you."

"Is it really so bad being a fraud?" asked Jimmy, which got a nervous laugh. "Seriously, I don't know how to change."

"I'd be worried if you didn't want to keep fooling people," Meg replied. "It's taken years to get your act down pat. But the disciple thinks you're ready, all of you."

"I'll bite," Galen said. He hadn't tossed in a complaint, because he didn't really have one. The light had treated him more carefully than the rest.

Meg felt a silent agreement all around. If they had hesitated, she was prepared to make the same promise Father Aloysius once made to her: "One taste of the light isn't the same as living there. When you live there, you won't need hope or faith. You'll know everything."

Back then, her anxiety wasn't assuaged. "I don't want to know everything."

"Yes, you do. You just don't realize it yet," he told her.

The golden shrine was sitting in its customary place in the center of the table. Meg placed her hands on it. The others followed her lead without being told. The room began to fade away. The shift into another reality happened smoothly this time, although they had no idea what would greet them on the other side.

This is what they saw. The thirteenth disciple was traveling on a road in the desert, empty in both directions. An old servant was leading the sleepy donkey she rode on, its clip-clop sending up puffs of dust. Spring had come into full bloom around Jerusalem. For a magical three weeks, splashes of yellow and purple brought joy to the landscape. But here the only vegetation was drab, low scrub.

"The place must be near," she said anxiously.

The servant shrugged his shoulders. "Who can say?"

This stretch of the road to Tyre was usually filled with traders and their caravans. Trade attracted bandits. But there were no hills or cliff faces for them to hide in for the next few miles, and Jerusalem could still be seen in the distance, a hazy blue mirage.

The servant eyed the sun's position in the sky. "If we don't see a house soon, we'll have to turn back." He didn't want to suffer the consequences if his mistress got waylaid.

Where could a house hide in such flat, unsheltered land? The answer came around the next bend—a deep ravine intersected the road like a slash in the skin.

"There," she said, pointing to a trail that led into the ravine.

The servant looked perplexed. "There's nothing down there but snakes and devils."

"In a few minutes there will be snakes, devils, and us."

Grunting, the servant goaded the donkey with a switch. The trail wound its way around rocky outcroppings. Once they reached the dry floor of the ravine, which had been cut by centuries of flash floods, the bed veered away from the road.

Ten minutes later they came upon their first human being, a man sitting on a sandstone boulder whittling on a stick. The servant wondered if the point of this activity was to show that the man had a knife.

When they were in close range, the man spoke cryptically. "I had a feeling."

The thirteenth disciple didn't hesitate. "Me too."

The man got to his feet, revealing how tall he was. His robe, tied with a sash at the waist, was good-quality hemp, but not the fine-spun linen the girl wore. He had a neatly trimmed beard and eyes that studied her with sharp clarity.

"Do we need to speak alone?" he asked, eyeing the servant, who didn't exactly seem pleased with their encounter.

"I'm staying," the servant insisted.

"It's all right," she said. The girl knew that age had made him somewhat deaf. Her father's granaries and fields were too busy at planting time to spare any of the young men. He wouldn't have sent anyone if he'd known she was going to hunt for one of Jesus's disciples. The miracle rabbi had caused trouble among the Jews, which tightened the Roman grip. Killing him only made the occupiers search harder for more of his kind.

She dismounted and approached the man. "What shall I call you?"

"Simeon. Or if you are more Roman than Jew, Simeonus."

"Simeon, then. Do you have a hiding place nearby?"

"Yes. Bandits dug out some caves. With everything stirred up, rebels use them now. You're safer here." Simeon gestured toward

the boulder he'd been sitting on, the only thing that could pass for a seat. The girl perched herself on it while he sat cross-legged in the dust.

"I've seen everything," she began. "Just as I saw how to find you today."

She was sparing his feelings. In a vision she had seen Simeon run away when the Roman soldiers seized Jesus. He hid in a hole in the poorest slums of the city, weeping uncontrollably. But that's what attracted the girl to him. She had wept uncontrollably too.

"What do you want from me?" he asked.

"I wish I didn't want anything. My family should be offering you a hiding place, someone as holy as you."

He shook his head. "You think I'm holy? I betrayed the one I promised never to betray. Now I have no way to go in the world. I used to fish in Galilee, but that's too far behind me."

"So you live as God pleases," she said.

Simeon sat back. "I live as my master taught, because I know he forgives me."

He spoke with total sincerity, and this encouraged the thirteenth disciple. The donkey wandered toward a tuft of grass lodged in a crevice, and the old servant sat in the shade with his straw hat pulled down over his eyes.

"I spoke with Jesus," the thirteenth disciple said. She took a deep breath. "He was on the cross when he came to me."

She expected Simeon to jump to his feet, in either anger or amazement. But he remained calm. "What did he tell you?"

"He told me he was the light of the world. Do you know what he meant?"

"He meant what he said."

Simeon spread his arms out. "All this, and everything we can see, is light. When the spirit completely fills us, we are the light. Jesus taught this."

"So you could become the same as God?"

He was alarmed. "Those words are blasphemous."

"Your whole life is blasphemous. I don't care. Let me follow you."

Simeon shook his head. "Someday I'll return to Jerusalem, God willing. I don't want your father stoning me for ruining his daughter."

"How can you ruin me?" She asked the question without flinching, staring directly into his eyes.

"By taking away your faith. With faith, you can still be a Jew."

"No, I'm like you. Neither of us can go back to how we were."

Simeon frowned. He'd never heard a woman speak like this. She could have explained to him about listening behind a curtain while the rabbis taught her brothers. She could have pointed to her heart, which many days was like a burning ball of fire. But there was no time.

He said, "It's rare to see a woman on the cross, but not impossible. You must go. I have nothing more to tell you."

The sun had already sunk below the lip of the ravine. She stood up, brushing the pale desert dust from her shift and sandals. "I know what I've seen. Whether I'm cursed or blessed, I'm one of you."

"Then I pity you." Simeon's eyes grew moist. "Jesus may never return to us. Don't put yourself in danger. Just go."

He saw how crestfallen she looked, and his voice softened. "If you're one of us, the Lord will guide you. Even in the shadow of the death."

She paused. "I know why you're sick at heart. It's not because you betrayed your master. It's because he left you behind. You blame him. You think it's unfair."

How did you know? he thought. To be so blessed when the master was alive and then abandoned like a stray spark blown from a bonfire into the night. How could she know?

When he didn't reply, her tone turned grim. "As long as you wallow in grief, you have no master, and no hope."

Her words would come back to haunt him in all the tomorrows leading to his death. Simeon waited while she woke up her drowsy old servant. He accompanied them to the trailhead and watched the donkey climb to the road. The little party had to make it back to Jerusalem before the night and its lurking dangers swallowed them up.

With one impulse, they all took their hands off the golden shrine. As often as the disciple had taken them back in time, it was still hard to believe. Lilith looked at the others. Did they realize that the hunted fugitive in the ravine was Simon Peter? Or that he would only meet his master by being crucified in Rome? All the disciples died violent deaths. If the girl shared their life, she must have shared their doom. Lilith decided not to mention any of this. She steered the group in a different direction.

"You said that going back there would help us make a choice," she reminded Meg. "What is it?"

"Living as God pleases," Meg replied, quoting the disciple. "Without doubt or fear."

Her words were meant to inspire them, but that wasn't the outcome. Jimmy looked anxious. "It sounds too hard," he said. "Look at them squatting in a ditch. They were miserable."

"And hunted down," Galen added. There was a general murmur of agreement. "The disciples were promised heaven, and then overnight they're criminals on the run."

Lilith was irritated. "For pity's sake, why can't you see past that?"

"Maybe I do," Galen shot back. "I'm sorry horrible things happened. But history is a nightmare we spend our whole lives trying to forget."

This was perhaps the deepest thought any of them had expressed, certainly the gloomiest. Jimmy felt sorry for Galen. But his gloominess wasn't the only way.

"If everything's so horrible, maybe it doesn't have to be," Jimmy said. "I'm an optimist."

"For how long? Eternal optimism is insanity if nothing ever changes," Galen declared.

When Jimmy didn't respond, Meg said, "You're looking at the world from darkness. But the light never abandoned us—we abandoned it. Is that what you want?"

She wasn't throwing a challenge in their faces, but one was implied.

Frank put into words what they were all thinking. "Okay, so I look into the light and say, 'Come and get me.' Is it going to make me crazy again?"

"I'm not a fortune-teller," Meg replied. "In this new life, every day is an unknown. The alternative is totally predictable. You stay behind bars."

They could tell she meant business, but they couldn't see where she was taking them. Meg didn't know either. Ever since Father Aloysius died, she had abided alone in a deserted kingdom. She was the queen of her own solitude. Now the kingdom was beginning to be populated. Five shipwrecked travelers had washed ashore by the light of the moon. They had no idea if they belonged in this strange land. It was time they found out.

Meg looked around the table, sizing up each castaway. "When you see me, do you see somebody who's like you?" She didn't wait for a reply. "I'm no different from you, I promise. Except in one thing. When the disciple says, 'Live as God pleases,' I get it."

She reached into her handbag and took out a small change purse. "Enough talk. There are five pennies inside this purse, one for each of you." She spilled the coins out; they clinked as they landed on the table. "Take one, and regard it as precious. If you lose it, that means you want to go back to your old life."

In silence the pennies were passed around. Galen eyed his, then he flipped it in the air. "Heads. Now what?"

"It's not a game," Meg warned. "The disciple gave plastic sunglasses a secret power. She's done the same here."

Frank shook his head. "This whole thing about walking away. It sounds like a threat."

"It's not," Meg insisted. "The instructions are simple. Carry your penny around for a week, and when you return, you'll be changed."

Galen was annoyed. "Every time you explain things, nothing gets explained."

If he expected more clues, Meg didn't offer any. "You're on your own," she said. "Just don't lose your penny, no matter what. If you do, don't bother to come back."

The group dispersed, going their separate ways in the fading twilight, more bewildered and fretful than ever.

CHAPTER *20*

That night Galen slept fitfully and woke up tangled in the sheets. He had twisted them tighter trying to burrow into the bed, like an animal digging its way out of danger. The meetings did that to him, and he hated it. But there was nowhere else to turn. His days were empty without the mystery school.

Standing in the bathroom, he looked at himself in the mirror, saddened by the puffy roundness of his face, his absent hairline, and his bloodshot eyes. *Why was nothing working?*

Nobody owes you anything, he reminded himself. *Get a grip.*

Back in the bedroom he pulled on the pants and shirt he'd flung over a chair. A bright spot glinted out of the corner of his eye. He leaned over and picked up the penny, which had fallen out of his khakis.

Really? he thought. It wasn't clear what another dose of magic would do. He'd already floated through the universe. He was tempted to throw it away the minute he got to the hospital parking lot. Galen had a deep suspicion of magic. It was primitive and mindless. As a child, he recalled random visits from a whiskery, smelly uncle, the last of the farming stock his mother came from. When Galen was ten, Uncle Rodney pulled him aside and produced a dollar bill from his wallet.

"I got somethin' real important to show you," he said. His tone was conspiratorial. He pushed the boy's hand away when Galen reached for the money. "This isn't for you, no sir."

Uncle Rodney gave the bill a snap. "This is the first dollar I ever made. It's sacred to me. If I ever lose it, Lord knows what will happen."

"You'd have one less dollar," said Galen.

"No! Much worse. I'd probably go bust."

"Why?"

His uncle frowned. "What do you mean why? Don't you believe in luck?" His breath smelled of chewing tobacco and bad teeth.

Galen turned and fled, much to his uncle's disgust. The only luck was bad luck—the boy knew that very well. Fortune was a secret enemy, and no matter how often you begged her to be kind, her treachery could never be appeased.

This recollection distracted him from throwing the penny away. He thoughtlessly pocketed it along with the rest of his loose change, which he'd neatly laid out in rows on the dresser. The winter sun was bright and high in the sky. Time to go out.

Because he was sulky and absent-minded, he didn't notice that he was headed in the wrong direction, away from the bus stop. Galen hung his head, mechanically counting his steps, when a stranger bumped into him. The next second, he felt something wet and hot. The man had spilled coffee down Galen's front.

"Watch it!" Galen snapped. He looked up, and it was no stranger. It was Malcolm, the kid reporter, who had rushed out of a Starbucks without looking where he was going.

"Jeez, are you okay, man?"

"I don't know." The coffee wasn't boiling hot, but it was Galen's habit to make someone else squirm for a change when he had the chance.

Malcolm looked genuinely apologetic. "Listen, I have a little time. Can I get you something to eat? How have you been?"

What is this? Galen thought. The last person who had said a kind word to him was Iris. The memory brought a stab of pain. His natural instinct was to brush the kid off and scurry down the street.

Before he could do this, Malcolm said, "You've been keeping out of trouble, I hope."

Malcolm's cell phone rang. He held up his hand, saying, "Just a second," and answered it.

Galen's hand wandered into his pocket, touching the change he was carrying. At that moment an unusual thought came into his head.

This kid pities you. Is he wrong?

Galen didn't know how to react. Malcolm's call was brief, and when he said good-bye, his face had fallen.

"I guess I have more time on my hands than I thought," he muttered. "They cancelled my assignment."

Galen's hand lingered in his pocket. In the back of his mind he knew he was touching the magic penny.

Without a second thought he said, "You're going to be fired tomorrow."

"What?" The kid backed away a step.

"Tomorrow morning the city editor is going to let you go. That's why he took your story away."

"Jesus." Malcolm looked badly shaken. He had a sinking feeling that he was hearing the truth. "What am I going to do?"

The words came out involuntarily. The last person on earth he wanted to share his trouble with was the nut job from the museum fiasco.

"I know you think I'm a loser," said Galen, "but I can help. Come back here after they fire you." He saw the doubt written on

Malcolm's face. "Sometimes weird people like me actually know something. You and me, we're a lot alike," he added.

"Wow, it's that bad?" Malcolm mourned. Galen was older than his father. He resembled a dumpling in wrinkled khakis. He probably had nothing to do but wander around all day pestering people. How could they be alike?

But by then Malcolm was starting to feel panicky. He turned away mumbling, "I have to make some calls" as he punched numbers into his cell phone. He wandered down the sidewalk without saying good-bye.

The voice in Galen's head said, *He'll be back.*

Which wasn't good news. Galen was almost as shaken as the kid. Some impulse he couldn't control had taken over. Why else had he said those things? He wasn't the kind to meddle in other people's affairs, ever.

Retracing his steps, Galen scurried home to clean the coffee stains off his jacket and scarf. This took only a few minutes, and afterward he didn't feel like mingling with the crowd at the mall anymore. *Who does that anyway, besides losers?*

The next morning he went back to the corner where the Starbucks stood. It took half an hour to talk himself into going; this time the only coin he put in his pocket was the penny. The day was gray and windy. There were gusts of sleet, and Galen almost turned back. A lifetime of missed opportunities told him not to.

Amazingly, Malcolm was there, sitting on the steps of the coffee shop. He looked miserable. "All right, I got sacked. So tell me the wisdom of the weird."

He followed Galen inside. As they stood in line, neither spoke. Galen felt cold with panic. Why had he lured this kid into meeting him?

The voice in his head returned. *Don't worry. It will be like talking to your double.*

Galen laughed, and Malcolm whipped around. "Something funny?" He looked irritated and as nervous as Galen.

"Potentially," Galen replied. "We'll have to wait and see."

After they took a table, Malcolm didn't make eye contact. He gulped his coffee until Galen said, "Slow down. No one's keeping you here."

"I've been thrashing this out in my mind," Malcolm said. "You took a lucky guess yesterday, didn't you?"

It would have been easy to say yes, and that would have been the end of it. But Galen remembered Meg's image of living behind bars. For the first time in his life, he asked for guidance.

Malcolm mistook his silence. "I thought so," he said, pushing his coffee away and starting to get up. "It was nice knowing you."

"If you stay, you'll get your job back."

"Bull."

"What have you got to lose?"

"I dunno, my self-respect?" Malcolm hesitated, perplexed, but he sat back down again. "What's the plan?"

Galen clasped his hands together under the table to keep them from trembling. "Go back to the paper. But you have to take me with you."

"Now?"

"Yes." Galen managed what he hoped was a confident smile. "I'll know what to do when we get there."

"Because you've run your life so spectacularly that way, right? Jesus!"

Malcolm didn't mute his insolence. He felt entitled to it, being young and employed. Except that the second part wasn't true anymore. The gap between them was closing. Wearily he got up and let Galen follow him out of the coffee shop, not looking over his shoulder.

They drove in silence through the cold, gray day. In the newspaper parking lot, Galen expected the kid to get cold feet, but

he marched the two of them upstairs to the newsroom. The city editor's desk had several reporters gathered around it, drinking coffee and shooting the breeze. No one looked Malcolm's way.

Coming to his senses, he shook his head. "This is ridiculous. Why did I listen to you?"

Without replying, Galen walked up to the desk. "I'm Malcolm's father. He's sick of being on obits, but he didn't want to tell you."

The city editor was Galen's age, but robust-looking, as red-faced as an Irish boxer. Behind him on a coatrack hung a trench coat and a fedora. He thought of himself as an old-school newspaperman.

"He should have had the guts to come to me himself," he said.

"He was afraid he'd get fired," Galen said.

"Fired?" The editor pointed to the circle of men around his desk. "These hacks would go first."

He grinned wickedly at the reporter lounging on the corner of the desk. "Isn't that right, Nicky?" The man stood up, faking a smile. No one looked very happy.

By this time Malcolm had walked up. He couldn't believe what Galen was trying to pull off.

"This isn't my fault," he said apologetically.

His editor looked annoyed. "You call in sick yesterday, and now I don't see any copy coming across my terminal." He tapped the computer screen in front of him. "Your old man's got a point. Forget obits. Someone else can pick up the slack. I want the story on police corruption you promised me."

He seemed oblivious of the fact that he'd fired Malcolm earlier that morning. The reporters around the desk had all witnessed the scene, had watched Malcolm clear out his desk. Without comment they drifted back to their cubicles.

To keep the kid from opening his mouth, Galen dragged him away. It wasn't easy.

"He doesn't remember a thing," Malcolm whispered. He sounded very agitated.

"Do you want him to remember?" Galen hissed.

"I want an explanation."

Galen searched his mind for one. "He can't remember because it never happened."

"You're crazy."

"I must be." Galen had no idea why such a bizarre explanation had come out of him. "Keep moving, and close your mouth. You'll catch flies."

Malcolm could have said, "It's winter, there are no flies." But he was dazed. Galen dragged him through the nearest door, which opened onto a stairwell. They both felt weak and sank down on the steps.

"This goes a lot farther than weird. Really. I guess I should be thanking you," Malcolm managed to say.

Galen shook his head. "I didn't do anything. I was just there."

"So you're not, like, a shaman or whatever?" Malcolm took a hard look at Galen and laughed. "Of course you're not." He got to his feet. "I meant that in the best possible way."

Galen shrugged. "I doubt it."

Malcolm opened the door to the newsroom, anxious to get back to work before his job vaporized again. He bit his lip, trying to think of something else to say. Nothing came, so he smiled weakly and left, letting the stairwell door bang shut behind him.

Galen took the magic penny out of his pocket and held it up to the light. It looked completely innocent, and the voice in his head said, *Sometimes being here is all it takes.*

CHAPTER *21*

The morning after the meeting Frank woke up in his bed and looked over at Mare, who was still asleep. They spent two or three nights a week together now, alternating between his place and hers. Each made room for the other's toothbrush and emptied half a drawer. It wasn't the first time for either of them. Frank got up and started a pot of coffee in the small galley kitchen. A bouquet of last week's flowers, daisy mums he'd bought half price at the supermarket, needed throwing out. The penny lay on the kitchen counter where he'd left it, looking harmless. But the sight of it bothered him.

"You're tricky, aren't you? You've given me a way to bail out. What if I take it? You don't control me."

Who was he speaking to—the disciple, God, Meg? He didn't have a good reason to drop out of the mystery school. Seeing is believing, and Frank had seen things he couldn't wrap his mind around. So he didn't try. That was the long and the short of it. He drifted with the group, waiting for a flash from God. For all he knew, the line was dead.

Mare came in, yawning and drowsy. She noticed Frank staring at the penny.

"A penny for your thoughts," she said. Her temp agency hadn't left a message on her cell, so she had the day off. She could curl up in bed again after Frank went to work.

"I don't know where we go from here," he mumbled. The coffeemaker beeped, and he poured two cups without looking into Mare's eyes. If he dropped out, he was sure that Mare would stop seeing him.

She didn't answer immediately, making a small business of dosing her coffee with milk and sugar.

"No one's putting pressure on you," she said, sounding as reasonable as she could.

He took her hand. "It's not just us. It's everything. We're on a roller coaster with a brick windshield. We can't see an inch ahead."

"Maybe we're not meant to," she said.

"So you aren't the least little bit worried?"

Mare picked up the penny. "Don't make any decisions until you've given it a chance. Meg promised it wouldn't make us crazy."

She put the coin in his hand and closed his fingers around it. Perhaps she also kissed him on the cheek, but Frank didn't notice. As soon as the penny touched his hand, disturbing images filled his mind, moving as fast as a movie spooling on a berserk projector. The coffee cup almost slipped from his hand. The images were gone in two seconds; he felt dizzy. He snatched his hand away and dropped the penny back on the counter.

"You're right. Listen, I'm late. Let me jump in the shower." He got the words out with difficulty.

For some reason Mare, who noticed everything, didn't question his behavior. She had already moved away and was sitting at the little breakfast table that caught the best morning sun. Her fingers absently picked through the droopy bouquet, looking for any flowers that might be worth saving.

Frank made his getaway and popped into the shower, running the water as cold as he could stand it. The flickering images didn't return. The stinging cold of the water made him shiver. By the time he got out, his body was numb enough to dull his brain. He no longer saw the mangled children's bodies, the blood on the road, the police cars. The wail of ambulance sirens was now so faint that he could barely hear it.

The drive to the paper usually took ten minutes, only there was roadwork, and traffic was diverted to the bypass. As soon as he pulled onto it, Frank became anxious, and by the time he'd merged into the center lane, his hands were shaking on the wheel. He reached into his jacket pocket where he stashed a cigarette for emergencies. He pulled out the penny instead. He hadn't put it there. His intention was to pretend that he'd forgotten it rushing off to work. This had to be Mare.

Before he could think, a low-sounding horn blasted in his ear. Frank had drifted half out of his lane, and he quickly swerved back as a tractor trailer bombed past on the left. In front of him was a gray minivan. Two little girls in the back turned around and waved. Frank started to sweat. He saw that the driver was a woman, perhaps a soccer mom taking her kids to school. Frank leaned on his horn.

"Pull over!" he shouted, waving his arm toward the shoulder of the road to show the driver what he wanted. The woman sped up, ignoring him. Frank gunned ahead, moving closer. The kids were still looking at him, no longer smiling.

"Pull over!"

This time the woman listened. When she stopped on the shoulder, Frank pulled in behind her. He didn't get out. There was no way to tell if the two girls were the mangled bodies he'd seen. The woman emerged from the minivan, looking perplexed. She walked to the back of her vehicle, checking the tires and the tail lights. Her face wore an exasperated look. She shot

Frank a rude gesture with her middle finger, got back in, and sped away.

God help you, Frank thought. After a few minutes he had settled down, but he felt nauseous. He was late to work, but he didn't get back on the road. In thirty seconds, he thought, the stream of traffic would suddenly slow. In a minute and a half the first patrol car would fly past, moving cars out of the way with its sirens. The ambulance would be close behind.

Actually, it was forty seconds before traffic slowed, but everything else unfolded just as he saw it. Frank's nausea grew worse. He could have gotten out and talked to her, given the woman his bizarre explanation and not worried that she would call him a lunatic.

If he stayed there on the shoulder, a cop would check what was going on. Reluctantly Frank pulled back on the highway. Traffic was moving again, slowly. After a mile he saw the flashing blue and red lights of the patrol cars. An officer was waving everyone into one lane. The tractor trailer had jackknifed, blocking the rest of the road. Frank wanted to close his eyes, but he kept looking, and as the single file of cars crawled past the accident site like a makeshift funeral cortege, he saw two crumpled sedans. A bewildered man stood beside a stretcher that was being hoisted into the back of an ambulance.

But that was it. No blood on the pavement, no mangled children. The gray minivan was nowhere in sight.

The security guard stationed beside the reception desk always nodded when Frank came in. This time he said, "You okay, buddy?"

"I'm great, I think," Frank muttered.

The guard, a retired policeman with a gray buzz cut, laughed. "You're the one who'd know," he said, rather puzzled.

Frank didn't stop to chat. Feeling dizzy, he got to his desk in the newsroom and sank into the chair. *What the hell?* His confused

thoughts whirled around, trying to make sense of what had happened. It was like being at the Laundromat watching clothes tumble in a dryer. Only in this case he was tumbling with them. The only thought he could seize onto said, *I told you so.* Frank knew exactly what this meant. The moment he agreed to join the mystery school, something bizarre would drag him under, a freak occurrence that would ruin his chance for a normal life.

He felt afraid, more afraid than he had a right to be. Wasn't he some kind of hero? He'd saved two little girls from a horrible death. Frank wanted to feel good about that, but his fear wouldn't let him. He took the penny out of his pocket and stared at it. Maybe if he threw it away immediately, he'd be safe.

At that moment the buzz of voices in the newsroom, which was always there like background static, dropped out. Very clearly Frank heard two reporters talking from twenty feet away.

"Anything on the police scanner?"

"Not really. A truck jackknifed on the bypass."

"Anybody killed?"

"Nah. There's no story."

"Too bad. Better luck next time."

The two reporters went back to work, and the buzz of voices in the newsroom rose again. Frank was disgusted. "Too bad." "Better luck next time." It could have been him talking. He regarded the penny again, this time with uncertainty. The two reporters were wrong. There was a story, but Frank couldn't tell it.

From behind him a voice spoke. "Why tell a story when you can live it?"

He knew it was Lilith before he turned around. No one else did that annoying mind-reading trick.

"Don't throw the penny away. You're just getting the hang of it," she said.

Frank had no reply. He was too fixated on how Lilith looked. In place of the gray tweed suit he'd always seen her in, she was

decked out in bright pink, with a wide-brimmed yellow hat and a feathery thing he thought was called a boa.

Lilith laughed and did a twirl. "Who doesn't like the circus?" she said.

Frank could see out of the corner of his eye that people were staring. A few at the far corner of the newsroom stood on their chairs for a better look.

"We weren't supposed to go crazy," he reminded her in an undertone. "You're not yourself."

"Thank God." Lilith laughed again, a bright sound that was as strange coming from her as the outlandish outfit. She raised her voice so that everyone could hear. "Come with me, darling. When the going gets tough, the tough go to lunch. My treat."

He followed helplessly as she swanned her way past the cubicles. At least they'd be out of sight in a minute. He had to hope that his editor was on the phone in his office and wasn't viewing the spectacle.

At the reception desk, the girl on duty said, "How did you get in?"

Lilith didn't stop, trailing an answer behind her. "Magic, my child. Magic."

Frank seriously considered phoning for medical help, but as soon as they were outside, Lilith dropped the act. "The things I do for you," she muttered in her normal starchy tone.

"For me?" Frank was astonished.

"You were wavering. I didn't want to lose you."

She seemed amused by his doubts, which annoyed him. "I can make up my own mind. I'm a big boy."

"Lucky for you. Rusty never got to be a big boy, did he?"

This enigmatic question had an astounding effect on Frank. His face turned white, and a tremor shook his body.

"You couldn't know about that," he said in a strangulated voice.

"But I do."

He leaned against the wall next to the exit, trying to catch his breath. A flood of half-buried images filled his mind. It was the summer he turned fourteen, and his father took Frank and his younger brother, Rusty, fishing. He roused them early in the morning, saying the bass wouldn't wait, and a few minutes later the brothers were in the backseat of the family Jeep, still trying to wake up. Rusty, who was ten, whined about it. He leaned against Frank, trying to use his shoulder as a pillow, but Frank pushed him away roughly.

The lake was as smooth as glass when they got into the canoe, and Frank was proud at how well he could balance standing up to push them away from the shore. His ankle socks had gotten wet running through the dewy grass—why did he remember that? The morning chill quickly turned into midday heat. Frank enjoyed fishing with his dad, and Rusty had fallen asleep at the other end of the canoe.

Neither of them, Frank or his father, paid attention when a shadow passed over the sun. The fish were biting too good. But then the shadow didn't pass, and looking up, they saw thunderheads approaching.

"Start paddling," his father said. They were pretty far out from shore; the dock was at least five minutes away. The storm didn't care. It was upon them in no time, bringing a sharp wind that roughed the surface of the lake. Frank saw his father's jaw set; they started paddling harder. The first clap of thunder woke Rusty up, and Frank knew that his younger brother had an undue fear of lightning.

"Fraidy cat," he teased.

Is that what caused Rusty to jump to his feet? It was such a strange, impulsive thing to do. He lost his balance as a wave rocked the boat. Frank saw the little boy's mouth form a silent "Oh!" before Rusty went over the side. His father, sitting up front, hadn't seen it.

"Dad!" Frank's shout pierced the wind, which had started to howl.

When he turned his head and grasped the situation, his father dropped his paddle and jumped into the water, where Rusty was flailing, his wide, frightened eyes showing white. If only Frank hadn't felt the same surge of adrenaline as his dad, but he did, and they dove into the water at the same instant. His father reached Rusty first, holding his head above the waves.

"Just breathe. It's going to be okay," he said. The little boy clung to him, gasping and spitting out water.

Frank didn't see fate closing in. The whole thing was disguised by tiny coincidences. Here, there were three. The canoe was empty, making it hard to climb back in. The mountain-fed lake was frigid in early June. His father had gained twenty pounds over the winter and was out of shape. Very innocent coincidences, really, but the result was inexorable. Their first attempt to climb into the canoe tipped it over. There was no bucket to bail it out with—everything inside the boat sank out of sight the minute it capsized—and when they righted it, the canoe rode too low because of the water it had taken on.

The rest happened in slow motion as Frank experienced it. Rusty started crying, whining about how cold he was. His father, who wasn't a good swimmer to begin with, used all his strength to hold his boy and the side of the canoe at the same time, but the cold water made his hands go numb. He lost his grip with the next big gust of wind. Rusty's panicked eyes landed on Frank, who was clinging to the other side of the boat. They didn't accuse him or say good-bye. It was just the gaze of a scared child, who then slipped away, leaving one last sight of his hair waving like seaweed in the current before disappearing.

Frank was the strongest swimmer in the family, and he dove repeatedly to find his brother, over and over until he was so exhausted there was a chance he might drown too. By then the sun

had come out again, and the surface of the lake calmed down, as if nothing catastrophic had occurred.

"Come back," said Lilith sharply.

The sound of her voice pulled Frank up from the depths of memory. "Why is this happening?" he asked. He wore a pained expression, which Lilith ignored.

"If you're going to walk away, you need to see what your choice is really about," she said.

"It's about leaving the rest of you high and dry," Frank snapped. What right did Lilith have to stir up his worst memory? "Be honest. That's why you came here."

She shook her head, pressing on. "Do you really think you survived that day? You lost everything. Can you even remember when you had faith or hope?"

"I don't need faith," said Frank, trying to sound defiant.

"All right," said Lilith. "But you need something besides guilt. It's led you in the wrong direction. You've become a bystander to your own life."

"That's not true." Her words felt cruel, as if she were prying open an oyster while it squirmed inside its shell.

"You learned how to wear a mask. What other choice did a kid your age have? But masks have a funny way of fooling the people who wear them, don't they?"

Frank wanted desperately to run away, but he felt weak and shaky. "Don't," he pleaded. Deep down, he was shocked that he could fall apart so completely.

"I know you feel blindsided," said Lilith, watching him closely. "We're on a fast track to the truth, the whole group. Did you really think you'd get left out?"

Frank heaved a sigh. His mind started to clear; he didn't feel as if the ground was wobbling under him. It would be solid in a minute, safe to stand on again. "I want to be left alone. Why can't you see that?" he said.

"Because it's not what God has in mind," Lilith replied.

Frank turned his head away. Lilith knew he didn't read the Bible, so he wouldn't know a phrase she had grown up with: "For He is like a refiner's fire." The divine flame had a long reach, and now it had touched another stranded soul.

CHAPTER *22*

Much had already happened that day before Lilith went to the newspaper to find Frank. She came down to breakfast in the morning wearing her outlandish pink and yellow outfit. She had dug it out of a box in the attic where the girls' old Halloween costumes were stored.

Herb looked up from the *Wall Street Journal* and faintly raised an eyebrow. "That's nice," he said. He was a cautious soul.

Lilith stroked the moth-eaten feather boa draped around her neck. "I needed a change."

No more was said, which was for the best.

Lilith had gone to bed anticipating that something wondrous would happen. Instead, she woke up feeling grumpy. There was no magic in the air. She waited, staring at the ceiling. Nothing. Getting dressed, she did feel something unusual, but it was trivial. She felt dissatisfied with the clothes in her closet. Going up to the attic was almost an afterthought. What could she possibly find there? Yet she was guided to poke through the old Halloween trunk, and as soon as she saw the boa, pink dress, and yellow hat, she had to try them on, even though this impulse was completely perplexing.

As she looked in the mirror, she thought, *I'm a cross between a drag queen and the Easter parade.* The fact that she didn't immediately take off the absurd costume must have been the penny's fault. With the same feeling of being guided, she got in the car after breakfast and started driving. It surprised her when she arrived at the hospital parking lot. She almost didn't get out. A voice inside warned her that she was about to make a fool of herself.

"Enough of that," she muttered. "Get on with it."

She walked briskly to the ER entrance and went inside. The waiting room was jammed already, and it wasn't even ten. Everyone was sunk in their own problems, so the only ones staring at her outfit were kids who had been dragged along by a sick parent. One little girl who was four or five pointed at Lilith and began to laugh loudly, a piercing bratty laugh that embarrassed her mother.

"Don't point," she scolded. The mother turned to the woman next to her, who was idly thumbing through a magazine. "Looks like somebody's off their meds." The two women followed Lilith with their eyes as she found an empty seat in the corner.

Lilith ignored their stares. Her attention was caught by the grayness that enveloped the room. The smell of sickness was mixed with apprehension. Everyone was braced for bad news, and not a small number would be getting it when their name was called. Lilith sat down, finding it hard to meet anyone's eyes. She resisted the urge to consult the magic penny for clues; it was safely nestled in her purse, wrapped in a handkerchief.

Then the waiting room became dead quiet. No one talked or moved. Before Lilith could register how strange this was, time stopped. The woman who had been reading a magazine was frozen with a page half-turned. The bratty little girl was posed bending over to grab her doll, which had fallen on the floor. The charge nurse at the front desk who was lifting the phone receiver to her ear never got it there.

Lilith was so startled that she leaped to her feet, which proved two things at once. She could move, and when she did, the freeze-frame stayed the same. She eyed everyone in the room, as if suspecting that somebody might be faking. But they remained eerily still. Lilith wasn't easily shaken, much less frightened. The scene fascinated her. She walked over to the bratty little girl, picked up her doll, and placed it beside her on the next chair. The child didn't stir. Lilith touched her hair, which was short and blonde. The hair moved like silk stands at Lilith's touch.

She took her hand away quickly. It felt wrong to disturb anyone. At that moment she heard footsteps approaching down a hall. Someone else was able to move, and Lilith suspected it could only be one person. A set of swinging doors swept open, and she was right.

"Did you do this?" Jimmy said. He was dressed for work in blue scrubs tied at the waist.

"It just happened," Lilith replied.

Jimmy nodded. Joining her in the middle of the room, he held up his penny with a puzzled smile. "What now?"

Lilith thought for a moment. "Let's see what the rest of the world is doing."

They went to the nearest window, which looked out over the parking lot. No one was visible. In the far distance cars were moving on the four-lane road that fed into the hospital.

"So it's just us. What if someone comes?" Jimmy said.

"They won't. Not for a while." Lilith looked around the room again. "We're in this alone, however long it lasts."

"Okay." This didn't seem like a satisfactory reaction, so Jimmy added, "There must be something we need to see. What are we missing here?"

"Missing?" All Lilith saw was a tightly packed room of department-store mannequins.

"Like that," said Jimmy. He walked closer to the little group with the bratty girl, her mother, and the woman flipping through a magazine.

"See? They're not all the same. Look closely."

It took Lilith a second, but she saw. The girl was brighter than the two women, like a photograph printed two shades lighter. The effect wasn't noticeable unless you looked for it. But once you did, you could see that the two women were slightly gray and dull.

"That's odd," Lilith murmured. She had witnessed a light when the spirit left the body. So had Jimmy, but not this.

Jimmy gazed around the room. "They're all so gray, except for the kids." He was right. The children in the waiting room weren't grayed out like the adults. They shone from within. Suddenly the freeze-frame didn't feel creepy anymore. These were souls on display, and the reason for stopping time was that it made it easier to notice, the way a sleeping person looks peaceful when the cares of the day are lifted.

Jimmy moved closer to the mother and held his hands above her head.

"What are you doing?" Lilith asked.

"I don't know. I just feel this urge."

He didn't touch the woman, but instead swept his hands in one motion down her body, beginning at her head and ending at her toes.

"There," he said. "Better."

Wisps of gray like tangled threads were now gathered around her feet, and the woman looked a fraction brighter. Jimmy kicked away the gray threads, which dissolved into dust. Then he did the same sweep for the woman holding the magazine, and it had the same effect. Grayness gathered at her feet, and her frozen image became visibly brighter.

Lilith hadn't moved.

"Go ahead," he said. "You try."

She leaned in close to the mother, examining her neck, where a dark irregular mole was visible. "That's why they came to the ER," Lilith murmured. "Cancer?"

Jimmy nodded. "Poor woman."

Lilith bit her lip, feeling a moment of indecision. Then with a fingertip she rubbed the dark mole. When she took her finger away, it was gone, like a blot erased from a sheet of paper.

"Wow," Jimmy exclaimed softly.

Lilith spotted an old man across the room, bent over in his seat leaning on a walking cane. She went over and saw that his knuckles were lumpy and red.

"Arthritis," she said. She started to smooth out his fingers, as if reshaping modeling clay. Jimmy watched until every inflamed bump was gone.

"That's incredible," he said.

Lilith stood back and examined her handiwork. "Indeed."

Jimmy did a silent head count. "There must be sixty people here. Are we supposed to do them all?"

Lilith might have said yes, but she didn't get a chance. Without warning the freeze-frame ended. The waiting room became animated. The old man leaning on his cane looked up at Lilith with surprise.

"Is it my turn yet?" he asked, mistaking her for a nurse.

"You've had your turn," Lilith replied, walking away quickly. The old man paid no attention. With a bemused look on his face, he was rubbing his fingers. They were smooth, just as she'd left them.

Jimmy followed Lilith to the exit. They faced each other in the bright winter morning.

"Why didn't we finish?" he asked.

She shook her head. "I'm not sure. Maybe it was just a demonstration."

"Of what?"

She held up her hand. "Don't talk. Let it sink in."

They sat down on the bench used by people waiting for a taxi. Jimmy's thin cotton scrubs gave no protection from the cold, but he wasn't shivering. A car pulled up to the entrance, and an old woman was helped out of the front seat into a wheelchair. She wore a woolen cap pulled down over her ears; her eyes were rimed with red.

This was something Jimmy saw every day, but now it looked unreal.

Lilith read his thoughts. "We were sent into the miracle zone," she said, "just for a moment."

"To see if we want to stay?"

"Something like that."

Lilith got to her feet. "I have to go. Frank is wavering. He can't stand this much truth. I'm going to try something drastic."

Jimmy nodded. "Is that why you're dressed like cotton candy with a banana on top?"

Lilith smiled. "Maybe I wanted them to see me coming."

"Or God did," said Jimmy. But Lilith was already hurrying across the parking lot to her car. Suddenly he realized how cold it was outside. The electric doors to the ER whooshed open, and he went inside, rushing to get back to work. Everything had returned to normal. People sat around waiting, staring at their watches or going up to hassle the nurse at the reception desk. There were no signs that the miracle zone had ever existed, except for the gray tinge that lingered on everyone he passed.

CHAPTER *23*

After the door closed behind Frank, Mare went back to bed, but she couldn't fall asleep again. She was too uneasy. The rising sun cast a shadow of windowpanes across the coverlet. Frank's apartment had the creaking floors and peeling paint of a veteran in the rental market, but Mare loved the elaborate plaster work on the ceiling. If you had the imagination, you could pretend you were in a Paris hotel.

She stared at it now, pondering. The magic penny would change Frank's life. Mare foresaw this, which was why she had slipped it into his pocket unawares. It would reveal things that would shake him to the core. She knew this too, because knowing came easily to Mare, all her life. As a girl she had laughed out loud one evening when a movie title came on television: *I Know What You Did Last Summer.*

I Know What You Did Next Summer, she thought. *That's a much better title.*

She opened the drawer of the bedside table, where she'd placed her penny. She couldn't help averting her eyes. She was afraid of its magic, because it spelled the end of her secret. Mare had skillfully kept her secret hidden even as so many others were coming to light. She'd only slipped up once, when she was at the bus

stop, seeing the light in every passenger who got on the bus. "I've found my calling," she said before Meg shushed her.

The time for secrets was over, but what about Frank? That was more complicated. It had been easy to keep things from the two or three serious boyfriends who came into her life and left again. Like them, Frank had felt like an intruder at first, but Mare had grown to love him. He was confused and hurt whenever she kept her distance.

"We spend the night, and then you don't call for days," he complained. "Why?"

Because I have to, she thought.

If she married him, her gift would become a threat, and not just to Frank. She had no control over her far-seeing. What if she saw that he would cheat on her? It would make for strange vows at the altar: "I do thee wed, for better or for worse, in sickness and in health, until you step out with Debbie from the gym."

Mare pushed the thought out of her mind. She took the magic penny from the drawer and folded her palm over it. She might as well face whatever it wanted to show or say. There was a message, but it wasn't magical: *Throw me away.* With a sigh of relief she got out of bed and tossed the coin into the wastebasket. It was like a last-minute reprieve.

But almost immediately a voice in her head said, *This is your test.* What did that mean? Mare anxiously waited for more, but nothing came. She suddenly knew that she had to act. Her test would mean something crucial for the whole group.

Quickly throwing on some clothes, she walked outside into the bright, brisk winter morning. She paused, peering up and down the street. Where was she supposed to go? It was entirely her choice, but the test consisted of making the right choice. She closed her eyes. Nothing appeared. She couldn't wander at random.

How do you find the route to an unknown destination?

Mare waited for an answer. Nothing.

All right, a clue, then?

Again nothing, no puff of wind, no glint of sunlight off a car windshield, no chance remark from a passing stranger. These were signs she had followed all her life. The world spoke to her, and it was time for Mare to realize that it didn't speak to everyone. To a normal person, looking for signs was like believing in omens—not something you did if you wanted to appear sane.

She would have to create her own clues. Mare looked inward, this time expecting nothing. And a faint image came through. She saw a gleaming silver thread lying across her palm. She took a step to the right, and the gleam grew dull. She took a step to the left, and it became brighter. So left it was. She'd stop at every corner to check which way to go next. It was a start.

When she was four, riding in the front seat of the car, her mother came to a lurching stop when another driver cut her off. Instinctively she reached out with her right arm to hold Mare back in her seat, forgetting that she was wearing a seatbelt. A few days later, when the car came to another sudden stop, Mare reached over from the passenger side to hold her mother back.

"What are you doing, honey?" her mother asked.

"Keeping Mommy safe."

Her mother laughed, but was strangely touched. Protecting Mommy became a little game between them. Her mother didn't notice that Mare was reaching out before the brakes were hit. She anticipated what was about to happen. The only one who saw this was Aunt Meg when her car wouldn't start one morning and she needed a ride to work, but she said nothing.

Lost in memory, Mare was forgetting to consult the silver thread. She looked down at her palm, and the thread had turned a dull gray. She had to retrace her steps a couple of blocks until it began to brighten again. It pointed down a broad thoroughfare leading to one of the swanky parts of town. Feeling tense, she quickened her pace. But for some reason memory wouldn't release her. It kept pulling her back to the past.

At some point when she was a child, Mare's gift started to betray her. She couldn't remember what finally caused her to bury it. Maybe she said something wildly inappropriate, like telling one of her mother's friends that she would never have children. Stuck in her recollection, though, were sharp looks directed her way. She felt different, but not special, the girl who burst out laughing before a joke reached the punch line.

She was secretly relieved when she grew up to be pretty. It was the best of disguises. She could go on a date with the high-school quarterback and cheer for him even when she knew the game would be lost. Behind a shy façade, Mare learned about human nature in all its unpredictability, which for her was entirely predictable.

She heard the word "psychic" for the first time in a psychology class in college, where the professor said the paranormal didn't exist. It was a fiction to mask neurosis. "Given the choice between feeling magical and feeling crazy," he said, "most people choose magical." By that time Mare had let her gift wither, so she didn't care if it was unreal. The important thing was that it was gone—until the day she went to the convent in search of her dead aunt.

Mare returned to her test. An hour dragged by as she followed the silver thread. Mare didn't know this part of town very well; most of its houses were built by old money. Where the money stuck around, the three-story brownstones were expensively kept up. Where the money flew away, old people lingered in tattered gentility and stashed bottles of gin. Deep into this mossy territory, which felt vaguely like a damp forest, Mare felt something new. The silver thread burned, and its glow turned almost incandescent.

It wanted her to stop. She looked around, but nothing unusual stood out. The neighborhood was empty, quietly moldering. Then a teenage boy in a hoodie and cargo shorts pedaled up the

street on a bicycle with a bag of groceries in the front basket. He stopped at the corner opposite Mare, not glancing her way, and rang the bell beside a wrought-iron gate with brick pillars as big as phone booths. After a few seconds someone buzzed the gate, and the delivery boy pushed it open.

Go. Now!

The voice in her head was urgent. Mare took off. Five seconds, and she'd be too late. She caught the gate just as it was about to click shut. The delivery boy turned around, startled.

"Those are for me," Mare said, reaching to take the brown paper bag from him. Stalks of celery and a baguette of French bread stuck out the top.

"You live here?" The delivery boy sounded more confused than suspicious.

"Yes. I didn't want to search for my keys. It's okay."

He wouldn't let go of the groceries. "I always give them to her, the older lady."

"My aunt," said Mare, hurriedly reaching in her purse. She needed to get rid of him before Meg answered the door.

"Here." She produced a twenty-dollar bill from her wallet. The delivery boy gave her the grocery bag just as Mare saw, over his shoulder, the heavy oak front door begin to open.

"Neatly executed," said Meg. She stood in the doorway dressed in a suit, as if she were going to her job at the bank. She didn't look the least bit surprised to see Mare. "This was the only time today I would have answered the doorbell." She gave a thin smile. "A person has to eat."

She turned back into the dimly lit house, leaving Mare to shut the door behind her and follow. The drawing room was immense and forlorn, the furniture shrouded in dusty sheets. The dining room table was uncovered, set for one. A massive silver candelabra sat in the middle. Mare gawked.

"You get used to it," said Meg.

The kitchen was laid out with a scullery, a butler's pantry, and zinc sinks big enough to bathe a sheepdog in. Meg put the groceries down on a massive butcher-block table. "Do you want lunch? You've been walking for hours."

Mare shook her head. "I'm too nervous."

"Don't I know it? When I was new at the convent, meals were the worst. A sister would say, 'Pass the ketchup,' and I'd hear, 'We all know you're a fraud.' I was lucky to keep anything down."

She caught the look on Mare's face. "Don't feel sorry for me. I was a kind of spiritual con artist, pretending to be a good Catholic."

"Did you ever fit in?"

"No. A nun may be many things. Disobedient isn't one of them. I did all the right things. My disobedience was of the heart."

Meg started unpacking the groceries, speaking as casually as if the whole situation wasn't extraordinary. "I really didn't know what to expect, but I had to be there, you see."

Mare fell into the rhythm of putting vegetables in the refrigerator and canned goods in the pantry. It seemed pointless to ask how her aunt acquired the huge mansion. "Why did you have to be there?"

Meg looked bemused. "For the longest time I had no idea. But now I see. It all led to this moment. You understand? No, how could you?"

Suddenly Mare felt a wave of resentment. "We're family. Why have you been hiding from us? My mother is worried sick. I can't tell her you're not dead without producing you."

"She's not all that worried. She just doesn't like surprises."

Meg took a seat at the butcher-block table and waited for Mare to sit down. "I kept myself hidden, so that you could pass this test. If you already knew where I lived, there would be no test." She paused. "Are you sure you won't eat something? Here." Meg pushed a bowl of apples across the table.

"In a minute," Mare replied. She wasn't satisfied with the

answers she was hearing. "You don't have a right to do all these things to us—not just me, the whole group. We're like rats in a maze." She caught herself. "That didn't come out right. I don't want you to feel guilty."

Meg gave a curt laugh. "Guilty? That's all I could feel when this began. I saw ordinary people thrown on a magical mystery tour, with no idea where they were going. It was outrageous."

"Maybe it was a power trip for you."

For the first time since Meg had reappeared, she was offended. "Watch yourself," she said sharply. "And eat. You're tired and cranky."

Reluctantly Mare picked out an apple and bit into it, while Meg went into the pantry and returned with a bag of potato chips. She watched her niece pick at them without enthusiasm. At the far end of the table was a lead-crystal vase with white roses picked from the garden. Meg gave them a sidelong glance. She waited to see if Mare would follow the glance. She did.

The roses had begun to glow, just as the golden shrine did. A soft radiance surrounded them. Mare stared, her mouth forming a silent "Oh."

"You can do that?"

"Who else? I'm not who you think I am."

The glow subsided, and the roses went back to normal. Mare sat back, stunned. A surreal image came to her. She saw Aunt Meg radiating the same white light, then vanishing into nothingness.

"All along, I thought—"

"That a magical talisman had dropped out of the sky? I've told you before, all of you, the shrine is just a distraction."

"But you didn't tell us it was a distraction from you."

Meg laughed. "The shrine isn't really old, probably Victorian. Someone I dearly loved, an old priest, bought it at an antique store and had it plated gold. He probably ruined its value."

While revealing this, Meg closely watched Mare's expression.

"You feel cheated, don't you? You wanted miracles, and now you think I'm some sort of illusionist."

"I don't know what I think."

"If it's any help, I'll tell you what an old priest told me. 'Either nothing is a miracle or everything is.' You understand?"

Mare shook her head.

Meg reached down the table and plucked a white rose from the vase. "This flower is made of light. If it weren't, I couldn't make it glow. A miracle exposes the light inside all things."

She didn't wait for Mare to reply. "I'm not telling you something you don't already know. You're a seer. Pushing it out of sight like dust under the carpet doesn't change the fact."

Mare felt a tremor of fear run through her. "I don't want to be a seer."

"Really, after all this? Frankly, I'm disappointed."

Meg stood up, tossing the rose on the table. "At the next meeting, tell the others it's over."

"You don't mean that!" Mare exclaimed.

Meg's face looked stern. "What do you care? The magical mystery tour stops here. All passengers off the bus, please."

Mare was bewildered. "Why?"

"Because there's somewhere I have to be."

Her aunt was about to pull a third vanishing act? Mare was about to get angry when Meg seemed to relent. "I'll let you come with me. When you get back, you can decide about the group."

Abruptly she left the kitchen, and when she returned, Meg had a sheaf of papers in her hand. "Sign these first. I'm giving you the house and the money that comes with it." Meg held out a pen. "Where I'm going, I won't need them."

Mare felt a fresh wave of anxiety. "You're making me dizzy." She wanted to get up from the table, but her knees felt watery. "Let me come back tomorrow. Once I think this over—"

Meg didn't let her finish. "There's no need. You passed the test.

If you could follow the invisible trail that led to here, you're the rightful owner."

She pointed to the first places where Mare needed to sign. Feeling helpless, Mare picked up the pen and scrawled her signature.

When the signing was done, Meg looked satisfied. "Now, then, shall we go?" She reached across the table and took Mare's hands in hers. "You know how by now."

Mare didn't hesitate. If everything was about Meg, she had to be trusted.

"One thing will be different," said Meg as their hands locked in a firm clasp. "This time we can talk to each other."

The kitchen vanished and was replaced by a long-ago scene. They were on a bustling street in Jerusalem, and Meg had been right. Mare could see her standing there. But the passing crowd took no notice of either of them. They were invisible, as before.

"Notice something?" asked Meg. "Look in their eyes."

Mare looked first at a fruit vendor ten feet away and his customer, hurriedly putting figs into a sack. She looked at a mother dragging her two small children into a side street, then at a bearded rabbi with a silver chain around his neck.

"They're all afraid," she said.

"All but one."

Meg led the way, weaving in and out of the crowd. She walked briskly; it was all Mare could do to keep up.

"Why are they all so scared?"

"It's like dogs getting frightened just before an earthquake. They can feel destruction coming."

At the end of the street, where it opened on a small plaza with a stone well in the center, there were no women drawing water. Instead, a squad of Roman soldiers guarded the well, scowling at anyone who came near.

Meg nodded toward them without stopping. "There have been rumors about the Jews poisoning the city's water supply."

Now Mare was beginning to see images in her mind's eye. A Roman soldier committing a sacrilege on the grounds of the temple. Jews running riot, the city boiling over. A veil of blood covered these images.

"Are we here to stop it?" she asked.

"No, Jerusalem will fall."

Meg stopped before an imposing two-story house on the corner, surrounded by a stone wall with well-tended olive trees beyond it. "I'm almost afraid to go in," she murmured.

"Why? Who lives there?"

"Who do you think?"

The iron gate in front of the house was slightly ajar, which made no sense amid the restless fear in the streets. Meg slipped through it and waited for Mare before locking the gate behind them. The courtyard contained a lush garden with a fountain and flowers planted in neat square beds. *A paradise garden,* Mare thought, dredging up the name from some distant memory.

Meg didn't give the garden a glance, but hurried to the front door. It too was slightly ajar. She and Mare entered and were met by a rush of cool perfumed air. A smaller inner courtyard faced them, bathed in sunlight, enclosed by a gallery of fretted marble.

"So beautiful," Mare whispered.

"It's her home." Meg pointed to an alcove nearby where the disciple sat, contemplating. The girl they knew was almost unrecognizable. She looked older now, middle-aged; but it was her, and the way she raised her head made Mare believe she knew they were there.

If we talk to her, she'll be able to hear us, Mare thought. Immediately a warning voice in her head said, *Don't.*

Meg barely glanced at the disciple before turning away. She retreated to a dark corner at the far end of the gallery. After a moment the disciple sighed deeply, stood up, and left, her purple silk skirts rustling as she walked.

Once it was safe to talk, Mare said, "You were right. She doesn't look afraid."

"She can see ahead, past the danger."

"So she'll save herself in time?"

Meg shrugged. "She's not worried about herself. She's past all that."

"I want to talk to her." Impulsively, Mare started to follow the disciple's footsteps into the depth of the house. Meg held her back.

"You've been talking to her the whole time," she said.

"What?"

Meg held her hand up, asking for silence. Her voice was already far away, and as dim as the shadows were in the cool, sheltered gallery. Mare saw doubt in her face. Her aunt had come to a crossroads, and she couldn't decide which way to go.

The silence didn't last long. "We part here," Meg said decisively. "You can embrace me. I believe that's customary."

The strangeness of these words made Mare go cold. "You're leaving me?"

"I'm staying here. It's not the same thing."

The blood drained from Mare's body. "You can't!" she exclaimed. Weak as she felt, her voice was loud, ringing down the marble halls of the gallery.

"That's right, shout some more," Meg murmured. "Shout all you want."

Mare might have, but she froze, hearing the approach of running feet. From around the corner came the disciple. Someone was following her—a servant?—but she waved him away. Now she could definitely see them, and the sight made her pause.

"It is done," said Meg.

The disciple nodded and began to approach.

"You see," Meg said, "I sent myself on a mission." She waited for the disciple to come nearer. "It took ten years in the convent to realize that. You couldn't expect me to believe it, not for a long time."

"Please," Mare pleaded, "just tell me what this is all about." She was suddenly overcome by a sense of loss.

Meg pointed to the disciple. "I am her. Now do you understand?"

Then she stepped forward, quickly covering the short distance between her and the disciple, who stood motionless, expectant. Just before there would have been a collision, Meg's body was transformed. It turned into pure light, like a movie image being replaced by the light of the projector. This took barely a second, and then there was only the disciple. She trembled slightly, making no sound.

"You," Mare whispered.

The disciple hadn't acknowledged that she was there, and even now she did no more than raise her hand. A farewell? A blessing? Mare couldn't tell, her sight blurred with tears. Suddenly there were voices approaching. They sounded alarmed. The disciple spoke sharply in Hebrew (Mare supposed) and strode toward them. She disappeared into a clutch of servants coming from deep inside the house.

Now Mare's tears flowed freely. Meg had been like a visitation, poised between two lifetimes. There was no way to explain how such a thing can occur. A breeze blew across Mare's cheek from the inner courtyard. She blinked to clear her eyes. A neat rectangle of white roses stood close by, and they began to glow.

Before Mare could blink again, she was back in the kitchen at the butcher-block table. She looked down. A half-eaten apple was starting to turn brown beside a withered white rose. Time had passed, but how much? Hours? Days? She couldn't tell. She could only tell that she'd come back a different person. Her secret gift, all the hiding, her dead aunt who wasn't dead but a conveyor of wonders—none of it mattered anymore. Something did, though, the one truth Mare could live by without fear or doubt.

Either nothing is a miracle or everything is.

CHAPTER *24*

When Frank arrived for the next meeting, the door was ajar. Inside he found the room dark and empty. Before he could turn on the lights, a voice said, "Please don't."

"Mare?"

The sound of her voice rattled him. "Where have you been?"

She wasn't at his apartment when Frank came home. That was two days ago. She didn't answer her cell phone or return any of his messages. He was getting more and more worried. "You didn't want to talk to me?"

"I needed to be by myself."

"I thought everything was good with us."

"It's more than us."

This cryptic exchange told him nothing. "Listen, talking in the dark is creeping me out. I'm turning the lights on."

Frank flicked the wall switch, and the buzzing fluorescent fixtures came on, casting a greenish pallor everywhere. He saw Mare seated at the head of the table where Meg always sat. The golden shrine was in front of her.

"Did Meg tell you to bring it?" he asked.

"In a way. She's not coming back."

Mare didn't wait to see if this news upset him. She already knew it wouldn't. "You're not coming back either, are you? None of you are. You just want out."

Frank was bewildered. "How did you find out? Have the rest of them been talking to you?" A note of suspicion crept into his voice. "I don't like this, not one bit."

Mare spoke insistently. "Does it matter? In an hour there won't be a mystery school."

"Jesus." This wasn't remotely what Frank expected.

"It won't be long now," Mare said. "Try and calm down."

She was asking the impossible. After his experience with the magic penny, bringing back the boating accident that had ruined Frank's life, his mind was reeling. He couldn't come to terms with anything, not his work or Mare or the past. Every night when he tried to sleep, he kept seeing Rusty's pale, frightened face sinking out of sight. Frank felt stranded, and the woman he needed to be there wasn't. His dark mood attracted comment in the newsroom, but it didn't improve. Everyone gave him a wide berth, even Malcolm.

The only solution, he finally decided, was to walk away from the mystery school. It led into too many weird and painful places. Maybe he still had a chance for a normal life.

"You couldn't at least answer my messages?" Frank asked.

Mare held up her hand to keep him from asking more questions. "Everything will be settled once the others are here."

Her calm tone was eerie. *You're not yourself,* he thought, staring at the woman who had been sharing his bed three nights ago. Just thinking about her, he felt the warmth of her skin.

"Why are you acting this way? You're treating me like a stranger."

"I care about you, but this isn't the time."

Mare looked deep into Frank's eyes, trying to communicate that he had nothing to be afraid of. It didn't work. He threw himself into a chair and pounded the table with his fist.

"You're leaving me. I knew it!" His hurt flared into anger. "And don't sell me some crap that it's more than us." He was already exhausted, and this outburst spent his last ounce of energy. Heaving a ragged sigh, he lowered his head in sorrow.

Maybe none of them will understand, Mare thought. *Even after all that's happened.*

She remembered that she had almost given up too. She didn't want to be a seer. Meg had replied, "Frankly, I'm disappointed," but Mare wasn't going to show that Frank had disappointed her. An invisible force had taken over, immense, powerful, beyond emotion. *The way being alone at sea must feel,* Mare thought, *when the wind has died and the moonless sky falls away to infinity.* Pure wonder pulled her away.

"You two don't look like happy campers."

Sunk in their own thoughts, they hadn't noticed Galen appear in the doorway. He was smirking, but he didn't follow up his remark with a jibe at Frank.

Not that it mattered. Frank was beyond caring. In a dull voice he said, "Take a seat, little guy. Mare's cooked us the last supper."

Warily Galen walked around the table and sat down away from Frank. "I don't get the joke."

"It's not a joke," Mare said. "This is our last meeting. Aren't you here to say you've had enough?"

Galen didn't ask how she knew. "I haven't made up my mind yet."

She smiled. "You have, but you wanted to shock the group. They won't be."

Now they heard footsteps in the corridor, and after a moment Lilith and Jimmy appeared. If they were about to say something, the tension in the room stopped them. The two newcomers exchanged glances and sat down at Mare's end of the table.

"You've all had a magical week," Mare said. "So have I. I went where I never imagined I could go. Coming back has been

a hard adjustment. I don't know how to live in the normal world again."

Was she talking about the journeys they took with the golden shrine? Why her alone? The very fact that Mare had usurped Meg's place was baffling.

"I need details," Lilith said. "Did all this happen because of the magic penny?"

Before Mare could answer, Galen interrupted. "Wait, I was gypped." He reached into his pocket and produced his penny. "Mine only worked once."

"Stop," Lilith said irritably. "Your situation isn't on the table right now."

Frank spoke up. "I'm with Galen. Mine lost its juice too." Not that he sounded sorry.

"Stop!" Lilith repeated, louder this time.

"It's okay," Mare said. "The penny was only meant to work once."

"How do you know?" asked Jimmy. He was upset and voiced the question bothering all of them. "Where's Meg, anyway?"

"Mare's not saying," Frank grumbled. "She's the new quarterback, and that's it."

No one was ready to believe this.

"You really should tell us what's happened," Lilith said, trying to sound reasonable. She took Jimmy's hand to reassure him, but she was hiding her own insecurity. It felt like the whole situation could unravel.

Mare surveyed their anxious faces. Reaching down, she found the canvas bag resting at her feet. She took out a hammer and rose to her feet. There was barely time for anyone to guess what she was about to do. With a swift, decisive motion she raised her arm and brought the hammer down hard. It struck the golden shrine in the center of the roof, midway between the four spires. With an agonized noise, halfway between a metallic screech and

a groan, the roof imploded, and the walls of the miniature church crumpled.

"Oh, my God," Lilith whispered, horrified. The others were too stunned to speak. The shrine was their only link to another reality.

"All of you wanted out," Mare declared. "Now you're free."

"What are you talking about?" Jimmy exclaimed. None of them realized that they had all come to the same decision. Strong magic had touched them, and the aftershock was too much to bear.

"It was our choice," Lilith protested. "Who gave you the right to smash the shrine?" They waited for what Mare would say next.

"I found Meg in her hiding place," she began. "She has a big house on the other side of town. We talked, and then she took me on a journey, back to the disciple." She paused with a doubtful expression.

"And then what?" Galen snapped impatiently.

"I left her there."

It was an answer that told them something and nothing at the same time. Before the room could fill with questions, Mare continued. "Is it possible for someone to vanish into the past? That's what I'm telling you. Meg isn't dead; she didn't run away."

Frank interrupted before she could explain further. "It's all pointless. Meg started something, and now she's not here to see it through. That's what you're telling us." He got up with an exaggerated shrug of indifference. "Anyone who wants to join me in a beer, I'm buying."

"Wait, there's another way," said Mare. "It doesn't have to end like this."

"Meaning what?" Frank demanded, on the verge of turning belligerent. He made no move to sit back down again.

"Meg didn't bring the mystery school down," she said. "Smashing the shrine didn't either."

Jimmy looked forlorn. "It was us. We did it."

"No, it also wasn't you," Mare replied.

Everyone was quiet, waiting tensely. Instead of more explanation, Mare said, "It's time for one last journey. You don't have to go. You can walk out the door this minute, but if you do, the mystery school is over for you."

Jimmy pointed to the crumpled shrine. "How can we go anywhere? You let the disciple out."

"I don't think it's like Aladdin's lamp," Frank said drily.

"Maybe it is. You don't know," replied Jimmy defiantly.

"We can take this journey by ourselves, without the shrine," said Mare. "Trust me."

The group was confused. How could they trust someone who had barely participated in the past, who seemed to go along meekly with whatever Meg said? Mare hadn't explained her sudden change. They felt as if they barely knew her.

There might have been an argument, but Lilith, who sat closest to Mare at the end of the table, took her hand. "I'm willing." She gestured for the others. "One last time? It's only fitting."

They all knew what she meant. Traveling back to the time of the disciple was the one thing that bound them together. After a moment a circle was formed, with everyone holding hands. In the middle stood the golden shrine, smashed like a toy in the hands of a spoiled child throwing a tantrum. It gave off no radiance, but as Mare had promised, there was no need.

First they heard the screeching cry of seagulls, followed instantly by the glare of sunlight over the water. They were standing on the crest of a hill, with the ocean half a mile down below. Was it the coast of an island or the mainland? It was impossible to tell. The hill was crossed by a narrow footpath. A pair of gulls sat on tilted posts that were once part of a fence. They didn't fly away when the group appeared or even stare at them inquisitively.

"We're invisible," said Galen.

This they were used to, but the absence of human life was puzzling. It took a moment before there was any indication of people coming up the path, and then it wasn't foot travelers, but a litter being carried by two panting servants. At first a speck, the conveyance grew larger as it approached. The servants dripped with sweat; the headbands they wore couldn't keep it from streaming down their faces as they pushed their way up the hill.

The litter was brightly painted, and the wood finely carved with deer and foxes and other animals. Whoever rode inside was hidden from view by drawn curtains. A woman's voice spoke in Hebrew, sounding urgent.

"She's telling them to hurry. There's little time," said Mare.

"How do you know what she said?" asked Frank.

"I just do." Mare couldn't explain why she could suddenly understand a foreign tongue, but there was no time for discussion. "We have to follow them."

Once the litter crested the hill, the bearers carried their mistress faster. The group trailed behind under the bright hot sun. Even without a burden they began to sweat and pant.

The members of the mystery school followed for more than half an hour without saying a word. Around a bend blocked by a thick grove of trees, they suddenly spied their destination, a huddled collection of docks used by local fisherman.

The woman in the litter parted a curtain and peered out. She was gray-haired and aristocratic looking, although much of her face was wrapped in a white linen shawl pulled around her head. The shawl was covered in a thin layer of dust, implying that they had been traveling since morning. She barked an order, and the message was clear to everyone. "Faster!"

The bearers nodded, but were too exhausted to pick up the pace. One man was much older than the other. Perhaps they were father and son. Galen sank to the ground in the shade of the trees. Frank looked at him over his shoulder. "Don't quit on us," he

said. Back in the meeting room he was ready to walk out, but now he was caught up in the adventure.

"Forgive me for not being young. My mistake," said Galen. He waved at the parting litter. "Let them go. They're dog-tired. We can catch up."

Frank might have tried to jerk Galen to his feet, but Mare said, "It's all right. We're all tired. Let's take a minute."

They gathered together, some sitting on the ground, others leaning against tree trunks. It was a relief to be out of the sun.

"As long as we're invisible," Jimmy said, "I wish we'd brought some invisible water."

"I know," said Mare, but her mind was on something else. "You saw who the old woman was, didn't you?"

"The disciple," said Lilith. Not that this was a surprise. "What has she been doing all these years?"

Lilith had studied about the early Christians, and she knew that women at first could preach in the churches alongside the men. Did the disciple do that? Or had she fled Jerusalem on an endless journey to escape the persecution that doomed the other disciples to violent deaths?

"Think about it," said Jimmy. "If we're here, somebody had to start the mystery school. It must have been her."

Mare nodded. Jimmy's reasoning was logical, but he'd missed something. She said, "There's a crisis. She's racing to find someone before he sails. Everything's at stake, for her and for us."

The group exchanged glances. Apparently this was another thing Mare just knew. To keep from being cross-examined, she got to her feet and started quickly down the path. Everyone followed. Galen, who could have used another ten minutes in the shade, brought up the rear. The walking was downhill, but they were drenched in sweat by the time they caught up with the litter, which was now less than a hundred yards from the water.

The two bearers showed signs of buckling, with the younger one muttering encouragement to the older. The disciple suddenly rapped on the roof of her compartment and jumped out almost before the bearers came to a stop. She ran the rest of the way to the water, kicking up dust with her slim lambskin sandals.

"Jonas, Jonas!" she called.

"Her son," Mare explained, running after her.

At the docks several fishing boats were moored, but only the largest, whose square-rigged sail was being raised by two sun-baked fishermen, was getting ready to depart. At first no one else was visible, and then from around the edge of the rising sailcloth a head appeared. The man was middle-aged, and as he stepped forward he frowned.

"He wanted to get away without facing her," said Mare.

The disciple stopped, her way blocked by the large scattered rocks on the shore. Mother and son faced each other silently for a moment before he barked an order to the fishermen, who stopped hauling up the sail. Looking angry, Jonas leaped from the prow of the boat into the water, not bothering with the rickety dock. He waded knee-deep until he reached the sand, then made his way to the disciple. Once he was close, she began to speak, not raising her voice but sounding very intense. There was an offshore breeze that carried her words out to sea; only some of it could be heard from where the group stood.

"She's begging him not to leave," said Mare.

"That's pretty obvious," Frank snapped. "What's the point? It's not like we can stop him."

Mare ignored this. "I need to get closer. You don't have to come if you don't want to."

With some reluctance they straggled behind her.

It was slow going to get nearer. The shore rocks were packed close together, inviting a twisted ankle if your foot slipped the

wrong way. But they could see that the conversation was becoming heated. The disciple's son grew red in the face.

From inside his tunic, which was cinched at the waist, he pulled out a rolled parchment. One could see that he wasn't young, his hair already thinning, crow's feet around his eyes wrinkling as he squinted in the bright sunlight. He unrolled the scroll and started reading aloud. From the way he barely glanced at the writing, he must have had it memorized.

Mare wasn't close enough to catch what he was saying. The wind swallowed his words. But a voice in her head began to recite with him. Unbelievably, she knew the text from childhood.

> And behold a pale horse, and he that sat upon him, his
> name was Death, and hell followed him. And power
> was given to him over the four parts of the earth.

The thirteenth disciple looked distressed and tried to grab the scroll from his hands. Her son snatched it back, turned, and marched into the sea. It was shallow along the beach. He waded through the water until he reached the boat. The two fishermen leaned over the bow and pulled him up. The disciple's face filled with tears. She didn't wait for the sail to be raised, but picked her way back to her litter. The two bearers had come to her side by now and helped her over the rocks. They stumbled several times before reaching open ground.

Mare stood and watched them for a moment.

As vigorous as she had looked before, the disciple suddenly seemed very frail. She paused, as if sensing a presence. Her gaze met Mare's. Did she recognize her? It was impossible to tell, for a second later the old woman looked away.

Meg's not there, Mare thought. She felt a pang in her heart. At least it was good to know; Mare no longer had a reason to look back.

The two bearers exchanged worried glances as the disciple collapsed into the cushioned seat inside the litter. She was panting and had no strength to pull the curtains. They did it for her, then took their places front and back between the poles. The litter was lifted, and the bearers retraced their steps up the winding dusty path.

Mare regarded the fishing boat, which was now rigged and ready. One fisherman minded the rope line that tied the boat to the dock, the other sat at the tiller. The disciple's son, still scowling, said nothing. He held on to the mast as some strong swells moved in, rocking the craft. For a moment he seemed hesitant, but his resolve quickly returned. He nodded, the mooring was loosed, and the fisherman on the dock pushed the nose of the boat away before jumping in.

This was all Mare needed to see. "The disciple will never convince him," she told the others. "He thinks God has a message for him. There's a new cause, and he can't wait to join it." Her instinct made her certain of this, even if she couldn't explain why.

Now that the excitement was over, Galen's doubt wasn't going to be squelched. He swept his arm over the landscape. "We don't belong here. None of this fits anything."

"Would it fit if this was the island of Patmos?" asked Mare quietly.

A flicker of recognition lit in Lilith's face. "It's where St. John wrote the book of Revelation."

"So what?" asked Frank. "That's just a legend. There probably wasn't a St. John. The church needed a scare tactic to keep the sheep in line."

Mare pointed at the departing boat, which had caught the wind and was moving quickly with bellied sail. "He's sure the final days are near. It makes him feel incredibly strong. He's going to be one of the saved, and it infuriates him that his mother doesn't believe him."

At that moment they heard the unmistakable buzz of fluorescent lights, and instantly they were back in the meeting room, sitting in a circle with joined hands. It took a moment to get their bearings. Galen wore the same dissatisfied look that he wore by the sea.

"Her son may be an idiot and a fanatic," he declared. "But his side won."

Frank chimed in. "Absolutely. The crazies came up with a bizarre myth about the end of the world. He raced off to hear the last trumpet, and his kind are still packed and ready for doomsday. Armageddon has them pumped."

This was a harsh indictment, but no one contradicted it. After a moment, Jimmy weakly muttered, "I still believe."

"It's over," Galen shot back. "The disciple failed. Her own son wouldn't follow her. We were there, we saw it."

"We did see it," Mare acknowledged. "Now you have a send-off, which is what you wanted, isn't it?"

Her tone was cutting, something no one had ever heard from her. They stared as she stood up in front of the smashed shrine. "Fairy tales don't always have happy endings. So leave. If anybody wants to stay behind, I know the real ending."

"We're not stupid," Galen grumbled. "You're baiting the hook." There was general dissatisfaction, but none of them moved toward the door.

Mare waited to see that everyone really intended to stay. "The disciple didn't fail that day. What did we really see, one woman against the force of history? The odds against one woman would be impossible."

Lilith was the first to catch on. "So she had to find another way. She had to go around history if she wanted to beat the odds."

With a beatific smile, Mare spread out her arms. "She found a way. It's us."

They'd never heard her be sarcastic; it was much weirder to see her being grandiose.

"Careful," Lilith murmured.

But Mare had kept her secret too long; she was bursting to tell them everything. "It took forever, but I pieced it all together. Don't you see? Every piece of the puzzle fits."

Galen slouched back in his chair, arms folded across his chest. "I must be stupid, because I don't see anything."

"It's quite astounding," Mare said. "God was sending revelations, but the disciples became confused. They were constantly fighting over what the messages meant. But the thirteenth disciple caught on. Everything was about the light. When a vision of Armageddon appeared, it came from fear. The light never promotes fear. Once the whole thing was revealed to me, I got incredibly agitated. Did everything really come down to us five? There's no other explanation for why we were called. I was blown away. That's why none of you has seen me."

She shot Frank a significant look.

He glared back with hostility. "I'm sorry, but if it's your revelation against theirs, you can keep 'em both."

He jumped to his feet and made for the door. On the threshold he turned back, hoping to get a sign from Mare. Did she want him to go or stay? But she gave no sign. Her eyes glistened with the secret knowledge that wanted to be told.

Frank shook his head in disgust. "If you want to call me, it's okay. Just don't expect me to come running."

His footsteps clattered angrily in the corridor before fading away.

"And then there were four," said Galen mockingly.

Mare turned on him. "You want to be next?" She spat out the question.

He was abashed. "No. Who said I did?"

She didn't relent. "Stop sniping. It's either go or stay."

"Okay, okay." Galen took a breath. "If I hear you out, can I still leave?"

Mare nodded.

"Okay, then," he said, starting to feel secure again. "Shoot."

The air was vibrating with suspense now. Quietly Mare said, "It all revolved around Meg. I was the last one to see her. All of you deserve to know what happened."

She told them the story of Meg's last day, including the journey they took together and the ominous scene as Jerusalem was about to be torn apart. No one interrupted. When Mare was finished, though, each person had a different interpretation.

"You can't prove Meg is the disciple," Galen objected. "The house was empty when you came to. She might just be a spinster aunt who couldn't stay in one place."

"Maybe she was a spirit," said Jimmy.

"Or a saint," Lilith added.

Mare didn't try to convince them otherwise. For two days she had been agitated—she hadn't lied when she told the others that—but it wasn't the agitation of grief. When she found herself alone in the dark mansion, she went from room to room turning on the lights. She didn't call out Meg's name or expect to find her hiding under a bed. Her vanishing act, Mare knew, was final this time. Throwing open the curtains, snatching off the sheets that covered the furniture and pictures, Mare felt driven. The house needed to be filled with light, because she was.

The light inside her didn't burn, but it was incredibly intense and impossible to sustain for more than a few minutes. When she got to the main bedroom, Mare's energy was spent. She collapsed on the bed and immediately fell asleep even though the curtains were pulled open and the sun shone directly in. When she woke up, night had fallen. Normal reactions started to set in. Doubt about what had really happened. Anxiety about Meg and

her strange fate. Disbelief that she would leave the house and a great sum of money to Mare. But when Mare rushed back to the kitchen, the legal papers were lying there on the butcher-block table, just where Meg had left them.

Now Mare looked at each face in the group. All the secrets had flown out of the cupboard, and she felt calm. "I'm not going to try and prove anything. We've shared the same journeys. You've formed your own version of events. Every version could be the truth, if it's true for you."

"No, it couldn't," Galen protested. "There are facts, and there are fantasies."

"You're forgetting faith," Jimmy said.

Lilith had nothing to say. She was the one whose dream had set everything in motion. Facts, fantasies, faith—who knows how they're woven into the tapestry of reality? In the end, she had no idea.

With a loud smack, Lilith slammed her hands on the table and stood up. "Meeting adjourned. I'm sure we all have places to go." No one could deny it. They made motions to leave.

"You're all welcome to come to Meg's house anytime you want," Mare said. "Even if the school is over, we need to keep in touch."

"Why?" Galen asked.

She smiled. "Because we're the same now."

"How can you say that? We argued all the time. We're still arguing."

"I know. But do you think anyone out there in the real world would believe a word of it? We're the only ones who understand."

"For now," said Jimmy, ever the optimist.

Somehow a group hug wasn't in the cards. They straggled out separately into the hospital parking lot, lit by yellowish halos from sodium streetlamps. Standing under one made a person's skin look zombified. Mare waited by the lamp closest to her car. She knew that Lilith would want to talk to her.

It took ten minutes before she appeared. She must have been turning everything over in her mind.

"So it was going to be you all the time. Who could have guessed?" she said.

"I'm sorry Meg didn't tell you good-bye," Mare replied.

Lilith shrugged. "It's just like her. It's her way of making me find her again. And I will, no matter how long it takes. You see, I get it now."

"You get what?"

"What Meg discovered years ago. Everything happens in the mind of God. The world, you and me, the march of history. It's all in the mind of God. Once you know that, nothing can stop you. It never stopped her."

A wave of emotion swept over them, and for the first time since her aunt disappeared, Mare began to cry. She brushed away the tears with the back of her hand.

"Doesn't this light make us look horrible?"

"Ghastly," Lilith said, managing to laugh. She turned away to go back to her car, and Mare got into hers.

The ride home was lonesome. In her mind's eye, Mare went around the table, singling out each one in turn. The light had turned them into something they could never have imagined, the souls they really were. Galen was a mental wizard. He could shut his eyes, make a wish, and reality obeyed his desire. Jimmy was a healer who could conquer death. Lilith became all-knowing, seeing through people's defenses like through glass. And Frank? He was a truth-teller, although his view was more obscured than the others. The light could only show them who they were; it couldn't force them to accept it.

It would take a while before any of them knocked on the thick oak door of Father Aloysius's mansion. Frank would be the last. Mare couldn't see where their relationship would go, but she knew his parting shot was wrong. He wanted to come running

back. His wounded pride wouldn't let him. It was all right. Frank was more than his pride.

The empty mansion was just as it was the day Meg left. All the lights were on and the curtains wide open. Mare had stopped off at the supermarket. A person has to eat, as Meg reminded her.

"Quite right," Mare said to no one in particular.

She finished putting the groceries away. She'd bought roses—red ones this time—which had to be put in water. She climbed the stairs to the maids' quarters at the top of the house. She preferred sleeping there to the huge main bedroom and its ticking French clock smothered in gilded cherubs. Once the clock ran down, she wasn't going to wind it up again.

Father Aloysius had kept one maid in the house for the long periods he wasn't there. She'd left behind a neat, clean bedchamber under the dormer roof. Mare went inside and began to undress. When she pulled back the sheets, she saw a small envelope. *No package this time,* she thought.

She wasn't surprised, but her hands still trembled slightly as she opened the envelope and unfolded the note inside.

Dear Mare,

Don't waver. Be strong. There is only one thing to live by, and now you know it. "I am the way and the light and the life." Remember me.

Yours in Christ,
Meg

As Mare nodded off, the wind picked up outside, and the leaves of an ancient sycamore brushed lightly across the windowpane. It sounded soft and gentle, like the angel of mercy passing over the face of the earth.

Afterword:
The Mystery and You

If I've created any magic around the mystery school in this story, I hope readers are thinking, "Can I join?" Before writing the book, I had heard about mystery schools that still exist. Rumors floated around with the following contour: a friend of a friend (usually unnamed) was walking down the street of a major city (Los Angeles, New York, San Francisco), when a total stranger came up and said, "You are meant to be in a mystery school. I can tell by your aura. Accept now, or I walk away."

This snippet of a rumor became the starting point for a tale about ordinary people who become inducted into life-changing spiritual mysteries. I thought this was a perfect symbol of our time. We live in a secular society where mystery has been pushed to the fringes. It's not part of the official culture. Even the term "spiritual mystery" will annoy a wide spectrum of people—skeptics, rationalists, scientists, and many regular churchgoers. Yet their disapproval only makes the mystery more enticing.

My tale is fiction, but mystery schools are anything but. Whether they existed in ancient Greece or the Christian Middle Ages, mystery schools shared the same purpose: to enter the reality of God. God's reality, being invisible, isn't easy to enter.

What does it take? Here most, if not all, religions agree. It takes obedience to the rules of that particular religion. Do what you're told and a higher, divine reality will open up its gates. You will see God. Don't do what you're told, and access to God will be closed to you. (If your faith includes a vengeful God, you can also expect harsh punishment for your disobedience.)

The decline of faith in our time indicates that obedience is out of fashion. But spiritual yearning isn't. Let's imagine, then, that you are that friend of a friend who is approached by a perfect stranger and invited to join a mystery school. What happens next? How do you get from a street corner in Los Angeles or New York to God's reality? Clearly a path is implied, which means a process. Once you begin the process, there are obstacles and challenges. Some people will refuse to go forward—as the New Testament says, many are called, but few are chosen (Matt. 22:14). Those who survive the challenges and overcome the obstacles reach the goal. They are with God; they live in his light.

I can't tap you on the shoulder and invite you to join the school of the thirteenth disciple, but the path followed by Meg, Mare, Lilith, Galen, Frank, and Jimmy in the novel is open to you in reality. The process they undergo transformed them, and that process has been thoroughly mapped out in the world's wisdom traditions. In outline it's quite simple, in fact. The path from here to God looks like a "reality sandwich," as shown in the diagram below.

God's Reality = the Light

Transition Zone

Ordinary Reality = the Illusion

The bottom layer of the sandwich is the everyday reality we all inhabit, the world of the five senses, physical objects, and daily

events. Being invisible, God doesn't appear in this reality (miracles, if they exist, are the exception). The top layer is God's reality, the realm of light, where "light" implies many things: truth, beauty, freedom from the darkness of pain and ignorance, and perfect love.

In between is some kind of transition zone. What is it like? The characters in our story find themselves in transition once they enter the mystery school and touch the golden shrine. They feel confused, but also enticed and intrigued. Galen, the rationalist, is awakened by love. Frank, the cynic, finds something of higher value to believe in. Jimmy, one of the socially downtrodden, finds in himself the spark of a healer. They each, in their own way, get a glimpse of the light, yet they also feel the pull to return to their normal lives. This push-pull motion is what the transition zone always feels like; spiritual growth comes with bewilderment.

Sri Aurobindo was one of the most educated twentieth-century gurus in India. He said that enlightenment would be easy if all it took was for people to be inspired. Truth isn't a hard sell. Children hearing about Jesus in Sunday school are inspired by a vision of heaven and the good shepherd gathering his flock. Even though the stories differ from culture to culture, with Krishna, Buddha, or Muhammad replacing Jesus as the spiritual ideal, there's a universal yearning to believe in a higher reality, which is what spiritual truth is about.

Where the problems arise, as Aurobindo also pointed out, is at the lower levels of life, where hard realities clash with inspiration. Peace is inspiring; violence is not. Gazing heavenward is inspiring; slogging through the mud isn't. Because the world is a place where we must confront violence, where slogging through the mud occupies far too much of daily existence, the transition zone between here and God is troublesome. Having entered it, our fictional characters encounter fear, anxiety, anger, confusion, sex, ambition, ego—the same things everyone in real life regularly encounters.

Joining a mystery school, then, is only a first step, a knock at the door. In the distance is the goal, which Meg states in her parting note to Mare: "I am the way and the light and the life." This is an intentional conflation of two of Jesus's most enduring statements—"I am the way and the truth and the life" (John 14:6), and "I am the light of the world" (8:12). In other words, the goal is a way of life that exists in the light of God.

Translating these words into a process, we can break it down into three components:

1. The way

2. The light

3. The life

With the way, you find a path that leads to God.

With the light, you begin to see the light of God.

With the life, you merge your present life with the life of God.

All three steps can be accomplished, and since "the way, the light, and the life" are familiar Christian terms in the West, we can stay with them while bringing in a few explanatory terms from other wisdom traditions.

THE WAY

Today finding the way to God is a do-it-yourself project. This is a radical change from the past, when the way to heaven was much more organized and collective, and yet a tiny band of outsiders—savants, saints, mystics, and visionaries—followed their own path. Today, the situation is reversed. Millions of people—modern-day seekers—crave spiritual growth on their own terms, which causes

them to turn in many directions. This can't help but be bewildering, but all paths are about one thing: experience. Experiencing yourself getting closer to the goal is the only measure of success.

I can imagine a cooking school set up for people who, lacking taste buds, cannot taste anything, but I doubt it would stay in business very long. Having faith that your cooking is delicious is no substitute for actually tasting it yourself. What does it mean to taste God's reality? Such an experience is actually extremely common. God is defined as infinite joy, love, compassion, and peace. Everyone has experienced these things. But no one told us that these very experiences could be the first steps on the path to God.

The problem with any single experience, however beautiful, is that it fades away and is lost. It's as if Jesus said, "Knock and the door will be opened—for a few minutes." The reason people seek unconditional love, eternal peace, or lasting bliss is rooted in frustration with how fickle and temporary love, peace, and bliss seem. The reason even the most beautiful experiences last only a short while—maybe moments, maybe days or months— isn't mysterious. We move on. We are pulled down to earth by everyday realities: families to raise, jobs to pursue, groceries to buy. Someone once said, "Ecstasy is great, but I wouldn't want it around the house." The practicalities of life aren't compatible with higher reality.

That's why a path is necessary, to get from here to there. Trying to pencil in God when you have a spare moment doesn't work. Remembering the last time you felt love, peace, and bliss doesn't work either. The experience of God must happen in the present moment, and then, like pearls, the moments can be strung together into a necklace. Eventually, to continue the metaphor, the pearls turn into a continuous strand that has no end. Instead of God here and there, God is everywhere.

What makes this process, which is true spiritual growth, possible? To begin with, your brain. No experience exists without a

brain to process it. A saint who sees God in every grain of sand exists on the same playing field as you or me when it comes to the brain. The difference is like an exquisitely fine-tuned radio that picks up the faintest signals and a radio filled with static that receives only the crudest signals. The better the receiver, the clearer the music.

When the Old Testament says, "Be still, and know that I am God" (Ps. 46:10), it is referring to a brain state. A brain that's restless, excited, distracted by the outside world, preoccupied with work, and so on—which pretty well describes the brain as you and I use it in everyday life—cannot be still. No matter how much faith you have that an FM station is broadcasting Mozart's beautiful music, if your radio can't pick up the signal, faith will be of little use.

What this means, in practical terms, is that the spiritual path is a positive lifestyle choice. The kind of lifestyle that fine-tunes the brain is far from mystical. It has five basic elements, which we can call the five pillars:

Sleep

Meditation

Movement

Food, air, and water

Emotions

These five pillars are basic for a balanced state of mind and body; therefore, they are basic for spiritual experience. Spiritual seekers, it turns out, must first pay attention to their well-being, and especially the well-being of the brain:

Good sleep keeps the brain alert and allows it to balance the entire mind-body system.

Meditation quiets the mind and trains the brain to operate at a very subtle level.

Movement keeps the system flexible and dynamic.

Pure food, air, and water nourish the system without impurities and toxins.

Emotions register joy, love, and bliss as personal experiences.

As you improve in each of these areas, your brain will shift, because you are giving it better input to work with. Your quality of experience, including spiritual experience, will improve. The five pillars work together to create a state of well-being, and it's this state that allows you to perceive finer signals from the source, which is God.

Kabir, a medieval mystical poet of India, who is beloved by people of all faiths, worked as a weaver. His view of spirituality rings with common sense, something I've appreciated since childhood. Here are two of his aphorisms:

Why run around sprinkling holy water?
There's an ocean inside you, and when you're ready
You'll drink.

A drop melting into the ocean—
That you can see.
The ocean melting into a drop—
Who sees that?

Linking the everyday with the sacred is critical. Kabir does just that through poetry. In another verse he says that he traveled to the sacred temples, bathed in the holy pools, and read the scriptures, but he found God in none of them. Only after he looked within did the divine reveal itself.

No great spiritual teacher has ever disagreed with him. What's been added in our day is that we now understand that "looking within" requires the use of a brain that's tuned to the subtle levels of experience where God is woven into the everyday. It isn't necessary to set aside holy places that work magic on the worshipper or to bathe in sacred waters or even to read scripture, although sacred writings do have their place—they offer inspiration, which is itself a subtle experience, the kind that points the way to the divine. These forces become amplified, so to speak, when your brain is trained to notice them.

THE LIGHT

No word is more important in the New Testament than "light." Even "love," the word that instantly comes to mind when thinking about Jesus, comes second. Once you realize that the light is a synonym for awareness, you understand that nothing is real unless we are aware of it. I'm sure you've heard someone say, "My father never told me that he loved me," which feels like a great loss. Silent love is love that creates doubt. You don't know if you can rely on it. You fear that it might not even be there. We're only human, and it takes hearing the words "I love you" to know for sure that we're actually loved.

Similarly, God has to enter your awareness in order to be real. Once the brain is attuned, the first step taken, the second step is focusing on the light. This is the only way to see past the illusion. In a movie theater, the romance, thrills, danger, and adventure on the screen are the illusion. The light that projects them is the reality. When Jesus tells his disciples, "You are the light of the world" (Matt. 5:14), we can accept him at his literal word. This is not a metaphor. Each of us is the light that projects the world.

You and I were born at the wrong time for this truth to sink in. Materialism rules. When I was twenty-something, I read Plato's

famous "Allegory of the Cave," where he compares ordinary life to people huddled in a cave watching shadows play on the wall. They mistake the shadows for reality and can only awaken if they turn around to see the light that's projecting them. I knew what the image meant, but it made no difference to me. I firmly believed in the physical world and knew no one who didn't. The allegory can be updated. Instead of a cave, the audience can be seated in a Cineplex entranced by Hollywood glamour on the screen, unaware that a projector sits behind them, casting the illusion through incandescent white light.

It's still a huge leap to believe that the entire world is a projection, and an even bigger leap to realize that you are watching the movie and projecting it at the same time. Magicians don't believe in their illusions, after all. Apparently we do. We are gullible magicians. When you can separate the two roles, everything changes. Instead of loving the illusion, you become fascinated by the creator, which is yourself. Only a creator has enough freedom to alter creation.

We pay a high price for being gullible magicians. We feel imprisoned in daily life by anxiety, fear, limited opportunities, financial strain, and unfulfilling relationships, and since we don't accept these as our own creation, our immediate response is to struggle with the outer picture. We try to upgrade the illusion, which is possible to do, of course. You can see a doctor for your anxiety, find a better paying job, and walk away from an unloving relationship.

No matter how successful you are in upgrading the illusion, however, you will never be free of it. The rich buy into their movie as much as the poor. The well-loved feel as bereft as the unloved when the person who loves them goes away. The illusion is the level of the problem. The light is the level of the solution, in fact of all solutions, which is why Jesus said, "Seek first the kingdom of God, which is within you" (Matt. 6:33; Luke 17:21).

But going within is exactly what most people dislike and even fear, because it is "in here" where anxiety, insecurity, past traumas, and old conditioning reside. So the mind is called on to heal the mind. How is that accomplished? The answer is obvious, though it is too often overlooked. If you want to escape the illusion, stop creating it.

How? Refuse the story told by false consciousness. False consciousness says, "Get with the program. The world is a hard place. The universe is vast. The forces of nature are fixed. You are a speck in this infinitely huge scene." When all of society is based on such a story, as our age certainly is, dismantling it means shifting into a completely new worldview.

The world's wisdom traditions tell a different story, which I've encapsulated in Jesus's statement: "You are the light of the world." Identify with the light, and you will never again fear the enticing images on the movie screen, even when they are projected eighty feet high.

False consciousness is a net woven from many strands, the most critical being your core beliefs. Among the most destructive of these beliefs are the following:

I'm alone and isolated, disconnected from the universe.

I'm weak and powerless compared with the huge forces arrayed against me.

My life is bounded by this package of skin and bones called the body.

I exist in linear time, which squeezes my being into the short span between birth and death.

I'm not in control of my life.

My choices are limited by my circumstances.

I will experience love in very temporary, imperfect
ways that can't be counted on.

Life is unfair and events are random—these are the
hard realities.

The best way to deal with my insecurity and anxiety
is to push them down out of sight.

If people knew the real me, they'd be repelled.

I have a right to blame others as much as or more than
I blame myself.

God may be real, but he's not paying any attention
to me.

This is quite a long list, because illusion affects every aspect
of life. If you had to overcome every belief on the list, a lifetime
wouldn't be enough, and in the end there would be no guarantee
of success. I'm only underlining the point that the level of the
problem isn't the level of the solution.

The level of the solution is awareness, the "light." Much of
Jesus's teaching can be interpreted as pointing to this solution.
That's what the characters learn in this book. The golden shrine
literally gives off celestial light. Jesus sees the Shekinah, the light
of the soul, when the thirteenth disciple approaches down a dark
alley. When Galen makes a wish and Malcolm hasn't lost his job,
he is manipulating a movie that everyone else accepts as reality.
The magic sunglasses are symbolic of the new vision that alters
their view of reality. I've magnified the effect by using magical
realism. A brilliant show is nice, but the spiritual path has only
one aim: to realize who you really are.

If you could see your true self, the more obscure parts of the New
Testament would become clear, even self-evident. This especially

applies to the portions of the Sermon on the Mount where Jesus tells his audience to do the following (Matt. 6:25–33; 5:5):

Rely on Providence for everything.

Don't plan for the future.

Don't worry about tomorrow. Let every day's problems take care of themselves.

Don't store up treasure, not even food.

Be assured that the meek will one day have all the power.

None of this advice, though, is realistic as a way to conduct daily life, and therefore Christianity has joined other idealistic faiths that hold out the impossible as a promise from God. There is a schism between the ideal and the real, succinctly captured in the Arabic proverb (which might be someone's clever invention), "Trust in God, but tie up your camel."

Many of Jesus's other teachings are impossible, from loving your neighbor as yourself to turning the other cheek. What makes them impossible isn't a flaw in Jesus's wisdom—it's in our own level of awareness. When we don't see ourselves as pure light, the creators and authors of our own existence, we can't access any of the ideals of the world's wisdom traditions. Buddha's pure detachment, the cure for pain and suffering, for instance, is just as removed from real life as Jesus's teaching of universal love. Islam's ideal of divine peace descending to earth, which is embedded in its very name, is unattainable in a violent world.

Nothing short of complete transformation will make the ideal a living reality. So confronting the illusion of false consciousness is the key to every problem, if what we want is a permanent, lasting solution. The true self isn't something you create, work toward, or have faith in. It's a reality that hides in plain sight.

In a movie theater, the projector is hiding in plain sight too; the pictures it creates are an enticing distraction that prevents us from turning around. I deliberately describe Meg's vision of the Crucifixion as feeling like a movie, to set the stage for her ten-year journey into the light. She's as bewildered as the rest of us, but she comes through.

Let's assume that you are leading the kind of life that gives your brain a chance to absorb new input at a subtler level, which I've called "the way." What is your brain supposed to notice? At first, it will notice occasional glimpses of the true self, and when that happens, there will be moments when the illusion falls away. These are unpredictable, because every life is unique, but we can say that in such moments a piece of false belief is exposed. Returning to the long list above, we can—and do—experience the reverse of each false belief. True belief rests on personal experience. So how does it feel to be in this light? The experience is profoundly different from everyday existence:

You feel connected to everything around you.

The forces of nature support you.

Your body extends beyond its visible boundaries, as if it is seamlessly connected to everything.

You experience the timeless, which removes the fear of death.

You feel in control, without effort or struggle.

You feel free. Your choices expand, despite the limitations of your present circumstances.

You experience love as an innate part of life, not something to be won or lost.

Events that once seemed random or unfair now begin to fit into a pattern that makes sense and contains meaning.

You feel secure in yourself, and this allows you to confront negative emotions, past hurts, and outworn conditioning.

There is increasing harmony with other people.

You feel a sense of acceptance that makes blame and guilt pointless.

God feels real and close by.

The characters in the story experience these shifts, and I'd like to emphasize that this part isn't fantasy—quite the opposite. Shorn of imagery, what happens to the characters has happened to me personally. I mean both sides, dark and light. My first moment of despair occurred when I spent a joyous day at the movies with my grandfather, only to have him die that very night. My deepest cynicism occurred in medical school, where nothing seemed more real than suffering and death—God was an illusion to be mocked. My experiences in the light were moments of awakened awareness in meditation, and these began to illuminate the most ordinary experiences—looking out a train window on the Northeast corridor and feeling that the drab industrial landscape stretched to infinity, catching the glance of a passing stranger and seeing in it the salute of another soul.

Every life contains moments when a person sees beyond the illusion. The secret is to pay attention, because once the moment is gone, so is its power to change you. You must be open and alert to signals from your true self.

What this takes is a kind of second attention. First attention, which we're all familiar with, deals with the events in daily life.

You eat breakfast, go to work, pick up groceries, watch TV. None of this has intrinsic meaning. It can be good, bad, or neutral. When second attention enters, you keep doing the same things you always did, but you are aware of them in a new way. Eating breakfast, you might be aware of your inner contentment, or of the food's subtle tastes, or of gratitude for nature's abundance. Going to work, you may feel inner satisfaction, excitement about new possibilities, or empowerment. There is often no neat match between what first attention is noticing and what second attention is realizing.

But there is a common thread to everything in second attention. You are glimpsing the truth of who you are. You are an unbounded field of infinite possibilities. You are infinite consciousness manifesting in space-time. You are the play of light as it shapes itself into forms. There is no arena for realizing these things except normal everyday life. Like a moviegoer turned halfway to the screen and halfway to the projector, you can appreciate the movie (first attention) while knowing all the while that it's a projection of light (second attention).

You can go on the Internet and find countless first-person accounts of experiences that derive from second attention. These stories narrate what happens when the illusion, the mask of materialism, falls away. Some of these stories appear to be exotic, as when people go out of body, view remote events, have foreknowledge of the future, or pop into enlightenment. But the focus shouldn't be on the supernatural, because second attention is completely natural, and "going into the light" happens here and now, not just in near-death experiences.

The more often you notice what's happening to you through second attention, the more you train your brain to go toward this direction. "Light" is a metaphor; awareness is how we exist—nothing is more real. Research into higher states of consciousness keeps growing, although most of the focus has been on disproving

the skeptics by showing with solid data that the paranormal is real. It will be far more useful to have research on how consciousness expands, because as it does, there's a natural progression:

Physical: Your body feels less bounded and limited. There's a sense of lightness, along with the pleasant sensation of simple physical presence. Almost without noticing it, you experience your body as merged with everything around you.

Mental: Your thoughts become fewer as your mind quiets down of its own accord. The mind is no longer restless or scattered. It becomes easy to focus your attention; distractions don't affect you as much. The past doesn't intrude on the present. Old conditioning, which makes you stuck in unwanted habits, loosens its grip.

Psychological: You feel less constricted. Negative emotions like anxiety and hostility start to lessen. The whole emotional landscape is less dramatic—mood swings and depression, for example, are less likely. Your sense of who you are is no longer a source of doubt and insecurity. You find it possible to live in the present moment.

Spiritual: Whatever your spiritual beliefs happen to be, they start to become validated. You experience whatever your conception of God is, or isn't. There doesn't have to be a personal God whose presence is felt. You may experience unbounded inner freedom instead, or unconditional love, or compassion for all living things. The common element, however, is expanded awareness, which allows for experiences of transcendence. This "going beyond" opens up levels of reality that first attention cannot attain.

THE LIFE

Since we are approaching this in stages, let's say that you have taken the first two steps. You've found a way to live that makes your brain capable of subtle experience, and you've learned to apply second attention, which reveals the light as the essence of everything. If these two steps are in place, an inner transformation begins. You are being ushered into "the life." For countless people, life is the opposite of death, but here life means eternal unbounded existence. Jesus promises eternal life, and he is continually taken literally by the Christian faithful. Fundamentalists, for instance, believe heaven is a physical destination; on Judgment Day, their bodies will rise from the grave and join Christ somewhere above the clouds.

When I consulted the *Catholic Encyclopedia* online, the entry under "heaven" explicitly states that it isn't a physical place, but a state of being attained through grace. A picture of green meadows with blue skies, baby animals, and children at play is the most common image of heaven that people bring back from near-death experiences, and so we must face the fact that heaven as a non-place isn't easy to accept. How do we go about it?

One opening comes from Erwin Schrödinger, one of the most brilliant pioneers in quantum physics, who turned his attention later in life to consciousness and its possibilities. Schrödinger said something very revealing about time: "For eternally and always there is only now, one and the same now; the present is the only thing that has no end."

This is a new definition of eternal life, which exists in the present moment. What makes the new eternal is that it is endlessly renewing itself. We can go farther and say that God (or the soul or grace) can only be encountered in the present moment. Finding eternal life in the present moment is the ultimate challenge. Looking at your own life, what happens from moment to

moment? A great many things, which we can arrange vertically, one on top of the other, like layers in an archaeological dig or noodles in a pan of lasagna. Every present moment contains seven layers. The first three are visible; those below the dividing line are buried out of sight:

> An event "out there" in the physical world
> The sights and sounds of the event
> A mental reaction
> ———————————————————
> The opening of a new possibility
> A level of quiet untouched by the outer event
> Pure awareness
> Pure Being

It's quite astonishing that you can answer the phone, decide to take a vacation, or catch a chance remark in an elevator, and far beneath the surface of this experience a hidden world is waiting to be revealed. In our story, Galen and Frank don't want to lift the rug, so to speak, to see what lies beneath. Lilith and Meg are the opposite. They were born to dive deep into their own consciousness. But all the characters are eventually pulled deeper and deeper.

You can take a knife and slice through all the layers of a chocolate cake at once, but most people experience the present moment only in the top two or three layers of their awareness. The deeper layers are unconscious.

They are the province of second attention. This is where Jesus was pointing when he said that the kingdom of heaven is within. The reason that we go within but don't find heaven is that our awareness is confined to the upper layers of experience. This can—and does—change as awareness expands.

Some examples will help. Imagine that you see a child starting to cross the street as you are driving. You stop to let the child go across, and then you move on. The event is superficial. If it is your own child you see, there's a deeper response. You care more about the child's welfare. There are moments when the sight of your child brings a wave of love—now your experience is starting to dip below the line. Something more profound, love, has entered. Can you go deeper? There may be a moment when you experience love for all children and compassion for all those in need. This may lead to a sense that you are connected to all of humanity. By going deeper and deeper, the same simple experience—the sight of a child—acquires new meaning.

Now comes the crucial challenge. Can you catch a glimpse of yourself in the mirror and see your true self? This is the challenge Jesus posed. He wanted his followers to see themselves in the light of love and compassion and then of all of humanity. Such an experience dives far under the line that divides everyday experience from what we call spiritual experience. If you can take a look at yourself as Jesus asked, you are seeing with the eyes of the soul.

One can also call it a journey into pure Being. For me, the greatest spiritual mystery is that existence *is* God. Every other secret springs from this one. If you allow your mind to find its source in silence, simply resting into existence, the simple state of being here is enough. The voice of the soul is silent. Yet as you attune yourself, you find that there is enormous power at the source, because silent awareness is the womb of love, creativity, intelligence, and organizing power. Invisible forces uphold your life. All of creation, including everything in the universe, is projected from the Godhead, which is found inside you.

As mystical as this may sound, it is grounded in ancient wisdom and modern science. In their teachings on higher consciousness, the world's wisdom traditions draw a flowchart of creation that's very different from the one in the book of Genesis and yet still

compatible with it. In Genesis, God is the uncreated. He exists outside time and space, with no need for anyone to create him, because he is eternal.

In this precreated state, there is nothing but emptiness, a formless void. What emerges in the metaphorical seven days are time, space, physical objects, worlds, and life. Living things take on the qualities of their Creator, who is alive, sentient, and—by definition—creative. This flowchart, which moves from nothing to something, from a state of possibilities into a state of manifestation, fits the scheme of quantum physics very neatly. Before the big bang, according to physicists, the precreated state was outside space-time, but contained the potential for everything that has emerged since the big bang. It's rather like pointing out that Einstein's mind contained the potential for great thoughts before they were expressed.

What's astonishing is that the entire flowchart of creation exists in the present moment. In the world "out there," every physical object consists of atoms that are made of subatomic particles. These, in turn, are formed from energy states, and energy states are constantly bubbling up in the quantum foam, as it's called.

Similarly, the flowchart "in here" produces thoughts, sensations, images, and feelings: from the potential of silent mind, faint stirrings of consciousness move upward, then take shape as they emerge into the active mind. Note that the flow moves from the bottom up. Being comes first (the ground state, with no apparent activity). Then the mind becomes aware of itself as silence. Self-awareness is alert; it wants to engage with life. So it creates a new possibility, and from there comes the constant activity we call the stream of consciousness.

Can a person live in the eternal now? Yes, but only when awareness is expanded enough to embrace all the layers of the mind, right down to its source. All the beautiful truths expressed by the great spiritual teachers have gotten obscured by hoping and

wishing that they are real, when what's needed is actually simple and natural: the expansion of consciousness. For me, that's the secret to the New Testament. It's a manual for higher consciousness, and Jesus, in his clarity of mind, knew precisely what it means to live in the highest state of consciousness where "I and the Father are one" (John 10:30). I have opened the New Testament at random, spotted a famous passage, and immediately felt a wave of Being emanate from the page.

What is happening is an experience of the eternal now, because an ordinary moment in my day is suddenly filled with light. If only people didn't place spirituality into a compartment marked "mystical." The only portal to God is the door opened by the present moment. That's why Mare learns a profound truth when she realizes that either nothing is a miracle or everything is a miracle. Actually, both are true. Nothing is a miracle when you see the world through first attention; everything is a miracle when you see it through second attention. You are in a position to make your life miraculous, then, simply by the kind of attention you pay to it.

In the end, this book comes down to something simple. It's an invitation to make the right choice, just as the characters in the story were invited to. In a moment of choosing, the process of transformation can begin, and once it does, you have taken the first and most important step into God's reality.

It would be fitting to give the last word to a poet. Kabir takes us to the place where God has always been:

> He is the tree, the fruit, and the shade
> He is the sun, the light, and the dream
> The word and its meaning
> A point in the All
> Form in the formless
> Infinity in a void.

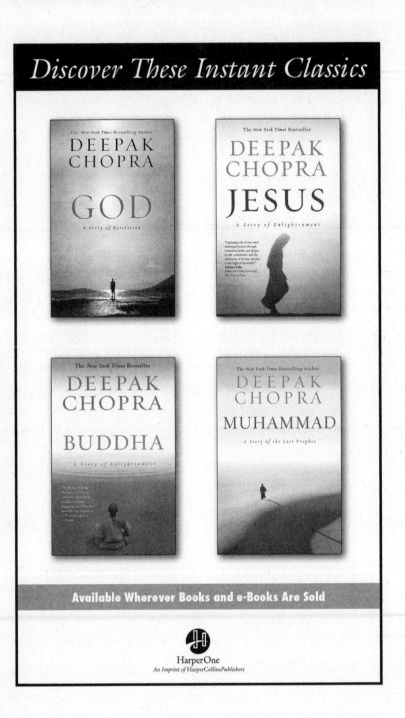